WOMEN
AND MASS
COMMUNICATIONS

**Recent Titles in
Bibliographies and Indexes in Women's Studies**

Women in China: A Selected and Annotated Bibliography
Karen T. Wei

Women Writers of Spain: An Annotated Bio-Bibliographical Guide
Carolyn L. Galerstein and Kathleen McNerney, editors

The Equal Rights Amendment: An Annotated Bibliography of the Issues, 1976-1985
Renee Feinberg, compiler

Childbearing Among Hispanics in the United States: An Annotated Bibliography
Katherine F. Darabi, compiler

Women Writers of Spanish America: An Annotated Bio-Bibliographical Guide
Diane E. Marting, editor

Women in Ireland: An Annotated Bibliography
Anna Brady, compiler

Psychological and Medical Aspects of Induced Abortion:
A Selective, Annotated Bibliography, 1970-1986
Eugenia B. Winter, compiler

Women Writers of Germany, Austria, and Switzerland: An Annotated Bio-Bibliographical Guide
Elke Frederiksen, editor

Immigrant Women in the United States: A Selectively Annotated Multidisciplinary Bibliography
Donna Gabaccia, compiler

Women and the Literature of the Seventeenth Century: An Annotated Bibliography Based on Wing's *Short Title Catalogue*
Hilda Smith and Susan Cardinale, compilers

REF
Z
5633
.W65
L45
1991

WOMEN AND MASS COMMUNICATIONS

An International Annotated Bibliography

Compiled by
JOHN A. LENT

Bibliographies and Indexes in Women's Studies,
Number 11

GREENWOOD PRESS
New York • Westport, Connecticut • London

Poynter Institute for Media Studies
Library

FEB 26 92

Library of Congress Cataloging-in-Publication Data

Lent, John A.
   Women and mass communications : an international annotated
bibliography / compiled by John A. Lent.
     p. cm.—(Bibliographies and indexes in women's studies,
ISSN 0742-6941 ; no. 11)
   Includes bibliographical references and indexes.
   ISBN 0-313-26579-8 (alk. paper)
   1. Mass media and women—Bibliography. I. Title. II. Series.
Z5633.W65L45   1991
[P94.5.W65]
016.30223'082—dc20   90-23780

British Library Cataloguing in Publication Data is available.

Copyright © 1991 by John A. Lent

All rights reserved. No portion of this book may be
reproduced, by any process or technique, without the
express written consent of the publisher.

Library of Congress Catalog Card Number: 90-23780
ISBN: 0-313-26579-8
ISSN: 0742-6941

First published in 1991

Greenwood Press, 88 Post Road West, Westport, CT 06881
An imprint of Greenwood Publishing Group, Inc.

Printed in the United States of America

The paper used in this book complies with the
Permanent Paper Standard issued by the National
Information Standards Organization (Z39.48-1984).

10 9 8 7 6 5 4 3 2 1

CONTENTS

PREFACE	vii
ACKNOWLEDGMENTS	xix
1. WOMEN AND MASS COMMUNICATIONS: GLOBAL AND COMPARATIVE PERSPECTIVES	3
General Studies	3
Historical Studies	26
Images of Women	27
Women As Audience	34
Women Practitioners	37
Women's Media	44
2. AFRICA AND THE MIDDLE EAST	49
General Studies	49
Africa	49
The Middle East	57
3. ASIA, AUSTRALIA, AND OCEANIA	61
General Studies	61
Asia	61
Australia and Oceania	112
4. EUROPE	122
Eastern Europe	122
Western Europe	126
5. LATIN AMERICA AND THE CARIBBEAN	172
General Studies	172
Caribbean	177
Central America	181
South America	184

6. NORTH AMERICA	190
General Studies	190
Canada	191
United States	200
APPENDIX: ORGANIZATIONS, PERIODICALS, OTHER RESOURCES	411
AUTHOR INDEX	419
SUBJECT INDEX	454

PREFACE

The roles and images of women in mass communications became topics of considerable importance after the 1960s. In nearly every part of the world women created alternative channels of communication, media monitoring groups, and professional organizations. They challenged the established media through requests, demands, suits, and boycotts, seeking more positive media portrayals and more equitable working conditions.

In Australia, Ireland, Sweden, and the United States, they formed their own pressure groups within traditional media organizations. Committees looking after media women's interests also developed in academic and professional organizations, such as the International Association for Mass Communication Research, International Communication Association, and Association for Education in Journalism and Mass Communication.

Additionally, women formed their own professional associations in England (Women in Media), Zimbabwe (Federation of African Media Women), Canada (World Association of Women Journalists and Writers), and the United States (Journalism and Women Symposium, Women in Film, American Women in Radio and Television, and Women's Institute for Freedom of the Press).

To ensure fair portrayals, women set up groups that regularly monitored media content. This was the case in England (AFFIRM), France (Association Internationales des Journalistes de Presse Féminine et Familiale), Germany (Deutscher Frauenrat), Canada (National Watch on Images of Women in the Media), India (Manushi Collective), and Sri Lanka (Voice of Women Group). Women also launched many alternative media to disseminate their views, including *Scarlet Woman* of Australia, *Especial-Mujer* and *Mujer/Fempress* of Chile, *Manushi* of India, *Broadsheet* of New Zealand, *Feminist Japan,* Cine Mujer of Colombia, and *Ms., The Tribune: A Women and Development Quarterly, Women's Studies Newsletter, Feminist Studies,* among many others in the United States. Women started academic and professional mass communication journals and newsletters to present a woman's perspective: *Camera Obscura, Media Report to Women, Gender: Art, Literature, Film, History, The Professional Communicator, Women's*

Studies in Communication, Press Woman, and *Women and Film,* all in the United States; *Frauen und Film,* Germany; *Gender and Mass Media Newsletter,* Sweden; *Serpentine,* Netherlands; and *Mujer y Comunicación,* Venezuela.

History of the Literature

Women initiated their own media journals because their presence was virtually non-existent in the already-established professional and academic periodicals until well into the 1970s. Previously, most publications did not consider women and mass communications a topic worthy of even an article a year, and the few articles that did appear usually dealt with women's pages, exceptional women journalists, and "newshens" invading the male domain of the newsroom. Articles that surveyed both males and females were apt to emphasize the former, as in the headline over a 1962 *Journalism Quarterly* article: "The Front-Page Teen-Ager: How 11 Dailies Treated Him."

Not until 1977 did the *Journalism Quarterly* annual index carry the category "minorities," which included women. That year, a record eight articles on women and mass communications appeared. In its first 40 years, *Journalism Quarterly* published fewer than 10 articles remotely related to women (the earliest in 1925). The periodical did not do much better in the 1960s and 1970s when the women's movement came to the forefront. For example, no articles appeared in the years 1964, 1968, 1970, 1971; one article appeared in 1965, 1966, 1967, 1973; and two articles appeared in 1969, 1978, 1981, 1982. Three articles on women and mass communications were published in 1972, four each in 1974 and 1976, five in 1980, and seven in 1975.

Other mass communications journals and their contributors also ignored the topic. The Amsterdam-based *Gazette* did not have a single article on women between 1967 and 1981, only one of the 25-year-old *Journalism Monographs* dealt specifically with women, and the three National Association of Educational Broadcasters journals (*PTR, NAEB Journal,* and *Educational Broadcasting Review*) offered five articles (of which three were tangentially related) between 1957 and 1979. Analyzing a 10-year period (1977-87) of speech- and communication-related journals, Foss and Foss (1989) found many articles on women and communications, but only a few on mass communications: one article of 13 in *Quarterly Journal of Speech,* no articles of the 15 in *Communication Monographs,* three articles of the three in *Critical Studies in Mass Communication,* one article of the 10 in *Human Communication Research,* and four articles of the 57 in *Women's Studies in Communication.* At least 23 of 32 women-oriented articles in the *Journal of Communication* dealt with mass communications. Although not part of the Foss and Foss study, *Communication Abstracts* has surveyed much literature on women and mass communications.

Among the professional magazines, *The Quill,* a monthly of the Society of Professional Journalists, carried only six articles between 1957 and 1971, featuring the topics of a female Alaskan editor, women invading the newsroom (1965), "A word about women," college editor Annette Buchanan, media keeping women in their place (1968), and "(News)hen" coops (1971). The annual, *Proceedings*, of the American Society of Newspaper Editors, which featured a potpourri of topics such as sports, Marilyn Monroe, the atomic bomb, water, the Korean War, and Joseph McCarthy, had nothing specific about women in 33 issues between 1937 and 1977. The five items that appeared about women between 1923 and 1937 involved the newspaper women's page.

Even the critical *Columbia Journalism Review* had only one article on women and journalism from its 1961 beginning until 1971; and only seven other stories appeared between 1971 and 1977. *Democratic Journalist*, the monthly trade magazine of the International Organization of Journalists in Prague, did better, with approximately 20 articles between 1968 and 1989. In the mid-1980s, *Democratic Journalist* began an irregularly run "women and media" feature.

Objectives and Emphases

Women and Mass Communications is an international survey of all types of literature on women and mass communications. The survey includes all mass media, such as publishing, radio, television, film, magazines, newspapers, and video, and affiliates such as advertising, public relations, and wire services. Omitted are speech communication, language and communication, and interpersonal communication, except for a few items that relate specifically to mass communications.

The book is organized by continental and regional arrangements: Africa and the Middle East; Asia, Australia, and Oceania (islands of both the Pacific and Indian Oceans); Europe (Eastern and Western sections, since this is an historical survey); Latin America and the Caribbean; and North America. An attempt has been made to include items on a wide range of countries, and this has meant including some "fugitive" and ephemeral items if not much else has been written about a country's media and women.

The first chapter takes a global perspective and subsumes comparative analyses, non-country specific material, special issues of journals, long-run representations of journals' contents, and edited volumes. The appendix is a descriptive list of resources (periodicals, collections, and associations) dealing with women and mass communications.

Topically, the chapters are divided into general studies, historical studies, images of women, women as an audience, women practitioners, and women's media. The images of women category encompasses sex-roles, sex stereotyping, treatment, portrayal, and coverage of women in media, and pornography. The women practitioners' category includes women working in mass media -- their experiences, anecdotes, successes, and struggles for job equality. Categories under the much larger United States section were expanded to include advertising and public relations, broadcasting, film, and print media under each of the six main topics.

x   Preface

The emphasis in this book is on the period from the early 1960s to the 1990s, but many pre-1960 works of historical or other significance are covered as well. Thus nineteenth-century books on journalism and women are included, along with sources on women and broadcasting published in the 1920s and 1930s because they were probably the first of their kind.

A serious effort was made to compile a bibliography that would cover the most important literature on women in mass communications and yet would present a careful representation of the types of materials, and provide an overview that would be comprehensive in encompassing the field and the significant literature on the topic under study. In selecting, many materials were excluded, of course, including thousands of items in the popular press that were not worthy of inclusion. Some items from nationally oriented newspapers and magazines (*Time, Newsweek,* The London *Times,* The *New York Times,* for example) were chosen because they had historical or other value, or because they might alert the reader to the reservoir of materials in certain periodicals.

The bibliography is representative in covering all genres of publications (books, periodicals, dissertations, conference papers, etc.), writing formats and styles, time periods, geographical areas, and languages. Although the bibliography consists mainly of English-language publications, hundreds of citations appear from other languages. The bibliography is comprehensive in encompassing a broad range of topics, areas all over the world, and different time periods. In the author's estimation, the bibliography provides an overall survey of the most important materials on women and mass communications.

More than 85 percent of the citations are annotated, descriptively and succinctly, without evaluative comments. The preparation of the annotations followed a careful reading of the works or their abstracts. Fuller annotations were provided for edited volumes, listing the contributors and their chapters, and for topics or countries about which not much is otherwise known. The citations are arranged alphabetically by author, or by article title when an author is not listed, and are numbered consecutively.

Search Process

Most of the search was manual because much of the literature is not in computerized databases. Even under ideal conditions, computerized bibliographies only pick up a fraction of the available material. The keywords "women and media" were searched in Sociofile, 1974 through December 1989, and ERIC (Educational Resources Information Clearinghouse), 1966 through December 1989. Sociofile yielded 219 items, about 45 percent of which were pertinent and not already in the bibliography, while ERIC had about 700 abstracts, many of which were usable.

Many bibliographies, indices, and bibliographic periodicals were used -- far too numerous to list here. Especially valuable were *Communication Booknotes* and *Communication Abstracts,* edited for the most part by Christopher Sterling and

Robert Roberts, respectively, and *Index to Journals in Communication Studies through 1979*, compiled by Ronald J. Matlon. *Communication Booknotes* and *Communication Abstracts* provide thousands of European, Australian, North and South American citations since their editors -- and in the case of *Booknotes*, its contributors also -- scrutinize hundreds of periodicals and book publisher lists on a regular basis. Matlon's book is a photocopy of all tables of contents in 13 journals: *Association for Communication Administration Bulletin, Central States Speech Journal, Communication Monographs, Communication Quarterly, Human Communication Research, Journalism Quarterly, Journal of American Forensic Association, Journal of Broadcasting, Journal of Communication, Philosophy and Rhetoric, Quarterly Journal of Speech, Southern Speech Communication Education,* and *Western Journal of Communication Education.*

All numbers of the following periodicals were scanned: *Cinema India International, Cinema Vision India, Cinemaya, Comics Journal, Communicate!, Communication Abstracts, Communication and Development, Communication Booknotes, Communication Research Trends, Critical Studies in Mass Communication, Development Dialogue, East-West Film Journal, Gannett Center Journal, Indian Journal of Communication Arts, Indian Press, Intermedia, Journal of Broadcasting and Electronic Media, Journal of Communication, Journal of Newspaper and Periodical History, Journalism History, Journalism Monographs, Journalism Quarterly, Keio Communication Review, Mass Comm Review, Media Asia, Media Development, Media History Digest, Media Monitor, Nordicom Review, Sex-Roles within Massmedia Newsletter, Studies in Latin American Popular Culture, Studies of Broadcasting, Target, Third Channel, WittyWorld, Women's Studies Abstracts, Women's Studies in Communication, Women Studies International Quarterly,* and *Women, Work and Development.*

The author surveyed the majority of issues of the following journals: *Abstracts of Popular Culture, American Heritage, Camera Obscura, Cine Cubano, Columbia Journalism Review, Communication in Africa, Communication Monographs, Communicatio Socialis Yearbook, Communicator, Democratic Journalist, Educational Broadcasting Review, European Journal of Communication, Feminist Studies, Forerunner, Gazette, Grassroots Editor, Human Communication Research, International Journal of Women's Studies, International Popular Culture, Isis Women's International Bulletin, Journal of Film and Video, Journal of Popular Culture, Journalism Educator, Matrix, Media and Values, Media, Culture and Society, Media Information Australia, Media Report to Women, Michigan Occasional Papers on Women's Studies, NAEB Journal, off our backs, Press Woman, Problems of Journalism, Professional Communicator, Psychology of Women Quarterly, Public Telecommunications Review, Publizistik, Quarterly Journal of Speech, Quill, RFD/DRF, Vidura, Wide Angle, Women and Film, Women and Politics, Women of Europe, Women's Studies Quarterly,* and *The Word.*

Literally hundreds of other journal titles were scanned over the years in the fields of mass communications, women's studies, sex research, social psychology, marketing, advertising, sociology, history, area studies, anthropology, and critical studies. The literature has been published on every continent.

"Fugitive" materials, such as dissertations not indexed through the University of Michigan program, theses, conference papers, and pamphlets, make up part of the bibliography for a number of reasons. First, conference papers presented between 1987 and 1990 probably have not often been published. Yet, they contain valuable information that should be available to researchers willing to contact the associations where they were presented. Second, "fugitive" documents are sometimes the only sources on women and mass communications in some countries. Third, unpublished dissertations and theses, if properly supervised, are oftentimes some of the best work on a topic. There are not very many times in a researcher's life when virtually all of his/her time and energy are concentrated on a single project that is being guided by at least five other professionals.

A number of conference papers are regularly abstracted in *Gender and Mass Communications Newsletter* (formerly *Sex-Roles within Massmedia Newsletter*), and because many involve topics and countries not commonly studied or available elsewhere, they have been transferred to this bibliography.

Organization of Book

The first chapter cuts across geographical boundaries, providing global and comparative perspectives. Some of the features of this section include edited books of a cross-national and/or cross-discipline nature; listings of all, or representative, articles in periodicals (e.g. *Camera Obscura, Media Report to Women, Sex-Roles within Massmedia Newsletter*), and thematic issues of journals (e.g. *Canadian Journal of Communication, Medie/Kultur*).

Africa and the Middle East make up the second chapter. Of all of the geographical regions, Africa and the Middle East were the most sparsely covered in the women and mass communications literature that I surveyed. However, conferences on the topic in Nigeria, Senegal, Tanzania, and Zambia yielded information, as did a United Nations report, a few dissertations, and scattered periodical articles. Associations such as the Federation of African Media Women and the Association of Media Women in Kenya also added some sources. This chapter has items that describe women and media in many countries (e.g. Congo, Gabon, Sudan, Tunisia), Nigerian chapbook (pamphlet) heroines, Egypt's weekly women's magazine, *Hawa*, Iranian women movie directors, and feminist publishing in Israel. Much of the limited research shows a negative situation for women in mass communications. An optimistic note was sounded by one source that reported the emergence of women in media management positions in Egypt.

The next chapter is subdivided into Asia, Australia, and Oceania. The valuable roles that women have played in mass communications in Asia are documented in many sources, including at least a half-dozen books and a rather large number of seminars, a few of which were in Thailand (1975), Hong Kong (1976), Malaysia (1980), Pakistan (1980, 1984), Indonesia (1983, 1984), the Philippines (1984), and Singapore (1987).

Preface xiii

The literature speaks of a long connection between women and mass communications, documenting early printings of women's periodicals in the Philippines (1891), Korea (1905), and China (1902). In 1958, DZWS was set up as a woman's station in Manila. More recently, China has a new "Women's Cinema," and India a television serial meant to raise women's status. Other sources discuss the prominence some Asian women have achieved in media, notably as film directors (such as Peries of Sri Lanka, Sangeeta of Pakistan, Mehta and Sen of India, and Diaz-Abaya of the Philippines) and as administrators who have published the *Philippines Daily Inquirer*, edited the Chinese-language *Reader's Digest*, or headed broadcasting stations in Hong Kong or Manila. A group of Philippine women journalists of the 1980s, called the "Bulletin Girls," who suffered painful consequences of defying the Marcos dynasty, is featured in some sources.

Despite these successes, the overall picture of, and for, women in Asian mass media is not very encouraging. Sources in this section show that a recent survey of 950 Indian journalists found only 88 women among them; that in Japan, women recently petitioned the broadcasting stations to promote sexual equality; and that in many countries, women still tried to move beyond the "lipstick" beat. Similarly, this section has many studies on the images of women in mass media: in the films of India, Japan, Malaysia, and Sri Lanka, women served a patriarchal order, held lower positions, were self-sacrificing, and were cast in the extreme roles of whore/virgin, whore/wife, or vamp/victim; on Indian and Philippine television, women were used to "evoke pity" and as sales bait, respectively; in Pakistani media, generally, they were stereotyped as housewives, mothers, or consumers of advertised products.

Australian literature discusses women journalists of the nineteenth century, early filmmaker Elsa Chauvel, the woman chief executive of Radio New Zealand, and the images of women in print media, television, and drug advertisements. A few recent works from the Office of the Status of Women and the Office of Women's Affairs provide guidelines on the treatment of women in the media, and others from the Australian Broadcasting Corporation, Australian Film Commission, and Australian Film and Television School recommend affirmative action and professionalization activities.

The fourth chapter covers Eastern and Western Europe and the USSR. That continent's body of work has been enhanced by reports of equality working groups at National Union of Journalists of England, Radio Telefís Eirann, and the Swedish Broadcasting Corporation, among others, and the frequent writings of Ulla Abrahamsson, Helen Baehr, Kevin Durkin, Marian Flick, Margaret Gallagher, Barrie Gunter, Oga Tokgöz, and Janice Winship.

The European female tradition in mass communications is historically rich, as reflected in this bibliography. It embraces Mary de la Rivière Manley and Elizabeth Mallet, British editors in the first decade of the eighteenth century; Marie Duval, eighteenth century cartoonist; periodicals such as France's *Le Journal des Dames* (1750s), England's *The Lady's Magazine* (1770s), *The Female Spectator*, and *Lady's Museum*. According to some authors, other countries, such as

Germany and Russia, also had women's journals in the early eighteenth century. An 1864 citation published in the *English Woman's Journal* describes the first six years of that periodical.

Women more recently involved in mass communications are profiled in this chapter, including filmmakers Shepitko, Duras, Riefenstahl, von Trotta, Sanders-Brahms, Akman, Varda, Downs, Wertmüller, and Lokkeberg; journalists Lazareff, Fallaci, and Klimova; as well as French, German, and other cartoonists. Other sources deal with women's magazines and feminist presses in England, France, Italy, Iceland, Spain, Netherlands, Greece, and Ireland, to name a few, as well as media groups such as Frauen-Film Produktion and Aktion Klartext, both of which are from Germany.

Most European evidence reveals a negative and inferior image of women in mass media. A Swedish/Danish study of 1983 concluded that women's presence in broadcasting had not yet left its mark, while another work declared that Swedish television cannot promote gender equality until more domestic programs are made. A Dutch study of 1986 stated that women's absence from television news production and content affected television content; another source pointed out that independent British radio was completely out of touch with contemporary women; other reports showed that men dominated Hungarian television and British radio; and a Danish work analyzed television's role as a gender influence upon children. Other items dealt with women's images in East German and Polish television, Spanish, French, and German comics, and Soviet, East and West German children's books.

A study of Belgian media showed an overall image of women as objects of men, while an Austrian source said women were depicted in that country's media in "trivialized and sensational capacities." A series of papers in a German journal concluded that media contributed to the "symbolic annihilation of women"; a content analysis of Hungarian commercial photographs found that women were shown "very far from looking real," and an Italian survey reported that women did not feel positive about their image in the feminist press. The story does not change much from country to country: images of women in Swiss media were of "dumb housewives" or "eternal seduction"; in Danish family magazines, the perception was either of what women should be or do, or as "mistress or self-dependent"; in Greek movies, "bad" girls were portrayed as poor, "good" girls as rich; in French news journalism, women were "mostly non-existent."

There are the bright spots. One is the number of equality groups attached to various media. Another relates to some optimistic study findings: in a year's period of the 1980s, the number of women newsreaders on British television doubled; over a 10-year period in Norway, the number of women broadcasting producers increased, and between 1965 and 1985, portrayals of women in Norwegian magazines changed for the better.

The fifth chapter concentrates on women and mass communications of the Caribbean, Central America, and South America. This region also has held conferences on the topic, with reports and papers, in Colombia (1978), Jamaica (1981), Mexico (1982), Cuba, Costa Rica, and Ecuador (all in 1984), and Nicaragua (1986), among others.

The favorite study topics concerning the region, as reflected in this bibliography, are roles of alternative media and the images of women in various media. A number of items cover *fotonovelas* and *telenovelas* as cultural/media forms aimed at a female audience. The alternative media have played vital roles in legitimizing women's movements and providing outlets for different views. They have published monographs and bulletins, produced films, operated their own radio stations, and made media available for the promotion of women. Various authors have described the functions of organizations such as ILET, Mujer-Fempress, FEM, Unidad de Comunicación Alternativa de la Mujer, Lilith Video Collective, Rede Mulher, Mujer Tec, and the Caribbean Women's Features Syndicate, and media such as Rádio-Mulher, *Mulherio, Nueva Mujer, Mujer,* or *La Tortuga.*

Other writers have looked at Latin American women's magazines (part of the "culture of feminine oppression" according to Michèle Mattelart), described as providing an "anglicized, consumerist" view of women in Mexico, and a false sense of women's liberation (equating it with sexual liberation) in Venezuela. A few works analyzed the impact of the United States women's magazine, *Cosmopolitan,* upon Latin American women.

Image studies were conducted of all types of media forms in the region -- Mexican television, Latin American magazine fiction, Bolivian and Costa Rican media, Brazilian advertisements, Trinidadian calypso, Mexican *telenovelas* and comic books, and Chilean *fotonovelas.* However, the results were the expected. Working women on Puerto Rican television were different from those in real life, and working women in Peru were not portrayed positively in that country's media; women in Puerto Rican television advertising were depicted as sex objects, the "harassing woman," or the "hysterical woman"; in Mexican comic books women were shown as being submissive, passive, long-sacrificing, and dependent, with few options outside of marriage; in Mexican cinema, women were shown as the bedrock of the family unit, and in roles as Virgin, virgin, mother, or whore; in Caribbean newspapers well after the 1950s, Caribbean women were portrayed in the image of foreign white women. One study found that heroines shown in Colombian news resembled the mother of Christ. Other works looked at eroticism in four Brazilian magazines and in Brazilian cinema (claiming 1919 as a starting date), and at Mexican television stereotypes from the perspective of psychologists, journalists, and others.

The history of Latin America and the Caribbean is replete with examples of women journalists and women's media, some of which are subjects of works listed in this book. For example, the three Stockdale sisters ran the first Bermudian newspaper nearly two centuries ago, Gertrudis Gómez de Avellaneda edited a Cuban women's magazine in 1860, and *O Jorno das Senhoras* and *Jornal das Famílias* were published for Brazilian women in 1852 and 1863, respectively.

Portraits were done of contemporary women media practitioners such as Dominican editor Allfrey, Mexican actress Félix, Nicaraguan chief censor Blandon and publisher Violeta Chamorro, Cuban filmmakers Arguelles, Vilasis, and Trujillo, and Peruvian director de Izcue.

Studies also were completed on the more general status of women media practitioners in Brazil, Ecuador, Mexico, and Uruguay. The Brazilian report was a bit encouraging, pointing out that women compose one-third of the newspaper editorial staffs (though they did not hold many managerial positions); the Mexican source said that women occupied only 20 to 25 percent of the broadcasting jobs, although they made up 60 percent of the communications student body.

Chapter Six, dealing with Canada and the United States, is disproportionately larger because of the tremendous volume of work developed by American researchers and writers in recent years.

A rather substantial number of sources on Canadian women and mass communications was generated by government, industry, and other private monitoring groups. For example, the Canadian Radio-Television and Telecommunications Commission, Canadian Broadcasting Corporation, Canadian Association of Broadcasters, Canadian Advertising Foundation, and Canadian Advertising Advisory Board all issued guidelines on non-sexist advertising and broadcasting, and reports on job equality and sex stereotyping. Other documents emanated from groups such as the Toronto Women's Media Committee, MediaWatch, Manitoba Action Committee on the Status of Women, and the Quebec YMCA "Sexism in Advertising" Committee.

Women practitioners and women's media were the subjects of a few reports, although as one source noted, women's status as employees in Canadian communications received less attention than their images in the media. One study in Quebec showed that female journalists were younger and less educated than their male counterparts. Among media personnel profiled were Kit Coleman, a foreign correspondent at the turn of the twentieth century, Sara J. Duncan, filmmaker Dorothy Hénaut, and award winning cartoonist Lynn Johnston. Some women's media described were Co-op Radio of Vancouver, Vidéo Femmes of Quebec, Studio D, *Webspinner,* and *Fireweed.*

Nearly every possible aspect of women and mass communications was covered in the United States section. Special issues of many journals, source books, bibliographies and other references, government, industry, citizen group documents, and many other items dealt with a diverse range of topics: doing research on women's communications, writing for the homemaker, feminine strategies in political advertising, sexual politics, women and consumerism, etc. Particularly popular topics were feminism and mass communications, pornography/violence, soap operas, sex roles, and sex stereotyping.

A number of individuals have taken up the task of documenting the history of women practitioners and women's media. Hundreds of sources relate to the media careers of pioneers such as Nuthead, Timothy, or Goddard in publishing; Blache and Cooper in film; Mills, Tucker, Hammersley, Waller, or Sioussat in broadcasting; Rayne, Grinstead, or Patterson in journalism education; Dumm in cartooning, and Benjamin in foreign correspondence. Many others -- some historical, some more contemporary figures -- were highlighted, including those in women's suffrage journalism (e.g. Woodhull, Stanton, or Hauser), muckraking (Tarbell), photography (Bourke-White), magazines (Hale or Fuller), and foreign and war reporting (Chapelle, Higgins, or Deepe).

Images of women were discussed in historical, descriptive, and experimental analyses. Some of the broader topics were sex roles and stereotyping in comics, soap operas, music videos, children's television, advertising, and other genres of mass communications; equal rights and feminist movement coverage in the media; and the effects of mass media exposure to filmed violence against women.

ACKNOWLEDGMENTS

I am indebted to many for helping me conceptualize and compile this book: numerous women practitioners in more than a dozen Asian and Caribbean countries who granted me interviews; the many librarians who helped me gather primary and secondary research materials during my 27 years of international research; those fellow academicians, such as Chris Sterling, Mike Kittross, Ken Harwood, and the late Jim Carty, who continue to think that bibliographies are important; and those institutions and publishers, notably Greenwood Press, which continue to keep printed bibliographies alive in this age of on-line databases.

I am especially grateful to Robin Larsen, who searched Philadelphia libraries, copied hundreds of items, and made me aware of new works; to Morris Dukuly, who organized an earlier set of cards for this bibliography, and Fei Zhengxing, Chuck W. Elliott, and Ellen Peskin who also added much in the search of sources.

Most of all, I wish to thank Robert Roberts, associate editor of *Communication Abstracts* and Temple University communications librarian. Bob is a dedicated bibliographer and caring colleague, without whose services, my work would be much more difficult, as would be the work of other faculty members and most students. Without any disrespect, I consider Bob to be our school's most valuable asset.

WOMEN
AND MASS
COMMUNICATIONS

1
WOMEN AND MASS COMMUNICATIONS: GLOBAL AND COMPARATIVE PERSPECTIVES

GENERAL STUDIES

1. ACCT. *A la recherche du temps des femmes: communication, éducation, rythmes de vie.* Paris: Agence de coopération culturelle et technique and groupe d'initiative femmes et développement, 1986, 188 pp.
    Includes research on mass media, mass communication, advertising, and textbooks in such countries as Iran, India, Greece, Niger, Burkina Faso, Senegal, Zambia, and Benin.

2. *Action*, London.
    Monthly newsletter of the World Association for Christian Communications has included brief articles on women and the media: Anjali Monteiro, "Our Story -- The Story of Womanhood. Report on Slide Tape Production for Bombay Slum Women," September 1983, p. 4; "Mulherio Speaks out for Women," August 1984, p. 3; "Women's News in China," October 1984, p. 7; and "Mexican Women's Paper Thrives Against All Odds," October 1987, p. 3.

3. Ashley, Barbara Renchkovsky, and David Ashley, eds. "Sex as Violence: The Body Against Intimacy." *International Journal of Women's Studies.* September-October 1984, pp. 352-371.
    Reviews pornography in view of feminist critiques.

4. Baehr, Helen. "The Impact of Feminism on Media Studies." In *Men's Studies Modified*, edited by Dale Spender. Toronto: Pergamon Press, 1981.

5. Baehr, Helen, ed. "Women and Media." *Women's Studies International Quarterly.* 3:1 (1980), pp. 1-133.
    Includes: Helen Baehr, "Editorial," p. v; Barbara M. Eddings, "Women in Broadcasting (U.S.) de jure, de facto," pp. 1-14; Jane Booth, "Watching the Family," pp. 15-28; Helen Baehr, "The 'Liberated Woman' in Television Drama," pp. 29-40; Anne Karpf, "Women and Radio," pp. 41-54; Pen Dalton, "Feminist Art Practice and the Mass Media: A 'Personal' Account," pp. 55-58; Diane Tammes, "Camerawoman Obscura: A 'Personal' Account," pp. 59-62; Joy Leman, "'The Advice of a Real Friend.' Codes of Intimacy and Oppression in Women's

Magazines 1937-1955," pp. 63-78; Nona Glazer, "Overworking the Working Woman: The Double Day in a Mass Magazine," pp. 79-94; Cornelia Butler Flora, "Women in Latin American Fotonovelas: From Cinderella to Mata Hari," pp. 95-104; Penni Stewart, "He Admits...But She Confesses," pp. 105-114; "Reports," pp. 115-122; "Book Reviews," pp. 123-133.

6. Baehr, Helen and Gillian Dyer. *Boxed In: Women and Television.* Winchester, Massachusetts: Unwin Hyman, and New York: Methuen, 1988, 241 pp.

    Eight essays discuss how women are represented on and behind the screen. Looks at women's relationship to television as performers, writers, program makers, and viewers. Questions how the communication revolution of video, cable, and satellite technology will affect programming and women's jobs in the industry.

7. Balaguer-Callejon, M. Luisa. *La mujer y los medios de comunicación: El caso de la publicidad en televisión.* Malaga: Agruval, 1985, 112 pp.

8. Barrowclough, Susan. "Not a Love Story." *Screen.* 23:5 (1982), pp. 26-36.

9. Baruch, Grace and Debra Renee Kaufman. "Interpreting the Data: Women, Developmental Research and the Media." *Journal of Thought.* Spring 1987, pp. 53-57.

    Media overemphasize social science research findings while paying little attention to methodology. Uses examples from research on women.

10. Beauchamp, Collette. *Le silence des media, les femmes, les hommes et l'information.* Montreal: Les Editions du remue-menage, 1987.

    A French feminist analysis of information in media, including chapters on women's images; absence of women's information and attacks in media on women; women, journalism, and power, and women journalists and feminism.

11. Benston, Margaret. "Worlds Apart: Women, Men and Technology." *Media and Values.* Winter 1989, pp. 16-17.

    Technology is gender-typed; the "whole realm of technology and the communication around it reinforces the idea of women's powerlessness."

12. Boserup, Ester and Christina Liljencrantz. "Integration of Women in Development Proposals for Action." *Literacy Discussion.* 6:4 (1976), pp. 141-148.

    Women's integration into development proposals worldwide, looking at communication and mass media, among other topics.

13. Bouillon, Antoine. "Discursive Power and Domination." *Communications.* 28 (1978), pp. 29-43.

    Among specific topics analyzed is soap operas and the social and economic functions of women.

14. Brie, Sonja. "College of Solidarity Holds Two Colloquys on Women." *Democratic Journalist*. May 1978, pp. 12-15.

    Held in East Berlin at the end of 1977, one dealt with mass media tasks in implementing equality for women. Includes information on women and media in Ghana, People's Democratic Republic of Yemen, India, Angola, Ethiopia, Iraq, Syria, Bangladesh, and Egypt.

15. Brown, Mary Ellen, ed. *Television and Women's Culture: The Politics of the Popular*. Newbury Park, California: Sage, 1989, 256 pp.

    International group of cultural critics show how television can offer women opportunities of negotiating their own media meanings. Chapters are: Mary Ellen Brown, "Feminist Culturalist Television Criticism: Culture, Theory, Practice"; Virginia Nightingale, "Women as Audiences"; Caren Deming, "For Television-Centred Television Criticism: Lessons from Feminism"; Dorothy Hobson, "Women Audiences and the Workplace"; Ien Ang, "Melodramatic Identification: Television Fiction and Women's Fantasy"; Lisa Lewis, "Consumer Girl Culture: How Music Video Appeals to Girls"; Sally Stockbridge, "Rock Video: Pleasure and Resistance"; Danae Clark, "*Cagney and Lacey*: Feminine Strategies of Detection"; John Fiske, "Women and Quiz Shows: Consumerism, Patriarchy and Resisting Pleasures"; Beverly Poynten and John Hartley, "Male Gazing: Australian Rules Football, Gender and Television"; Andrea Press, "Class, Gender and the Female Viewer: Women's Responses to *Dynasty*"; Mary Ellen Brown and Linda Barwick, "Motley Moments: Soap Opera, Carnival, Gossip and the Power of the Utterance," and Mary Ellen Brown, "Conclusion: Consumption and Resistance: The Problem of Pleasure."

16. Buck, Macky, Cindy Deitch, Dale Melcher, Lydia Nettler, Ann Wassell, Edie Spielman. "Socialist-Feminist Women's Unions: Past and Present." *Socialist Review*. March-April 1978, pp. 37-57.

    Evaluation of future directions of socialist-feminism: communications networks between groups and women's cultural activities, including media.

17. *Camera Obscura*.

    Contents include: Nos. 3-4 -- Jacqueline Suter, "Feminine Discourse in *Christopher Strong*"; Lyon, "Discourse and Difference"; Bergstrom, "Enunciation and Sexual Difference"; Raymond Bellour, "Psychosis, Neurosis, Perversion"; Freude, "Notes on Distribution."

    No. 5 -- Kuntzel, "The Film-Work/2"; Penley, "The Story of Anna O."; Cowie, "The Song of the Shirt"; Potter and Weinstock on "Thriller."

    No. 6 -- Marc Silberman, "Catalog of Women Filmmakers in West Germany"; Lyon, "The Cinema of Lol V. Stein"; Duras on "India Song"; Rodowick, "Vision, Desire and the Film-Text"; Kuntzel, "Sight, Insight, Power"; Bergstrom on "The Dancing Soul of the Walking People."

    No. 7 -- Lea Jacobs, "*Now Voyager*: Some Problems of Enunciation and Sexual Difference"; Penley, "Introduction to Metaphor/Metonymy"; Augst Metz, "Metaphor/Metonymy, or the Imaginary Referent"; Hamilton, "Psycholanalysis and Film Theory."

    Nos. 8-9-10 -- Special issue on Jean-Luc Godard. Includes: Lyon, "La Passion, c'est pas ça"; Penley, "Pornography, Eroticism"; Bergstrom, "Violence and Enunciation"; Penley, "Les Enfants de la Patrie"; Bellour on "Sauve qui peut (la vie)"; Aumont on "La Chinoise"; Williams, "Godard's Use of Sound"; "The Economics of Film Criticism: Godard/Kael Debate."

No. 11 -- Doane, "Gilda: Epistemology as Striptease"; Bellour, "Thierry Kuntzel and the Return of Writing"; Reisman on Marjorie Keller; McCarroll, "The Body Human: The Sexes"; Silberman, "Women Filmmakers in West Germany: A Catalog (Part 2)."

No. 12 -- Mann, "Staggering Toward Modern Times"; interview with Max Almy; Morris, "Identity Anecdotes"; Dolan on Marie-Claire Ropars and Film Theory; Turim on Lyotard: *Desire in Art and Politics*; Lyotard, "Philosophy and Painting in the Age of Their Experimentation."

Nos. 13-14 -- Kirby, "Fassbinder's Debt to Poussin"; Duguet, "The Luminous Image"; Aumont, "Eisenstein: Notes Toward a Biography"; Godard and Beauviala, "Genesis of a Camera"; special section on "Documentary/Documentation"; Trinh T. Minh-ha, "Reassemblage"; Solomon-Godeau, "Reconstructing Documentary"; Mary Kelly and Paul Smith, "No Essential Femininity."

No. 15 -- Special issue on "Science Fiction and Sexual Difference." Includes: Sobchack, "Child/Alien/Father: Patriarchal Crisis and Generic Exchange"; Bergstrom, "Androids and Androgyng"; Penley, "Time Travel, Primal Scene, and the Critical Dystopia"; Greenberg, "Reimaging the Gargoyle: Psychoanalytic Notes on Alien"; Bellour, "Ideal Halady"; Dadoun, "Metropolis: Mother-City -- 'Mittler' -- Hitler"; Patalas, "Metropolis, Scene 103."

No. 16 -- Special issue on "Television and the Female Consumer." Includes: George Lipsitz, "The Meaning of Memory: Family, Class and Ethnicity in Early Network Television Programs"; Lynn Spiegel, "Installing the Television Set: Popular Discourses on Television and Domestic Space, 1948-1955"; Denise Mann, "The Television Star vs. the Hollywood Star: Comedy-Variety and Its Mode of Reception, 1946-1956"; Lynne Joyrich, "All That Television Allows: TV Melodrama, Postmodernism, and Consumer Culture"; Robert Deming, "*Kate and Allie*: 'New' Women and the Audience's Television Archives"; Sandy Flitterman-Lewis, "All's Well That Doesn't End Well: Soap Operas and the Marriage Motif"; Dan Einstein et al., "Source Guide to TV Melodrama: The Family Drama and Situation Comedy -- 1950 to 1970."

18. *Canadian Journal of Communication.* September 1989.

Thematic issue on "Women's Voices in Media Research" includes: "Guest Editor's Introduction," pp. iv-vii; Donna Gill, "REAL Women and the Press: An Ideological Alliance of Convenience," pp. 1-16; Sheila Petty, "Images of Women and Oppression in 'Francophone' West African Film," pp. 17-28; Elspeth Probyn, "TV's Local: The Exigency of Gender in Media Research, " pp. 29-41; Michèle Martin, "Capitalizing on the 'Feminine' Voice, " pp. 42-61; Peggy Kelly, "When Women Try to Work with Television Technology," pp. 63-75; Jocelyn Denault, "Conference Report from the Society of Cinema Studies: Viewing Feminist Films," pp. 76-81; Francine Pelletier et al., "Les femmes journalistes: Le pouvoir? Quel pouvoir?" pp. 82-96.

19. Ceulemans, Mieke and Guido Fauconnier. *Mass Media: The Image, Role, and Social Conditions of Women. A Collection and Analysis of Research Materials.* Paris: Unesco, Reports and Papers on Mass Communications No. 84, 1979, 78 pp.

Broken into two main sections -- "The Images of Women in the Mass Media" and "The Professional Status of Women in Mass Media," this is a summary of international and U.S. research of various media and their portrayal of women. Women were depicted as housewives and sex objects in advertising and programming, appeared less frequently and in lower roles than men, and were underrepresented either as news presenters or newsmakers.

20. *Cinema India-International.* October-December 1986.

    Includes Thomas Radecki, "Pornography in Cinema," pp. 12-13, and Nirmala, "Women's Films Exposing the Brutality of Man," pp. 16-18.

21. Cirksena, Kathryn. "Women's Liberation from Spirals of Silence: The Need for Feminist Studies in Mass Communication Research." In *Communications at the Crossroads: The Gender Gap Connection*, edited by Ramona Rush and Donna Allen, pp. 46-58. Norwood, New Jersey: Ablex, 1989.

    The growth of feminist communication studies, giving example of spiral of silence theory of Germany's Elisabeth Noelle-Neumann.

22. *Communication.* 10:3/4 (1988).

    Thematic issue on "Postmodernism/Marxism/Feminism" includes Anne Balsamo, "Reading Cyborgs Writing Feminism" and Nancy Fraser, "Social Criticism without Philosophy: An Encounter Betweeen Feminism and Postmodernism."

23. *Communication Quarterly.* Spring 1983.

    Thematic issue on "Women and Communication: An Introduction to the Issues," the title of the lead article by Julia T. Wood. Others are Karlyn Kohrs Campbell, "Femininity and Feminism: To Be or Not To Be a Woman"; Martha Solomon, "Stopping ERA: A Pyrrhic Victory"; Paula A. Treichler and Cheris Kramarae, "Women's Talk in the Ivory Tower"; Fern L. Johnson, "Political and Pedagogical Implications of Attitudes Towards Women's Language"; Becky Swanson Kroll, "From Small Group to Public View: Mainstreaming the Women's Movement"; Gretchen S. Barbatis, Martin R. Wong, and Gregory M. Herek, "A Struggle for Dominance: Relational Communication Patterns"; Ellen M. Murray, "Channels to the Top: An Exploration of Sex Role and Information Source"; Carol Simpson Stern, "Parties as Reflectors of the Feminine Sensibility"; Susan B. Shimanoff, "The Role of Gender in Linguistic References to Emotive States," and Marty M. Slater, Deborah Weider-Hatfield, and Donald L. Rubin, "Generic Pronoun Use and Perceived Speaker Credibility."

24. *Communication Research Trends.* 10:1 (1990).

    Thematic issue on "Soap Opera," edited by Gerlinde Frey-Vor; included "What Are Soap Operas and Telenovelas?" which discussed U.S., England, Latin America, France, India, and West Germany, and "Studying the Content of Soap Operas and Telenovelas."

25. *Communication Research Trends.* 10:2 (1990).

    Thematic issue on "More on Soaps," edited by Gerlinde Frey-Vor; included "The Production of Soap Operas/Telenovelas," "Soap Opera Part of National or International Media Culture?" and "Soap Operas and Telenovelas for Education and Development."

26. Cotten-Huston, A.L. "Gender Communication." In *Human Communication as a Field of Study*, edited by S.S. King, pp. 127-134. Albany: State University of New York Press, 1989.
    Gender communication analyzed through verbal and non-verbal messages.

27. Cottingham, Jane. "ISIS: A Decade of International Networking." In *Communications at the Crossroads: The Gender Gap Connection*, edited by Ramona Rush and Donna Allen, pp. 238-250. Norwood, New Jersey: Ablex, 1989.
    The development of ISIS from the mid-1970s, with discussions of *International Bulletin*, documentation center and information service, International Feminist Network, women in development project, and exchange program.

28. Dalton, Pen. "Feminist Art Practice and the Mass Media: A 'Personal Account.'" *Women's Studies International Quarterly*. 3:1 (1980), pp. 55-58.
    Male artists have moved their work to the mass media, away from the gallery, leaving female artists behind.

29. Davies, Margery. "Woman's Place is at the Typewriter: The Feminization of the Clerical Labor Force." In *Capitalist Patriarchy and the Case for Socialist Feminism*, edited by Zillah R. Eisenstein, pp. 248-266. New York: Monthly Review Press, 1979.
    Feminization of the nineteenth century office.

30. de la Luz Hurtado, Maria. *La telenovela: Mundo de realidades invertidas*. Santiago de Chile: Maria de la Luz Hurtado, 1976, 199 pp.
    The ideological nature of the world-view of melodramatic telenovelas.

31. De Lauretis, Teresa. *Alice Doesn't: Feminism, Semiotics, Cinema*. Bloomington: Indiana University Press, 1984, 232 pp.
    Feminist and other theories used in looking at feminism and cinema. By the same author and press: *Technologies of Gender: Essays on Theory, Film and Fiction* (1987, 160 pp).

32. Dervin, Brenda. "The Potential Contribution of Feminist Scholarship to the Field of Communication." *Journal of Communication*. Autumn 1987, pp. 107-120.
    How and why there can be or should be more feminist scholarship for women aiming to work in communications.

33. *Development Communication Report*.
    Among issues numbered 40 through 54, the following appeared: "Women, Communication, and Primary Health Care," No. 54, p. 11; "Video: A Development Tool for Women," No. 53, p. 4; "Radio Improving the Status of Women in Nepal," No. 41, p. 5.

34. Dworkin, Andrea. *Pornography: Men Possessing Women*. London: The Women's Press, 1981.

35. Eakins, B.W. and R.G. Eakins. *Sex Differences in Human Communication.* Boston: Houghton Mifflin, 1978, 217 pp.

   Chapters deal with cultural and genetic differences between the sexes; power, sex, and talk; talk -- structure and models -- and communication between the sexes; sex patterns in sound; ways language deals with sexes differently, and sex and sex differences in nonverbal communication.

36. *Estudios sobre las culturas contemporaneas.* February 1988.

   Thematic issue on the telenovela included articles on Latin America and India.

37. Fejes, Fred, ed. "Gender Studies and Communication." *Critical Studies in Mass Communication.* June 1989, pp. 195-221.

   Four review essays on the relation between the study of gender and communication. Andrea Press reviewed main features of feminist and communication theories and called for a feminist "critique"; Cathy Schwichtenberg examined British and U.S. cultural studies as an "example of work that combines an approach to communication within an overall feminist context"; Lana Rakow addressed roles of feminist scholars in the field of communication, and Fejes looked at the growing critique of the gender system by male scholars.

38. *Framework.* No. 2, 1976.

   Includes "Lina Werthmuller and Entertainment" and "The International Convention of Women in the Cinema."

39. Gallagher, Margaret. "Feminism, Communication and the Politics of Knowledge." Paper presented at International Communication Association, Honolulu, Hawaii, May 23-27, 1985, 22 pp.

   From a feminist perspective, very little research within critical research paradigms has questioned the "basic assumptions, conventional wisdom, media myths and the accepted way of doing things" that permeate gender relations.

40. Gallagher, Margaret. "Parallels and Paradoxes of Women and the NWICO." *Media Development.* February 1984, pp. 2-6.

   The direction of change in international and national policies, especially in regard to communication and economics, remains a male monopoly.

41. Gallagher, Margaret. "Women and NWICO." In *Communication for All: The Church and the New World Information and Communication Order*, edited by Philip Lee, pp. 77-99. Maryknoll, New York: Orbis, n.d.

   Literature reviewed relating to "Women's Status and the Role of Information," "Communicating the Status of Women," "Women's Status and Communication Systems: Structural Relationships," "Global Issues," and " Women and the Composition of Knowledge, Information, and Communication."

42. Gallagher, Margaret. "Women and the Cultural Industries." In *Cultural Industries: A Challenge for the Future of Culture*, pp. 78-95. Paris: Unesco, 1982.

   Worldwide characteristics of women's relationship to cultural industries, the socialization process and media images of women, functional roles and media's portrayal of women, women working in media, the relation between media women and the media output, the impact of media portrayals of women, and media portrayals and the social reality of women.

43. Gallagher, Margaret. "Women and the Mass Media: Industrialization and Development." *Educational Broadcasting International*. December 1979, pp. 148-152.

   The representation of women in mass media, women's employment trends, attitude changes, and the social climate internationally.

44. Gallagher, Margaret. "Women and the Media World." *Isis International Bulletin*. No. 18, 1981, pp. 4-7.

   Extracted from author's *The Portrayal and Participation of Women in the Media* (Institute of Educational Technology, The Open University, UK, 1979). The status of women in media internationally, dealing with women as participants and subjects. Data from Kenya, India, Egypt, Arab States, other countries of Eastern and Western Europe, Asia, Africa, Latin America and Caribbean.

45. Gallagher, Margaret. "Women at the Centre and the Periphery of International Communication." In *Communication and Social Development: A Fundamental Human Right*, edited by Paul Ansah. London: CSCC/World Association for Christian Communication, 1985.

46. Geist, Kathe. "Report on the Hawaii International Film Festival 1988." *Asian Cinema*. 4:1/2, 1988-89, pp. 22-24.

   Synopsis of papers presented, most with family themes: Indian women film directors, "video mom," family and films in Korea, China, USA, and the Philippines.

47. *Gender and Mass Media Newsletter*. No. 10, Nov. 1989.

   Includes abstracts of papers presented at Ninth Nordic Conference on Mass Communication Research in Borgholm, Sweden; gender roles in Norwegian advertising; images of women in 19th century Swedish newspaper; a simplistic theory of women and news; defining the image of women in Norwegian newspapers; feminine strategies in journalism; women and the news. Other reports on conferences on gender and new information technologies, woman/man in text and reading, women in China. Presents proposal to International Association for Mass Communication Research for a new section on sex roles and mass media; article on broadcast regulation and sex-role stereotyping in U.S. and Canada; abstract of a report on women and television in Europe. Other reports on the changing face of U.S. newsrooms, pay and power gap for U.S. media women, the British code of practice on sexism, and Canadian sex-role stereotyping guidelines.

48. Guida alla Mostra Internazionale dei Cartoonists. Rapallo, Italy: 1976.

   Includes: Chantal Mareuil, "La Femme dans la Bande Dessinée"; Maria-Grazia Perini, "Sexus Sequior"; and Mort Walker, "Do Women Have a Sense of Humor?"

49. Henley, Nancy M. *Body Politics. Power, Sex, and Nonverbal Communication.* Englewood Cliffs, New Jersey: Prentice-Hall, 1977.
    Body language is not "composed only of messages about friendship and sex; it is *body politics* also." Author's concerns with women's issues reflected.

50. International Association for Mass Communication Research. Congress. Prague, Czechoslovakia. August 1984. [Summary in *Sex-Roles within Massmedia Newsletter.* November 1984.]
    Sessions of working group on "Sex Roles and the Mass Media" included: Addy Kaiser, "Who is News? Sex Roles in Dutch Newspapers -- in Photos and in Text"; Lies Jansen, "A Look Behind the Scene in Dutch Broadcasting"; Angela Spindler-Brown, "Transforming Television: Feminist Experience in the U.K."; Marian Flick, "Journalists and Their Role in the New Women's Movement: An Interview Study of Norwegian Journalists"; Oya Tokgöz, "Sex-Role Differences Among Children in Interpreting the 'Selling Intent' and the 'Persuasive Intent' of Television Commercials in Turkey"; Vibeke Pedersen, "The Male Gaze and Female Strategies"; Barrie Gunter, "Television Viewing and Perceptions of Women and Men on Television and in Real Life"; Marta Hoffman, "Gender Advertisements in Hungary"; Ila Pathak and Amina Amin, "Ahmedabad Women's Action Group"; Margaret Gallagher, "Communication, Control and the Problem of Gender," and Else Jensen, "Video and Sex-Specific Socialization."

51. International Association for Mass Communication Research. Congress. New Delhi, India. August 1986. [Summary in *Sex-Roles within Massmedia Newsletter.* December 1986.]
    Sessions of working group on "Sex Roles and Mass Media" included: Leela Rao and M.N. Vani, "A Cultural Enigma -- Portrayal of Women in Indian Television"; Prabha Krishnan, Anita Dighe, and Purnima Rao, "Affirmation and Denial -- Sex Roles Patterns on Delhi's Doordarshan"; S.R. Joshi, "Participation of Women in Higher Decision Making Levels of Doordarshan -- The Television Authority of India"; Tannis MacBeth Williams, "The Portrayal of Sex Roles on Canadian and U.S. Television"; Uta Meier, "Masculinity and Feminity [sic] in Television Drama"; Addy Kaiser, "If Room at the Press-Table -- An Inquiry into the Formal and Informal Position of Female Journalists at Dutch Daily Newspapers"; Liesbet Van Zoonen, "Rethinking Women and the News"; Else Jensen, "Mass Media and the Cultural Life of Young Girls"; H. Leslie Steeves, "Feminism, Communication and Development: Complementary Goals in the Context of East Africa," and Charles Okigbo, "Male-Female Differences in Perceptions of Media Professionalism."

52. International Women's Tribune Center. *Guide to "Forward-Looking Strategies."* New York: International Women's Tribune Center, 1988.
    Guide to strategies developed at the United Nations' Third Conference on Women, Nairobi, 1985. Decisions concerning media and communication that governments agreed to.

53. *Isis International Bulletin.* Rome.
    No. 2, October 1976, "Women in the Daily Press"; No. 16, 1981, "The Feminist Press in Western Europe"; No. 18, 1981, "Women and the Media"; No. 24, 1982, "Women and New Technology"; No. 27, 1983, "Women and Visual Images"; No. 28, 1983, "International Women and New Technology Conference."

54. *Isis International Bulletin.* No. 18, 1981.

   Thematic issue on "Women and the Media" includes: Margaret Gallagher, "Women and the Media World," pp. 4-7; Manushi Collective, "The Media Game," pp. 7-13; "Images of Women in Indian Films," pp. 14-15; Magaly Pineda, "Telenovelas: Just Entertainment," pp. 16-18; Adriana Santa Cruz and Viviana Erazo, "Media as Manipulation," pp. 18-22; "Liberated Women in Television Serials," pp. 22-24; Roxanne Claire, "Women and Pornography," pp. 24-25; Marilee Karl, "Alternative World Communication," pp. 26-29; "Real Alternatives: Women Organizing in Media," pp. 30-36; "Resources," pp. 36-39. The Spanish edition of the Bulletin (*Isis Boletín Internacional*), No. 4, 1980, carried the theme, "Mujeres y Medios de Comunicación." Besides some of the above articles, others were included that dealt specifically with Latin America.

55. *Isis International Bulletin.* No. 27, June 1983.

   Thematic issue on "Women and Visual Images" includes: "An Interview with Margarethe Van Trotter," p. 5; "Women in Film," p. 7; "Nora the Filmmaker," p. 9; "The Celluloid Image," p. 10; "Video in the Village," p. 12; "What Does the Term Women's Films Mean to You?" p. 13; "Claude's Circus: A Modern Fairy Tale in Three Parts," p. 14; "Lesbians and Films," p. 16; "Audiovisual Resources," p. 17.

56. Jelinkova, L. "Women and Media: 1985: End of the U.N. Decade for Women." *Democratic Journalist.* June 1985, p. 25.

   The world conferences of the U.N. relative to women; includes role of media.

57. *Journal of Film and Video, The.* Spring, 1985.

   Thematic issue on "Sexual Difference" includes: Gaylyn Studlar, "Visual Pleasure and the Masochistic Aesthetic," pp. 5-27; Marcia Landy, "The Narrative of Conversion and Representations of Men in the Italian Pre-War Cinema," pp. 27-40; Ellen Seiter, "The Political Is Personal: Margarethe Von Trotta's Marianne and Juliane," pp. 41-46; Charlotte Delorme, "On the Film Marianne and Juliane by Margarethe Von Trotta," pp. 47-52; Ruth Perlmutter, "Rear Window: A 'Construction Story,'" pp. 53-65, and Patricia R. Zimmermann, "Good Girls, Bad Women: The Role of Older Women on Dynasty," pp. 66-74.

58. *Journal of Film and Video, The.* Fall, 1987.

   Thematic issue on "Spectatorship, Narrativity, and Feminist Revision" includes: Linda Mizejewski, "Women, Monsters, and the Masochistic Aesthetic in Fosse's Cabaret," pp. 5-17; Karen Hollinger, "'The Look,' Narrativity, and the Female Spectator in Vertigo," pp. 18-27, and Gorham A. Kindem, "Norway's New Generation of Women Directors: Anja Breien, Vibeke Lokkeberg, and Gorham A. Kindem," pp. 28-42.

59. Kaplan, E. Ann. *Women and Film: Both Sides of the Camera.* London: Methuen, 1983. 272 pp.

   The "controlling power of the male gaze as it works to relegate women to absence, silence and marginality." Four films analyzed to show how women have been represented by Hollywood; case studies of independent women's films and the work of U.S., French, German, and British filmmakers, as well as the work of one Third World director.

60. Kaplan, E. Ann. *Psychoanalysis and Cinema*. New York: Routledge, 1989. 256 pp.

    These fifteen essays demonstrate the vitality and variety of psychoanalytic film criticism, as well as the crucial role feminist theory has played in its development. Among films discussed are "Duel in the Sun," "The Best Years of Our Lives," "Now, Voyager," "Marnie," "Three Faces of Eve," "Tender is the Night," "Pandora's Box," "Secrets of the Soul," "Adynata," and the works of Jacques Tourneur (director of "The Cat People" and other features). The contributors are: Laura Mulvey, Anne Friedberg, Mary Ann Doane, Claire Johnston, Deborah Linderman, Raymond Bellour, Kaja Silverman, E. Ann Kaplan, Janet Walker, Janet Bergstrom, Linda Peckham, Yvonne Rainer, and Guy Rosolato.

61. Kaplan, E. Ann, ed. *Regarding Television. Critical Approaches*. Frederick, Maryland: University Publications of America, 1983.

    Includes Robert Allen, "On Reading Soaps: A Semiotic Primer"; Charlotte Brunsdon, "Crossroads: Notes on Soap Opera," and Tania Modleski, "The Rhythms of Reception: Daytime Television and Women's Work."

62. Karpf, Anne. "Women and Radio." *Women's Studies International Quarterly*. 3:1 (1980), pp. 41-54.

    The state of women and radio from the perspectives of programming, ownership, and international efforts to make radio more responsive to feminist movements.

63. Klenicki, Ana. R. and Deborah Ziska. "The Need for Increased Participation and Utilization of Mass Media by Women." Paper prepared for NGO Pre-Nairobi Conference Consultation, Vienna, 1984.

64. Knight, Annette. *A Women's Studies Select Bibliography (with a Third World Emphasis)*. St. Augustine, Trinidad: University of West Indies, The Women and Development Studies Group, 1988. 81 pp.

    Small section on mass media.

65. Kramarae, Cheris, ed. *Technology and Women's Voices: Keeping in Touch*. New York: Routledge and Kegan Paul, 1988. 246 pp.

    Women's talk as part of the "technological environment," contending that technological progress has an important impact on women's communication. Includes M.L. Bentson, "Women's Voices/Men's Voices: Technology as Language," pp. 15-28; A. McKay, "Speaking Up: Voice Amplification and Women's Struggle for Public Expression," pp. 187-207.

66. Krichmar, Albert, et. al. *The Women's Movement in the Seventies: An International English-Language Bibliography*. Metuchen, New Jersey: Scarecrow Press, 1977. 891 pp.

    More than 8,600 items concerning women's status in nearly 100 countries, arranged by continent and subject, including sexism in textbooks, affirmative action, and negative images of women in literature and media.

67. Lefanu, Sarah. *Feminism and Science Fiction*. Bloomington: Indiana University Press, 1989.

Themes and individual writers on feminism and science fiction.

68. Limbacher, James L. *Sexuality in World Cinema*. 2 vols. Metuchen, New Jersey: Scarecrow Press, 1983. 1,535 pp.

69. Lindsay, Beverly, ed. *Comparative Perspectives of Third World Women: The Impact of Race, Sex and Class*. New York: Praeger, 1980.

   Includes: Nora Jacquez Wieser, "Ancient Song, New Melody in Latin America: Women and Film," pp. 179-199; Johnetta B. Cole, "Women in Cuba: The Revolution within the Revolution," pp. 162-178; Gail P. Kelly, "The Schooling of Vietnamese Immigrants: Internal Colonialism and its Impact on Women," pp. 276-296.

70. Longreen, Hanne, Birgitte Tufte, Else F. Jensen, and Vibeke Pedersen. "From the Introduction of the Conference Report." *Sex-Roles within Massmedia Newsletter*. December 1986, pp. 8-9.

   Papers presented at the "Women and Electronic Mass Media" conference in Copenhagen, April 1986. Themes treated were the role of feminist women in media research and the development of media research on depiction of women, women as electronic media consumers, and the position of women in media institutions. Includes U.S., Canadian, Swedish, Danish, South American, English, Norwegian, and Italian perspectives.

71. McRobbie, Angela. "The Politics of Feminist Research: Between Talk, Text and Action." *Feminist Review*. October 1982, pp. 46-57.

   Women must exploit their skills, not disguise them, and must study communication, their own and that of others.

72. Martin, Michèle. "Capitalizing on the 'Feminine' Voice." *Canadian Journal of Communication*. September 1989, pp. 42-62.

   Sources of "gender differentiation in cultural practices within the capitalist production of communication"; topics include feminist studies in communication, the art of talking over the telephone, the voice of "authority," and voicing their silence. The issue of women's voices relative to communication is important.

73. Martineau, Barbara Halpern. "Paris/Chicago: Women's Film Festivals 1974." *Women and Film*. 2:7 (1975), pp. 10-27.

   Fourteen short articles on problems and possibilities of women's film festivals: female stereotypes, lesbian/straight conflicts, women's vision, social commentary film, and revolutionary filmmaking.

74. Mattelart, Michèle. "Women and the Cultural Industries." *Media, Culture and Society*. 4:2 (1982), pp. 133-151.

   Topics of "Everyday Life, the Media and Women's Reality," "Invisible Work," "The Exception Confirms the Rule -- Adventure Consecrates Routine," "On the Consumer Process," and "Where Pleasure Poses a Problem." Appendix summarized the French serial, "Les Amours des Années Folles."

75. Mattelart, Michèle. *Women, Media and Crisis. Femininity and Disorder.* London: Comedia, 1986. 123 pp.

    The changing role of women in Western and Third World societies; the impact of the women's movements and women and media. Economic crises cannot be understood in isolation from a moral and political crisis centering around femininity and the family. The role of media is analyzed throughout, especially in chapters on media and women's reality, women as consumers, information versus fiction, and the media and Chile's revolutionary crisis. An advisor to the Allende government before the 1973 coup, the author spoke from first-hand experience.

76. *Media Development,* London. 2 (1984).

    Thematic issue on "Women and Media" includes: "Cosmetics Changes for Women and Media," p. 1; Margaret Gallagher, "Parallels and Paradoxes of Women and the NWICO," pp. 2-6; Marjorie T. Carty, "Women Challenging the Status Quo of Mass Media," p. 7-10; Marlene Cuthbert, "'Woman Day a Come': Mass Media and Development in the Caribbean," pp. 18-21; Marcy Amba Oduyoye, "A New Community of Women and Men in Africa," pp. 25-28; Elsa Tamez, "La mujer que complicó la historia de la salvación," pp. 28-33; "Full Equality for Women in Communication and Society," p. 34; Margaret Gallagher, "Bibliography on Women and Media," p. 36.

77. *Media Report to Women.*

    A sampling of articles from 1973 to 1989 includes: "Feminist Journalism," May 1973, p. 3; "Sexism in the Country's Largest Newspaper, the New York Daily News," January 1974, p. 11; "Women Relative to Men in TV Commercials: A Screen Actors Guild Study," March 1975, p. 6; "How Would a Woman Shoot a Story Differently Than a Man?" April 1975, p. 5; "'Branching Out' -- New Canadian Magazine for Awareness of Feminine Culture," August 1975, p. 7; "Children Watching Public TV Are Being Taught That Girls Have Limited Roles," January 1976, p. 4; "Image of Women in the Media," p. 8, "June Arnold Notes Language Writing Changes in Women's Press," p. 10, "How Are News Decisions Made and by Whom," p. 7, "Movie Shows Men Cutting up Women's Bodies," p. 1, all April 1976; "New Paper -- Hudson Valley Women's Times: 'Little Known, but Vital, Information,'" August 1976, p. 7; "Fran Hosken Reports on Women's Communication Networks in Africa," September 1977, pp. 12-13; "Comision interamericana de mujeres (CIM): Resolution Passed at the Seminar on Mass Communication Media and Their Influence on the Image of Women, Santa Domingo, August 1977," October 1977, pp. 1, 4-5; "A Medium To Let Women Speak for Themselves," April 1979, p. 10; "Women in East Africa Media were 1% of Total; Now are 5% to 10%," January 1980, p. 6; "Feminist Journalism," April 1980, p. 4; "Radio Women's Show Follows Feminist Principles," October 1981, p. 11; "124 Attend World Feminist Media Conference . . .," May 1982, pp. 1-2, 7; "Shere Hite Sues Nobile $15 Million for His Campaign of Attacks on Her Integrity," pp. 1, 15, " *N.Y. Times* Women's Caucus Goes Back to Court to Get Compliance with 1978 Agreement," pp. 1, 14, "Minority Preference in Broadcast Ownership Should Also Apply to Women: A.W.R.T.," pp. 3, 13, "Newspaper Editors Indicate They Don't Believe the Rape Myths," pp. 10-11, "New *Women's Review of Books*," p. 16, all in March-April 1984; "'Preying Mantis' Women in Actions to Break Silence and Start Public Discussion on Pornography," pp. 1, 10, "West German Women's Monthly Magazine, *Courage*, To Become a 24-Page Weekly Newspaper," p. 1, "Australian Minister and Shadow Minister Cooperate on Guidelines for Positive Portrayal of Women in Media," pp. 1, 9, "Journalism Schools are 2/3rds Women," p. 3, "Jean Wilson Hears Women Expected To Rise," pp. 4-5, "Media Increasingly Show Violence to Women," p. 6, "Sandy Boucher on How Media's Massive Outreach Shapes Us," p. 7, "Eleanor Bader Sees Us Once Again Facing Mass Media's Outreach for Its 'Feminine Mystique' of the 1950s," p. 8, "Rediscovery of Sadie Miller, Photojournalist Who Made *Leslies' Weekly* Famous and Successful," p. 12, "Women's Bookstores," pp. 14-15, all in March-April 1984; "For Women Politically, Today is Different from the 1920s in Two Significant Media Respects," July-August 1984, p. 16; "Women Monitor Fairness of Ferraro News Coverage," pp. 1,5, "Joan Tobin Describes How Media Try To Turn Word 'Feminist' Into Something Bad," p. 7, "Dr Carol Oukrop Survey Brings Women's Rape Reporting Concerns Together with Editors' Viewpoints," pp. 12-13, all September-October 1984; "Few Women in Media in Eastern Countries," p. 7, "Nurses Begin 'Media Watch' for Accurate Professional Portrayal Instead of Media's Romantic and Sexual Image," p. 11, "Paper in Japan Uses World Periodical Exchange Network To Spread Word of Victory Against Sexist Ad," p. 12, all November-December 1984; "Progress of Women into Top Editor Positions on U.S. Dailies Is at Standstill in 1984," pp. 1, 6, "Critical Support Medium: Their Own Newspapers Needed for Women of Color to Speak for Themselves," 5; "IWTC Sees 'Wealth of Information' in Women's Publications Worldwide," p. 6, "Diane Silver Study Shows High Ranking Women State Officials Received Nearly Equal News Coverage as Men," p. 9, all January-February 1985; "Face Pornographers' Unequal First Amendment Rights, Women Work To Be Heard," pp. 1, 7, "Less Than Quarter of Page One By-Lines Are by Women; *USA Today* Highest in Study; *New York Times* Worst," p. 3; "ISIS *Journal* Goal is Building Communication Among Women Internationally; Links Third World Networks," p. 5; *New York Times* Tells Women To Use Free Speech, But Reports It Erroneously When They Do," p. 7, "Massive Pornography Comes to Israel in Last Five Years, Reports Judith Bat-Ada in *Lilith*," pp. 9-10, *SAGE* Is Scholarly Journal for Black Women To Speak for Themselves," p. 15, all May-June 1985; "Women's International News Service Forms To Obtain News Coverage of World Conference of Women," pp. 1, 3, "Women's Movement Publishers Meet in 70 Workshops," p. 4, "Marlene Sanders: White Male Private Club Atmosphere Also Operates in Media To Hold Women Down," p. 6, "Male Media View of Women Results in Propagation of Myths, Stereotypes Denigrating Women: Caryl Rivers," p. 7, "Marvel Comics Gave the Task to Male Artists," p. 7, all July-August 1985; "Press Coverage of World Conference of Women To Be Examined in International Study," p. 1, "90% of TV News Directors are Men, 82% in Radio," p. 7, "*License To Rape* Notes Power of Mass Media When and If They (Not We) Choose To Cover Our Issues," p. 8, "New Videotape, *Still Sane*, Celebrates Women in Focus' First Ten Years as Feminist Arts and Media Centre," p. 9, "Dr. Helen R. Wheeler's First Prize Media-and-Women Course," p. 10, "Womyn's Braille Press Records First Books, Periodicals," p. 11, all September-October 1985; "Journalism Schools Asked To Adapt to Different World Reality for 'New Majority' of Women Going into Media," pp. 1, 7-8, "Co-Anchor Christine Craft Asks Supreme Court to Review Circuit Court Reversal of Her Two Jury Awards," pp. 3, 6, all January-February 1986; "World Women Leaders Meet to Discuss 'Media' as a Women's Issue," pp. 1, 3, Dorothy Jurney, "Women Top Editors, 11.1% in 1984, Rise Only to 11.7% in 1985," p. 7, all March-April 1986; "For 5 Days WEFT Will Be Totally Women's Radio," p. 1, "Thesaurus is First Step to New Media for Women's Experience and Information Using Latest Technology," pp. 1, 4, "Women at ABC Negotiating for Equal Treatment," p. 3, "Men in

Broadcasting Had To Be Forced To Change, Marlene Sanders Observed from the 1950s to the '80s," p. 6, "Women of Color 'Speak Out' on Discrimination in Media," p. 7, "No Higher Percent of Women Newsmaker Photos in *Time*, *Newsweek* in 1980 Than in 1940 or 1960," p. 7, "Publishing Industry's Monopoly on Means of Reaching Mass Audience Affects Black Women Writers," p. 8, "Japanese Ad Agency Has All-Woman Subsidiary," p. 9, "Women Journalists in India Send Team To Investigate Women's Question in Crisis Situations in the News," p. 9, "Cartys Report Women in Top Level Puerto Rico Media Jobs," pp. 9-10, "*Belles Lettres* Is New Book Review Paper To Keep Up with Hundreds of Women's Books," p. 11, all May-June 1986; "Canadian Commission Takes Next Step in Plan To Eliminate Sex Role Stereotyping from Broadcasting," p. 5, "UAE Women Rising into Media Work; Now Nearly 10%," p. 6, all July-August 1986; "Low Employment, and Only 344 Women Film Directors of 7,800 DGA Members, Spark Full Page Ads," p. 4, "Swedish Broadcasting Reports Affirmative Action Progress," pp. 5, 6, "Male Monopoly of Mass Media Makes It Possible To Present Pornographers' View as Only Correct One," pp. 7-8, all September-October 1986; "FCC Sees No Greater Programming Diversity Would Result from More Minority or Women Station Owners," pp. 1, 5, "HERA Prints Names and Sex-Crime Charges," pp. 1, 4, "Fifty International Media Women Meet with U.S. Counterparts (and Each Other) on Status in the Industry," pp. 1, 3, "*Chicago Tribune* Begins 'TempoWoman' as Sunday Supplement," p. 3, "At BBC Policy-Making Level: 6 Women and 159 Men," p. 6, all November-December 1986; "Women's Movement in U.S. and Abroad Finds Its Media Outreach Enough To Counter Mass Media Manipulation," pp. 1, 7, "International Women's Network Objects to Documentaries That Omit Women's Part in Public Life," p. 5, "Unlike 1950s, Women Now Have Own Strong Media Networks To Expose Mass Media Manipulation," p. 7, "JAWS (Journalism and Women Symposium) To Continue," p. 8, "Lebanese Women Meet on Media Image," pp. 8-9, "Dorothy Jurney Sums Up 10 Years of Women in Policy-Making Newspaper Jobs; Top Editors Still 87.6% Male," pp. 9-10, "NCWW Notes TV Changes But Some Serious Inaccuracies in Portrayal of Working Women," pp. 11-12, "Diane Wyndham Paper Describes Status of Self-Regulation of Advertising Industry in Australia," pp. 12-13, "Canadian Women Save U.S. from Sexist Ads Promoting Tourism to Canada," p. 13, "Women in Publishing Are Analyzing Book Reviewing," p. 15, "Barbara Freeman: Canadian Women Journalists Organize Press Club in 1966 To Support Their Rights," p. 16, "INSTRAW Sees Communication and Networking as Key to Success of Programs for Advancement of Women," p. 18, "Icelandic Women Depend on Their Own Newspapers to Coordinate Their Political Support," p. 19, all January-February and March-April 1987; "Professors, Media, and Women Cooperate To Produce Guide for News Reporting of Sexual Assault," pp. 1, 15, "Rape Crisis Newsletter Is Sued by Assaulter for Identifying Him, Causing Him 'Emotional Distress,'" pp. 1, 15, "Third World Women Journalists Begin 'Women's Feature Service' for News Media from Feminist Perspective," pp. 3-4, "UN Radio Service Has 8 Women-and-Media Programs," p. 4, "Women in the News (WIN) Using Settlement Funds for Precedent-Setting Suits in Employment Rights," p. 6; "Women Journalists 'Severely Underrepresented' in European News; Only 1.4% of News Is on Female Issues," p. 7, "MediaWatch Study Measures Broadcast Favoring of Men Teaching Children; Men More Important Than Women," pp. 9-11, "NCWW Finds Portrayal of Older Women on TV Still Doesn't Fit Reality: 26% Are Millionaires," p. 12, all May-June and July-August 1987; "Room for Improvement, Says TV Executive," pp. 1, 4; "First Woman President of ASNE To Help Promote Women and Minorities in Media," p. 1, "Women's Feature Service Bridges Gap Between Nations," p. 3, "Veteran Journalist Marlene Sanders Reflects on 'Pioneer Days,'" p. 4, "Zambian Women Explore New Media Opportunity," p. 6, "Philippine Radio Celebrates International Women's Day," p. 7, all September 1987; "NOW Charges *Washington Post* of Non-Coverage of Events," p. 1, "European Study Indicates Portrayal of Women Related to Numbers in Media Management," p. 3, "Are Literary Women Really Ascending to Publishers' Row? *Savvy* Thinks So," p. 4, "New Study Proves Women Still Stereotyped on Primetime Television," p. 4, "Carbine Says Sale of *Ms.* to Australian Will Open New Opportunities for the Magazine," p. 4, "Argentine Women Target Sexism in TV Spots," p. 6, "Korean Women's Study on Media Portrayal Stimulates Monitoring Programs," p. 6, "Thai Women Journalists Use Survey To Demonstrate Inequality in News," p. 6, "Philippine Women's Page Editors Aim for More Issues, Less Fluff," p. 6, "Belgium Television Program Features Sexual Equality," p. 7, "China Media Women Begin Networking," p. 7, "New Magazine Proposed for Arab Women," p. 10, all November-December 1987; "$10 Million Sex Discrimination Suit Filed Against NBC Network News," pp. 1-3, "Female News Directors Are Younger, Lower Paid," p. 3, "Fewer Women in Leading Roles in This Fall's TV Season," p. 4, "Women Hold over Half of Jobs in PR, But Still Making Less Than Men," p.5, "Journalism School Research Shows Unequal Treatment for Women Faculty," p. 5, "Feminine Product Ads Not Sexist, Says Canadian Women's Organization," p. 6, all January-February 1988; "Ad Age Report Zeroes in on Problems in Marketing to Women," p. 1, "Anti-Pornography Battles Continue, with Police Help (in India), Handbooks, and Tapes," p. 2, "USIA Loses Hiring and Promotion Discrimination Case, Must Pay Damages," p. 3, "New Equity Pay Law in Ontario Will Affect Women in Newspaper Work," p. 3, "Women in Television Still Fight Uphill Battles, Says Journalist," pp. 3-4, "Women's Magazines More Intimate, Caring, and Open Than Men's, Study Shows," p. 4, "Women Writing More Front-Page News, But Not Making It, Study Says," p. 7, "Numbers Not There for Media Employment of Women, Wilson Says," p. 11, all March-April 1988; "Women J-School Heads Now Earn More, Junior Faculty Earn Less Than Men," pp. 2-3, "VP's Office Says Bush Did Not Insist That Interviewer Be Male," p. 3, "11 Media Firms Are Listed as Best Places of Employment for Women," pp. 3-4, *Washington Woman* Shareholders Set Meeting To Discuss Magazine's Fate," p. 4, "Local News Teams Double Number of Women in 10 Years, Study Shows," p. 5, "Australian Women Debate Sexual Politics in the News Media," p. 6, "Australian TV Training Fund Targets Industry Women," pp. 6-7, "Australian Notes on Women and Media," p. 7, "Asian Women Plan Media Strategy," p. 7, "Three Women Reporters Win 1988 Pulitzer Prizes," p. 9, all May-June 1988; "CBS Producer Says Women in TV Don't Experience Special Pressures," pp. 2-3, "Minneapolis Ad Agency Loses Account After Insulting Feminist Critic," p. 3, "Replication of 1972 Ad Study Shows Women's Roles Have Changed Little," p. 4, "'Tabloid TV' Finds Many Viewers among Women 18-49," p. 5, "Women Business Reporters and Editors Still Small Minority at Top Publications," pp. 6-7, "Sexism in Children's Television Results in Low Ratings, More Scrutiny," p. 7, "Canadian Groups Develop Guidelines To Eliminate Sex-Role Stereotyping," p. 7, "Canadian Report Documents Inequities For Women in Film," p. 8, "South Asian Women Formulate Plan To Counter Media Discrimination," p. 8, all July-August 1988; "Newspaper Guild Files Discrimination Complaint Against *Washington Post*," p. 1, "PR and Advertising Salaries for Women Still Lower Than Men's, Survey Shows," pp. 2, 3, "Vermont Newspaper Runs Rape Victim's Letter on Front Page," pp. 3-4, "MediaWatch Angry Over Watered-Down Language in Canadian Broadcasting Act," p. 5, "Women Athletes Challenge Coverage by *Sports Illustrated* and NBC Sports," pp. 5-6, "Washington Press Club Foundation Traces Careers of 60

Journalists," pp. 6-7, "St. Louis Study Shows Women Are Underrepresented in TV Management," p. 8, all September-October 1988; "WICI National Meeting Shows Continuing Conflict Between Career, Personal Life," pp. 1, 3, "Minority Women Trail Minority Men, White Women and Men in Newspaper Industry," p. 4, "APME Report: Journalists Find It Harder To Balance Family, Career," p. 6, "Women's Bylines in Short Supply on Washington Post's Front Page," p. 5, "Younger Women, Older Men Taking Anchor Slots at TV Networks, Local Stations," pp. 6-7, "NOW To Analyze Coverage of Women by Major Dailies," p. 7, all November-December 1988; "Newscaster Wins Pay After Quitting Over Being Object of On-Air Sex Jokes," p. 1, "TV Portrayal of Teen Girls Lacks Realism, Depth, NCWW/WOW Study Says," pp. 1-2, "*Advertising Age* Picks 100 Best and Brightest Ad Women," pp. 3-4, "Gender Analysis of Ads in Men's, Women's Magazines Shows Women To Be Subordinate," p. 4, "Portrayal of Women by European Media Still 'Excessively Traditional,'" pp. 4-5, all January-February 1989; "Pay Gap/Power Gap Still Apparent for Media Women, Studies Show," pp. 3-5, "Woodhull: If Press Doesn't Cover You, The Perception Is That You Don't Exist," pp. 5-6, "Pan Am Cancels Ad in Response to Charges of Sexism, Vulgarity," pp. 7-8, "On 15th Birthday, New Words Is Highest-Grossing Women's Bookstore in U.S.," p. 8, all May-June 1989; "Philadelphia TV Stations Are Targets of Petitions To Deny Relicensing," p. 1, "'Seven Sisters' Magazines Continue To Lose Readers to Newcomers," p. 3, "More Than 1,000 Women Found for Class Action Settlement from USIA," pp. 3-4, "Annual 'Visibility' Study of TV Reports Shows Women Lagging," p. 6, "To Break Radio's 'Glass Ceiling': Take Risks, Be Tough, Play Golf," p. 7, all September-October 1989.

78. *Medie/Kultur*. 4 (1986).

    Devoted to women and electronic media, this 240-page issue includes papers from the Nordic/International Conference on Women and Electronic Mass Media, held in Copenhagen in 1986: Sissel Lund, "Mass Media Fail To Inform Women"; Birgitte Tufte, "Girls and Electronic Mass Media -- Something That Could Really Happen"; Else Fabricius Jensen, "The Cultural Life of Young Girls"; Vibeke Pedersen, "The Male Gaze and Feminine Strategies -- On the Literary Program 'Bazar'"; E. Ann Kaplan, "Feminist Criticism in Television Studies"; Michèle Mattelart, "Sex Differences in Program Policy -- On the South American Soap Operas: Telenovelas"; Charlotte Brunsdon, "Women Watching Television"; Gioia Longo, "Aerobic Hostesses in Talk Shows -- The Commercial Influence in State Television"; Gertrude J. Robinson, "Mass Media Research on Women -- The Feminist Paradigm in Historical Perspective"; Helen Baehr, "The Impact of Feminism on Media Studies -- Just Another Commercial Break?" Margaret Gallagher, "Ten Years of Equal Opportunity: Myth and Reality in Women's Employment in Broadcasting"; Ulla B. Abrahamsson, "Strategies and Results of Equality of the Sexes Program in Swedish Broadcasting," and Michèle Mattelart, "The Genre 'Telenovela' and the Female Notion of Time."

79. *Medium*. 8:12 (1978).

    Thematic issue on "Medien und Frauen, Frauen und Medien," pp. 1-45, includes topics: "Feministische Presse," "Frauenzeitschriften," "Frauengruppen im Rundfunk," "Blick über Grenzen: USA, Italien, CSSR," "Hörfunkprogramme für Frauen," "Frauenfilm: feministischer Film," "Eine gewöhnliche Tagesschau," and "Frauenbilder im Fernsehprogramm."

80. Modleski, Tania. "Femininity as Mas(s)querade: A Feminist Approach to Mass Culture." *High Theory/Low Culture: Analyzing Popular Television and Film*, edited by Colin McCabe, pp. 37-52. New York: St. Martin's Press, 1986.

   Although women have spoken their points of view, they have not fully been heard.

81. Newland, Kathleen. *The Sisterhood of Man*. New York: W. W. Norton, 1979. 247 pp.

   The changing roles of women, with a section on mass media.

82. Noelle-Neumann, Elisabeth. "The Spiral of Silence: A Theory of Public Opinion." *Journal of Communication*. Spring 1974, pp. 43-51.

   The willingness to speak out varies with sex, age, occupation, and residence; women and lower-income groups speak less. By the same author: *The Spiral of Silence: Public Opinion -- Our Social Skin*. Chicago: University of Chicago Press, 1984.

83. Nordic/International Conference on Women and Electronic Mass Media. Copenhagen, Denmark. April 1986. *Report*. Aalborg, Denmark: Mediekultur, Universitetscenter, 1986. 240 pp.

   Includes Sissel Lund, "Mass Media Fail To Inform Women"; Birgitte Tufte, "Girls and Electronic Mass Media -- Something That Could Really Happen"; Else Fabricius Jensen, "The Cultural Life of Young Girls"; Vibeke Pedersen, "The Male Gaze and Feminine Strategies -- On the Literary Program 'Bazar'"; E. Ann Kaplan, "Feminist Criticism in Television Studies"; Michèle Mattelart, "Sex Differences in Program Policy -- On the South American Soap Operas: Telenovelas"; Charlotte Brunsdon, "Women Watching Television"; Gioia Longo, "Aerobic Hostesses in Talk Shows -- The Commercial Influence in State Television"; Gertrude J. Robinson, "Mass Media Research on Women -- The Feminist Paradigm in Historical Perspective"; Helen Baehr, "The Impact of Feminism on Media Studies -- Just Another Commercial Break?" Margaret Gallagher, "Ten Years of Equal Opportunity: Myth and Reality in Women's Employment in Broadcasting," and Ulla B. Abrahamsson, "Strategies and Results of Equality of the Sexes Program in Swedish Broadcasting."

84. Oehler, Carolyn Henninger. "Rediscovering Community Through Awareness of Language." *Media Development*. February 1984, pp. 22-24.

   At the heart of the call for non-sexist language is the growing recognition of linguistic, historical, and theological biases against women.

85. Prevratilova, Gabriela. "Women and Media: Problems Persist." *Democratic Journalist*. November 1985, pp. 9-10.

   Proceedings of the 1985 Nairobi Conference in relationship to women and media; big mass media of the world did not play a positive role relative to women and their problems between 1976 and 1985.

86. *Quarterly Review of Film Studies.*
    Has had special sections on women and film, such as Beverle Houston's "Feminist and Ideological Criticism."

87. *Quest: A Feminist Quarterly.* Fall 1976.
    Special issue on "Communications and Control," pp. 3-10, 31-40.

88. "Resources." *Isis International Bulletin.* No. 18, 1981, pp. 36-39.
    Lists of organizations, newsletters, books, and other sources on women and the media.

89. "Resources and Networks." *Isis International Women's Journal.* December 1984, pp. 122-132.
    List, by country, of organizations and media dealing with various facets of the woman's movement, including media and women.

90. Roberts, Helen, ed. *Doing Feminist Research.* London: Routledge and Kegan Paul, 1981.
    Includes A. Oakley, "Interviewing Women: A Contradiction in Terms," pp. 30-61, and Dale Spender, "The Gatekeepers: A Feminist Critique of Academic Publishing," pp. 186-202.

91. Robinson, Gertrude J. "Feminism and Communication Studies." *Sex-Roles within Massmedia Newsletter.* November 1988, pp. 22-23.
    Critique of four approaches (liberal feminism, radical feminism, traditional Marxism, and socialist Marxism) to the study of women.

92. Robinson, Gertrude J. "The Female/Male Equation in Broadcasting: Future Perspectives." Unpublished paper, ASCRIT Convention, Montreal, Canada, 1986.

93. Robinson, Lillian S. "Dwelling in Decencies: Radical Criticism and the Feminist Perspective." In *Sex, Class and Culture*, edited by Lillian S. Robinson, pp. 310-342. Bloomington: Indiana University Press, 1978.
    This critical analysis applies to Eisenstein's theories of cinema but not to his films.

94. Root, Jane. *Open the Box: About Television.* London: Comedia, 1986. 128 pp.
    The social context and history of prejudices against television ("the box"); the role of television in family life and ideas of good and bad television.

95. Rush, Ramona R. "From Silent Scream to Silent Scheme: The Role of Women in International Communications." In *International Communication. In Whose Interest?* edited by Graeme Osborne and Margaret Madrigal, pp. 489-452. Canberra: University of Canberra, Centre for Communication and Information Research, 1989.
    Many works cited to show women are relatively silent in many spheres.

96. Rush, Ramona and Donna Allen, eds. *Communications at the Crossroads: The Gender Gap Connection.* Norwood, New Jersey: Ablex, 1989. 316 pp.

   Broken into parts on "Women and the Communication Process," "The Media Model: 'Fits' for Women," "Issue-Raising Globally and Locally: A Flow-Keeping Agenda," and "Crossroads Ahead!" Twenty-three contributions on women and media in U.S., Norway, Latin America, and Caribbean; topics such as women and hi-tech media, fiction writing, international networking, telecommunication, and feminist studies and women's media.

97. Sandler, Joanne. *It's Our Move Now: A Community Action Guide to the UN Nairobi Forward-Looking Strategies for the Advancement of Women.* New York: International Women's Tribune Centre, 1987. 229 pp.

   Strategy implementation for the advancement of women, developed by the 1985 UN World Conference in Nairobi; the longest section deals in part with media and communications.

98. Saunders, Eileen. "Teaching Media and Gender." *Canadian Journal of Communication.* Winter 1985, pp. 35-50.

   How a critical perspective can inform the construction of a course in media studies centered around the gender issue; selected books and articles to use in such a course.

99. *Sex-Roles within Massmedia Newsletter.* August 1981.

   Summary of research on women and media by eight scholars from West Germany, Sweden, Hungary, U.S., Canada, and Norway; report on the equality project of the Swedish Broadcasting Corporation.

100. *Sex-Roles within Massmedia Newsletter.* March 8, 1982.

   Includes "Working Party on Women in Broadcasting: Report to the Radio Telefís Eireann Authority -- April 1981," p. 5; reviews; summaries of work by 18 researchers from Hungary, Holland, India, Turkey, U.S., Lebanon, Finland, Jamaica, Argentina, Brazil, Colombia, Australia, Korea, Japan, Pakistan, and Sri Lanka.

101. *Sex-Roles within Massmedia Newsletter.* March 8, 1983.

   Brief reports from conferences and abstracts of research on gender portrayal on TV in Japan, Korea, the Philippines, U.S., and Great Britain; Danish TV newscasts in a woman's perspective; implicit gender messages to teenaged TV viewers in Denmark; semiotics as a tool for qualitative analysis of sex-role stereotypes; women in Swiss mass media; working women of West Deutsche Rundfunk; Australian women in advertisements; and attitudes towards roles of women in Arabic mass media.

102. *Sex-Roles within Massmedia Newsletter.* December 1983.

   Summary of papers presented at a Nordic Conference on Mass Communication Research, dealing with women and media in Finland, Norway, and Denmark; abstracts of research projects on images of women in Finnish youth magazines, women in community radio in Europe, images of men and women in Japanese TV, role of women in Danish and Swedish TV, women's role in the New

World Information and Communication Order, and a bibliography for women in media research.

103. *Sex-Roles within Massmedia Newsletter.* November 1984.
Reports of conferences of International Association for Mass Communication Research, European Seminar on Women and Media, and Indian Council for Communication, Training, and Research; abstracts of research projects on media and sex roles in India, journalists and their role in the New Women's Movement, the picture of women on Hungarian TV, youth radio and sex-roles, the male gaze and female strategies, the equality group of Swedish TV, sex role differences among Turkish children in interpreting TV commercials, and women working in Norwegian broadcasting.

104. *Sex-Roles within Massmedia Newsletter.* November 1985.
Reports of EBU Workshop on Sex-Roles (Seville), seminar on women and television (Brussels), consultation on "Women and the Media, Strategies for Change" (Lusaka), world conference to review and appraise achievements of the UN Decade for Women (Nairobi), and Nordic conference (Denmark); abstracts of research projects on accessibility of women to mass media in Zambia, sex-roles in Dutch drama productions and talk shows, and action research in Swedish local radio.

105. *Sex-Roles within Massmedia Newsletter.* December 1986.
Reports from conferences of "Women and Electronic Mass Media" in Copenhagen, and International Association for Mass Communication Research in New Delhi; other articles on women and the media of India; a number of book, report, and article reviews; other materials dealing with women and the media in U.S., Europe, Asia, Hungary, Canada, Latin America, Korea, Australia, Sweden, and more.

106. *Sex-Roles within Massmedia Newsletter.* November 1987.
Reports of conferences and abstracts of papers on Dutch feminist television shows, women in Dutch broadcasting, women's presence in Spanish radio and television, television aesthetics and the representation of women, gender images in Japanese TV drama, television and discrimination against women in Japan, Canadian broadcasting and women, Australian bibliography on women and media.

107. *Sex-Roles within Massmedia Newsletter.* November 1988.
Abstracts of papers of the International Association for Mass Communication Research conference in Barcelona: women in Danish family magazines; Spain's *Hymsa* magazine; wedding photographs in Hungary; images of women in Pakistani media, Madonna character, Indian TV, Nigerian press, and Indian advertising; feminists sexuality in British TV advertising; advertisements and Norwegian feminism; "porn-vertising"; women media administrators in Turkey; individual aspirations of Swiss women journalists; professional socialization of Dutch feminist journalists; Dutch TV melodrama and gender; gender role biases in Indian television; journalism, gender and German youth; feminism and communication studies; women and alternative media in Tanzania; women and communication in West Africa; and the portrayal of women workers on Peruvian TV. Shorter abstracts of proceedings dealing with women and media at

Asia/Pacific Regional seminar on Women and the Media, World Association for Christian Communication, Asia-Pacific Developmment Centre, Asian Women Journalists Seminar, National Women's Studies Association, and Association for Education in Journalism and Mass Communication. '88 Tokyo Symposium on Women abstracts included Japanese women in television, representations of women in Philippine television, women and Philippine media, women in Israel's broadcasting media, Indian women in mass media, women in U.S. media, and Swedish women and broadcast equality.

108. Shimanoff, S.B. "Sex as a Variable in Communication Research 1970-1976: An Annotated Bibliography." *Women's Studies in Communication*. 1 (1977), pp. 8-20.

109. Silverman, Kaja. *The Acoustic Mirror: The Female Voice in Psychoanalysis and Cinema*. Bloomington: Indiana University Press, 1988. 288 pp.
     The intersection of feminism, film theory, and psychoanalysis.

110. Smith, Dorothy. "A Peculiar Eclipsing: Women's Exclusion from Man's Culture." *Women's Studies International Quarterly*. 1 (1978), pp. 281-295.
     Women's exclusion from the communicative work of society, the silencing of women.

111. Sofia, Zoe. "Masculine Excess and the Metaphysics of Vision: Some Problems in Feminist Film Theory." *Continuum*. 2:2 (1989), pp. 116-128.
     The focus is "primarily psychoanalytic and content-oriented, dealing with specific organ-symbols and metaphors which are excessive to the conventional representations of Man as a phallocentric, rational, unitary-speaking subject."

112. Spender, Dale. *Man Made Language*. Boston: Routledge and Kegan Pual, 1980. 250 pp.
     For women, language is man-made. Literature on language and sex role socialization surveyed to see how language structures reality. Also by same author: *Men's Studies Modified: The Impact of Feminism on the Academic Disciplines*, Oxford: Pergamon Press, 1981.

113. Spender, Lynne. *Intruders on the Rights of Men: Women's Unpublished Heritage*. London: Pandora Press, 1983.

114. Unesco. *Communication in the Service of Women: A Report on Action and Research Programmes, 1980-1985*. Paris: Unesco, 1985. 170 pp.
     Document prepared for World Conference to Review and Appraise the Achievements of the United Nations Decade for Women, Nairobi; based on replies of 95 governments. The various parts explore Unesco activities concerning women and communication between 1980 and 1985; officials, government perceptions of change in media content, employment, and policy concerning women; and developments and research in the area of women and communication.

115. Unesco. *Mass Media: The Image, Role and Social Conditions of Women. A Collection and Analysis of Research Materials*. Paris: Unesco, 1979. 78 pp.

Divided into sections of "The Image of Women in Mass Media," "The Professional Status of Women in Mass Media," and "Conclusions, Implications, Recommendations" and subheadings of regions or continents.

116. Unesco. *Unesco Publications Concerning the Status of Women: Annotated Bibliography for the Period 1965-1985.* Paris: Unesco, 1986. 134 pp.

    Stereotypes, textbooks, mass media, and cultural role included among topics.

117. Unesco. *World Communication Report.* Paris: Unesco, 1989. 551 pp.

    Many mentions of women and media, including Women's Community Video Group, Women's Features Service, Women's Information Network for Asia and the Pacific, Women's Radio Collective, Women in Broadcasting Technology, and Women Make Movies, Inc.; women in communication relative to Africa, the Arab States, Caribbean, Europe, Latin America, and North America; women's education through mass media in Africa, Arab States, Asia and the Pacific, Europe, North and Latin America, and the Caribbean; and women's employment in media in Africa, Arab States, Asia and the Pacific, Europe, and North America.

118. United Nations. "Influence of Mass Communication Media on the Formation of a New Attitude Towards the Role of Women in Present-Day Society." New York: United Nations Economic and Social Council Commission on the Status of Women, January 1974.

119. United Nations. "Women and the Media." *Sex-Roles within Massmedia Newsletter,* November 1985, pp. 46-49.

    Recommendations about women and media set down by an "expert" group meeting in Vienna in 1981.

120. United Nations. "Women and the Media: Report of an Expert Group Meeting." New York: United Nations, 1982. 19 pp.

121. United Nations. World Conference of the United Nations Decade for Women: Equality, Development and Peace. Copenhagen, Denmark, July 14-30, 1980. New York: United Nations, 1980.

    Papers include "Information and Communication as Development Resources for the Advancement of Women," A/CONF. 94/27; and "Programme of Action for the Second Half of the United Nations Decade for Women: Equality, Development and Peace," A/CONF. 94/34.

122. United Nations. World Conference of the United Nations Decade for Women. "International Seminar on Women and the Media." New York, May 20-23, 1980. New York: United Nations, 1980.

    Includes Conference Background Paper and National Report Submitted by Indonesia.

123. United States Congress. Committee on Foreign Relations. *Women in Development: Looking to the Future.* Hearing Before Committee on

Foreign Relations. United States Senate, Ninety-Eighth Congress, Second Session. Washington, D.C.:: U.S. Congress, 1984. 162 pp.

The roles of various sectors, including the media, in furthering the enhancement of women in the economic development of the Third World.

124. Wartella, Ellen, D. Charles Whitney, and Sven Windahl, eds. *Mass Communication Review Yearbook*. Beverly Hills, California: Sage, 1983.

Includes part on "Feminism and the Media," with contributions by Mary Ann Yodelis Smith, Gertrude Robinson, Angela McRobbie, and Thelma McCormack.

125. Wober, Mallory. "Cinderella Comes Out, Showing TV's Hits Are Its Myths." *Media, Culture and Society*. 6:1 (1984), pp. 65-71.

Review of three books on soap operas -- Dorothy Hobson's *Crossroads -- The Drama of a Soap Opera*, Muriel G. Cantor and Suzanne Pingree's *The Soap Opera*, and Mary Cassata and Thomas Skill's *Life on Daytime Television: Tuning in to Serial Drama*.

126. "Women and Representation." *Jump/Cut*. No. 29 (1984), pp. 25-48.

Twelve essays dealing with various aspects of women's representation in film and other media, including black women filmmakers and critiques of a number of films and books dealing with women. European, Puerto Rican, and other U.S. films discussed, as well as lesbianism, work in a white man's world, and "movies with women in them."

127. World Association for Christian Communications. First World Congress '89, Manila, October 15-19, 1989. Papers. London: WACC, 1989.

Includes Rita Monteiro, "Communication To Build Community Through Stri Mukti (Women's Liberation, India)"; Nancy Mwendamseke, "The Female Image in the Mass Media (of Tanzania)"; Karen Hurt, "Smashing the Mirror: The Image of Women in Mass Media (of South Africa)."

128. World Association for Christian Communication. "Women in the Media: The Beirut Consultation. Beirut, Lebanon, February 19-24, 1978." London: World Association for Christian Communication, 1978. 38 pp.

Summary of the experiences of 20 women from various cultures on the role of women in media, the responsible use of media, and the image of women; includes a presentation on women in ecumenical communications work and reports from Sweden, the Arab world, Asia, the Philippines, Caribbean, and Africa.

HISTORICAL STUDIES

129. Armatage, Kay and Linda Beath. "Women in Film." *Isis International Bulletin*. June 1983, pp. 7-8.

Traces role of women in film from 1896, incorporating examples from U.S., Soviet Union, Austria, Canada, France, and Czechoslovakia.

130. Buckmann, Peter. *All for Love: A Study in Soap Opera.* London: Secker and Warburg, 1984.
History of U.S. and British soap operas.

131. Fergus, Jan. "Women, Class, and the Growth of Magazine Readership in the Provinces, 1746-80." In *Studies in Eighteenth-Century Culture* 16, edited by O.M. Brack, Jr., pp. 41-56. Madison: University of Wisconsin Press, 1986.

132. Grilikhes, Alexandra. "Films by Women 1928-1971." *Film Library Quarterly.* Winter 1972-73, pp. 8-11, 47.
How the author started Philadelphia's first international festival of films by women in 1972. Some of the women film pioneers whose work was shown: French director Germaine Dulac, Leontine Sagan, and Marie Menken.

133. Sloan, Kay. "Sexual Warfare in the Silent Cinema: Comedies and Melodramas of Women Suffragism." *American Quarterly.* Fall 1981, pp. 412-436.
As early as 1898, silent films spoke clearly of sexual politics. A number of U.S. (and some British) films studied; a "brazen young film industry stepped without hesitation into the midst of the conflict [concerning suffrage] for both profit and propaganda."

IMAGES OF WOMEN

134. Adams, C. and R. Laurikietis. *The Gender Trap. A Closer Look At Sex Roles. Book 3: Messages and Images.* London: Virago, 1976.

135. Agardy, Susanna. "Problems with Flick's Model." *Media Information Australia.* November 1984, pp. 35-36.
Cautions that Flick's model of looking at women in electronic media should be used only with due regard to issues of context, sample, and final impression.

136. Arboleda Cueva, Esmeralda. "Women in the Media." *World Health.* June 1980, n.p.
Calls on media to portray women more positively.

137. Berckman, Edward M. "Images of Women in the Comics -- American and Chinese." In *Abstracts of Popular Culture.* Bowling Green, Ohio: Bowling Green State University, 1976(?).
U.S. comics had sexist distortion; Chinese comics defined women in relationship to society, rather than to men.

138. Betterton, Rosemary, ed. *Looking On: Images of Femininity in the Visual Arts and Media.* London: Pandora Press, 1987, 293 pp.

Images of women from a feminist view in 22 essays. Ways women in advertising, magazines, fine art, fashion, and British pornography influence commonly-held perceptions of femininity and female sexuality.

139. Binford, Mira Reym. "Half the Sky: Women's Worlds on Film." *International Development Review*. 1, 1976, pp. 37-40.

Eight documentary films showing the worlds of women in Asia, Latin America, or Africa. Seven of these had U.S. funding, and five were made by men. Contends that "while a film is not solely a function of its maker's gender, passport, or funding, these factors do influence its stance and quality."

140. Brown, Mary Ellen and Linda Barwick. "Soap Opera and Women's Culture." *Continuum*. 1:2 (1988), pp. 71-82.

What is shocking about TV soap opera is that it "makes public the domestic and affirms the centrality of talking and intimacy as positive values in women's lives." Also by the senior author: "The Politics of Soaps: Pleasure and Feminine Empowerment," *Australian Journal of Cultural Studies*, 4:2 (1987), pp. 1-25, and "Soap Opera and Women's Culture: Politics and the Popular," In *Doing Research on Women's Communication: Perspectives on Theory and Method*, edited by Kathryn Carter and Carole Spitzack, pp. 161-190, Norwood, N.J.: Ablex, 1989.

141. Christopher, R. "Holy Heroines!" *Macleans*. November 13, 1978, pp. 58-59.

Women in comics.

142. Claire, Roxanne. "Women and Pornography." *Isis International Bulletin*. No. 18, 1981, pp. 24-25.

Pornography attacked as the dehumanization of women. Includes lists of groups fighting pornography and books which explore arguments against pornography.

143. Cook, Pam and Claire Johnston. "The Place of Women in the Cinema of Raoul Walsh." In *Raoul Walsh*, edited by Phil Hardy. Colchester: Vineyard Press, 1974.

Claude Levi-Strauss theories applied to the representation of women in film.

144. Cowie, Elizabeth. "Women, Representation and the Image." *Screen Education*. Summer, 1977, pp. 15-23.

The "images of women" concept needs to be replaced with the idea of women as "signifier in ideological discourse."

145. Cutrufelli, Maria Rosa. *L'invenzione della donna -- miti e teeniche di uno sfruttamento*. Milan: Edizioni Mazzotta, 1974.

Through mass media examples from Europe and the U.S., demonstrates the "making" of women and the exploitation of such images.

146. Davies, Katherine, Julienne Dickey, and Teresa Stratford, eds. *Out of Focus: Writings on Women and the Media.* London: The Women's Press, 1987. 230 pp.

    Collection of about 40 articles providing briefings on media and women, with reference to special areas of race, age, class, sexuality, disability; discusses violence, romance, health, the domestic sphere, and images of tradeswomen, nurses, secretaries, and prominent women.

147. Derry, Charles. "Television Soap Opera: Incest, Bigamy, and Fatal Disease." *Journal of the University Film and Video Association.* Winter 1983, pp. 4-16.

148. Derryck, Vivian Lowery. "The Differential Impact of Educational Innovations on Girls and Women: Media-Based Instruction and Curriculum Revision. Phase II, Curriculum Revision as If Women Mattered." Washington, D.C.: Office of Women in Development, Agency for International Development, 1979. 16 pp.

    Curriculum revision in the formal education structure of developing countries to eliminate bias against women.

149. Dickey, Julienne. *Women in Focus: Guidelines for Eliminating Media Sexism.* London: Campaign for Press and Broadcasting Freedom, 1985.

150. Dijkstra, Bram. *Idols of Perversity: Fantasies of Feminine Evil In Fin-De-Siecle.* New York: Oxford, 1986.

    Images of a woman presented as a "sexless, mindless, helpless creature," who becomes a monstrous evil if she rejects this nature.

151. Doane, Mary Ann. "The Economy of Desire: The Commodity Form in/of the Cinema." *Quarterly Review of Film and Video.* 11 (1989), pp. 23-33.

    The cinematic image for women is "both shop window and mirror, the one simply a means of access to the other"; the female subject "of the consumer look in the cinematic arena becomes ... the industry's own merchandizing asset."

152. Eubben, M.C. and C. Vanderhaeghen. "Feminine and Masculine Stereotypes in Motion Pictures for French-Speaking Children and Adolescents." *Revue de l'institut de Sociologie.* No. 3-4 (1982), pp. 433-458.

153. Flick, Marian. "Women in Advertisements: Comments on Susanna Agardy's Views." *Media Information Australia.* May 1985, p. 44.

154. Flora, Cornelia Butler. "Changes in Women's Status in Women's Magazine Fiction: Differences by Social Class." *Social Problems.* June 1979, pp. 558-569.

    Images of women in magazine fiction compared between middle-class and working-class women's magazines, 1970 and 1975.

155. Flora, Cornelia Butler. "Maids in the Mexican Photonovel." *Studies in Latin American Popular Culture.* 4 (1985), pp. 84-94.

　　Twenty percent of 150 Mexican *fotonovelas* included maids. Only in Mexico, did *fotonovelas* show maids in major roles; maids as heroines or villainesses were absent in *fotonovelas* of Italy, Spain, Colombia, and Venezuela.

156. Flora, Cornelia Butler. "The Passive Female: Her Comparative Image by Class and Culture In Women's Magazine Fiction." *Journal of Marriage and the Family.* August 1971, pp. 435-444.

　　With passivity indicators drawn from a sample of women's magazine fiction of working and middle-class audiences in the U.S. and Latin America, upheld the concept of female passivity. Latin American fiction stressed passivity more than that of U.S.

157. Gabor, Mark. *The Illustrated History of Girlie Magazines. From National Police Gazette to the Present.* New York: Harmony Books, 1983. 181 pp.

　　"Girlie" magazines of the nineteenth century discussed but concentration is on the 1960s through 1970s. Examples from Europe and Asia.

158. Gallagher, Margaret. *The Image Reflected by Mass Media: Stereotypes. b) Images of Women. Images of Women in the Mass Media.* Paris: Unesco, International Commission for the Study of Communication Problems, n.d., ca. 1980. 27 pp.

　　How radio, television, film, press, and books portrayed women throughout the world. Poorly. "Media treatment of women is at best narrow and at worst manipulative or discriminatory"; news values consider women and their problems unnewsworthy; in entertainment content, women appear as "passive, dependent creatures with few concerns outside the domestic or the romantic"; as the target of much advertising, women are manipulated and patronized; women are seen as subordinate to men.

159. Gaspar-Ruppert, Walburga. "The Media and the 'Nairobi' Future Strategies for the Advancement of Women." *Osterreichische Zeitschrift fu soziologie.* 14:2 (1989), pp. 68-72.

　　Summary of the results of a worldwide United Nations study; mass media tended to present traditional stereotypes and to reinforce opposition to change.

160. Gilly, Mary C. "Sex Roles in Advertising: A Comparison of Television Advertisements in Australia, Mexico, and the United States." *Journal of Marketing.* April 1988, pp. 75-85.

　　All three reflected stereotypes of male-female roles.

161. Gunter, Barrie. *Television and Sex Role Stereotyping.* London: John Libbey, 1986. 89 pp.

　　Examination of the description of the sexes in TV adult and children's programming. Divided into four parts: portrayals of the sexes on TV, perceptions of the sexes by children and adults, social effects of TV and sex stereotyping, and counter-stereotyping through television. By the same author and Mallory Wober:

"Television Viewing and Perceptions of Women's Roles on Television and in Real Life," *Current Psychological Research*. 2 (1982), pp. 277-288.

162. Halonen, Irma Kaarina. "Women and The News." *Gender and Mass Media Newsletter*. November 1989, p. 8.

    Strategies about the construction of news from women's viewpoints.

163. Hamlin, John E. "Who's the Victim: Women, Control, and Consciousness." *Women's Studies International Forum*. 11:3 (1988), pp. 223-233.

    Press coverage of rape cases; criticism of media for sensationalizing certain rapes; myths about rape.

164. Jaddou, Liliane and Jon Williams. "A Theoretical Contribution to the Struggle Against the Dominant Representations of Women." *Media, Culture and Society*. April 1981, pp. 105-124.

    The two dominant theoretical frameworks to study media and women -- derivatives of content analysis and structuralist psychoanalysis -- have proved inadequate. Use of content analysis has "identified imbalances in the number and types of representation of women in media output" but not located the nature and origins of such imbalances. The structuralist approach has a seriously flawed theoretical framework.

165. *Journal of Communication*. Winter 1976.

    Thematic symposium on "Explicit Sex -- Liberation or Exploitation?" includes: Don D. Smith, "The Social Content of Pornography," pp. 16-24; John Stauffer and Richard Frost, "Male and Female Interest in Sexually-Oriented Magazines," pp. 24-30; John C. Carlin, "The Rise and Fall of Topless Radio," pp. 31-37; Marie Shear, "Free Meat Talks Back," pp. 38-39; and Victor Bachy, "Danish 'Permissiveness' Revisited," pp. 40-43.

166. Karl, Marilee. "Alternative World Communication." *Isis International Bulletin*. No. 18, 1981, pp. 26-29.

    General research findings relating to media presentation of women in industrialized and developing countries: they are nearly absent from the "important" news; very little media coverage is given to women's work, needs, and accomplishments; media perpetuate stereotypes of women; media distort and ridicule when women step out of their traditional roles, and women lack access to information.

167. Kleberg, Madeleine. "Sex Roles With the Focus on Women -- Current Research." *The Nordicom Review*. 2, 1984, pp. 18-21.

    A summary of papers presented at the 1984 conference of the International Association for Mass Communication Research, with the theme of sex roles in mass media.

168. Kong, A.C. "Sex Roles on Television: A Comparison of Eastern and Western Media." *International Journal of Inter-Cultural Relations*. 3 (1979), pp. 437-445.

169. Kotz, Liz. "Striptease East and West: Sexual Representation in Documentary Film." *Afterimage.* October 1989, pp. 13-18.

170. Kuhn, Annette. *The Power of the Image: Essays on Representation and Sexuality.* London: Routledge and Kegan Paul, 1985. 146 pp.

   Two essays reprinted from *Wide Angle* and *Camerawork* and three original ones analyzing many films by exploring how they create cultural images. Discusses films and photographs, glamour, pornography, crossdressing, censorship, and presentation of sexuality in VD propaganda features.

171. Laner, Mary R. "Make-Believe Mistresses: Photo-Essay Models in the Candy Sex Magazines." *Sociological Symposium.* Spring 1976, pp. 81-98.

   A sample of "candy-sex" magazines, focusing on the occupations of photo-essay models. Despite publishers' lip service, the magazines present models in "truncated occupational terms."

172. Loree, M. "L'image de la femme dans la publicite nord-américaine et française." In *Femmes, sexisme et sociétés,* edited by Andree Michel, pp. 133-145. Paris: Presses Universitaires de France, 1977.

   A comparison of women's images in U.S. and French advertising.

173. MacBride, Sean, et al. *Many Voices, One World.* London/New York/Paris: Kogan Page/Unipub/Unesco, 1980.

   Final report of the International Commission for the Study of Communication Problems deals with women and media in only a few pages. Women's rights are discussed on pages 189-190 and 266. Concludes that: "The achievement of full equality for women is a matter of justice and of human rights; it is also necessary so that society can mobilize all its forces for social progress and especially for efforts of development. The world cannot afford to waste the great resources represented by the abilities and talents of women. This is the thought that should be constantly in the minds of those responsible for decisions in communication."

174. Maykovich, M.K. "Comparison of Soap Opera Families in Japan and the United States." *International Journal of Sociology of the Family.* Autumn 1975, pp. 135-149.

175. *Media Information Australia.* February 1989.

   Issue includes four articles on women and media. Roberta Perkins' "'Wicked Women or Working Girls': The Prostitute on the Silver Screen" (pp. 28-35) claimed prostitute characters in European and U.S. movies reveal scientific and social images of real prostitutes; J.H. Bell and U.S. Pandey's "Gender-Role Stereotypes in Australian Farm Advertising" (pp. 45-59) reported on a content analysis of advertisements featuring men and women in 42 numbers of *The Land,* the nation's leading farm magazine; Patricia Mann's "Portrayal of Women in Advertising" (pp. 50-55) looked at women as portrayed in European advertisements, and Diana Wyndham's "The Portrayal of Women in Advertising: Surveys and Forum" (pp. 58-60) reported on a 1988 Australian forum on the topic. Other articles included, Suzanne Keeler's "Non-Sexist Ads? We've Only

Just Begun" (pp. 56-57) and Henry Mayer's "Women's Portrayal in Advertisements: OSW Forum: More Responses" (p. 64).

176. Newland, Kathleen. "As Others See Us." *Development Forum*. January-February 1979, p. 11.
    Women rarely appeared in "hard" news, and when they did, their appearance and family status were reported. Using the example of the Latin American soap opera and *fotonovela*, "Simplemente Maria," the author said that magazines often prescribe "appropriate" behavior for women; some women's periodicals such as Japan's *Watashi Wa Onna*, address themselves to collective awareness and common problems of women.

177. Newton, Barbara J. and Elizabeth B. Buck. "Television as Significant Other: Its Relationship to Self-Descriptors in Five Countries." *Journal of Cross-Cultural Psychology*. September 1985, pp. 289-312.
    Sex-role values of parents and their children, as well as portrayal of sex-roles on television in Japan, Korea, Philippines, U.S., and Britain.

178. Peeradina, Saleem. "Women in World Cinema." *Indian Journal of Communication Arts*. April 1976, pp. 15-20.
    Concentrates in Western and some Indian films. An edited reprint from *Fulcrum*.

179. Perloff, Richard M., Jane Delano Brown, and M. Mark Miller. "Mass Media and Sex-typing: Research Perspectives and Policy Implications." *International Journal of Women's Studies*. May-June 1982, pp. 265-273.
    New directions for, and policy implications of, research on mass media and sex roles.

180. Putnam, Linda L. "In Search of Gender: A Critique of Communication and Sex-Roles Research." *Women's Studies in Communication*. Spring 1982, pp. 1-9.
    Sex-role research critiqued; a call for alternative feminist media to deflect people's attention from cultural and institutional structures that maintain sexual differences.

181. Rihani, M. *Development as if Women Mattered: An Annotated Bibliography with a Third World Focus*. Washington, D.C.: Overseas Development Council, 1978. 137 pp.
    Includes 287 study citations, mostly from 1976-77, divided into categories, among which are women's informal social and communication networks and image of women in the mass media.

182. Root, Jane. *Pictures of Women: Sexuality*. Winchester, Massachusetts: Unwin and Hyman and Pandora Press, 1984. 128 pp.
    Analysis and critique of the commercialization of women's bodies. Edited volume by the same author: *Women's Film and Video List*, London: British Film Institute, 1986.

183. Ross, Andrew. "*Miami Vice*: Selling in." *Communication.* 9:3/4 (1987), pp. 305-334.

    Sexual politics in the British magazine, *Tomorrow: Politics and High Fashion*, and the U.S. television show, "Miami Vice."

184. Rupp, Leila J. *Mobilizing Women for War. German and American Propaganda, 1939-1945.* Princeton, New Jersey: Princeton University Press, 1978. 243 pp.

    The images of women in Nazi ideology ("mother of the *volk*") and in the U.S. (housewife) before the war; their changes to "Rosie the Riveter" or "Mrs. Casey Jones" in the U.S. and to soldiers' mothers or wives who supported the war through work outside the home in Germany. Also see her "Woman's Place Is in the War: Propaganda and Public Opinion in the U.S. and Germany, 1939-1945." In *Feminist Frontiers*, edited by L. Richardson and V. Taylor. Reading, Ma.: Addison-Wesley, 1983.

185. Sargent, Alice G. *Beyond Sex Roles.* New York: West Publishing Co., 1977. 475 pp.

    Includes parts on "Toward Androgyny" and "Awareness of Sex-Role Stereotypes"; among the latter is Nancy Henley and Barrie Thorne, "Womanspeak and Manspeak: Sex Differences and Sexism in Communication, Verbal and Non-Verbal," pp. 201-218.

186. "Struggling for Space." *Isis International Women's Journal.* December 1984, pp. 26-31.

    The results of surveys done in France and Japan on stereotyped images of women and anti-feminine prejudices in children's books. Much stereotyping of sex roles, femininity and masculinity, mother's role, and women's occupations.

187. "The Celluloid Image." *Isis International Bulletin.* June 1983, pp. 10-11.

    Stereotyping of women in the male-monopolized film industry for over 50 years.

188. *Unesco Courier*, Paris. July 1980.

    Thematic issue on women includes Margaret Gallagher, "Male Chauvinism in the Mass Media," pp. 20-21, 24-25.

WOMEN AS AUDIENCE

189. Ang, Ien. *Watching Dallas: Soap Opera and the Melodramatic Imagination.* New York and London: Methuen, 1985. 136 pp.

    Points to the soap opera's contributions to the regulation of women's lives. Last chapter is a feminist analysis.

190. Bahi, Sushil. "The New Woman Consumer." *Solus.* July 1989, pp. 13-15.

191. Bartos, Rena. *Marketing to Women Around the World.* Boston: Harvard Business School Press, 1989. 320 pp.

    Applies her "New Demographic Framework" to ten countries of North America, Asia, Latin America, and Europe to help marketers target female consumers.

192. Bartos, Rena. *The Moving Target: What Every Marketer Should Know about Women.* New York: Free Press, 1982. 304 pp.

    How advertisers streamline appeals for women -- where women are and where they are likely to be.

193. Bartos, Rena. "Women and Advertising." *International Journal of Advertising.* 2:1 (1983), pp. 22-45.

194. Clift, Elayne. "Women, Communication, and Primary Health Care." *Development Communication Report.* Summer 1986, p. 11.

195. Colle, Royal D. *Reaching Rural Women: Case Studies and Strategies.* New York: United Nations Social Development Centre, 1977. 62 pp.

196. De La Roche, Catherine. "That Feminine Angle." *Penguin Film Review.* January 1949, pp. 25-34.

    The difference of appeal to men and women in film audiences.

197. Doane, Mary Ann. "Film and the Masquerade -- Theorising the Female Spectator." *Screen.* 23:3/4 (1983), pp. 74-84.

198. Epstein, T. Scarlett. "Women's Access to Rural Services." *Assignment Children.* April-June 1977, pp. 27-38.

    Access to rural services; the need to use mass media to emphasize rural problems.

199. Jensen, Else. "Mass Media and the Cultural Life of Young Girls." *Sex-Roles within Massmedia Newsletter.* December 1986, pp. 23-24.

    The development of youth follows a pattern determined by both class and sex; this pattern influenced by the use of TV and video, is different for girls than for boys.

200. Kippax, Susan. "Women as Audience: The Experience of Unwaged Women of the Performing Arts." *Media, Culture and Society.* January 1988, pp. 5-21.

    The ways in which women's experiences of art are generated within their social lives.

201. Kokohiwa, Milda. *Reaching for Rural Women: The Promise of Radio Mass Campaigns.* East Lansing, Michigan: Michigan State University Educational Information Center, College of Education, 1978.

202. Mattelart, Michèle. *Les femmes et les industries culturelles.* Paris: Développement Culturel: Dossier Documentaire 23, 1981.

History and present situation of women as prime targets for advertisers and marketers of consumer goods; women were expected to adopt the images media developed for them.

203. Mattelart, Michèle. "Notes on Modernity." In *Communication and Class Struggle, Vol. 1,* edited by A. Mattelart and S. Siegelaus, pp. 158-170. New York: International General, 1979.

Myths of modernity and newness as they are related in advertising and women's magazines; examples of consumer massification. States that women are at the center of strategies for action concerning modernity.

204. Miles, Virginia. "The New Woman, Her Importance to Marketing." *International Advertiser.* Fall 1971, pp. 13-16.

205. Reimann, Helga. "The Influence of Mass Media on Women in Developing Areas." *Communications.* 7:2/3 (1981), pp. 215-225.

Critical of traditional sociological and communication researchers for neglecting the consideration of women in their work. To study the influence of the mass media on women, one must realize the interrelations of the development stage of a society, the status of women therein, and the corresponding communication structure of this society.

206. Seiter, Ellen, et al., eds. *Remote Control: Television Audiences and Cultural Power.* London/New York: Routledge, 1989.

Includes: Dorothy Hobson, "Soap Operas at Work"; Ellen Seiter et al., "Don't Treat Us Like We're Stupid and Naive: Towards an Ethnography of Soap Opera Viewers"; Robert C. Allen, "Bursting Bubbles: 'Soap Opera,' Audiences, and the Limits of Genre"; Charlotte Brunsdon, "Text and Gender," and Tamar Liebes and Elihu Katz, "On the Critical Abilities of Soap Viewers."

207. Stromquist, Nelly P. "Women and Literacy: Promises and Constraints." *Media Development.* 1 (1990), pp. 10-13.

Women and illiteracy in Africa, Asia, Latin America, and the Caribbean.

208. Stuart, Martha. "Social Change Through Human Exchange: Listening Moves People More Than Telling." In *Communications at the Crossroads: The Gender Gap Connection,* edited by Ramona Rush and Donna Allen, pp. 177-192. Norwood, New Jersey: Ablex, 1989.

Her strategies and techniques in development communication; experiences mainly from Indonesia.

209. Wiio, Osmo A. and Linda McCallister. "Sex and Communication Uncertainty: A Comparison of American European Organizations." Helsinki: Department of Communication, University of Helsinki, 1981. 32 pp.

The effect of sex on organizational communication; questions such as "Are communication variables that affect women different from communication variables that affect men?" "Are communication needs of women different?" "What situational variables are most affected by sex and communication?"

210. "Women and Literacy: Yesterday, Today, and Tomorrow" Symposium. Hasselby Slott, Sweden, June 8-10, 1989.

    Papers included: Agneta Lind, "Literacy: A Tool for the Empowerment of Women"; Swarna Jayaweera, "Women and Literacy: The Sri Lanka Experience"; Francoise Caillods, "Women's Literacy for Development: A Brief Overview of The Situation Today"; Samora Gaborone, "Gender and Literacy: The Case of Botswana," and Aikael Kweka, "Women in Literacy Programmes and Underdevelopment: The Case of Tanzania."

WOMEN PRACTITIONERS

211. Bate, Barbara and Anita Taylor, eds. *Women Communicating: Studies of Women's Talk*. Norwood, New Jersey: Ablex, 1988. 336 pp.

    Original inquiries into women communicating with other women, a neglected field. Deals with recording, film, women in sports, business, family, clinics, drama, guild, research teams, feminist humor, feminist bookstore, and implementing feminist principles in the National Film Board of Canada Studio D.

212. Brown, Mary Ellen. "The Politics of Soaps: Pleasure and Feminine Empowerment." *Australian Journal of Cultural Studies*. 4:2 (1987).

    In U.S. and Australia.

213. Cadman, Eileen, Gail Chester and Agnes Pivot. *Rolling Our Own: Women as Printers, Publishers and Distributors*. London: Minority Press Group, 1981. 120 pp.

    Provides inspiration and guidance to women who wish to print and publish. Sections include women writers and feminism, women in publishing, self publishing, pamphlets, newsletters, periodicals, illustrators, typesetting, printing, distribution, sexism in the radical press, and useful resources and organizations. Provocative topics dealt with such as women printers and unions and why work with men.

214. Carty, Marjorie, T. "Women Challenging the Status Quo of Mass Media." *Media Development*. February 1984, pp. 7-10.

    Based on a survey of the numbers of women working in the media in different countries and the work they do.

215. Chen, Anne M. Cooper. "Can a Woman Deliver the News?" *Media and Values*. Spring 1990, pp. 18-19.

    Abstracted from author's *Television's Invisible Women: A Five-Nation Study of Anchors, Reporters and Correspondents*, dealing with Colombia, Jamaica, Japan, Sri Lanka, and the U.S.

216. *Cineaste*.

    Various issues have included women filmmakers: Agnes Varda, 8:3; Anne-Clair Poirier, 10:3; Molly Haskell, 11:3; Bonnie Sherr Klein, 12:3; Ann Hui, 13:2; "Sexual Politics in Fassbinder and Pasolini," Margarethe von Trotta, 13:4; Maria

Luisa Bemberg, 14:3; "Feminist Heroines," 14:4; Donna Deitch, Agnes Varda, 15:4; Julie Christie, 15:2; Lizzie Borden, 15:3; "Who's Who of Women Filmmakers," 16:1/2; Patricia Rosema, Larissa Shepitko, 16:3; "Hollywood's Women's Films," 17:1.

217. *Cine Cubano*. (Havana)
Contains many articles about women in the film industry, mostly non-Cuban. On France's Agnes Varda, articles appeared in 2:6, 1962, (pp. 13-65; pp. 66-67), September 1965 (pp. 16-26), and July 1963 (pp. 1-8); U.S.'s Jane Fonda, August-October 1967 (pp. 45-46) and July-December 1970 (pp. 63-65), Greta Garbo in May-August 1969 (pp. 72-77), Marilyn Monroe, 1962 (pp. 18-20); Cuba's Norma Martinez in May 1965 (pp. 23-24); Czechoslovakia's Dana Smutna in June 1963 (pp. 28-32) and Karla Chadimova in March 1965 (pp. 5-10) and June 1963 (pp. 33-37); Greece's Melina Mercouri in August-October 1967 (pp. 45-46); England's Julie Christie in March 1967 (pp. 29-31), Natasha Parry in June 1961 (pp. 48-49), Vanessa Redgrave in September 1966 (p. 1), and April 1967 (pp. 24-27); Soviet Union's Natalia Bondarchuk in June-December 1972 (pp. 40-43), as well as Marguerite Duras in August-October 1967 (pp. 65-69), Rita Montaner in 1962 (pp. 38-40), Violeta Parra in January-March 1972 (pp. 166-169), among others.

218. *Cinema India - International*. January-March 1986, pp. 29-50.
With theme of "Hail Women Directors of the World!" profiles Tizuka Yamasaki (Brazil), Mary McMurray (Britain), Micheline Lanctot (Canada), Zhang Nuanxin (China), Margarethe von Trotta (FRG), Agnes Varda (France), Iris Gusher and Evelyn Schmidt (GDR), Ann Hui (Hong Kong), Vijayanirmala, Suprabha Debi, Prema Karath, Sai Paranjpye, Parvati Ghosh, Bhanumathi, Aparna Sen (all India), Lillian Cavani (Italy), Sangeeta (Pakistan), Susan Seidelman (USA), and Larisa Shepitko (USSR). Same issue includes "Women of World Film-makers at London Fest," pp. 60-62; "*Bandhana* Advocates Women's Lib" (India), p. 76; "Woman Film-maker (Clare Downs of Britain) Forges Ahead," p. 88; "Love and Hatred Have the Same Roots" (on Helma Sanders-Brahms of Germany), p. 90; "Best Film of the Year" (on Agnes Varda of France), p. 91.

219. "Claude's Circus. A Modern Fairy Story of Filmland in Three Parts." *Isis International Bulletin*. June 1983, pp. 14-17.
Satirization of the plight of feminist directors attempting to sell their TV programs at the MIPTV in Cannes.

220. Cooper, Anne M. "Television's Invisible Women: A Five-Nation Study of Anchors, Reporters, and Correspondents." Paper presented at Association for Education in Journalism, Portland, Oregan, July 2-5, 1988. 28 pp.
Visibility and participation of women working in U.S. television compared with those in Japan, Sri Lanka, Colombia, and Jamaica. In all five countries, no women reported on any of the five biggest stories of the week; the number of women on the major U.S. network newscasts declined between 1979 and 1986.

221. Cornwell, Regina. "Maya Deren and Germaine Dulac: Activists of the Avant-Garde." *Film Library Quarterly*. Winter 1971-72, pp. 29-38.
Women directors within the avant-garde -- Maya Deren of the U.S. and Germaine Dulac of France. Also see: Wanda Bershen, "Departmental Paper:

The Films of Maya Deren," Master's thesis, Yale Univeristy, 1971; "Germaine Dulac," in *Anthologie du Cinema. IV*, edited by Jacques Charriere, pp. 6-7, Paris: 1968.

222. Dawson, Bonita. "'Fly Me to Toronto ... Oberhausen ... and Sinking Creek.' Our Correspondents Report: Women and Film International Festival '73 in Toronto." *Film Library Quarterly*. Fall 1973, pp. 36-38.

    A number of films shown at the Toronto festival reviewed, such as the works of Canadians, Mireille Dansereau, Sylvia Spring, and Claudia Weill; Julia Alvarez of Colombia; Joyce Weiland, and others.

223. Dewey, Langdon. "Three Lady Iconoclasts." *Film*. Spring 1970, pp. 20-21.

    The work of Directors Agnes Varda, Vera Chytilová, and Mai Zetterling.

224. Eddings, Barbara. "Women in Broadcasting." *Women's Studies International Quarterly*. 3:1 (1980), pp. 1-13.

225. "Empowering Women Through Media." *Group Media Journal*. 7:2 (1988).

    Under this theme, the Sonolux periodical featured seven women who discussed the need for alternative channels of communication "which lay open unjust social structures." Contributors from Nigeria, England, Peru, Tanzania, Kenya, and the Philippines wrote on "Women and NWICO," "The Role of Women in Media," "Women and Religion," and "Women as Producers and Communicators." Includes interviews with women communicators and a reading list.

226. Feldman, Joseph and Harry Feldman. "Women Directors." *Films in Review*. November 1960, pp. 9-12.

    Sketches of the careers of Dorothy Arzner (U.S.), Margarita Barskaya (USSR), Leni Riefenstahl (Germany), Leontine Sagan (Germany), Germaine Dulac (France), Wanda Jakubowska (Poland), and Ida Lupino (U.S.).

227. *Film Library Quarterly*. Winter 1971-72.

    Thematic issue on "Women in Film" includes: Janet Sternberg, "Revealing Herself," pp. 7-13; Lillian Gerard, "Belles, Sirens, Sisters," pp. 14-21; Lora Hays, "From the Frying Pan to the Trim-bin," pp. 22-25; "Man's World, Woman's Place," pp. 26-28; Regina Cornwell, "Maya Deren and Germaine Dulac," pp.29-38; "Madeline Anderson on 'I Am Somebody,'" pp. 39-41; Madeline Friedlander, "Struggle for Equality," pp. 42-45; "Films by and about Women -- Reviews," pp. 46-54. The latter reviews films illuminating aspects of the women's movement, problems frequently encountered by women, and "creative, forceful, original female personalities."

228. Gallagher, Margaret. *Unequal Opportunities: The Case of Women and the Media*. Paris: Unesco, 1981. 221 pp.

    Studies throughout the world on the relationship between women and the media reviewed. Invariably, women were underrepresented and did not have many central roles.

229. Gallagher, Margaret. *Women and Media Decision-Making: The Invisible Barriers.* Paris: Unesco, 1987. 121 pp.

Women's employment, sex discrimination, women's status, and other issues in television and radio of India, Ecuador, Nigeria, Egypt, and Canada.

230. Gentile, Mary C. *Film Feminisms: Theory and Practice.* Westport, Connecticut: Greenwood Press, 1985. 210 pp.

A rejection of the view that feminist film theory differs from and is in opposition to traditional film theories. Author introduces alternate views while analyzing differences and similarities. Part One investigates interrelation of ideology and subjectivity as evidenced in the work of Jacques Lacan and Louis Althusser. Part Two applies the theory to works of women film directors, such as Marta Meszaros, Helke Sauder, Yvonne Rainer, and Marlene Gorris. Author's Ph.D. dissertation: "Reel Alternatives: Feminist Film Theory and Practice," State University of New York at Buffalo, 1983, 204 pp.

231. Grewe-Partsch, Marianne and Gertrude J. Robinson. *Women, Communication and Careers.* Munich: K. G. Saur Verlag, 1980.

232. Halliday, Jon, ed. *Sirk on Sirk: Interview with Jon Halliday.* London: Secker and Warburg, 1971.

233. Hardy, Phil, ed. *Raoul Walsh.* Edinburgh: Edinburgh Film Festival, 1974.

Includes Pam Cook and Claire Johnston, "The Place of Women in the Cinema of Raoul Walsh."

234. Heck-Rabi, Louise. *Women Filmmakers: A Critical Reception.* Metuchen, New Jersey: Scarecrow Press, 1984. 408 pp.

Guide to films of major women directors and producers and bibliography on women's films. Eleven filmmakers discussed, including Germaine Dulac, Alice Guy Blache, Ida Lupino, Shirley Clarke, Dorothy Asner, and Agnes Varda.

235. Hirschfeld, Mary. "Women Journalists Elsewhere." *The Quill.* September 1973, pp. 23-25.

Important women journalists in Hong Kong, Iran, Korea, Chile, and Peru, with background on each.

236. *Isis International Bulletin.* September 1982.

Thematic issue on "Women and New Technology" includes: "Editorial," pp. 4-6; "Women and Electronics," p. 7; "The Micro Revolution," pp. 8-10; "How It Is Done," p. 11; "Overview of Women Industrial Workers in Malaysia," pp. 12-18; "Health and Profit in the Electronics Industry," p. 19; "Maquiladoras," p. 20; "Growing Resistance," pp. 21-22; "Technology and Employment: Women's Job Displacement," pp. 23-26; "Is Even Patriarchy Not Sacred?" p. 27; "Domestic Technology -- Liberator or Enslaver?" pp. 28-29; "International Solidarity," p. 30; "Women's Network on Global Corporations," pp. 30-31; "Pushing Our Own Buttons: The Feminist Computer Technology Project," pp. 32-33; "Are Computers Feminist?" p. 34; "Feminist Groups on New Technology," p. 35; "Groups Working on Multinationals," pp. 35-37; and "Selected Literature Resources," p. 38.

237. Kay, Karyn and Gerald Peary, eds. *Women and the Cinema: A Critical Anthology*. New York: E. P. Dutton, 1977. 464 pp.

    Forty-five articles and film reviews about women's contributions to the culture. Among contributions is E. Ann Kaplan, "Interview with British Cine-Feminists," pp. 393-406.

238. Knightley, Phillip. *The First Casualty*. London: Harcourt, Brace, Jovanovich, 1975. 465 pp.

    A number of profiles of women war correspondents, from Winston Churchill's aunt, Lady Sarah Wilson, the *Daily Mail*'s Boer War reporter, to Madeleine Riffaud, the only woman correspondent with the Vietcong.

239. McGillivray, Katherine. "Women in Advertising." In *Mother Was Not a Person*, compiled by Margaret Anderson, pp. 71-73. Montreal: Content Publishing Ltd. and Black Rose Books, 1972.

240. *Matrix*.

    Sampling of the early 1970s included: Marlene Sanders, "From the Networks -- An Overnight Success -- After 16 Years of Hard Work," Fall 1971, pp. 10-11, 23; Mary A. Gardner, "The Press Women of Chile," Winter 1972/73, pp. 6-7, 22-23; Jerry Knudson, "Press Women of Bolivia," Winter 1973-74, pp. 8-10; Ethel L. Payne, "Minority Women in Communication," Spring 1974, pp. 4-5; Hilda Avilade O'Farrill, "Mexico's Media Women," Summer 1974, pp. 10-11, 22; Jackie Lapin, "A New Generation of Sportswriters in the Press Box," Summer 1975, pp. 5-9; "A Winding Path (on Marguerite Cartwright)," Fall 1975, p. 10; Julie Blakely, "Copley Hopes To Share Attitude," Fall 1975, pp. 6-7, 15; Nancy Popkin, "Plan for Parity," Fall 1975, pp. 19-25; "Success with Wit and Ambition," Fall 1975, p. 11; Blythe Foote Finke, "UN Women Correspondents," Winter 1975, pp. 18-20; and Jean E. Collins, "Kathleen McLaughlin, Journalist: An Oral History," Spring 1976, pp. 19-21, 29.

241. Mattelart, Michèle. "Mujer, politica, cultura, los desafíos de los años 80." *Media Development*. 2, 1984, pp. 14-17.

    The problems of women and their opportunity to speak through mass communication in the construction of a different society.

242. *Millennium*.

    Includes extensive interviews with women film personalities, such as Laura Mulvey (No. 4/5) and Carolee Schneemann (No. 7/8/9).

243. Mrazkova, Daniela. "Woman with a Camera: Leena Saraste." *Democratic Journalist*. October 1987, pp. 27-29.

    Leena Saraste, known for her photographs of the massacre committed by Israelis on Lebanon refugee camps in 1982.

244. Okigbo, Charles. "Sex in the Newsroom: Male-Female Differences in Perceptions of Media Professionalism." *Sex-Roles within Massmedia Newsletter*. December 1986, p. 26.

Differences between women and men in terms of "accepted concepts of media professionalism"; women did not differ much professionally from their male counterparts.

245. Penley, Constance, ed. *Feminism and Film Theory*. New York: Routledge, 1988. 272 pp.

Ten women in 15 chapters deal with various women filmmakers, such as Raoul Walsh and Dorothy Arzner, and topics related to feminism or film theory. Prominent as contributors are Claire Johnson, Jacqueline Rose, Janet Bergstrom, and Laura Mulvey. Also by the same author: *The Future of an Illusion: Film, Feminism, and Psychoanalysis*, Minneapolis: University of Minnesota Press, 1989.

246. Place J. and J. Burston. "Feminist Film Criticism." *Movie*. Spring 1976, pp. 53-62.

247. Pribram, E. Deidre, ed. *Female Spectators: Looking at Film and Television*. London: Verso, 1988. 199 pp.

A state-of-the-art picture of feminist film criticism in the 1980s, from U.S. and European perspectives. Includes readings of individual films and TV shows and insights from women in the business. Contributors are Linda Williams, Michele Citron, Christine Gledhill, Jackie Byars, E. Ann Kaplan, Alile Sharon Larkin, and Teresa De Lauretis.

248. "Producers." *Isis International Bulletin*. June 1983, pp. 19-21.

Films made about women by women in Brazil; mention of women film producers in Sweden, Finland, Denmark, Norway, India, Israel, Canada, Egypt, Tunisia, Nicaragua, Peru, New Zealand, Netherlands, England, Yugoslavia, Poland, and USSR.

249. Quart, Barbara K. *Women Directors: The Emergence of a New Cinema*. New York: Praeger, 1989. 284 pp.

The major contemporary women directors of feature films -- their themes, art, and circumstances of work; ties between women directors, rather "than on a survey of women who direct films." Discussed are U.S., Western and Eastern Europe, and Third World directors: Alice Guy-Blache, Germaine Dulac, Lois Weber, Dorothy Arzner, Ida Lupino, Lina Wertmuller, Elaine May, Joan Micklin Silver, Claudia Weill, Susan Seidelman, Joyce Chopra, Martha Coolidge, Donna Deitch, Barbra Streisand, Goldie Hawn, Margarethe von Trotta, Doris Dorrie, Agnes Varda, Diane Kurys, Gunnel Lindblom, Marleen Gorris, Marta Meszaros, Larisa Shepitko, Vera Chytilová, Agnieszka Holland, Euzhan Palcy, Lu Xiaoya, Zhang Nuanxin, Ann Hui, Sachiko Hidari, Aparna Sen, Prema Karanth, Maria Luisa Bemberg, Susana Amaral, and others.

250. "Real Alternatives: Women Organizing in Media." *Isis International Bulletin*. No. 18, 1981, pp. 30-36.

Discussion of women and broadcasting taken from *The Report of the Women and Media Conference*, held in Bristol, United Kingdom, July 6, 1974.

251. Seligman, Ruth. "Video: A New Development Tool." *Cooperation South*. No. 3, 1988, pp. 16-17.

Use of video networks for development purposes in India and Guyana, with some mention of Video SEWA, a branch of the Self-Employed Women's Association of India.

252. Smith, Prudence, ed. *Women and Film Biography.* London: British Film Institute, 1986.

253. Spender, Dale. *The Writing or the Sex? Or Why You Don't Have To Read Women's Writing To Know It's No Good.* Elmsford, New York: Pergamon Athene Series, 1989. 256 pp.

   Men have been in charge of giving value to literature and they found the writings of their own sex superior. Chapter on "Publishing: Damned If You Do, and Damned If You Don't."

254. Spender, Lynne. "The Politics of Publishing: Selection and Rejection of Women's Words in Print." *Women's Studies International Forum.* 6:5 (1983), pp. 469-473.

   Part of special issue on "Gatekeeping: The Denial, Dismissal and Distortion of Women." Commercial publishing is dominated by men who claim to produce materials that are universal, but who support the male view of the world; feminist publishing compete poorly in this milieu.

255. *Take One.*

   Carried a regular column on "Women in Film" by variously, Kay Armatage, Barbara Martineau, and Sandra Lowell, as well as a single-topic issue, January 1972, devoted to "Women in Film." Included in the latter were an interview with Shirley Clarke, views of women on film, and "Canadian Women Directors: A Filmography," compiled by Alison Reid. Also see: "Women on Women in Films," November-December 1970, pp. 10-14; Barbara Martineau, "Thoughts about the Objectification of Women," November-December 1970, pp. 15-18.

256. "The UN System Can't Survive Without Media." *Democratic Journalist.* January 1990, pp. 12-15.

   Interview with Thérèse Pacquet-Sévigny, under secretary-general for public information of the United Nations.

257. Todd, Alexandra Dundas and Sue Fisher, eds. *Gender and Discourse: The Power of Talk.* Norwood, New Jersey: Ablex, 1988. 320 pp.

   Different theories and insights into the relationship between gender and discourse; includes Cheris Kramarae, "Censorship of Women's Voices on Radio."

258. Unesco. *Women in the Media.* Paris: Unesco, 1980. 119 pp.

   Result of a group set up by Unesco and the International Film and Television Council during International Women's Year. The first part deals with participation of women in radio, television, and film in Australia, Canada, United Kingdom, and the U.S.; the second part, "Women in Cinema," presents the findings of a Unesco International Symposium on Women in Cinema, convened in Italy in 1975.

259. "Women and the Media." *Intermedia.* October-November 1989, pp. 25-29.

    Report of a conference, "Media and Women in a North-South Perspective," held in 1988. Participants from 18 countries discussed the problems and opportunities for women in media. Extracts from the following papers: Joyce Ayree, "Women in the Media -- Ghana," pp. 26-27; Patricia de la Peña, "Women in Television -- Mexico," pp. 27-28; Cecilia L. Lazaro, "Women in Television -- The Philippines," p. 28; Nanise Fifita, "Women in the Media -- The Pacific," p. 29.

260. "Women in Broadcasting ... in Africa ... and in the Caribbean." *COMBROAD.* October-December 1987, pp. 18-24, 28.

    A report on seminars held in Nairobi and Barbados to discuss the roles of women in broadcasting media in the Commonwealth. Problems at the African seminar included those at the recruitment stage and others having to do with women broadcasters' domestic duties and "lack of personality and drive." Eleven recommendations included. At the Caribbean seminar, 16 recommendations were offered.

261. "Women in Journalism, 1987." *Gender and Mass Media Newsletter.* November 1989, p. 29.

    Data on 13 countries (mainly in Europe, plus Australia, Canada, Brazil, Nigeria, New Zealand, and U.S.) that show, with the exception of West Germany, the proportion of female journalism students is "very much higher" than the percentage of female working journalists.

262. "Women Journalists on the Move." *Democratic Journalist.* April 1989, p. 29.

    Excerpts of materials illustrating the current status of women journalists in several parts of the world. In San Francisco, the first news agency for women (WINGS) was set up; in Beijing, women journalists from 12 countries met to discuss their roles; in Sweden, a newsletter, *Sex-Roles within Massmedia*, was launched. Asian countries decided to support the creation of a regional women and media information exchange network.

263. Women's History Research Center. *Films by and/or about Women: Directory of Filmmakers, Films, and Distributors Internationally, Past and Present.* Berkeley, California: Women's History Research Center, 1972.

264. "World's Top Women Journalists To Meet in 1986 on Women's Role and Participation in Communication." *Media Report to Women.* January-February 1986, pp. 1, 4-5.

    Gathering in Washington of journalists from 15 countries.

WOMEN'S MEDIA

265. Brunsdon, Charlotte, ed. *Films for Women.* London: British Film Institute, 1986. 236 pp.

Twenty-three articles scan women's representation in cinema, those produced and directed by women. Divided into documentary, fictions, Hollywood, and distribution and exhibition. Also by this author: "Writing about Soap Opera," in *Television Mythologies*, edited by L. Masterman, pp. 82-87, London: Comedia, 1984.

266. Byerly, Carolyn M. "Through a Lens Clearly: Women and the Evolution of World News." Paper presented at Association for Education in Journalism and Mass Communication, Minneapolis, Minnesota, August 1990.

Ways the Unesco-funded women's feature service addresses women's issues with world news.

267. *Connexions*. Spring 1985.

Special issue on women and media with articles on making documentaries in New Zealand, book publishing in Zimbabwe, censorship in West Germany, alternative radio programs in Mexico, and feminist archives in Denmark.

268. Consultation on "Women and the Media, Strategies for Change." Lusaka, Zambia. June 1985. [Summary in *Sex-Roles within Massmedia Newsletter*. November 1985.]

Includes Gwendoline Konie, "Opening Remarks"; Margaret Gallagher, "Women and the Media"; Elizabeth Okwenje, "Media as a Tool for Change"; Eunice Njambi Mathu, "Publishing a Woman's Magazine: Strategies for Success"; Margaret Adams, "Promotion and Marketing of a Publication"; and Margaret Waller, "Photography -- Visual Literacy."

269. Dancyger, Irene. *A World of Women: An Illustrated History of Women's Magazines*. Dublin: Gilland MacMillan, 1978.

270. "Distributors." *Isis International Bulletin*. June 1983, pp. 22-28.

Distributors of women's films in Brazil, Mexico, England, U.S., Switzerland, Canada, and Japan. Sections on "Libraries," "Audiovisuals," "Action Groups," "Training," "Photography, Graphics, and Posters," and "Publications."

271. Dominguez Juan, Milagros. "Prensa femenina y reproducción social." *Telos*. July-August 1988, pp. 52-56.

272. Ferguson, Marjorie. *Forever Feminine, Women's Magazines and the Cult of Femininity*. Exeter, New Hampshire: Heinemann Educational Books, 1983. 243 pp.

Women's magazine journalism from angles of who decides message content, readership, and scale of production.

273. Ferguson, Marjorie. "The Woman's Magazine Cover Photograph." In *The Sociology of Journalism and the Press*, edited by H. Christian, pp. 219-238. Totowa, New Jersey: Rowman and Littlefield, 1980.

The social world suggested by covers of traditionalist women's magazines.

274. "First UN All-Woman, International Staff Puts Out U.N. *Forum 85* Newspaper." *Media Report to Women.* September-October 1985, pp. 1, 4-5.
        The birth of the first all-woman newspaper at a UN conference.

275. Gaines, Jane M. and Charlotte Herzog, eds. *Fabrications: Costume and the Female Body.* New York: Routledge, 1990. 304 pp.
        Convergence of U.S. and British feminist theory; connections between female consumer and female viewer.

276. Gledhill, Christine, ed. *Home is Where the Heart Is: Studies in Melodrama and the Woman's Film.* London: BFI Publishing, 1987. 365 pp.
        Guide to feminist film criticism, popular culture, and role of melodrama in film; 18 papers by well-known authors who analyze production and consumption; fantasy and ideology in Hollywood cinema, etc. See her "Recent Developments in Feminist Criticism," *Quarterly Review of Film Studies*, Fall 1978.

277. Hodge, Esther. "A Women's International Quarterly over 30 Years. Are the Arguments to Be Feminine or Feminist?" *Women's Studies International Forum.* 7:4 (1984), pp. 265-273.
        Profile of *Women Speaking* (earlier called *Speaking of Women*) from 1951-1982.

278. Inoue, Teruko and Women's Magazines Research Group. *Josei Zassi wo Kaidoku-suru* (Reading the Message in Women's Magazines: COMPAREPOLITAN -- A Comparative Study of Japan, the U.S. and Mexico). Tokyo: Kakiuchi Publishing Co., 1989.

279. Isis International. *Powerful Images: A Women's Guide to Audiovisual Resources.* Rome: Isis International, 1986. 220 pp.
        Information on audiovisuals produced by and for women from 50 countries. More than 600 films, slides, tapes and videos listed. The guide also recounts women's experiences in producing the materials.

280. Johnston, Claire. *Notes on Women's Cinema.* London: Society for Education in Film and Television, 1975.

281. Johnston, Claire. "Women's Cinema as Counter-Cinema." In *Notes on Women's Cinema. Screen* Pamphlet No. 2. London: SEFT, 1973.

282. *Jump/Cut. A Review of Contemporary Media.*
        No. 14, special section on "Women, Power, and Violence"; Nos. 24/25 (1981), "Lesbians and Film"; No. 27 (1982), "Film and Feminism in Germany Today," pp. 41-52.

283. Kassell, Paula and Susan J. Kaufman. "Planning an International Communications System for Women." In *Communications at the Crossroads: The Gender Gap Connection*, edited by Ramona Rush and Donna Allen, pp. 222-237. Norwood, New Jersey: Ablex, 1989.

A report on the work towards setting up an international communications system for women, from initial talks about an international news service in 1979. Discussion at a meeting in Copenhagen in 1980, where concern about control prevented action being taken on an offer by the Inter Press Service of Rome to distribute women's news dispatches. The result was the Women's International News Service.

284. Kuhn, Annette. "Women's Genres." *Screen*. January-February 1984, pp. 18-28.

285. Kuhn, Annette. *Women's Picture: Feminism and Cinema*. Boston: Routledge and Kegan Paul, 1982. 226 pp.
    A stocktaking of feminist film, showing the conflict between opposition to "sexist" films and today's cultural values.

286. Lamphere, Louise. "Women in Film: An Introduction." *American Anthropologist*. March 1977, pp. 192-211.
    Review of a number of films on women in U.S., Canada, Europe, Asia, and Africa.

287. Lesage, Julia. "Feminist Film Criticism: Theory and Practice." *Women and Film*. 1:5/6 (1974), pp. 12-19.
    A theoretical framework for criticism which sees film as a process including the milieu of the filmmaker, the maker, the film, the audience, the audience milieu, and the relations of production and distribution. Reprinted in: Patricia Erens, ed., *Sexual Stratagems: The World of Women in Film*, New York: Horizon Press, 1979.

288. McGarry, Eileen. "Documentary, Realism and Women's Cinema." *Women and Film*. 2:7 (1975), pp. 50-59.
    An attack on the assumption that documentary films on women escape stereotyping.

289. Mayer, Henry. "New Women's Publications." *Media Information Australia*. November 1984, pp. 37-40.
    Eight books on women reviewed, a few of which have to do with communications.

290. Millum, Trevor. *Images of Women: Advertising in Women's Magazines*. London: Chatto and Windus, and Totowa, New Jersey: Rowan and Littlefield, 1975.

291. Ramazanova, Nelia. "Women's Press Calls for Peace and Truth." *Democratic Journalist*. November 1987, pp. 13-14.
    Various women's periodicals call for the promotion of world peace.

292. *Resources for Feminist Research*. November 1980.
    Includes: "*La Presse Feministe*: Deaths at Publications at Risk," pp. 8-13; Sharon Batt, "Feminist Publishing: Where Small Is Not So Beautiful," pp. 13-14;

Susan Bazilli, "Feminist Print Media Conference (Ottawa, Canada, June 26-29, 1980)"; "A Brief History of *Feminist* (Japanese periodical)," pp. 15-16.

293. Rush, Ramona and Christine L. Ogan. "Communication and Development: The Female Connection." In *Communications at the Crossroads: The Gender Gap Connection*, edited by Ramona Rush and Donna Allen, pp. 265-278. Norwood, New Jersey: Ablex, 1989.

Women's efforts in communication and development, with the example of Women's Features Services.

294. Sullivan, Kaye. *Films For, By and About Women. Series II*. Metuchen, New Jersey: Scarecrow, 1985. 790 pp.

Approximately 3,200 film titles with brief descriptions; continuation of 1980 volume of same title by same compiler.

295. Winship, Janice. *Inside Women's Magazines*. Winchester, Massachusetts: Unwin and Hyman, 1987. 210 pp.

The women's magazine market from the 1950s to 1980s; relationship between magazine editors and readers, importance of illustrations, ideological frameworks, and limits of feminism in commercial magazines.

296. *Women's Studies International Quarterly (Women's Studies International Forum* with Vol. 5), London.

Has included: Elaine Morgan, "Writing for Television: Women's Contribution," 2:2 (1979), pp. 209-214; Lynne Spender, "The Politics of Publishing: Selection and Rejection of Women's Words in Print," pp. 469-474, Felicity Hunt, "The London Trade in the Printing and Binding of Books: An Experience in Exclusion, Dilution and Deskilling for Women Workers," pp. 517-524, Andrea Fleck Clardy, "Creating the Space: Feminist Publications Outside the Mainstream," pp. 545-546, all 6:5 (1983); Beth Nelson, "Lady Elinor Davies: The Prophet as Publisher," 8:5 (1985), pp. 403-410; and David T.J. Doughan, "Periodicals By, For, and About Women in Britain," 10:3 (1987), pp. 261-274.

297. Zavitz, Carol and Hans Kleipool. "International Guide to Women's Periodicals and Resources, 1981/2." *RFR/DRF*. December 1981/January 1982, pp. 33-96.

A listing by continent and country of women's periodicals and resources, with essential information; includes periodicals that ceased to exist or were "missing in action."

298. Ziska, Deborah. "Video: A Development Communication Report. Spring 1986, p. 4.

Advantages, disadvantages of the used video for women's development as brought out at a 1985 conference in Kenya.

2
AFRICA AND THE MIDDLE EAST

GENERAL STUDIES

299. Accad, E. *Veil of Shame: The Role of Women in the Contemporary Fiction of North Africa and the Arab World.* Sherbrooke, Canada: Editions Naaman, 1978.

300. Al-Abd, Atif Adli. "The Image of Women in School Books and the Foreign Media." *Al-Fann Al-Idhai.* July 1980, pp. 51-60.

301. Al-Qazzaz, Ayad. *Women in the Middle East and North Africa: An Annotated Bibliography.* Austin, Texas: University of Texas Center for Middle Eastern Studies, Middle East Monographs No. 2, 1977.
    No specific topic on mass media but includes sex roles and others tangentially connected.

302. Ata, A.W. "Impact of Westernization and Other Factors on the Changing Status of Moslem Women." *Eastern Anthropologist.* April-June 1984, pp. 95-126.
    Mentions role of media as looks at changes in the status of women in Muslim societies as products of Westernization.

AFRICA

General Studies

303. AAWORD Working Groups. "Women and the Mass Media in Africa." *Sex-Roles Within Massmedia Newsletter.* November 1987, pp. 32-33.
    Details papers of a 1986 working group on research held in Zambia: Myriam Traore, "Place and Image in Selected Radio and Television Programmes in Mali"; Pierrette Herzberger-Fofana, "Image of Women in Senegalese Literature Authored by Women"; Kayissan Dravie, "Media in Togo"; Josina N. Kaunda, "Accessibility of Women to the Media of Zambia"; Mounira Chelli, "The Image

of Women in Tunisian Television Films"; Soha Abdel Kader, "Images of Women in Egyptian Television Drama"; Ayesha Imam, "The Role of Mass Media in the Construction of Gender Ideologies in Northern Nigeria"; Penina Mlama, "Women and Communication: Popular Theater as an Alternative Medium." These proceedings also appeared in *Echo*, AAWORD's newsletter. AAWORD, B.P. 3304. Dakar, Senegal.

304. Abdul-Rahman, Asma; Faiza Shawkat, and Mariam Osman. *The Sudanese Woman in Mass Media*. Report prepared for the Arab Women Journalists' Seminar, Algeria, 1981. See *Al-Raida*, Vol. 5, no. 20, 1982.

305. Bullwinkle, Davis A., comp. *African Women: A General Bibliography, 1976-1985*. Westport, Connecticut: Greenwood Press, 1989. 354 pp.

Among 32 subject categories are "Arts," "Cultural Roles," and "Mass Media." The latter contained seven sources.

306. Bullwinkle, Davis A., comp. *Women of Eastern and Southern Africa: A Bibliography, 1976-1985*. Westport, Connecticut: Greenwood Press, 1989. 570 pp.

English-language publications about women in Eastern and Southern Africa, broken into regional, national, and general subject categories. Mass media on pages 13, 222, 247, 418, covering Tanzania, Uganda, and South Africa.

307. Bullwinkle, Davis A., comp. *Women of Northern, Western, and Central Africa: A Bibliography, 1976-1985*. Westport, Connecticut: Greenwood Press, 1989. 628 pp.

Sources on women of Northern, Western, and Central Africa divided by chapters taking regional, national, and general subject approaches. Mass media is a category of entries under Egypt (p. 104), Ghana (p. 280), Nigeria (p. 431), and Sierra Leone (p. 493).

308. Cooper, Anne M. "Covering Kenya." *Press Woman*. September 1985, pp. 1-3.

The UN International Women's Decade conference in Nairobi.

309. Cutrufelli, Maria Rosa. *Women of Africa. Roots of Oppression*. London: Zed Press, 1983.

310. Hall, Susan. "African Women on Film." *Africa Report*. January-February 1977, pp. 15-17.

311. Karoui, Naima. "La notion d'emancipation de la femme à travers la presse: Ebauche d'une analyse de contenue." *Revue Tunisienne de Sciences Sociales*. 47 (1976), pp. 93-124.

312. Koumba-Tessa, Albertine. *Les femmes et les medias au Gabon*. Paris: Universite de Droit, n.d.

313. Kurtz, Camille and Daniel G. Matthews. *"Africa Speaks, America Responds": A Report on the African Council on Communication Education Dialogue, "Communication Education/Training Needs in Africa."* April 11-13, 1979, Washington, D.C. Washington, D.C.: African Bibliographic Center, 1979. 129 pp.
A priority concerning women and the media discussed.

314. McCaffrey, Kathleen M. "African Women on the Screen." *Africa Report.* March-April 1981, pp. 56-58.

315. Mhaiki, P.J. "Political Education and Adult Education." *Convergence.* 6:1 (1973), pp. 15-21.
The equality of women and the mass media's importance in the Third World from a Tanzanian perspective.

316. *Proceedings of the African Women's Features Services Workshop.* Marandellas, Zimbabwe: Regional Population Communication Unit for Africa, 1981.
Includes: Molefi Kete Asante, "Mass Media in Raising Public Awareness of Women's Issues in Zimbabwe," pp. 25-29; Alem Seged Herouy, "An Overview of the Mass Media in Ethiopia and the Role of Women," pp. 38-40; Hilda I. Kundya, "The State of Mass Media in Tanzania Mainland," pp. 52-53.

317. Toyo, Rose "La situation de la Congolaise." Paper presented at conference, "Femmes, developpement, communications: Quelles perspectives?" Dakar, Senegal, n.d.
Women in the Congo were being censured; urged to stand up for what they thought was right.

318. "Women and Media: East and West Africa." *WIN News.* May 1977. 10 pp.

319. Workshop on Women's Studies and Development. Dar-es-Salaam, Tanzania: Bureau of Resource Assessment and Land Use Planning, University of Tanzania, September 24-29, 1979.
Among papers presented were: R.M. Besha, "The Mass Media and Entertainment," No. 34; Deborah Bryceson, "Notes on the Educational Potential of the Mass Media Vis-a-Vis Women's Roles in Tanzanian Society," No. 23, 10 pp.; Agnes Kyaruzi, "Women's Images in Mass Media: Newspapers," No. 45, 4 pp.; Deborah Mwenda, "The Women's Image in the Tanzanian Mass Media: Radio," No. 38, 5 pp.

Images of Women

320. Adeogun, Modupe F. "Attitudes of Nigerian Mass Media Towards Women." Paper presented at the Women and Education Conference, Port Harcourt, Nigeria, April 1984.

321. Akpan, Emmanuel D. "News Photos and Stories: Men's and Women's Roles in Two Nigerian Newspapers." Ph.D. dissertation, Ohio State University, 1979. 144 pp.

322. Akudinobi, Emmanuel. "Men Still Lionized on Nigerian TV." *Media and Values*. Fall 1989, pp. 19-20.

    Nigerian television mirrors a society that is patrilineal and patriarchal; examples given.

323. Anani, Elma L., Alkaly M. Keita, and Awatef A. Rahman. *Women and the Mass Media in Africa: Case Studies from Sierra Leone, the Niger and Egypt*. Addis Ababa, Ethiopia: United Nations Economic Commission for Africa, African Training and Research Centre for Women, 1981. 38 pp.

    Discusses women's media image and the small number of women in policy-making media positions in Africa. Content analyses of media in the three countries.

324. Bop, Codou. "Les femmes et les medias en Afrique." Paper presented at conference, "Femme, Developpement, Communication: Quelles Perspectives?" Dakar, Senegal, n.d.

    Women are portrayed as socially and economically dependent as children, dominated by their sentiments and with status only as wife and mother. A study of picture books in Senegal found: "All the action revolved around the men. The heroine represents purity and is ready to sacrifice all for the hero. The women are materially rich and live a western life-style. If they work they are secretaries and are shown to be more interested in office romance than office politics."

325. Frenkel, C. "Sensual ... But Not Too Far From Innocent: A Critical Theory of Sexism in Advertising." *Critical Arts*. March 1980.

    See author's 1980 B.A. honors dissertation at the University of the Witwatersrand, Johannesburg, South Africa: "A Comparison of the Images of Black and White Women in South African Magazine Advertisements."

326. Glazer Schuster, Isa. *New Women of Lusaka*. Palo Alto, California: Mayfield, 1979.

    Women are trivialized or sensationalized when they do make Zambian news.

327. Isaacs, Gayla C. "Women in Southern Africa: The Media and the Ideal Women." *Africa Report*. March-April 1983, pp. 48-51.

328. Kyaruzi, Agnes. "Women's Images in the Tanzanian Mass Media: Newspapers." Paper presented at the BRALUP (Bureau of Resource Assessment and Land Use Planning), University of Dar es Salaam, 1975.

    Gross misrepresentation of women in Tanzanian media.

329. Lazreg, Marnia. "Prisoners of the Mirror: Representations of Women in the Algerian Media." *Sex-Roles within Massmedia Newsletter*. November 1988, pp. 33-34.

French men during colonial times "eroticized" the Algerian woman's body; film dealing with women focus on love, men's desire for women, and feminist themes, and TV and radio are the most popular media for women.

330. Lemmer, Eleanor M. "Invisible Barriers: Attitudes Toward Women in South Africa." *Suid Afrikaanse Tydskrif vir Sosiologie.* February 1989, pp. 30-37.

Special attention to the position of middle class white women, the female image propagated by media, and the effect of religious views.

331. Lihamba, Amandina. "Media Reinforce the Oppression of Women in Tanzania." *Media Development.* 35:1 (1988), pp. 36-37.

A detailed examination of women's portrayal in Tanzanian media advocated, to arrive at conclusions and suggest changes.

332. Lindfors, Bernth. "Nigerian Chapbook Heroines." *Journal of Popular Culture.* Winter 1968, pp. 441-450.

Nigerian chapbooks (pamphlets) yield unreliable data and "nothing truthful about Nigerian women."

333. McCaffrey, Kathleen M. "Images of Women in West African Literature and Film: A Struggle Against Dual Colonization." *International Journal of Women's Studies.* January/February 1980, pp. 76-88.

West African woman's relationship to language, her body, and work as reflected in literature and film of Ghana and Senegal.

334. McLellan, Iain. *Television for Development: The African Experiment.* Ottawa: International Development Research Centre, 1986. 157 pp.

"African Women and TV: Changing Images and Progress Through Access," pp. 85-101; controllers of media are men who "perpetuate certain myths and images regarding women."

335. Madjdi, Sofia. "The Image of Women in the Egyptian Cinema: Description of Forms of Behaviour Through Social Roles." *Egyptians on Screen: Studies and Seminar Discussions, Al-Hay a Al-Misraya Al-Amma li'l-Kitab.* Cairo: 1986.

336. Nlomo, Jacqueline Abema. "La situation de la femme camerounaise et son image dans les media." Paper presented at conference, "Femmes, Developpement, Communication: Quelles Perspectives?" Dakar, Senegal, n.d.

Her study showed two media images of Cameroon women: "dedicated, hardworking, good mother and faithful wife and ... the young, beautiful sex object who is either unfaithful or a prostitute."

337. Okigbo, Charles. "Gender Representation in the Nigerian Press." *Sex-Roles within Massmedia Newsletter.* November 1988, p. 15.

Three studies to determine how men and women perceived media professionalism; women were still largely underrepresented in journalism schools.

338. Petersen, Angela. "Die uitbeelding van die vroulike rol in advertensies in Suid-Afrikaanse vrouetydskrifte." *Communicare*. November 1989, pp. 40-52.

Women in South African magazine ads were depicted free from stereotyped images and traditional roles.

339. Petty, Sheila. "Images of Women and Oppression in 'Francophone' West African Film." *Canadian Journal of Communication*. September 1989, pp. 17-28.

The analysis of film content and structure to examine images of women and oppression in West African film; strategies for examining images of women and oppression in African film, specificity of African women film characters and images of women in pre-colonial society and post-colonial society.

340. Schmidt, Nancy J. "Nigerian Chapbook Heroines: A Reply to Bernth Lindfors." *Journal of Popular Culture*. Winter 1968, pp. 451-456.

Scholars should look at Nigerian chapbooks and their heroine portrayals within a Nigerian literary context.

341. Steeves, H. Leslie. "Feminism, Communication and Development: Complementary Goals in the Context of East Africa." *Sex-Roles within Massmedia Newsletter*. December 1986, pp. 25-26.

An attempt to develop a theoretical and methodological model for evaluating gender consideration in East African development projects. Data on mass communications in East Africa, particularly Kenya and Tanzania.

342. Wattz, Susan. "Gender Role Rigidities and the Media in Tunisia." Paper presented at Third Annual Third World Conference, University of Nebraska at Omaha, October 1979.

343. Zinn, Deborah. "Women's Role Portrayal in the South African Print Media." B.A. honors dissertation, University of the Witwatersrand, Johannesburg, South Africa, 1983.

Women as Audience

344. Dawit, T. "Mass Media and Rural Women in Africa." *Assignment Children* (UNICEF). April-June 1977, pp. 64-70.

African women's access to education and information had not been proportionate to their responsibilities for development. Analysis of six African dailies for one month found "only a few" articles on urban women.

345. Fougeyrollas, Pierre. *Television and the Social Education of Women, A First Report on the UNESCO - Senegal Pilot Project at Dakar*. Paris: Unesco, Reports and Papers on Mass Communication No. 50, 1967, 37 pp.

Attitude changes among illiterate African women brought about in 1965 by educational television.

346. Mlama, Penina M. "Culture, Women and the Media." In *Communication and Culture: African Perspectives*, edited by S.T. Kwame Boafo, pp. 11-18. Nairobi: Africa Church Information Service, 1989.

    The cultural reasons for the constraints women face as communicators in, and as audiences of, African (mainly Tanzanian) media.

347. Ndulo, Winnie N. "The Accessibility of Women to the Mass Media in Zambia." *Sex-Roles within Massmedia Newsletter*. November 1985, pp. 29-30.

    Media content, accessibility of women to media, gatekeepers, and audiences; very few women find employment in media, and those who do are not in management positions likely to influence the image of women portrayed.

Women Practitioners

348. Andoh, Isaac Fritz. "Problems of Women in the Media in Ghana." *Democratic Journalist*. May 1989, p. 10.

    In workshop on role of women in media, male participants believed women were not reliable employees.

349. Ayree, Joyce. "Women in the Media -- Ghana." *Intermedia*. October-November 1989, pp. 26-27.

    Women of Ghana lack influence in media. At four media, 45 women were in the work force of 322; none was in a position higher than third in rank, and all were kept away from news, current affairs, economics, and politics.

350. Berrian, B. *Bibliography of African Women Writers and Journalists*. Washington, D.C.: Three Continents Press, 1985.

351. DeMott, John and Nihal Naga. "Egyptian Women Emerging as Force in Modern Communications World." *Press Woman*. January 1984, pp. 8-9.

    For many years, women have been involved in Egyptian communications, but they were emerging by the 1980s: the "best news announcers are female and TV is managed by a woman .... In radio, announcers are usually women .... Out of the seven main advertising agencies in Cairo, three are run or owned by women."

352. Fahim, Fawzia. "Professional Women in Egyptian Radio and Television." In *Women and Media Decision-Making: The Invisible Barriers*, edited by Margaret Gallagher, pp. 81-94. Paris: Unesco, 1987.

    Women's participation, decision-making, and career development; sex distribution and sex discrimination, relative to radio and television in Egypt.

353. Federation of African Media Women. "Seminar on Women in Media." Kampala, Uganda, 1983.

    Among papers presented were Eunice Njambi Mathu, "Media Women in Private Enterprise"; Rebecca Katumba, "Media Women in Uganda."

354. Irukwu, Enoh. "Women in Nigerian Broadcasting: A Study of Their Access to Decision-Making Positions." In *Women and Media Decision-Making: The Invisible Barriers*, edited by Margaret Gallagher, pp. 63-80. Paris: Unesco, 1987.
   Women's status, employment; sex discrimination; employment policy; communication administration of Nigerian broadcasting.

355. Katana, Kazungu. "African Women Demand Larger Role in Media." *World Broadcast News*. June 1985, p. 12.
   Meeting of 54 African women journalists in Addis Ababa.

356. Kodesh, Wolfie. "Ruth First and *New Age*." *Democratic Journalist*. July-August 1983, pp. 44-45.
   The virtues of journalist Ruth First of South Africa's *New Age*; her murder for writing against apartheid.

357. Nasha, Margaret. "Women in the Media in Botswana." *COMBROAD*. July-September 1985, pp. 15-17.
   Director of information and broadcasting of Botswana, Margaret Nasha, describes the role of women journalists, information training of journalists, and media portrayals of women.

358. Nozkova, Marta. "Women Journalists in Botswana: A Minority That Is Becoming Accepted." *Democratic Journalist*. February 1990, p. 28.
   The overall percentage of female to male journalists in Botswana is 45 to 55, with men holding most senior media positions. One women's magazine, *Mosadi*, exists.

359. Opole, Monica and Prabha Shardwaj, eds. *Directory of Media Women in Kenya*. Nairobi: Association of Media Women in Kenya, 1985.
   The association (AMWIK) and strides made in women's roles in Kenyan mass media. Review of the book appeared in *Sex-Roles within Massmedia Newsletter*, November 1985, pp. 54-59.

360. Sassi, Sinikka. "Woman and Communication in a West-African Society." *Sex-Roles within Massmedia Newsletter*. November 1988, p. 23.
   The role of women in communication.

361. Unesco. *Report of the Regional Seminar on Women and Decision-Making in the Media*. Addis Ababa: Economic Commission for Africa/Unesco, 1985. 21 pp.

362. "Women Demand More Top Media Posts." *Africom*. March/April/May 1977, pp. 1-3.

363. *Women in Nigeria Today*. London: Zed Press, 1985.
   Includes: T. Nweke, "The Role of Women in Nigerian Society: The Media," pp. 201-207, and H.S. Dangugo, "Women in Electronic Media," pp. 208-211.

Women's Media

364. Alloo, Fatma. "Women and Alternative Media." *Sex-Roles within Massmedia Newsletter.* November 1988, pp. 23-24.
    Alternative media have emerged as a "powerful tool of enpowerment" in Africa, with women making increasing use of them.

365. Black, Maggie, ed. "On the People's Wavelength: Communication for Social Change." *UNICEF News.* 114 (1982), 37 pp.
    Among articles dealing with communication in development programs is one on facilitating communication through the use of photographs made by illiterate village women in Tanzania.

366. Doumbia, Terez and Tiana Hanitra. "What Price Dreams?" *Democratic Journalist.* July 1989, pp. 23-25.
    Women's magazines published in Africa and Paris, aimed for African women, offer "fine Dutch fabrics that drape your figure elegantly ..., threadlike braids of synthetic hair produced in the West, Lancome and Christian Dior cosmetics and Renault cars." Authors, from Senegal and Madagascar, claimed, "Women's magazines that display a sophisticated attitude to family problems and interpersonal relations and ignore Islamic dogmas and the taboos imposed on some subjects are a distinctive product of the 1980s." Women's magazines devote too much space to the promotion of status symbols.

367. "Moroccan Women's Magazine Halts Publication To Protest Censorship." *Media Report to Women.* September-October 1989, p. 8.
    Kalima, founded in 1985, closed to protest government censorship.

THE MIDDLE EAST

Images of Women

368. Abdel-Rahman, Awatef. *Image of the Egyptian Woman in the Mass Media.* Cairo: University of Cairo, 1978.

369. Al-Abd, Atif Adli. "The Image of Women in the Media." *Al-Buhuth.* December 1985, pp. 141-156.

370. Al-Hadeedy, Muna. "Image of Women in the Egyptian Cinema." Cairo: University of Cairo, 1977.

371. *Al-Raida*, Beirut.
    Articles on women include: Richard Allouche, "Woman's Image in the Lebanese Press 1935-1975," Vol, 3, No. 14, 1980, pp. 12-13; Abdelkader Hammouche, "Image of Woman in the Press and Television," Vol. 7, Nos. 27-28, 1984, pp. 12-13. Institute for Women's Studies in the Arab World, P.O. Box 11-4080, Beirut University College, Beirut, Lebanon.

372. Bahri, Muna Vonnis. "Values Related to Women in President Saddam Hussein's Addresses to Women." *Sex-Roles within Massmedia Newsletter.* November 1985, pp. 34-36.

   In six speeches of president of Iraq, the chief values pertaining to women that were addressed were "love of family," "women's liberation," "the new position of women," and "injustice for women."

373. Baraka, Iqbal. "The Influence of Contemporary Arab Thought on the Women's Movement." In *Women of the Arab World*, edited by Nahid Toubia, pp. 45-55. London: Zed Books, 1988. 168 pp.

   Discusses first book in Arabic dealing with women's position. Section on "The Image of Women in the Cinema and Novels," pp. 52-54, states that the "germ of bias and mistrust" in Arab novels infects large parts of the population as these works are adapted to radio, TV, and film.

374. Bat-Ada, Judith. "Porn in the Promised Land." *Lilith.* Fall-Winter 1983, pp. 9-14.

   Israel has moved far from the egalitarianism of its founders to a state that degrades and threatens its women as pornography has become rampant.

375. Doneson, Judith E. "The Jew as a Female Figure in Holocaust Films." *Shoah.* No. 1, 1979, pp. 11-13, 18.

376. Efrat, Roni Ben. "The Image of the Press in the 'Only Democracy in the Middle East.'" *Democratic Journalist.* January 1990, pp. 16-19.

   Author recounts her problems, and those of journalists generally, in operating in Israel. Employed by *Derech Hanitzotz*, Efrat was arrested for reporting upon certain spheres of interest in the Occupied Territories.

377. El Saadawi, Nawal. *The Hidden Face of Eve: Women in the Arab World.* London: Zed Press, 1980.

378. Eyal, C.H. "Sources of Abstract and Symbolic Modeling: The Presentation of Social Roles in Two Israeli Children's Magazines." *Gazette.* 37:1/2 (1986), pp. 103-122.

   Magazines *Ha'aretz Shelanu* and *Mishmar Li 'Yladim* studied in 1980; among categories analyzed was the story protagonist's sex.

379. Graham-Brown, Sarah. *Images of Women. The Portrayal of Women in Photography of the Middle East 1860-1950.* New York: Columbia University Press, 1988.

   Eight chapters showing Middle East women's depiction in photographs.

380. Mikhail, M.N. *Images of Arab Women.* Washington, D.C.: Three Centuries Press, 1979.

381. Shinar, Dov, Adrian Tomer, and Ayala Biber. "Images of Old Age in Television Drama Imported to Israel." *Journal of Communication.* 30:1 (1980), pp. 50-55.

In seven weeks of 1976 programs televised in Israel, the percentage of female characters decreased with age.

382. Weimann, Gabriel and Gideon Fishman. "Attribution of Responsibility: Sex-based Bias in Press Reports on Crime." *European Journal of Communication.* December 1988, pp. 415-430.

In Israeli dailies, female criminality was treated as a result of social/psychological factors; however, attribution of responsibility was very dependent upon the crime involved.

Women as Audience

383. Bagheri, Abbas S. "Precipitating Factors of Neurotic Reactions in Middle and Upper-Middle Class Persian Women." *International Journal of Social Psychiatry.* Spring 1981, pp. 47-51.

Discusses media's role in developing confusion that heightened the negative effects of factors contributing to neuroses among Persian women in 1973-1974.

384. Cohen, Akiba A. and Judith Dotan. "Communication in the Family as a Function of Stress During War and Peace." *Journal of Marriage and the Family.* February 1976, pp. 141-148.

Effects of war-related stress on family communication patterns during the October 1973 Middle East war. Two sets of interviews with a sample of women.

385. Ramzi, Nahid. "Social Responsibility for the Means of Communication and Changing the Social Position of Women in Arab Society." *Shu'un Arabiya.* September 1983, pp. 72-88.

386. Tohamy, Mochtar. "Media Research on the 'Mass Role about Rural Women'; Rural Women and Development Seminar, Middle East Centre." Cairo: Ein Shams University, 1980.

387. Tomeh, Aida K. "On the Cumulative Nature of Social Participation and Mass Media in Lebanon." *International Journal of Contemporary Sociology.* January-April 1975, pp. 95-112.

A test of 434 women students in Lebanon to find out, among other things, if joiners of clubs make more use of mass media than non-joiners; the answer was generally yes.

Women Practitioners and Media

388. Dajani, Karen Finlon. "Magazine for Arab Women: *Hawa.*" *Journalism Quarterly.* Spring 1982, pp. 116-118.

History and description of *Hawa* (Eve), weekly women's magazine published in Cairo, Egypt. Magazine has had very little competition in women's field, not many problems politically (although it has been censored), and a "liberal" stand in the Arab, Moslem world.

389. Freedman, Marcia. "Feminist Publishing in Israel." *Women's Studies Newsletter.* Winter 1980 pp. 29-30.
Feminist bookshops, presses, and books.

390. Golmakani, Houshang. "Iranian Women Directors." *Cinemaya.* Spring 1989, pp. 26-27.
The careers and films of Iran's three women movie directors -- Tahmineh Ardakani, Rakhshan Bani Etemad, and Puran Derakhshandeh.

391. "The Seminar on Women's Programmes on Radio and Television." *ASBU (Arab States Broadcasting Union).* January 1976, pp. 45-52.

392. Tidhar, Chava E. "Women in Israel's Broadcasting Media and on Israel Television." *Sex-Roles within Massmedia Newsletter.* November 1988, p. 36.
Women had high positions, and a number of them, on Israel's television station, IETV; however, they were underrepresented on IBA. Men appeared six times more frequently in news programs than did women.

393. *WIN (Women's International Network) News.* Autumn 1985.
Includes an address by the delegation of the United Arab Emirates to the U.N. World Conference of Women, July 1985, pointing out UAE women had risen to 10 percent of the media workforce.

3
ASIA, AUSTRALIA, AND OCEANIA

GENERAL STUDIES

394. Asia-Pacific Institute for Broadcasting Development. Regional Seminar on Women and the Media, 1980. *Papers.* Kuala Lumpur: APIBD, 1980.
      Includes: Najma Athar, "Women and Media in Bangladesh"; Cakau Cockburn, "Women and Media in Fiji"; Neera Desai, "Indian Women and Media," Hema Goonatilake, "The Direction of Women in the Mass Media: Myth and Reality."

395. "Asia-Pacific Call for Action on Population and Development: Guidelines for the Formulation of Responsive Policy Measures." *Asian-Pacific Population Programme News.* 12:2 (1983), pp. 17-23.
      Presents four reports related to population and development, one of which is about ways to maximize effectiveness of information, education, and communication relative to women.

396. United Nations. *Women's Information Network for Asia and the Pacific.* New York: United Nations Economic and Social Commission for Asia and the Pacific, 1987. 139 pp.

ASIA

General Studies

397. A.D. and S.M. "Media and Women." *Mainstream.* December 10, 1983, p. 30.
      In India.

398. Agarwal, Bina and Kamla Bhasin. "Group Action for Change in India." *Isis International Women's Journal.* December 1984, pp. 109-113.
      Profiles and describes activities of Delhi-based Committee on the Portrayal of Women in the Media, constituted in 1983.

399. Agarwal, Bina and Kamla Bhasin, eds. "Women and Media: Analysis, Alternatives and Action." *Isis International Women's Journal.* December 1984, pp. 1-132.

   Includes: Kamla Bhasin, "Women, Development and Media," pp. 8-18; Sujata Madhok, "Struggling for Space," pp. 19-25; "Roles of Women as Portrayed in Children's Books (Sri Lanka)," pp. 26-31; "Packaged for Consumption: The Abuse of Women in Advertising (Malayasia)[sic]," pp. 31-36; Aruna Vasudev, "The Woman: Vamp or Victim," pp. 37-43; Ira Bhaskar, "Mother Goddess Ascendant: Ghatak's *Meghe Dhaka Tara*," pp. 44-47; Lee Jones, "Push-button Pornography: Some Thoughts on Video Pornography and Its Effects on Women in Australia," pp. 48-54; Shahnaz Anklesaria, "Obscenity, Media and the Law," pp. 55-60; Akhila Ghosh, "Media and Rural Women," pp. 63-68; "Manushi: A Journal about Women and Society," pp. 69-73; Ila Pathak, "AWAG's Battle Against the Media," pp. 74-77; "Consumer Education for Women," pp. 78-81; Farida Shaheed, "Creating One's Own Media," pp. 82-88; Sunila Abeysekera, "Voices of Women: Media Alternatives in Sri Lanka," pp. 89-91; Roushan Jahan, "Exploring the Outreach: The Video Project of Women for Women," pp. 92-93; Amrita Chhachhi, "Media as a Political Statement: Two Attempts by Women's Groups," pp. 94-100; Chandralekha, "Screenprinting Workshops," pp. 101-105; "The Magazine of the Friends of Women Group (Thailand)," pp. 106-108; Bina Agarwal and Kamla Bhasin, "Group Action for Change in India," pp. 109-113; Urvashi Butalia, "Making News: Asian Women in the West," pp. 114-119; Vibhuti Patel, "Songs of Solidarity," pp. 120-121; "Resources and Networks," pp. 122-132.

400. Anklesaria, Shahnaz. "Obscenity, Media and the Law." *Isis International Women's Journal.* December 1984, pp. 55-60.

   Claims Indian legislation does not acknowledge the impact of obscenity on women and offers suggestions on what is to be done.

401. Anuradha, Sushma Kepoor. *Women and Media in Development.* New Delhi: Centre for Development of Instructional Technology, 1986. 65 pp.

402. Asian Broadcasting Union and Unesco. *Report.* "Seminar on the Role of Broadcasting in International Women's Year." Bangkok, September 8-12, 1975. Kuala Lumpur: ABU, 1975.

403. Association of Women for Action and Research. *The Singapore Woman.* Singapore: AWARE, 1988.

   Thought-provoking comments on the social and economic status of Singapore women.

404. Banerji, Prava. "Portrait of Women in Media." *Communicator.* April-July 1985, pp. 33-35.

   Highlights of book, *Women and Media: Analysis, Alternatives, and Action,* edited by Kamla Bhasin and Bina Agarwal.

405. Chandiram, Jai. "Media: The Challenge for Women in the Asia-Pacific." *Media in Education and Development.* June 1984, pp. 111-112.

406. Chandiram, Jai and Binod C. Agrawal. "Towards Equality: Women in Indian Television." *Media Asia*. 9:3 (1982), pp. 161-164.

   An attempt to analyze television programming for rural and urban women in information, entertainment, education, and development; synthesize results of various impact studies of women's responses to the programs directed towards them; describe the portrayal of women and the status of women employed in television, and raise specific issues related to television studies on Indian women.

407. Chandralekha. "Screenprinting Workshops: A Step Towards Control over Media." *Isis International Women's Journal*. December 1984, pp. 101-105.

   A Madras-based group SKILLS, has made people aware of their capacities to handle cultural and media forms. Describes SKILLS workshop on the use of posters, held for the National Conference of Women Against Oppression.

408. *Countermedia. Investigating Journalism.* 1:4 (1987).

   Thematic issue of this Indian periodical on "Women and the Media, in the Media, on the Media." The 32-page issue leads off with Vimal Balasubrahmanyam's "Beyond Sexism," followed by "Women in the Media," "The Ad-Film Culture," "Ways of Seeing" (women's magazines), "Mechanical Dolls" (regional media), "Doordarshan and Women," and "Downhill in Hindi Movies."

409. Daswani, T.C. "Women in Media and Attitudes." *Vidura*. October 1984, pp. 243-246.

   An attempt at understanding roles and behavior patterns of Indian TV through interviews with ten TV directors and 50 women viewers and by content analysis. Women were pictured as romantic or family inclined, as being very young or very old. Men outnumbered women four to one on TV. Women felt they were not interviewed in expert roles on TV.

410. Desai, Neera. "Indian Women and Media." Bombay: Vithaldas Vidya Vihar SNDT Women's University, Research Unit on Women's Studies, ca. 1980. 34 pp.

   After discussing women's roles in India and the country's communication policy, author deals with broadcasting and women, television and women, and women and cinema. In each case, she shows the role women play in those industries and their projection by the media. She concludes the media show traditional images of women -- actually reality -- as docile, submissive, and suppressed individuals.

411. *East-West Film Journal.* December 1989.

   Special issue on "The Family and Cinema" includes articles on Chinese family melodrama, family life and Philippine cinema, Morita's *The Family Game*, and Ozu's films, all with allusions to the role of women.

412. Eisen, Arlene. *Women and Revolution in Viet Nam.* London: Zed Books Ltd., 1984.

   Some information on mass media.

413. Feliciano, Gloria D. "Influence of Mass Communication Media on the Formation of a New Attitude Towards the Role of Woman in Present-

Day Society." Quezon City: University of the Philippines, Institute of Mass Communication, 1973. 7 pp.

Roles of education, economics, social influences, and mass media in encouraging attitudes towards the present-day status of women in society.

414. Gokhale, L.N. "Towards 'Another Development with Women' and Mass Media Experience." *Vidura*. October 1984, pp. 246-248.

The rate and amount of communication increased many-fold in this century, but the development and status of Indian women did not.

415. Goonatilake, Hema. "Women and the Media." In *The UN Decade for Women: Progress and Achievements of Women in Sri Lanka*, pp. 181-216. Colombo: CENWOR, 1985. 218 pp.

416. Ide, Sachiko. "Language, Women, and the Mass Media in Japan." *Press Woman*. September 1978, pp. 8-9.

Most Japanese media were in the hands of men; of 12,621 newspaper writers, only 121 were female. Language in mass media showed male domination: on social pages, women were described as belonging to their husbands; interviews were usually done by men and when the interviewee was a woman, her dress and looks were mentioned. An earlier version was presented at the 1977 Women in Communication Seminar, East-West Communication Center, Honolulu.

417. Indian Council for Communication, Training and Research. Seminar on "Media Utilization for the Development of Women and Children." New Delhi, India. September 11-12, 1984. [Summary in *Sex-Roles within Massmedia Newsletter*. November 1984, pp. 13-15.]

Includes: Manzurul Amin, "Television Programmes for Women and Children"; L.N. Gokhale, "Toward 'Another Development with Women' and Mass Media Experience"; T.C. Daswani, "Women in Media and Attitudes"; R.A. Khileshwari, "Use of Television for Development of Women"; U.K. Srivastava, "The Cost of Doordarshan Programmes for Women and Children: Some Preliminary Estimates"; Mira B. Aghi, "How Research Can Improve Television Programmes"; Binod C. Agrawal, "Communication Research Related to Women and Children"; Tara Gopaldas, "Women's Needs: Health and Nutrition," and Rina Gill, "Television for Children."

418. *Indian Journal of Adult Education*.

Has had articles on women and media, including, K. Sharma, "Women and the Media: A Case for Critical Correction," 46 (1985), pp. 27-30, and R. Shyam, "Women in Rural Newspapers," 47:7-8 (1984), pp. 49-50.

419. *Indian Women in Media: Focus on Women's Issues*. N.p.: Lithouse Press, 1984. 62 pp.

Essays on women in the press, journals, Bengali literature, mass media in Kerala, and television.

420. International Group for the Study of Women. "Can Women's Participation in Broadcasting Change the Media? Case Studies of Japanese Women in

Television." *Sex-Roles within Massmedia Newsletter.* November 1988, pp. 31-33.

    Data on Japanese media showed women were big users, but information provided for them did not help them understand their social environment. Women only made up 13 percent of the 44,000 broadcast employees, 5 percent of the employees of Tokyo's three main papers. Interviews conducted with Japanese women who work in media.

421. Jabbar, Javed. "Media, Madams and Messages." Paper presented at Seminar on Women and Media, Karachi, Pakistan, October 18-20, 1984. 23 pp.

    Women and Pakistan mass media.

422. "Japanese Call for Equality in Broadcasting." *Asian Media Alert.* Spring 1990, pp. 8-9.

    Group of 72 people petition all Japanese broadcasting stations to promote sexual equality.

423. Jimenez David, Rina. "Women in Media in the Philippines." Presented at seminar organized by PILIPINA, Davao City, Philippines, 1984.

424. Joshi, S.R. and Hansa Joshi. "Women and Television: ISRO Experiences." In *Communication Research for Development: The ISRO Experience*, edited by Binod C. Agrawal, S.R. Joshi, and Arbind Sinha, pp. 22-33. New Delhi: Concept Publishing Co., 1986.

    Issues of women and media in India: women as an audience, projection of women's issues and images on TV, and research in women's program production.

425. Kishwar, Madhu. "The Bihar Press Bill: Impact on Women's Lives and Women's Movements." *Manushi.* 3:1 (1982), pp. 11-14.

    In India.

426. Kulkarni, V.G. "Of the Men, by the Men, Mostly for the Men." *Media.* May 1976, pp. 20-21.

    Based on Kulkarni's report to the 1976 women and media seminar in Hong Kong.

427. Lanot, Marra P. "The Absentee Woman in Local Cinema." *Diliman Review.* November-December 1982, pp. 1, 18-22.

    In the Philippines.

428. Lebra, Joyce, Joy Paulson, and Elizabeth Powers, eds. *Women in Changing Japan.* Boulder, Colorado: Westview Press, 1976. 322 pp.

    Mass media included.

429. Lent, John A. "Women and Mass Communications: The Asian Literature." *Gazette.* 35 (1985), pp. 123-142.

Bibliography of women as journalists and as audience, images of women, and women's media in Asia.

430. Lent, John A. *Women and Mass Media in Asia: An Annotated Bibliography.* Singapore: AMIC, 1985. 54 pp.

An attempt to sythesize literature pertaining to women in Asian media found by author in his 20 years of bibliographic research on Asian mass communications. About 200 items are presented, most annotated, and at least 16 countries are represented. Appendices added by publisher include additional items found in AMIC Documentation Unit, National Library of Singapore, University of the Philippines Institute of Mass Communication, Indian Institute of Mass Communication, and National University of Singapore.

431. Lim, Linda Y.C. *Women Workers in Multinational Corporations: The Case of the Electronics Industry in Malaysia and Singapore.* Ann Arbor: University of Michigan, Michigan Occasional Paper IX, Women Studies Program, 1978. 66 pp.

Based on the author's Ph.D. dissertation at the University of Michigan, this study concludes, among other points, that "employment of Third World women in offshore manufacturing plants of multinational electronics corporations is based on the higher degree of exploitation to which these women may be subjected compared to other workers in the world."

432. Matsuzawa, Kazuko and George L. Olson. "Church Women and the Media." *Japan Christian Quarterly.* Winter 1985, pp. 24-29.

433. *Media Asia*, Singapore. 14:4 (1987).

Thematic issue on women and media in Asia includes: Doreen G. Fernandez, "Women in Media in the Philippines"; Mohd. Hamdan Adnan, "Women and the Media in Malaysia"; Ruriko Hatano, "Japanese Women in Media"; Sima Sharma, Irvin Weerackody, Narendra R. Panday, Sharif Al Mujahid, and A.B.M. Musa, "Women and Media in South Asia"; Park Yong-Sang, "Women in the Mass Media (South Korea)"; Shailaja Ganguly, "Who Are the Change Makers and How Much Has Been Achieved So Far?"

434. Moslem, Shima. "Women and the Media in Bangladesh: A Case Study." *Media Asia.* 16:3 (1989), pp. 148-153.

A survey of 20 Bangladeshi women journalists and a content analysis of four national dailies discovered that women only got two percent of the total newpaper space. Only 34 women were among the 900 journalists of Dhaka.

435. Mulhern, Chieko. "Japanese Television Drama by, for, and about Women." Paper presented at Association for Asian Studies, Washington, D.C., March 25, 1984.

Gender figures prominently not only in the issues, themes, and plots of Japanese TV drama, but also in the titles of weekly episodes. Housewives are the prized television viewers in Japan; television "provides a grand stage and ample opportunities for talented women."

436. Muramatsu, Yasuko. "Of Women by Women for Women?: Japanese Media Today." *Studies of Broadcasting*. 1990, pp. 83-104.

   Topics included: "The Situation of Japanese Media and Women -- Women as the Target," "Information for and of Women in the Media," "Women as Creators and Communicators in the Media," and "In Search of Media for Both Women and Men."

437. Office of Media Affairs, Philippines. *A Study on the Role of Women in Philippine Movies*. Manila: Office of Media Affairs, Planning Service, 1980.

438. Office of Media Affairs, Philippines. *A Study on the Role of Women in Print Media*. Manila: Office of Media Affairs, Planning Service, 1980.

439. Pakistan Women's Institute. Seminar on Women and Media, 1980. *Papers*. Lahore: 1980.

   Includes: Saleema Khanum, "Broadcasting -- A Profession for Women," and Shireen Pasha, "Television and Women."

440. Park Yong-Sang. "Women in the Mass Media." *Media Asia*. 14:4 (1987), pp. 228-231.

   Review of the sparse literature on women and the media in South Korea; recommendations on areas requiring study.

441. Phadnis, Urmila. "Indian Women in Mass Media." *Sex-Roles within Massmedia Newsletter*. November 1988, pp. 37-38.

   For the mass of illiterate Indian women, print media have hardly any relevance. In one survey of 950 Indian journalists, only 38 were women. Space and coverage given to women's issues increased, but sex-role stereotypes and sexual exploitation of women's bodies in media persisted.

442. Press Foundation of Asia. Media Seminar on Women, Children, and Population, 2nd Jakarta, 30 October-5 November 1983. *Papers*. Manila: Press Foundation of Asia, 1983.

443. Press Institute of India. "Report of the Seminar on the Role of the Mass Media in Changing Social Attitudes and Practices Towards Women." New Delhi: Indian Institute of Mass Communication and Indian Council of Social Science Research, 1975.

   Hindi periodicals over the previous 30 years declined in their discussion of women's issues. Discussed most frequently, relative to women, were traditional concerns such as food, fashion and beauty.

444. "Pressing for Women's Lib." *Asian Mass Communcation Bulletin*. March 1980, p. 6.

   Originally a Depthnews feature by Estella Carreon, reporting on a Unesco-sponsored study by Tokiko Fukao and V.G. Kulkarni. Women of Japan were stereotyped; needed were more female journalists and a strong protest from women readers. Hong Kong English-language dailies did not focus on the women's movement; a possible solution was to concentrate on "development aspects with special emphasis on equality between the sexes."

445. Rao, Punima. *Towards Breaking the Silence: Women and the Media in South Asia.* New Delhi: FFHC/AD, United Nations Food and Agricultural Organization, 1986.

446. Schodt, Frederik L. *Manga! Manga! The World of Japanese Comics.* New York: Kodansha, 1983. 260 pp.
    "Flowers and Dreams," pp. 88-105, treats comics for girls, including a subsection on women comic artists.

447. "Seminar on the Role of Broadcasting in International Women's Year, Bangkok, 8-12 September 1975. Report and Recommendations." *HBF Newsletter.* May 1976, pp. 21-24.

448. Seminar on 'Women and Media,' 1984, Karachi. *Report; Sponsored by Women's Division, Government of Pakistan.* Islamabad: Print Corporation of Pakistan Press, 1985. 123 pp.

449. "Seminar on Women and Media in Asia." *Asian Mass Communication Bulletin.* January-February 1987, pp. 8-9.
    Seminar sponsored by the Asian Mass Communication Research and Information Centre in Singapore.

450. Sharma, Sima, Irvin Weerackody, Narendra R. Panday, Sharif Al Mujahid, and A.B.M. Musa. "Women and the Media in South Asia." *Media Asia.* 14:4 (1987), pp. 218-227, 235.
    Urban South Asian women employed in various media were few, and although more women had been joining the media in the last few decades, social attitudes needed to change before greater participation was achieved. Region broken by countries of India, Nepal, Sri Lanka, Pakistan, and Bangladesh. Each country treated under subheadings of access to media and media training, status of women in media, skills development needs, and portrayal of women in media.

451. Shrivastava, K.M. *Radio and T.V. Journalism.* New Delhi: Sterling Publishers, 1989. 287 pp.
    Women in Indian broadcasting media, their employment and image, pp. 222-224.

452. Song, Yu-jae. "La femme et les médias en Corée." *Revue de Corée.* Summer 1985, pp. 77-105.

453. Southerwood, Marion. *Information Resources on Women in Singapore: Survey and Bibliography.* Singapore: Ministry of Social Affairs, 1983.
    Facilities and resources in libraries and other information centers dealing with women in Singapore.

454. Szanton, Cristina Blanc. "The Philippines: Femme Fatalism Panel." *Asian Cinema*. 5:1 (1990), pp. 16-17.

    Report of a panel at Asian CineVision's Asian Film Series, December 1988. Panelists discussed two films based on women's lives, recounted the history of Philippine cinema, and showed the role women have played in film.

455. "The Multi-Media Resource Kit." *Broadcaster*. March 1990, p. 11.

    Report on an Asian Institute for Broadcasting Development seminar, "Broadcasting for Women's Development."

456. "The Omnipresent Voice." *Manushi*. 3:5 (1983), pp. 10-13.

    In India.

457. *Times of India*, New Delhi.

    Has articles dealing with women and media, as do other Indian newspapers. A few are listed here: Jaina Gomes, "Women and Mass Media," March 26, 1976; Geeti Sen, "Sex and Fantasy in India," May 6, 1984. From the *Indian Express:* Rami Chhabra, "Women and the Media: A Feminist Viewpoint," February 23, 1980; Rami Chhabra, "Women and the Media," January 28, 1983. From the *Hindustan Times*: Chidananda Dasgupta, "Indian Women in Ray's Cinema," February 24, 1980; Ranjana Sengupta, "Women in Indian Cinema," October 12, 1980; Neelam Dutta, "Women in Cinema," October 26, 1980; Rama Shanker Lal," Women in Cinema," November 9, 1980. Others include: Rami Chhabra, "Media and Women," *Statesman*, July 2, 1980; Mehmood Hammeluddin, "Does Sex Sell?" *Youth Times*, February 21, 1975, pp. 12-13; F. de Souza, "Images of Women in Cinema," *Economic Times*, November 5, 1978.

458. Turim, Maureen. "Panels on Women in Asian Film -- Parts I and II." *Asian Cinema*. 4:1/2 (1988-89), pp. 18-21.

    Panels at the Conference on Asian Cinema, Athens, Ohio, October 6-8, 1988; women and film in India, Sri Lanka, China, Taiwan, Philippines, and Japan represented.

459. *Vidura*. February-March 1976, pp. 3-48.

    Special number on "Women and the Reluctant Media" of India approached the topic in 15 articles, from newsworthiness of women to women's magazines, TV images of women, and women and broadcasting, advertising, films, and textbooks.

460. *Vidura*. October 1984.

    Thematic issue on women included: T.C. Daswani, "Women in Media and Attitudes," pp. 243-246; L.N. Gokhale, "Towards 'Another Development With Women' and Mass Media Experience," pp. 246-248; Binod C. Agrawal, "Communication Research Related to Women and Children," pp. 249-253.

461. *Voice of Women*, Sri Lanka. 2:2 (1983).

    Includes Jane Cregeen, "Advertising in Sri Lanka: The Place of Women in the Future," p. 22; Selvy Thiruchandran, "Image of Women in Sri Lankan Films," pp. 11-13; Amila Weerasinghe, "Creation of Myths Through the Media: A Survey of the Five Women's Weekly Newspapers in Sri Lanka," pp. 23-25.

462. Wahab, Eileen. "Women and Communication in the Asia/Pacific Region." *Communication Broadcast*. April-June 1987, pp. 13-15.

463. "Women and the Media Spotlighted in Taiwan." *Gender and Mass Media Newsletter*. November 1989, p. 11.

    Abstracted from *Asia Media Alert* (Summer 1989, p. 7) on a one-day seminar on "Women and the Media" held in Taiwan, December 31, 1988. Some participants found that women were participating in TV news more often and that such women had to remain flexible and "strive against stereotypes" showing them as beautiful faces without depth."

464. "Women in the Press." *Asian Mass Communication Bulletin*. 16:5 (1986), p. 7.

    In Thailand.

465. Wood, Ananda. *Knowledge Before Printing and After: The Indian Tradition in Changing Kerala*. Delhi: Oxford University Press, 1985. 199 pp.

    Revision of author's University of Chicago dissertation on traditional education and knowledge, with a section on women.

466. Yeo, Mary Chuan-Hua. "The Cultural Implications of Multinational Corporations for Singapore Women: An Exploratory Study." Unpublished thesis, University of Singapore, Department of Sociology, 1980.

467. Yu, Timothy and Leonard L. Chu, eds. *Women and Media in Asia*. Hong Kong: Center for Communication Studies, Chinese University of Hong King, 1977. 251 pp.

    Proceedings of a 1976 "Asian Consultation on Women and Media," held in Hong Kong. Divided into four sections: "Inaugural Sections," with opening and keynote addresses; "Regional Reports: Philippines, Singapore, Taiwan, Thailand, and Hong Kong; "Regional Reports: Access to Education and Employment in Mass Media for Asian Women," with reports from Japan, Korea, Malaysia, Philippines, Singapore, Taiwan, Thailand, and Hong Kong, and "Position Papers" of V.G. Kulkarni, "Asian Social Consciousness of Women's Role in Mass Media," Tokiko Fukao, "Contributions Women Make for National Development in Asia Through Mass Media," Alicia M.L. Coseteng, "Opportunities for Training Women for Media Careers in Asia/Teaching Opportunities," and Hamima Dona Mustafa, "Sensitization and Mobilization of Resources for Wider Involvement of Women."

Historical Studies

468. Beahan, Charlotte L. "Feminism and Nationalism in the Chinese Women's Press, 1902-1911." *Modern China*. October 1975, pp. 379-416.

    Discusses women's education, journalism for sisterhood, nationalism and women's press, Chen Xie-fen and the *Journal of Women's Studies*, Ding Chuo-o and *Women's World*, Qiu Jin and the *Chinese Women's Journal*, Chen Rujin and the second *Women's World*, Lo Yan-bin and the *Journal of the New Woman of China*, Jang Jan-yun and the *Peking Women's News*, and He Zhen and *Tianyi*.

Concluded that these women editors firmly believed their feminism was an integral part of nationalism.

469. Ching, Liu Mei. "Women and the Media in China: An Historical Perspective." *Journalism Quarterly.* Spring 1985, pp. 45-52.

   Women entered Chinese media in 1902, but the women's emancipation efforts of Ch-iu Chin in 1905 spurred on women's journalism. Her publication in 1907 of *Women's Monthly* was followed by many other periodicals.

470. Croll, Elisabeth. *Feminism and Socialism in China.* London: Routledge and Kegan Paul, 1978.

   The role of the Chinese press in reflecting the development of feminism and political concerns from the early twentieth century. By same author: *Chinese Women Since Mao*, London: Zed Books, 1983, and *Women in Rural Development: The People's Republic of China*, Geneva: International Labor Organization, 1979.

471. Croll, Elisabeth. "The Anti-Lin Piao and Confucian Campaign: A New Stage in the Ideological Revolution of Women." *Australian and New Zealand Journal of Sociology.* February 1976, pp. 35-42.

   Contents of Chinese media show that the early 1970s' effort was the most analytical to "integrate the redefinition of the female role into a nation-wide effort to change the self-image and expectations of men and women."

472. "Getting the Printed Word Before the Public Eye." *Weekly Women's Magazine.* May 16, 1958, pp. 58-60.

   Women contributed to journalism in the Philippines for years; even on the revolutionary *La Solidaridad* in the 1890s, where Rosa Sevilla de Alvero and Florentina Nable de Avellano wrote.

473. Jayamanne, Laleen. "Positions of Women in the Sri Lankan Cinema 1947-1979." Ph.D. dissertation, New South Wales University, 1981.

474. Lee Kyong-ja. "A Historical Approach to Magazines for Women in Korea; Based Particularly on Magazines Published Before 1945." Master's thesis, Seoul National University, 1971. 132 pp.

   Korean Woman's Magazine analyzed for years 1905-1945; a content analysis of 18 women's magazines found to promote self-consciousness and modernization among women.

475. Logarta, Lita Torralba. "The Distaff Side of Journalism in the Philippines." *Saturday Mirror Magazine.* February 19, 1955, pp. 5-7.

   No women's magazines existed in the Philippines until *El Bello Sexo* in 1891, an illustrated weekly of fashions, morals, literature and history. Another periodical for women appeared in 1892, but the first real women's journal was *El Hogar* (The Home) in 1893, whose entire staff was female.

476. Malay, Armando. "Filipino Women in Journalism." *Weekly Women's Magazine.* May 2, 1952.

Author refutes critical comments of his writing on women's journalsim. Women's agitation for their rights brought out the first women's magazines in 1912, among which were *The Outlook* and *The Dawn*. Also see May 23, 1952 issue of this Manila magazine.

477. *Millard's Review of the Far East.*
Includes: "A Magazine for Chinese Women," May 7, 1921, pp. 520-522; "Chinese Women Now Have a 'Ladies Home Journal,'" September 21, 1918, p. 112; "Miss Wong Chen Quan Edits Women's Weekly," October 11, 1919, pp. 248-249.

478. Mulhern, Chieko Irie. "Japan's First Newspaperwoman: Hani Motoko." *Japan Interpreter.* Summer 1979, pp. 310-329.
Hani Motoko (1873-1957) was unique in the history of Japanese women as she built her reputation as a journalist and educator on her own merits. Her journalistic work on *Hochi Shinbun* and *Fujin no tomo* was unusual at a time when women were not thought to have opinions or convictions of their own. See also Yoshimi Kaneko, "Hani Motoko," *Jinbutsu Nihon no joseishi.* XII, p. 205.

479. Nakashira, Tumiko. "My Experience As a Woman-Journalist Who Was Misled Because of the Weakness of the Feminine Nature." *Chuo Koron.* May 1916.

480. Soh Mi-ja. "A Historical Study on the Korean Film Actresses Between 1903 and 1946." Masters thesis, Chungang University, 1971. 98 pp.
Social and artistic characteristics of Korean actresses for a 43-year period of Japanese occupation; chronological list of films from 1921 to 1961 included.

481. "Woman in P.I. Radio." *Saturday Mirror Magazine.* October 25, 1952, pp. 12-14.
In the late 1930s, women such as Lina Flor and Luz Mat Castro first went on the air in the Philippines; they emceed and played drama roles, but did not announce. By 1952, about 20 women announcers worked in the Philippines.

482. "Women Reporters in Tokyo." *Chuo Koron.* July 1913.

483. Yau, Esther C.M. "Cultural and Economic Dislocations: Filmic Phantasies of Chinese Women in the 1980s." *Wide Angle.* 11:2 (1989), pp. 6-21.
Revolutionary heroines of film in the 1950s to 1970s; gender and Chinese film of the 1980s. The "representations of women suggest a socialist emancipation which ultimately put Chinese women in a more privileged position of power, in contrast to Hollywood."

484. Yonezawa, Yoshihiro. *Sengo Shojo Mangashi* (A Postwar History of Girls' Comics). Tokyo: Shimpyosha, 1980.

Images of Women

485. Amin, Amina. "Commercial Ads and Insult and Injury to Women." Paper presented at inauguration of display on advertising, organized by the Ahmedabad Women's Action Group (AWAG), Ahmedabad, 1981.

486. Amin, Amina. "Commerical Ads and the Great Health Robbery of Women and Children." Paper presented at Seminar of the Voluntary Health Association of India, Ahmedabad, 1982.

487. Anand, Anita. "Asia-Pacific: Bringing Women Together To Break the Media Role Model." *Sex-Roles within Massmedia Newsletter.* November 1988, pp. 27-28.
    Summarizes reports to and actions of a Kuala Lumpur meeting of Asian women media specialists.

488. Anu, Mini and Shashi Joshi. "Old Poison in New Bottles." *Manushi.* March-April 1979, pp. 51-54.
    Indian films portray a double image of women, mother or whore.

489. Asian Institute of Journalism. *A Course Guide in Development Journalism.* Manila: AIJ, 1983.
    "Women in the Media," pp. 49-52.

490. Azarcon-dela Cruz, Pennie S. *Images of Women in the Philippine Media.* Manila: The Asian Social Institute in cooperation with World Association for Christian Communication, 1988. 136 pp.
    Outgrowth of Women's Research Collective of 1984 and its Alternative Country Report. Hard data and research were later provided by the Research and Publications Office and Maryknoll College students. Chapters cover radio and TV ads, print ads, newspapers and tabloids, weekly magazines, *komiks* and porno magazines, TV shows, radio serials, and Tagalog movies. Findings show women and men in traditional roles. Data are from mid-1980s; changes have been made as women are publishers now and others have moved beyond the "lipstick" beat. TV shows such as "Woman Watch," "Public Forum," and "Probe" deal with women's issues; women have assumed prominent positions in television. But not much has changed with radio serials or Tagalog movies. Plots of radio "soaps" still revolve around family strife, with women "typically martyr, victim and superwoman keeping her disintegrating family together against all odds." Movies, though somewhat improved, generally show women as "weak-willed, passionate and emotional ... easily swayed by unbridled sexuality, by family and by lovers."

491. Banks, Asiah Sarji. "Film and Change: The Portrayal of Women in Malay Film." Paper presented at symposium, "Film and Social Change: East-West Approaches to Cinema," Maui, Hawaii, November 26-30, 1985.
    Explores position of women in society as portrayed in five films of the 1950s and 1960s, directed by famous Malaysian director, P. Ramlee. In all, women were portrayed as "supportive mothers, submissive and sacrificial wives and bereaved widows." Includes tables of characterizations, references, and synopses.

492. Barrett, Gregory. *Archetypes in Japanese Film. The Sociopolitical and Religious Significance of the Principal Heroes and Heroines.* Selinsgrove, Pennsylvania: Susquehanna University Press, 1989. 252 pp.

Filmic role of women in works of Japanese masters, especially in chapters, "All-Suffering Female and Weak Passive Male," and "Prodigal Son, Forgiving Parent, Self-Sacrificing Sister," pp. 118-159.

493. Bautista, Paulina F. "Women's News Reporting of Four Philippine National Daily Newspapers." Quezon City: University of the Philippines, Institute of Mass Communications, 1965. Unpaged.

Content analysis of July 1965 issues of *Manila Times, Manila Daily Bulletin, Manila Chronicle,* and *Philippines Herald* to find total number of pages devoted to women's news.

494. Behera, Sunil Kanta. "Gender Role Biases in the Indian Television Programmes." *Sex-Roles within Massmedia Newsletter.* November 1988, pp. 21-22.

How women and their concerns are portrayed in the media, the extent to which special shows for women represent women's realities, and the pattern of women's representation in TV programs.

495. Behera, Sunil K. "Gender Role Biases on Indian Television." *Media Asia.* 16:3 (1989), pp. 119-124.

Sexual discrimination in Indian television programs and commercials has caused an "alarming degradation of the image of womanhood"; women are useful in media "only for evoking pity."

496. Benegal, Shyam and Marilou Diaz-Abaya. "Women in Cinema: What Change?" *Asiaweek.* February 23, 1986, p. 74.

Contending that women have gradually made inroads into Asia's male-dominated movie industry -- in being made directors and into strong, central characters, *Asiaweek* set up a dialogue between Indian director Benegal and Philippine director Diaz-Abaya. The topic: how much have traditional social attitudes concerning women changed within cinema? Both agreed women's roles had not changed very much. They also discussed "heroine-oriented" films, capability of film to change social attitudes, and women's participation in cinema.

497. Bhasin, Kamla. "Women, Development and Media." *Isis International Women's Journal.* December 1984, pp. 8-18.

Development communication media remain silent about the role of women as professionals. Indian media distort women's social and self images and reinforce the conservative view of women. Women must create alternatives in different media and use them to empower women.

498. Bhasin, Kamla and Bina Agarwal. "Radio Ads: Reinforcing Sexist Stereotypes." *Voice of Women.* 2:2 (1983), pp. 14-15.

499. Bhaskar, Ira. "Mother Goddess Ascendant: Ghatak's *Meghe Dhaka Tara.*" *Isis International Women's Journal.* December 1984, pp. 44-47.

The myth of the Mother Goddess is powerful in Hindu mythology. Director Ritwik Ghatak was one of the very few filmmakers who made the protagonist of his film, "Meghe Dhaka Tara," an archetypal Mother Goddess.

500. Bowser, Pearl, ed. *In Color: Sixty Years of Images of Minority Women in the Media, 1921-1981.* New York: Third World Newsreel, 1983.
Includes Renee Tajima, "Asian Women's Images in Film: The Past Sixty Years," pp. 26-29.

501. Chang, Sung-Ja. "Feminists Hit Typecasting in Korean TV." *DEPTHNEWS Women's Feature.* March 1987.
Research of the Korean Women's Development Institute that looked at televised gender roles in 21 shows and 80 commercials. Men were shown in high-level occupational roles and women in lower ones and home environments, but men and women appeared almost equally in numbers, and the depiction of career women increased.

502. Chatterji, Jyotsna. "Women in Relation to Communication and Community." In *Communication and Community and Prophecy*, edited by James Massey, pp. 112-120. New Delhi: Asia Region, World Association for Christian Communications, 1989.
Images of women in Indian media.

503. Chatterji, Shoma A. "Identity and Status of Women in Bimal Roy's Films." *Cinema India-International.* July-October 1985, pp. 24, 26.
Women's portrayal in Indian cinema elicited much criticism of stereotyping in the mid-1980s, but director Bimal Roy took great pains to show women with dignity and charm.

504. Consumer's Association of Penang. *Abuse of Women in the Media.* Penang: Consumer's Association of Penang, 1982. 85 pp.
How media have been used to portray Malaysian and Third World women as inferior or as sex objects. This theme is examined in advertising, pornography, sex tourism, women's magazines, paperback romances, humor, television programs, films, and press coverage.

505. Council on Interracial Books for Children. "Children's Books from the New China." In *Racist and Sexist Images in Children's Books*, pp. 30-34. New York: Council on Interracial Books for Children, 1975.
Challenges to traditional Western stereotypes of women's roles and positive models concerning China.

506. Coxon, Kirby. "Taiwan Embraces Sexy Advertising." *Asian Advertising and Marketing.* September 1989, pp. 22-24.

507. Cronberg, Tarja and Inga-Lisa Sangregorio. "More of the Same: The Impact of Information Technology on Domestic Life in Japan." *Development Dialogue.* 2, 1981, pp. 68-78.

The impact that new information technology had upon two Japanese towns was to reinforce existing social patterns, including the role of women, rather than test out imaginative ways for social change.

508. Dasgupta, Shibani. "How Newsworthy are Women?" *Vidura*. February-March 1976, pp. 16-19.

    Sunday editions of four English dailies in 1975 carried women's articles which were mainly serious. Two points needed attention: the limited range of themes, not reflecting many of the economic and political realities in women's lives and the bias towards middle class women over those in rural areas.

509. Dayal, Abha. "Images of Women in Advertising." *Vidura*. June 1981, pp. 177-181, 187.

    Analysis of the image of women in Indian magazines, radio, television, and advertising leads to the view that women are used only as commodities; their bodies, smiles, and curves sell goods.

510. Desser, David. "From Feminisuto to Feminism: Women in the Films of Mizoguchi Kenji and Imamura Shohei." Paper presented at Association for Asian Studies, Philadelphia, Pennsylvania, March 1985. 18 pp.

511. Dua, M.R. "Violence and Sex in Advertising." *Indian Press*. September 1979, pp. 54-57.

    Of women images in Indian advertising, author asks, "what has a boob-dangling luscious thing got to do in the interior of a loco."

512. Elvinia, Lutgarda R. "Women in Communication for Peace and Development." *Communicate!* January-June 1989, pp. 56-61.

    A high level of sexism in Philippine mass media cited, including the very-popular radio dramas that spewed violence against women, the voice-overs in TV advertisements that were mainly those of males, the portrayals of women that implied that they keep themselves fresh, clean, and attractive to catch males' attention, and tabloid dailies' headlines that featured women as victims of crime and torture, as criminals, or as rape victims.

513. "En Chine: La réalité d'une contre-révolution bureaucratique." *Des femmes en mouvement hebdo*. June 27, 1980, pp. 24-31.

    With China's emphasis on "modernization," foreign images were creeping into advertising. After a 1980 visit, Des femmes en mouvement reported they saw, "billboards full of advertisements for cashmere sweaters and beauty creams (modelled by curly-headed, blond, slant-eyed 'Chinese')."

514. Forum for Children's Television. "Women and Informationalized Television in Japan." *Sex-Roles within Massmedia Newsletter*. November 1985, pp. 36-38.

    "Biased Information," "The Disappearing Boundary," and "Deep-Rooted Gender Stereotyping" addressed.

515. F.R. "In a Women's World: Women in Advertising." *Beautiful.* November 1978, pp. 24-25.
   In India.

516. Freiberg, Freda. *Women in Mizoguchi's Films.* Melbourne: Papers of the Japanese Studies Centre, 1981.
   Japanese director Kenji Mizoguchi's films from a feminist viewpoint. Mizoguchi women are self-sacrificing, serving the patriarchal order.

517. Gallagher, Margaret. "Broadcasting for Women's Development: Defining and Meeting a Need." *Asia Calling.* March 1985, pp. 8-10.
   Needs of women in Asia related at a regional seminar on "Broadcasting for Women's Development" in Kuala Lumpur. Asia media ignore or stereotype women; broadcasters seldom scrutinize program content to see what it might be telling audiences about women.

518. Ganguly, Shailaja. "Who Are the Change Makers and How Much Has Been Achieved So Far? A Brief Analysis of the Portrayal of Women in the Media." *Media Asia.* 14:4 (1987), pp. 232-235.
   The roles of women's groups and advertising associations in setting codes on the portrayal of women. Some attention to India's Indecent Representation of Women (Prohibition) Bill 1986.

519. Girija, Devi. "Women in Indian Films." *Women's Era.* June 1, 1978, pp. 46-53.

520. Goonatilake, Hema. "Women in Creative Arts and Mass Media." In *Status of Women in Sri Lanka*, pp. 45-188. Colombo: University of Colombo, 1980.
   Women in Sri Lanka cinema in 1979 were shown as either good or bad (the double image), and seldom in outside-the-home work experiences. On radio, women's programs were very romantic with almost nil discussion or analysis of problems. In 18 newspapers, women newsmakers only made up eight per cent of the news; women's appearances in photographs, only 20 per cent. With an exception or two, the women's columns discussed traditional topics -- fashions, cooking, child-rearing, etc. Magazines for women were also closely tied to this formula. Same author also wrote: "Media Reactions to a Journalists' Workshop on Women and Development: A Case Study," paper presented at UNITAR Seminar on "Creative Women in Changing Societies," Oslo, Norway, 1980; and "The Depiction of Women in the Mass Media: Myth and Reality," paper presented at regional seminar on "Women and the Media," Kuala Lumpur, Malaysia, 1980.

521. Gosling, L.A. Peter. "Sob-sisters and Sirens: Images of Women on Television." *Commentary.* October 1981, pp. 82-85.

522. Grjebine, Lois, ed. *Reporting on Prostitution: The Media, Women and Prostitution in India, Malaysia and the Philippines.* Paris: Unesco, Communication and Society Document #18, 1987. 106 pp.

Includes papers delivered at a 1986 Consultation on "Women, Media and Prostitution" in New Delhi. Analysis of media's attitudes towards the many facets of prostitution, including sex tourism. Among questions raised: Why have mass media remained silent about women's problems? What are the underlying attitudes of media people, and what is the ideal role of the media as seen by communications professors?

523. Gupta, J.P. "Women Life and TV As a Medium for Development. An Impact Study." Lucknow: Audience Research Unit, Doordarshan Kendra, 1980. Manuscript.

524. Habib, Miriam. "Women and the Media in Pakistan." Paper presented at International Women's Year Seminar, Islamabad, 1975.

Pakistani media stereotyped women in roles of housewife, mother, and consumer of advertised products. As far as development was concerned, women seldom were spokespersons for their own problems. Author also wrote 1980 paper for seminar on Women and Media (Pakistan Women's Institute, Lahore) entitled, "Women in the Communication Workforce."

525. Ide, Sachiko. "Language, Women, and Mass Media in Japan." *Feminist Japan*. 4:1 (1978), pp. 22-24.

The trivializing or sensationalizing of women shown in Japanese media.

526. "Images of Women in Indian Films." *Isis International Bulletin*. No. 18, 1981, pp. 14-15.

Extracted from *Images of the Woman in Indian Films* (Woman's Group, Ahmedabad, India). Twelve Hindi and six Gujarati films of 1976 analyzed; the emphasis was on "woman's beauty, her emotionality and her timidness," submissiveness, and irrationality.

527. Imamura, Taihei. "Comparative Study of Comics: American and Japanese -- Sazae-san and Blondie." In *Japanese Popular Culture*, edited by Hidetoshi Kato, pp. 87-102. Cambridge: M.I.T. Press, 1959.

First published in *Me* magazine, February 1953, this study compared two heroines in newspaper comics in two different cultures. *Sazae-san* (Mrs. Sazae), created by Machiko Hasegawa for *Asahi Shimbun*, worked on the theme that, "as drunkenness makes men active, the lack of rational thinking makes contemporary women active."

528. "Indian Media Are Slow in Helping Change That Society's Conflicting Views of Women." *Media Report to Women*. March/April 1988, pp. 6-7.

Indian media are playing only a minor role in conflicting ideas of "new" and "traditional" woman.

529. Ishikawa, S. "Shinbun no Terebi Bangumi-ran ni Mirareru Sei-hyogen" (Sexual Expressions in the TV Program Columns on the Newspaper). *Hoso Kenkyu to Chosa (The NHK Monthly Report on Broadcasting Research)*. August 1987, pp. 14-29.

530. Iwao, S. "Gaikoku-jin Moderu Kiyo no Jittai" (Content Anaylsis of Japanese Advertisements with Foreign Models). *Keio Gijuku Daigaku Shinbun Kenkyusho Nenpo (The Bulletin of the Institute of Communications Research).* No. 23, 1984, pp. 81-92.

531. Jaschok, Maria. "Images of Women in Chinese Cinema." *China Now.* November-December 1982.

532. Kaplan, E. Ann. "Problematizing Cross-Cultural Analysis: The Case of Women in the Recent Chinese Cinema." *Wide Angle.* 11:2 (1989), pp. 40-50.

   "The Legend of Tian Yun Mountain" compared with "Army Nurse." There is a "new moment" in China, reflected in recent films: "It is not by accident that female directors and writers are central in dealing with the change: since women's situation's the more extreme, they are the ones making the strongest demands for subjectivity."

533. Kaur, Anita. "Can Advertising Survive Without Women?" *Communicator.* July 1979, pp. 39-41.

   Although other Indian communication forms have exploited women, advertising has done the opposite, "projecting the super-liberated woman, who couldn't care a hang to keep within the bounds of tradition."

534. Kim Sook-hyun. "An Analytical Study of Women's Articles As Carried in the Korean Newspapers." Masters' thesis, Seoul National University, 1973. 49 pp.

   Dong-A Ilbo issues for March, June, September and December 1923, 1928, 1963 and 1968 were analyzed to see attitudes of the newspaper towards women. Of the 783 articles concerning women, 14.1 per cent were on clothing, 7.2 per cent on child rearing, 10.8 per cent on female activities, 22.4 per cent on culture and ethics, 1.5 per cent on fine arts, and 1.8 per cent on household accounting. Space devoted to women issues was 3.2 per cent of the total newshole in the 1920s; 2.2 per cent in the 1960s.

535. Kishwar, Madhu. "Family Planning or Birth Control." *Manushi.* January 1979, pp. 24-26.

   In Indian government films promoting family planning, a heavy sexist bias was present: emphasis on the importance of sons over daughters, the passive nature of women, and promotion of family planning as a duty of women.

536. Kodama, M. *Janarizumu no Josei-kan (Images of Women in Journalism).* Tokyo: Gakubun-sha Publishing Co., 1989.

537. Korabik, Karen. "Women at Work in China: The Struggle for Equality in a Changing Society." *Resources for Feminist Research.* December 1987, pp. 33-34.

   Chinese women have advantages over those of North America, including less sex-stereotyping in the media.

538. Krippendorff, Sultana. *Women's Education in Bangladesh: Needs and Issues. Part II.* Dacca: The Foundation for Research on Educational Planning and Development, 1977. 58 pp.

Contents of school textbooks (the *Bangla Readers*) in Bangladesh to ascertain ideas and attitudes about women that were taught to children. Questions arranged by the representation of women and the social value and capabilities of women. The textbooks were "clearly biased" against women in both categories.

539. Krishnan, Prabha, Anita Dighe, and Purnima Rao. "Affirmation and Denial -- Sex Role Patterns on Delhi Doordarshan ." *Sex-Roles within Massmedia Newsletter.* December 1986, pp. 13-14.

A 1984 survey of Indian media content revealed an increasing commonality in images of different media and a trend toward more negative portrayals of women. Study of Doordarshan Television's portrayals of women in July 1986 found that the main trends were those of affirmation and denial -- affirming her role in the home and deriving her existence from her husband and denying her struggles for economic and political autonomy.

540. Lebra, Joyce and Joy Paulson. *Chinese Women in Southeast Asia.* Singapore: Times Books International, 1980, pp. 171-177.

Southeast Asia media systematically discriminate against woman employees in pay and upward mobility. Section on images of women in the media.

541. Ledden, Sean and Fred Fejes. "Female Gender Role Patterns in Japanese Comic Magazines." *Journal of Popular Culture.* Summer 1987, pp. 155-176.

Female gender role patterns in Japanese comic magazines under categories of dimorphic, bimorphic, and amorphic. The majority of the women in stories fell in the dimorphic category.

542. Locher-Scholten, Elsbeth and Anke Niehof, eds. *Indonesian Women in Focus. Past and Present Notions.* Leiden, Netherlands: Koninklijk Instituut Voor Taal-, Land-en Volkenkunde, 1987. 264 pp.

Papers of a 1984 symposium on "Images and Ideas Concerning Women and the Feminine in the Indonesian Archipelago." Includes: T. Hellwig, "Rape in Two Indonesian Pop Novels: An Analysis of the Female Image."

543. Madhok, Sujata. "Struggling for Space." *Isis International Women's Journal.* December 1984, pp. 19-25.

Indian media have trivialized wife-battering and rape issues and neglected women as front page or headline news.

544. Makita, Tetsuo and Yasuko Muramatsu. "Changing Themes and Gender Images in Japanese TV Dramas, 1974-1984." *Studies of Broadcasting.* 1987, pp. 51-72.

Catering to the majority of their viewers, TV dramas focus on the women of the baby-boom generation. Rather than sacrifice themselves for those around, female characters in recent dramas show a strong sense of self regard. But many traditional sex role stereotypes remain, especially among supporting characters.

545. Makita, Tetsuo and Yasuko Muramatsu. "Ima, Terebi Dorama wa Nani wo egaiteiruka (2) Tojo-jinbutsu no Tokusei ni tsuite" (What TV Dramas Are Portraying Today -- A Detailed Analysis of Characters). *Hoso Kenkyu to Chosa (The NHK Monthly Report on Broadcasting Research)*. October 1985, pp. 26-37.

546. Marchetti, Gina. "'Four Hundred Years in a Convent, Fifty in Hollywood': Sexual Identity and Dissent in Contemporary Philippine Cinema." *East-West Film Journal*. June 1988, pp. 24-48.
    Marcos period films to understand the nature of cultural change and political resistance. Discussion of anti-Marcos filmmakers, a number of whom dealt with the interrelationship of sexuality and political dissent, and specific films: Lino Brocka's *Bona, Manila: In the Claws of Neon*, and *Jaguar*, Mike de Leon's *Moments in a Stolen Dream*; Lupita A. Concio's *Once a Moth*; Marilou Diaz-Abaya's *Moral* and others.

547. Marquez, Floredelindo T. "A Comparative Analysis of Culture and the Cultural Content of Printed-Media Advertising in the Philippines and Thailand." Ph.D. dissertation, University of Wisconsin, 1973. 333 pp.
    An analysis of eight periodicals -- two dailies and two magazines from Thailand and the Philippines -- to determine nine "cultural parameters," including male-female roles and concept of masculinity and femininity, in advertising; male-female roles and the concept of femininity and masculinity in both Thai and Filipino advertising were indicative of the presence of Western influence. By the same author: "The Relationship of Advertising and Culture in the Philippines," *Journalism Quarterly*, 52:3 (1975), pp. 436-442.

548. Mashita, Shin'ichi and Jun Fukuda. *Eiga no naka no josei-zo*. Tokyo: Kawade Shinsho, 1956.
    Japanese cinematic images of women.

549. Matsui, Y. "Contempt for Women and Asians in the Japanese Press." *Feminist Japan*. February 1978, pp. 12-14.
    Analysis of the Japanese press revealed a tendency in news reporting to provoke hostility towards women who move outside traditional roles and to approve of women who "stay in their place."

550. Mehta, Subhash C. "Effects of Sexual Illustrations on Brand-Products Recall." *Vikalpa*. October 1979, pp. 307-317.
    In India.

551. Mellen, Joan. *The Waves at Genji's Door. Japan Through Its Cinema*. New York: Pantheon, 1976. 463 pp.
    The role of women in Japanese film included in chapters: "The Japanese Woman," "Kurosawa's Woman," "Mizoguchi: *Woman As Slave*," "Tadashi Imai: *Woman Under Feudalism*," "Hani's Awakened Women," and "Shohei Imamura: Woman as Survivor." Directors treated women differently; Ozu is a "traditionalist and through his films we perceive the feudal, pre-World War II evaluation of the Japanese woman," while Kurosawa, respecting individual conscience, is more sympathetic to "psychic enslavement of the Japanese woman."

552. Mellen, Joan. *Voices from the Japanese Cinema.* New York: Liveright, 1975.
 A look at 15 Japanese film directors; women's portrayal in, and work with, media such as film.

553. Mellen, Joan. *Women and Their Sexuality in the New Film.* New York: Horizon Press, 1973.
 The "wife or whore" dichotomy was most frequently the pattern of portrayal of women in author's study of a few Japanese film directors.

554. Mohd. Hamdan Adnan. "Portrayal of Women in Malaysian Print Media." *Pengguna.* March 1984, pp. 31-34.

555. Monji, Jana. "Nightingale in a Cage: Japanese Women in the Media." Paper presented at "Facing East/Facing West: North America and the Asia/Pacific Region in the 1990s," Kalamazoo, Michigan, September 15, 1990.

556. Mulay, Vijaya. "Women in Indian Films." *Vidura.* February-March 1976, pp. 33, 35.
 A review of Feroze Rangoonwala's study of women in Indian cinema, which showed that cinema continues to portray women in traditional ways, that a few films tried to popularize women beating as a form of taming or romancing. The films of Ray, Ghatak, Sen, and Benegal portrayed women more realistically.

557. Muramatsu, Yasuko. "Images of Men and Women in Japanese TV and Sex-Role Attitude of People." *Sex-Roles within Massmedia Newsletter.* December 1983, pp. 21-24.
 Programs project images which almost correspond to those held of real men and women.

558. Muramatsu, Yasuko. "Terebi Dorama no Egaku Josei-zo" (The Portrayal of Women in TV Dramas). *Bunken Geppo (The NHK Monthly Report on Broadcasting Research).* October 1975, pp. 10-29.
 Analysis of 32 evening dramas of 1974; 11 of 13 home dramas showed broken families or families with unusual relationships. Most characters were in the 20s age group, and the proportion of working women "was higher than expected."

559. Muramatsu, Yasuko. "The Image of Women in Japanese Television Dramas." Tokyo: Nippon Hoso Kyokai, 1977. Mimeographed.
 Japanese television dramas portrayed women as young, in traditionally feminine occupations, seeking an identity through love or marriage, "with a passive attitude to the solution of problems, diligently home-oriented, self-sacrificing and dependable." Some change was evident.

560. Nathan, D.V. "Let's Stop This Insult and Injury to Womanhood." *Indian Press.* December 1976, pp. 43, 45.

Condemnation of the exploitation of women in Indian advertisements; "A product must sell by its quality and not with the aid of semi-exposed breasts, big bosoms or the hind parts of a young woman."

561. National Commission on the Role of Filipino Women. "A Study of the Image of the Filipino Woman in Mass Media. Interim Report." Manila: 1978.

The values associated with women in a sample of ten Tagalog films did not coincide with those of a sample of female college students. Of 19 traditional to modern values, five were emphasized in the films: respect for the old, double-standard of morality, loyalty to loved one, service to others, and self-sacrifice.

562. National Commission on the Role of Filipino Women. "Image and Reality Among Filipino Women: A Comparative Study of the Values Portrayed by the Female Lead Characters in Tagalog Films and the Values Held by Female College Students." Manila: NCRFW, 1978. Mimeographed.

563. National Commission on the Role of Filipino Women. "Stereotyping of Women in Prime Time Television Commercials." Manila: NCRFW, 1978. Mimeographed.

Almost 60 percent of TV commercials either used women as sales bait or addressed them as consumers; women were over-represented in advertisements for home and personal care, and as ornaments to ads for liquor, cars, and cigarettes.

564. National Commission on the Role of Filipino Women. "The Image of Filipino Women in Newspaper Advertising." Manila: NCRFW, 1978. Mimeographed.

Women were used in only 30 percent of the newspaper advertisements, probably because women made up a small part of the newspaper reading public.

565. "Packaged for Consumption: The Abuse of Women in Advertising (Malayasia)[sic]." *Isis International Women's Journal.* December 1984, pp. 31-36.

A number of ads from Malaysia used to display sexism -- e.g. Anchor beer, National Radio Cassette, and washing machines.

566. Patel, Vibhuti. "Songs of Solidarity." *Isis International Women's Journal.* December 1984, pp. 120-121.

Songs written by Indian women to promote their campaigns against stereotyping, rape, etc.

567. Pathak, Ila. "Reporting Rape Cases." *Vidura.* February 1981, pp. 10-11, 76.

The manner in which Indian dailies treated rape was abhorrent to many women, especially the great detail and imagination used in discussing the subject. The author asks, "Why did the journalists see rape cases as merely spicy stories?" and gives a number of examples where newsmen and copywriters treated rape in a humorous, callous or otherwise unsympathetic manner.

568. Pathak, Ila. "The Relevance of the Image of the Woman Reflected in the Women's Sections of the Dailies Printed in Ahmedabad." Ahmedabad: The Women's Group, 1979. Mimeographed.

   A three-month study of weekly women's sections of two Gujarati dailies revealed that editors did not want to tackle women's problems seriously.

569. Pathak, Ila, et al. "The Images of the Woman in Indian Hindi and Gujarati Films." Ahmedabad: The Women's Group, 1977.

   Analysis of women's roles in 12 Hindi and six Gujarati films of 1976 showed an emphasis on young, beautiful and sexually attractive women; the portrayal of women in terms of their relationship to men, in traditional female occupations, as overwhelmingly emotional, dependent, superstitious and irrational, and in marriage. Among other papers presented by the author were: "Media and Sex Roles," with Amina Amin, Ahmedabad: Women's Action Group, n.d.; "Role of Doordarshan Television in Women's Equality and Development," New Delhi: Doordarshan, 1983, and "Women and Media" Ahmedabad: Indian Institute of Management Seminar, 1982.

570. Pervez, Seema. "Image of Women in Media." *Sex-Roles within Massmedia Newsletter*. November 1988, p. 13.

   In fiction parts of Pakistani mass media, women characters portrayed the image of a woman who "wants to be an affiliate, calls for help, has a low self-concept, resigns to fate, is passive, humble, and modest." Also by the same author: *Analysis of Mass Media Appealing to Women*, Islamabad: Government of Pakistan Women's Division, 1982.

571. Powers, Janet. "The Media's Portrayal of the Women's Movement in India." Paper presented at Mid-Atlantic Region, Association for Asian Studies, October 1987.

   An assessment of the response of the mass media to certain efforts of the Indian Women's Movement.

572. Punwani, Jyoti. "Advertising and Women." *Debonair*. April 1980, pp. 53-56.

   In India.

573. Rao, Leela. "Woman in Indian Films -- A Paradigm of Continuity and Change." *Media, Culture and Society*. October 1989, pp. 443-458.

   Major trends in Hindi films relative to portrayals of women; history compressed into eras of "Silent Heroines," the "Dream Girls," and the "New Woman."

574. Rao, Leela and M.N. Vani. "A Cultural Enigma -- Portrayal of Women in Indian Television." *Sex-Roles within Massmedia Newsletter*. December 1986, pp. 12-13.

   Two very popular Indian TV serials, "Hunlog" and "Khandaan," personified women characters, reflecting the "irreconcilable areas of social and cultural values."

575. Rayns, Tony. "The Position of Women in New Chinese Cinema." In *Cinema and Cultural Identity: Reflections on Films from Japan, India, and China*, edited by Wimal Dissanayake, pp. 185-198. Washington, D.C.: University Press of America, 1988.

The tensions and contradictions in the depiction of women in "some recent" Chinese cinema, all dealing with "New Wave." Films were "formularly" and entrenched; radical-feminist Chinese film was not possible yet; strategies in creating new images of women were limited. Originally in *East-West Film Journal*, June 1987, pp. 32-44.

576. Reid, Thomas R. "Where the Singer May Be Slender, Pretty and Nude." *TV Guide*. July 6-12, 1974, pp. 10-12.

Japanese audiences were hooked to television through a nightly show, "11 P.M.," in which women were shown naked.

577. Reyes, Emmanuel A. *Notes on Philippine Cinema*. Manila: De La Salle University Press, 1989.

Includes "The Women on Her Shoulders: Women in Melodrama," pp. 43-50.

578. Richter, Linda K. and William L. Richer. "Analysis of Female Images in Five Indian Magazines." *South Asia Papers*. September-December 1977, pp. 25-55.

An analysis of fiction in two general readership magazines, *The Illustrated Weekly* and *Dharmayug*, and three women's periodicals, *Eve's Weekly*, *Femina*, and *Sarita*, showed that women were overwhelmingly shown at home, either unemployed or doing their own housework, and more passively than men.

579. Riti, M.D. "'Bandhana' Advocates Women's Lib." *Cinema India-International*. January-March 1986, p. 76.

"Bandhana," an Indian film.

580. Sasidharan, Rekha M. "The Advertised Image of Indian Women." *Sex-Roles within Massmedia Newsletter*. November 1988, pp. 17-18.

Forty graduate students objected to advertisers' clinging to sex-role stereotyping in about 100 TV commercials and "some" English-language magazines.

581. Sato, Tadao. "Change in the Image of Mother in Japanese Cinema." In *Cinema and Cultural Identity: Reflections on Films in Japan, India, and China*, edited by Wimal Dissanayake, pp. 63-70. Washington, D.C.: University Press of America, 1988.

Mother dramas in Japanese films, historical and contemporary perspectives; Japanese film of the 1980s had not created the type of heroine portrayed before, as in *Oshin*.

582. *Seminar*, New Delhi. August 1984.

Thematic issue on "The Sexist Media" includes: Modhumita Mojumdar, "The Problem," pp. 12-14; Prabha Krishnan, "Hidden Face of Patriarchy," pp. 15-18; Nina Kapoor, "Re-Marketing the Whore," pp. 19-25; Asha Ramesh, "The

Magazine Scene," pp. 26-28; Sujati Madhok, "Struggling for Space," pp. 29-33; Anjali Deshpande, "Hindi Journals," pp. 34-37; Bina Agarwal and Kamla Bhasin, "Action for Change," pp. 38-42.

583. Sethi, Renu. "Advertisers' Obsession with the Female Figure." *Indian Press*. December 1976, pp. 47, 49, 58.

    Indian advertisers got this obsession from the West; disccussion of the 20 obscenity complaints in the press before the Indian Press Council, 1968-1973. Examples given of advertisements which use women's figures in an unethical manner. Also see H. Mahmood, "Selling Sex or Products?" *Indian Press*, No. 10, 1974.

584. Singhpatboonporn, Urai. "Newshens Decry Sexist Bias in Thai Media." *DEPTHNEWS Women's Feature*. February 1987.

    If women made the front pages of Thai dailies, it was not on the basis of what they accomplished, but rather on what had happened to them (e.g. as victims of crimes). Results of a seminar of women journalists in Thailand given.

585. Siu, Yvonne. "TV Images of Chinese Women." *Asian Messenger*. Winter 1981, pp. 39-42.

    Excerpted from the author's M. Phil. thesis at Chinese University of Hong Kong; the image of Chinese women in contemporary drama on China's Guangdong TV and Taiwan's Networks, CTV, TTV, and CTS, from January 7 to March 9, 1980. One significant finding was the "salience of female major characters in the single-girl status both in the sampled mainland China and Taiwan programs. These young women, more than women of the older generation, were the active members of society; their attitudes and outlooks could contribute and influence the prospect of their society at large, their spirit of outwardness and non-passivity were particularly worthy of note."

586. Song, Yu-jae. "The Role and Image of Women in Korean Television Drama Programs." *Women's Studies Review* (Korean Women's Institute, Ewha Woman's University). 1 (1984), pp. 92-93.

587. Srinivasan, K.S. "Advertising and Women." *Vidura*. February-March 1976, pp. 31-32.

    The demeaning manner in which women are portrayed in advertisements, without giving much detail on the situation in India.

588. Suzuki, Midori F. "Television and Discrimination Against Women." *Sex-Roles within Massmedia Newsletter*. November 1987, p. 16.

    Gender stereotyping on Japanese television and the "commercialization of sex."

589. Tanwar, Taruna. "Sex Roles and Indian Cinema." Paper presented at International Association for Mass Communication Research, Paris, France, September 1982.

590. "Terebi Nyusu no Naiyo ni tsuite" (The Content of TV News). Tokyo: Nihon University, TV News Research Group, College of Art, 1988.

591. "Textbooks and Sexist Messages." *Vidura.* February-March 1976, pp. 39, 41.

Report of a study of the All India Women's Conference, in which textbooks in the "Let's Learn English" series were analyzed; few women were cast as central characters; instead, they were shown as either mothers or teachers.

592. "Textbooks and TV Shows Still Reflect Gender Bias." *Korean Woman Today.* Spring 1986, pp. 65-66.

Korean television shows and elementary school textbooks portray biased attitudes toward women. Abstracted in *Sex-Roles within Massmedia Newsletter*, December 1986, pp. 65-66.

593. Tokyo Paper's Editors Note Different Perspectives and Effects of Males v. Females on Media Content." *Media Report to Women.* September-October 1985, p. 7.

Taken from articles by Audrey E. Lockwood and Maki Yoshida in April and May 1985 issues of *Feminist Forum* of Tokyo.

594. Valicha, Kishore. "Sex and the Indian Film." *Cinema India-International.* 3 (1988), pp. 22-24.

Indian cinema had not evolved an adequate idiom to express frank sexual meaning; reasons given on why man-woman relations were difficult to portray.

595. Vanderwey, Judy K. "The Filipina in Life and in Film: A Comparison of the Typical Filipino Woman As Viewed by Sociologists and As Viewed by Film Makers." MA thesis, University of the Philippines, 1978. 201 pp.

596. Vasudev, Aruna. "Policy Parameters and Ideological Directives of Programming in Third World Broadcasts -- India." *Third Channel.* May 1988, pp. 857-861.

How Doordarshan, India's television channel, and films have portrayed women unfavorably.

597. Vasudev, Aruna. "The Woman: Myth and Reality in the Indian Cinema." In *Cinema and Cultural Identity: Reflections on Films From Japan, India, and China*, edited by Wimal Dissanayake, pp. 107-126. Washington, D.C.: University Press of America, 1988.

Role of women in Indian cinema historically and by regions and types -- within the family, beyond the family, courtesan, women at work, and sex object.

598. Vasudev, Aruna. "The Woman: Vamp or Victim." *Isis International Women's Journal.* December 1984, pp. 37-43.

Adapted from an article in *Indian Cinema Superbazaar* (New Delhi: Vikas, 1983); Indian cinema portrays women within the family as wife and mother, beyond the family as courtesan, at work, as a sex object.

599. Verghese, Joseph. "The Female Form in Our Advertising." *Indian Press.* September 1979, pp. 59-61.

The "female form" had become commonplace in Indian advertising; it must be handled with "great care and good taste."

600. Vibas, Danny T. "Celso Ad: Pro-Women or a Film Sexploiter?" *Malaya*. January 14, 1986, p. 7.

Film by Philippine director, Celso Ad. Castillo was supposed to be feminist.

601. Vilanilam, J.V. "Portrayal of Women in Malayalam Movies." *Mainstream* (New Delhi). December 22, 1984, pp. 24-27.

As a member of the Kerala State Film Award Committee, the author viewed 27 Malayalam feature films in 1984; many portrayed woman as "cheap, dumb and incapable of making decisions affecting her own life." Three movies were exceptions to this norm.

602. Wang, Yeujin. "Mixing Memory and Desire: *Red Sorghum,* A Chinese Version of Masculinity and Femininity." *Public Culture*. Fall 1989, pp. 31-53.

Aspects of female sexuality portrayed in the Chinese film, "Red Sorghum."

603. "War Against Sexism Is Global Struggle." *Media and Values*. Winter 1989, p. 20.

MediaWatch Collective in the Philippines and its findings concerning images of women in Philippine media.

604. Wheeler, Helen Rippier. "Japan-America Connections: Knowing about Japanese Women." Washington, D.C.: Women's Institute for Freedom of the Press, 1985. 26 pp.

Description of a semester-long, interdisciplinary course on Japanese women and feminism, portrayed in the media.

605. *Wide Angle*. 11:2 (1989).

Thematic issue on Chinese cinema includes Esther C.M. Yau, "Cultural and Economic Dislocations: Filmic Phantasies of Chinese Women in the 1980s," and E. Ann Kaplan, "Problematizing Cross-Cultural Analysis: The Case of Women in the Recent Chinese Cinema."

606. Willer, Thomas. "Perceptions of Women in Singapore: A Computerized Analysis of Newspaper Coverage." *Studies in Third World Societies*. December 1979, pp. 65-78.

Analysis of the *Straits Times*, 1972 and 1977; the "vast majority" of women's articles focused on Singaporean females, rather than on foreigners; there was positive movement in treatment of women outside their traditional roles in the family, kinship, and marriage, and a spillover effect from the Western women's rights movement.

607. Wilson, Rosalind. "Change at A.I.R.?" *Vidura*. February-March 1976, pp. 28-29.

In 1975, All India Radio, which carried women's programs for years, tried to get problems, issues, and interests concerning women projected through the whole range of broadcasting. A difficulty was that AIR tried to do this without a separate budget for women's programming.

608. "Women's Group Against Sexist Ads." *Asian Mass Communication Bulletin.* 17:1 (1987), p. 4.
In Singapore.

609. Yau, Esther C.M. "Yellow Earth: Western Analysis and a Non-Western Text." *Film Quarterly.* Winter 1987-88, pp. 22-33.
Analysis of position of contemporary Chinese women in film, "Yellow Earth."

Women as Audience

610. Agrawal, Binod C. "Communication Research Related to Women and Children." *Vidura.* October 1984, pp. 249-253.
Describes Indian TV research with emphasis on women and children; reviews audience studies of Indian women and makes recommendations.

611. Agrawal, Binod C. and Kumkum Rai. *Women Television and Rural Development.* New Delhi: National Publishing House, 1988. 99 pp.
Field-based anthropological techniques provide an understanding of how rural Indian women react to development messages relayed by satellites. By same authors: "Women Television and Rural Development: An Evaluative Study of SITE in a Rajasthan Village," Ahmedabad: Space Application Centre, 1980.

612. Agreda, Consuela C. "Availability and Use of Communication Media by Homemakers in Mass Media Barrios." Los Baños, Laguna: College of Agriculture, University of the Philippines, 1964. 36 pp.

613. Akhileshwari, R. "TV Should Enhance Role of Women in India." *COMBROAD.* January-March 1986, pp. 12-17.
Looks at print, radio, television, films and concludes reach of Indian media among women is low as result of illiteracy, inaccessibility, lack of respite from household duties, inconvenient program times, and traditionally-imposed inhibitions restricting the movement of women. Men are the readers and media viewers; women are stereotyped, even by women in women's magazines. Women producers of TV and films, Class 1 women officers of All India Radio and women print journalists are few.

614. Ali, S. M. "The Courtship of Housewives." *Media* (Hong Kong). January 1976, p. 7.
Discusses need to court non-English speaking, "sophisticated" housewives in Southeast Asian advertising campaigns.

615. All India Radio, Allahabad. "Women's Programmes of AIR Allahabad: A Mail Survey Report (June 1950-July 1960)." Allahabad: Listeners' Research Unit, AIR, 1960. 25 pp.

   Mail questionnaire results showed the majority of respondents listened to the women's shows, but only one-fourth listened regularly, while most listened occasionally. The majority of respondents thought noon was the best time for women's programs.

616. Bajaj, S.S. and Ishwar Banchare. "Research in Agricultural Communication: A Neglected Area -- Farm Women." In *Communication and Indian Agriculture*, edited by Ronald E. Ostman, pp. 271-276. New Delhi: Sage, 1989.

   Despite women's important role in Indian farming, they have not been studied by extension researchers.

617. Begum, Hasna. "Mass Media and Women in Bangladesh." *South Asia: Journal of South Asian Studies*. June 1986, pp. 15-23.

   Assesses each medium, pointing out strengths and weaknesses and providing generalizations about women. The "closed society" of Bangladesh gives few opportunities for women to benefit from anything mass media offer. Sufficient media exposure does not exist because of women's lack of literacy skills and financial resources.

618. Bhagat, Rekha. "Communicating Home Science to Rural Women." *Communicator*. April-July 1985, pp. 25-27.

   The use of a combination of media will lead to better communication of messages to rural women. Highlights the effect of communication factors in the transfer of home science technology to rural women.

619. Bhagat, Rekha and P.N. Mathur. "Impact of Mass Media on Farm Women's Opinion on Social Issues." *Interaction*. 3:1/2 (1985), pp. 72-82.

   Indian media play an important role in shaping lifestyles, influencing women's thinking on socio-economic issues.

620. Bhagat, Rekha and P.N. Mathur. *Mass Media and Farm Women*. New Delhi: Intellectual, 1989.

   Focuses on villages near Delhi and films, radio, TV, print media. By the senior author: "Impact of Mass Media on Rural Women," Ph.D. dissertation, IARS, New Delhi, 1983.

621. Bharti. "Political Consciousness of White Collar Working Women: A Case of the Capital City of Madhya Pradesh." *Journal of Sociological Studies*. January 1989, pp. 139-148.

   Media exposure, among other variables, was significantly related to political consciousness of the white-collar women in Bhopal, India.

622. "Career Women Boost Magazine Sales." *Free China Journal*. June 23, 1985, p. 3.

A survey indicated that career women in the Republic of China spent an average of 7.78 percent of their total incomes, or more than $10 million, monthly on self-education through books, magazines, newspapers, and extended courses.

623. Carreon, B.A. "Komiks Even Mothers Enjoy." *Woman's Home Companion* (Manila). April 25, 1974, pp. 26-27.
Appeal of comic magazines in the Philippines.

624. "Consumer Education for Women." *Isis International Women's Journal.* December 1984, pp. 78-81.
Advertising, consumer education, and women in Malaysia, through the declaration and resolutions adopted by the Seminar on Consumer Education for Women, held in Penang. The work of the Consumers' Association of Penang discussed.

625. Corpuz, Lavinia F. "TV Exposure and Attitude of Bagong Baryo Housewives Towards Luxury Commodities." AB thesis, University of the Philippines, 1974. 34 pp.

626. Council for Better Programming, Tokyo. "Housewives and Morning TV Shows." *The Annual Report of the Council for Better Programming.* 1970, pp. 38-48.
A 1969 survey revealed that housewives watched TV 3½ hours daily, in the process being the most enthusiastic viewers in the country. About one-third of the housewives' viewing time was devoted to dramatic programs, 13 percent to other entertainment, 17 percent to news, and ten percent to sports.

627. Fewster, W. Jean. "Reaching and Teaching Women by Radio." *Indian Journal of Communication Arts.* December 1975, pp. 14-21.
How women can be taught by radio in India. Reprinted from *Nutrition Newsletter*, January-March 1970.

628. Forum for Children's Television. *Joho-ka suru Asa no Terebi to Shufu-tachi* (Information-Oriented Morning Television and Housewives: The FCT's Fourth Report). Tokyo: Forum for Children's Television, 1985.

629. Ghosh, Akhila. "Media and Rural Women." *Isis International Women's Journal.* December 1984, pp. 63-68.
The impact of about 100 government films on family planning upon women of northern India.

630. Goodman, Kathleen and Mana Wagley. "Radio Improving Status of Women in Nepal." *Development Communication Report.* March 1983, pp. 5-6.
Radio Education Teacher Training Project (RETT), sponsored by U.S. AID, found women underrepresented in the Nepalese educational system; has strategies of radio training for women primary teachers, characterization of women in RETT broadcast and written materials, special programming for women,

programming to increase female student participation, and increased participation by women as staff members in RETT.

631. Hamima Dona Mustafa. "Communication and Change: A Comparison of Malay Women in Three Squatter Villages." Ph.D. dissertation, University of Washington, 1985. 216 pp.

Problems and changes in lives of Malay women who left their squatter villages to work in the city. Interpersonal, not mass media, communication was considered useful in solving their problems.

632. Hartmann, Paul, B.R. Patil, Anita Dighe, et al. *The Mass Media and Village Life: An Indian Study.* Leicester, England: University of Leicester, Centre for Mass Communication Research, 1983.

Includes the role of women in, and use by women of, mass media in India. Short sections are entitled, "Women's Campaign," "Marriage and the Family," and "Women, Youth and Others."

633. Hino, Jiro. "The Impact of TV Upon Housewives and Children." *Commercial Broadcasting Research.* No. 9, 1957, pp. 18-29.

Tokyo Broadcasting System tried to see effects of TV, after the first three years of telecasting, on family life. The findings of the 1,533 questionnaires showed that 32.5 percent of housewives regularly watched cooking lessons and 42.3 occasionally; other findings sought housewives' views on what TV had done to family life.

634. Johnson, Lynda D. "Magazine Use of Middle-Class English-Speaking Indians in New Delhi, India." Paper presented at Association for Education in Journalism, East Lansing, Michigan, August 8-11, 1981. 25 pp.

Survey of 200 residents of New Delhi found that age and gender made a difference in the number and types of magazines read. Women read more than men; feminist magazines ranked low.

635. Joshi, Ila S. "The Interpretation of Objectives of Television Programmes by the Employees of the Indian Television in the Light of Gender Equality." *Sex-Roles within Massmedia Newsletter.* November 1988, pp. 13-14.

Interviews with Indian television employees revealed that males did not give importance to the issue of women's development and both males and females believed that except for films and commercials, the portrayal of women on TV was positive.

636. Jung Yung-ae. "A Study of the Influence of Mass Communication and Personal Communication in the Purchasing Behaviors of Korean Urban Females." Masters' thesis, Seoul National University, 1972. 86 pp.

Application of five Western-originated communication hypotheses to Korean buying habits.

Asia, Australia, and Oceania 93

637. Karkal, Malini. *Mass Media Communication and Leadership Among Women in Six Rural Areas of Maharashtra.* Bombay: Demographic Training and Research Centre, 1968. 38 pp.

    An attempt to determine women's exposure to mass media and to identify leadership in a village in Thana district, February 1968.

638. Kaur, Ranbir. "Impact of Television on Farm Women." Masters' thesis, Indian Institute of Agricultural Research, 1970. 84 pp.

    A survey of three villages of Delhi Territory showed that as a result of TV exposure, women gained significant knowledge that was retained at a high degree.

639. Mallick, Amal Kumar. "Age and Sex as Factors in Newspaper Reading in India." *Journalism Quarterly.* Autumn 1963, pp. 602-604.

    A survey of subscribers to an Indian newspaper distributing agency revealed the main initiator of interest in females is news in general; in males, it is sports.

640. Mathai, Rabia. "A Study of Communication Patterns and Key Communicators Among Rural Women with Reference to Adoption of Family Planning Practices." Ph.D. dissertation, Indian Agricultural Research Institute, New Delhi, 1971. 192 pp.

    A large majority of the respondents were aware of various family planning methods; key communicators were found in all socio-economic classes in high-adoption villages and only in higher classes in low-adoption villages.

641. Mathur J.C. *Adult Education for Farmers in a Developing Society.* New Delhi: Indian Adult Education Association, 1972. 242 pp.

    Women farmers and the need for mass media and literacy to function together.

642. Matsuzawa, Kazuko. "Survey of Women in the Mass Media and Church." Tokyo: Lutheran Office of Communication, 1983.

    A sample of about 1,000 Lutheran women in Japan, found they preferred more culturally highbrow television programs than Japanese women in general, were not attracted to entertainment programs, and preferred serious magazines.

643. Mazumdar, Vina. "Women, Development and the Press." *Vidura.* February-March, 1976, pp. 3-5.

    The Indian press played a considerable role in improving women's status in earlier years, but, too much of the concentration was on problems and achievements of urban, middle class women.

644. Miyazaki, Toshiko. "Housewives and Daytime Serials in Japan: A Uses and Gratifications Perspective." *Communication Research.* July 1981, pp. 323-341.

    The average daily consumption of television by Japanese housewives is four hours and 29 minutes. Among these programs, serials ("hirumelo") have been criticized for stereotpying and scandalous content. A sample of 183 housewives of a Tokyo suburb showed no significant association between social participation and social use.

645. Movido, Monica S. "Comics -- Magazine Exposure and Family Planning, Knowledge, Attitudes, and Practices among Murphy Libis Housewives." *Philippine Journal of Communication Studies*. September 1971, pp. 44-59.

    The results of an experiment using Philippine comics to change housewives' views on family planning.

646. Muramatsu, Yasuko. "TV Drama and Women." *The Annual Bulletin of NHK Radio and TV Culture Research*. No. 23, 1978, pp. 59-109.

    A study of 2,000 women in Tokyo in 1977, found that 75.9 percent watched dramas regularly, 69.1 percent watched TV with another person, and 28.8 percent alone. They preferred plots rather than the actor/actresses, and took part less in social activities. By the same author: "Images of Man and Woman in Japanese TV and Sex-Role Attitude of People," *Hoso Bunko Foundation Newsletter*, May 1982.

647. Murthy, P.V.S. "Role of Women in Decision-Making at the Farm Operational Level." *Behavioral Sciences and Community Development*. September 1976, pp. 100-106.

    The interrelationships of the attitudes of Indian men towards women studied with other variables, including mass media contact.

648. Nakajima, Iwao. "Katei-fujin ni yoku mirarete iru terebi bangumi." (Television Programs Popular Among Housewives). *Bunken Geppo*. January 1964.

    In Japan.

649. "Newspaper Ads and Japanese Housewives." *Asian Mass Communication Bulletin*. November-December 1985, p. 4.

    Report on Japanese survey conducted annually since 1976; the eighth (1983) of 11,000 housewives found that the average housewife read a paper for 34.9 minutes daily.

650. Nuita, Yoko. "Impact of Audio-Visual Media on Socio-Cultural Behaviour of Women in Japan." Paris: Unesco, 1979. Mimeographed.

    Television dramas depicted women as housekeepers and men as wage earners, although some slight changes to show women outside the home existed.

651. Ohashi, Terue. "How Do The Mass Media Affect Women's Consciousness Formation?" *Soshioroji*. February 1984, pp. 117-137.

652. Pernito, Virgilio L. "Soap Opera Exposure and the Sexual Knowledge and Attitudes of Housewives." BA thesis, University of the Philippines, 1972.

653. Pervez, Seema. *Analysis of Mass Media Appealing to Women*. Islamabad: Government of Pakistan, Women's Division, 1982.

Final report of a project carried out by the National Institute of Psychology, Islamabad for the Women's Division of the Government of Pakistan.

654. Red, Isagani V. "Mass Media Exposure and Attitude Towards the Socio-Political Leadership of Women." AB thesis, University of the Philippines, 1974. 25 pp.

655. Saito, Kenji. "Housewives As TV Audience." *The NHK Report on Broadcast Research.* December 1975, pp. 10-15.

   Average TV exposure of Japanese housewives was 4 hours, 28 minutes, spread evenly through all three periods of the day. They watched more TV in the morning and afternoon than did American housewives.

656. Sohoni, A.W. "Broadcasting for Rural Mothers by All India Radio." *COMBROAD.* June 1985, pp. 37-38.

   How All India Radio, through workshops, attempted to ascertain the level of comprehension of rural mothers.

657. Stuart, Martha. "Are You Listening/Japanese Young Women?" *HBF Newsletter.* November 1983, pp. 39-41.

658. Taiwan. Ministry of Economic Affairs. Textile Industry Development Section. "A Study of the Housewives' Media Exposure in Taiwan." By Textile Industry Development Section of the Ministry of Economic Affairs and the Public Opinion Survey Center of the National Chengchi University. Taipei, 1969. 130 pp.

   Results of a questionnaire administered to 900 housewives illustrated their exposure to newspapers, radio, and television; media exposure correlated with economic status, education, husband's profession, residence, etc.

659. TV Entertainment Study Group. "How Do Housewives Feel about TV Entertainment?" *The NHK Report on Broadcast Research.* July 1977, pp. 27-42.

   Entertainment was most preferred in this Tokyo survey; amusement needs, rather than needs for self advancement, were met by TV.

660. Verbrugge, Lois M. "Peers as Recruiters: Family Planning Communications of West Malaysian Acceptors." *Journal of Health and Social Behavior.* March 1978, pp. 51-68.

   Whether personal or mass media communications was effective in recruiting 2,605 Malaysian women to use contraception.

661. Wartovo, John. "Planning and Production of Radio Programmes for Rural Women." *Broadcaster.* June 1989, p. 5.

   In Asia.

662. Wells, Troth and Foo Gaik Sim. *T'ill They Have Faces: Women as Consumers.* Penang: International Organization of Consumers Unions and Isis International, 1987. 142 pp.

The central role of women as consumers of health services, technology, food, housing, hazardous products, and credit facilities; women's needs and the actions taken in all of these areas.

663. "Women Are Greater Media Consumers." *Asian Mass Communication Bulletin.* June 1973.

Report of a Japanese survey that showed women watch television five hours and 18 minutes daily, listen to the radio for nearly one hour, read the newspaper for over an hour, magazines over half an hour, and books, 20 minutes. About 17,500 persons from 6,800 families were surveyed by a team headed by Yujiro Hayashi of Tokyo Institute of Technology.

664. Yadava, J.S. "Exposure of Women to Mass Media." New Delhi: Indian Institute of Mass Communication, 1976.

665. Yonezawa, Hiroshi. "Fujin wa dono yo ni terebi o miru ka." (Television Viewing Among Women). *Bunken Geppo.* October 1965.

666. Yu, Jen. "A Study on the Motivation of Housewives in Watching TV Serials." National Chengchi University Graduate School of Journalism, *Mass Communication Research.* May 1973, pp. 81-226.

A sample of 100 housewives in 1973 showed they had developed a strong habit of watching television serials, that social prestige was not a motive for doing so, that they watched the serials for entertainment, nostalgia, emotional release, substitutional participation, and as a reference for daily life.

667. Zhao, Xiaoyan. "Effects of Foreign Media Use, Government and Traditional Influences on Chinese Women's Values." *Revue Européenne des Sciences Sociales.* 27:84 (1989), pp. 239-251.

Sampled women in 11 universities and research institutes in three Chinese cities to determine effects of foreign media on values of social contribution, family, and self-realization; foreign media had negligible effects.

Women Practitioners

668. Ancheta, Herminia M. and Michaela B. Gonzalez. *Filipino Women in Nation Building.* Quezon City: Phoenix Press, 1984. 357 pp.

Women media personalities featured: Dolores H. Vera, Atang de la Rama-Hernandez, Katy de la Cruz, Daisy Hontiveros-Avellana, Maria Anson-Roa, in films; Trinidad Tarrosa-Subido, Carolina Flores-Trinidad, Estrella D. Alfon, Carmen Guerrero-Nakpil, Kerima Polotan-Tuvera, Rosalinda L. Orosa, in journalism. Marred by a boot-licking spread on Imelda R. Marcos.

669. Bahadur, Satish and Shyamala Vanarase. "The Personal and Professional Problems of a Woman Performer." *Cinema Vision India.* January 1980, pp. 22-25.

Interview with Indian actress, Kamalabai Gokhale, whose career began in the 1914 film, "Bhasmasur Mohini."

670. Baytion, Maria Corazon E. "Women and Media: The Philippine Case." *Sex-Roles within Massmedia Newsletter.* November 1988, pp. 34-35.

TV management was dominated by women, while they represented 32.16 percent of the total staff in seven dailies. Despite strong occupational roles, women continued to be stereotyped by media.

671. "Breaking Free." *Asiaweek.* July 18, 1980, pp. 20-26.

Cover story on women's successes in Asia, claiming the "old stereotype of the downtrodden Asian woman, subservient in all things to an insensitive male whose chattel she is, is largely untrue." Features as women leaders, Aw Sian, Hong Kong publishing tycoon, and Marina Samad, communications manager of Malaysia Esso's public affairs division.

672. Butalia, Urvashi. "Women and the Media." *Vidura.* June 1980, pp. 183, 185, 187, 189.

Indian journalism is male-dominated; therefore, women are discouraged from entering the field. Sought to find out why "the role that women play in the media, their professional status in it, and the images of women projected by the media are inextricably linked."

673. Careem, Nicky. "A New World for Nancy Kwan." *Media.* January 1977, pp. 12-15.

Star of "The World of Suzie Wong" entered a different part of film industry, becoming a producer and director of films with her Nancy Kwan Films Ltd. in Hong Kong.

674. Carty, James W., jr. "Female Journalists in Asian Countries Show Wide Range from 1% to 40% of Total." *Media Report to Women.* May-June 1983, p. 6.

"The numerical strength, status, salary, significance, and scope of Asian women communicators is small -- but not surprisingly so in view of the persisting traditions of the masculine-oriented cultures," according to Carty. The percentage of women in media was one in Bangladesh, 1.4 in Japan and Nepal, 10 in Pakistan and South Korea, 15 in Hong Kong and Malaysia, 20 in Sri lanka, 35 in Taiwan, and 40 in Thailand.

675. Chang, Gypsy. "The Woman Behind Chinese *Reader's Digest.*" *Sinorama.* March 1988, pp. 42-45.

Lin Tai-yi, editor-in-chief of the Chinese-language *Reader's Digest* for 23 years.

676. Chatterji, Shoma A. "Life and Times of Vijaya Mehta: 'It Has Been an Exciting Challenge' -- Vijaya Mehta." *Cinema India-International.* 5:2 (1988), pp. 39-48.

Indian woman theatre personality who became a film director is interviewed about differences between theatre and cinema work, the combining of economics and aesthetics in cinema, her beginnings as a director, methods of directing, and reasons for doing films the way she does. Includes synopsis of her *Pestonjee* with excerpts, stills, and a review.

677. Cheung Man-Yee. "Profiles of Women in Commonwealth Broadcasting." *COMBROAD.* July-September 1989, pp. 17-18.

Interview with director of broadcasting, Radio Television Hong Kong, and president of the Commonwealth Broadcasting Association, Cheung Man-Yee.

678. Chhabra, Rami. "Where Is the Communication Gap?" *Vidura.* February-March 1976, pp. 11-13.

An Indian seminar on women and the media is portrayed as an exercise in futility because senior women journalists were not present and the women represented almost a "closed door feminist meet."

679. *Cinema India-International.* July-September 1986.

Cover story devoted to "Raosaheb," a film made by Indian director, Vijaya Mehta. Her work is reviewed by Iqbal Masud, "Raosaheb: Triumph of Neurosis," pp. 19-20; V.P. Sathe, "A Socially Relevant Film," pp. 21-22; Shoma A. Chatterji, "A Salute to Vijaya Mehta," p. 23.

680. *Cinema India-International.* 3, 1988.

Cover story of Indian film director, Mira Nair, who won numerous awards for her work, especially "Salaam Bombay!" Includes Madhavi Purohit, "Mira Nair Scores a Unique Triumph," pp. 32-34; "World Press Reviews *Salaam Bombay!*" p. 35; Sooni Taraporevala, "Street Kids Philosophise!" pp. 36-38; Madhavi Purohit and Sangita Parmar, "'Many Stories in India Are Just Crying Out To Be Made' -- Mira Nair," pp. 39-41.

681. *Cinema Vision India.* 2:2 (1982).

Theme of "Moral Men, Immortal Melodies: The Golden Age of Hindi Film Music," which includes much on women, including, "When a Song Paid Fifty and Petrol was Six Annas a Gallon: Singer Rajkumari Talks to Ashok Ranade," pp. 16-19; Sumit Mitra, "O Indisputable and Indispensable Queen," pp. 38-45; Lata Mangeskar, "Lata on Others," pp. 46-47; Indu Bishnoi, "Portrait of a Melody Queen," pp. 48-50; Shashikant Kinikar, "Lasting Lady, Khurshid-Saraswati," pp. 70-72.

682. Coke, Andree and Meg Thompson, eds. *Asian-American Women Journalists' Conference.* East-West Center, Honolulu, Hawaii, May 24-28, 1965. Honolulu: East-West Center, 1965. 49 pp.

Twenty-two papers under headings of status of women journalists, role of women journalists in interpreting social change, role of women journalists in nation building, and creativity include the Pacific, U.S., Asia generally, Japan, and other regions.

683. Cong Cong. "A Series of Introduction of Well-Known Chinese Actresses. Part 6. Shangguan Yunzhu." *China Screen.* 4, 1989, pp. 32-33.

Screen career of Shangguan Yunzhu, from 1941 until her suicide, at age 48, during the Cultural Revolution of 1968.

684. deLeon, Anna Leah. "The Status and Role of Women in Philippine Television." *Sex-Roles within Massmedia Newsletter.* November 1988, p. 35.

Women have played important roles in Philippine television but not in the technical area. Women's Media Circle Foundation is working to change that with training courses.

685. Deocampo, Nick. "Women and Their Role in the Philippine Movie Industry." *Asian Cinema*. 4:1/2, 1988-89, pp. 3-5.

    Philippine cinema projects itself as male-dominated, but historically, the female presence exerted tremendous influence on the industry.

686. Dissanayake, Wimal. "Questions of Female Subjectivity, Patriarchy, and Family: Perceptions of Three Indian Women Film Directors." *East-West Film Journal*. June 1989, pp. 74-90.

    Three Indian women film directors closely associated with New Indian Cinema: Prema Karanth, Vijaya Mehta, and Aprana Sen. A number of their films analyzed to show cultural differences related to gendered subjectivity.

687. "Distaff of Communication." *Asian Messenger*. Spring 1976, pp. 24-26.

    Australia, China, Hong Kong, Taiwan, Japan, and Malaysia as brief case studies to discuss the various problems facing women in communications.

688. Dutt, Prabha and Coomi Kapoor. "Woman Reporter." *Vidura*. February-March 1976, pp. 14-15.

    Women reporters separately tell their difficulties of being "token" females in male-dominated newspapers.

689. Duus, Masayo. *Tokyo Rose: Orphan of the Pacific*. Tokyo: Kodansha International, 1979. 248 pp.

    Iva Toguri d'Aquino's life and role in Japanese propaganda to U.S. GIs; the myth of one "Tokyo Rose."

690. Estabaya, D.M. "Cebu's Crusading Newspaperwomen." *Kislap Graphic*. February 25, 1959, pp. 22-23.

691. Fernandez, Doreen. "Women in Media in the Philippines: From Stereotype to Liberation." *Media Asia*. 14:4 (1987), pp. 183-193.

    Though well represented in the print media, Filipino women journalists paid a high price for their current position. Certain areas of electronic media are still exclusively male dominated. Portrayal of women by Philippine media fall short of reality.

692. "First Woman Editor Resigns." *IPI Report*. March 1990, pp. 16-17.

    The first woman editor of a national daily in Pakistan, *The Muslim*, resigned when the management changed editorial policies.

693. Gajendragadkar, Nikhil. "Lata Mangeshkar: The Nightingale of India." *Cinema India-International*. 3/4 (1989) and 1 (1990), pp. 24-27.

    Prolific female singer of Hindi films.

694. Gunawardene, Hema. "Women Journalists' Role in Sri Lanka." *Vidura.* December 1973, pp. 429, 431.

    Of all professions, the one in which women are most underrepresented in Sri Lanka is journalism; not more than two dozen women work as journalists.

695. Habib, Miriam. "Women in the Communication Workforce: A Profile of Lahore. Perspective Paper for UN/Unesco Seminar on Women and the Media." New York: United Nations, 1980. Mimeographed.

    Formula films of Pakistan usually show women in stereotyped roles -- "deserted heroine," "shrewish mother-in-law."

696. Harris, Anne. "Leading Lady of Taiwan Publishing Faces New Challenge." *Asian Advertising and Marketing.* May 1989, pp. 14-17.

697. Hatano, Ruriko. "Japanese Women in Media." *Media Asia.* 14:4 (1987), pp. 216-217, 239.

    Some improvements in hiring of women have occurred; before 1986, legislation did not allow women in most Japanese occupations to work after 10 p.m. While media are no longer legally hindered from employing more women, reservations remain.

698. Hulston, Linda. "Not Just a Passing Vision." *Horizons.* 17:11, n.d., pp. 32-35.

    Profile of Khun Nilawan Pintong of Thailand who, in 1945, started the first "thinking" magazine for women, *Satri Sarn.* Although an editor for women, she did not consider herself a "firebrand feminist."

699. Hutnik, Nimmi. "Why Women Can't Give Their Best to Media." *Media Monitor.* July-August 1986, pp. 32-33. Reprinted in *Sex-Roles within Massmedia Newsletter.* December 1986, pp. 32-33.

    Gender equality in Indian mass media; media organizations had not been "adaptive enough" to the arrival of female employees. They expected women to be "but shadows" of men, to conform to standards of "maleness."

700. Ijaz Gul. "Women Directors Turn Out Hits." *Cinema India-International.* October-December 1984, p. 77.

    The directorial work of Pakistani women in 1984, among whom were Sangeeta and Shamin Ara.

701. "Indispensable Queen." *Time.* August 31, 1959, pp. 52-53.

    The woman who provides the singing voice for Indian actresses.

702. Inoue, Teruko. "Women's Journalism." *Japanese Journalism Review.* March 1985.

703. International Organization of Journalists. *Les femmes et la presse.* Prague: IOJ, 1975. 44 pp.

Nguyen Thi Than Huong, editor of *Femmes du Viet-Nam*, described that periodical's role in Vietnam's development on pages 20-21, while others reported on Poland, USSR, Czechoslovakia, and East Germany.

704. Jang, Hoonsoon Kim. "An Orientation Toward Tradition in Contemporary Korean Film Narrative and Structure: A Study of a Western Medium Produced in a Non-Western Culture." Ph.D. dissertation, Temple University, 1990. 176 pp.

 Women led men as major characters in contemporary top-grossing Korean films.

705. Joshi, S.R. "Invisible Barriers: Women at Senior Levels in Indian Television." In *Women and Media Decision-making: The Invisible Barriers*, edited by Margaret Gallagher, pp. 17-43. Paris: Unesco, 1987.

 Women's employment, status, and participation; general sex distribution, and sex discrimination relative to Indian television.

706. Joshi, S.R. "Participation of Women in Higher Decision-Making Levels of Doordarshan -- The Television Authority of India." Paper presented at International Association for Mass Communication Research biannual meeting, New Delhi, 1986.

 Gender bias and "invisible barriers" are not legally allowed in India, but they do exist. An exploratory study about the role played by women at higher decision-making levels in the Indian national TV network.

707. Katsutoshi, Yamashita. "Pure, Sweet and Slightly Dangerous -- Japanese Actresses." *Japan Quarterly*. April-June 1983, pp. 169-172.

708. Kumar, Jai. "'Play the Game' -- Shabana Azmi." *Cinema India-International*. 1, 1989, pp. 34-38.

 Interview with Indian actress, Shabana Azmi, a champion of small budget, quality films.

709. Lazaro, Cecilia L. "Women in Television -- The Philippines." *Intermedia*. October-November 1989, pp. 28-29.

 The bravery of women journalists who rebelled against Marcos. Women have increased their stake in mid-management positions in television, the highest held by women in 1989 being deputy network manager and senior vice president.

710. Lent, John A. "Bulletin Girls Who Left the 'Safe Zone.'" *IPI Report*. August 1986, pp. 8-10.

 Contributions of a group of women journalists at the *Manila Daily Bulletin* toward providing alternative views during the Marcos regime.

711. Lesage, Julia. "Interview with Deepa Dhanraj: Feminist Documentary in India." *Jump/Cut*. No. 31, 1986, pp. 40-42.

 Deepa Dhanraj, who makes films in Bangalore, India, discusses Indian films, the industry, censorship, and her feminist films.

712. Li Li. "I Don't Want To Be an Actress in My Next Life-- An Interview with Xu Shouli." *China Screen.* 4 (1989), pp. 10-11.
Profile of one of China's famous actresses.

713. McCormick, Ruth and Bill Thompson. "Feminism in the Japanese Cinema: An Interview with Sachiko Hidari." *Cineaste.* Spring 1979, pp. 26-30.
On her feminist portrayals in films such as "Bride of the Andes" and "The Far Road."

714. Madhok, Sujata. "Women in Journalism." *Democratic Journalist.* April 1986, pp. 9-11.
A "startling" rise in the number of Indian women journalists during the previous decade; magazine journalism attracted a large number. Not many women in managerial posts because of their late entry in the profession and the high dropout rate. Women settled for dead-end jobs because of the double burden of domestic and professional work. Trade unions must be more alive to the implications of the increasing recruitment of women.

715. Makhijani, Savitri. "It's Difficult for Women." *Vidura.* February 1982, pp. 49-50.
Difficulties women face as freelance writers in India: broken promises, returned commissioned work, etc.

716. Malay, Armando J. "Women of the Press." *Malaya.* September 1, 1985, pp. 4-5.

717. "Management and Production Recommend...." *Broadcaster.* June 1988, p. 12.
Fifteen recommendations of the 1988 Commonwealth Broadcasting Association - Radio Television Malaysia seminar on "Women in Broadcast Management and Production." Includes recruitment and training, working conditions, programming and research, and future cooperation.

718. Mohd. Hamdan Adnan. "Women and the Media in Malaysia." *Media Asia.* 14:4 (1987), pp. 194-203.
More women are enrolled in schools of mass communication than men, yet, few of them are in the highest levels of the media hierarchy. Various media portray women negatively.

719. Moslem, Shima. "Bangladesh: Distorted Image." *Democratic Journalist.* May 1990, pp. 8-9.
The position of Bangladeshi women journalists in the print media; how women are portrayed in the media, and role of women's pages. Abstracted in *IOJ Newsletter*, May 1990, p. 4.

720. Muramatsu, Yasuko, et al. "Can Women's Participation in Broadcasting Change the Media? -- Case Studies of Japanese Women in Television." In *Proceedings of '88 Tokyo Symposium on Women: Women and*

Communication in an Age of Science and Technology, pp. 79-98. Tokyo, 1988.

721. Nathan, D.V. "Women in Indian Journalism." *Indian Press.* October 1975, pp. 44-45.

    Using as an example, Annie Besant, who 58 years before, became the first woman editor in India, the author said one cannot find another woman journalist with the same power today. Women's editors today are assigned to women's journals, film periodicals, or children's papers.

722. National Press Club. *The Philippine Press Under Siege. Volume II.* Manila: 1985. 208 pp.

    Women journalists figured prominently in the fight for Philippine freedom, as reflected in sections on: "*Panorama* and *Bulletin Today*: Women Writers under Siege," pp. 53-106; "Forced Resignations, Arrest and Detention of Journalists," pp. 107-138; "Military Interrogations of Eight Women Journalists...," pp. 139-159.

723. "Nepal's Farmers Learn from the 'Old Lady.'" *World Broadcast News.* March 1981, pp. 10-11.

    A radio farm show that used "The Old Lady" to transmit development messages; the program was successful because the woman announcer effectively related to farmers' problems.

724. Neumann, A. Lin. "Ferdinand and Imelda, Ink." *The Quill.* September 1983, pp. 21-27.

    Considerable space to women journalists who opposed the Marcos Dynasty in their writings; especially the "Bulletin Girls," who braved the wrath of the presidential palace and their own publisher, Hans Menzi.

725. Nevard, Jacques. "Quemoy Speaks to Its Defenders and Besiegers in a Girl's Voice." *New York Times.* March 6, 1960, p. 17.

    Taiwan's use of 12 female disk jockeys to broadcast propaganda to China.

726. Ohkum, Yukiko. "Women Journalists: Their Lives and Opinions." *Journalism Research* (Japan). August 1973, pp. 28-40.

727. "Our Women Not Confined to Conventional Role." *Asian Messenger.* Autumn 1979/Spring 1980, pp. 56-57.

    Reprint from *The Mirror,* Sept. 3, 1979, claims that 37 percent of the journalists working for Singapore's four largest dailies and radio-television were women who were not assigned to producing only women's and children's fare but to covering political, economic, international, and general news.

728. Pham-Tung. "SVN Female Journalists, 'Vanguard Women' of a Country at War." *JESCOMEA Newsletter.* July 31, 1972, pp. 10-11.

    In the early 1970s, 30 South Vietnamese women were journalists, most of them metropolitan news editors and reporters. The number made up one-fifth of the Vietnamese Journalist Union membership. An official of the Information Ministry said of them: "They are the vanguard women of the weaker sex in

South Vietnam and no matter how their professional output is, we must be proud of them."

729. Quimpo, Candy. "The Fearless Publisher." *Asia Magazine.* January 8, 1989, pp. 26-28.

　　Eugenia Apostol spent 20 years editing women's pages at newspapers and magazines before becoming publisher of the defiant *Mr. and Ms.* during the Marcos years. She now publishes *Philippine Daily Inquirer.*

730. Ratnavibhushana, Ashley. "Sumitra Peries Speaks Out." *Cinema India-International.* 5:2 (1988), pp. 69-70.

　　Interview with Sri Lankan woman film director, Sumitra Peries, on her background and aims and feminist cinema in Sri Lanka; short filmography included.

731. Sharma, Sheila. "Women Journalists in India." *Democratic Journalist.* October 1968, p. 213.

732. Sherwood, Peter. "Stop Talking About Just Me -- Chow." *Media.* April 1978.

　　Selina Chow, successful television personality of Hong Kong, and her move to CTV in an attempt to save that station.

733. Sicam, Paulynn P. "Women in Philippine Journalism After 1972." *Diliman Review.* July-August 1982, pp. 28-31.

　　Before martial law in 1972, women journalists were a "safe and predictable entity"; they covered society or less active beats such as health, science, and education. After martial law, women asserted themselves as journalists on publications such as *Panorama* and *Bulletin Today.*

734. Soriano, Marcelo B. *The Quiet Revolt of the Philippine Press.* Manila: We Forum, 1981. 114 pp.

　　Attempts in the late 1970s and early 1980s to reinstall a free press in the Philippines; the forced resignation of *Panorama* editor, Letty Jimenez-Magsanoc, discussed, as were other women journalists who fought against Marcos repression.

735. Tolentino, Mercy Therese S. "A Case Study on Women in Journalism: Changing Status." AB thesis, Institute of Mass Communications, University of the Philippines, Quezon City, 1975. 73 pp.

　　Questionnaires and interviews used to determine the attitudes of Filipino women journalists towards sex equality. The results showed the changing status of Filipino women journalists as shown by the assertion equality among the majority of respondents. However, the author concludes that women in the Philippines have not yet established "a strong foothold in print media and in modernism."

736. Torrevillas-Suarez, Domini. *Sounds of Silence, Sounds of Fury.* Quezon City: New Day, 1989. 110 pp.

Writings of Philippine newspaper columnist who made up part of the corps of women journalists famous for taking on the Marcos government.

737. "TV News." *Asiaweek.* September 12, 1980, pp. 25-26.
Profiles women television reporters, Michelle Han of Hong Kong TVB and Tina Monzon Palma of Manila's Channel 7.

738. Van Zandt, Lydia. "Young Taiwanese Wife, Mother is Founder, Editor of Magazine." *Christian Science Monitor.* July 19, 1976, p. 18.
Linda Wu, editor of *Echo Magazine.*

739. Vasudev, Aruna. "Indonesia's Christine Hakim." *Cinemaya.* Autumn 1989, pp. 46-47.
Career of Indonesian actress, Christine Hakim, from her film debut in "Cinta Pertama" in 1973 to "Tjoet Nja Dhien" in 1988.

740. Ward, Lea. "How One Girl Grew Up in the Communication Business." *Media.* July 1979, pp. 13-14.
Profile of head of television programs for government's Radio Television Hong Kong, Cheung Man-yee.

741. "Women Writers Can Shock." *Asiaweek.* November 25, 1983, p. 68.

742. "Workshop To Equip Women Journalists for Senior Posts." *Asian Mass Communication Bulletin.* March-April 1990, p. 16.
In South Asian media.

Women's Media

743. Abeysekera, Sunila. "Voices of Women: Media Alternatives in Sri Lanka." *Isis International Women's Journal.* December 1984, pp. 89-91.
Media alternatives for women in Sri Lanka: *Kantha Maga* (Progressive Women's Front) and *Kantha Handa* (Voice of Women).

744. Agrawal, Binod C. and Arbind K. Sinha. "Challenges of Production and Research for Women and Children." In *SITE to INSAT.* New Delhi: Concept Publishing Company, 1986.
Contends that Indian TV's programs for women are of poor quality in content and presentation and cannot solve misapprehensions by rural women.

745. Agrawal, Binod C. and Arbind K. Sinha. "Instructional TV for Rural Women: Observations from Kheda." *Vidura.* August 1983, pp. 206-208.
Describes the weekly one-half hour of television devoted to women in India's Kheda district as important, because they had little access to other media.

746. *ASPBAE Courier.* "Women's Information Centre, Bangkok, Thailand." April 1988, pp. 3-22.

Shows how the center deals with creating modules for professional skills training, etc.

747. Awasthy, G.C. *Broadcasting in India.* New Delhi: Allied Publishers Pvt. Ltd, 1965. 268 pp.

Women's programs on All India Radio (pp. 96-98) started in 1940, with discussion on whether separate programs for women were necessary.

748. Bal, Vidya. "Women's Magazines and Social Purpose." *Vidura.* February-March 1976, pp. 21-24.

Advertisements and readers' rigid point of view towards retaining traditional feminine images of women influence women magazines' social purpose. Most Indian women's magazines lack a social purpose. Reprinted in *Media*, April 1976, pp. 16-17. By same author: "What Women's Journals Can Do," *Vidura*, October 1972.

749. Berry, Chris. "Chinese 'Women's Cinema.'" *Camera Obscura.* September 1988, pp. 5-52.

Interviews with Zhang Nuanxin, Peng Xiaolian, and Hu Mei, an introduction, and an article on "China's new 'Women's Cinema,'" all written by Berry. "Women's cinema" surfaced in 1986.

750. Brady, Kate. "From Fantasy to Reality: Magazines for Women." *Feminist International.* No. 2, 1980, pp. 5-8.

An examination of Japanese, general interest, women's magazines, showed that "the younger the group of women for whom the magazine was designed, the further removed from reality are its contents." The magazines minimize problems and look at life in idealistic terms. Housewife magazines reinforce the status quo; "all share a narrow vision of the world."

751. Butalia, Urvashi. "Making News: Asian Women in the West." *Isis International Women's Journal.* December 1984, pp. 114-119.

Examples of media for Asian women (BBC's program, "Ghar Bar," the women's newspaper *Outwrite*, the Indian magazine for Asian women, *Mukti*).

752. Butalia, Urvashi. "On the Absence (So Far) of Feminist Book Publishing in India." *Women's World.* No. 2, 1984, pp. 26-27.

753. Chhachhi, Amrita. "Media as a Political Statement: Two Attempts by Women's Groups." *Isis International Women's Journal.* December 1984, pp. 94-100.

Alternative media forms developed by Indian women featured: the feminist journal *Manushi*, posters, a calendar, street plays, and exhibition.

754. Constantino, Renato. "The Society Page." *Sunday Chronicle Magazine* (Philippines). December 7, 1958, pp. 10-12, 14-15.

Next to comics, society pages were the most widely read of Philippine newspaper fare. The author believed one could gauge the culture through society pages and attempted to do that for the Spanish, American, and post independence periods in the Philippines.

755. Cruz, Neal H. "The Most Useless Part." *Press Forum*. September 1964, pp. 5, 8.

    Newspaper editor discussed a Philippines controversy at the time: Is the society page necessary? Catalyst for the controversy was a Philippine Press Institute seminar on society pages. Manila newspapers carried numerous articles: *Manila Times*, September 22, 23, 25, 28, 1964; *Daily Mirror*, September 24, 25, 26, 1964; *Evening News*, September 22, 23, 24, 1964; *Philippines Herald*, May 29, 1965, p. 4; *Manila Bulletin*, September 24, 25, 26, 28, 1964; *Philippines Free Press*, April 3, 1965, p. 19; *Manila Chronicle*, September 24, 1964.

756. "DZWS, Women's Radio Station on Air." *Manila Times*. August 11, 1958, pp. 1, 14.

    Labeled itself the first radio station in the world strictly devoted to women.

757. Gloria, Amelia J. "The Content and Readership of the *Women's Journal*: A Case Study." AB thesis, University of the Philippines, 1973. 33 pp.

758. "Happy 30th Birthday, *Women of China*." *Media Report to Women*. January-February and March-April 1987, p. 18.

    History of *Women of China*, quarterly of All-China Women's Federation.

759. "How Good Are Our Women's Journals." *Vidura*. February 1972, pp. 35-37.

    Report on a seminar, "Writing for Women's Journals," held in India in 1971; among the conclusions, magazines had turned women's liberation into a joke.

760. Jahan, Roushan. "Exploring the Outreach: The Video Project of Women for Women." *Isis International Women's Journal*. December 1984, pp. 92-93.

    Activities of the Bangladeshi body, Women for Women: A Research and Study Group, especially its project to train women to use video for their betterment.

761. Japan Broadcasting Co. "Educational Broadcasts of NHK." Special issue of *NHK Today and Tomorrow*. Tokyo: Nippon Hoso Kyokai, 1975. 35 pp.

    Open-circuit and classroom broadcasts, including description of programs for women.

762. Josephine. "Importance of Film Medium in Social Change: A Study of Women's Films Made in India During the International Women's Decade, 1976-1985." Ph.D. dissertation, University of Madras, 1989. 205 pp.

    Six Indian films made during the International Women's Decade analyzed. Films were considered progressive with strong women characters. Chapters on the history of Indian cinema, "Women: Framed in Society, on Screen," "Towards a

Feminist Media Criticism from Stereotype to Liberation," and "A Totempole of Women's Films."

763. J.V.H. "India's Women Raise Their Voice." *South*. September 1984, pp. 109-111.
   The 1979 birth of the Indian women's magazine, *Manushi*, described with excerpts on its campaigns against the dowry system.

764. Kalwachwala, Dinaz. "Nari Tu Narayani: A Retrospective Look (A Television Serial on Women)." Ahmedabad: Development and Educational Communication Unit/ISRO, 1990. 109 pp.
   The process of making the TV serial, "Nari Tu Narayani," aimed at raising the status of women.

765. Karlekar, Malavika. "What Are Women's Magazines About?" *Vidura*. February-March 1976, pp. 25-28.
   Analysis of *Femina* and *Eve's Weekly*, Indian women's magazines, showed the Indian woman as a "winsome doe-like creature who questions little; or where she does, she works off steam by opening a boutique, designing clothes *a la Vogue*, or occasionally turning to administration."

766. Kim Jae Hee. "A New Challenge for Women's Editors -- the Expansion of Women's Page in Korean Press." Presented at First International Congress of Women Journalists, Washington, D.C., 1971.

767. Kon, Hidemi. "Women's Magazines Are Much Read by Japanese." *The Peiping Chronicle*. October 4, 1940.

768. Kurokochi, Paul. "Society Page in Japanese Newspapers." Presented at Philippine Press Institute "Seminar for Society and Women's Page Editors and Writers," Manila, September 21-25, 1964.
   An analysis of Japanese society pages by a staff member of the Japanese Embassy in Manila. Includes an appendix that translated the "Home" page of *Asahi Shimbun* for July 21, 1964, and "Women" page of *Yomiuri Shimbun* for July 15, 1964.

769. Lee Myong-ha and Shin Young-Il. "Woman Column in the Korean Newspaper." *Journalism Research* (Korea). March 1972, pp. 7-27.

770. Lee Wai Keong and Venugopal. "Impressionistic Content Analysis of Women's Magazines of Malaysia (*Her World, Wanita, Women* and *New Women*)." Unpublished paper, Universiti Sains Malaysia, 1974.
   Content analysis and interviews of young women who preferred foreign to local women's magazines. Popular local magazines were *Her World, Wanita, New Women*, and *Women*, whose contents revealed an interest in advancing commercialism.

771. Levin, Tobe. "Introducing Manushi: An Indian Feminist Journal." *Women's Studies Newsletter*. Winter 1980, pp. 30-31.

772. Malay, Armando. "Of Women, by Women, for Women." *Weekly Women's Magazine.* May 2, 1952, p. 6.
   In the Philippines.

773. "*Manushi*: A Journal about Women and Society." *Isis International Women's Journal.* December 1984, pp. 69-73.
   Manushi from its 1977-78 conception as a post-Emergency political journal dealing with women's issues; its operation and readership.

774. Manushi Collective. "The Media Game." *Isis International Bulletin.* No. 18, 1981, pp. 7-13.
   In capitalist societies, mass media brainwash people and force a distorted self-view down women's throats. Three Indian women's magazines for 1978-79 pushed competition among women, consumerism through sexist ads, fashion, etc. Originally published as "The Media Game: Modernising Oppression," *Manushi*, May/June 1980, pp. 37-46.

775. Nakpil, Carmen Guerrero. "Are Society Pages Necessary?" *Orient.* March 1964, p. 33.
   Yes, because front pages are terrifying and other pages are too cold and serious; the society page tells the public about the people in the big house on the hill.

776. "New Links for Pacific Women." *Asia Calling.* March 1985, pp. 3-4.
   Proposals of a workshop on planning radio programs for women of the Pacific Islands, including proposed monthly show, "Pacific Women."

777. Nirmala. "Women's Films Exposing the Brutality of Man." *Cinema India-International.* October-December 1986, p. 16.
   Indian films done by women, showing the extent to which women were abused at home and at work.

778. "On the Air: First Women's Radio Station in the World." *Weekly Women's Magazine.* August 22, 1958, pp. 40-41.
   In the Philippines.

779. Pathak, Ila. "AWAG's Battle Against the Media." *Isis International Women's Journal.* December 1984, pp. 74-77.
   The Ahmedabad Women's Action Group of India (established 1981) and its actions against mass media. AWAG has done indepth analyses of images of women in film, ads (*Commercial Ads: The Great Health Robbery of Women and Children*), print media, textbooks, stage plays, and TV shows.

780. Pathak, Ila. "Women's Pages of Gujarati Dailies." *Vidura.* August 1981, pp. 278-281, 288.
   A capsulized version of the previously mentioned 1979 Women's Group study.

781. Ramanathan, Kamala. "Do Women's Journals Click?" *The Word.* December 1972, pp. 15-17.

Indian women's journals had a total circulation of 383,000, of which, 212,000 was for English-language magazines. *Femina* in 1970 was the fifth largest English-language periodical in India. Author analyzed *Femina* and *Eve's Weekly* and asked 52 respondents in five different socio-economic categories their opinions of the two magazines. Everyone read the magazines, although they were not "starry-eyed" about them.

782. Ribeiro, Jorge. "Japan's World of Women." *Asiaweek.* July 6, 1984, pp. 41-42.

There appeared to be no end in sight to the proliferation of women's magazines in Japan.

783. Salmon, Claudine. "Presse feminine ou feminists." *Archipel.* 13, 1977.

Indonesian women's magazines, including a chronological listing.

784. Shaheed, Farida. "Creating One's Own Media." *Isis International Women's Journal.* December 1984, pp. 82-88.

The work of the Women's Action Forum (Khawateen Mahaz-e-Amal) of Pakistan, formed in 1981 to raise consciousness about women's issues; the role of media discussed.

785. Sidharta, Myra. "Women's Magazines in Indonesia: Between Hopes and Realities." *Prisma: The Indonesian Indicator.* March 1982, pp. 69-77.

The development of Indonesian magazines from their first appearance under the Dutch at the turn of the century.

786. "Society Pages Merely 'Puff the Image.'" *Press Forum.* March 1969, pp. 5, 8.

A survey of four Manila dailies in 1958 and 1968 showed society pages merely puffed images; were "pallid compendiums of weddings, engagements and social comings and goings." The 1968 pages were made up of fewer features, more social items, advertisements, blown-up photographs, and column inches.

787. Srivastava, U.K. *The Cost of Doordarshan Programmes for Women and Children: Some Preliminary Estimates.* Ahmedabad: Indian Institute of Management Working Paper 526, 1984.

788. Suyoko, Threes S. "Lembaran Wanita Dalam Surat-surat Kabar Indonesia." *Pers Indonesia.* December 1974, pp. 48-50.

Women's pages in Indonesian newspapers.

789. Takemiya, Keiko and Hagio Moto. *Shojo Mangaki ni Nareru Hon* (How To Become a Girls' Comic Artist). Tokyo: Futami Shobo, 1980.

790. "The Magazine of the Friends of Women Group (Thailand)." *Isis International Women's Journal.* December 1984, pp. 106-108.

Friends of Women, published by Puen Ying (Friends of Women Group) of Thailand, was formed in 1980. Contents of the first three numbers were described; the first issue of May-June 1983 was devoted to "Women and the Mass Media," with interviews of women in media, articles on media's view of women, book reviews, and data on the effectiveness of advertising laws.

791. "Third World Women's Film Programme." *Cinema India-International.* January-March 1986, pp. 127-128.

    At Filmotsav '86, Hyderabad, India.

792. Tipace, Amada R. "A Study of the *Weekly Women's Magazine*." Masters thesis, Syracuse University, 1966.

    All issues of *Weekly Women's Magazine* analyzed from 1951 to 1964, tracing a number of factors, especially development of editorial content.

793. "Trade War in Magazines for Women." *Free China Weekly.* September 26, 1976, p. 4.

    The emergence of "instant" publishers to scramble for the women's consumer dollar in Taiwan; more than 20 magazines for women existed. Reasons for this boom were the social progress of women, the large number of young women at marriageable ages, and the belief that advertisements in women's magazines had more impact than those in general interest newspapers.

794. Valenzuela, Carmen and Minnie Narciso. "*Women's Daily* Puts Women's News on the Front Pages." *Press Forum.* April 1972, pp. 1-2.

    Women's Daily came into existence "to give today's women a newspaper that will abet her growing interest in her environment, the historical period she is in, and the shifting social milieu."

795. Villamar, Sonia S. "Woman's Home Companion: A Case Study." AB thesis, University of the Philippines, 1977. 67 pp.

796. Wen, Wendy H.L. "Foreign Influences on the Media in Taiwan: The Case of *The Woman*." Masters thesis, University of Florida, 1979. 54 pp.

    Content analysis of all 1977 issues of Taipei monthly, *The Woman*, tested a number of hypotheses concerning foreign images: That foreign terms are presented more frequently as being superior to native models rather than as inferior (supported); that "America" is the nation looked upon as the foreign culture to be emulated (supported); that most of the foreign-oriented content materials are written or sponsored by Chinese instead of foreigners (supported).

797. Yem Chan-Huy. "A Structural Analysis of Korean Realism Films -- With Five Representative Films Produced Since 1970s." Masters thesis, Seoul National University, 1986.

    Analysis of narrative structure of five Korean women's films of 1970s and 1980s. Article resulted that was published in *Ready Go*, Vol. 2, 1988, pp. 32-57.

AUSTRALIA AND OCEANIA

General Studies

798. Branningan, A. and A. Kapardis. "The Controversy over Pornography and Sex Crimes: The Criminological Evidence and Beyond." *Australian and New Zealand Journal of Criminology.* December 1986, pp. 259-284.

    Other characteristics were considered as explanations of variations in rates of rape than circulation of pornography.

799. Mathew, Rae and Alfreda Stressac. *The Directory of Women.* Melbourne: Dent, 1987. 329 pp.

    Over 800 listings in more than 100 occupational categories, including advertising, bookshops, film/TV, image, journalist, librarian, direct mail, marketing, media, publicity/PR, and publishing.

800. *New Journalist,* Sydney. September 1976.

    Women Media Workers' issue, which contains "The Amazing Invisible Woman," "Rape and Media Hypocrisy," and "Guidelines for Non-Sexist Journalism." January 1978 issue dealt with the presentation of women in the news.

801. NSW Women's Advisory Council. *Organizations for Women in New South Wales. Directory.* Sydney: 1986.

    Information on the Australian Women's Broadcasting Co-Operative, Women's Film Fund, Sydney Women's Radio Group, and Women in Film and Television.

802. Tulloch, John and Albert Moran. *A Country Practice: "Quality Soap."* Sydney: Currency Press, 1986. 303 pp.

    Australian medical soap opera, "A Country Practice."

803. Wyndham, Diana. "A Select Bibliography/Contact List of Australian Articles/Research on Women and Media." *Sex-Roles within Massmedia Newsletter.* November 1987, pp. 23-30.

    Official reports, as well as popular and academic treatments; discussion of a volume by this author under the identical title, published in North Ryde (Australia) by the Australian Film, Television and Radio School (1987).

Historical Studies

804. Chauvel Carlsson, Susanne. *Charles and Elsa Chauvel: Movie Pioneers.* St. Lucia, Australia: University of Queensland Press, 1988.

    Thirty years of filmmaking (1925-1955) by Australia's pioneering filmmakers, Charles and Elsa Chauvel. Elsa Chauvel's important role is given long-overdue attention.

805. Clarke, Patricia. *Pen Portraits: Women Writers and Journalists in Nineteenth Century Australia.* Sydney: Allen and Unwin, 1988. 289 pp.

Asia, Australia, and Oceania   113

The lives of Australian women journalists on newspapers and magazines. Biographical data are organized under "Most Moral and Earnest," "New Women in Print," and other broad categories.

806. Richardson, John. "New and Strange Ways: The Radio Broadcasts of Irene Greenwood." *Continuum.* 2:2 (1989), pp. 50-76.

Examination of a number of radio scripts written by West Australian women's activist, Irene Adelaide Greenwood, between the mid-1930s and the mid-1950s.

807. Teale, Ruth, ed. *Colonial Eve. Sources on Women in Australia, 1788-1914.* Melbourne: Oxford University Press, 1978. 288 pp.

The section on advertising, pp. 104-118, stated that despite the few women with separate incomes, much advertising was directed at them -- in the home. Women journalists of the 1890s and 1900s were discussed on pp. 224-226.

Images of Women

808. Alford, Katrina. "Academic and Media Views of Married Women's Employment." In *Australian Women: Feminist Perspectives*, edited by Norma Grieve and Patricia Grimshaw, pp. 205-212. London: Oxford University Press, 1981. 333 pp.

Australian media criticized working married women with the "frequency and intensity" of a "campaign."

809. Bell, J.H. and U.S. Pandey. "Gender-Role Stereotypes in Australian Farm Advertising." *Media Information Australia.* February 1989, pp. 45-49.

Of 778 ads in *The Land*, 81 percent portrayed men only; none of the ads showing women only depicted them as farmers.

810. Bunce, Jenny. "Far From the Ivory Tower: A Review of Research on Women and Education in New Zealand." Paper presented at National Conference of the New Zealand Association for Research in Education," Wellington, New Zealand, December 7-10, 1979. 24 pp.

A brief part on the effects of sex stereotyping in mass media and children's books.

811. Cousins, Jane. "Gender and Genre: 'The Summer of the Seventeenth Doll.'" *Continuum.* 1:1 (1987), pp. 121-139.

The Australian play-film of 1955, "The Summer of the Seventeenth Doll," from a feminist perspective.

812. Dowling, G.R. "Female Role Portrayal: An Exploratory Analysis of Australian Television Advertising." *Media Information Australia.* August 1980, pp. 3-7.

Analysis of 239 Australian TV ads; the most sex-role stereotypes were for women's grooming, non-prescriptive health care, and household products.

813. Edgar, Patricia. *Sex Type Socialization and Television Family Comedy Programs*. Bundoora, Australia: La Trobe University, Centre for the Study of Educational Communication and Media, 1977. 50 pp.

    TV shows in Australia and their imagery of women; most of the shows were from the U.S.

814. Edgar, Patricia and Hilary McPhee. *Media She*. St. Kilda, Victoria, Australia: Heinemann Australia, 1974.

    Contribution of media, as well as the family, education, and the workplace, considered in the socialization into sex roles of women and men.

815. Jones, Lee. "Push-Button Pornography: Some Thoughts on Video Pornography and Its Effects on Women in Australia." *Isis International Women's Journal*. December 1984, pp. 48-54.

    The thoughts and feelings of a group of women opposing the spread of pornography through Australian video. The group, Women Against Violence and Exploitation, WAVE, described linkages between sexism in media and soft and hard core pornography.

816. Keeler, Suzanne. "Non Sexist Ads? We've Only Just Begun." *Media Information Australia*. February 1989, pp. 56-58.

817. Leder, Gilah C. "Fear of Success Imagery in the Print Media." *Journal of Psychology*. May 1988, pp. 305-307.

    Update of earlier study; of 57 articles in 1986 sample, 60 percent contained fear-of-success imagery.

818. Leder, Gilah C. "Successful Females: Print Media Profiles and Their Implications." *Journal of Psychology*. May 1986, pp. 239-248.

    How outstanding women are pictured by Australian print media. Do the portrayals reflect government proposals to stop discrimination against women?

819. Mann, Patricia. "Portrayal of Women in Advertising: Self-Regulation and Other Options." *Media Information Australia*. February 1989, pp. 50-55.

    Women must be portrayed in advertising with a plurality of roles and self-perceptions.

820. Mant, Andrea and Dorothy B. Darroch. "Media Images and Medical Images." *Social Science and Medicine*. November-December 1975, pp. 613-618.

    The image of women in drug advertisements contrasted with that of men in a seven-year sample of the *Medical Journal* of Australia and *Australian Family Physician*.

821. Mayer, Henry. "Women in TV Advertising: Melbourne Survey." *Media Information Australia*. August 1980, pp. 30-32.

    Women continued to be portrayed negatively or decoratively in Australian TV ads.

Asia, Australia, and Oceania   115

822. Mayer, Henry. "Women's Portrayal in Advertisements: OSW Forum: More Responses." *Media Information Australia.* February 1989, pp. 64-65.

823. Office of the Status of Women, Canberra. *Fair Exposure: Guidelines for the Constructive and Positive Portrayal and Presentation of Women in the Media.* Canberra. 1983.
   How to portray women constructively and positively in advertisements and media.

824. Office of the Status of Women, Canberra. *The Portrayal of Women in Advertisements.* Canberra, 1988.
   Two studies summarized at an Australian forum in 1988: Saulwick Weller, *Sex Roles Portrayal of Women in Advertisements: A Content Analysis,* 1987, 83 pp., and Sally Hartnett, *The Portrayal of Women in Advertisements: Stage 2: Women's Views about the Way They Are Portrayed in Television Advertising,* 1988, 87 pp. Weller analyzed the content of TV, radio, newspaper, and magazine ads, while Hartnett used a telephone survey and interviews with agencies.

825. Office of Women's Affairs, Canberra. *Towards Non-Sexist Guidelines for the Media. A Compilation of Suggestions for Change in the Media's Portrayal of Women.* Canberra: Department of Home Affairs, Office of Women's Affairs, 1980.
   Research, policy reports, and other Australian documentation on non-sexist guidelines in programming and advertising.

826. Pauwels, Anne, ed. *Women and Language in Australian and New Zealand Society.* Mosman, Australia: Australian Professional Publications, 1987. 171 pp.
   Eight chapters on language and gender in Australia and New Zealand; Lesley Stirling, "Language and Gender in Australia Newspapers," and the use of "ms." and gender in children's first school books.

827. Perkins, Roberta. "Wicked Women or Working Girls: The Prostitute on the Silver Screen." *Media Information Australia.* No. 51, 1989, pp. 28-34.

828. Schaffer, Kay. *Women and the Bush: Forces of Desire in the Australian Cultural Traditions.* Cambridge: Cambridge University Press, 1988. 229 pp.
   The Australian identity debate and the masculinity and femininity that underlie it; how cultural myths about gender are constructed and circulated in narratives of exploration and settlement, nationalistic literature of the 1890s, historical studies, modes of landscape representation, films, TV and press news.

829. Stocker, Laura J. "Songs of Our Future: Feminist Representation of Technology in Science Fiction." *Media Information Australia.* November 1989, pp. 49-52.

The portrayal of technology in three works of feminist science fiction: Charlotte Perkins Kilman's *Herland* (1915), Marge Piercy's *Women on the Edge of Time* (1976), and Sally Miller Gearhart's *The Wanderground* (1979).

830. Wyndham, Diana. "Ad Men, Subtract Women: Profit Without Honor." *Media Information Australia.* August 1987, pp. 52-58.

Although Australia and 65 other countries signed a United Nations agreement to eliminate all forms of discrimination against women, obstacles stand in the way because of portrayals of women in advertisements and the media. Examination of the shortcomings in the measures designed to eliminate discrimination from advertising and media, using Canadian and Australian experiences.

831. Wyndham, Diana. "Advertisers' Woman, 80s Woman: Which Twin is the Phony?" *Media Information Australia.* February 1984, pp. 26-33.

Despite studies (in at least Australia and Canada) which showed how to treat women fairly in ads, it was "unfortunate that most advertisers' women are phonies."

832. Wyndham, Diana. "Sexism Complaints Checklist." Sydney: New South Wales Anti-Discrimination Board, 1986.

833. Wyndham, Diana. "The Portrayal of Women in Advertising: Surveys and Forum." *Media Information Australia.* February 1989, pp. 58-61.

Women as Audience

834. Edgar, Patricia. "Social and Personality Factors Influencing Learning from Film and Television." Paper presented at American Educational Research Association, New Orleans, Louisiana, February 25-March 1, 1973. 25 pp.

Australian children and their reaction to film and TV violence. An analysis of male and female children on the basis of their self-esteem, found females preferred fantasy shows with female protagonists, and low-esteem females preferred them more than high-esteem females.

835. Herbert, Ralph, Michael Emmison, and Clare Burton. "Social Contacts Amongst Suburban Housewives." *Australian Journal of Social Issues.* November 1977, pp. 307-315.

Among Brisbane housewives, the dissatisfaction with the housewife role as expressed in the media may be overstated.

836. March, Robert M. and Margaret W. Tebbutt. "Housewife Product Communication Activity Patterns." *Journal of Social Psychology.* February 1979, pp. 63-69.

Communication behavior of Australian housewives to test hypotheses about four types of communication: leaders, followers, exchangers, and isolates. Opinion exchange between housewives was the dominant pattern for household products.

837. Palmer, Patricia. *Girls and Television.* Sydney: NSW Ministry of Education, Social Policy Unit, 1986.
   More than 50 Australian girls tell the role TV plays in teenagers' lives; TV programs are more immediate and involving than school.

838. "South Pacific Women Discuss by Satellite Their News/Information Media Needs." *Media Report to Women.* April 1, 1982, pp. 8-9.
   Women's needs for information on nine South Pacific islands.

839. Taylor, Sandra. "Days of Their Lives?: Popular Culture, Femininity and Education." *Continuum.* 2:2 (1989), pp. 143-162.
   The place of popular culture (especially soap operas) in the lives of Australian teenage girls and young women, and the "relevance of media in the social construction of femininity in contemporary Australia."

Women Practitioners

840. Alexander, Sandra. *Stop Organising...Be Creative. Report of the Organisation of Training Courses for Women in Film and Television Production Conducted by the Film and Television School, Open Program.* Sydney: Australian Film and Television School, 1979.
   Pamphlet inviting applications for the women's training course held in 1977.

841. Atkin, Elsa. *Equal Employment Opportunity Report. A Report on Equal Employment Opportunity Based on a Survey of Staff in the ABC.* Sydney: Australian Broadcasting Commission, 1982.
   Includes 41 recommendations (pp. 163-206), stating objectives, specific actions, responsibilities, target dates, and evaluation procedures.

842. Australia Council. *The Artist in Australia Today: Report of the Committee for the Individual Artists Inquiry (The Throsby Report).* Sydney: Australia Council, 1983.
   Identifies by name and address 25,000 artists in all artistic endeavors, excluding filmmaking.

843. Australian Broadcasting Corporation (ABC). *Report on the Work of the Equal Opportunities Unit.* Sydney: ABC, 1984.

844. Australian Film Commission. *Affirmative Action Program Report, Including an Equal Employment Opportunity Management Plan.* Sydney: AFC, March 1986.
   Detailed analysis and statistical documentation of employment patterns in AFC with reference to recruitment, training, and working conditions.

845. Australian Film Commission. *Women in Australian Film Video and Television Production.* Canberra: Australian Film Commission, 1987

846. Australian Film and Television School. "Selected Case Studies of Women Working in the Australian Mass Media. Background Paper for the Unesco Women in the Media Seminar and the Women Media Workers Seminar, May 1976." Sydney: AFTS, 1976.
   Includes: Babette Smith, "Television -- The Way In"; Suzanne Baker, "Women's Editor"; Patience Thoms, "Women's Pages"; Lana Wells, "Wire Service"; Pat Walter, "Cinecamera"; Pat Hudson, "Talk-back Radio"; Dorothy Drain, "Women's Magazines."

847. Australian Film and Television School. *The Media as a Profession for Women: Problems and Perspectives. Papers and Resolutions of the 1976 Unesco Seminar*. Sydney: Australian Film and Television School, Research and Information, 1976.
   Includes keynote address by Jerzy Toeplitz and presentations on TV and radio, press, film, and media's view of women (Mary Falloon, Barbara McGough, Helen Care), and the resolutions.

848. Australian Film and Television School. *The Professional Participation of Women in the Media*. Sydney: Australian Film and Television School, 1976.
   Part of a Unesco world survey for International Women's Year. Deals with role and status of women in radio, TV, and film. Includes results of 1975 survey. Also see Sara Pantzer. "Women and Media Action," *Media Information Australia*, Oct. 1976, pp. 8-9.

849. Australian Women's Broadcasting Co-operative (AWBC). *Corporate Policy in the ABC*. Sydney: ABC, 1984.

850. Baldwin, Wayne. "Kaz Cooke: The Modern Cartoonist." *Inkspot*. Spring 1989, pp. 34-38.
   One of Australia's first women cartoonists, who did strips for the *Sydney Morning Herald* and *The Eye* magazine.

851. Baranay, Inez. "Report on Participation of Women in Top Level Decision Making in Film and Television." *Media Information Australia*. November 1983, pp. 13-22.
   Reports on research trying to find out who determines film and TV content and who selects producers and directors and the role women play.

852. Blonski, Annette, Barbara Creed, and Freda Freiburg, eds. *Don't Shoot Darling: Women's Independent Filmmaking in Australia*. Richmond, Australia: Greenhouse, 1987. 400 pp.
   The historical, economic, and political factors influencing cinema and the achievements and limitations of affirmative action training schemes for women filmmakers are examined. Women filmmakers speak about their experiences and attitudes.

853. *Cinema Papers.* Sydney.
Two-part study of Australian women directors, June-July and September-October 1976; Daniela Torsh, "National Industry Training Scheme [AFC 1981-82]," October 1982, pp. 435-437; Victoria Treole, "Susan Lambert -- Interviewed by," pp. 37-39, and Vicki Molloy, "Women in Australian Film," p. 101, both March-April 1984; Christine Cremen, "Interview of Sophia Turkiewicz," August 1984, pp. 237-239.

854. Fernon, Christine. *Australian Women in Newsprint 1986.* Canberra: Vida Publications, 1987. 239 pp.
Indices of items on women found in major Australian newspapers.

855. Fifita, Nanise. "Women in the Media -- The Pacific." *Intermedia.* October-November 1989, p. 29.
A survey of Pacific nations showed that the newsroom of Tonga's broadcasting service was completely female; the announcing and programming staffs were 90 percent female. Radio Tuvalu had an all-female newsroom; one-fourth of the newsroom of Papua New Guinea's broadcasting was feminine, and Fiji and Western Samoa had more male than female reporters.

856. Lealand, Geoff. "Young, Trained, Female: A Survey of New Zealand Journalists." *Australian Journalism Review.* January-February 1988, pp. 93-99.
A 1987 survey that showed education levels of New Zealand journalists had risen dramatically in the previous 15 years; considerably more women had joined the profession.

857. Majumder, Kumar Sankar. "A Woman's Struggle for Dignity." *India Currents.* October 1989, pp. 18, 64.
Interview with "Spices" ("Mirch Masala") film writer Shafi Hakim.

858. Pip, Chris and Marion Marsh. *Women in Australian Film, Video and Television Production: 1987 Report.* Sydney: Australian Film Commission, 1987.
A full and long-range data base for research on the position of women in the film and other media industries.

859. Speed, Sally. "Women Film Makers in Australia." BA honors thesis, Australian National University, 1984.
Through search of library records, archives, and trade journals, tries to answer why women filmmakers existed in the 1920s but not subsequently.

860. Still, L.V. "Women Managers in Advertising: An Exploratory Study." *Media Information Australia.* May 1986, pp. 24-30.
Sixty-two Australian agencies had a total of 660 women employees, 52.7 percent of the entire workforce. Only 15.5 percent of the women held management jobs; women received less remuneration than men.

861. Wakem, Beverley. "Profiles of Women in Commonwealth Broadcasting." *COMBROAD*. April-June 1989, pp. 15-17.
    Chief executive of Radio New Zealand and president of the Asia-Pacific Broadcasting Union interviewed.

862. Watanabe, Haruko K. "Unesco Study on Women in the Pacific Media: Evaluation of the Needs/Requirements in Recruitment, Advancement and Working Conditions for Professional Media Women Throughout the Pacific Region." Paris: Unesco, 1984.

863. *Women Australia*. October-November 1985.
    Includes: Margaret Fink, "Calling the Shots in the Film Industry"; Vicki Molloy, "Australian Film Commission," and "Women in the Australian Film Industry."

864. Women's Film Fund. *Women in Australian Film Production*. Sydney: Australian Film Commission, 1983.
    In 146 feature films made between 1974 and 1983, male producers outnumbered female producers six to one, and male screenwriters outnumbered women eight to one. Also, the number of women in creative technical jobs, such as camera work and editing, was minimal. Also see report synopsis in *Sex-Roles within Massmedia Newsletter*, November 1985.

865. Wood, J. *Employment of Women in Radio and Television Stations in Australia, 1981*. Canberra: Office of Women's Affairs, 1982.

866. Wyndham, Diana. "On the Job Training Scheme for Women: Evaluation." Sydney: Australian Film and Television School, June 1986.
    Film and television's first on-the-job training scheme for women; 97 percent of the employers said working relationships were excellent or good, and 88 percent of the trainees had jobs three months after their training.

Women's Media

867. Brophy, Chris, comp., and Annette Blonski, ed. *Australian Women's Film and Video: A Catalogue of Films and Videos Produced or Directed by Australian Women*. Australian Film Institute, 1988. 104 pp.
    Films and videos produced or directed by Australian women, about women, on issues of concern to women. Can be used as bibliography, supplier directory, title listing of films and videos, index of subjects, producers, and directors.

868. Dunne, Carolyn. "Why the 'Coming Out Show' Keeps on Coming." *Look and Listen*. November 1984, pp. 23-25.
    Discussion of broadcast show and the Australian Women's Broadcasting Cooperative.

Asia, Australia, and Oceania 121

869. Harris, Rosemary J. "The Politics of the Women's Pages." *Sex-Roles within Massmedia Newsletter.* November 1985, pp. 38-39.

   How Australia's *Courier-Mail* (Brisbane) converted its women's pages into "living and leisure" pages. Interviews with staff and content analysis of four weeks of the newspaper.

870. "Korean Women's Magazines Surge in Popularity." *Asian Mass Communications Bulletin.* May-June 1990, p. 5.

   Number of women's monthlies has increased to huge proportions; 30 new magazines recently. Circulations of monthlies about 70,000 to 80,000 each.

871. "Rosemary Harris Surveys Journalists: Male Editors Make Decisions on, Without Understanding, Women's News." *Media Report to Women.* November-December 1984, p. 8.

   In the Australian press, especially the *Courier-Mail* of Brisbane. Continued in July-August 1985 issue, page 6.

4
EUROPE

EASTERN EUROPE

General Studies

872. Bosanac, Gordana and Mirjana Pocek Matic. "Problem komunikacije seksualiteta u masovnom mediju." *Zena.* 1-2 (1973), pp. 11-28.

873. Drakulich, Slavenka. "Wanted: A Nude *Glasnost.*" *The Nation.* June 20, 1987, pp. 846-847.
   Discussion of women's magazines in the Soviet Union in light of the launching of a Soviet edition of the West German fashion magazine, *Burda Moden.*

874. International Organization of Journalists. *Women and Media.* Prague: IOJ, 1984. 29 pp.
   Report of the European seminar in Warsaw, October 1984, sixth in a series of Unesco regional seminars for professional journalists. Recommended that a series of regional meetings be held to sensitize media managers to the disadvantaged state of women as an audience and as media personnel.

875. *Jel-Kép.* Special Edition. August 1984.
   Includes following on women and media: Róbert Angelusz, Ferenc Békés, Márta Nagy, and János Timár, "The Hungarian Journalist Community in 1981," pp. 96-138; Eva Foldvári, "Why a Medical Advice Column in the Press?" pp. 86-95, and Katalin Hanák, "Male and Female Communicators on the Screen," pp. 156-177.

876. Lewartowska, Zofia. "Prasa Kobieca i rodzinna" (Women's and Family Newspapers and Magazines). *Zeszyty Prasoznawcze.* 16:4 (1975), pp. 65-70.

877. Mamonova, Tatyana, ed. *Women and Russia: Feminist Writings from the Soviet Union.* Boston: Beacon Press, 1984. 273 pp.

Media discussed, including *Woman and Russia: An Almanac to Women about Women.*

878. Unesco. "Women and Media." European Seminar, 2-5 October 1984, Warsaw. Prague: International Organization of Journalists, 1985. 29 pp.

879. Varga, Karoly. "Motivational Background of the Mass Communication Behavior." *Magyar Pszichologiai Szemle.* 32:6 (1975), pp. 567-580.
    Study of a 69 male and 43 female TV-radio audience panel of Hungary to discover the intensity and mood direction of their achievement and affiliation motives.

880. "Women and Media: European Seminar in Warsaw, Poland, October 2-5, 1984." *Democratic Journalist.* January 1985, pp. 19-21.
    Discussions and actions of first all-European seminar on "Women and Media," held in Poland. Other Unesco-sponsored regional seminars of this nature had been held in Jamaica, Malaysia, Mexico, Fiji, and Tunisia. Some views of European participants and three recommendations for media organizations and four for research institutions.

Images of Women

881. Andrassy, Maria. *The Impact of Cultural Industries in the Field of Audio-Visual Media on the Socio-Cultural Behavior of Women in Hungary.* Paris: Unesco, 1980. 95 pp.
    Status of Hungarian women and their image in media.

882. Hanák, Katalin. "The Image of Women in the Radio." *Jel Kép.* Special Edition, August 1982, pp. 97-126.
    Content analysis of radio and television programs braodcast in Hungary for one week in 1979. In the main program types of radio, the predominance of men was clearly visible, however not so excessive as in Western radio. About 60 percent of the radio programs broadcast during the week did not contain any woman image worth evaluation.

883. Hanák, Katalin. "The Picture of Women on Television." *Sex-Roles within Massmedia Newsletter.* November 1984, p. 21.
    In a week of Hungarian TV, two-thirds of the people portrayed were men; in fiction programs, the story and dramatic situations were attached to the life of men.

884. Hoffmann, Márta. "Gender Advertisements in Hungary." Paper presented at International Association for Mass Communication Research, Prague, Czechoslovakia, August 1984.
    In 50 commercial photographs (mostly posters) from 1981-83, Hungarian women were "very far from looking real," looked directly into the camera, and wore an "opaque, uncertain smile" on their faces.

885. *Jel-Kép*. Special Edition. August 1982.
Includes: Zoltán Jakab and Márta Hoffmann, "A Society as It Appears on the Air," pp. 83-96, and Katalin Hanák, "The Image of Women in the Radio," pp. 97-127.

886. Knopp, S. "Sexism in the Pictures of Children's Readers: East and West Germany Compared." *Sex Roles*. April 1980, pp. 189-205.
Children's readers (grades 1-5) in East and West Germany. West German books of the 1970s were more biased than those of the 1960s, and both countries' books discriminated against women, those of West Germany significantly more so.

887. Mamonova, Tatyana. *Russian Women's Studies. Essays on Sexism in Soviet Culture*. New York: Pergamon Press, 1988. 198 pp.
Includes: "Elements of Feminism in Soviet Films," pp. 112-120; "Women in the USSR from the Points of View of the Official and Unofficial Presses," pp. 138-146.

888. Rosenham, Mollie. "Images of Male and Female in Soviet Children's Readers." In *Women in Russia*, edited by D. Atkinson. Palo Alto, California: Stanford University Press, 1977.

889. Semenoz, V.S. "Obszory Braka i Ljubvi v Moladeznyh Zurnalov" (Survey of Marriage and Love in Periodicals for the Young). In *Moladez Obrazovanie, Vospitanle, Professional'naja Dejatel'nost*, pp. 164-170. Leningrad: 1973.

890. Sokologska, Magdalena. "The Social Role of Women" (According to Materials from Public Opinion Research in Poland). *Sotsiologicheskie Issledovaniya*. July-September 1978, pp. 87-90.
Findings of a 1974 study of perceptions of women in Poland; for years, the media portrayed a variety of views of women's roles.

891. Sokologska, Magdalena. "The Woman Image in the Awareness of Contemporary Polish Society." *Polish Sociological Bulletin*. 3:35 (1976), pp. 41-50.

892. Szilágyi, Erzsébet. "Women in the Hungarian Film in the Seventies and Eighties." *Sex-Roles within Massmedia Newsletter*. December 1986, p. 51.
Female main characters were not very frequent in Hungarian films before 1970. However, between 1970 and 1979, 13 percent of the films had female characters "capable of creating their own lot actively." In the 1980s, the cultural-economic changes of society appeared as changes in feminine behavior.

Women Practitioners

893. Abdullayeva, Irada. "If the Husband Is Not a Journalist." *Democratic Journalist*. July-August 1985, p. 36.

How a Soviet woman journalist decides about advancing her career or saving her marriage.

894. Bolle, Hans-Jurgen. "Im Vormarsch." *Journalist.* 28:11 (1978), pp. 51-52.
Mentions women in the mass media of the Democratic Republic of Germany.

895. Hanák, Katalin. "Male and Female Communicators on the Screen." *Jel-Kép.* Special Edition, August 1984, pp. 156-177.
In Hungary.

896. Hansson, Carola and Karin Liden. *Moscow Women.* London: Allison & Busby, 1984.

897. Kinross, Felicity. "A Woman's View on Women in the Mass Media." *Democratic Journalist.* February 1989, pp. 24-25.
President of International Association of Women in Radio and Television discussed the organization's formation in 1951. IAWRT was to heal the divisions of World War II in Europe, the belief being women, including those in broadcasting, could do that best.

898. McReynolds, Louise. "Female Journalists in Prerevolutionary Russia." *Journalism History.* Winter 1987, pp. 104-110.
The roles of women reporters in Russia from the eighteenth century, attributing origins to Catherine the Great's 1774 satirical journal. The first successful woman's journal appeared in 1823; by 1864, a *Petersburg Leaf* female reporter unmasked a crooked employment firm in the style of the U.S.'s Nellie Bly 20 years later.

899. Quart, Barbara K. "Between Materialism and Mysticism: The Films of Larissa Shepitko." *Cineaste.* 16:3 (1988), pp. 4-11.
The work of aspiring USSR filmmaker, Larissa Shepitko, killed in an automobile accident in 1979.

900. Ramazanova, Nelia. "A Chance in Journalism." *Democratic Journalist.* June 1987, pp. 12-13.
The gains made by women in U.S. and USSR mass media.

901. Vasikova, Irina. "Chiefs of Soviet Diplomatic and Intelligence Agencies Questioned by Women Journalists." *Democratic Journalist.* April 1990, pp. 24-25.
Activities of the international press club, 33 Women and One Man, founded in Moscow in 1989.

902. Wilhelm, Klaus. "Frauenbilder im Programm des DDR-Fernsehens. Konzepte, Konstruktion und Realität." In *Audiovisuelle Medien in der*

politischen Bildung. Zweimal Deutschland seit 1945 im Film und Fernsehen, pp. 197-221. Munich: 1985.

Women in broadcasting programs in the Democratic Republic of Germany.

WESTERN EUROPE

General Studies

903. AAVV. *Donna e Tecnologie*. Rome: Commissione Nazionale per la Parita, Presidenza del Consiglio, 1986.

904. Abrahamsson, Ulla B. "Equality of Men and Women." *Audience and Programme Research*. June 1990, p. 1.
    Summary of ten years' activities of Equality Committee of Sveriges Radio.

905. Abrahamsson, Ulla B., Gunilla Boethius, and Maria Modig. *Nyheter för Kvinnor och Män?* Stockholm: Sveriges Radio Publik- och Programforskningsavdelningen, 1983.

906. *Analisi*. No. 9, 1984.
    Dossier on "El folletín por entregas y el serial," pp. 142-166, which summarized a roundtable discussion on soap operas held in San Sebastian.

907. Ashworth, Georgina and Lucy Bonnerjea, eds. *The Invisible Decade: UK Women and the UN Decade, 1976-1985*. Brookfield, Vermont: Gower, 1985. 162 pp.
    Includes Claire Crowther, "The Media: Power and Presentation," pp. 32-49.

908. Association FEM. *Les femmes vivent la téchnique; Les nouvelles technologies dans la vie professionnelle et la vie domestique*. Paris, 1987.
    Two reports resulting from a conference held in France on "New Technologies of Professional and Domestic Life out of a Gender Perspective."

909. Baehr, Helen and Michele Ryan. *Shut Up and Listen! Women and Local Radio: A View from the Inside*. London: Comedia, 1984. 64 pp.
    Ryan worked for Cardiff Broadcasting Company, the first independent local radio station to be partly owned by the community it serves. She and Baehr describe decisions and actions taken at the station and offer a number of alternatives on programming, uses, and listening. They conclude that local independent radio has grown increasingly out of touch with the experiences of women in the 1980s.

910. Benoît, N., E. Morin, and B. Paillard. *La femme majeure. Nouvelle féminité nouveau féminisme*. Paris: Seuil, 1973.
    Includes Benoît's "La nouvelle féminité," pp. 39-89.

911. Bermann, Tamar. *Kvinneperspektiv pa Dagspressen.* Fra et arbeidsmiljoprosjekt i norsk presse. Oslo: Arbeidspsykologisk Institutt, 1981.

912. Ceulemans, Mieke. "Het vrouwbeeld in de reclame." *Communicatie.* Autumn 1977, pp. 1-8; Winter 1977-78, pp. 9-14.

913. Commission of the European Communities. *Women and Television in Europe.* Women of Europe Supplement No. 28. Brussels: Commission of the European Communities, Women's Information Service, September 1988. 45 pp.

 Changing media environment, how women are represented in European media, women's employment in TV, and the future for women and the media.

914. Commission of the European Communities. *Women in Portugal.* Supplement No. 11 to *Women of Europe.* Burssels: 1984.
 "Women and Advertising," p. 50.

915. Darschin, Wolfgang. "Ältere Frauen sind das treueste Publikum von Frauensendungen. Ergebnisse einer Sonderuntersuchung zum Schverhalten der Frauen." *Notizen zum ARD Programm.* 4 (1978), pp. 1-3.

916. Diekerhof, Els, Mirjam Elias, and Marjan Sax. *Voor Zover Plaats aan de Perstafel: Vrouwen in de Dagladjournalistiek: Vroeger en Nu.* Amsterdam: Meulenhoff Informatief, 1986.

917. Eckersley, Robyn. "Whither the Feminist Campaign?: An Evaluation of Feminist Critiques of Pornography." *International Journal of the Sociology of Law.* May 1987, pp. 149-178.

 Reasons given for the feminists' entry into the pornography debates; the public debate on pornography in the United Kingdom.

918. *Femmes Suisses*, Geneva. October 1980.

 Gives some information on the images of Swiss women in country's media (dumb housewives or "eternal seduction") and women's participation in news presentation or reporting. B.P. 194, 1227 Carouge, Geneva, Switzerland.

919. *Fernsehen und Bildung.* Munich. 14:1/2 (1980).

 Includes: Hildegard Scholand, "Fernsehnachrichten gegen Fraueninteressen?" pp. 90-101; Elisabeth Berg and May Britt Ruths, "Ist Rundfunk in der Bundesrepublik Deutschland Mannersache?" pp. 135-145; Gerda Kanzleiter and Irene Neverla, "Frauen in einem Mannerberuf," pp. 148-173; Anna-Luise Heygster, "Die 'Aktion Klartext' in der BRD," pp. 174-175; Elke Baur, "Ans der 'Erhebung uber Anzahl und Positionen von Frauen in den Privaten Film - und Fernseh - Produktionsbetrieben in der BRD," pp. 176-185. Surveys women's role in television, pointing out non-occupational factors which affect their work and the sex-stereotyped stories they are assigned. Written by women professionals of Germany, England, France, Australia, and the U.S. All reach the conclusion that media contribute to the "symbolic annihilation of women." Worldwide bibliography. Rundfunkplatz 1, 8000 Munich 2, West Germany.

920. *Fraue-Zitig*, Zurich. December 1980/February 1981.
Thematic part on women and film -- films made about and by women. Most of contents featured Swiss women. Discussed three films; interviewed four film directors. Spitalgasse 8, CH-8001 Zurich, Switzerland.

921. Gallagher, Margaret. "Shifting Focus: Women and Broadcasting in the European Community." *Studies of Broadcasting.* 1990, pp. 61-82.
Topics covered for most of Europe: "Women and the Information Revolution," "Women's Responses: The Options Available," "Media Research and Action," "The Employment of Women in Broadcasting," and "An Action Programme: The Commission of the European Communities."

922. Gallagher, Margaret. "Unequal Opportunities." *Media in Education and Development.* December 1983, pp. 172-175.
Interview with Gallagher.

923. Gallagher, Margaret. *Women and Television in Europe.* Women of Europe Supplements No. 28, September 1988. Brussels: Commission of the European Communities, Women's Information Service, 1988.
Three studies from 1982-1985: analysis of images of women projected in popular TV shows by Gabriel Thoveron, et al., 1985; assessment of "alternative" programs of mainstream stations by Eliane Vogel-Polsky, 1984, and study of women's employment in European TV by Margaret Gallagher, 1984, 1986.

924. Geissbler, Rainer. "The Political Opinion Leader: Ideas and Propositions" (Politische Meinungsfuhrer: Begriffe und Theorieansatze). *Soziale Welt.* 23:4 (1973), pp. 482-496.
A la Lazarsfeld, when personal influence channels were researched, women were influenced by men.

925. Gibbons, Keith and Tonya K. Gwynn. "A New Theory of Fashion Change: A Test of Some Predictions." *British Journal of Social and Clinical Psychology.* February 1975, pp. 1-9.
Clothes as a means of communication.

926. Hall, Stuart, Dorothy Hobson, Andrew Lowe, and Paul Willis, eds. *Culture, Media, Language.* Working Papers in Cultural Studies, 1972-79. London: Hutchinson, in association with the University of Birmingham, Centre for Contemporary Cultural Studies, 1980.
Includes Dorothy Hobson, "Housewives and the Mass Media," pp. 105-114, and Janice Winship, "Sexuality for Sale," pp. 217-223.

927. Harms, Joan. "Yleisradion Selonteko Yk: N Kansainvalisen Nairsten Vuosikymen Suomemn Ohjelmaan" (Report of the Finnish Broadcasting Company for the International Women's Decade Programme). Helsinki, 1978.

928. Henstra, P. and L. Pinckaers. "Het beeld van de vrouw in de reclame: 1965-1975." Paper presented at the conference on Advertising and Women, Erasmus University, Rotterdam, February 25, 1976.

929. *HFF.* November 1983.
Monthly publication of the radio/TV/film trade union of West Germany includes Gisela Gassen's "Media and Equality," calling for media support of the equality of the sexes.

930. Holopainen, Irma, et al. *"Good Evening, Our Main Item Tonight Is ... Women": A Preliminary Study on the Role of Women in Television.* Helsinki: Oy. Yleisradio Ab., Planning and Research Department, 1984. 31 pp.
The role of women as provided in pictures by news and current affairs programs. Are women equally represented among television program editorial staffs and do they receive equal television time?

931. International Association for Mass Communication Research. Congress. Paris, France. August 1982.
Papers presented included Lies Janssen, "The Women's Emancipation Project in the Dutch Broadcasting System"; Else Jensen, "Television Newscasts in a Women's Persepctive," and Margaret Gallagher, "Television Content and Gender: What It Portrays and How It Is Perceived."

932. Jensen, Else and Madeleine Kleberg. *Kvinnors Roll i TV-Nyheter och Underhallningsprogram.* Stockholm: NORD, 1982.

933. Juno, Pia. "Kvinder i en Mandeverden." In *Danmarks Journalisthojskole 1982*, edited by Thorkild Behrens, pp. 28-31. Arhus: Danmarks Journalisthojskole, 1982.

934. Kerns, Ruth. "Selected Women's Issues in England, 1978-81." *RFR/DRF.* December 1982/January 1983, pp. 428-440.
Media is among the issues.

935. *Kirche and Rundfunk.* Nos. 70/71 (1978), pp. 1-27.
Symposium on "Frauen und Medien" includes: Lore Walb, "Sie haben ja einen Mann, der verdient"; Jutta Szostak, "Ihr Auseres hat störend von der Moderatorin abgelenkt"; Annemarie Mevissen, "Neue Einsichten, die fur die Zukunft hoffen lassen," and Gerda Kanzleiter and Irene Neverla, "Die Situation der Frau im Journalismus."

936. Kuchenhoff, E. *Die Darstellung der Frau und die Behandlung von Frauenfragen im Fernsehen.* Eine empirische Untersuchung einer Forschungsgruppe der Universität Münster u.l.v. (Band 34, Schriftenreihe des Bundesministers für Jugend, Familie und Gesundheit). Stuttgart: Verlag W. Kohlhammer, 1975.

937. Kuhn, Annette. *Cinema, Censorship and Sexuality: 1909-1925.* New York: Routledge and Kegan Paul, 1988. 252 pp.
Censorship exists in British films. By analysing three case histories about commercial features, author offers a view of censorship as a set of processes under conflicting forces.

938. *La Revue du Cinéma. Image et son.* April 1974.
Thematic issue on "Les femmes et le cinéma."

939. Lavaerts, C. "Kwantitatieve en Kwalitatieve analyse van de Belgische Nederlandstalige gespecialiseerde vrouwenper i.v.m. de problematiek vrouwenarbeid." Licentiaats thesis, Catholic University of Leuven, 1975.

940. *Les femmes: guide établi par la Bibliothèque de la Documentation Française* (Women: A Bibliographic Guide by the Library of French Documentation). Paris: La Documentation Française, 1975. Vol. 1.
An annotated listing of 1,466 books and articles in the library, arranged by seven categories, including women and the press. Vol. 2 is an update of 366 items received in 1974.

941. Lilli, Laura. "La Stampa Femminile." In *La Stampa Italiana del Neocapitalismo*, edited by V. Castronovo and N. Tranfaglia, pp. 253-311. Bari: Editori Laterza, 1976.

942. Maes, L. "De journalisten van de geschreven pers in België. Een sociologisch onderzoek." Licentiaats thesis, University of Gent 1973.

943. *Media, Culture and Society*, (London). April 1981.
Thematic issue on "Women and Media" includes: Liliane Jaddou and Jon Williams, "A Theoretical Contribution to the Struggle Against the Dominant Representations of Women," pp. 105-124; and Helen Baehr, "Women's Employment in British Television: Programming the Future?" pp. 125-134.

944. Mercadier, Marthe; Jeanne Maud Voyenne, Michèle Cabau, Anne Polini, and Franck Peyrinaud. *Les Femmes et l'Audiovisuel.* Rapport demandé par la Ministère des Droits de la Femme, Paris, 1983.

945. Michel, Andrée. "Multinationales et Inégalités de Classe et de Sexe." *Current Sociology.* 31:1 (1983), pp. 1-211.

946. Müller, Jutta. "Frauen-Fragen. Was Frauen denken, fühlen und erleben. Porträt einer Sendereihe im WDF." *WDR Print.* No. 115, 1985, p. 3.

947. Mulvey, Laura. *Visual and Other Pleasures.* Bloomington: Indiana University Press, 1988. 224 pp.
Collection of essays of Britain's foremost feminist film theorist provides an outline of an intellectual era within the changing context of the feminism and film cultures of the 1970s-1980s. By the same author: "Visual Pleasure and Narrative Cinema," *Screen*, Autumn 1975, pp. 6-18.

948. Muskens, G. J. "Journalist als beroep. Een sociologische analyse van de leden van de Nederlandse Vereniging van Journalisten." Band I, Verslag van het onderzoek. Nijmegen: Sociologisch Instituut, 1968.

949. "19 Sprecher und Fünfmal Dagmar Berghoff." *Courage.* January 1981.
    Reports on a women's meeting in Cologne (1980), dealing with women in media and representation by media and criticizes how women report on women. The December 1980 *Courage* discusses Frauen-Film Produktion, a German group of professional and non-professional women experimenting with filmmaking.

950. Nordiske Konferanse for Massekommunikasjonsforskning (Nordic Conference on Mass Communication Research). Volda, Norway. August 1983. (Summarized in *Sex-Roles within Massmedia Newsletter*, December 1983.)
    Working group on "Women and the Media" included: Else Jensen, "The Importance of Television and Video Film Medium as Influencing Factors in Terms of Gender Identification of Children and Youth [in Denmark]"; Sissel Lund, "Women's Mass Media Usage -- A New Field of Research into Women"; Marjan Flick, "The New Women's Movement and Mass Media"; and Irma Holopainen, et al., "The Role of Women in Finnish TV-Programmes."

951. Palmegiano, E.M. "Women and British Periodicals 1832-1867: A Bibliography." *Victorian Periodicals Newsletter.* 9:1 (1976), pp. 1-36.

952. *Papers: Revista de Sociología de la Universidad Autónoma de Barcelona. Mujer y Sociedad.*
    Includes: M. Isabel Marrades, "Feminismo, prensa y sociedad en España," No. 9, 1978, pp. 39-134, and Adolfo Perinat and M.I. Marrades, "El Cambio de Imagen del Rol Político de la Mujer a través de un Siglo de Prensa Femenina Española," No. 11, 1979, pp. 145-167.

953. "Promoting Equality Is Broadcasting's Responsibility as Opinion-Makers, Says Report." *Media Report to Women.* October 1, 1981, pp. 4-5.
    Excerpts from *Men and Women in Broadcasting, Working Towards Equality at Sveriges Radio*, Sweden. After the Swedish Broadcasting Corporation had a 1975 workshop on sex roles, an Equality Project was set up by union and management; this report, which devoted 23 pages to descriptions of things tried and listed 69 recommendations, was the result.

954. Radio Telefís Eireann (RTE), Working Party on Women in Broadcasting. *Report to the Radio Telefís Eireann Authority.* Dublin: RTE, 1981.
    Gross misrepresentation of women in Irish broadcasting.

955. Radio Telefís Eireann (RTE), Women in Broadcasting Study Group. *Women and RTE: A Question of Balance.* Report presented to Radio Telefís Eireann, Dublin, RTE, 1980.

956. Rinnert, Ulrike. "Frauen in den Medien." *Journalist.* 28:10 (1978), pp. 12-15.

957. Sadoul, Jacques. *Les Filles de Papier.* Paris: J.-J. Pauvert, 1971.

958. *Schriftenreihe zur Sozialen und Beruflichen Stellung der Frau.* No. 14. Vienna: Bundesministerium fur Soziale Verwaltung, 1983.
    Includes the following on women and Austrian media: Dorothea Gaudart, "Frau und Medien: Internationale Impulse -- Nationale Aktivitäten," pp. 5-21; Christine Leinfellner, "Frau und Berufswelt im Osterreichischen Fernsehen," pp. 22-52; Wolfgang Schulz, "Die Kommunikation über Ausbildung und Beruf der Frau in den Druckmedien," pp. 52-57.

959. Sheehan, Helena. *Irish Television Drama: A Society and Its Stories.* Dublin: Radio Telefís Eireann, 1987.
    Soap operas.

960. Skard, Torild. *Det Koster a Vaere Kar - Saerlig Nar en er Kvinne.* Fredrikstad: Instituut for Journalistik, 1984.

961. Straube, Gabi. "Frauen: Kolleginnen für 'Ecken und Nischen'?" *Journalisten-Jahrbuch '86.* Munich: 1985, pp. 153-155.

962. Summerhill, Audrey. "Feminism and Film." In *Feminist Action I,* edited by Joy Holland, pp. 162-179. London: Battle Axe Books, 1984.
    Mainly about the British scene.

963. Szostak, Jutta. "Klischees die ganze Woche lang. Frauen im Fernsehen -- wie sie dargestellt werden, was sie darstellen können." In *Frauen heute -- Jahrhundertthema Gleichberechtigung,* pp. 146-161. Cologne and Frankfurt: 1978.

964. *Telos,* Madrid. March-May 1980.
    Telecommunications journal carried seven articles dealing with Spanish women and aspects of technology in a special section, "La mujer ante el cambio tecnológico." Among the writers were Victoria Camps, Pilar Escario, Inés Alberdi, M. Cristina Lasagni, Judith Astelarra, Paola Piva, and Rosa Franquet.

965. "The Role of Women in Television News and Entertainment Programmes. A Danish-Swedish Study of Equality of the Sexes and Mass Media." *Nordicom Review.* No. 1, 1983, pp. 9-11.
    Interviews with working women journalists and content analyses of programs on Swedish and Danish TV; women's presence in broadcasting had not yet left its mark.

966. *The Times,* London.
    Has carried occasional articles, such as: Caroline Moorehead, "Women in Advertising," February 26, 1980, p. 9; Patricia Jones, "Hypocrisy and the Nymphet Trade," May 3, 1981, p. 36; "Anna Ford Condemns 'Dolly' Image," July 10, 1980, p. 2. Also see other British dailies such as *The Guardian, The Observer,* and *The Daily Telegraph.*

967. Trades Union Congress (TUC). *Images of Inequality: the Portrayal of Women in the Media and Advertising.* London: TUC, 1984.

Media image and employment in British newspapers, broadcasting, and advertising; one chapter on achieving change and an appendix with the National Union of Journalists' *Equality Style Guide.*

968. Trommsdorff, G. "Kommunikationsstrategie sechs Westdeutscher Frauenzeitschriften: Einkommenshöhe der Leserin als beschränkender Einfluss auf ihre soziale Orientierungsmöglichkeiten." *Kölner Zeitschrift für Soziologie und Sozialpsychologie.* 21 (1969), pp. 60-92.

969. Tunstall, Jeremy. *The Media in Britain.* London: Constable, 1983. 304 pp.

Includes employment of women in program production, pp. 215-16; feminist publications, p. 107; media bias against women, pp. 141, 143, 148-150; women's magazines, 86, 91, 93, 101-103, 128, 178; women in ads, 102, 103; others.

970. Van de Maele, B. *Met beeld van de vrouw in de reclame van de nederlandstalige vrouwen bladen: een inhoudsanayse.* Leuven: Catholic University of Leuven, 1978.

971. Van Zoonen, Liesbet. "Rethinking Women and the News." *European Journal of Communication.* March 1988, pp. 35-53.

A call for changing the way research is conducted on mass media and women in the Netherlands.

972. Van Zoonen, Liesbet. "Rethinking Women and the News." *Sex-Roles within Massmedia Newsletter.* December 1986, pp. 21-23.

Assumption that women's absence from news production and content of Dutch television affects news content; different meanings of change, assumptions behind news production, and dimensions behind women and news. Several ways suggested to improve women's roles in news production and news content.

973. Vervaet-Clays, Els. "Women in Media." *EBU Review.* January 1987.

Summary of some work done on women and media in various parts of Europe.

974. Vorlat, E. "Waar Houdt de verleider zich schuil? Het taalspel in de reclame." *Streven.* June 1976, pp. 773-786.

975. Wassenaar, I. *Vrouwenbladen. Spiegels van een mannenmaatschappij.* Amsterdam: Wetenschappelijke Uitgeverij, 1976.

976. "Women in Austria, 1975-85." *Sex-Roles within Massmedia Newsletter.* November 1985, pp. 60-61.

Extracted from a report done for the UN Decade for Women with a section on "Media and Opinion Formation, Culture, and the Arts."

977. Women's Study Group. *Women Take Issue.* Birmingham: University of Birmingham/Centre for Contemporary Cultural Studies, Hutchinson, 1978.

Development of the feminist cultural studies tradition in Britain and on the Continent. In Britain, feminists had to challenge male-dominated studies to make themselves heard. By the same center: *Images of Women in the Media*, 1974.

Historical Studies

978. Adburgham, Alison. *Women in Print: Writing Women and Women's Magazines from the Restoration to the Accession of Victoria.* London: George Allen and Unwin Ltd., 1972.

Little known history of women writers and publications in Britain, using pre-Victorian periodicals and "undisturbed sources." Begins with Aphra Behn, author of many licentious plays before her death in 1689.

979. Albistur, Maïté and Daniel Armogathe. *Histoire du féminisme français du moyen âge à nos jours.* Paris: Éditions des Femmes, 1977. 508 pp.

Includes "Journaux féminins et féministes," pp. 230-232; "Les femmes, le cinéma," pp. 470-475.

980. Anderson, Paul Bunyon. "The History and Authorship of Mrs. Crackenthorpe's *Female Tatler*." *Modern Philology*. 28 (1931), pp. 354-360.

981. Bennett, Arnold. *The Savour of Life. Essays in Gusto.* Garden City, New York: Doubleday, Doran and Co., 1928.

"Editing a Woman's Paper," pp. 169-183, relates author's editorship after 1896, of *Woman*, a penny illustrated weekly for women in the vanguard of progressive movements.

982. Bennett, E.A. *Journalism for Women: A Practical Guide.* London: John Lane, 1898. 98 pp.

One of first journalism books designed for women states that journalism is "strictly a place of business."

983. Bennett, Shelley M. "Changing Images of Women in Late-Eighteenth-Century England: The 'Lady's Magazine,' 1770-1810." *Arts Magazine*. May 1981, pp. 138-141.

984. Blanchard, Rae. "Richard Steele and the Status of Women." *Studies in Philology*. 26 (1929), pp. 325-355.

985. Bostick, Theodora P. "Women's Suffrage, the Press, and the Reform Bill of 1867." *International Journal of Women's Studies*. 3:4 (1980), pp. 373-390.

Analyzes the female suffrage votes of 1832 and 1867 in England through looking at 50 influential newspapers and journals of opinion.

986. Bussy Genevois, Danielle. "Problemas de aprehension de la vida cotidiana de las mujeres Españolas a traves de la prensa femenina y familiar (1931-1936)." In *La mujer en la historia de España. Actas de las 11 jornadas de investigación interdisciplinaria*, pp. 263-278. Madrid: Universidad Autonoma de Madrid, 1984.
Women and other topics as viewed in seven Spanish periodicals.

987. Crawshay, Myfanwy. *Journalism for Women.* London: Fleet Publications, 1932.

988. Doane, Mary Ann. "Remembering Women." *Continuum.* 1:2 (1988), pp. 3-14.
Max Ophul's 1934 film, "La Signora di tutti" analyzed because it makes "uncannily explicit many of the most crucial themes of contemporary feminist film theory."

989. Evans, Richard J. *The Feminist Movement in Germany 1894-1933.* Beverly Hills, California: Sage Publications, 1976. 310 pp.
Includes "Propaganda and Practice, 1905-1908," pp. 123-130.

990. Faithfull, Emily. "The Victoria Press (1860)." In *Strong-Minded Women and Other Lost Voices from Nineteenth-Century England,* edited by Janet Horowitz Murray. New York: Pantheon, 1982.
Originally in National Association for the Promotion of Social Science *Transactions*, 1 (1860), pp. 819-882.

991. Gelbart, Nina Rattner. *Feminine and Opposition Journalism in Old Regime France: Le Journal des Dames.* Berkeley: University of California Press, 1987. 354 pp.
History of the pioneer women's journal, *Le Journal des Dames*, published from 1759 to 1778. First edited by a 21-year-old man, the magazine contended with royal censors, although later Marie Antoinette became royal protectress. After some men editors, Madam de Montanclos took over the periodical. In its last years, *Le Journal* took on a number of opposition causes.

992. Grieve, Mary. *Millions Made My Story.* London: Gollancz, 1964. 242 pp.
Author's editorship of the British magazine, *Woman*, from its beginnings to her 1962 retirement.

993. Harrison, Brian. *Prudent Revolutionaries: Portraits of British Feminists Between the Wars.* Oxford: Clarendon Press, 1987. 362 pp.
Includes "Publicist and Communicator: Nancy Astor," pp. 73-98.

994. Herd, Harold. *A Press Gallery.* London: Fleet, 1958. 144 pp.
Careers of nine British journalists, including Mary de la Riviere Manley of *New Atalantis* (1709).

995. Hodges, James. "*The Female Spectator:* A Courtesy Publication." In *Studies in the Early English Periodical*, edited by Richmond Bond. Chapel Hill: University of North Carolina Press, 1957.

996. Hunt, Margaret. "Hawkers, Bawlers, and the Mercuries: Women and the London Press in the Early Enlightenment." *Women and History*. 9 (1984), pp. 41-68.

997. Hunter, Jean. "The Eighteenth-Century Englishwoman: According to *The Gentleman's Magazine*." In *Woman in the Eighteenth Century and Other Essays*, edited by Paul Fritz and Richard Morton. Toronto: McMaster University Association for Eighteenth-Century Studies 4, 1976.

998. Joubert, Jacqueline. *Lettre à Emma* (A Letter to Emma). Paris: Hachette, 1980. 221 pp.
Joubert, who started working in French TV in 1949, tells its history to her granddaughter, Emma.

999. Koon, Helene. "Eliza Haywood and the *Female Spectator*." *Huntington Library Quarterly*. 42 (1978), pp. 43-55.

1000. Kunzle, David. "Marie Duval: A Caricaturist Rediscovered." *Woman's Art Journal*. Spring-Summer 1986, pp. 26-31.
Creator of England's nineteenth century comic strip, "Ally Sloper."

1001. Kunzle, David. *The History of Comic Strip. The Nineteenth Century*. Berkeley: University of California Press, 1990. 411 pp.
Europe's first enduring serialized comic strip, "Ally Sloper" -- 1867-1879, was drawn by Marie Duval. The strip and its creator are discussed on pp. 316-322.

1002. Lee, Marilyn. "First English Daily Shy on Local News." *Media History Digest*. Fall-Winter 1989, pp. 13-22, 46.
Contents of *Daily Courant*, first English daily, published in London and edited by Elizabeth Mallet.

1003. Lee, Marilyn. "Will the Real E. Mallet Stand Up?" *Media History Digest*. Fall-Winter 1989, p. 22.
The name on the first English daily of the world, the London *Daily Courant*, stood for Elizabeth Mallet, not Edward Mallet, as a few writers contended.

1004. Leman, Joy. "'The Advice of a Real Friend': Codes of Intimacy and Oppression in Women's Magazines 1937-1955." *Women's Studies International Quarterly*. 3:1 (1980), pp. 63-78.
A code of intimacy in the language of women's magazines is assumed, developing a "sisterly" relationship between the magazine and reader. Analysis of British women's magazines of the late 1930s to the early 1950s.

1005. Levy, Darline, Harriet B. Applewhite, and Mary D. Johnson, comps. *Women in Revolutionary Paris 1978-1795.* Urbana, Illinois: University of Illinois Press, 1979. 325 pp.

   Includes an attempt of a liberal journalist to integrate the insurrectionary deeds of women and women in the popular press.

1006. Lott, Sylvia. *Die Frauenzeitschriften von Huffzky und John Jahr: Zur Geschichte der deutschen Frauenzeitschrift zwischen 1933 und 1970* (The Women's Magazines of Hans Huffzky and John Jahr: Towards the History of the German Women's Magazine 1933-1970). Berlin: Spiess, 1985. 740 pp.

   The history of women's magazines of the Third Reich compared with the Federal Republic of Germany; the leading, large circulation magazines of various genres.

1007. Parkes, Bessie Rayner. "A Review of the Last Six Years." *English Woman's Journal.* October 1864, p. 364.

   A short account of the author's work as editor of the British periodical credited with launching the feminist movement in the 1860s. A description of her initial experience with the *English Woman's Journal* is in her: "A Year's Experience in Women's Work," *English Woman's Journal*, October 1860, pp. 113-114.

1008. Petersson, Birgit. "Images of Women and Women's Lives: An Analysis of Advertisements in a Nineteenth-Century Provincial Newspaper." *Gender and Mass Media Newsletter.* November 1989, p. 6.

   Advertisements in Sweden's *Sundsvalls Tidning*, betwen 1845-1890, the period of Öffentlichkeit that the Liberal press opened up; women played a very minor role.

1009. Petro, Patrice. *Joyless Streets: Women and Melodramatic Representation in Weimar Germany.* Princeton, New Jersey: Princeton University Press, 1989. 248 pp.

   The conventional assessment of German film history, which sees classical films as responding solely to male fears, is challenged. Weimar Germany had a commercially viable female audience for films and magazines, interested in looking at traditional images of women.

1010. Reynolds, Kimberley. *Girls Only? Gender and Popular Children's Fiction in Britain, 1880-1910.* Philadelphia, Pennsylvania: Temple University Press, 1990. 208 pp.

   How publishing practices established in late nineteenth century have been perpetuated to the present.

1011. Scholtz-Klink, Gertrud. *Die Frau im Dritten Reich.* Tübingen: Grabert Verlag, 1978. 546 pp.

   Women and the press, propaganda, broadcasting, and film of Third Reich Germany, pp. 82-103.

1012. Shevelow, Kathryn. "C.L. to Mrs. Stanhope: A Preview of Charlotte Lennox's the *Lady's Museum*." *Tulsa Studies in Women's Literature*. 1:1 (1982), pp. 83-86.

1013. Shevelow, Kathryn. "Fathers and Daughters: Women as Readers of the *Tatler*." In *Gender and Reading: Essays on Readers, Texts, and Contexts*, edited by Elizabeth A. Flynn and Petrocinio P. Schweickart, pp. 107-123. Baltimore, Maryland: Johns Hopkins University Press, 1986.

1014. Shevelow, Kathryn. *Women and Print Culture: The Construction of Femininity in the Early Periodical*. London: Routledge, 1989. 235 pp.

Delineation of the "process of simultaneous enfranchisement and restriction that marked women's visible entrance into print culture" by analyzing eighteenth century British periodicals, such as *Athenian Mercury, London Mercury, Tatler, Spectator, Free-Thinker, Visiter, Female Spectator,* and *Lady's Museum*. Includes analyses of women's letters to editors of the *Tatler* and *Spectator*, the *Tatler's* introduction of a writer known as "Jenny Distaff," and periodicals for women.

1015. Stearns, Bertha. "Early English Periodicals for Ladies." *Proceedings of the Modern Language Association*. 48 (1933), pp. 38-60.

1016. Stearns, Bertha. "The First English Periodical for Women." *Modern Philology*. 28 (1930), pp. 45-59.

1017. Sullerot, Evelyne. *Histoire de la presse feminine des origines á 1948*. Paris: Armand Colin, 1966. 228 pp.

History of magazines and newspapers aimed at women with comprehensive bibliography.

1018. "The Press and the Launching of the Woman's Suffrage Movement, 1866-1867." *Victorian Periodicals Review*. Winter 1980, pp. 125-131.

1019. "The *Saturday Review* and the *English Woman's Journal*." *English Woman's Journal*. May 1858, p. 202.

1020. Waller, Jane and Michael Vaughan-Rees. *Women in Wartime: The Role of Women's Magazines 1939-1945*. London: Macdonald & Co., 1987. 128 pp.

Commentary on home life during World War II as depicted in women's magazines. Includes reprinted features, fashion tips, morale-boosting stories, mottoes, recipes, and advertisements that reflect the shifting roles of women during this period.

1021. Webb, R.K. *Harriet Martineau, A Radical Victorian*. London: Heinemann, 1960. 385 pp.

Newspaper work of Harriet Martineau in nineteenth century England.

1022. Weiner, Joel H., ed. *Innovators and Preachers: The Role of the Editor in Victorian England.* London: Greenwood Press, 1985.
Includes: Charlotte C. Watkins, "Editing a 'Class Journal': Four Decades of the *Queen*," pp. 185-199 and Sheila R. Herstein, "The *English Woman's Journal* and the Langham Place Circle: A Feminist Forum and Its Women Editors," pp. 61-76.

1023. Wischermann, Ulla. *Frauenfrage und Presse: Frauenarbeit und Frauenbewegung in der illustrierten Presse des 19 Jahrhunderts* (Women's Question and the Press: Women's Work and Women's Movement in the Illustrated Press of the 19th Century). Munchen: Saur, 1983. 222 pp.
The texts and illustrations of two chief German magazines of the nineteenth century, *Illustrierte Zeitung Leipzig* and *Gartenlaube*; were they supportive or repressive of women's rights?

Images of Women

1024. Abrahamsson, Ulla B. "Hidden Messages to Girls and Boys: I. Sex Roles in Children's Programmes." *EBU Review.* January 1985, pp. 8-9.
Calls for balanced programming depicting gender. Relates findings of a Swedish sample of TV fiction shows for children where men dominated the roles. Discusses similar findings from other studies of Swedish radio and television.

1025. Abrahamsson, Ulla B. *The Sex-Roles in Televised Fiction: A Swedish Frame of Reference.* Stockholm: Swedish Broadcasting Corporation, 1980. 25 pp.
Reports on sex roles in Swedish TV and the type of reality TV has to people in U.S. and Sweden.

1026. Abrahamsson, Ulla B. *TV-Program för Kvinnor och Män?* Stockholm: Sveriges Radio Equality Working Group, 1982.

1027. Abrahamsson, Ulla B. *TV-Världen och Verkligheten. Delrapport 1: Människor och Samhälle i TV-Fiktion för Barn och Ungdom.* Stockholm: Sveriges Radio Publik-och Programforskningsavdelningen, 1983.

1028. Abrahamsson, Ulla B. "Women and Men in Televised Drama and Film." *Sex-Roles within Massmedia Newsletter.* November 1985, p. 43.
A greater volume of domestic TV production is needed for Swedish television to promote gender equality.

1029. Advertising Standards Authority. *Herself Appraised.* London: Advertising Standards Authority, 1982.

1030. Agger, Gunhild. "Covers and Counterparts: Images of Women in Danish Family Magazines From the First Part of the Twentieth Century" *Sex-Roles within Massmedia Newsletter.* November 1988, pp. 10-11.
Two kinds of women images dominate: What women should be and do, and women as mistresses or self-dependent.

1031. Amadieu, Georges. "L'eternel féminin triomphe dans les bandes dessinées." *V-Magazine* (Paris). Winter 1968.
French comics and women.

1032. Andrén, Gunnar. "On the Study of Casual Connections Between Patterns of Culture and Other Societal Structures -- With an Illustration Concerning Gender Structures in Advertising and Reality." *The Nordicom Review.* No. 2, 1984, pp. 2-8.
Traditional sex roles continue to be communiated and advocated by advertising. Scandinavian viewpoint.

1033. Andrén, Gunnar and Kiell Andrén. "Gender Structures in Swedish Magazine Advertising 1950-1975." Stockholm: University of Stockholm, 1978.

1034. Arbeitsgruppe Frauenmaul. *Ich Hab' dir keinen Rosengarten Versprochen: Das Bild der Frau in vier Oesterreichischen Tageszeitungen -- eine Dokumentation.* Vienna: Frischfleisch und Löwenmaul, 1979.
Reports Austrian women are pictured in trivialized or sensational capacities in media.

1035. Association of Cinematograph, Television and Allied Technicians, United Kingdom. "Code of Practice on Sexism." *Gender and Mass Media Newsletter.* November 1989, pp. 30-31.
ACTT's code dealing with representation of women in media, attitudes toward women in the workplace, and employment practices. Also by ACTT: *Patterns of Discrimination Against Women in the Film and Television Industries,* 1975.

1036. Baehr, Helen. "The 'Liberated Woman' in Television Drama." *Women's Studies International Quarterly.* 3:1 (1980), pp. 29-39.
The agenda set by mass media reinforces patriarchal culture. Looks at England's television drama series "Plays for Today."

1037. Baehr, Helen, ed. *Women and Media.* Oxford: Pergamon, 1980. 137 pp.
Addresses the need to consider problems and issues around media representation of feminism and media employment. Examines decisive role media perform in transmitting patriarchal culture, with accounts by women journalists.

1038. Baerns, Barbara. "Journalism and Gender -- As Perceived by German High School Graduates Planning a Career in Journalism." *Sex-Roles within Massmedia Newsletter.* November 1988, p. 22.
Career decisions made by female high school graduates and the relationship between the image and everyday reality of the female journalist.

1039. Barreno, M.I. *A imagen de mulher na imprensa.* Lisbon: Comissão de Condição Femenina, 1976.

1040. Beardsell, Susan. "The Uses and Possible Consequences of Female Sexuality in British Television Advertising." *Sex-Roles within Massmedia Newsletter.* November 1988, pp. 18-19.
    In British TV ads aimed at females, the use of female sexuality constituted a "distinct sub-set, not only in terms of images of women, but in overall structure and production."

1041. Berlan, Martine. "Farmers' Wives in Protest: A Theatre of Contradictions." *Sociologia Ruralis.* 26:3/4 (1986), pp. 285-303.
    The media coverage of 1967 public protest actions by French farm women.

1042. Booth, Jane. "Watching the Family." *Women's Studies International Quarterly.* 3:1 (1980), pp. 15-27.
    The BBC TV series of 1953, "Pattern of Marriage," and how it showed the "happy family" as the norm.

1043. Bruggerman, Theodor. "Das Bild der Frau in der Comics." *Studien zur Jugendliteratur.* 1956.
    Women in German comics.

1044. Buch, Hans-Christoph. "Sex-Revolte im Comic-Strip." *Pardon.* No. 12, 1966.

1045. Buonanno, Milly. *Cultura di Massa e Identità Femminile: L'Immagine della Donna in Televisione.* Turin: ERI, 1983.

1046. Chambon, Jacques. "Statut de la femme dans les bandes dessinées d'avant-garde." *Mercury.* No. 7, 1965.
    In France.

1047. *Chronique Feministe.* September-October 1988.
    Special issue of this Belgian journal includes articles analyzing functions of advertising, cinema, and television, whereby women are shown as "objects in a society dominated by masculine powers and concerns." Also explores women's images in documentary work and fiction and their role as professional media workers.

1048. Curran, James. "The Impact of Advertising on British Mass Media." *Media, Culture and Society.* January 1981, pp. 43-69.
    Women's portrayal included as part of larger study of the immense power advertisers exert over British media.

1049. Curry, T.J. and A.C. Clarke. "Developing Visual Literacy: Use of Magazine Advertisements Depicting Gender Roles." *Teaching Sociology.* April 1983, pp. 361-369.
    Classroom strategies for analyzing depictions of femininity and masculinity through magazine ads.

1050. De Keyser, E. "L'image de la femme dans la publicité." *Cahiers du Centre d'Etudes Jacques Georgin.* 3:1, pp. 81-90.

1051. De Kunst, R. "Sociale aspekten van de vrouwenpers" (Naar een nieuw beeld van de vrouwenbladen). Licentiaats thesis, Catholic University of Leuven, 1978.

1052. di Stadio, Patrizia. "Una singolare 'rapresentazione collettiva': l"imago' delladonna in Roma (atteggimenti ed opinioni di una centuria di romane ed il modello proposto dalla stampa femminile)." *Revista del Instituto de Ciencias Sociales.* 24 (1974), pp. 211-228.

About 49 percent of 100 Roman women surveyed about the image of women in leading feminist publications did not feel positive about the feminist press.

1053. Downing, John. *The Media Machine.* London: Pluto Press, 1980. 237 pp.

Class exploitation in British work, racism, and sexism. Chapter 5 covers sexism, looking at women's position in capitalism; Chapter 6 reveals the media's role in promoting sexist, stereotypical images of women.

1054. Durkin, Kevin. "Sex Roles and Television Roles: Can a Woman Be Seen To Tell the Weather as Well as a Man?" *International Review of Applied Psychology.* April 1985, pp. 191-201.

British TV weather forecasters are competent in science, and not simply "entertainers." Until 1980, TV weather forecasting was exclusively presented by males. This study analyzes 40 people's responses to a video recording of either a male or female weather forecaster; the sex of the forecaster was not a main predictor of negative evaluations.

1055. Durkin, Kevin. "Television and Sex-role Acquisition 1: Content." *British Journal of Social Psychology.* June 1985, pp. 101-113.

Broken into parts on adult and children's television; both adult and children's TV portray men as dominant, women as nurturant and complementary.

1056. Durkin, Kevin. "Television and Sex-role Acquisition 2: Effects." *British Journal of Social Psychology.* September 1984, pp. 191-210.

Effects of TV sex-role content on young viewers have been assumed, rather than proven.

1057. Durkin, Kevin. "Television and Sex-role Acquisition 3: Counter Stereotyping." *British Journal of Social Psychology.* September 1985, pp. 211-222.

The prospects of using TV as a social change agent in counter stereotyping.

1058. Durkin, Kevin. *Television, Sex Roles and Children.* Milton Keynes: Open University Press, 1985.

Chapters on theories of sex roles and television, the sex role content of television, children's reactions to counter-stereotyped sex role themes in television, and television, sex roles and children: towards a developmental social psychological theory.

1059. Easton, G. and C. Toner. "Women in Industrial Advertisement." *Industrial Marketing Management.* April 1983, pp. 145-149.

Sample of 71 issues of British commercial, industrial, and business magazines found that images of men dominated industrial advertising much more than consumer advertising and men and women equally were represented in participant and decorative roles. The working roles women were portrayed in were white collar.

1060. Eide, Elisabeth. "How To Define the Image of Women? Methodological Problems Relating to Identifying Masculine-Feminine in Norwegian Newspapers." *Gender and Mass Media Newsletter.* November 1989, p. 7.

The "first" study to describe women and men as presented in Norwegian newspapers consists of questions addressed to editors and journalists, and quantitative and qualitative content analyses of newspapers.

1061. Equality Group of the Swedish Television Co. "News for Women and Men?" *Sex-Roles within Massmedia Newsletter.* November 1984, pp. 25-27.

Men still dominated in news programs; most of the news was aimed at men; and women were invisible in programs. Results of a 1983 survey showed proportion of female reporters doubled during previous seven years.

1062. Ergas, Yasmine. "Subjectivity and Women's Work." *Sociologia e Ricerca Sociale.* April 1981, pp. 129-137.

Women's place in the Italian labor market that was facing a crisis in 1981. The impact of media images of working women considered.

1063. Fagoaga, Concha and Petra Maria Secanella. *Umbral de Presencia de la Mujeres en la Prensa Española.* Madrid and Barcelona: Institute of Women, Complutense University of Madrid/Autonomous University of Barcelona, 1987.

1064. Fasting, Kari and Jan O. Tangen. "Gender and Sport in Norwegian Mass Media." *International Review of Sport Sociology.* 18:1 (1983), pp. 61-70.

An attempt to determine bias toward female athletes in Norwegian newspapers and TV. In newspapers, coverage of women's sports increased from 5 percent in 1973 to 10 percent in 1980-1981.

1065. Fasting, Kari and Jan O. Tangen. "Kvinneidrett i massemediene" (Women's Sports in the Mass Media). In *Kvinner og idrett, Fra myte til virkelighet* (Women and Sports, from Myth to Reality), edited by G. Lippe. Oslo: Gyldendal Norsk Forlag, 1982.

1066. "Fernsehen/Frauen: Hubsches Beiwerk." *Der Spiegel.* October 27, 1975, pp. 67-68.

Government study on the image of women in German television showed prejudice in every area.

1067. Flick, Marian. "Advertisements and Feminism: Gadfly or Revolution?" *Sex-Roles within Massmedia Newsletter.* November 1988, p. 18.

Norwegian magazines changed the images of women in ads between 1965 and 1985.

1068. Flick, Marian. "Advertising Manipulates Women's Lib." In *Marketing and Semiotics: New Directions in the Study of Signs for Sale*, edited by Jean Umiker-Sebeok. Berlin: Mouton de Gruyter, 1987.

Summary of different theoretical approaches to study of gender roles in advertisements. Presents guidelines suggested in a Norwegian government White Paper (Advertising and Gender/Reklame og kjonn, NOU 1981:34), against which ads should be evaluated.

1069. Flick, Marian. "Gender Roles in Norwegian Advertising 1965-1985." *Gender and Mass Media Newsletter.* November 1989, p. 5.

Theories and results of a study the author was completing on gender roles in Norwegian advertising: *The Year You Can Dare Anything, Try Anything ... Study of Gender Roles in Advertisements of Norwegian Weeklies 1965-1985*, Forthcoming, 1990.

1070. Flick, Marian. "Images of Women in the Media." *Nordicom Review.* No. 2, 1986, pp.46-47.

The "Images of Women in Mass Media" project at the University of Bergen, Norway, consists of two parts: "Sex Roles in Advertising" and "The New Women's Movement and the Mass Media."

1071. Flick, Marian. "Invisible or Lovely: Women in Advertisements." *Media Information Australia.* November 1984, pp. 23-34.

Ads in three Dutch and three Norwegian magazines analyzed for 1965-73/76, with an eye on the gender roles depicted. Among results is: "When looking at the product to be sold, the *market forces* influencing women's appearance are cross-culturally the same," but the symbols and social situations depicted are different.

1072. Flick, Marian. *Kvinner i ramme: En innholdsanalyse av kjonnsroller i ukebladreklame.* Bergen: University of Bergen, Department of Sociology, 1978.

Content analysis of gender roles in magazine advertisements.

1073. Flick, Marian. "Marketing Manipulates Women's Lib." *Sex-Roles within Massmedia Newsletter.* December 1986, pp. 53-54.

Regulation of advertising concerning portrayal of women differs from country to country. Originally presented at a symposium in Bergen, Norway, October 1986, the paper reports that in European Economic Community states, gender specification in job announcement is forbidden.

1074. Flick, Marian. "Norway: Impact of the Women's Movement on the Mass Media." In *Communications at the Crossroads: The Gender Gap Connection*, edited by Ramona Rush and Donna Allen, pp. 142-148. Norwood, New Jersey: Ablex, 1989.
    Twenty female journalists and two women's researchers asked what impact the new women's movement had on media content. All believed that the media cover women's issues well, partly because of pressure from women.

1075. Flick, Marian. *Political Socialization: The Social Function of Sex Roles in Advertisements. Design of a Comparative Study of the Netherlands and Norway*. Bergen, Norway: University of Bergen, Center for Mass Communication Research, Institute of Sociology, April 1977.

1076. Flick, Marian. "The New Women's Movement and the Mass Media." Bergen: University of Bergen, Institute of Sociology, 1983.

1077. Flick, Marian. "We gaan weer in eerlijke dingen geloven. Verkennende studie naar man -- vrouw rollen in tijdschriftreklame." Amsterdam: University of Amsterdam, Baschwitz Institute for Mass Psychology and Public Opinion, 1976.
    Study of gender roles in magazine advertising in Norway and the Netherlands.

1078. Flick, Marian and J. Lied. "Sex Roles in Advertisements. Selling Soap or Statesmen: The Use of Evaluative Sales in Picture Analysis." *Sex Roles in Advertisements Working Papers No. 9*. Bergen: University of Bergen, Centre for Mass Communications Research, 1979. 17 pp.
    Randomly samples three popular Norwegian magazines in 1965 and 1976 and comparatively analyzes newspaper and magazine advertisements run by five Norwegian political parties to determine gender roles.

1079. Flitterman, Sandra. "Women, Representation, and Cinematic Discourse: The Example of French Cinema." Ph.D. dissertation, University of California - Berkeley, 1982. 322 pp.

1080. Fries, M. "Feminae Populi: Popular Images of Women in Medieval Literature." *Journal of Popular Culture*. Summer 1980, pp. 79-86.
    The duality of women in medieval literature -- virgins or whores.

1081. Fulle, Isis. *Image de la Femme dans les Annonces Publicitaires*. Brussels: Commission of the European Communities, 1984.

1082. Fulle, Isis. *Image de la Femme dans les Feuilletons Européens à la Télévision*. Brussels: Commission of the European Communities, 1984.

1083. Furian, M., ed. *Kinder and Jugendliche im Spannungsfeld der Massenmedien*. Stuttgart: Bonz Verlag, 1977.
    Includes E. Kuchendoff, "Die Darstellung der Frau im Fernsehen."

1084. Furnham, A. and S. Schofield. "Sex-role Stereotyping in British Radio Advertisements." *British Journal of Social Psychology.* June 1986, pp. 165-171.
      Analysis of Capital Radio (London) advertisements; typical stereotypes of males as dominant, females as dependent. Females portrayed more often in the home.

1085. Furnham, Adrian and Virginia Voli. "Gender Stereotypes in Italian Television Advertisements." *Journal of Broadcasting and Electronic Media.* Spring 1989, pp. 175-185.
      Replication of U.S., Canadian, and British studies on portrayal of men and women in TV commercials. From content analysis of 333 commercials, determined that "gender stereotyping in Italy was constant across time-of-day and more apparent than in America, but as frequent as in England."

1086. Gallagher, Margaret. "Television Content and Gender: What It Portrays and How It Is Perceived." *Sex-Roles within Massmedia Newsletter.* March 8, 1983, pp. 8-10.
      The British component of a 5-country study showed British TV numerically underrepresented women, depicted them as younger and less authoritative than men and less identified with the work force. In the shows, most conversations occurred between men.

1087. Gallagher, Margaret. "Why Can't a Man Be More Like a Woman?" Honolulu: East-West Center, Institute of Culture and Communication, 1983.
      The British part of a cross-cultural study of sex-role attitudes, perceptions and television viewing.

1088. Gasca, Luis. *Mujeres Fantásticas.* Barcelona: Editorial Lumen, 1969.
      In the comics.

1089. Gunter, Barrie. "Television Viewing and Perceptions of Women and Men on Television and in Real Life." London: Independent Broadcasting Authority, Research Department, 1984.
      Presented at International Association for Mass Communication Research, Prague, Czechoslovakia, August 1984.

1090. Gunter, B. and A. Furnham. "Androgyny and the Perception of Television Violence as Perpetrated by Males and Females." *Human Relations.* June 1985, pp. 535-549.
      British viewers' judgments of violent television scenes examined; male violence on a female victim was rated more serious than the opposite in British crime drama.

1091. Halonen, A. and Irma Kaarina Halonen. "The Image of Women in Finnish Mass Media." *Nordicom Review.* 1 (1988), pp. 41-43.
      Women are "mostly non-existent" in ordinary Finnish news journalism; when they appear, they fit into seven negative categories.

1092. Hamilton, Robert, Brian Haworth, and Nazli Sardar. *Adman and Eve.* London: Equal Opportunities Commission, 1982.

1093. Hansson, Lennart and Bosse Jersenius. *Does Youth Radio Change Sex-Roles?* Gothenburg, Sweden: University of Gothenburg, Department of Sociology, 1983.
Abstracted under same title in *Sex-Roles within Massmedia Newsletter*, November 1984, p. 22.

1094. Harris, P.R. and J. Stobart. "Sex-role Stereotyping in British Television Advertisements at Different Times of the Day: An Extension and Refinement of Manstead and McCulloch (1981)." *British Journal of Social Psychology.* June 1986, pp. 155-164.
Replication of 1981 study carried out in 1983.

1095. Heiskala, Risto. "Sex and Gender in the Semiotic Perspective: Male and Female Cultural Identities in Finnish Cultural Products from the 1950's to the 1980's." *Acta Sociologica.* 30:2 (1987), pp. 207-211.
Popular Finnish cultural products of films, hits, magazines, and novels.

1096. Hering, Heide. *Weibs-Bilder -- Zeugnisse zum öffentlichen Ansehen der Frau Ein Hässliches Bilderbuch.* Reinbek bei Hamburg: Rowohlt Taschenbuch Verlag GmbH, 1979.
The misrepresentation of women in the German press, advertising, and the comics.

1097. Holopainen, Irma, et al. "The Role of Women in Finnish TV-Programmes." *Sex-Roles within Massmedia Newsletter.* December 1983, pp. 16-17.
The results corresponded with those of other Nordic countries: the choice of subject in both news and current affairs programs emphasized the spheres of life of the male culture. The world of women was not rated highly as a topic of news and current affairs.

1098. Horn, Maurice. "Défense et illustration de la pin-up dans la bande dessinée," *V-Magazine.* Fall 1965.
In France.

1099. Jensen, Else. "Video and Sex-Specific Socialization." Paper presented at International Association for Mass Communication Research, Prague, 1984.

1100. Kalonen, Irma Kaarina. "The Image of Women in Finnish Mass Media." *Nordicom Communication Review.* 1 (1988), pp. 41-43.
The role of women in Finnish TV programs, primarily with reference to the image provided by news and current affairs programs. The conclusion: The greater the control women have exerted over popular culture images, the less passive and domestic they have been shown and the more reflective of women's works and commitments outside the home.

1101. Kettner, Britta. "Austrian Seminar on Stereotyped Portrayal of Women on Television." *Sex-Roles within Massmedia Newsletter*. March 8, 1983, pp. 21-22.

   A report on a seminar which revealed that women accounted for more than one-half of the ORF (radio-TV) staff, but only 20 of them had reached high qualification job categories.

1102. King, J. and M. Stott, eds. *Is This Your Life? Images of Women in the Media*. London: Virago, 1977.

   Includes: M. Ross, "Radio," pp. 5-35; C. Faulder, "Advertising," pp.37-64; P. Barr, "Newspapers," pp. 67-81; C. Brayfield, "Films," pp. 107-121; C. Koerber, "Television," pp. 123-142; T. Goddard, J. Pollock, and M. Fudger, "Popular Music," pp. 143-159, and C. Faulder, "Women's Magazines," pp. 173-194.

1103. Klein, Marie Luise. "Women in the Discourse of Sports Reports." *International Review for the Sociology of Sport*. 23:2 (1988), pp. 139-152.

   Analysis of 3,000 sports reports and photographs from four national West German newspapers showed the press functioning as a normalizing agent; legitimized the marginal position of women in sport.

1104. Kotelmann, Joachim and Lothar Mikos. *Frühjahrsputz und Südseezauber: Die Darstellung und das Bewusstsein von Zuschauerinnen* (Spring Cleaning and the Magic of the South Seas: The Portrayal of Women in Television Advertising and the Consciousness of the Female Viewers). Baden-Baden: Baur, 1981. 243 pp.

   Publication of "Aktion Klartext," a women's organization of journalists. Their first books were on women's employment in German media; this one looks at roles of women in TV commercials, using content analysis.

1105. Kuusela, Leila. *A Study of the Images of Women and Men Conveyed by Commercial Youth Magazines*. Helsinki: Council for Equality Between Men and Women. 1983.

1106. Laine, P. *La femme et ses images*. Paris: Stock, 1974.

1107. Lavoisier, Bénédicte. *Mon corps, ton corps, leur corps, le corps de la femme dans la publicité*. Paris: Editions Seghers, 1978. 256 pp.

   Interviews with women and men about the images of women that are advertised.

1108. Levelt, Peter. "Hidden Messages to Girls and Boys: II. Effects on Children and Their Development." *EBU Review*. January 1985, pp. 9-12.

   Examples and studies from the Netherlands to answer the questions: "Does the sexist television world increase sexism in the audience?" "Are there indications that non-traditional programmes can change things?" "Women and girls are absent: are children satisfied with this symbolic annihilation?"

1109. "Liberated Women in Television Serials." *Isis International Bulletin.* No. 18, 1981, pp. 22-24.

   A "new woman" had appeared in films, TV, and advertising; she was active, aggressive, liberated, and feminine, but never a feminist. Discussion of BBC's "Play for Today," a serious drama that did deal with liberated women.

1110. Longo di Cristofaro, Gioia. *Immagine Donna. Modelli di Donna Emergenti nei Mezzi di Comunicazione di Massa.* (Women Patterns in Mass Communications Media). Rome: Commissione Nazionale per la Parita, Prezidenza del Consiglio, 1986.

1111. Lysonski, S. "Role Portrayals in British Magazine Advertisements." *European Journal of Marketing.* 19:7 (1985), pp. 37-55.

   Analysis of 15 British magazines, 1976 and 1982-83; themes of "concerned about physical attractiveness" (50 percent), "sex object" (17 percent), and "housewife" (10 percent) most prevalent.

1112. Manduit, Jean. "Des rôles, des figures, des masques." *La Nef.* January-March 1976, pp. 63-70.

   Images of women in the press.

1113. Manns, Ulla. "The Image of Women in Front-Page Copy: A Preliminary Study of Dagens Nyheter." *Sex-Roles within Massmedia Newsletter.* November 1985, pp. 26-27.

   The presence of women and men in front-page news in this Swedish daily; women were "strongly underrepresented," and when mentioned, it was in the context of the masculine world.

1114. Manstead, A.S.R. and Caroline McCullough. "Sex-Role Stereotyping in British Television Advertisements." *British Journal of Social Psychology.* September 1981, pp. 171-180.

   The portrayal of men and women in a sample of 170 British television advertisements, to determine if, and how, they were depicted differently: women were more often product users, in dependent roles and at home, providing no arguments in favor of advertised products, and appearing in conjunction with domestic products.

1115. Martinelli, Adriana, Caterian Porcu Sanna, and Stefania Giacomini. *Progetto di una Ricerca sul Lavoro Femminile Dentro la Radiotelevisione Italiana, e sulla Immagine che ne Consegue.* Rome: RAI, 1981.

1116. Mauriac, Claude. "De Modesty Blaise à Polly Maggoo." *Le Figaro Littéraire.* October 27, 1966.

   Women in comics.

1117. Mawby, Rob I. and Judith Brown, eds. "Newspaper Images of the Victim: A British Study." *Victimology.* 9:1 (1984), pp. 82-94.

British press coverage of crime; young, female and high status victims were overrepresented in crime news, suggesting "press selectivity was framed by the need for newsworthy, atypical, and entertaining stories."

1118. Meier, Uta. "Analysis of Sex-Roles in Dutch Drama Productions and Talk-Shows." *Sex-Roles within Massmedia Newsletter*. November 1985, pp. 30-31.
Semiologic and content analytic points of view applied to the topic.

1119. Mikos, Lothar. "Familienserien - Familienbilder." In *Familien im Mediennetz*, edited by Dieter Baacke and Jurgen Lauffer. Opladen: 1988.
Images of families in serials of West Germany.

1120. National Union of Journalists. Equality Working Party. *Non-Sexist Code of Practice for Book Publishing*. London: National Union of Journalists, 1975.

1121. Natkin, Ritva. "The Public Image of Women and the Disfiguring Effect of Alcohol." *Alkoholipolitiikka*. 49:4 (1984), pp. 208-213.
Media publicize a strong moralistic bias when dealing with women's use of alcohol in Finland.

1122. Nicholls, Jill and Pat Moan. "What Offends One of Us Won't Offend the Next Chap." *Spare Rib*. July 1978, p. 19.
Critical of the British Advertising Standards Authority, where sexism fits only under the category of "decency." The watchdog role of AFFIRM relative to ads, articles, and images exploiting women is described.

1123. Portuges, Catherine E. "Cinema and Psyche: A Psychoanalytical View of the Representation of Women in Three French Film Directors of the 1960s." Ph.D. dissertation, University of California, Los Angeles, 1982. 287 pp.

1124. Reynolds, Lessie M. "The Journey Toward Liberation for Fellini's Women." Paper presented at Speech Communication Association, New York, November 8-11, 1973. 10 pp.
States that the characterizations of women in three of Federico Fellini's films can be used to demonstrate the process of self-actualization real women experience during the fulfillment of the promises of the women's liberation movement.

1125. Robertson, E. Arnot. "Women and the Film." *Penguin Film Review*. August 1947, pp. 31-35.
A complaint about British film treatment of love, mothers, and old age.

1126. Rocard, G. and C. Gutman. *Sois belle et achète. La publicité et les femmes*. Paris: Ed. Gonthier, 1968.
Women and advertising in France.

1127. Rolland, Asle. "On Women, Sex Roles, Equality of the Sexes and Mass Media." *Sex-Roles within Massmedia Newsletter.* November 1985, p. 28.

    Quantitative survey of Nordic research, 1975-82, based on bibliographies produced by NORDICOM; the literature on these subjects expanded in recent years.

1128. Safilios-Rothschild, Constantina. "'Good' and 'Bad' Girls in Modern Greek Movies." *Journal of Marriage and the Family.* August 1968, pp. 527-531.

    In 25 modern Greek movies, "bad" girls (more emancipated, independent) were portrayed as rich; "good" girls (who love unconditionally) as poor.

1129. Salber, Wilhelm. *Film und Sexualitat: Untersuchungen zur Filmpsychologie* (Films and Sexuality: Investigations Concerning Film Psychology). Bonn: H. Bouvier, 1970.

1130. Sepstrup, P. "En undersagelse of mands og kvindebilledet i den danske magasin og dagspresseannoncering" (Report on Sex Roles in Advertising). Report to Danish Consumer Ombudsman, Copenhagen, 1978.

1131. Sklar, Robert and Charles Musser, eds. *Resisting Images: Essays on Cinema and History.* Philadelphia, Pennsylvania: Temple University Press, 1990. 320 pp.

    Included is Antonia Lant, "The Female Spy: Gender and Nationality in World War II British Film."

1132. Thoveron, Gabriel. *Place and Role of Women in Certain Television Programmes in EEC Countries. Final Review.* Brussels: Commission of the European Communities, 1984.

    One of three reports issued by the Commission on "Sex Roles and Mass Media." Analyzed 25 channels in 10 EEC countries and found women severely underrepresented on TV. Article from this research, "European Televised Women" appeared in *European Journal of Communication* (Vol. 1, No. 3).

1133. Towler, Robert. *Gender on Television and Gender in Real Life.* London: Independent Broadcasting Authority, Research Department, 1984.

1134. Towler, Robert. "The Sexes on Television." *Airwaves.* Spring 1985, pp. 10-11.

1135. Tsudor, A. "Mediation of Sex Roles: the Case of Norwegian Television." Oslo: University of Oslo, 1975.

1136. Vogel, Jean and Lydia Zaid. *How Women Are Presented in Television Programmes in the EEC. Part Two. Positive Action and Strategies: Evaluation of and Lessons To Be Learned from Alternative Programmes.* Brussels: Commission of the European Communities, 1984.

    The origin of and the original model of alternative programs, the difficulties and crises they encountered, possible ways to revive them, and key questions that govern further advances.

1137. Walkowitz, Judith R. "Jack the Ripper and the Myth of Male Violence." *Feminist Studies.* Fall 1982, pp. 542-574.

>A review of the 1988 Jack the Ripper murders in London with analyses of media images, including those of women.

1138. Werner, Anita. "A Case of Sex and Class Socialization." *Journal of Communication.* Autumn 1975, pp. 45-50.

>A Norwegian study that analyzed a campaign to influence the buying of children's books through a TV promotion; parents seemed more interested in the intellectual development of their sons.

1139. "Who Does the Talking on Norwegian Radio and TV?" *Gender and Mass Media Newsletter.* November 1989, pp. 24-25.

>Update of 1973 and 1983 studies on women's participation in Norwegian Broadcasting Corporation (NRK). The 1988 survey found that in the previous five years, women's share of NRK program producers rose by 8 percent (to a total of 35 percent) and there was a "heartening" increase in the number of women participating in radio programming (+ 5 percent).

1140. Williamson, Judith. *Decoding Advertisements: Ideology and Meaning in Advertising.* London: Marion Royars, 1978.

1141. Winship, Janice. "Handling Sex." *Media, Culture and Society.* 3 (1981), pp. 25-41.

>Analysis of women's and men's hands in ads to tackle the question of representation of femininity and masculinity.

1142. Winship, Janice. "Sexuality for Sale." In *Culture, Media, Language,* edited by Stuart Hall, et al., pp. 217-223. London: Hutchinson, 1980.

>Analysis of women in advertisements in *Cosmo, 19,* and *Honey,* all British periodicals; women are nothing more than the commodities they wear.

1143. "Women and Men in Televised Drama." *Audience and Programme Research.* December 1985, p. 1.

>A greater volume of domestic TV production is necessary for Swedish Television to perform its duty of promoting equality between the sexes.

1144. "Women and Television in Europe." *Gender and Mass Media Newsletter.* November 1989, pp. 17-20.

>Findings of studies on images of women in European TV shows and a study dealing with women's employment in European media; all reported in the monograph, *Women and Television in Europe.*

1145. "Women in the Federal Republic of Germany." Bonn: Federal Minister for Youth, Family Affairs and Health, 1985.

>Brochure contending women were poorly represented in German media; 9.3 percent of 431 committee members of ARD were women.

1146. Women Working at Norwegian Broadcasting Corporation. "Who Speaks in Norwegian Radio and Television?" *Sex-Roles within Massmedia Newsletter*. November 1984, pp. 28-29.

    Comparison of 1973 and 1983 surveys to show that in the former year, 21.5 percent of those who spoke in radio were women, 25.3 percent in TV. In 1983, 24.9 percent of those who spoke on radio were women, 27 percent in TV.

Women as Audience

1147. Bulcher, Graf. "Información: De donde saca el ciudadano su información?" (Information: Where Does the Citizen Obtain His Information?). *Revista Española de la Opinion Publica*. April-June 1973, pp. 249-265.

    Education and sex as related to knowledge of current events: with men, oral information dominates; with women, visual information.

1148. Carter, Erica. "Alice in the Consumer Wonderland: West German Case Studies in Gender and Consumer Culture." In *Gender and Generation*, edited by Angela McRobbie and Mica Nava, pp. 185-214. London: Macmillan, 1984.

1149. Gunter, B., A. Furnham, and G. Gietson. "Memory for the News as a Function of the Channel of Communication." *Human Learning*. October-December 1984, pp. 265-271.

    In a sample of 128 teenagers on their cued recall of news stories presented to them, males recalled more than females.

1150. Hjort, Anne. "The Appeal of TV and TV-Series to Women." *Sex-Roles within Massmedia Newsletter*. November 1985, pp. 24-25.

    The U.S. TV series, "Dallas," and its popularity in Denmark.

1151. Hobson, Dorothy. *Crossroads: The Drama of a Soap Opera*. London: Methuen, 1982.

    An analysis of soap operas to understand the popularity of the British series, "Crossroads." Studying viewers in their homes, she looked at how the program fit into the structure of their own homes. Women identified with particular characters or recognized problems they knew were common among women.

1152. Hobson, Dorothy. "Housewives and the Mass Media." In *Culture, Media, Language*, edited by Stuart Hall, et al., pp. 105-114. London: Hutchinson, 1980.

    Radio and TV programs used by British housewives: preference for popular drama and light entertainment, rejection of the news programs. Radio is integral to their working day.

1153. Larsson, Lisbeth. *En annan historia. Om Kvinnors läsning och svensk veckopress* (Another Story. On Women's Reading and Swedish Weeklies). Dr. dissertation, Symposion Bokförlag, 1989. 342 pp.

The history of Swedish weeklies, with particular emphasis on the gender inscription.

1154. Larsson, Lisbeth. "Women's Reading." *Women's Studies International Quarterly*. No. 1, 1980, pp. 227-283.

Women's reading in Sweden from the perspectives of formal and practical considerations under which they read and the form and structure of what they read.

1155. Lund, Sissel. *Mass Media Fail To Inform Women*. Oslo: Norwegian Broadcasting, Research Department, 1986. 8 pp. (Nordic/International Conference on Women and Electronic Mass Media, 7-11 April 1986, Copenhagen, Denmark.)

Reference to earlier research which shows that women are more ignorant than men, and systematically prefer mass media with less informative content, even when their stated aim is to seek information on specified issues. Explains that content and form in the informative media are strongly masculine in orientation, both by concentrating on information from the public sphere and essentially presenting a male world.

1156. Lund, Sissel. "The Media Let Women Down." *Sex-Roles within Massmedia Newsletter*. November 1985, pp. 25-26.

Norwegian men and women on their use of media; women considered TV as the best source of information about new subjects, while men chose newspapers. It was more difficult for women than for men to find media subjects useful to their lives.

1157. Mann, Margaret. *The Reading Habits of Adults: A Selected Annotated Bibliography*. British National Bibliography Research Fund Report 1. London: British Library, Research and Development Department, 1977. 65 pp.

Includes 609 entries on the public's reading behavior; one of the nine sections deals in part with women readers.

1158. Meier, Uta. "Watching Television: Melodrama in the Living Room." *Sex-Roles within Massmedia Newsletter*. November 1988, p. 21.

A telephone survey of 700 males and females and 40 Dutch and 20 Turkish women in their homes, about TV viewing. Showed "remarkable" differences between the sexes in program preferences, selectivity, valuation, amount of viewing attention, and uses of remote control and video.

1159. Rossler, Patrick. *Dallas und Schwarzwaldklinik: Eine Programmstudie uber Seifenopern im deutschen Fernsehen* (Dallas and Schwarzwaldklinik: A Study of Soap Operas in Germany). Munich: Richard Fischer, 1988. 186 pp.

The uses and gratifications of people watching German TV serials.

1160. Tokgöz, Oya. "Televizyonun Kadinin Siyasallasmasina Etkisi." *Siyasal Bilgiler Fakültesi Dergisi*. 31:1-4 (1978).

The political impact on women voters of the first political newscasts allowed on the air during a Turkish general election (1971). By the same author on this research: "Siyasal Haberlesme ve Karar Verme," *Amme Idaresi Dergisi*, 10:4 (1977), and "1973 Genel Secimlerinde Radyo Propagandasinin Rolü ve Önemi," *Seha Meray Armagani* (in print).

Women Practitioners

1161. Abrahamsson, Ulla B. "Working Towards Equality in a Broadcasting Corporation." *Sex-Roles within Massmedia Newsletter*. November 1988, pp. 39-40.

    Talks about the company-wide Committee for Equality between the sexes at Swedish Broadcasting Corporation since 1980. Discusses continuing problems of unequal representation. Originally presented at '88 Tokyo Symposium on Women.

1162. Agren, Annika, ed. *Something Has Happened, Equality Work at the Swedish Broadcasting Corporation*. Stockholm: Swedish Broadcasting Corporation, Equality Committee, 1986.

    Summarzies four years of work toward equality of sexes, 1980-83.

1163. "Aktion Klartext -- gleichstellung der Frauen in den Medien." *Funk Report*. No. 16, 1978, pp. 1-4.

    Interview with Hilde Junkerseeliger on women in German media.

1164. Baehr, Helen. "Out of Focus." *The Guardian*. May 6, 1980.

    Reports that only 14 percent of news reporters and six percent of current affairs producers of BBC Television were women.

1165. Baehr, Helen. "Women's Employment in British Television: Programming the Future?" *Media, Culture and Society*. April 1981, pp.125-134.

    In previous year, the number of women newsreaders in Britain television almost doubled, but the number in decision-making jobs remained the same. By showing more women on the screen, the myth arises that equality for one has meant equality for all.

1166. Baldes, Ingrid. "Women in the Swiss Mass Media." *Sex-Roles within Massmedia Newsletter*. March 8, 1983, p. 16.

    Samples 87 women and 437 men working in Swiss media, focusing on employer, occupation, qualifications, and social security. Finds that women journalists are a minority; most are young, unmarried, childless, working in fields "traditionally regarded as female." They are highly-qualified but underpaid.

1167. Baldes, Ingrid. "Woman Journalist -- Dream Profession?" *Sex-Roles within Massmedia Newsletter*. November 1985, p. 42.

    Sample of Swiss journalists yielded only 17 percent women. Abstract from 1984 German report, "Journalistin ein Traumberuf?"

1168. Barat, François and Joël Farges, eds. *Marguerite Duras*. Paris: Editions Albatros, 1975.
Life and work of French filmmaker.

1169. Bargh, Liz, Jack Cosgrave, and Fiona Edwards-Stuart. *Equalising Job Opportunities for Women in Printing and Publishing*. London: The Printing and Publishing Industry Training Board, 1982.

1170. Bernheim, Nicole-Lise. *Marguerite Duras tourne un film*. Paris: Editions Albatros, 1974.
French filmmaker, Marguerite Duras.

1171. Blanchard, Simon and David Morley, eds. *What's This Channel Four?* London: Comedia, 1982.
A look at Britain's Channel Four, with some feminine perspectives, such as Lesley Hilton, "Women Command the Flagship?" pp. 94-102; Women's Advisory and Referral Service Action Group, "Opporutnity Knocks (But Not Very Hard)," pp. 104-109; Sue Clayton, "Cherchez la femme," pp. 151-156.

1172. Bossart, Louis, et al. *Frauen und Massenmedien: Eine Bestandsaufnahme* (Women and Mass Media: Taking an Inventory). Aarau: Sauerländer, 1988. 174 pp.
Eight articles on many aspects of Swiss women and media -- their occupational roles in media, images of women on Swiss TV and in advertising, women as audience.

1173. Bruno, Giuliana and Maria Nadotti, eds. *Offscreen: Woman and Film in Italy*. New York: Routledge, 1988. 160 pp.
Women's involvement with political theory and filmmaking in Italy -- how women chose to represent themselves, how they were represented, and how they deal with the cinematic apparatus as subjects of production, objects of representation, and spectators.

1174. Burchfield, Stephanie. "The New Journalism of Oriana Fallaci." Masters thesis, California State University, Northridge, 1984.

1175. Clifton, T. "The Fallaci Treatment." *Newsweek*. January 22, 1973, pp. 83-84.
Italian journalist, Oriana Fallaci.

1176. Coordination Office for Emancipation Policy. *Vrouw in beel, een vademecum van vrouwelijke deskundigen* (Women in Pictures -- A Guide to Female Experience). Hilversum, The Netherlands: Coordination Office for Emancipation Policy, 1988.
Directory of 1,111 women in variety of media fields, particularly television.

1177. Corboud, Adrienne and Michael Schanne. "Women Journalists and Feminist Consciousness: Collective Strategy and Individual Aspirations of the Swiss Women Journalists." *Sex-Roles within Massmedia Newsletter.* November 1988, p. 16.

A survey of 402 Swiss women journalists in 1985 showed their situation was improving and their feeling of being discriminated against was on the wane. For details, see Adrienne Corboud, "The Situation of Swiss Women Journalists: A Study of the Problems of the Majority of Swiss Women Journalists," Institut de Journalisme et des Communications Sociales, Université Fribourg-Suisse, 1986.

1178. Daisley, Jenny. "Women's Development in the BBC." *COMBROAD.* July-September 1989, pp. 26-28.

The British Broadcasting Corporation and women's development through a series of three workshops.

1179. Dubois-Jallais, Denise. *La tzarine: Hélène Lazareff et l'adventure de "Elle"* (The Czarina: Hélène Lazareff and the Story of "Elle"). Paris: Laffont, 1984. 2523 pp.

Hélène Lazareff created *Elle* magazine in 1945.

1180. Emancipation Committee in Dutch Broadcasting. *Vrouwen in Operationele Beroepen.* Hilversum: NOS, 1983.

1181. "Entretien avec Michel Foucault." *Cahiers du Cinéma.* Nos. 251-252.

1182. Feinstein, Adam. "Pilar Miró ... a Woman at the Helm of Spanish Television." *IPI Report.* March 1987, p. 13.

Miró, the director-general of RTVE, Spain's state-run radio and television network.

1183. Flick, Marian. "Journalists and Their Role in the New Women's Movement: An Interview Study of Norwegian Journalists." *Sex-Roles within Massmedia Newsletter.* November 1984, pp. 18-19.

Coverage of New Women's Movement worldwide, but focus on Norway. Only 21 percent of all Norwegian journalists are women, usually designated by editors to cover the movement for their papers.

1184. Fogarty, Michael P., Isobel Allen, and Patricia Walters. *Women in Top Jobs 1968-1979.* London: Heinemann Educational Books, 1981.

1185. Françoise and Benedicte. "Les femmes et la technique du cinéma." *La Revue du Cinéma. Image et Son.* April 1974, pp. 23-29.

1186. Franks, Lucinda. "Behind the Fallaci Image." *Saturday Review.* January 1981, pp. 18-22.

Italian newswoman Oriana Fallaci.

1187. Freise, H. and J. Drath. *Die Rundfunk Journalistin.* Berlin: Verlag Volker Spiess, 1977.

1188. Gallagher, Margaret. *Employment and Positive Action for Women in the Television Organizations of the EEC Member States.* Brussels: Commission of the European Communities, 1984. 204 pp.

    Results of project to review the position of women working in television broadcasting organizations of EEC member states in 1984. Data gathered by questionnaires sent to 30 TV companies and interviews of 150 people in 25 of these organizations in nine countries. Reported by topics and countries. Number of recommendations, tables.

1189. Gallagher, Margaret. "Myth and Reality in Women's Employment in Broadcasting." *Medie/Kultur.* November 1986, pp. 202-209.

    How broadcasting systems of Western Europe use both the mirror and the animator roles to rationalize their unfair treatment of women broadcasters. Sixty percent of all women in television are in the administrative sector, but only 2 percent are in the top positions. By contrast, while only 15 percent of all men working in Western European television are in administration, 20 percent of them are in the top two tiers. When a job category is dominated by women, that job tends to be poorly paid.

1190. "German Film Women." *Jump/Cut.* No. 29 (1984), pp. 49-64.

    Twelve essays, including overview of German women's films, reviews of two German films, and interviews with Christina Perincioli, Erika Runge, Ula Stockl, Ulrike Ottinger, and Helke Sander. Follows up on symposium on women and film in Germany in No. 27 of *Jump/Cut*, which included an overview of German women's cinema, comparison of U.S. and German feminist movements, interviews with Helga Reidemeister, Jutta Bruckner, and Christina Perincioli, articles from German feminist film periodical *frauen und film*, and a theoretical essay by Gertrud Koch on why women go to the movies.

1191. Graham, Cooper C. *Leni Riefenstahl and Olympia.* Metuchen, New Jersey: Scarecrow Press, 1986. 347 pp.

    On the production of "Olympia," a film linked to National Socialism; not much on her career.

1192. Haagen, Bernd-Ulrich and Bettina Warken. "Grenzen der Galanterie, Die Frauen in den Funkmedien." *Kirche und Rundfunk.* No. 53 (1985), pp. 5-7.

    The situation of women in German broadcasting.

1193. Hays, Lora. "From the Frying Pan to the Trim-Bin." *Film Library Quarterly.* Winter 1971-72, pp. 22-25.

    A woman film editor's inside view of sexism in the cutting room. Author was an editor on scores of films. Talked about her work in making documentaries in "Glancing Backward ... Without Nostalgia," *Film Library Quarterly,* Summer 1971.

1194. Heinzelmann, Herbert. "Helma Sanders-Brahms' New Problem-Oriented Film." *Cinema India-International.* January-March 1986, p. 90.

    A film of West Germany's Helma Sanders-Brahms.

1195. Hinton, David B. *The Films of Leni Riefenstahl.* Metuchen, New Jersey: Scarecrow Press, 1978. 162 pp.
German director's entire film work, as actress and director, before and during the Nazi era.

1196. Hitchens, Gordon. "An Interview with a Legend." *Film Comment.* January 1964, pp. 4-25.
Leni Riefenstahl, Hitler's filmmaker; her story and biographical sketch, sound and picture outline of her "Triumph of the Will," program notes, review of a lesser Riefenstahl work.

1197. Holmlund, Christine Anne. "Destroy the Old, Suggest the New: Image, Sound and Text in Marguerite Duras' 'Detruire, Dit-Elle' Film." Ph.D. dissertation, University of Wisconsin-Madison, 1984. 314 pp.

1198. Holy, Renate. *Fernsehcutterinnen: Frauenarbeit in der Medienproduktion* (Female Cutters in Television: Female Work in Media Production). Frankfurt: Campus Verlag, 1981. 217 pp.
The work of a nearly unknown group of TV production female workers -- the cutters. The working conditions of women in TV production and effects upon their living conditions in Germany.

1199. Infield, Glenn B. *Leni Riefenstahl: The Fallen Film Goddess.* New York: Crowell, 1976. 278 pp.
World War II years and her Hitler-inspired documentaries for the Nazis.

1200. Jensen, Else. "Television Newscasts in a Womans [sic] Perspective." *Sex-Roles within Massmedia Newsletter.* March 8, 1983, pp. 11-12.
Interviews with women working on Danish TV newscasts in 1980 found that women worked on the bottom of the hierarchy and dissociated themselves from the character or role included in the executive job.

1201. Jensen, Else and Madeleine Kleberg. "The Role of Women in Television News and Entertainment Programmes: A Danish-Swedish Study of Equality of the Sexes and Mass Media." *Sex-Roles within Massmedia Newsletter.* December 1983, pp. 24-25.
Women in these two countries "have not yet left their mark on television in any decisive way." The number of women in TV increased markedly during the previous decade, but they did not change the norms of the medium.

1202. Johannesson, Jan and Lars Söderström. *Dagstidningsjournalister i Malmö.* Lund: Lunds Universitet, 1971.

1203. Johnston, Claire. *The Work of Dorothy Arzner. Towards a Feminist Cinema.* London: British Film Institute, 1975.

1204. Journalisthögskolan. *Journalistkaren i Sverige.* Stockholm: Almqvist and Wiksell, 1970.

1205. Jyrkiainen, Jyrki. *City, Way of Life, Social Functions of Mass Communication: Report.* Tampere: University of Tampere, 1986. 84 pp.

Report of Finnish/Soviet Seminar on Problems of Communication Research, 4th, Tampere, 1985. Women is a topic in the report: Marja Jarvela, "Urbanization and Women in Wage Employment."

1206. Kaiser, Addy. "If Room at the Press-Table." *Sex-Roles within Massmedia Newsletter.* December 1986, pp. 20-21.

In Dutch daily newspapers, women change newspaper or position less often than men; journalism has a labor culture that is definitely male, to which women must adapt, and women journalists are "emphatically judged as women."

1207. Kindem, Gorham A. "Norway's New Generation of Women Directors: Anja Breien, Vibeke Lokkeberg, and Laila Mikkelsen." *The Journal of Film and Video.* Fall 1987, pp. 28-42.

These Norwegian women directors, who made important contributions to the country's cinema and feminist film practice, distinguished themselves by their criticism of patriarchal forms of discrimination within Norwegian society, their enunciation of feminist points of view, and the development of alternative and oppositional values and forms of expression to those of Hollywood.

1208. Kleberg, Madeleine. "Women and News: A Simplistic Theory in Practice." *Gender and Mass Media Newsletter.* November 1989, pp. 6-7.

Recent research on Swedish Television, showing that more female reporters appeared on television during the previous 15 years.

1209. "*Lidové Noviny* -- Coming Out into the Open." *IPI Report.* January 1990, pp. 6-7.

Interview with Rita Klimova, leading member of editorial staff of Czech underground paper, *Lidové Noviny.*

1210. Liehm, Mira. *Passion and Defiance: Film in Italy from 1942 to the Present.* Los Angeles: University of California Press, 1984. 396 pp.

Important era in Italian cinema traced; emergence of important female directors such as Liliana Cavani and Lina Wertmüller.

1211. "Lilli Palmer: Eine Frau bleibt eine Frau. Drei Autoren über eine Sendung." *Das Palament.* 28:3 (1978), p. 20.

1212. Linden-van Ruiten, Ank. "Women and the Mass Media: Trace Back the Messages and Act!" *Sex-Roles within Massmedia Newsletter.* November 1984, pp. 23-24.

In Holland, women who are depicted as "media-output" underestimate social reality; women are underrepresented in policy making and production sectors of mass media.

1213. Linné, Olga. "Why Do Female Media Professionals Produce Male Messages?" *Sex-Roles within Massmedia Newsletter.* December 1986, pp. 52-53.

Although women professionals primarily produce male messages, in Scandinavia, they are beginning to find "their own profile in media production." Appeared as Chapter 23 in *Communication and Domination Essays to Honor Herbert I. Schiller*, edited by Jorg Becker, et al.

1214. Lyon, Elisabeth. "Discours et Désir: L'Oeuvre de Marguerite Duras." Masters thesis, University of California, Berkeley, 1978.
French filmmaker, Marguerite Duras.

1215. Martin, Marcel. "Agnes Varda's 'Without a Roof Nor Law.'" *Cinema India-International*. January-March 1986, p. 91.
French director Agnes Varda and her prize-winning "Without a Roof Nor Law."

1216. Menezes, Ervell E. "Woman Film-maker Forges Ahead." *Cinema India-International*. January-March 1986, p. 88.
The success of England's Claire Downs.

1217. Michel, Andrée. "Le role novateur des femmes dans les societes industrieles advancees" (The Innovative Role of Women in Advanced Industrial Societies). *Centre National Recherche Scientifique Supplement*. December 1978, pp. 495-506.
French women have made "radical cultural innovations" in producing culture (creating publishing houses, feminist journals, magazines, films, radio, and TV), or in changing how they are viewed in media. Edited by the same author: *La féminisme*, Paris: Presses Universitaires de France, 1979.

1218. Möhrmann, Renate. *Die Frau mit der Kamera*. Munich: Carl Hauser Verlag, 1980.
German women filmmakers.

1219. Morgan, Janice M. "Marguerite Duras: The Novelist as Filmmaker." Ph.D. dissertation, Indiana University, Bloomington, 1982. 211 pp.

1220. Muir, Anne Ross. *A Woman's Guide to Jobs in Film and Television*. London: Pandora Press, 1987. 342 pp.
Based on the experiences of several hundred women already working in the media; facts and figures, personal accounts, advice on problems such as sexual harassment and discrimination, and British industry addresses.

1221. National Union of Journalists (NUJ). "Fleet St: Still a Male Preserve." *Free Press* (Journal of the Campaign for Press and Broadcasting Freedom). July-August 1984, p. 4.
NUJ survey of journalists in England.

1222. Neverla, Irene and Gerda Kanzleiter. *Journalistinnen: Frauen in einem Mannerberuf* (Women Journalists: Women in a Men's Profession). Frankfurt: Campus Verlag, 1984. 218 pp.

Interviews with 100 female journalists of Germany showed inequalities of opportunities.

1223. *News from Neasden*, London. Spring 1979.
Thematic issue on "Women and Publishing" in England.

1224. Padgaonkar, Latika. "The Triumphant Woman: An Interview with Nisan Akman." *Cinemaya*. Autumn 1989, pp. 36-37.
Nisan Akman, one of Turkey's female film directors, on the role of women directors and the nature of their work.

1225. Penolidis, Tina. *Place et rôle de la femme dans les journaux télévisés*. Brussels: Commission of the European Communities, 1984.

1226. Pierre. "'I'm Not a Radical Feminist' -- Margarethe Von Trotta." *Cinema India-International*. April-June 1984, pp. 28-29.
An interview with German, husband-wife, filmmaking team, Volker Schloendorff and Margarethe Von Trotta.

1227. "Playboy Interview: Oriana Fallaci." *Playboy*. November 1981, pp. 77-108.
Italian newswoman noted for her tough questioning of world dignitaries.

1228. Ray, Michèle. *The Two Shares of Hell*. New York: McKay, 1968. 217 pp.
The story of this French journalist who drove through South Vietnam in 1966-67.

1229. Reumann, K. and W. Schulz. "Journalist." In *Publizistik*, edited by E. Noelle-Neumann and W. Schulz. Frankfurt-am-Main: Fischer Tachenbuch Verlag, 1971.

1230. Robarts, Sadie. *Account of the Thames Positive Action Project, 1980-1981*. London: Thames Television, 1981.

1231. Robinson, Gertrude J., ed. *Emotional Effects of Media: The Works of Hertha Sturm*. Montreal: Working Papers in Communication, Graduate Program in Communication, McGill University, 1987. 90 pp.
Pulls together the work of German scholars Hertha Sturm and Marianne Grewe-Partsch on media research effects. Sturm is a psychologist who applied Piagetian learning theory to media effects. Among articles are "Piaget's Theory of Intellectual Development Applied to Radio and Television," "The Missing Half-Second," "The Recipient-Oriented Approach," and "Television -- The Emotional Medium: Results from Three Studies."

1232. Romero, Patricia W. *E. Sylvia Pankhurst: Portrait of a Radical*. New Haven, Connecticut: Yale University Press, 1987. 334 pp.
This British radical's journalistic career was featured in chapters on "Author and Journalist," pp. 178-196, and "Radical Propagandist," pp. 239-264.

1233. Sagan, Leontine. "Courage in Production." *Cinema Quarterly.* Spring 1933, pp. 140-143.
German female director's views on directing films.

1234. Sanford, David. "Two Women: The Lady of the Tapes." *Esquire.* June 1975, pp. 102-105.
Italian journalist, Oriana Fallaci.

1235. Schwarzer, Alice. "An Interview with Margarethe von Trotta." *Isis International Bulletin.* June 1983, pp. 5-7.
Background of this German film director and her motivations for making films; unabridged German version appeared in January 1982 *Emma*.

1236. Seiter, Ellen. "The Political Is Personal: Margarethe von Trotta's *Marianne and Juliane*." *Journal of Film and Video.* Spring 1985. pp. 41-46.
The German films of Margarethe von Trotta offer an "exploration of primary relationships between women, where the tension reflects the difficulties for women in securing an identity in a culture where they are devalued."

1237. Silberman, Marc. "Cine-Feminists in West Berlin." *Quarterly Review of Film Studies.* Spring 1980, pp. 217-232.
Discusses work of a number of German women filmmakers.

1238. Sims, Monica. "Women in BBC Management." *COMBROAD.* September 1985, pp. 11-14.
Report of author showed only six out of 165 senior management positions at BBC were filled by women. Reasons given.

1239. Skard, Torild. "It's Hard To Be a Man -- Especially When You're a Woman." *Sex-Roles within Massmedia Newsletter.* November 1985, p. 41.
Every fifth Norwegian journalist is a woman, not a significant increase in recent years. On the working conditions of Norwegian newspaper journalists in 1979, the author said women were under particularly "hard pressure." A follow-up study resulted in the book, *The Lives and Working Conditions of Women in Journalism*, 1984, Norwegian.

1240. Skard, Torild. "Norway: Two Edged S(word)s for Women Journalists." In *Communications at the Crossroads: The Gender Gap Connection,* edited by Ramona Rush and Donna Allen, pp. 132-141. Norwood, New Jersey: Ablex, 1989.
A qualitative analysis of the lives and working conditions of 50 women journalists in Norway during the early 1980s; the media presented a biased image of reality because most journalists were men.

1241. Skard, Torild. *You Pay the Price To Be a Tough Guy -- Particularly If You Are a Woman.* Fredrikstad, Norway: Institute of Work Psychology and Norwegian Journalist Association, 1984.

Working conditions of 50 women journalists in Norwegian press and broadcasting.

1242. Smith, R. "Images and Equality: Women and the National Press." In *The Sociology of Journalism and the Press*, edited by H. Christian, pp. 239-258. Totowa, New Jersey: Rowman and Littlefield, 1980.

The British national press is a male preserve and if women reached the upper levels of newspaper management, not much would change because of external pressures.

1243. Spain, Nancy. *Why I'm Not a Millionaire.* London: Hutchinson, 1956. 264 pp.

Author's career as reporter and critic for the *London Daily Sketch.*

1244. Strzyz, Klaus. "A Successful Female Cartoonist Looks for Topics in Everyday Life." *WittyWorld.* Autumn 1988, pp. 30-31.

One of the three leading German female cartoonists, Doris Lerche, who uses an unspectacular drawing style with everyday subjects.

1245. Sveriges Radio. *Men and Women in Broadcasting: Working Towards Equality at Sveriges Radio.* Stockholm: Sveriges Radio Forlag, 1981. 104 pp.

Report on Sveriges Radio's efforts to achieve equality between the sexes; analyses of current situation and proposals.

1246. Sveriges Radio, Equality Working Group. *Nagonting har Hänt.* Evaluation of the Sveriges Radio Equality Project, 1980-1983. Stockholm: Sveriges Radio, 1984.

1247. Swedish Broadcasting Corporation. "Something Has Happened: Equality Work at the Swedish Broadcasting Corporation." *Sex-Roles within Massmedia Newsletter.* December 1986, pp. 70-73.

Progress report on the Equality Project of Swedish Broadcasting Corporation; of 69 points, 24 were completed, three were in progress, five were not started, and nine were no longer relevant between 1980-1983.

1248. Tammes, Diane. "Camerawoman Obscura: A 'Personal Account.'" *Women's Studies International Quarterly.* 3:1 (1980), pp. 59-62.

Her camerawoman experiences with British film and television.

1249. Thompson, Kim. "Claire Bretécher: Triumphant Despite Traitorous Translation." *Comics Journal.* October 1978, pp. 40-41.

French cartoonist Claire Bretécher and her strips, some of which appeared in her books, *Les Frustrés* and *Les Frustrés 2.*

1250. Thunberg, Anne-Marie, Kjell Nowak, Karl Erik Rosengren, and Bengt Sigurd. *Communication and Equality: A Swedish Perspective.* Stockholm: Almqvist and Wiksell International, 1984.

Communication provides power to individuals against authoritarian information systems.

1251. Tielens, M., L. Vankeirsbilck, and M. Ceulemans. "De professionale status van vrouwen in de nieuwsmedia." *Communicatie.* Spring 1978.

1252. Tiercelin, Marie-France. "Les télécom au féminin." *Revue française des télécommunications.* April 1976, pp. 28-32.
   One-half of the 120,000 employees of French telecommunications were women.

1253. Tokgöz, Oya. "Women as Administrators in Mass Media: A Case Study in Turkey." *Sex-Roles within Massmedia Newsletter.* November 1988, pp. 14-15.
   Women make up one-third of Turkey's media personnel and one-third of the journalism students; 15 women interviewed on their roles, needs, and responsibilities as media administrators.

1254. Trömel-Plotz, Senta. "'Es ist nicht mehr meine Haut.' Semantik eines Fernsehgesprächs: Rudolf Augstein und Alice Schwarzer." *Medium.* 15:3 (1985), pp. 6-15.

1255. Tuchman, Gaye and Nina E. Fortin. *Edging Women Out: Victorian Novelists, Publishers, and Social Change.* New Haven, Connecticut: Yale University Press, 1989. 266 pp.
   How men redefined a British cultural form and took over an occupation previously the domain of women.

1256. Tunstall, Jeremy. "British Communicator Occupations." Paper presented at Association for Education in Journalism, Seattle, Washington, August 13-16, 1978. 23 pp.
   Includes the role of women and minorities in the British media.

1257. Van Zoonen, Liesbet. "Deviant Behavior? Professional Socialisation of Dutch Feminist Journalists." *Sex-Roles within Massmedia Newsletter.* November 1988, p. 17.
   The meaning and potential of feminist professional values in Dutch journalism; by the time feminist journalists entered paid journalism, they knew what the limits of feminism in journalism were.

1258. Vergne, E. "Les métiers du cinéma: Script-girl." *La Revue du Cinéma. Image et Son.* April 1974, pp. 30-32.

1259. Werner, Anita. *Norsk Journalister.* Oslo: Universitetsforlaget, 1966.

1260. Whitehouse, Mary. *A Most Dangerous Woman?* Tring, Herts: Lion Publishing, 1982. 256 pp.
   Author's motivations and struggles in her campaigns for morality in British media.

1261. Willis, Sharon. *Marguerite Duras: Writing on the Body.* Urbana: University of Illinois Press, 1987. 204 pp.
   Treatment of Duras' cinematic and literary production.

1262. Wistrand, Birgitta. "'Swedish Women on the Move' -- But Still Scorned by the Press." *Media Report to Women.* November 1, 1981, pp. 5, 7.
   Taken from her 1981 book, *Swedish Women on the Move* (Swedish Institute, Stockholm), which had a chapter entitled, "Sex Roles in the Mass Media and Literature"; men dominated the top positions in the press, weeklies reinforced stereotypes, some magazines fostered in boys and men a contemptuous and scornful attitude about women, and advertising promoted stereotypes, although they no longer used nudes.

1263. Zilliacus-Tikkanen, Henrika. "Feminine Strategies in Journalism." *Gender and Mass Media Newsletter.* November 1989, pp. 7-8.
   Strategies female journalists apply in their work as determined in interviews with 40 female radio and TV journalists, both Finnish - and Swedish-speaking, within Finnish Broadcasting Company.

1264. Zilliacus-Tikkanen, Henrika. "Kvinnlig och Manlig Journalistik - nyhetsvärdering ur jämställdhetssynvinkel." Masters thesis, University of Helsinki, 1982.

Women's Media

1265. Anant, Victor. "A Woman's Own View." *New Society.* January 1, 1976, pp. 12-14.
   Compares Britain's woman's journal, *Woman's Own,* in 1958 and mid-1970s.

1266. Arens, Agna, Anja Meulenbelt, Mrijke Rawie, Ynske Rodenhuis, eds. *Gelukkig Kan Je Er Nu Over Praten* (Fortunately We Can Talk About It Now). Amsterdam: Sara, 1979. 240 pp.
   Textual review of a Dutch TV series for women with reactions from women who appeared on TV.

1267. *Ariel.* June 5, 1985.
   Includes a report commissioned by the British Broadcasting Corporation Board of Governors on women's attaining top positions. Monica Sims reports on "Paving the Way for Women" in the same issue of the staff newspaper of the BBC.

1268. Barrell, Joan and Brian Braithwaite. *The Business of Women's Magazines.* 2nd ed. London: Kogan Page, 1988. 219 pp.
   History, organization, and management of women's magazine publishing with topics such as the initial concept, editorial content, marketing, launching, advertising, production, and distribution.

1269. Bonvoisin, S.M. and M. Maignien. *La presse féminine* (Women's Magazines). Paris: Presses universitaires de France, No. 2305, 1986. 128 pp.
   Much data on French magazines for women.

1270. Bouraoui, H.A. "La Femme Révoltée: A Contrastive Cultural Study." *Journal of Popular Culture*. Spring 1969, pp. 592-614.
   Analysis of Betty Friedan's *The Feminine Mystique* and Simone de Beauvoir's *Le Deuxième Sexe*. Particularly useful is the analysis of the French magazine, *Marie-Claire* which gave the "impression that all one need do to keep a Frenchwoman happy is talk to her about fashion, or, better still, buy her something from the 'new collections.'"

1271. *CinémAction*. No. 9.
   Devoted to "Le cinéma au féminisme."

1272. Clardy, Andrea Fleck. "Creating the Space: Feminist Publications Outside the Mainstream." *Women's Studies International Forum*. 6:5 (1983), pp. 545-546.
   The Crossing Press which insists on the necessity and value of small publishers who can publish and promote feminist writing.

1273. Dardigna, Anne-Marie. *La presse "feminine": fonction idéologique*. Paris: Maspéro, 1978. 248 pp.
   Critically appraises wide gamut of French women's magazines, showing how they adapted to the women's liberation movements. Sequel to author's *Femmes-femmes sur papier glacé*, Paris: F. Maspéro, 1974.

1274. de Claricini, S. "Women's Weeklies in Italy." *Gazette*. 11:1 (1965), pp. 43-56.
   The field of woman's magazines in Italy, consisting of 20 weeklies with over 7 million circulation and oriented to fashion, topical subjects, photo-romances, and topics "in-between." Editors did not think of women as interested in politics.

1275. de Grass, Jan. "Reckoning in Reykjavik, the Icelandic Women's Movement Takes Power." *Herizons*. March 1986.
   Women's newspaper, *Kvennalistinn*, described.

1276. Delorme, Charlotte. "On the Film *Marianne and Juliane* by Margarethe von Trotta." *Journal of Film and Video*. Spring 1985, pp. 47-51.
   Critical of von Trotta's German film as not representative of what it claimed to be. Instead, the film is "nothing but the illustration of various kinds of subjugation and dependency" with a justification of "not standing up for what is right with an appeal to be left alone." Translated by Ellen Seiter from *Frauen und Film 31*, 1982.

1277. Doughan, David T. "Periodicals By, For, and About Women in Britain." *Women's Studies International Forum*. 10:3 (1987), pp. 261-273.

Two centuries of British commercial women's magazines, women's organization periodicals, and feminist publications.

1278. Drotner, Kirsten. "Schoolgirls, Madcaps, and Air Aces: English Girls and Their Magazine Reading Between the Wars." *Feminist Studies*. Spring 1983, pp. 33-52.

The development of popular magazines for girls, tracing their history to *School Friend*, 1919-40, and the fictional transitions that made certain themes popular.

1279. Earnshaw, Stella. "Advertising and the Media: The Case of Women's Magazines." *Media, Culture and Society*. October 1984, pp. 412-421.

Women's magazines in Britain are controlled by advertisers, whose desires have shaped the occupational practices and assumptions of journalists, editors, and production staffers.

1280. Earnshaw, Stella. "Women's Magazines: Culture, Ideology, and the Oppression of Women." Ph.D. dissertation, Liverpool University, 1982.

1281. Fallon, Martine. "Le procès de la mode dans deux magazines féminins." *Revue de l'Institut de Sociologie*. Brussels University Libre. No. 3, 1977, pp. 261-270.

Analysis of U.S. and French women's magazines, *Cosmopolitan* and *Marie Claire*.

1282. *Feminari: Dona i Cultura de Masses*, Barcelona. "Prensa para mujeres o el discurso de lo privado: El caso del grupo hymsa." *Sex-Roles within Massmedia Newsletter*. November 1988, pp. 11-12.

"Women's magazine as the portrayal of the private life: A case study of Hymsa" deals with a family enterprise, Hymsa, that has produced women's publications since the early twentieth century.

1283. *Feminisme in de Mediamangel* (Feminism as Exploited by the Media), Amsterdam.

First issue (1979) of this Dutch feminist journal produced by De Strijdijzers deals with the role of media in announcing/denouncing feminism and the "ridiculing and commercialization of the women's movement."

1284. Ferguson, Marjorie. "Learning To Be a Woman's Woman." *New Society*. 64:1066 (1983), pp. 94-97.

The theme of "getting and keeping your man" and the roles of mother and wife dominated British women's magazines from 1949-1974.

1285. Fernández, Norman. "La trampa que no es mujer." *El Wendigo*. Autumn/Winter 1989-90, pp. 13-15.

The comics, *La Mujer Trampa*, published in France.

1286. "First Women's Paper in Mediterranean: To Establish Our Own Forum for Our Voices To Be Heard on Region." *Media Report to Women.* November-December 1984, pp. 1, 13.
Excerpts from prospectus of first number of *Mediterranean Women* of Athens, Greece.

1287. Frazer, Elizabeth. "Teenage Girls Reading *Jackie*." *Media, Culture and Society.* October 1987, pp. 407-425.
Empirical data on seven groups of British girls and their reaction to a photo-story in *Jackie*, the teenage magazine. Readers took a critical stand vis-à-vis texts.

1288. Fritz, Leah. "Publishing and Flourishing." *Women's Review of Books.* February 1986, pp. 16-17; September 1986, pp. 14-15.
Two-part portrayal of England's feminist publishing scene.

1289. Grunwald, Mary. "West German Feminist Book Publishers." *Women's Studies Newsletter.* Winter 1979, pp. 23-24.
Feminist publishers were *the* sensation in the German book trade; discussion of some major ones -- Frauenoffensive Verlag, Frauenbuchverlag, Frauenselbstverlag, Amazonen-Frauenverlag, and Verlag Frauenpolitik.

1290. Hermes, Joke and Liesbet van Zoonen. "Fun or Serious Business? Dutch Feminist Television Programmes in the Past Fifteen Years." *Sex-Roles within Massmedia Newsletter.* November 1987, p. 7.
How solutions were found to problems of how to present feminist shows on Dutch TV.

1291. *Isis International Bulletin.* No. 16, 1981.
A resource issue on "The Feminist Press in Western Europe," listing more than 250 feminist publications, presses, bookshops, and archives in 18 European countries: Austria, Belgium, Denmark, France, Germany, Greece, Iceland, Ireland, Italy, the Netherlands, Norway, Portugal, Spain, Sweden, Switzerland, England, Northern Ireland, and Scotland.

1292. McClelland, W.D. "Women's Press in Britain." *Gazette.* 11:2/3 (1965), pp. 148-165.
The part of the press that is edited and published exclusively for women; the women's press in Britain has immense power, but enjoys varying fortunes and faces a volatile market where one in two publications fails.

1293. McRobbie, Angela. "Jackie: An Ideology of Adolescent Femininity." In *Popular Culture: Past and Present*, edited by Bernard Waites, Tony Bennett, and Graham Martin, pp. 263-283. London: Croom Helm, 1982.
British teen magazine, *Jackie*, popular with girls, and how it is read.

1294. McRobbie, Angela and Trisha McCabe, eds. *Feminism for Girls: An Adventure Story.* London: Routledge and Kegan Paul, 1981.

1295. Mayne, Judith. "The Woman at the Keyhole: Women's Cinema and Feminist Criticism." *New German Critique.* Summer 1981, pp. 40-41.

1296. Melville, Joy. "I'm Not a Feminist, But..." *New Society.* June 7, 1984, pp. 391-392.
   The feminist publishing world of Great Britain.

1297. Neustatter, Angela. *Hyenas in Petticoats.* London: Harrap, 1989.
   Women's pages of newspapers and feminist periodicals in England; includes "The Medium and the Message -- Feminism in the Theatre and the Visual Arts," pp. 115-144; "Stay Out of the Harem -- Women and Journalism," pp. 145-160.

1298. Nye, Russel B. "Miroir de la vie: The French Photoroman and Its Audience." *Journal of Popular Culture.* Spring 1977, pp. 744-751.
   The photoroman, a successful type of "presse du coeur" which is an offshoot of the general woman's magazine; its story, related to dramatic serial, has deeper roots than twentieth century women's magazines.

1299. "Radio Donna -- Frauenradio in Rom." *Medienarbeit.* Nos. 17/18, 1978, pp. 52-56.
   The private radio station, Radio Donna, devoted to women.

1300. Sempere, Pedro. *Semiologia del infortunio: Lenguaje e ideologia de la fotonovela.* (Semiology of Misfortune: Language and Ideology of the Photonovel). Madrid: Ediciones Felmar, 1976. 171 pp.
   Mass culture primarily addressed to women, especially Spain's popular "Lucecita," which appeared as a radio drama and photonovel in 1975.

1301. Smyth, Ailbhe. "Ireland's New Rebels." *Women's Review of Books.* April 1987, pp. 16-18.
   Role of feminist publishing in Irish women's struggle for autonomy.

1302. Stanley, Liz, with Ann Morley. *The Life and Death of Emily Wilding Davison.* London: The Women's Press, 1988.
   The origins of the Woman's Press of England in "Will the First Woman's Press Stand Up, Please?" pp. 81-95.

1303. Struck, Karin. "Weg von den Müttern." *Der Spiegel.* November 26, 1973, pp. 163-166.
   Critical of the first international women's film festival, held in Berlin; films shown were too simplistic, narrow, and reactionary.

1304. Taylor, D.B. "The Information Content of Women's Magazine Advertising in the UK." *European Journal of Marketing.* 17:5 (1983), pp. 28-32.
   The information content of advertisements in British women's magazines -- *Woman, Woman's Weekly, Woman's Own,* and *Woman's Realm*; 83 percent of the ads contained at least one informative cue.

1305. van Dijck, Bernadette and Anneke Smelik. "Dutch Women's Movies: Developments and Interrelations." In *Historiography of Women's Cultural Traditions,* edited by Maaike Meijer and Jetty Schaap, pp. 119-128. Providence, Rhode Island: Foris Publications, 1987.

   Categorization of about 150 films made by women directors between 1966 and 1985; deals with "Female Culture" and "Female Pleasure."

1306. White, Cynthia Leslie. *Women's Magazines, 1963-1968.* London: Michael Joseph, 1971. 348 pp.

   The development of women's magazines in Britain from sociological and economic perspectives; the last chapter is about U.S. women's periodicals. By the same author: *The Women's Periodical Press in Britain 1946-1976,* London: Her Majesty's Stationery Office, 1977.

1307. Winship, Janice. "A Woman's World: 'Woman' -- An Ideology of Femininity." *Working Papers on Cultural Studies.* 11 (1978), pp. 133-154.

   A feminist assessment of the ideological presentations of femininity by women's magazines in England.

1308. Winship, Janice. "'Options -- For the Way You Want to Live Now', or a Magazine for Superwoman." *Theory, Culture and Society.* 1:3 (1983), pp. 44-65.

1309. "Women's Magazines Hot Properties in International Media Markets." *Media Report to Women.* November-December 1988, pp. 7-8.

   European publishers were very interested in the women's market; discussion of *Prima, Best, Essentials,* and *Hello!*

1310. Zagarell, Sandra Abelson. "Courage, Emma: You Can Read Two Feminist Magazines Each Month in the Federal Republic of Germany." *Women's Studies Newsletter.* Winter 1979, pp. 25-26.

   German feminist magazines, *Courage* and *Emma.*

5
LATIN AMERICA AND THE CARIBBEAN

GENERAL STUDIES

1311. Barreto, Marien S. "La imagen de la mujer en las telenovelas." In *La imagen de la mujer en los medios de comunicación*, pp. 29-34. San Juan: Comision para el mejoramiento de los derechos de la mujer, 1978.

1312. Bonilla de Ramos, Elssy, coordinator. *Memorias del encuentro sobre la mujer y los medios masivos de comunicación. Documentos y discusiones.* Bogota: Documento No. 058, CEDE, 1979. 152 pp.
    Documents and discussions of a seminar on "Mass Media and the Participation of Women in Development," Bogota, November 1978.

1313. Byrne, Pamela R. and Suzanne R. Ontiveros, eds. *Women in the Third World: A Historical Bibliography.* Santa Barbara, California: ABC-CLIO, 1986. 152 pp.
    Not many citations on media, but see pp. 459 and 494 on Argentina and Mexico.

1314. Calderon, Carola Garcia. *Revistas femininas: La mujer como objeto de consumo.* Mexico: Ediciones El Caballito, 1980.

1315. Carty, James W., jr. and Marjorie T. Carty. "Notes on Latin American Women in the Media: A Mid-1980s Sample of Voices and Groups." *Studies in Latin American Popular Culture.* No. 6, 1987, pp. 311-341.
    Survey of women journalists and leaders of feminist organizations of Latin America categorizes women journalists as traditionalists and transformers. Countries covered were Cuba, Mexico, Puerto Rico, Costa Rica, Honduras, Guatemala, Uruguay, Colombia, Peru, Argentina, and Brazil.

1316. *Chasqui.* (Quito). July, August, September, 1982.
    Special thematic issue on "La Mujer en Los Medios de Información y Comunicación" (Women in the Media of Information and Communication).

Published by CIESPAL (Centro Internacional de Estudios Superiores de Comunicación para América Latina -- International Center of Higher Studies of Communication for Latin America).

1317. Conferencia Cristiana por la Paz de Latinoamérica y el Caribe. *La mujer, taller de la vida: constructora de la nueva sociedad.* Mantanzas, Cuba: Centro de Información y Documentación "Augusto Cotto," ca. 1983.

   Under section on women and institutions, the chapter, "La Mujer y los Medios Masivos de Comunicación," by Migdaléder Mazuera of Venezuela.

1318. de Guevara, Licenciada Miriam Lynch and Estela Marip Minervini. *Los medios de comunicación de masas y imagen de la mujer en algunos países de América* (Means of Mass Communication and Image of Women in Some American Nations). Cordoba, Argentina: Centro Multinacional de la Mujer de Investigación y Capacitación de la Comisión Interamericana de Mujeres, 1982. 16 pp.

1319. Díaz de Landa, Marta and Carlos Alberto Lista. "La imagen de la mujer y los medios de comunicación de masas. Focos de interes femeninos y masculinos en el espacio periodistico de las revistas de actualidad." Washington, D.C.: Organization of American States, Comision Interamericana de Mujeres, Serie: Estudios No. 9, Cuaderno No. 2, 1983. 43 pp.

   Part of a series on women and communication in Latin America, based on content analysis. Others in the series include: No. 1, "La mujer de la publicidad: Qué se le ofiece y cómo sela representa"; No. 3, "Análisis de las figuras reales en las revistas de actualidad: Estudio de los estereotipos sexuales"; No. 4, "La imagen de la mujer en las fotonovelas"; No. 5, "La participación de la mujer en la comunicación social como formadora de opinión y comunicadora social."

1320. Flora, Cornelia Butler. "Roasting Donald Duck: Alternative Comics and Photonovels in Latin America." *Journal of Popular Culture.* Summer 1984, pp. 163-182.

1321. Flora, Cornelia Butler. "The Passive Female and Social Change: A Cross-Cultural Comparison on Women's Magazine Fiction." In *Female and Male in Latin America*, edited by Ann Pescatello, pp. 59-85. Pittsburgh, Pennsylvania: University of Pittsburgh Press, 1973.

1322. Flora, Cornelia Butler. "Women in Latin American Fotonovelas: From Cinderella to Mata Hari." *Women's Studies International Quarterly.* 3:1 (1980), pp. 95-104.

   Shifts in Latin American *fotonovelas* in 1970s -- to *novela suave* and *novela roja* -- and implications for women's passivity.

1323. García Flores, Margarita. "Las mujeres y la publicidad: Mujeres kitsch en lugar de seres reales?" In *Mujer y Sociedad en América Latina*, edited by Lucia Guerra-Cunningham, pp. 63-76. Irvine: Editorial del Pacifico and University of California, Irvine. 1980.

Mainly on images of women in media (primarily TV) in Mexico and Bolivia.

1324. Gay, Jill. "Sweet Darlings in the Media." *Multinational Monitor.* August 1983, pp. 19-21.

Growing transnational corporate domination of media in Third World; data on Latin America where Hearst's *Good Housekeeping* and *Cosmopolitan* have the largest circulation.

1325. Herrera, Alicia. "Estela bravo y sus documentales." *UPEC.* March-April 1985, pp. 20-23.

Work of Latin American documentary film director, Estela Bravo.

1326. ILET-Unesco. "Seminario ILET-Unesco: La comunicación alternativa de la mujer en América Latina. Documento final y conclusiones." Mexico City: ILET, 1982. 20 pp.

Summary of a conference on alternative communication of Latin American women, sponsored by ILET, including a list of participants, the titles of 17 papers, and the conclusions.

1327. Instituto Italo Latinoamericano. Rome. Conference "La Donna, la Comunicazione e lo Sviluppo in America Latina," 1983.

Papers included: Adelia Borges, "Intentande romper los estereotipos: Relato di una experiencia de comunicación alternativa en América Latina"; Estela Erausquin, "Ni cenicienta, ni mujer maravilla: la prensa feminina en Argentina"; Maria Isabel Garcia, "Condición, mujer. Oficio, periodista"; Maricla Sellari, "Annotazioni su una Esperienza alla Televisione Italiana, negli anni 1975-1982"; Vanda M. Silva Torres, "A mulher na gerencia dos meios de comunicaçao: Relato de experiencia en Brasil"; Rosario Utreras, "La mujer y los medios de comunicación en el Ecuador"; Marcela Fernández Violante, "La Partecipazione della Donna nella Industria Cinematografica Messicana."

1328. Laverde Toscano, María Cristina. "Mujeres y hombres luchan juntamente." *Media Development.* 3, 1980, pp. 38-39.

Mass communication and popular communication in the context of Latin American women.

1329. McCracken, Ellen. "In Search of the Female Consumer: Latin American Women's Magazines and the Transnational Model." *Studies in Latin American Popular Culture.* Vol. 2, 1983, pp. 226-233.

A review of Santa Cruz and Erazo's *Compropolitan: El orden transnacional y su modelo femenino* and García Calderón's *Revistas Femeninas: La mujer como objeto de consumo*; her own insights are offered.

1330. Mattelart, Michèle. *La Cultura de la Opresión femenina* (The Culture of Feminine Oppression). Mexico: Editorial Era, 1977. 207 pp.

The "culture of feminine oppression" in Latin America, ranging from women's magazines to *fotonovelas*. These essays represented three distinct periods related to the 1970-73 Popular Unity: a pre-Allende analysis of *fotonovelas*, a 1971 study of pseudo-modernity in women's magazines, and a study of organized protest by women against the Popular Unity government, published in 1974.

1331. Mazuera, Migdaléder. "La mujer y los medios masivos de comunicación." In *II Encuentro continental de mujeres Cristianas por la paz. La mujer, taller de la vida: constructora de la nueva sociedad*, pp. 65-78. Matanzas, Cuba: Centro de Información y Documentación, 1983.

   Profiles of Latin American media; reactions of women to media portrayals of them.

1332. Miller, Francesca. "Internationalist Politics and Women's Journalism." Paper presented at Latin American Studies Association, Miami, Florida, December 1989. 9 pp.

   A hallmark of the Latin American women's movement is the sustained production of feminist journals; examples from a number of countries.

1333. Organization of American States. *La imagen de la mujer y los medios de comunicación de masas: Focos de interés femeninos y masculinos en el espacio periodístico de las revistas de actualidad.* Cuaderno No. 2, Series: Studio Nu. 9 (Image of Women and Means of Mass Communication: Foci of Feminine and Masculine Interests in Journalistic Space in Current Magazines). Washington, D.C.: OAS, 1983. 43 pp.

1334. Pescatello, Ann, ed. *Female and Male in Latin America.* Pittsburgh, Pennsylvania: University of Pittsburgh Press, 1973.

   Includes Cornelia B. Flora, "The Passive Female and Social Change: A Cross-Cultural Study of Women's Magazine Fiction," pp. 59-85, and Evelyn P. Stephens, "Marianismo: The Other Face of Machismo in Latin America," pp. 89-102.

1335. Randall, Margaret. "El mensaje y la mujer: Los medios masivos de comunicación como arma imperialiste, y su influencia sobre la mujer en América Latina." Presented at seminar, "La participación de la mujer en el desarrollo rural y sus consecuencias en el ámbito urbano," Managua, Nicaragua, September 1-7, 1981.

   Methods U.S. media corporations, especially Hearst, use to alienate women and give false values; Latin America is discussed in detail.

1336. Rodríguez Calderón, Mirta. "For Truthful Information about Women's Struggles." *CEMEDIM.* September-October 1986, pp. 1-3.

   Eighty-nine women journalists from 16 Latin American countries, plus guests from Denmark, Norway, Switzerland, and the U.S. met in Managua to formulate specific proposals concerning an agenda whose first demand consisted of having those who work in communications promote truthful information about women's struggles.

1337. Rodríguez Calderón, Mirta. "To Speak Out and Act So There'll Be a Year 2000." *CEMEDIM.* March-April 1985, p. 1.

Discussions at a 1984 meeting in Havana of non-governmental women's organizations on women's use of formal and clandestine communications means. Also see in same issue: "Declaration on the Mass Media and Their Impact on Women," p. 2.

1338. Rush, Ramona R. and Sonia Gutierrez y Villalobos. "Images of Women in Latin America and Other Gender and Communication Issues." Paper presented at Association for Education in Journalism and Mass Communication, Minneapolis, Minnesota, August 1990.

Latin American women viewed within global issues of gender and communication.

1339. Santa Cruz, Adriana. "Alternative Communication and Latin American Women." In *Communications at the Crossroads: The Gender Gap Connection*, edited by Ramona Rush and Donna Allen, pp. 251-261. Norwood, New Jersey: Ablex, 1989.

The levels and influences of alternative communication for women, concentrating on Mujer-FEMPRESS. The bulletin, *Mujer*, is sent to 840 subscribers in 21 Latin American countries.

1340. Santa Cruz, Adriana. "Media Images of Latin American Women." *Media Information Australia.* February 1988, pp. 50-55.

The oppression and manipulation of Latin American women were still there, and media were major tools in maintaining this system.

1341. Santa Cruz, Adriana. "Mujer y comunicación: Nuevas voces en la búsqueda de una democracia auténtica." In *Comunicación alternativa y búsquedas democraticas*, edited by Fernando Reyes-Matta, pp. 71-86. Mexico City: Instituto Latinoamericano de Estudios Transnacionales and Friedrich-Ebert-Stiftung, 1983.

Women's communication projects as alternatives in Latin America, citing Unidad de Comunicación Alternativa de la Mujer, FEM, *Nueva Mujer, Mulherio*, ILET, among others. Examples are given from Brazil, Peru, Mexico, Dominican Republic, and other countries.

1342. Santa Cruz, Adriana and Viviana Erazo. "Media as Manipulation." *Isis International Bulletin.* No. 18, 1981, pp. 18-22.

Abstract of authors' 1980 book; the way transnationals' "structure of communication plays on the culture of the region in order to involve and alienate Latin American women, through the message carried by women's popular magazines."

1343. Unidad de Comunicación Alternativa de la Mujer. *Coleccion Comunicación Alternativa de la Mujer*, Mexico City.

Series of monographs that began in the early 1980s assesses women in Latin American mass media; most deal with a specific medium and are based on interviews. Includes: "La mujer en *El Mundo* (Mexico)," "*Suplemento La Mujer*

(Argentina)," "La Tribuna (Mexico)," "La barra de mujeres, Radio Educación México," "Publicaciones alternativas, de Grupos de Mujeres en América Latina," "Red Radiofónica de Mujeres, América Latina," "*La Mala Vida*: revista feminista Venezuela," "*La Cacerola*: boletín de mujeres, Uruguay," "*Viva*" (Peru), "Spots antisexistas: T.V. Argentina," "*Mulherio* (Brazil)," "*Maria, Liberacion del Pueblo* (Mexico)," "*Nueva Mujer* (Ecuador)," "*Fem* (Mexico)," "*ISIS* (Italy)," "Club Mencia (Dominican Republic)," "La Causa de las Mujeres (Mexico)," and "Colectivo ven/seremos (Mexico)."

1344. Viezzer, Moema. "Alternative Communication for Women's Movements in Latin America." In *The Myth of the Information Revolution*, edited by Michael Traber, pp. 117-125. Beverly Hills, California: Sage Publications, 1986.

   The activities of alternative systems of communication among women, such as, Rede Mulher of Brazil, Latin American Network for Women's Education, and Isis International.

1345. Villar-Gaviria, Alvaro. "Housewife's Neurosis." *Revista Colombiana de Psiquiatria*. July 1975, pp. 285-296.

   Discussion of "housewife's neurosis," found among the middle class. Attitudes endemic to the neurosis were encouraged by TV and radio advertising.

1346. Zornosa, Anna Lucia. "Collaboration and Modernization: Case-Study of a Transitional Magazine." *Studies in Latin American Popular Culture*. 2 (1983), pp. 24-35.

   Comparison of U.S. and Mexican editions of the women's magazine, *Cosmopolitan*; collaborations between publishers in the U.S. and Latin America significantly affected the magazine's content and allowed the Mexican editions to be subtly altered to include messages more appealing to the Latin American audience.

CARIBBEAN

General Studies

1347. Candelas, Laura. "Propaganda publicitaria y la mujer en las sociedad de consumo." *Mi Ruta*. October-November 1982, p. 23.

   Puerto Rican advertising and women in a consumer society.

1348. Cuthbert, Marlene. "Caribbean Women, Self-Reliance and the Information Industry." In *Development Communication in the Commonwealth Caribbean*, pp. 50-63. Ottawa: Canadian Foundation for Caribbean Development and Cooperation, 1984.

1349. Cuthbert, Marlene. *The Impact of Audio-Visual Media on the Socio-Cultural Behavior of Women in Jamaica*. Paris: Unesco, 1979.

1350. Ellis, Pat, ed. *Women of the Caribbean.* London: Zed Books, 1986.
Includes Claudette Earl, "Media Concepts for Human Development in the Caribbean with Special Reference to Women," pp. 115-118, and Elma Reyes, "Women in Calypso," pp. 119-121.

1351. Hodge, Merle. "C'bean Women Face Conflicting Contradictory Codes." *Caribbean Contact.* January 1985, pp. 11, 13.
Role of media discussed.

1352. Pineda, Magaly. "Telenovelas: Just Entertainment?" *Isis International Bulletin.* No. 18, 1981, pp. 16-18.
Originally published in the magazine *Ahora* of Dominican Republic. The goal of telenovelas is to "defuse the potential of women for united action in social organization, and to reinforce traditional roles and the particular attributes of the 'ideal woman.'"

1353. Poteet Bussard, Lavonne C. "Feminist Publications in the Caribbean." Presented at Latin American Studies Association, Washington, D.C. March 6, 1982.

1354. Santiago-Marazzi, Rosa. "La mujer y su experiencia cultural en Puerto Rico." *Homines.* January-June 1982, pp. 118-126.

Historical Studies

1355. Escoto, José Augusto. *Gertrudis Gómez de Avellaneda. Cartas inéditas y documentos relativos a su vida en Cuba de 1859 a 1864.* Matanzas: Imprenta La Pluma de Oro, 1911.
Life of Gómez de Avellaneda, famous literary figure and editor of a short-lived women's periodical in Cuba, *Album Cubano de lo Bueno y lo Bello.*

1356. Lent, John A. "Pioneer Women Editors -- The Stockdale Sisters of Bermuda." *Printing History.* 10:1 (1988), pp. 36-39.
One of early instances when women edited a Caribbean newspaper. Sisters Priscilla, Frances, and Sarah Stockdale edited the *Bermuda Gazette* for a number of years after their father, Joseph, died in the early nineteenth century.

1357. Miller, Beth. "Gertrude the Great. Avellaneda, Nineteenth-Century Feminist." In *Women in Hispanic Literature: Icons and Fallen Idols*, edited by Beth Miller, pp. 201-214. Berkeley: University of California Press, 1983.
Gertrudis Gómez de Avellaneda, who, among other things, edited a woman's magazine in Cuba in 1860.

1358. Picon Garfield, Evelyn. "Political Literature for Women in Mid-Nineteenth Century Cuba: The Case of Gertrudis Gómez de Avellaneda's *Album Cubano de lo Bueno y lo Bello.*" Paper presented at Latin American Studies Association, Miami, Florida, December 1989. 24 pp.

Gómez de Avellaneda's bi-monthly periodical for women, published in Havana between February 15, and August 12, 1860.

Images of Women

1359. Aho, William R. "The Treatment of Women in Trinidad's Calypsoes, 1969-1979." *Sex Roles.* 10:1/2, 1984, pp. 141-148.
Empirical evidence of Trinidadian calypso and its treatment of women through analysis of 311 songs. About one-fourth of all calypsoes deal centrally with women and nearly all in negative ways.

1360. Alegría Ortega, Idsa E. "La representacion de la mujer trabajadora en la television en Puerto Rico." *Homines.* February 1987, pp. 289-293.
Differences between working women in real life and as depicted on Puerto Rican television.

1361. Brodber, E. *Perceptions of Caribbean Women: Towards a Documentation of Stereotypes.* Cave Hill: Barbados: University of the West Indies, Institute of Social and Economic Research, 1982.
Print media historically have had similar sex-role stereotyping from country to country. In 1800s, Caribbean papers showed women as beautiful, frail, nervous, sickly homebodies. Until well after the 1950s, images of women were mainly those of foreign white women.

1362. Cuthbert, Marlene. "'Woman Day a Come': Mass Media and Development in the Caribbean." *Media Development.* February 1984, pp. 18-21.
Important changes in the situation of Caribbean women and mass media have taken place. Yet the image of women as portrayed in the press, on radio and television, and particularly in music lyrics is still that of the stereotype.

1363. Cuthbert, Marlene. "'Woman Day a Come': Women and Communication Channels in the Caribbean." In *Communications at the Crossroads: The Gender Gap Connection,* edited by Ramona Rush and Donna Allen, pp. 149-159. Norwood, New Jersey: Ablex, 1989.
Women's images in the press, radio, recording industry, television, film, and advertising, and participation of women in Caribbean media.

1364. Cuthbert, Marlene, ed. *Caribbean Women in Communication for Development.* Barbados: Cedar Press, 1975. 62 pp.
Essays on the use of print media to project problems of underdeveloped women and law in Barbados, Jamaica women and media, and development support communication.

1365. Hernández Torres, Elizabeth. "Images of Women in Mass Media." *Homines.* February 1987, pp. 296-300.
Puerto Rican TV and advertising portrayed women as sex objects, the "harassing woman," and the "hysterical woman."

1366. *Homines*, Puerto Rico. February 1987.
Thematic issue on "Mujeres Puertoriqueñas, protagonistas en el Caribe" includes: Idsa E. Alegría Ortega, "La representacion de la mujer trabajadora en la television en Puerto Rico," pp. 289-293; Gladys Crescioni, "Mujer Puertorriqueña: Fuente y caudal," pp. 294-295; Elizabeth Hernández Torres, "Images of Women in Mass Media," pp. 296-300, and Jesús Vera Irizarry, "La mujer en los medios de comunicacion. Problemas de ellas o de todos?" pp. 301-303.

Women Practitioners

1367. Alegría, Idsa and Isabel Picó. *La mujer en los medios de comunicación social.* San Juan: Centro de Investigaciones Sociales, Universidad de Puerto Rico, 1980.

1368. Andujar, Sonia. "Mujer-Tec: An Appropriate Intervention." *Development Communication Report.* June 1982, p. 15.
Mujer Tec is an action and advocacy group in the Dominican Republic, devoted to promoting community action through media use. Its activities are focused on the development of women's technical and leadership roles in the media.

1369. Caribbean Institute of Mass Communication (CARIMAC). "Regional Seminar on Women and Media Decision-Making." Kingston, Jamaica. 1981.
Papers presented include: Peggy Antrobus, "Caribbean Women in the Media"; Marlene Cuthbert, "A Survey of Women Professionals in Jamaican Electronic Media"; Marlene Cuthbert, "What Makes News? (Why Women Don't)"; Sandra Edwards, "Caribbean Women's Features Syndicate"; Vic Fernandes and Harold Hoyte, "Perceptions on Recruitment, Training, Salaries, Working Conditions and Promotion of Women in Media"; Barbara Glouden, "How Media Values Affect Caribbean Women"; Lorna Gordon, "The Portrayal and Participation of Women in the Caribbean Mass Media: A Socio-Economic Perspective"; George John, "News Values and Women: A Media Manager's Perspective"; Corina Meeks, "Women in the Public Information Services in Jamaica"; Nora E. Peacocke, "Recruitment, Training,, Salaries and Promotion of Women in the Media"; Gloria Royale, "Images of Women in Caribbean TV Ads: A Case Study," and Heather Royes, "Communication Policy and Development: Women's Work."

1370. Cudjoe, Selwyn R. *Caribbean Women Writers: Essays from the First International Conference.* Wellesley, Massachusetts: Calaloux Publications, 1990. 272 pp.
Works of women journalists such as Phyllis Allfrey included.

1371. Cuthbert, Marlene, ed. *Women and Media Decision-making in the Caribbean: CARIMAC/Unesco Seminar, Kingston, Jamaica, Sept. 28-30, 1981.* Kingston: Caribbean Institute of Mass Communication, 1981.

1372. Deming, Caren. J. "Mujeres cubanas y la revolución: Using Media to Improve the Status of Women." Paper presented at International Communication Association, Acapulco. San Francisco: San Francisco State University, Broadcast Communication Arts Department, 1980.

1373. Edwards, Sandra. "Women Assert Communcation Power in the Caribbean." *Media Development*. 28:1 (1981), pp. 29-31.

   How the Caribbean Women's Features Syndicate, established in Barbados in 1978, strives to focus on women's contributions to development; how women have been relegated to women's pages; how finding and motivating correspondents has been difficult.

1374. Fanshel, Susan, ed. *A Decade of Cuban Documentary Film, 1972-1982*. New York: Young Filmmakers, Inc., 1982.

   Includes "Three Women at ICAIC: An Interview with Gloria Arguelles, Mayra Vilasis, and Marisol Trujillo," pp. 25-28.

1375. Haniff, Nesha Z. *Blaze a Fire. Significant Contributions of Caribbean Women*. Toronto: Sister Vision, 1988. 220 pp.

   Discussion of women prominent in other areas with strong connections to mass media, particularly Louise Bennett, Jamaica *Gleaner* columnist, and Phyllis Shand Allfrey, editor of Dominica's *Star* and *Herald*.

CENTRAL AMERICA

Images of Women

1376. de la Peña Sobarzo, Patricia. "Mexico: Today Girls -- Looking Forward to Tomorrow." *Intermedia*. July-September 1987, pp. 12-16.

   Experiences concerning sex stereotyping in Mexican media, from views of a psychoanalyst, TV consumers, writers, journalists, and advertising creative directors. Findings and comments about media portrayals of women in other parts of the world.

1377. Hill, Jane H. and Carole Browner. "Gender Ambiguity and Class Stereotyping in the Mexican Fotonovela." *Studies in Latin American Popular Culture*. 1 (1982), pp. 43-64.

   In sample of 75 Mexican *fotonovelas* (comic book-size photo novels), 1973-79, looked at activity, evaluation, and gender; evaluation and punishment; male/female interchangeability, and class. Class roles and relations were depicted in "strong contrast, with rigid stereotyping," while gender roles and relations were handled in "blurred, complex, almost naturalistic detail."

1378. Hinds, Harold E., jr. and Charles Tatum. "Images of Women in Mexican Comic Books." *Journal of Popular Culture*. Summer 1984, pp. 146-162.

   The images of women in popular Mexican comic books, *Kaliman, Lagrimas, risas y amor, La familia Burrón*, and *El Payo*. Readers usually were subjected to portrayals of women as submissive, passive and long-suffering, dependent upon males for their self esteem.

1379. Korzenny, Betty Ann, Felipe Korzenny, and Gilda Sanchez de Rota. "Women's Communication in Mexican Organizations." *Sex Roles.* April 1985, pp. 667-676.

Forty-five women in 14 Mexican organizations were interviewed to derive a communication profile of women in Mexican private organizations. Women perceived themselves to differ from men on 18 of 40 verbal and nonverbal communication variables.

1380. Mora, Carl J. "Feminine Images in Mexican Cinema: The Family Melodrama; Sara García, 'The Mother of Mexico'; and the Prostitute." *Studies in Latin American Popular Culture.* 4 (1985), pp. 228-235.

The image of the mother is the bedrock of Mexico's cinematic family unit; Latin America's "favorite self-sacrificing mother figure" on film was Sara García.

1381. Quiroz, Teresita and Bárbara Larrain. *Imágen de la mujer que proyectan los medios de comunicación de masas en Costa Rica.* San José, Costa Rica: Universidad de Costa Rica, Instituto de Investigaciones Sociales, 1978.

1382. Ramírez Berg, Charles. "The Image of Women in Recent Mexican Cinema." *Studies of Latin American Popular Culture.* 8 (1989), pp. 156-181.

The stereotypical roles of virgin, Virgin, mother, and whore in Mexican films; since 1968, the thrust has been revisionist -- "re-evaluating the stereotypes, redefining the roles."

1383. Scantlebury, Marcia and Patricia Blanco. "La mujer y los medios de comunicación." Paper presented at first Congreso Universitario de la Mujer, Universidad de Costa Rica, San José, Costa Rica, May 1984. 4 pp.

Women and media generally, with some focus on Costa Rica.

1384. Steele, Cynthia. "Ideology and Mexican Mass Culture: The Case of *Sangre India: Chamula.*" *Studies in Latin American Popular Culture.* 2 (1983), pp. 14-23.

The role of women as portrayed in this Mexican comic book; "the objective alternatives to remaining in unhappy marriages" are few for women.

1385. Zornosa, Anna Lucia. "Sex Roles in Mexican Commercials: The Formation of a Transnational Feminine Model." Paper presented at Communication & Culture Conference, Temple University, Philadelphia, Pennsylvania, April 9-11, 1981.

Analysis of four nights of programs on Televisa's Channel 2; despite the differences betwen the countries, the commercial depiction of women in Mexican television was similar to that in the U.S. The majority of the women were anglos and middle class, confirming that commercials reflected North American race and class distinctions rather than those of Mexico.

Women Practitioners

1386. Carty, James W., jr. "Costa Rica Boasts Most Female Journalists." *Times of the Americas.* November 19, 1980, p. 6.

1387. Carty, James W., jr. "Women's Role in Mexican Media Rising." *Times of the Americas.* August 27, 1980, p. 8.

1388. de la Peña, Patricia. "Women in Television -- Mexico." *Intermedia.* October-November 1989, pp. 27-28.
    Sixty percent of the students in Mexico's communications schools are women, but only 20-25 percent of broadcasting employees. Although Mexican women occupy influential media positions, much has to change before women achieve the status they deserve.

1389. de O'Farrill, Hilda Avila. "Mexico's Media Women." *Matrix.* Summer 1974, pp. 10-11, 22.
    Women long have been part of the Mexican press. Profiles of some women journalists.

1390. Ellison, Katherine. "The Censor and the Censored." *The Quill.* November 1982, pp. 27-28.
    Profile of Nelba Blandon, chief newspaper censor for Nicaragua's Sandinista government.

1391. Moody, John. "Don't Call Her Comrade." *Time.* June 12, 1989, pp. 62-64.
    Violeta Chamorro, publisher of *La Prensa* and later president of Nicaragua, and the political cleavage in her family.

1392. Mrazkova, Daniela. "War Photographer Susan Meiselas." *Democratic Journalist.* November 1986, pp. 26-27.
    Her work mainly in Nicaragua.

1393. Taibo, Paco Ignacio. *María Félix: 47 pasos por el cine* (María Félix: 47 Steps Through the Movies). Mexico City: Editorial Joaquin Mortiz/Planeta, 1985. 316 pp.
    Mexican actress María Félix described as combining the sex appeal of Marilyn Monroe, the "brassiness" of Mae West, and the toughness of Bette Davis; her career chronolgically, interspersing comments on her acting, films, and life.

Women's Media

1394. García Calderón, Carola. *Revistas femininas: la mujer como objeto de consumo.* Mexico City: Ediciones El Caballito, 1980. 139 pp.
    Concerned with how women's magazines are distributed in Mexico and how they promote an "anglicized, consumerist" view of women.

1395. MacLachlan, Colin. "Modernization of Female Status in Mexico: The Image of Women's Magazines." *Revista/Review Interamericana*. 4 (1974), pp. 246-257.

Examination of Mexican women's magazines from perspective of the "needs they satisfy among readers in a developing society"; the editors were aware that they were addressing an audience looking for advice in a changing environment for women.

1396. Santa Cruz, Adriana and Viviana Erazo. *Compropolitan: El orden transnacional y su modelo femenino. Un estudio de las revistas femeninas en América Latina* (Consumopolitan: The Transnational Order and Its Feminine Model. A Study of Women's Magazines in Latin America). Mexico City: Editorial Nueva Imagen, 1980. 290 pp.

Gender-divided women's magazine of Mexico is linked with women's consumer habits. A discussion of the concentration of ownership of media in Mexico and other parts of Latin America and women's magazines' dependence upon advertising from transnational corporations. Same authors did *Reflexion en Toro a la Comunicación Alternativa de la Mujer*, published by Unidad de Comunicación Alternativa de la Mujer.

SOUTH AMERICA

General Studies

1397. Barrios, Leoncio. "Television, Telenovelas and Family Life in Venezuela." In *World Families Watch Television*, edited by James Lull. Newbury Park, California, Sage, 1988.

1398. Barros, Sonia Miceli Pessoa de. *Imitação de vida; pesquisa exploratória sobre a telenovela no Brasil*. São Paulo: Depto. de Ciências Sociais, Fac. de Filosofia, Letras e Ciências Humanas, University São Paulo, 1974. 156 pp.

Operating conditions of Brazilian TV, especially those of the telenovela.

1399. Colomina de Rivera, Marta. *La Celestina mecánica* (The Mechanical Celestina). Caracas: Monte Avila Editores, 1976. 435 pp.

Mass cultural forms primarily aimed at women, such as Venezuelan glossy magazines, romance novels, photonovels, and television soap operas First half is devoted to women's condition throughout history and in contemporary Latin American society, and role of media in maintaining that condition. In second half, some forms of women's mass culture were content analyzed.

1400. *Comunicación: Estudios Venezolanos de Comunicación Perspectiva Crítica y Alternativa*. Autumn 1984.

Thematic issue on the telenovela: "Telenovela: un juglar capitulado," "Telenovela nuestra de cada día," "La telenovela como genero popular femenino y como parte de su especifidad," "Imagen de la mujer en la telenovela," and "La radionovela Venezolana: Tres momentos y una muerte anunciada?"

1401. Covarrubias, Paz and Rolando Franco. *Chile: Mujer y sociedad.* Santiago: Alfabeta Impresores for UNICEF, 1978.

Includes Silvia Pellegrini, "La mujer y los medios de comunicación de masas," pp. 583-590; Israel Marshall, "La imagen femenina en la fotonovela amorosa," pp. 591-604; Naciones Unitas, "Utilización de los medios de comunicación de masas para ejercer influencia en las actividades respecto a la mujer," pp. 605-614.

1402. Fachel Leal, Ondina and Ruben G. Oliven. "Class Interpretations of a Soap Opera Narrative: The Case of the Brazilian Novela 'Summers Sun.'" *Theory, Culture and Society.* 5:1 (1988), pp. 80-99.

1403. Fundação Carols Chagas. *Mulher Brasileira. Bibliografia anotada.* 2 vols. São Paulo: Editora Brasiliense, 1979-81.

Emphasized are pre-1977 materials; particularly important is section on communications and the arts in 1981 volume, pp. 308-364.

1404. Habert, Angeluccia Bernardes. "A fotonovela: Forma e conteúdo." Dissertation, University of São Paulo, 1972. 133 pp.

Characteristics of 56 Brazilian fotonovelas.

1405. Haffey, Joan, Nancy Newton, and Blanca Figueroa. "Women Learn with Visual Aids: Experiences in Peru." *Development Communication Report.* Autumn 1986, p. 11.

Asociación Peru-Mujer, a private, non-profit organization designed to stimulate women's role in national development. Discussion of community-oriented activities of the group that effectively used visual aids.

1406. Mariño, Nery. "La mujer y los medios de comunicación social." In *Los Medios de Comunicación Social en Venezuela.* Caracas: Escuela de Comunicación Social, Universidad Central de Venezuela, 1979.

1407. Marques de Melo, Jose. "Las Telenovelas em São Paolo: Estudio do publico receptor." In *Comunicacão social; teoria e pesquisa*, pp. 247-254. Brazil, Vozes, 1971.

1408. Martin, Richard R., Olga J. Mayorca E., and Stan McDermott. *Women and the Mass Media in a Venezuelan City.* East Lansing, Michigan: Michigan State University, Department of Communications, 1976. 29 pp.

Prepared for International Communication Association, Portland, Oregon, April 1976.

1409. Nagelschmidt, Ana M. "Una medida de modernismo individual entre mujeres de Brazil" (A Measure of Individual Modernism in Brazilian Women). *Revista de la Asociacion Latinoamericana de Psicologia Social.* January-June 1981, pp. 63-74.

A study of 170 Brazilian women to determine machismo levels found that the machismo scale had a high negative correlation with mass media exposure.

1410. Peres, B. "Sexo e erotismo em revistas Brasileiras." *Paz e Terra.* August 1967, pp. 113-140.
Erotic material analyzed in four Brazilian periodicals -- *Realidade, Manchete, Cláudia,* and *Jóia.*

1411. Quiroz, María Teresa and Ana María Cano. "Los antecedentes y condiciones de la produccion de telenovelas en el Peru." *Estudios Sobre Las Culturas Contemporaneas.* February 1988, pp. 187-222.

1412. Santa Cruz, Adriana. "Mujer y medios de comunicación: Una perspectiva del caso Chileno." *Revista Signos.* May-June 1984, pp. 56-58.
Women and media in a few countries of Latin America, with concentration on Chile.

Historical Studies

1413. Azevedo, Christiane D. de. "Le 'Jornal das Famílias'; contribuition à l'étude de la presse féminine Brésilienne." Paris: Univ. Paris I, 1976. 121 pp.
Looks at 192 numbers of *Jornal das Famílias* (1863-1878), a Brazilian woman's periodical.

1414. Hahner, June E. *A mulher Brasileira e suas lutas socialis e políticas: 1850-1937.* São Paulo: Editora Brasiliense, 1981.
Much on the origins of the Brazilian feminist press from 1852, *O Jorno das Senhoras*: "O início da imprensa feminina," pp. 34-43; "Associações de Mulheres e o Movimento Abolicionista," pp. 44-50, which deals with *O Bello Sexo*; and "O feminismo e o desenvolvimento da imprensa feminina," pp. 51-65.

1415. Hahner, June E. "The Nineteenth-Century Feminist Press and Women's Rights in Brazil." In *Latin American Women: Historical Perspectives,* edited by Asunción Lavrin, pp. 254-285. Westport, Connecticut: Greenwood Press, 1978.
Use of a number of nineteenth century feminist periodicals to analyze feminist activities, demands, and goals in Brazil.

1416. Pereira, Regina Paranhos. "Erotismo e cinema Brasileiro." *Filme Cultura.* July 1968, pp. 29-37.
Eroticism in Brazilian cinema, as far back as 1919.

Images of Women

1417. Carlson, Marifran. *Feminismo!* Chicago: Academy Chicago Publishers, 1990. 225 pp.
Feminist movement in Argentina, with references to the role of the press.

1418. Harkness, Shirley and Cornelia B. Flora. "Women in the News: An Analysis of Media Images in Colombia." *Revista Interamericana.* 4 (1974), pp. 220-238.
   Colombian heroines were portrayed as Mary, the mother of Christ -- passive, self-abnegating.

1419. Mattelart, Michèle. "Chile: The Feminine Version of the Coup d'Etat." In *Sex and Class in Latin America: Women's Perspectives on Politics, Economics, and the Family in the Third World,* edited by June Nash and Helen Icken Safa, pp. 279-301. New York: J.F. Bergin Publishers, 1980.

1420. Mattelart, Michèle and Armand. *Le carneval des images: La fiction Bresilienne.* Paris: La Documentation Française, 1987. 163 pp.
   Section on telenovela production in Brazil.

1421. Padilla, Dolores. "Estrategias para defender la imagen de la mujer definen periodistas." *Mujer.* March 1984, p. 1.
   A meeting in Ecuador of 27 reporters and public relations personnel on the image of women.

1422. Santos, Rubens de Costa. "The Portrayal of Women in Brazilian Advertisements; An Exploratory Study." s.l. 1975. 54 pp. Mimeographed.
   The period, 1965 to 1975, in Brazilian periodicals.

1423. Vargas Roma, Maria Antonieta. "Sex Roles Approaches 1975-1985: The Portrayal of the Peruvian Woman Worker within Mass Media." *Sex-Roles within Massmedia Newsletter.* November 1988, p. 24.
   How media increased consumption patterns of Peruvian women workers.

1424. Zuñiga Escobar, Miriam. *La mujer del buzón sentimental.* Cali, Colombia: Universidad del Valle, 1980. 78 pp.
   The mythical image of woman presented by media as an agent of socialization; based on letters women sent to the Colombian paper, *El Espectador,* to seek help with their problems.

Women Practitioners

1425. Abramo, Lélia, Irede Cardoso, and Nanete Voltoline. "O Trabalho da Mulher nos Meios de Comunicação." *Cadernos do CEAS.* May-June 1982, pp. 5-15.
   Discusses their work in communication; two of the authors are Brazilian reporters, the third, a theatrical and TV actress.

1426. Augusto, Sérgio. "Divagações sobre as Estrelas, um Estudo do Divismo no Brasil." *Filme Cultura.* September-October 1970, pp. 32-41.
   Women and film in Brazil.

1427. Baum, Chris. "Women Approaching Parity with Men in Brazil's Newsrooms." *Press Woman.* November 1981, pp. 2-3.

   Women gained in employment on Brazilian dailies (about one-third of total staff) but not in management.

1428. de Camargo, Nelly. "Women in Media Management and Decision-making: A Case Study of Radio in Ecuador." In *Women and Media Decision-making: The Invisible Barriers,* edited by Margaret Gallagher, pp. 44-62. Paris: Unesco, 1987.

   Ecuadorean radio and women's participation, employment policy, career development, and stereotypes.

1429. Klimpel Alvarado, Felícitas. *La mujer Chilena (El aporte feminino al progreso de Chile) 1910-1960.* Santiago de Chile: Editorial Andrés Bello, 1962.

   Has short sections on women journalists, women in radio, and editors of periodicals in Chile.

1430. Luisi, Paulina. *La mujer Uruguaya reclama sus derechos politicos.* Montevideo: Editorial Apolo, 1929. 213 pp.

   Includes: Laura Cortinas, "La mujer escritora," pp. 115-126.

1431. *Mulherio*, São Paulo.

   The September-October 1984 issue discusses Brazilian journalist, Helena Silveira; March 1985, the experiences of Monica Nogueira Lima on *A Tribuna do Ribeira,* a newspaper of Brazil's interior.

1432. Pollarola, Giovanna. "Nora, the Filmmaker." *Isis International Bulletin.* June 1983 p. 9.

   An interview with Nora de Izcue, Peruvian filmmaker. Extracted from *Tortuga,* No. 4, 1982.

Women's Media

1433. Burton, Julianne and Julia Lesage. "Broadcast Feminism in Brazil: An Interview with the Lilith Video Collective." In *Global Television*, edited by Cynthia Schneider and Brian Wallis, pp. 224-229. Cambridge, Massachusetts: MIT Press, 1988.

   Conversational information about the first feminist series broadcast on Brazilian television, "Femininio Plural." Based in São Paulo, the Lilith Video began in 1983.

1434. Cardoso, Irede. "No ar um diálogo entre mulheres." *Audiência.* September 1976, pp. 44-46.

   Programs, audiences, and propaganda of Rádio-Mulher, a Brazilian woman's radio station.

1435. Clason, C. *La Compesina: Acción Cultural Popular Reaches Rural Women with Mixed-Media Program in Colombia. World Education Reports No. 10.* New York, December 1975.

1436. Cuenca de Herrera, Gloria. "La prensa feminina: Factor deformante de la mujer Venezolana." *Orbita.* 8 (1974), pp. 7-40.

    Four women's magazines described: two of Venezuela, *Kena* and *Páginas*, and two of the U.S., *Buenhogar* and *Cosmopolitan*. Venezuelan magazines reflected a false sense of women's liberation, equating it to sexual liberation.

1437. Dejanikus, Tacie. "Peruvian Magazine: The Tortoise Moves Forward." *off our backs.* June 1983, p. 11.

    About *La Tortuga*.

1438. Fempress, ILET. "Comunicación alternativa de la mujer presenta red radiofónica de mujeres II. América Latina." Santiago, Chile: Instituto Latinoamericano de Estudios Transnacionales, ca. 1984 or 1985. 26 pp.

    Details of radio programs for women in Argentina, Bolivia, Brazil, Chile, Paraguay, Peru, Uruguay, and Venezuela.

1439. Padilla, Dolores. "Communication Among Women." *Sex-Roles within Massmedia Newsletter.* December 1986, pp. 63-64.

    Reprinted from November 1985 *Mujer ILET*; a description of a women's group in Ecuador which uses communication as its principal tool. Centro de Información y Apoyo de la Mujer produces a magazine and radio shows and provides a discussion forum.

1440. Prieto de Zegarra, Judith. *Mujer, poder y desarrollo en el Peru. Tomo II.* Los Artesanos: Editorial Cientifica, n.d.

    Includes "Mujeres y ayudas al sostenimiento de periódicos," pp. 430-438.

6
NORTH AMERICA

GENERAL STUDIES

1441. Courtney, Alice E. and Thomas W. Whipple. "Women in TV Commercials." *Journal of Communication.* Spring 1974, pp. 110-118.

   Two studies in New York and one each in Toronto and Washington, D.C. verified that men and women are presented differently in TV advertising, each sex shown in traditional roles.

1442. Cristall, Ferne and Barbara Emanuel. *Images in Action: A Guide to Using Women's Film and Video.* Toronto: Between the Lines, 1986. 128 pp.

   Practical information on designing film programs and planning group showings; discusses feminist filmmaking and the women's movement, Hollywood images of women, and documentary filmmaking in North America.

1443. Epstein, Laurily Keir, ed. *Women and The News.* New York: Hastings House, 1978. 144 pp.

   Eight chapters on: "Public Response to the Daily News," "Agenda Setting: Are There Women's Perspectives?" "Women out of the Myths and into Focus," "An Overview of Access to the Media," "Access to the Media: Balancing Feminism and the First Amendment," "Women, Media Access and Social Control," "Defining News Organizationally," and "News Definitions and Their Effects on Women." Deals with U.S. and Canada; resulted from a 1977 conference on women and the news held in Washington.

1444. Robinson, Gertrude J. "Broadcast Regulation and Sex Role Stereotyping: In Canada and the United States." *Gender and Mass Media Newsletter.* November 1989, pp. 14 - 17.

   Whether women made a difference to broadcast programming in the two countries, looking at two linkages: that between diversified ownership and employment and that of production of diversified program content.

1445. Robinson, Gertrude J. "Changing Canadian and U.S. Magazine Portrayals of Women and Work: Growing Opportunities for Choice." In *Mass Communication Review Yearbook*, edited by Ellen Wartella, D. Charles

Whitney, and Sven Windahl, pp. 229-249. Beverly Hills, California: Sage, 1983.
Portrayals of women and work in Canadian and U.S. magazines; differences across time and national borders.

1446. Williams, Tannis MacBeth, Deneen Baron, Susana Phillips, Lisa Travis, and Darryl Jackson. "The Portrayal of Sex Roles on Canadian and U.S. Television." *Sex-Roles within Massmedia Newsletter.* December 1986, pp. 16-18.
In a 1985 week of Canadian television, attempted to find similarities and differences in the portrayals of women and men on Canadian and U.S. TV networks, government- and privately-owned networks, and networks with and without special guidelines for non-sexist portrayals.

CANADA

General Studies

1447. Burstyn, Varda, ed. *Women Against Censorship.* Vancouver: Douglas and McIntyre, 1985. 210 pp.
Essays by lawyers, filmmakers, artists, teachers, and journalists argue that Canadian feminists, favoring state action on censorship sided with the right wing.

1448. *Cinema Canada.* No. 51, 1978.
Section on "Women and Film" from a Canadian viewpoint.

1449. Fellman, Anita Clair. "Teaching with Tears: Soap Opera as a Tool in Teaching Women's Studies." *Signs: Journal of Women in Culture and Society.* 3:4 (1978), pp. 909-911.
The use of a soap opera written by the author, "Stress of Our Lives," to give students she teaches a look at the lives of Canadian women.

1450. "Film Violence Does Affect Men's Attitudes to Women." *New Scientist.* February 11, 1982, p. 374.
Abstracted from fuller study carried out at the University of Manitoba.

1451. *Hysteria.* Winter 1982-1983.
Thematic issue on "The Future: Science Fiction and Other Speculations," discussing media produced by, or that affected Canadian women.

1452. Jensen, Margaret Ann. *Love's Sweet Return: The Harlequin Story.* Toronto: The Women's Press, 1984. 188 pp.
Romance paperbacks and Harlequin Enterprises of Toronto *Star*, in particular. By this author: "Women and Romantic Fiction; A Case Study of Harlequin Enterprises, Romances, and Readers," dissertation, McMaster University, 1980.

1453. Nelson, Sharon H. "Sharon H. Nelson Describes Structures by Which Male Control of Culture in Canada Excludes Women." *Media Report to Women*. March-April 1984, pp. 4-6.
Reprinted from Winter 1972 *Fireweed*; deals with publishing, arts, book reviewing, women's books, and newspapers.

1454. *OptiMSt*, Yukon, Canada.
Includes Jane Woodhead, "Something Rotten in the Schools of Journalism," March 1984, and other pertinent articles.

1455. Robinson, Gertrude J. "The Future of Women in the Canadian Media." *McGill Journal of Education*. Spring 1977, pp. 123-133.

Historical Studies

1456. Ferguson, Ted. *Kit Coleman, Queen of Hearts*. Toronto: Doubleday, 1978.
Excerpts from "Woman's Kingdom" columns of Canadian woman journalist, Kathleen Blake Coleman of the *Toronto Mail*. Also about Coleman: Emily Weaver, "Kit, The Journalist," *Canadian Magazine*, August 1917; David MacDonald, "Queen of the Sob Sisters," *Maclean's*, January 1953, Kit Coleman, "The Vagaries of the Woman's Page," *Winnipeg Free Press*, June 9, 1906.

1457. Freeman, Barbara M. "A Canadian Woman Journalist Covers The Spanish-American War: 'Kit' in Cuba 1898." Paper presented at Association for Education in Journalism and Mass Communication, Washington, D.C., August 1989.
Adventures of Catherine Ferguson Willis, known as "Kit," who covered the Spanish-American War in Cuba for the *Toronto Mail*. Willis was against the war and saw through the U.S. propaganda that promoted it.

1458. Freeman, Barbara M. "'An Impertinent Fly': Canadian Journalist Kathleen Blake Watkins Covers the Spanish-American War." *Journalism History*. Winter 1988, pp. 132-140.
Wartime reporting and exploits of Canadian journalist Kathleen B. Watkins of Toronto *Mail and Empire*. Many excerpts from her writings.

1459. Freeman, Barbara M. "'Every Stroke Upward': Women Journalists in Canada 1880-1906." *Canadian Woman Studies*. Fall 1986.
Agnes Maule Machar, Kit Coleman, E. Cara Hind, and Kate Simpson Hayes discussed. Reprinted in Lawrence Steven, Douglas Parker, and Jack Lewis, eds., *From Reading to Writing: A Reader, Rhetoric and Handbook*, Toronto: Prentice Hall Canada, 1988.

1460. Freeman, Barbara M. *The Queen of Woman's Kingdom: The Journalism of Kathleen Blake Coleman ("Kit") 1889-1915*. Ottawa. Carleton University Press, 1990.
The career of the *Toronto Mail* reporter.

1461. Haig, Kenneth M. *Brave Harvest: The Life Story of E. Cara Hind.* Toronto: Thomas Allen, 1945.

1462. Lang, Marjory. "Separate Entrances: The First Generation of Canadian Women Journalists." In *Re (Dis)covering Our Foremothers: Nineteenth Century Canadian Women Writers*, edited by Lorraine McMullen. Ottawa: University of Ottawa Press, 1989.

1463. Martin, Michèle. "Feminization of Labour Power in Communication Industry: The Case of the Telephone Operators, 1876-1904." *Labour/Le Travail.* Fall 1988, pp. 1-23.

 The role of women as telephone operators, based on University of Toronto dissertation in 1987, entitled, "Communication and Social Forms: A Study of the Development of the Telephone System, 1876-1920."

Images of Women

1464. Aaron, D., *About Face: Towards a Positive Image of Women in Advertising.* Toronto: Ontario Status of Women Council, 1975. 35 pp.

 Reports on survey of 1,017 women on their portrayal in advertising -- their views on objectionable and offending product ads.

1465. Archibald, Linda, Leona Christian, Karen Deterding, and Dianne Hendrick. "Sex Biases in Newspaper Reporting: Press Treatment of Municipal Candidates." *Atlantis.* Spring 1980, pp. 177-184.

 Relates to "the communication of cues through the print media relating to the traditional sex-role stereotype and dependent status about women candidates in Canadian municipal politics."

1466. *Atlantis.*

 Has included: M. Susan Bland, "Henrietta the Homemaker and 'Rosie the Riveter': Images of Women in Advertising in *MacLean's* Magazine, 1939-1950," Spring 1982, pp. 61-86; Gertrude J. Robinson, "The Media and Social Change: Thirty Years of Magazine Coverage of Women and Work (1950-1977)," 8:2 (1983), pp. 87-111.

1467. Canadian Advertising Foundation. *Report to the Advertising Industry of Initiatives re Sex-role Stereotyping.* Toronto: Canadian Advertising Foundation, Advisory Division, 1988. 12 pp. and appendices.

 "Sex-Role Stereotyping Guidelines" that have gained interest elsewhere.

1468. Canadian Advertising Foundation. "Sex-Role Stereotyping Guidelines." *Gender and Mass Media Newsletter.* November 1989, pp. 31-32.

 Deals with authority, sexuality, decision-making, household, diversity, and language. Originally developed by a Canadian Radio-Television and Telecommunications Commission Task Force on Sex-role Stereotyping in the Broadcast Media in 1981; revised in July 1987.

194 Women and Mass Communications

1469. Canadian Radio-Television and Telecommunications Commission. *Images of Women* (Supply and Services). Ottawa: Canadian Government Publishing Centre, 1982. 189 pp.

    Includes: "The Portrayal of Women in CBC Television" (A Brief to the Canadian Radio-Television and Telecommunications Commission prepared by the National Action Committee on the Status of Women), 1978.

1470. Canadian Radio-Television and Telecommunications Commission. *Sex-Role Stereotyping in the Broadcast Media: A Report on Industry Self-Regulation*. Ottawa: Canadian Radio-Television and Telecommunications Commission, 1986. 240 pp.

    The concern expressed and progress made in Canada three years after the publication of a critical report on media images of women. Each chapter analyzes a part of the industry.

1471. "Canadian Special." *Sex-Roles within Massmedia Newsletter*. November 1987, pp. 17-22.

    A calendar of events concerning the Canadian Radio-Television and Telecommunications Commission and its role in sex-role stereotyping; 1986 policy statement on sex-role stereotyping issued by CRTC and information on the Canadian Broadcasting Corporation.

1472. "Canadian Women: Mandatory Stereotyping Guidelines and 52/48% Sex Ratio in All Broadcast Jobs at All Levels." *Media Report to Women*. July-August 1986, pp. 3, 5.

    After self-regulation experiment.

1473. "CRTC Makes Adherence to Industry Guidelines on Sex Stereotyping a Requirement for Broadcast License." *Media Report to Women*. May-June and July-August 1987, pp. 8-9.

    The origin of this Canadian broadcast policy.

1474. Gill, Donna. "REAL Women and The Press: An Ideological Alliance of Convenience." *Canadian Journal of Communication*. September 1989, pp. 1-16.

    How the Canadian press responded to the development of the antifeminist group REAL Women, a conservative organization whose appearance allowed the press to reconstruct the publicly available definitions of feminism.

1475. Griffith, Alison. "Reporting the Facts: Media Accounts of Single Parent Families." *Resources for Feminist Research*. 1 (1986), pp. 32-33.

    Canadian newspaper and magazine articles that address the "single parent family."

1476. Indra, Doreen. "The Invisible Mosaic: Women, Ethnicity and the Vancouver Press, 1905-1976." *Canadian Ethnic Studies*. 13:1 (1980).

    Between 1905 and 1976, Vancouver newspapers virtually omitted women from ethnic stereotypes.

1477. Junyk, Myra. "Using Rock Videos To Analyze MTV." *Media and Values.* Winter 1989, p. 19.

   Canadian high school teacher believes rock videos degrade women and calls upon teachers to make students aware of such sexism.

1478. Kimball, M.M. "Television and Sex-role Attitudes." In *The Impact of Television: A Natural Experiment in Three Communities*, edited by T.M. Williams, pp. 265-301. Orlando, Florida: Academic Press, 1986.

   Assessment of television's influence on children's sex-role attitudes in three Canadian towns.

1479. Manitoba Action Committee on the Status of Women. "Women and Aging." *Action.* June 1981.

   Special issue on women and aging includes role of media in perpetuating the obsession with youth.

1480. MediaWatch. *Adjusting The Image: Women in Canadian Broadcasting.* Vancouver: MediaWatch, 1988.

   Review of a 1987 conference on portrayal and employment of women in Canadian broadcasting recommended at least six additions to the Broadcasting Act of Canada to accommodate women in the media.

1481. "MediaWatch (for Over 500 Women's Groups) Meet on Canadian Government's Goal to End Sex Stereotyping." *Media Report to Women.* May-June and July-August 1987, pp. 1, 8-11.

   Discussion of the meeting of media monitoring groups in Canada on the topic, "Adjusting The Image."

1482. Palys, T. S. "Testing the Common Wisdom: The Social Content of Video Pornography." *Canadian Psychology.* January 1986, pp. 22-35.

   Of 150 sexually-oriented home videos obtained in Vancouver, "Triple-X" were more explicit, but mainstream films had more sexually aggressive content.

1483. Parkinson, Laura. "Women and the Media: The Broken Promise of Equality." Presented at "'Adjusting the Image,' A National Conference on Broadcasting Policy," Ottawa, Canada, March 20-22, 1987.

   A determination of the legal basis to challenge the "inferior treatment" of women by Canadian broadcasting.

1484. Posner, Judith. "Old and Female: The Double Whammy." In *Aging in Canada: Social Perspectives*, edited by V.W. Marshall, pp. 80-87. Toronto: Fitzhenry and Whiteside, 1980.

   The topic analyzed, partly through media depictions.

1485. Probyn, Elspeth. "TV's Local: The Exigency of Gender in Media Research." *Canadian Journal of Communication.* September 1989, p. 29-41.

Television analysis must consider the ways in which daytime television positions women in the home; TV talkshow viewing produces gendered and local interpretations.

1486. Pyke, S. W. and J. C. Stewart. "This Column Is About Women: Women and Television." *Ontario Psychologist*. 6:5 (1974), pp. 66-69.

   A week of all programs and commercials aired on three Canadian television stations; females made up 28 percent of the central characters; males shown as responsible, dominant, independent, and work-oriented and females as understanding, sexy, practical, and extrovert.

1487. *Sex-Role Stereotyping in the Broadcast Media: A Report on Industry Self-Regulation*. Ottawa: Canadian Radio-Television and Telecommunications Commission, 1986. 240 pp.

   Progress made in Canada in the three years since publication of a report critical of the images of women in the media. Included are the CRTC, CBC, Canadian Association of Broadcasters, stations and networks, and the advertising industry.

1488. Sigurdson, Karen and Lori Harrop. "The Invisible Pitchfork or the Portrayal of Farm Women in the Canadian Media." Presented at First National Farm Women's Conference, Ottawa, December 1980.

   Canadian farm women are given very little media coverage; when they are covered, traditional images are presented.

1489. Soderlund, Walter C., Stuart H. Surlin, and Walter I. Romanow. "Gender in Canadian Local Television News: Anchors and Reporters." *Journal of Broadcasting and Electronic Media*. Spring 1989, pp. 187-196.

   An examination of local TV news reporting on publicly-owned and private network stations found dramatic differences in number and use of women as anchors, suggesting that "government commitment to gender equality does make a difference." Same breakthrough was not evident in respect to reporters.

1490. "Survey of Broadcast Self-Regulation in Canada Notes Pay TV Programs Sanction Sexual Coercion of Women." *Media Report to Women*. March-April 1986, p. 8.

   Reports on Ana Wiggins' 225-page document, "Sex Role Stereotyping: A Content Analysis of Radio and Television Programs and Advertisements."

1491. Task Force on Women and Advertising. "Women and Advertising: Today's Messages -- Yesterday's Images?" Ottawa: Canadian Advertising Advisory Board, 1977.

1492. Toronto Women's Media Committee. "Study of the Image of Women in Toronto Area Television Commercials." Toronto: Toronto Women's Media Committee, 1973.

1493. Voumakis, Sophia E. and Richard V. Ericson. *News Accounts of Attacks on Women: A Comparison of Three Toronto Newspapers*. Toronto: University of Toronto Centre of Criminology, 1984. 98 pp.

> Analysis of the *Sun*, *Star*, and *Globe and Mail* of Toronto in 1982 and how attacks on women were reported according to headlines, amount of space, position on page, and sources.

1494. YMCA "Sexism in Advertising" Committee, Quebec. *Sexism in Advertising: Report of the Montreal YMCA "Sexism in Advertising" Committee*. Montreal: YMCA, December 1978. 39 pp.

> Definition of sexism, methods used, media chosen, and results obtained on sexism in Canadian advertising; translated from French version: *Rapport du comité 'publicité et sexisme' du YMCA de Montréal*, 1978.

1495. Zureik, Elia T. and Alan Frizzell. "Values in Canadian Magazine Fiction: A Test of the Social Control Thesis." *Journal of Popular Culture*. Fall 1976, pp. 359-376.

> Includes data showing that in Canadian magazines between 1930 and 1950, the proportion of employed heroines increased significantly; however, the magazine exercised a social control function between 1950 and 1970, showing a decline in the proportion of employed heroines.

Women Practitioners

1496. Canadian Broadcasting Corporation (CBC). Ottawa.

> *CBC Equal Employment Program: Report to the Commission of Inquiry on Equality in Employment*, 1983; *The Presence, Role and Image of Women in Prime Time on the English Television Network of the CBC*, 1982; *Report on the Action Taken by the CBC Further to the Report of the Task Force on Sex-Role Stereotyping in the Broadcasting Media (Images of Women)*, 1984; *Women in the CBC. Report of the CBC Task Force on the Status of Women*, 1975.

1497. Charney, Ann. "Who's Afraid of Canadian Women Filmmakers?" *Ms*. November 1984, pp. 39-40, 44.

> A few Canadian films by women directors which are described as not being slick, finished products, but agents of social change.

1498. Crean, Susan. *Newsworthy: The Lives of Media Women*. Toronto: Stoddart, 1985. 350 pp.

> History and summary of positions held by about 100 women in Canadian media (most in broadcasting). Author interviewed many of the journalists and uses a number of quotes in tracing paths of careers and obstacles in the way.

1499. Crean, Susan. "Piecing the Picture Together: Women and the Media in Canada." *Canadian Woman Studies*. 8:1 (1986), pp. 15-21.

> Researchers and management have theorized that first stage entry into the previously all-male occupations of media may be "shocking but it is not

dislocating." Women can be accommodated "relatively painlessly and their presence does not imply fundamental alternations to the job or environment."

1500. Crean, Susan M. "Women in Broadcast Management: A Case-Study of the Canadian Broadcasting Corporation's Programme of Equal Opportunity." In *Women and Media Decision-making: The Invisible Barriers*, edited by Margaret Gallagher, pp. 95-118. Paris: Unesco, 1987.

Canadian Broadcasting Corporation's equal opportunity program: women's status and the employer; sex discrimination; and sex stereotypes.

1501. de la Garde, Roger. "Profil sociodemographique des journalistes de la presse ecrite quebecoise" (Sociodemographic Profile of Journalists of the Press in Quebec). *Communication et Information*. August 1975, pp. 31-51.

In Quebec, female journalists were younger and less educated than men, and equal percentages of men and women belonged to journalistic groups.

1502. Emond, Ariane, Fabienne Julien, Raymonde Provencher, Gisele Tremblay, Françoise Guénette, and Francine Pelletier. "Les femmes journalistes: Le pouvoir? Quel pouvoir?" *Canadian Journal of Communication*. September 1989, pp. 82-96.

Women journalists of Quebec from interviews with 37 of them.

1503. Finlayson, A. "Cartoonist for Better or for Worse." *Macleans*. November 24, 1980, pp. 16+.

Woman cartoonist Lynn Johnston profiled.

1504. "For Better or For Worse by Lynn Johnston." *Canadian Cartoonist*. April 1989, pp. 2-6.

Philosophy and inspirations of Canadian cartoonist Lynn Johnston, who draws "For Better or For Worse."

1505. Johnston, Lynn. "Reuben Winner! For Better or For Worse." *Cartoonist PROfiles*. September 1986, pp. 38-43.

Successful woman cartoonist, Lynn Johnston of Canada, discusses her work.

1506. Kelly, Peggy. "When Women Try to Work With Television Technology...." *Canadian Journal of Communication*. September 1989, pp. 63-75.

The practices of a private, metropolitan television station in Ontario to support the contentions that television reflects society and that television "harbours the same systemic discrimination against women as does patriarchal culture."

1507. King, Linda. "Broadcasting Policy for Canadian Women." Presented at "Adjusting the Image," A National Conference on Canadian Broadcasting Policy, Ottawa, Canada, March 20-22, 1987.

Amendment of Broadcasting Act called for to accommodate equality for women, more employment, and women's right of access to the public.

1508. Lewis, Paula Gilbert, ed. *Traditionalism, Nationalism, and Feminism: Women Writers Of Quebec.* Westport, Connecticut: Greenwood Press, 1985. 305 pp.
Women's writing in Quebec from 1884 to 1982, in 17 critical essays. Each essay is by and about women and their roles in this French speaking culture.

1509. Nugent Andrea. "Canada's Silenced Communicators: A Report on Women in Journalism and Public Relations." *Atlantis.* Spring 1982, pp. 123-135.
Women's status as employees in Canadian communications has drawn much less attention than their media images. Research on women journalists reviewed.

1510. O'Bryan, K. and M. Raices. "Male and Female Roles in OECA Programming." Toronto: Ontario Educational Communications Authority, 1976.

1511. Robinson, Gertrude J. "Women Journalists in Canadian Dailies: A Social and Professional Minority Profile." Paper presented at the Association for Education in Journalism, Carleton University, Ottawa, August 16-19, 1975.
Published later as a McGill University Working Paper.

1512. Tauskey, Thomas, ed. *Sara Jeannette Duncan: Selected Journalism.* Ottawa: Tecumseh Press, 1978.

1513. *Vingt-cinq à la une. Biographies.* Montreal: La Presse, 1976. 192 pp.
Biographies of women journalists of Quebec.

1514. Williamson, Janice. "Firewords: Dorothy Hénaut, National Film Board, Studio D." *Resources for Feminist Research.* December 1986 - January 1987, pp. 22-24.
Review of three films made by Canadian filmmaker, Dorothy Hénaut, concerning three radical feminist Québecoise women writers.

Women's Media

1515. *Kinesis*, Vancouver.
November 1984 issue included articles about a women's Co-op Radio in Vancouver, written by Sharon Knapp and Jan DeGrass; May 1986 issue had a report on self-regulation of sex-role stereotyping at Canadian Radio-Television and Telecommunications Commission.

1516. Lamoureux, Diane. "Vidéo femmes: Les filles des vues." *Resources for Feminist Research.* December 1986 - January 1987, pp. 28-29.
Describes Vidéo Femmes, a video production and distribution collective in Quebec.

1517. McCullum, Pamela. "World Without Conflict: Magazines for Working Women." *Canadian Forum*. September 1975, pp. 42-44.

1518. "New Concept of People's Newspaper in Alberta: It Travels the Province -- Put out by Women in Each Area." *Media Report to Women*. May-June 1983, p. 22.

   Webspinner, a Canadian newspaper published by a working group of Alberta women.

1519. Shannon, Kathleen. "Real Issues in a Reel World." *Media and Values*. Winter 1989, pp. 14-15.

   Canadian feminist filmmaker and how to make films and use them to bring about change. Sidebar, entitled "Studio D: Canada Pioneers Women's Images," recounts the brief history of the Canadian women's film unit -- Studio D, and includes titles of some "powerful films" done by the unit.

1520. Silvera, Makeda. *Fireworks. The Best of Fireweed*. Toronto: Women's Press, 1986.

   Fireweed was an eight-year-old Canadian women's literary and cultural journal: the magazine's history as a forum for women writers, visual artists, and photographers; articles that appeared between 1978 and 1986 reprinted.

UNITED STATES

General Studies

1521. *American Behavioral Scientist*. January-February 1986, pp. 267-376.

   Thematic issue on "Gender and Communication" included five papers chosen from two conferences on the topic.

1522. Beasley, Maurine H. and Sheila Silver. *Women in Media: A Documentary Source Book*. Washington, D.C.: Women's Institute for Freedom of the Press, 1977.

   Short profiles of well-known women journalists, reports of publications or incidents affecting women journalists, and a bibliographical summary. Included are Mary Katherine Goddard, Ann Royall, Jane G. Swisshelm, Margaret Fuller, Sarah J. Hale, "Nelly Bly," Ida Tarbell, Rheta Childe Dorr, Ishbel Ross, Margaret Bourke-White, and Ruth Crane. Also covered: suffrage newspapers, *The Journalist*, women's magazines, journalism of women's liberation, *off our backs*, *Ms* magazine, challenging broadcast licenses, filing federal complaints, monitoring newspapers and primetime, public broadcasting, advertising, and publisher's guidelines. Second printing in 1979 lists Sheila Gibbons as secondary author.

1523. Beasley, Maurine H. and Kathryn Theus. *The New Majority: A Look at What the Preponderance of Women in Journalism Education Means to the Schools and to the Professions* Lanham, Maryland: University Press of America, 1988. 186 pp.

Book-length version of a report based on a case study of graduates of the University of Maryland College of Journalism. Topics discussed include: What happens when journalism enrollments change from predominantly male to predominantly female? What are the implications within the campus and the work place? Excerpts of a roundtable discussion by successful women in communications.

1524. Berryman, C.L. and V.A. Eman, eds. *Communications, Language and Sex*. Rowley, Massachusetts: Newbury House Publishers, 1980. 241 pp.
Proceedings of First Annual Conference on Communication, Language, and Sex, held in 1978 in Bowling Green, Ohio. The 16 articles treat sexism scaling in advertising, the construct of androgyny, lesbian humor, and the role of values in research on language, gender, and communication.

1525. Biagi, Shirley. *Media/Impact*. Belmont, California: Wadsworth, 1990. 411 pp.
Includes "Women's Role as Colonial Publishers," pp. 33-34; "The Alternative Press, " pp. 37-39; "Women's Issues [in Magazines]," pp. 67-69. "Ida Tarbell Uncovers John D. Rockefeller," pp. 74-75.

1526. Brown, J.D. "Adolescent Peer Groups Communication, Sex-role Norms and Decisions about Occupations." In *Communication Yearbook 4*, edited by D. Nimmo, pp. 659-678. New Brunswick, New Jersey: Transaction Books, 1980.
Sex-role norms and interpersonal communication patterns influenced decision-making among 588 undergraduates studied.

1527. Buhle, Paul, ed. *Popular Culture in America*. Minneapolis: University of Minnesota Press, 1987. 272 pp.
Sample of popular culture scholarship rooted in the social experience of the 1960's, including Ann D. Gordon, "Laughing Their Way: A Background to Women's Humor," pp. 46-51; Mary Bufwack and Bob Oermann, "Women in Country Music," pp. 91-101; Ann D. Gordon, "Janis Joplin Was No Rose," pp. 102-107; C.L.R. James, "Three Black Women Writers," pp. 232-239; Catherine Clinton, "Me and My Feminist Humor: All Alone and Feeling Blue," pp. 251-258.

1528. Burgard, Andrea M. *The Women's Information Center Project. Final Report*. College Park, Maryland: College of Library and Information Services, University of Maryland, n.d.
Study to determine the need for a special information center to serve women on University of Maryland campus.

1529. Busby, Linda Jean. "The Uses of Media To Improve the Status of Women on an International Scale." Paper presented at Speech Communication Association, Washington, D.C., December 1-4, 1977. 31 pp.
Advantages and disadvantages of various media for helping women evaluate and change their societal roles.

1530. Carr, E.A. "Feminism, Pornography, and the First Amendment: An Obscenity-Based Analysis of Proposed Antipornography Laws." *UCLA Law Review*. April 1987, pp. 1265-1304.

The proposed antipornography ordinances according to First Amendment considerations. A few concepts of the First Amendment-based criticism commonly cited against the ordinances are provided.

1531. Carter, Kathryn and Carole Spitzack, eds. *Doing Research on Women's Communication: Perspectives on Theory and Method*. Norwood, New Jersey: Ablex Publishing, 1989. 304 pp.

Guidelines for "coordinating applied research for women" and critical possibilities for gender and feminist communication researchers. Sections deal with problems of feminism and social science, "theoretics of feminism and communication studies," and methods of studying women's communication. Chapters on interviewing women, soap opera and women's culture, triangulation and gender research, and exposing masculine science.

1532. *Chicago Journalism Review*. July 1971.

Special issue on "Women and the Media" in this alternative periodical of journalists.

1533. Citizens Advisory Council on the Status of Women, Washington, D.C. *Women in 1975*. Transmitted to the President, March 1976. Washington, D.C.: U.S. Government Printing Office, 1976. 154 pp.

Women and the media discussed in the first part. See volume for 1974 (1975, 65 pp.)

1534. *Communication*. New York. 9:1 (1986).

Thematic issue on "Feminist Critiques of Popular Culture," edited by Ellen Wartella and Paula A. Treichler, includes: Paula A. Treichler and Ellen Wartella, "Interventions: Feminist Theory and Communication Studies"; Lana F. Rakow, "Feminist Approaches to Popular Culture: Giving Patriarchy Its Due"; Thelma McCormack, "The 'Wets' and the 'Drys': Binary Images of Women and Alcohol in Popular Culture"; Katie King, "The Situation of Lesbianism as Feminism's Magical Sign: Contests for Meaning and the U.S. Women's Movement, 1968-1972"; and Janice A. Radway, "Identifying Ideological Seams: Mass Culture, Analytical Method and Political Practice."

1535. Creedon, Pamela J., ed. *Women in Mass Communication. Challenging Gender Issues*. Newbury Park, California: Sage, 1989. 304 pp.

Eighteen chapters include: Pamela J. Creedon, "The Challenge of Re-Visioning Gender Values"; Susan Henry, "Changing Media History Through Women's History"; Carolyn Stewart Dyer, "Feminist Perspectives on Media Law: Or Media Law As If Women Mattered"; H. Leslie Steeves, "Gender and Mass Communication in a Global Context"; Jane Rhodes, "Strategies on Studying Women of Color in Mass Communication"; Paula Matabane, "Strategies for Research on Black Women and Mass Communications"; Larissa S. Grunig, "The 'Glass Ceiling' Effect on Mass Communication Students"; Linda Schamber, "Women in Mass Communication Education: Who Is Teaching Tomorrow's

Communicators?"; Sue Lafky, "Economic Equity and the Journalistic Work Force"; Maurine Beasley, "Newspapers: Is There a New Majority Defining the News?" Sammye Johnson, "Magazines: Women's Employment and Status in the Magazine Industry"; Judith A. Cramer, "Radio: A Woman's Place Is on the Air"; Conrad Smith, Eric S. Fredin, and Carroll Ann Ferguson Nardone, "Television: Sex Discrimination in the TV Newsroom -- Perception and Reality"; Linda Lazier-Smith, "A New Generation of Images to Women"; Alice Gagnard, "A Sociocultural Close-Up: Body Image in Advertising"; Carolyn Garrett, "Public Relations: The $1 Million Penalty for Being a Woman"; Marilyn Crafton Smith, "Women's Movement Media and Cultural Politics," and Lana F. Rakow, "A Bridge to the Future: Re-Visioning Gender in Communication."

1536. Donnerstein, Edward and David Linz. "Mass Media Sexual Violence and Male Viewers." *American Behavioral Scientist*. May/June 1986, pp. 601-618.
Research on aggressive pornography and non-pornographic media images of violence against women.

1537. Douglas, Ann. *The Feminization of American Culture*. New York: Alfred A. Knopf, 1977.

1538. Ellis, Dicki Lou, et al. *Women's Work and Women's Studies*. Pittsburgh, Pennsylvania: KNOW, Inc., 1972. 251 pp.
Scholarly research and lists of women's activist groups; an annual which includes categories of "media" and "sex-role socialization."

1539. Elsas, Diana, et al. "Women and Film/Television. Factfile No. 5." Washington, D.C.: American Film Institute, 1977. 12 pp.
List of basic reference sources relevant to women and television/film includes training centers, literature, and films concerning women in media.

1540. Ferrarotti, Franco. "From 'Guevarism' to 'Travoltism'? The Private as the Private Myth of the Mass Media." *Critica Sociologica*. October-December 1978-79, pp. 3-5.
The political movements of women and youth show that public and private cannot be separated.

1541. Fink, Conrad C. *Inside the Media*. New York: Longman, 1990. 398 pp.
Includes "Minorities and Women at Work in the Mainstream Media," pp. 259-262; personality profile of Carol Hope Reuppel, p. 228.

1542. Forte, Jeanie K. and Katherine Fishburn. "Women." In *Handbook of American Popular Culture*, edited by M. Thomas Inge, pp. 1425-1458. Westport, Connecticut: Greeenwood Press, 1989.
Women in popular culture must be re-articulated within categories of women as producers and consumers, and women as the very basis of conceptual foundation of popular culture. This chapter looks at the history of women in popular culture, reference works, research collections, history and criticism (with categories of general, popular fiction, magazines, film).

1543. Foss, Karen A. and Sonja K. Foss. "Incorporating the Feminist Perspective in Communication Scholarship: A Research Commentary." In *Doing Research on Women's Communication: Perspectives on Theory and Method*, edited by Kathryn Carter and Carole Spitzack, pp 65-91. Norwood, New Jersey: Albex, 1989.

   Literature on the topic reviewed and articles on women and communication listed that appeared in the *Quarterly Journal of Speech, Communication Monographs, Critical Studies in Mass Communication, Human Communication, Journal of Communication*, and *Women's Studies in Communication*.

1544. Foss, Sonja K. and Karen A. Foss, eds. *Women's Studies in Communication*. Fall 1987.

   Papers on communicating with female patients on contraception, training in argumentativeness for women, sex and occupational roles of women in children's picture books, and "Five Questions for Gender Research."

1545. Friedman, Barbara, ed. *Women's Work and Women's Studies, 1973-1974: A Bibliography*. Old Westbury, New York: The Feminist Press, 1975. 381 pp.

   Mass media is a major topic of this listing of 4,000 sources about women and feminism.

1546. Gaines, Jane M. "Women and Representation: Can We Enjoy Alternative Pleasure?" In *American Media and Mass Culture: Left Perspectives*, edited by Donald Lazere, pp. 357-372. Berkeley: University of California Press, 1987.

   Freudian and Marxist theory concerning the "relation of looking," using pornographic film as base.

1547. Gibbons, Sheila. "'Women in Media' Courses Continue To Grow Steadily." *Journalism Educator*. October 1979, pp. 17-18.

   Development of a women and mass media course at the University of Maryland.

1548. Glenn, Judith A., comp. *Holdings of the Women's Center Library at Oregon State University*. Corvallis, Oregon: Kerr Library Bibliographic Series No. 21, Oregon State University, 1987.

   Only seven citations on media/pop culture.

1549. Gordon, Thomas F. and Mary Ellen Verna. *Mass Communication Effects and Processes: A Comprehensive Bibliography, 1950-1975*. Beverly Hills, California: Sage, 1978. 227 pp.

   Fifty-four citations to work on women in advertising, magazines, and TV; images of women; newspapers and feminism; roles; and sexism.

1550. Grimshaw, Allen, et al. "What Ought Sociology To Be Doing? And Why Aren't We Doing It?" *American Sociologist*. May 1979, pp. 68-69.

Includes Phyllis Ewer's "Sociology through the Media," in which she states that sociologists have become material for discussion on what used to be the "woman's page."

1551. Henry, Susan. "Cathy Covert: 'I'm Right Here with You.'" *Journalism History*. Autumn/Winter 1983, pp. 54-56.
Journalism historian and teacher, Catherine L. Covert.

1552. Hiebert, Ray Eldon and Carol Reuss, eds. *Impact of Mass Media: Current Issues*. 2nd Ed. New York: Longman, 1988. 516 pp.
Section 12, "Mass Media and Women," includes, Terri Schultz-Brooks, "Getting There: Women in the Newsroom"; Caryl Rivers, "Mythogyny"; Sheila J. Gibbons, "Women's Magazines"; Lori Kessler, "Bringing the Moving Picture into Focus."

1553. Hole, Judith and Ellen Levine. *Rebirth of Feminism*. New York: Quadrangle Books, 1971.
Overview of women's liberation movement and the role of journalism included.

1554. Horowitz, D., M. Lerner, and C. Pyes, eds. *Counterculture and Revolution*. New York: Random House, 1972.
Includes "Rat Staff; Cock Rock: Men Always Seem To End Up on Top," pp. 96-102.

1555. Inge, M. Thomas, ed. *Handbook of American Popular Culture*. Westport, Connecticut: Greenwood Press, 1989. 1613 pp.
Includes section on women and popular culture.

1556. Jansen, Sue Curry. "Gender and the Information Society: A Socially Structured Silence." *Journal of Communication*. Summer 1989, pp. 196-215.
"The price paid for the price of a critical consciousness about gender in discussions of communications and technology is the reproduction of old patterns of power and privilege in the social distribution of knowledge."

1557. Johnson, Fern L. "Feminist Theory, Cultural Diversity, and Women's Communication." *Howard Journal of Communications*. Summer 1988, pp. 33-41.
The entwining of race, gender, and ethnicity in the study of communication.

1558. Johnstone, John W.C., Edward J. Slawski, and William W. Bowman. *The News People. A Sociological Portrait of American Journalists and Their Work*. Urbana: University of Illinois Press, 1976. 257 pp.
Women and their career aspirations and opportunities; education of women journalists; income levels, job functions, and job satisfaction of women journalists; women in various media; professional values; wage discrimination

against women, and women in alternative media. Data gathered from a nationwide survey of over 1,000 news organizations.

1559. *Journal of Communication.* Winter 1978.

Thematic symposium on "What Does 'She' Mean?" includes: Barbara Bate, "Nonsexist Language Use in Transition," pp. 139-149; Jeanne Marecek, et al., "Women as TV Experts: The Voice of Authority?" pp. 159-168; Matilda Butler and William Paisley, "Magazine Coverage of Women's Rights," pp. 183-186; and William J. O'Donnell and Karen J. O'Donnell, "Update: Sex-Role Messages in TV Commercials," pp. 156-158.

1560. *Journal of Communication.* Summer 1989.

Thematic issue on "The Information Gap" includes: Jean Brunet and Serge Proulx, "Formal versus Grass-Roots Training: Women, Work and Computers," pp. 77-84; Kathy Krendl, et al, "Children and Computers: Do Sex-Related Differences Persist?" pp. 85-93; and Sue Curry Jansen, "Gender and the Information Society: A Socially Structured Silence," pp. 196-215.

1561. *Journal of Communication Inquiry.* Winter 1987, pp. 8-117.

Thematic issue on "Feminism" includes: Nina Gregg, "Reflections on the Feminist Critique of Objectivity"; Kathryn Cirksena, "Politics and Difference: Radical Feminist Epistemological Premises for Communication Studies"; Gina Marchetti, "The Threat of Captivity: Hollywood and the Sexualization of Race Relations in *The Girls of the White Orchid* and *The Bitter Tears of General Yen*"; H. Leslie Steeves and Marilyn C. Smith, "Class and Gender in Prime-Time Television Entertainment: Observations from a Socialist Feminist Perspective"; Anne Balsamo, "Unwrapping the Postmodern: A Feminist Glance"; Lisa Lewis, "Female Address in Music Video"; Jane Banks and Patricia R. Zimmerman, "The Mary Kay Way: The Feminization of a Corporate Discourse"; Patricia A. Sullivan, "Campaign 1984: Geraldine Ferraro vs. The Catholic Church and One Master Motive"; Anne Cooper and Lucinda Davenport, "Media Coverage of the International Women's Decade: Feminism and Conflict"; and Karen E. Altman, "Conversing at the Margins: A Polemic, or Feminism and Communication Studies."

1562. Kramarae, Cheris. *Women and Men Speaking.* Rowley, Massachusetts: Newbury House, 1981.

Women must use their special skills and perspectives, especially in examining their (and others') communication.

1563. Krendl, Kathy A., Mary C. Broihier, and Cynthia Fleetwood. "Children and Computers: Do Sex-Related Differences Persist?" *Journal of Communication.* Summer 1989, pp. 85-93.

Three-year study of students revealed girls were less interested in computers and less confident in their skills.

1564. Kronhausen, Eberhard and Phyllis Kronhausen. *Pornography and the Law: The Psychology of Erotic Realism and Pornography.* New York: Ballantine, 1959. 317 pp.

The contention that pornography has no major ill effects upon readers.

1565. Leidholdt, Dorchen and Janice G. Raymond. *The Sexual Liberals and the Attack on Feminism.* Elmsford, New York: Pergamon Athene Series, 1989. 256 pp.
Radical feminists and topics such as pornography, incest, and reproduction.

1566. Lloyd, Jerome. "Ada Louise Huxtable: A Case Study." Masters thesis, University of Kansas, Lawrence, 1975.

1567. Lull, J., A. Mulac, and S.L. Rosen. "Feminism as a Predictor of Mass Media Use." *Sex Roles.* February 1983, pp. 165-177.
Survey of 523 residents of Santa Barbara, California found significant differences in how mass media were used among high and low feminists.

1568. McCormack, Thelma. "Machismo in Media Research: A Critical Review of Research on Violence and Pornography." In *Mass Communication Review Yearbook*, edited by Cleveland Wilhoit and Harold de Bock, pp. 574-585. Beverly Hills, California: Sage, 1980.
Examination of areas of pornography and violence, drawing on three studies -- The National Commission on the Causes and Prevention of Violence, Commission on Obscenity and Pornography, and the Surgeon General's Report on Television and Social Behavior.

1569. McGuigan, Dorothy G., ed. *New Research on Women and Sex Roles at the University of Michigan. Papers on Changing Sex Roles; Work, Family, and Change; Status, Power and Politics; Women and Men; In Marriage and Out; Women in Higher Education; Women in Literature; Women in Media; Directions and Needs of New Research on Women.* Ann Arbor: University of Michigan, Center for Continuing Education for Women, 1976. 403 pp.
Papers given at a 1975 conference on women and sex roles in society, held in Ann Arbor.

1570. *Mademoiselle.*
A sampling of articles on women and the media includes: Betty Anderson, "The Country Weekly," January 1947; "Getting on a Paper: 1949," August 1949; Vernon Small, "I Want To Be in Pictures," April 1950; "Jobs with the Press," September 1951, pp. 129-136; Gael Greene, "Wire Service Reporting," March 1957; Mary Ann Guitar, "The Eye, The Moment," December 1957; Mary Ann Guitar, "Is Anybody Not Listening?" March 1959; "Women in TV News Reporting," November 1960, pp. 151-152; "An Off-Camera Close-up," February 1963; "The Word Around the World: Jobs in International Radio and TV," February 1963; "Twelve Writing Jobs," March 1963; Patricia E. Davis, "Lady on the Beat," May 1968; Nancy A. Comer, "Magazine Jobs USA," September 1970; Helen Whitehead, "The Newsweeklies -- and Women," September 1970, pp. 36, 109; Catherine Calvert, "Five Women Filmmakers: How They Started, Where They're Going," November 1972, pp. 144-145, 195-197; Eleanor Perry, "Is There a Female Film Aesthetic?" November 1972, p. 145; Penelope Gilliatt, "On Women in Films and Women," November 1972, pp. 142-143; Nancy A. Comer, "Eleven Jobs in TV," November 1974.

1571. Malamuth, Neil M. and V. Billings. "Why Pornography? Models of Functions and Effects." *Journal of Communication.* Summer 1984, pp. 117-129.
   Different views and definitions of pornography: psychoanalytic, Marxist, social change, and feminist, the latter contending that pornography is a means for males to subjugate females.

1572. Malamuth, Neil M. and John Briere. "Sexual Violence and the Media: Indirect Effects on Aggression Against Women." *Journal of Social Issues.* 42:3 (1986), pp. 75-92.
   Use of a model to demonstrate how media portrayals of sexual violence might lead to violence committed against women.

1573. Marine, Gene. *A Male Guide to Women's Liberation.* New York: Holt, Rinehart, and Winston, 1972.
   Many references to media.

1574. Martin, Michèle. "'Rulers of the Wires'? Women's Contribution to the Structure of Means of Communication." *Journal of Communication Inquiry.* Summer 1988, pp. 89-103.
   Women's role as telephone operators and users; their contribution to the structure of the means of communication occurs in different forms according to their level of participation.

1575. Martyna, Wendy. "What Does 'He' Mean?: Use of the Generic Masculine." *Journal of Communication.* Winter 1978, pp. 131-138.
   The use of "he" when referring to sex-unspecified persons.

1576. Marzolf, Marion and Walter Ward, comps. "A Directory of Women and Minority Men in Academic Journalism and Mass Communication: A Two-Year Study." Paper presented at Association for Education in Journalism, San Diego, California, August 18-21, 1974. 90 pp.
   List of names, degrees, teaching experiences, and specialties of more than 400 teachers.

1577. Meade, M. "The Degradation of Women." In *The Sounds of Change,* edited by R.S. Denisoff and R.A. Peterson, pp. 173-177. Chicago: Rand McNally and Co., 1972.

1578. *Media and Values.* Fall 1989.
   Thematic issue on "Men, Myth and Media" has much to say about the role of women in television viewing patterns ("Home, Home on the Remote"), and as Asian-American TV anchors ("Why Are There No Asian Male News Anchors?").

1579. *Media and Values.* Winter 1989.
Thematic issue on "Redesigning Women" includes: Rosalind Silver, "The Many Faces of Media Women," pp. 2-4; "Prime-Time Girls Just Want To Have Fun," p. 5; Judith Posner, "Where's Mom?," pp. 6-7; Jean Kilbourne, "Beauty...and the Beast of Advertising," pp. 8-10; Junior Bridge, "No News Is Women's News," pp. 11-13; Kathleen Shannon, "Real Issues in a Reel World," pp. 14-15; Margaret Benston, "Worlds Apart: Women, Men and Technology," pp. 16-17; Reflection/Action," pp. 18-20; Linda Seger, "How To Evaluate Media Images of Women," p. 21; "Watch, Read, Listen: Resources for Follow-up," p. 23; Elizabeth Thoman, "Springboard to Action," p. 24.

1580. Morgan, Robin, ed. *Sisterhood Is Powerful.* New York: Vintage Books, 1970.
Includes Alice Embree, "Media Images I: Madison Avenue Brainwashing -- The Facts" and Florika, "Media Images II -- Body Odor and Social Order."

1581. *Ms Magazine.*
A sampling includes Margaret Sloan, "Keeping the Black Woman in Her Place," January 1974, pp. 30-31; Judith Hennessee, "Some News Is Good News," July 1974, pp. 25-29; Beth Gutcheon, "There Isn't Anything Wishy-Washy about Soaps," August 1974, pp. 42 +; Lindsy Van Gelder, "Women's Pages: You Can't Make News Out of a Silk Purse," November 1974, p. 112; Lee Israel, "Women in Film: Saving an Endangered Species," February 1975, pp. 51-57; Sara Sanborn, "Byline Mary McGrory," May 1975, pp. 59-61, 74-75; Stephanie Harrington, "Mary Hartman: The Unedited All American Unconscious," May 1976, pp. 53 +; Molly Haskell, "Meryl Streep: Hiding in the Spotlight," December 1988, pp. 68-72.

1582. Murphy, Sharon M. "'Well We Tried a Man, But He Didn't Work Out.'" *The Quill.* February 1990, pp. 26-28.
Changes in journalism education relative to women, looking at the Committee on the Status of Women in the Association for Education in Journalism and Mass Communication.

1583. Nadler, Lawrence B., Marjorie Keeshan Nadler, and William Todd-Mancillas, eds. *Advances in Gender and Communication Research.* Lanham, Maryland: University Press of American, 1987. 413 pp.
Twenty-three chapters deal with gender in organizational communication, journalism education, interpersonal and professional relationships, gender and advocacy, the communicative influence of gender on politics and culture, and gender communication pedagogy.

1584. National Commission on the Observance of International Women's Year. "Sexual Preference." Washington, D.C.: U.S. Government Printing Office, 1977. 65 pp.
Sexual preference as related to women, with attention to the role of media.

1585. North, Sandre. "Reporting the Movement." *Atlantic Monthly.* March 1970, pp. 105-106.

1586. Peirce, Kate and Emily D. Edwards. "Children's Construction of Fantasy Stories: Gender Differences in Conflict Resolution Strategies." *Sex Roles.* April 1988, pp. 393-404.

The influence of media sex-role stereotyping was in stories related by 266 students (aged 9 to 14).

1587. *Quill, The.* February 1990.

Special issue on "An Expanding Journalistic Universe: Getting a Fix on the Status of Women in the News Business" included: Kay Mills, "We've Come a Long Way, Maybe," pp. 20-22; Marlene Sanders, "Time: As Solutions Go, a Bad One," pp. 23-24; Georgie Anne Geyer, "Say 'No' to Adversarial Journalism," p. 25; Sharon Murphy, "'We Tried a Man, But He Didn't Work Out,'" pp. 26-27; Lucinda Davenport, "Will the Circle Remain Unbroken?" p. 28; Jean Gaddy Wilson, "At Sea in a Sea Change," p. 29; Nancy L. Green, "Advice From Women Who Have Made It," pp. 30-31; Peggy Simpson, "The Meek Shall Inherit the Newsroom," pp. 32-35; Junior Bridge, "The Somewhat Visible Woman," pp. 36-37; Barbara Reynolds, "Black Females: Presumed Incompetent," pp. 38-39; Bea Bourgeois, "She 'Fainted'; He 'Passed Out,'" pp. 40-41; Jane P. Marshall, "JAWS of Hope," pp. 42-43; Nan Siemer, "Get What You Deserve," pp. 44-45; Lynda McDonnell, "Family Track or Fast Track?" pp. 46-48; Judy VanSlyke Turk and Linda Anderman, "A Selected Bibliography," pp. 49-51.

1588. Rakow, Lana F. "Feminist Approaches to Popular Culture: Giving Patriarchy Its Due." *Communication.* 9:1 (1986), pp. 19-41.

Feminist approaches to popular culture constitute a serious social analysis; the approaches (images and representations, recovery and reappraisal, reception and experience, and cultural theory) "argue that popular culture plays a role in patriachal society."

1589. Rakow, Lana. "Feminist Perspectives on Popular Culture." In *Questioning The Media: A Critical Introduction*, edited by John Downing, Ali Mohammadi, and Annabelle Sreberny-Mohammadi, pp. 231-241. Newbury Park, California: Sage Publications, 1990.

Analysis of how women have developed media to communicate their reality and women as audience.

1590. Rakow, Lana F. "Rethinking Gender Research in Communication." *Journal of Communication.* Autumn 1986, pp. 11-26.

The history of the concept of sexual differences and the types of communication research it has encouraged suggests that "gender is a verb," created by and creating communication.

1591. Ray, L. "The American Woman in Mass Media: How Much Emancipation and What Does it Mean?" In *Towards a Sociology of Women*, edited by C. Safilios-Rothschild, pp. 41-62. Lexington, Massachusetts: Xerox College Publishing, 1972.

1592. Reed, Linda. "A Paradox: The Role of Women in Journalism." *Communications: Journalism Education Today.* 9 (1976), pp. 2-4.

Literature reviewed on women in the mass media in Educational Resources Information Center (ERIC).

1593. Rickel, Annette U. and Linda M. Grant. "Sex Role Stereotypes in the Mass Media and Schools: Five Consistent Themes." *International Journal of Women's Studies*. May-June 1979, pp. 164-179.
Content analyses of mass media, school curriculum, and other aspects of schools showed the messages presented "rigidly stereotyped sex role patterns which are more conservative than contemporary societal attitudes."

1594. Rubin, B., ed. *Small Voices and Great Trumpets: Minorities and the Media*. New York: Praeger, 1980. 295 pp.
Part 4 deals with women and the media, the elderly and the media, and immigrants and the media.

1595. Schiller, Patricia. "Effects of Mass Media on The Sexual Behavior of Adolescent Females." In *Technical Report of the Commission on Obscenity and Pornography: Preliminary Studies*, compiled by W.C. Wilson, pp. 191-195. Washington, D.C.: Government Printing Office, 1971.
That love and sex are closely associated for most young females was supported.

1596. Schreiber, E.M. "Education and Change in American Opinions on a Woman for President." *Public Opinion Quarterly*. Summer 1978, pp. 171-182.
Data on the willingness of Americans to vote for a woman for president with a catalogue of articles appearing in *Reader's Guide* as an indication of media content; the growing media coverage of women's issues was related to the public willingness to accept a woman for president.

1597. Schroeder Harold E. and Richard F. Rakos. "Effects of History on the Measurement of Assertion." *Behavior Therapy*. November 1978, pp. 965-966.
How exposure to information about assertiveness through media and other means influences people's self-reports about their own assertiveness; distinction made between women and men.

1598. Sellen, Betty-Carol and Patricia A. Young, eds. *Feminists, Pornography and the Law: An Annotated Bibliography of Conflict, 1970-1986*. Hamden, Connecticut: Library Professional Publications, 1987. 204 pp.
Bibliography, lists of periodicals, and a newspaper chronology.

1599. Senderowitz, Judith and Brenda Hebert. *Community Survey on the Status of Women*. Second Ed. Washington, D.C.: Population Institute, 1977. 44 pp.
How to conduct a survey on the positions women hold in occupational structures, including those of media.

1600. *Sex Roles.* April 1984.
Includes works on women and media, such as: F.L. Geis, et al., "TV Commercials as Achievement Scripts for Women," pp. 513-525; P.A. Kalisch and B.J. Kalisch, "Sex-Role Stereotyping of Nurses and Physicians on Prime-Time Television: A Dichotomy of Occupational Portrayals," pp. 533-553; J. Mills, "Self-Posed Behaviors of Females and Males in Photographs," pp. 633-637.

1601. Silbert, Mimi H. and Ayala M. Pines. "Pornography and Sexual Abuse of Women." *Sex Roles.* June 1984, pp. 857-868.
A survey of 200 prostitutes in the San Francisco Bay area revealed that many who had been sexually abused early in their lives pointed to pornography as a cause.

1602. Smith, Don. D. "The Social Content of Pornography." *Journal of Communication.* Winter 1976, pp. 16-23.
"Adults only" paperbacks between 1968-74 not surprisingly, were built around a "series of sex episodes tied together by transition pages of non-sexual activity."

1603. Smith, Mary Ann Yodelis. "Research Retrospective: Feminism and the Media." *Communication Research.* January 1983, pp. 145-160.
Review of eight books on women and the media and feminism. Despite its usefulness, most research on women and the media fails to bring in issues from communication theory. Reprinted in Ellen Wartella, D. Charles Whitney, and Sven Windahl, eds., *Mass Communication Review Yearbook*, Beverly Hills, Ca.: Sage, 1983, pp. 213-228.

1604. Spitzack, C. and K. Carter. "Women in Communication Studies: A Typology for Revision." *Quarterly Journal of Speech.* November 1987, pp. 401-423.
Five conceptualizations of women in communication research: womanless communication, great women communicators, woman as other, politics of woman as other, and women as communicators.

1605. Steeves, H. Leslie. "Feminist Theories and Media Studies." *Critical Studies in Mass Communication.* June 1987, pp. 95-135.
The assumptions underpinning radical, liberal, and socialist feminist theoretical frameworks; critique of feminist media research argues that liberal feminism, characteristic in U.S. mainstream media research, speaks only to white, heterosexual, middle and upper class women.

1606. Stevenson, Rosemary M. "Bibliography: Blacks in America Featuring the Black Experience in Latin America." *Black Scholar.* January-February 1985, pp. 49-53.
Works on Blacks in America in a number of categories, including media.

1607. Sutheim, S. "The Subversion of Betty Crocker." In *Marriage and the Family: A Critical Analysis and Proposals for Change*, edited by Carolyn Perrucci and Dena Targ, pp. 287-296. New York: McKay, 1974.

1608. Treichler, Paula A. and Ellen Wartella. "Interventions: Feminist Theory and Communication Studies." *Communication*. 9:1 (1986), pp. 1-18.

   Feminist theory and communication studies can "fruitfully" inform each other; a number of ways of doing this offered. Despite such potential intersections, feminist theory and communication studies have had little to do with each other. By the same authors: *Feminist Critiques of Popular Culture*, Urbana-Champaign: College of Communication, University of Illinois, 1986.

1609. Tysoe, Maryon. "The Porno Effect." *New Society*. March 7, 1985, p. 358.

   Discussion of the research of Edward Donnerstein who showed that students increased their insensitivity to women as victims after seeing commercially-released "slice 'n dice" films.

1610. United States Congress. Committee on Interstate and Foreign Commerce, Subcommittee on Communications and Power. *Films and Broadcasts Demeaning Ethnic, Racial, or Religious Groups*. Washington, D.C.: Government Printing Office, 1970, 1971.

   The results of 1969 and 1970 Congressional hearings on women and minority participation in television, and to a lesser degree, film.

1611. Valentine, Carol Ann and Nancy Hoar, eds. *Women and Communication Power: Theory, Research, and Practice*. Monograph developed from Speech Communication Association Seminar Series, Denver, Colorado, 1985. 132 pp.

   Ten essays on women and communicative power, conversation, women communication managers, communication strategies, NOW's media strategies, and feminist theory and public address.

1612. *Variety*, New York.

   Weekly newspaper of show business has included occasional articles on women in film, radio, or television. A sampling: "Women's Film Week To Screen Eight Pics," May 29, 1985, p. 52; Morry Roth, "Women Nix All-Male Newscasts," December 25, 1985, pp. 1, 50; Jim Robbins, "Hollywood Keeps Women in Front of Lens -- Not Behind It -- Say Cinetex Panelists," September 27 - October 3, 1989, p. 19; "More Famous Than the Emperor's Wife," March 28, 1990, p. 52. The latter profiles Japan's popular TV talk-show hostess Tetsuko Kuroyanagi.

1613. Walker, Nancy A. *A Very Serious Thing: Women's Humor and American Culture*. Minneapolis: University of Minnesota Press, 1988.

   U.S. women's humorous writing.

214 Women and Mass Communications

1614. Walters, Chris. "Does [sic] the Mass Media Influence Women's Attitudes about Nuclear War?" Paper presented at Western Social Science Association, Fort Worth, Texas, April 26, 1985. 35 pp.
   Yes.

1615. Wells, Alan. *Mass Media and Society.* Third Ed. Palo Alto, California: Mayfield, 1979.
   Includes: Charlotte G. O'Kelly and Linda Edwards Bloomquist, "Women and Blacks on TV," pp. 458-463; Muriel G. Cantor, "Women and Public Broadcasting," pp. 464-470; and Neil Vidmar and Milton Rokeach, "Archie Bunker's Bigotry," pp. 470-483.

1616. Wheeler, Helen Rippier. *Womanhood Media: Current Resources about Women.* Metuchen, New Jersey: Scarecrow Press, 1972.
   Includes a basic book collection, non-book resources, and directory of sources. Updated 1975 version by the same publisher: *Womanhood Media Supplement: Additional Current Resources About Women.*

1617. White, David Manning and John Pendleton, eds. *Popular Culture: Mirror of American Life.* Del Mar, California: Publisher's Inc., 1977. 360 pp.
   Supplemental reader for a 15-week newspaper course about popular culture in the U.S.; includes a section on the impact of television and movie images of women on the American public.

1618. *Women! A Journal of Liberation.*
   Includes articles of relevance, such as Jo Ann Gardner, "Sesame Street and Sex-Role Stereotypes," 1 (1970), p. 42; Jamie Kelem Frisof, "Textbooks and Channeling," 1 (1969), pp. 26-28, and Leah Heyn, "Children's Books," 1 (1969), pp. 22-25.

1619. Women's Equity Action League, Washington, D.C. "Decade for Women: World Plan of Action." Washington, D.C.: 1976. 18 pp.
   Condensation of the world plan of action for the Decade of Women with section on the media.

1620. *Women's Studies in Communication.*
   Numerous articles, of which these are a sampling: Sandra E. Purnell, "Women's Studies in Communication: Status Report," Summer 1978; Sheila J. Gibbons, "Covering Women: Women's Publications and the Mass Media," Summer 1979; and Mildred S. Myers, "Mary Cunningham and the Press: Who Said What and How?" Fall 1983.

1621. *Wonder Woman. A Ms. Book.* New York: Holt, Rinehart and Winston and Warner Books, 1972.
   An introduction by Gloria Steinem and Phyllis Chesler, "The Amazon Legacy."

1622. Zillman, Dolf and Jennings Bryant. "Pornography, Sexual Callousness, and the Trivialization of Rape." *Journal of Communication*. Fall 1982, pp. 10-21.

The consequences of long-term exposure to pornography on beliefs about sexuality and women; loss of compassion toward women rape victims and women generally. The discussion continued in : Ferrel Christensen, "Sexual Callousness Revisited," and Dolf Zillmann and Jennings Bryant, "Response," both in Winter 1986 *Journal of Communication*.

Advertising, Public Relations

1623. *Admap*.

Articles of relevance to women and media. M. Bird, "New Opportunities in Magazine Marketing," Mar. 1977, and "Innovation in Women's Magazines: The Fourth Dimension," Jan. 1979.

1624. *Advertising Age*. New York.

Weekly trade magazine of the U.S. advertising industry has included numerous articles on women, as evidenced in a sampling from the early 1970s: Maurine Christopher, "American Women To Spend a Bundle on Problems They Never Knew Existed," July 26, 1971, p. 27; "European Women Hit Mass Media Image of Being Robots, Sex Objects," Aug. 9, 1971, p. 26; Lorraine Baltera, "O and M and NOW Rap about Ads That Lib Group Finds Demeaning," July 10, 1972, p. 3; Midge Kovacs, "Where Is Woman's Place?" July 17, 1972, p. 48; Maurine Christopher, "Hush Hush Women's Products Grow Big in TV Ads," Nov. 20, 1972, pp. 27-28; Midge Kovacs, "Are Your Ads Reaching Those Millions of Women Who Work?" Dec. 4, 1972, p. 48; "Libs Have Had Little Effect on Ads to Women," Mar. 19, 1973, p. 44; J. Revett, "Bankamericard Sets Guides for Women," Mar. 26, 1973, p. 2; "Guard Changes Brochure for Women," June 25, 1973, p. 22; Henry R. Bernstein, "Women Come on Strong in Newest Video Shows," Sept. 24, 1973, p. 23; "NOW Says Drive Getting Heavy Media Support," Oct. 1, 1973, p. 23; "*Women's News* Set for 1974 Introduction," Oct. 1, 1973, p. 6; "*Time* Finds Working Gals Top Prospects," Oct. 15, 1973, p. 32; Tina Santi, "Today's Woman Explodes Yesterday's Ad Dream World," Mar 1, 1974, pp. 49-53; B. Donath, "*New York Woman* Hits the Streets in September," July 22, 1974, p. 76; Lorraine Baltera, "Working Woman's Come a Long Way, But Can Advertisers Find Her?" July 22, 1974, p. 2; Louis J. Haugh, "New Disposable Douches Enter Market in Wake of Summer's Eve Success," Sept. 30, 1974,, p. 1; Norma Green, "Women News Victim of Tight Economy," Oct. 28, 1974, p. 53; "*Woman Coach* To Bow," Oct. 28, 1974, p. 53; "Women's Magazines Moving Beyond Kitchen," Nov. 4, 1974, p. 30; "Savvy Marketers Will Improve Women's Ad Roles: JWT Exec, " Mar. 3, 1975, p. 53; "What's a Sexist Ad?" Mar. 17, 1975, p. 3; "Advertising Portraying or Directed to Women," Apr. 21, 1975, p. 72; "Women's Ad Guides Pegged Good Start, But No Panacea," May 12, 1975, p. 58; Fred Danzig, "Sales Exec Panel Tells Feminist Ad Obstacles," June 16, 1975, p. 27; "Working Women Market No Monolith, Admen Told," Nov. 3, 1975, pp. 22-23.

1625. *Adweek.*
May 7, 1984 issue devoted to "Women 1984," pp. 5-50. Some other articles: Katrine Ames, "Public Relations: The Velvet Ghetto," July 13, 1986, pp. W4-W5; Mark Dolliver, "The Sixth Annual Women's Survey," July 11, 1988, pp. W4-W8; Michael Winkleman, "The Seventh Annual Women's Survey," June 5, 1989, pp. W4-W12.

1626. Barthel, Diane. *"Putting on Appearances: Gender and Advertising.* Philadelphia: Temple University Press, 1988. 219 pp.
Gender identities in advertising and how ads create gendered relationships with consumers. Deals mainly with advertisements in women's beauty and glamor magazines and some men's periodicals.

1627. Bishop, Robert L., comp. *Public Relations: A Comprehensive Bibliography; Articles and Books on Rublic Relations, Communication Theory, Public Opinion, and Propaganda, 1964-1972.* New York: A.G. Leigh-James for Public Relations Society of America, 1974. 212 pp.
Lists 4,000 sources on numerous categories, including "women in public relations," p. 183.

1628. Cutlip, Scott M. *A Public Relations Bibliography.* Madison: University of Wisconsin Press, 1965.
Includes "Special Publics: Women," p. 159.

1629. Lonial, S.C. and S. Van Auken. "Wishful Identification with Fictional Characters: An Assessment of the Implications of Gender in Message Dissemination to Children." *Journal of Advertising.* 15:4 (1986), pp. 4-11.
Analysis of female and male children on the extent of differences in their wishful fictional character identification.

1630. *Public Relations Review, A Journal of Research and Comment.* Fall 1988.
Devoted to women in public relations with the following articles: Doug Newsom, "How Women Are Depicted in Annual Reports," pp. 3-5; David M. Dozier, "Breaking Public Relations' 'Glass Ceiling,'" pp. 6-14; Lynda J. Stewart, "Women in Foundation and Corporate PR," pp. 20-24; Wilma Mathews, "Women in PR: Progression or Retrogression?" pp. 24-29; Debra A. Miller, "Women in Public Relations Graduate Study," pp. 29-34; Elizabeth Lance Toth, "Making Peace with Gender Issues in Public Relations," pp. 36-45, and Larissa A. Grunig, "A Research Agenda for Women in Public Relations," pp. 48-57.

1631. Rossiter, John R. "Point of View: Brain Hemisphere Activity." *Journal of Advertising Research.* October 1980, pp. 75-76.
Commentary on a previous study that found no right-left hemispheric activity differences in response to print versus TV advertising; distinctions made between male and female.

1632. Wadsworth, A.J., et al. "'Masculine' vs. 'Feminine' Strategies in Political Advertisements: Implications for Female Candidates." *Journal of Applied Communication Research.* Spring/Fall 1987, pp. 77-94.

Aggressive strategy worked better for female candidates than did the family strategy.

1633. Whipple, Thomas W. and Alice E. Courtney. "How Men and Women Judge Humor: Advertising Guidelines for Action and Research." In *Current Issues and Research in Advertising 1981*, edited by J.H. Leigh and C.R. Martin, jr., pp. 43-56. Ann Arbor: University of Michigan, Graduate School of Business Administration, 1981.

The research and guidelines for the use of humor in advertising, working on the premise that men and women differ widely in their appreciation of humor.

Broadcasting

1634. Allen, Robert C. *Speaking of Soap Operas*. Chapel Hill and London: University of North Carolina Press, 1985. 245 pp.

1635. Allen, Robert C. "The Guiding Light: Soap Opera as Economic Product and Cultural Document." In *American History/American Television*, edited by John E. O'Connor, pp. 306-327. New York: Frederick Ungar, 1983.

1636. Avery, Robert K. et al. *Research Index for NAEB Journals: NAEB Journal, Educational Broadcasting Review, Public Telecommunications Review, 1957-1979*. Annandale, Virginia: Speech Communication Association, 1980. 171 pp.

Among 11 major topics, minorities/women/special interest groups.

1637. Baran, Stanley J. "Sex on TV and Adolescent Sexual Self-Image." *Journal of Broadcasting*. Winter 1976, pp. 61-68.

In test of public high school students to measure perceptions of television portrayals of sexual behavior, a correlation was found between the perception of television sex and coital satisfaction.

1638. Barrett, Marvin. "Broadcast Journalism Since Watergate." *Columbia Journalism Review*. March-April 1976, pp. 73-83.

1639. Bean, Susan. "Soap Operas: Sagas of American Kinship." In *The American Dimension: Cultural Myths and Social Realities*, edited by W. Arens and Susan Montague, pp. 80-98. Port Washington, New York: Alfred Publishing Co., 1976.

1640. Buck, E.B. and B.J. Newton. "Research on the Study of Television and Gender." In *Progress in Communication Sciences*, edited by Brenda Dervin and Melvin J. Voight, pp. 1-42. Norwood, New Jersey: Ablex, 1989.

Major theories on gender and television, broken into two parts -- dominant paradigm and focus on culture. Researchers working within the confines of different theories discussed gender and television accordingly.

1641. Buerkel-Rothfuss, Nancy L., with Sandra Mayes. "Soap Opera Viewing: The Cultivation Effect." *Journal of Communication.* Summer 1989, pp. 108-115.

About the relationship between exposure to U.S. television soap operas and perceptions about people and events in the real world; claims that, "As expected, exposure to soap operas was found to relate to perceptions of increased numbers of certain professionals and problems in the real world."

1642. Busby, Linda Jean. "Broadcast Education: Courses on Women, Minorities and the Mass Media." Paper presented at National Association of Educational Broadcasters, Washington, D.C., November 13-17, 1977. 22 pp.

Topics concerned with women and the media that are taught in broadcast education courses.

1643. Byars, Jackie. "Reading Feminine Discourse: Prime-Time Television in the U.S." *Communication.* 9:3/4 (1987), pp. 289-303.

Alternate theories of psychoanalysis espoused by Carol Gilligan and Nancy Chodorow, and ignored or dismissed by film theorists; aid in "identifying the gaps and exceptions where feminine discourses...challenge those patriarchal discourses now dominant." Discusses Chodorow's *The Reproduction of Mothering: Psychoanalysis and the Sociology of Gender* and Gilligan's *In a Different Voice: Psychological Theory and Women's Development.*

1644. Cantor, Muriel G. "Children's Television: Sex-Role Portrayals and Employment Discrimination." In *The Federal Role in Funding Children's Television Programming*, edited by Keith W. Mielke, Rolland C. Johnson, and Barry G. Cole. Bloomington, Indiana: Indiana University, Institute of Communication Research, 1975.

Males were much more visible (66 percent of characters and 75 percent of voice-overs) than females in a week's sample of children's programming in 1975. Public television does same sex-role stereotyping as commerical television.

1645. Cantor, Muriel G. and Suzanne Pingree. *The Soap Opera.* Beverly Hills, California: Sage Publications, 1983. 166 pp.

Background on U.S. soap operas -- radio, TV, content, audience, and predictions and analysis of one serial, "The Guiding Light," from 1948-1982.

1646. Cassata, Mary B., Thomas D. Skill, and Samuel Osei Boadu. "In Sickness and in Health." *Journal of Communication.* Autumn 1979, pp. 73-80.

A 1977 content analysis of 13 daytime TV soaps finds that "homicide is the number one killer, psychiatric disorders are the bane of females, and cardiovascular disease is the most common illness among the soap opera population."

1647. Edmondson, Madeleine and David Rounds. *From Mary Noble to Mary Hartman: The Complete Soap Opera Book.* New York: Stein and Day, 1976.

By these same authors: *The Soaps: Daytime Serials of Radio and TV,* New York: Stein and Day, 1972.

1648. *Feedback.* Spring 1984.
Issue devoted to women and broadcasting, including, John Abel, "Female Ownership of Broadcast Stations," pp. 1-18, and Catharine Heinz, "The Voice of Authority; or, Hurrah for Christine Craft," pp. 3-6.

1649. Fine, Marlene G. "Soap Opera Conversations: The Talk That Binds." *Journal of Communication.* Summer 1981, pp. 97-107.
Soap opera conversations and their relationships to conversations in daily life. "Although same-sex relationships on the soaps are similar to those in everyday life, the preponderance of male-female relationships and the intimacy of the conversations seem unlike the daily patterns of social interaction."

1650. Fischer, Raymond L. "Television Drops the Other Shoe -- Sex Replaces Violence." *USA Today.* July 1978, pp. 48-50.
In 1977-78, networks switched from crime/police shows to more sexually explicit ones. Congressional activities cited.

1651. Fiske, John. "*Cagney and Lacey*: Reading Character Structurally and Politically." *Communication.* 9:3/4 (1987), pp. 399-426.
"Reading" television is as ideological as producing it and "the reading strategy promoted by our dominant ideology is one realism which foregrounds the uniqueness of the self and body as the key to understanding both character and its representation." Character should be read structurally and discursively as in "Cagney and Lacey."

1652. Fiske, John. *Television Culture.* New York: Methuen, 1988.
Chapter 10, "Gendered Television: Femininity," looks at television as a popular culture agent."

1653. Franzblau, Susan, Joyce N. Sprafkin, and Eli A. Rubinstein. "Sex on TV: A Content Analysis." *Journal of Communication.* Spring 1977, pp. 164-170.
Part of six-article symposium on "Sex, Violence, and the Rules of the Game." Major finding was that "physical intimacy appeared most often in less sensuous forms than one would expect from the public criticism of the portrayal of sexuality on current television programming.

1654. Greenberg, Bradley S., Robert Abelman, and Kimberly Neuendorf. "Sex on the Soap Operas: Afternoon Delight." *Journal of Communication.* Summer 1981, pp. 83-89.
In 65 hours of U.S. television soap operas during the 1976, 1979, and 1980 seasons, hourly rates of occurrence of intimate sexual acts, and references to such acts, did not increase greatly.

1655. Greenfield, Thomas Allen. *Radio: A Reference Guide.* Westport, Connecticut: Greenwood Press, 1989. 172 pp.

Women in radio dealt with in the final chapter.

1656. Harp, D.A., S.H. Harp, and S.M. Stretch. "Apparel Impact on Viewer Responses to Television News Anchorwomen." *Southwestern Mass Communication Journal.* June 1985, pp. 49-60.

    Clothing style of news anchorwomen had no impact on news story retention.

1657. Intintoli, Michael J. *Taking Soaps Seriously: The World of Guiding Light.* New York: Praeger, 1984. 247 pp.

    Soap opera, "The Guiding Light."

1658. Isber, Caroline and Muriel Cantor. *Report of the Task Force on Women in Public Broadcasting.* Washington, D.C.: Corporation for Public Broadcasting, 1975. 141 pp.

    Discussions of women in programming, employment practices, recommendations. In a one-week sample of Public Broadcasting Service programs in 1974-75, women were generally excluded. Nine of ten programs had only male announcers; overall, 85 percent of all participants in PBS shows were male. Women were also underrepresented in children's series.

1659. Jeffrey, Liss. "Women and Television: Listen, We're Waiting To See The Results." *Scan.* March 1989, pp. 7-10.

1660. *Journal of Communication.* Autumn 1979.

    Thematic symposium on "Daytime Serial Drama" includes: Muriel G. Cantor, "Our Days and Our Nights on TV," pp. 66-72; Mary Cassata, Thomas D. Skill, and Samuel Osei Boadu, "In Sickness and in Health," pp. 73-80; Brian Rose, "Thickening the Plot," pp. 81-84; Philip Wander, "The Angst of the Upper Class," pp. 85-88.

1661. *Journal of Communication.* Summer 1981.

    Thematic issue on "Daytime Serial Drama: The Continuing Story" includes: Bradley S. Greenberg, et al, "Sex on the Soap Operas: Afternoon Delight," pp. 83-89; Dennis T Lowry, et al, "Sex on the Soap Operas: Patterns of Intimacy," pp. 90-96; Marlene G. Fine, "Soap Opera Conversations: The Talk That Binds," pp. 97-107, and Nancy L. Buerkel-Rothfuss, "Soap Opera Viewing: The Cultivation Effect," pp. 108-116.

1662. Katzman, Natan. "Television Soap Operas: What's Been Going on Anyway?" *Public Opinion Quarterly.* Summer 1972, pp. 200-212.

    The TV soap opera audience in the U.S. is "extremely large, predominantly female." Most of what appears on the screen is conversation.

1663. Kilguss, Anne F. "Using Soap Operas as a Therapeutic Tool." *Social Casework.* November 1974, pp. 525-530.

1664. La Guardia, Robert. *From Ma Perkins to Mary Hartman: An Illustrated History of Soap Operas.* New York: Ballantine Books, 1977.
Ranges from 1930 to 1970's, but mainly on TV soaps.

1665. Lewis, Cherie S. *Television License Renewal Challenges by Women's Groups: A Study of Citizen Activism and the Broadcast Industry.* Ann Arbor, Michigan: University Microfilms International, 1986. 232 pp.
Interviews with 58 government officials, legal scholars, political activists, communications attorneys, television station managers, and communications scholars produced discussions of the women's movement, media reform movement, major legal decisions, and impact of media reform activism on the television industry. Nine chapters included case studies and agreements signed by broadcasters.

1666. Lewis, Lisa A. "Female Address in Music Video." *Journal of Communication Inquiry.* Winter 1987, pp. 73-84.
Female address videos use the interrelated modes of address of access signs and discovery signs.

1667. Lieberman, Leslie and Leonard Lieberman. "The Family in the Tube: Potential Uses of Television." *The Family Coordinator.* July 1977, pp. 235-242.
Proposal to use television in classes on the family.

1668. Littell, Joseph F., ed. *Coping with Television.* Evanston, Illinois: McDougal, Littell and Co., 1973. 213 pp.
The image of women on TV, "The Content of Television."

1669. Lowry, Dennis T., Gail Love, and Malcolm Kirby. "Sex on the Soap Operas: Patterns of Intimacy." *Journal of Communication.* Summer 1981, pp. 90-96.
An attempt to determine the extent and nature of sexual behavior in daytime television soap operas. In all soap operas on all three networks for one week in 1979, erotic touching was the most frequent sexual activity; "intimate relations of all kinds were most likely to occur between unmarried partners."

1670. Matelski, Marilyn. *The Soap Opera Evolution: America's Enduring Romance with Daytime Drama.* Jefferson, North Carolina: McFarland and Co., 1987. 212 pp.
Plot development, audience, characters, and trends in 13 TV daytime dramas.

1671. *Media and Values.* Spring 1989.
Thematic issue on "The Birds, The Bees, and Broadcasting: What The Media Teaches Our Kids About Sex" includes "*Sassy* and *Seventeen*: Do Teen Magazines Reflect or Influence Sexual Attitudes?" and "Who's in the Dollhouse? Today's Toys Provide Children With Some Surprising Role Models."

1672. Messaris, Paul and Dennis Kerr. "Mothers' Comments About TV Relation to Family Communication Patterns." *Communication Research.* April 1983, pp. 175-194.
    The relationship between family communication style and the mothers' comments to children about TV content examined in sample of 336 mothers of elementary school children.

1673. Modleski, Tania. "The Search for Tomorrow in Today's Soap Operas." In *American Media and Mass Culture: Left Perspectives*, edited by Donald Lazere, pp. 266-278. Berkeley: University of California Press, 1987.
    Soap operas are stereotypical, provide through the villainness an outlet for feminine anger, and are antiprogressive. Recommendations for feminists in understanding soap operas. Reprinted from *Film Quarterly*, Fall 1979, pp. 12-21.

1674. National Institute of Mental Health. *Television and Behavior: Ten Years of Scientific Progress and Implications for the Eighties*, Vol. 2: Technical Reviews. Rockville, Maryland: National Institute of Mental Health, 1982.
    Includes Robert P. Hawkins and Suzanne Pingree, "Television's Influence on Social Reality," pp. 224-247.

1675. Press, Andrea. "Class and Gender in the Hegemonic Process: Class Differences in Women's Perceptions of Television Realism and Identification with Television Characters." *Media, Culture and Society.* 11:1 (1989), pp. 229-253.

1676. Roberts, Elizabeth J. "Television and Sexual Learning in Childhood." In *Television and Behavior: Ten Years of Scientific Progress and Implications for the Eighties*, edited by David Pearl, Lorraine Bouthilet, and Joyce Lazar, pp. 209-223. Washington, D.C.: Government Printing Office, 1982.
    An overview of U.S. television's "sexual curricula."

1677. Rose, Brian. "Thickening the Plot." *Journal of Communication.* Autumn 1979, pp. 81-89.
    Characterization of soap operas as not concealing much, never ending, and promoting interest through juxtaposition. Also see: Robert La Guardia, *The Wonderful World of TV Soap Operas*, New York: Ballantine Books, 1977; Frances Farmer Wilder, *Radio's Daytime Serial*, New York: CBS, 1945, and Ralph Stedman, *The Serials*, Norman, Oklahoma, 1977.

1678. Seiter, Ellen. "Promise and Contradiction: The Daytime Television Serials." *Film Reader.* Winter 1982, pp. 150-153.

1679. Spigel, Lynn and Denise Mann, eds. "Television and the Female Consumer." *Camera Obscura.* March 1988.
    Provides a number of historical and theoretical perspectives on television -- its intrusion into "private domestic havens," "mediation of ethnic tradition and homogenous consumer culture, reconstruction of the Hollywood actress and

narrative conventions, and respresentation of sexuality and family life." Special issue also includes a special guide to family comedy, drama, and soap opera from 1947-1970. Includes: George Lipsitz, "The Meaning of Memory: Family, Class and Ethnicity in Early Network Television Programs"; Lynn Spiegel, "Installing the Television Set: Popular Discourses on Television and Domestic Space, 1948-1955"; Denise Mann, "The Television Star Vs. the Hollywood Star: Comedy - Variety and Its Mode of Reception, 1946-1956"; Lynne Joyrich, "All That Television Allows: TV Melodrama, Post Modernism, and Consumer Culture"; Robert Deming, "*Kate and Allie*: 'New' Women and the Audience's Television Archives"; Sandy Flitterman-Lewis, "All's Well That Doesn't End Well: Soap Operas and the Marriage Motif"; and Dan Einstein, Nina Liebman, William Lafferty, and Sarah Berry, "Source Guide to TV Melodrama: The Family Drama and Situation Comedy -- 1950 to 1970."

1680. United States Commission on Civil Rights. *Window Dressing on the Set: Women and Minorities in Television*. Washington, D.C.: U.S. Government Printing Office, August 1977.

The underrepresentation of women as decision makers in media and as producers of media content and their stereotypical portrayal. In 1977, females made up 26 percent of network drama characters; were usually younger than males; less likely to be in serious roles, to be villains; more likely to be married without an occupation. In an analysis of TV network news, women made up 12 percent of the correspondents, reported only one of the first three stories each night, and covered health, education, and welfare. Only three of 230 reported stories related to women, and of 141 newsmakers on TV, only 13 percent were women.

1681. United States Commission on Civil Rights. *Window Dressing on the Set: An Update*. Washington, D.C.: Government Printing Office, January 1979.

Update of the 1977 study; females made up 28 percent of sample. Only major gains were made by non-white females; most other aspects stayed the same. In the news sample, less than two percent of the stories related to women and minorities, no minority female correspondents existed on the news shows, and women made up 10 percent of the correspondents. Only seven percent of the newsmakers were women.

1682. Wander, Philip. "The Angst of the Upper Class." *Journal of Communication*. Autumn 1979, pp. 85-89.

In the world of soap operas, personal happiness is the basis for human relationships, and it is anchored in family life and marriage.

1683. White, Paul. *News on the Air*. New York: Harcourt, Brace, 1947.
Section on "The Women, Bless 'Em," pp. 244-246.

1684. Women's Advisory Council. "WNBC News Monitory: Findings." New York: Women's Advisory Council, 1976.

1685. Women's Advisory Council to KDKA-TV. *Women on TV: Reflections in a Funhouse Mirror*. Pittsburgh, Pennsylvania: Women's Advisory Council to KDKA-TV, 1975.

Film

1686. Association of American Colleges. *Women and Film: A Resource Handbook*. Washington, D.C.: Association of American Colleges, Project on the Status and Education of Women, 1972. 27 pp.

    Media resources available to women, feature films relevant to women, and films shown at the international festival of women's films.

1687. Bathrick, Serafina Kent. "The True Woman and the Family Film: The Industrial Production of Memory." Ph.D. dissertation, University of Wisconsin, Madison, 1981.

1688. Bisplinghoff, Gretchen Deanna. "Codes of Feminine Madness in Film." Ph.D. dissertation, Northwestern University, 1984. 145 pp.

1689. Denault, Jocelyne. "Conference of the Society for Cinema Studies." *Canadian Journal of Communication*. September 1989, pp. 76-81.

    Women's roles in a society for cinema studies conference: 71 women gave presentations, 137 men. Although the U.S. has no specific center for feminist film studies, women continue to publish and present their findings in a number of places.

1690. Donnerstein, Edward. "Aggressive Erotica and Violence Against Women." *Journal of Personality and Social Psychology*. August 1980, pp. 269-277.

    Effects of aggressive-erotic stimuli on male aggression toward females.

1691. Donnerstein, Edward and Leonard Berkowitz. "Victim Reactions in Aggressive Erotic Films as a Factor in Violence Against Women." *Journal of Personality and Social Psychology*. 41:4 (1981), pp. 710-724.

    From two experiments, concluded, "angered male subjects were more aggressive toward female after viewing either aggressive erotic film but that only the positive-outcome aggressive film increased aggression in non-angered subjects."

1692. Epple, Ron. "Films By/About Women." *Media and Methods*. 11:6 (1975), pp. 36-37.

    Includes films and instructional materials.

1693. *Film Reader 5*. 1980.

    Includes a section of papers delivered at a feminist film criticism conference held at Northwestern University in 1980. Edited collectively by the Feminist Film Seminar of that university's Radio-Television-Film Department.

1694. Freyer, E. "Film: Three Films on Women." *Craft Horizons*. April 1974, p. 13.

1695. Gish, Lillian. *Dorothy and Lillian Gish*. New York: Scribner's, 1973. 320 pp.

    The sisters' film careers from 1912 to 1969, mainly in photos.

1696. Huyssen, Andreas. *After the Great Divide: Modernism, Mass Culture, Postmodernism*. Bloomington, Indiana: Indiana University Press, 1986.
A collection of essays detailing the recurring separation of high art and mass culture. Feminism and film theory play important roles in the analysis.

1697. Kaplan, E. Ann. "Feminist Film Criticism: Current Issues and Problems." *Studies in the Literary Imagination*. Spring 1986, pp. 7-20.

1698. Kernan, Margot. "Radical Voices: A Film Course Study Guide." New York: Grove Press Film Division, 1973. 28 pp.
Discussion of the films, "I Am Curious (Yellow)" and "Something Different," as examples of works showing women's efforts to free themselves from traditional social patterning.

1699. Kowalski, Rosemary Ribich. *Women and Film: A Bibliography*. Metuchen, New Jersey: Scarecrow Press, 1976. 289 pp.
As many as 2,300 annotated citations subdivided into: women as performers, women as filmmakers, screen images of women, and women columnists and critics.

1700. La Place, Maria. "Bette Davis and the Ideal of Consumption: A Look at Now Voyager." *Wide Angle*. 6:4 (1985), pp. 34-43.

1701. Linz, D., E. Donnerstein, and S. Penrod. "Effects of Long-Term Exposure to Violent and Sexually Degrading Depictions of Women." *Journal of Personality and Social Psychology*. November 1988, pp. 758-768.
An investigation of the effects of emotional desensitization to films of violence against women and the effects of violent and sexually degrading films on beliefs about rape.

1702. Linz, D., E. Donnerstein, and S. Penrod. "The Effects of Multiple Exposures to Filmed Violence Against Women." *Journal of Communication*. Summer 1984, pp. 130-147.
Fifty-two men exposed to large doses of filmed violence against women to see if desensitization set in. Prolonged exposure lowered emotional reactions, and the men seemed to be more likely to enjoy the films on the final day of viewing.

1703. Malamuth, Neil M. and James V.P. Check. "The Effects of Mass Media Exposure on Acceptance of Violence Against Women: A Field Experiment." *Journal of Research in Personality*. December 1981, pp. 436-446.
A test of 271 students on the effects of exposure to films that portray "sexual violence as having positive consequences"; such exposure increased male subjects' acceptance of "interpersonal violence against women."

1704. Mizejewski, Linda. "Women, Monsters and the Masochistic Aesthetic in Fosse's Cabaret." *The Journal of Film and Video*. Fall 1987, pp. 5-17.

1705. *Quarterly Review of Film and Video.* 11 (1989).
Thematic issue on "Female Representation and Consumer Culture," edited by Jane Gaines and Michael Renov, includes their introduction; Michael Renov, "Advertising/Photojournalism/Cinema: The Shifting Rhetoric of Forties Female Representation," pp. 1-21; Mary Ann Doane, "The Economy of Desire: The Commodity Form in/of the Cinema," pp. 23-33; Jane Gaines, "The Queen Christina Tie-ups: Convergence of Show Window and Screen," pp. 35-60; Mary Beth Haralovich, "Sitcoms and Suburbs: Positioning the 1950s Homemaker," pp. 63-83; Lynn Spigel and Denise Mann, "Women and Consumer Culture: A Selective Bibliography," pp. 85-105; Lynn Spigel, "The Riddle of the Reader in Mass-Produced 'Women's Fiction,'" pp. 107-112; Jeanne Allen, "Harlequins, Gothics, and Soap Operas: Addressing Needs and Masking Fears," pp. 113-115; Denise Mann, "Rosie the Riveter -- Construction or Reflection?" pp. 117-120.

1706. Reed, Rex. "Movies, Give Them Back to Women." *Vogue.* March 1975, pp. 130-131.

1707. Studlar, Gaylyn. "Visual Pleasure and the Masochistic Aesthetic." *Journal of Film and Video.* Spring 1985, pp. 5-26.
"Blind spots" in literature on the nature of "a specifically male spectatorial pleasure within cinema, the patriarchal limitations on female representation in film, and the problematic position of the female spectator." Gilles Deleuze in *Masochism: An Interpretion of Coldness and Cruelty* used as model.

1708. *The Velvet Light Trap.* Fall 1972.
Special issue on "Sexual Politics and Film."

1709. Turim, Maureen. "Designing Women: The Emergence of the New Sweetheart Line." *Wide Angle.* 6:2 (1984), pp. 4-11.

1710. Turim, Maureen. "Gentleman Consumes Blondes." *Wide Angle.* 1:1 (1976), pp. 68-77.
Reprinted in Bill Nichols, ed., *Movies and Methods II*, pp. 369-378. Berkeley: University of California Press, 1985.

1711. Tyler, Parker. *Sex, Psyche, Etcetera in The Film.* Baltimore, Maryland: Penguin Books, 1971.

Print Media

1712. Abramson, Paul R. and Mindy R. Mechanic. "Sex and the Media: Three Decades of Best-Selling Books and Major Motion Pictures." *Archives of Sexual Behavior.* June 1983, pp. 185-206.
Study of sexuality in best-selling novels and films, 1959, 1969, and 1979; sexual performance standards were exceedingly high.

1713. *Aegis, Magazine on Ending Violence Against Women.*
Some articles on media: Ginny NiCarty et al., "Going Public About Battering," February 1984; Judy Helfand, "Media Backlash," No. 40, 1986.

1714. Baird, Jo, Shirley Frank, and Beth Stafford. *Index to the First Ten Years 1972-1982*. Old Westbury, New York: The Feminist Press, 1984. 50 pp.

Index for *Women's Studies Newsletter, Women's Studies Quarterly*, and *Women's Studies International*. Includes Florence Howe's introduction, "The First Ten Years Are the Easiest," pp. 1-4, and a chronology and subject, author, title indices.

1715. Butler, Matilda and William Paisley. "Equal Rights Coverage in Magazines, Summer 1976." *Journalism Quarterly*. Spring 1978, pp 157-160.

In their magazine sample, the ERA was most frequently covered in *Ms., New Dawn, Playgirl*, and *Redbook*.

1716. Butler, Matilda and William Paisley. "Magazine Coverage of Women's Rights: What Does 'She' Mean." *Journal of Communication*. Winter 1978, pp. 183-186.

Use of *Reader's Guide to Periodical Literature* to determine frequency of articles dealing with women's rights in U.S. The 1920s and 1970s were high points in an otherwise fluctuating pattern of media attention.

1717. Campbell, Richard and Jimmie L. Reeves. "Covering the Homeless: The Joyce Brown Story." *Critical Studies in Mass Communication*. March 1989, pp. 21-42.

Interpretation of four news stories about a homeless New York woman institutionalized against her will.

1718. Carden, Maren Lockwood. *The New Feminist Movement*. New York: Russell Sage Foundation, 1974.

Overview of women's liberation movement and journalism's role within it. Updated in author's: *Feminism in the Mid-1970s: The Non-Establishment, the Establishment, and the Future*, New York: The Ford Foundation Office of Reports, 1977.

1719. Cardinale, Susan. *Special Issues of Serials About Women, 1965-1975*. Monticello, Illinois: Council of Planning Librarians, 1976.

1720. Christian, Harry. "The Sociology of Journalism and the Press: Introduction." *Sociological Review Monograph*. October 1980, pp. 5-17.

Includes "Women and the Press" among five categories.

1721. Cooper, Pamela, Lea P. Stewart, and Sheryl Friendly. "The Status of Women's Research in Communication Journals." Paper presented at International Communication Association, Honolulu, Hawaii, May 1985. 22 pp.

Women's research in communication journals from 1970-1984: females were underrepresented in terms of authorship; the area of women and communication needs more work.

228   Women and Mass Communications

1722.   *Editor and Publisher*, New York.

Weekly trade periodical of the journalism profession has included many articles on women practitioners, women's media, and coverage of women. Only a small sampling between 1970 and 1990 is given: Charles Smith, "New Lady IPI Chairman Runs Newspaper Group," Dec. 5, 1970; Lenora Williamson, "Maggie Kilgore Was There (in Vietnam)," Dec. 4, 1971, p. 24; Glenn A. Himebaugh, "Women's Lib Makes Headway on Many College Newspapers," June 17, 1972, p. 18; S. Kelly, "Editors Don't Drop Women from Paper's Women's Pages," July 15, 1972, p. 30; Frederick A. Raborg, "Bolder and Brighter Pages for Women Beckon to Men," Sept. 2, 1972, p. 15; June Almquest, "Another Newspaper Revamps Women's Section," Sept. 30, 1972, p. 42; "Women's Pages Undergo Change in Ames, Iowa," Mar. 24, 1973, p. 22; Lenora Williamson, "Women's Editors Express Concern with Content, Direction of Pages," Apr. 7, 1973, pp. 14-15; Gena Corea, "Writer Says Papers Biased in Covering News of Women," Apr. 21, 1973, p. 62; Gena Corea, "How Papers Can Conduct Serious Coverage of Women," Apr. 28, 1973, p. 28; Margaret Fisk, "Steinem Knocks Newspaper Coverage of Women's Issues," May 5, 1973, p. 11; June Almquest, "Women's Sections," May 12, 1973, p. 28; "Quebecor Introduces Women's Newspaper in U.S.," Oct. 13, 1973, p. 36; "Editors Tested for Women's Section Quality," Dec. 1, 1973, p. 30; Lenora Williamson, "Women's Page 'Relevancy' Stories Should Go to Subject Page," Apr. 6, 1974, pp. 10-11; Jane Levere, "Portrayal of Women in Ads Defended by Top Ad Women," June 8, 1974, p. 11; Jim Scott, "Women's Page Changes Noted by Three Editors," July 6, 1974, p. 21; Robert U. Brown, "Colonial Women Journalists," May 10, 1975, p. 72; "National Conference on Women and the Media," May 17, 1975, p. 10; Pamela Carlson, "Are Women's Pages Getting Better?" May 31, 1975, p. 11; Michael Davies, "Women's Pages," Nov. 1, 1975, p. 36; M.K. Guzda, "A Need To Reevaluate," June 30, 1984, p. 15; Linda Cunningham, "We've Come a Long Way, Baby," Nov. 24, 1984, p. 52; M.K. Guzda, "Exposing the Victim," Nov. 24, 1984, pp. 14-15; M.L. Stein, "Sexism in the Newsroom," July 4, 1987, p. 4; M.L. Stein, "Promotion Priorities Questioned," Aug. 15, 1987, pp. 14-15; Carole Rich, "A Close-Up Look at Women Journalists," Sept. 5, 1987, p. 56; Fred Burkhart, "When Readers Prefer Women," July 22, 1989, pp. 54+; Mark Fitzgerald, "'Gender Neutral' Pay Plans," July 22, 1989, pp. 22-24.

1723.   Ellis, Kate. "Gimme Shelter: Feminism, Fantasy, and Women's Popular Fiction." In *American Media and Mass Culture: Left Perspectives*, edited by Donald Lazere, pp. 216-230. Berkeley: University of California Press, 1987.

The "strains between evocations of precapitalist familial and sexual roles and accommodations to feminist advances" are traced by analyzing contemporary popular women's fiction.

1724.   Foss, Karen A. and Sonja K. Foss. "The Status of Research on Women and Communication." *Communication Quarterly*. Summer 1983, pp. 195-204.

Summary of the research on women, gender, and sex differences published in speech communication journals, categorized into historical treatments of women, sex differences, images of women in media, education and pedagogy, and surveys and integrative works. By the same authors: "Research in Communication and

Gender: Making the Link to Feminist Theory," *Women's Studies in Communication*, 7 (1984), pp. 83-85.

1725. "'Hell Hath' Just Ain't Good Enough." *American Society of Newspaper Editors Bulletin*. October 1971, pp. 3-7.

1726. Horn, Maurice. *Women in the Comics*. New York: Chelsea House, 1977. 229 pp.

　　　The portrayal of women in comics from 1897 to 1977. Final chapter provides author's view of the development of women in comics, entitled, "You've Come a Long Way, Baby." List of women cartoonists and bibliography.

1727. Johnson, Robert C. "'Blacks and Women': Naming American Hostages Released in Iran." *Journal of Communication*. Summer 1980, pp. 58-63.

　　　How U.S. newspapers used race/sex designations to describe hostages released by Iran in November 1979; these were not the best choices.

1728. Kirkendall, Lester, Gina Allen, Albert Ellis, and Helen Colton. "Sex Magazines and Feminism." *The Humanist*. November-December 1978, pp. 44-51.

　　　Symposium to answer questions: Are sex magazines pornographic? Do they demean women? What role do they play in society?

1729. MacDonald, Kenneth. "Should Newspapers Be Policing Sex?" *Columbia Journalism Review*. May-June 1978, pp. 14-15.

　　　If a product or service is to be banned, the "acceptable way" is through the democratic processes, not "arbitrary censorship."

1730. Malamuth, Neil M. and Barry Spinner. "A Longitudinal Content Analysis of Sexual Violence in the Best-Selling Erotic Magazines." *Journal of Sex Research*. August 1980, pp. 226-237.

　　　In *Playboy* and *Penthouse* magazines, 1973-1977, pictorial violent sexuality rose significantly, although by 1977, only 5 percent of the pictorials were rated sexually violent.

1731. Mills, Janet. "Self-Posed Behaviors of Females and Males in Photographs." *Sex Roles*. April 1984, pp. 633-637.

　　　How males and females pose themselves for photographs, with females smiling, canting, and orientating away from the camera more than males.

1732. Mueller, Carol, ed. *The Politics of the Gender Gap: The Social Construction of Political Influence*. Beverly Hills, California: Sage, 1988.

　　　Includes Kathleen A. Frankovic, "The Ferraro Factor: The Women's Movement, the Polls, and the Press," pp. 102-123, and Julio Borquez, Edie M. Goldenberg, and Kim Fridkin Kahn, "Press Portrayals of the Gender Gap," pp. 124-148.

1733. Mussell, K. *Fantasy and Recollection: Contemporary Formulas of Women's Romance Fiction.* Westport, Connecticut: Greenwood Press, 1984. 217 pp.

Romance fiction examined in light of changes in U.S. women's culture; identifies types of romantic fiction, constructs a typology of romance formulas, and points out trends in their popularity.

1734. Overstreet, Robert M. *The Comic Book Price Guide 1978-1979.* Cleveland, Tennessee: Robert Overstreet, 1978. 454 pp.

A section on "Women in Comics," including 14 pages of front covers of women's or girls' comics in full color; Bill Ward, "The Man Behind Torchy," pp. A40-A53; Carl Macek, "Women in Comics," pp. A-54-A-75; and Trina Robbins, "Tarpe' Mills -- An Appreciation," p. A-76. Also see Carl Macek, "Good Girl Art -- An Introduction" in the 1976 edition of *The Comic Book Price Guide.*

1735. Patterson, Elizabeth L. "Pornography, Publishing, and Preservation: A Womanist View." *Microform Review.* Winter 1990, pp. 20-23.

Telephone survey of microform service units of libraries to determine their collecting and preserving of sexually graphic material.

1736. Peterson, Robin T. and Charles W. Gross. "Social Rsponsibility in Magazine Advertisements." *Atlanta Economic Review.* March-April 1978, pp. 35-38.

A study of 17 magazines for 1967, 1972, and 1975 indicated increased involvement on the part of firms to be responsible, measured by the relative number of ads with socially responsible themes.

1737. Potkay, Charles R. and Catherine E. Potkay. "Perceptions of Female and Male Strip Characters II: Favorability and Identification Are Different Dimensions." *Sex Roles.* 10:1/2 (1984), pp. 119-128.

In the ratings of 20 daily newspaper comic strip characters, the prediction that male characters elicit greater identification than female ones was replicated.

1738. Potkay, Catherine E., Charles R. Potkay, Gregory J. Boynton, and Julie A. Klingbeil. "Perceptions of Male and Female Comic Strip Characters Using the Adjective Generation Technique (AGT)." *Sex Roles.* 8:2 (1982), pp. 185-200.

An "unexpected" pattern of equivalent or greater favorability resulted for female characters than for male ones.

1739. *Problems of Journalism.* Proceedings of the American Society of Newspaper Editors.

Includes these talks or panels: Julia Coburn, "That Woman's Page," 1935, pp. 79-90; Elizabeth Gilmer, Inez Robb, Doris Fleeson, "The Women's Hour," 1939, pp. 77-95; Malvina Lindsay, "Streamlining the Woman's Page," 1938, pp. 139-146; Anna Steele Richardson, "What I Think Women Want in a Newspaper,"

1936, pp. 20-30; Mary Stow, "The Woman's Page Changes Its Mind," 1938, pp. 147-152.

1740. Radway, Janice A. *Reading the Romance: Women, Patriarchy, and Popular Literature*. Chapel Hill: University of North Carolina Press, 1984. 274 pp.

The six chapters look at how romance novels are produced and distributed, the types of women who seek out romance titles, the significance of reading romances as determined by the 42 readers in this study, the basic desires that are the source of romance readers' search for perfect romance, the fears women handle by reading romance, and the language and narrative discourse of romance fiction. By the same author: "The Utopian Impulse in Popular Literature: Gothic Romances and 'Feminist Protest,'" *American Quarterly*, Summer 1981, pp. 140-162, and "Women Read The Romance: The Interaction of Text and Context," *Feminist Studies*, Spring 1983, pp. 53-78.

1741. Rawnsley, David E., comp. *A Comparison of Guides to Non-Print Media. Updated 1975*. Palo Alto, California: Stanford University, 1975. 50 pp.

Update of 1973 work, which listed guides and indices to non-print instructional media; women among subject areas.

1742. Richardson, Lou and Genevieve Callahan. *How To Write for Homemakers*. Ames: Iowa State University Press, 1962. 205 pp.

For writers in the homemaking field.

1743. Rodi, Rob. "Girls Just Wanna Survive." *Comics Journal*. April 1987, pp. 35-41.

A review of three U.S. comic books, *The World of Ginger Fox*, *The Ballad of Halo Jones*, and *Love and Rockets*.

1744. *Sojourner, the New England Women's Journal of News, Opinions, and the Arts*.

Includes: Molly Lovelock, "Persephone Press: Why Did It Die?" September 1983; Betsy Brown, "Censorship Isn't the Only Threat to Free Expression," November 1986.

1745. Sonenschein, David. "Progress in the Production of Popular Culture: The Romance Magazine." *Journal of Popular Culture*. 6:2 (1972), pp. 399-406.

The philosophies of romance magazine editors toward their jobs and audiences. Most editors are male and make decisions on the explicitness of their content, mainly for a female audience, based on sales.

Historical Studies

1746. Beasley, Maurine H. "Women in Journalism Education: The Formative Period, 1908-1930." *Journalism History*. Spring 1986, pp. 10-18.

Experiences of pioneer women in journalism education analyzed via questions: Were women graduates fully prepared to compete with their male counterparts? What led women to study at the first journalism schools?

1747. Boughner, Genevieve. "Some Semi-Journalistic Opportunities for Women Graduates of Journalism." *Journalism Quarterly*. June 1928, pp. 13-21.

While journalism enrollments among women increased, newspaper job opportunities for them dwindled. Proposes that women look elsewhere for jobs -- in retail advertising, fashion writing, publicity, and radio. Second article on women and the media to appear in *Journalism Quarterly*.

1748. Boughner, Genevieve Jackson. *Women in Journalism*. New York: Appleton, 1926. 348 pp.

Outdated guidance for women aspiring to journalism careers; however, useful as historical document, being one of the early volumes to consider women's journalism.

1749. Collins, Jean E. *She Was There: Stories of Pioneering Women Journalists*. New York: Julian Messner, 1980. 191 pp.

Careers of 15 widely known women newspaper reporters, photographers, critics, and radio reporters told through interviews with the author.

1750. Covert, Catherine L. "Journalism History and Women's Experience: A Problem in Conceptual Change." *Journalism History*. Spring 1981, pp. 2-6.

Journalism history has been recorded according to the patterns and values of white American males.

1751. Emery, Michael and Edwin Emery. *The Press and America*. Sixth Ed. Englewood Cliffs, New Jersey: Prentice Hall, 1988. 786 pp.

Numerous short sections on women in journalism that first editions neglected: colonial period, columnists, foreign correspondents; in advertising, broadcasting, magazines, newspapers, photography, press associations, and public relations.

1752. Hodson, Jeannette. "Propaganda Techniques Employed in the Women's Army Corps." *Journalism Quarterly*. June 1958, pp. 151-156.

Techniques the Women's Army Corps relied on to recruit young women: leaflets, the weekly *Army Talks* columns, the bi-monthly *Service Woman*, and posters.

1753. *Independent Woman*.

Carried many articles on women and the media, including: Rebecca Dare Scott, "Women on the Air," November 1926, pp. 9-11; Ishbel Ross, "Shall Women Inherit the Fourth Estate?" April 1937, pp. 106-107, 119-120; "What's in the News?" June 1937, pp. 162-163; Carmen McCormack Simpson, "Foreign Correspondent," January 1941, pp. 6-8, 26-27; Carmen McCormack Simpson, "They're Roving Newscasters," May 1941, pp. 135-136, 159; Michael Costello, "Red Flannel Magic," Fall 1941, pp 39, 53; Beatrice Oppenheim, "Tune in on Radio

Jobs," April 1943, pp. 104-106, 125; Sarah Fields Pfeiffer and Ralph D. Casey, "Now's Your Chance for That Newspaper Job," September 1943, pp. 264-265, 281-282; Doris Minney, "She Meets Such Interesting People," (on Bess Furman) October 1953, pp. 357, 381; Edna Robb Webster, "Tells the Story of Our Times in Photographs," (on Margaret Bourke-White) March 1955; James H. Rice, "Women Engineers Behind the VOICE," April 1955, pp. 140-142.

1754. *Journalism History.* Winter 1976-77.

Thematic issue on "The Literature of Women," includes: Maurine Beasley, "The Curious Career of Anne Royall," pp. 98-102; Lynne Masel-Walters, "A Burning Cloud by Day: The History and Content of the 'Woman's Journal'"; Mary E. Williamson, "Judith Cary Waller: Chicago Broadcasting Pioneer," pp. 111-115; Marion Marzolf, "The Literature of Women in Journalism History: A Supplement," pp. 116-119; Virginia Elwood, "A Preliminary Bibliography: Images of Women in the Media, 1971-1976," pp. 120-123; and Sherilyn C. Bennion, "Fremont Older: Advocate for Women," pp. 124-127.

1755. McBride, Mary Margaret. *A Long Way From Missouri.* New York: Putnam, 1959. 254 pp.

Author's career as a New York newspaper sob sister and a magazine writer. Her radio career of the 1920s and 1930s is portrayed in the second part of her autobiography: *Out of the Air*, Garden City, New York: Doubleday, 1961. 384 pp.

1756. Rush, Ramona R. "Patterson, Grinstead and Hostetter: Pioneer Journalism Educators." *Journalism History.* Winter 1974-75, pp. 129-132.

Three women who pioneered in journalism education, beginning in the 1920s -- Helen Patterson Hyde, Helen P. Hostetter, and Frances Grinstead; their experiences and struggles competing in the male world of university teaching, based on interviews.

1757. Rysman, Alexander. "How the 'Gossip' Became a Woman." *Journal of Communication.* Winter 1977, pp. 176-180.

Gossip associated with women as early as 1600; Chicano women's use of gossip for solidarity.

Advertising

1758. Endres, Kathleen L. "'Strictly Confidential': Birth Control Advertising in a 19th-Century City." *Journalism Quarterly.* Winter 1986, pp. 748-751.

Classified ads from *Cleveland* (Ohio) *Plain Dealer*, 1850 to 1880, concerning birth control.

1759. Lopate, Carol. "Selling to Ms. Consumer." *College English.* 38:8 (1977), pp. 824-834.

The history of consumerism, advertising, and their impact on women, 1890-1920.

1760. McBride, Genevieve G. "From the Pedestal to PR: Women Reformers and Public Relations, 1910-1920." Paper presented at Association for Education in Journalism and Mass Communication, Norman, Oklahoma, August 3-6, 1986. 44 pp.
   Public relations in the Wisconsin woman suffrage campaign, 1910-1920.

1761. Roberts, Nancy L. "Riveting for Victory: Women in Magazine Ads in World War II." Paper presented at Association for Education in Journalism, Houston, Texas, August 5-8, 1979. 21 pp.
   Magazine advertising played a major role in calling women into factories to help the war effort.

1762. Schudson, Michael. "Women, Cigarettes, and Advertising in the 1920s: A Study in the Sociology of Consumption." In *Mass Media Between the Wars*, edited by Catherine L. Covert and John D. Stevens, pp. 71-84. Syracuse, New York: Syracuse University Press, 1984.
   Advertisers cautiously began to address women as smokers in the 1920s; examples of cigarette campaigns.

1763. Spigel, Lynn and Denise Mann. "Women and Consumer Culture: A Selective Bibliography." *Quarterly Review of Film and Video*. 11 (1989), pp. 85-105.
   Authors hope to open up areas of research into the history of women and consumer culture. Literature from disparate fields subdivided into "Consumer Culture and Commodity Display," "Magazines," "Mass-Produced 'Women's Fiction,'" and "Writing the History of Women."

Broadcasting

1764. Altman, Karen. "Television as Gendered Technology: Advertising the American Television Set." *Journal of Popular Film and Television*. Summer 1989, pp. 46-56.
   How advertisers "placed" TV sets in U.S. homes after World War II, identifying them with femininity, masculinity, romance, sexuality, and family.

1765. Arell, Ruth. "Silent Voices in Radio." *Independent Woman*. November 1937, pp. 341-342, 362-363.

1766. Beasley, Maurine H. and Paul Belgrade. "Eleanor Roosevelt: First Lady As Radio Pioneer." *Journalism History*. Autumn/Winter 1984, pp. 42-45.
   Eleanor Roosevelt's radio career while she was First Lady of the U.S. and its significance as a "vehicle of political and personal influence important in the evolution of commercially-sponsored radio broadcasting."

1767. Berg, Gertrude. *Molly and Me*. New York: McGraw-Hill, 1961.
   Author's immigrant background in New York and career on radio's "The Rise of the Goldbergs." Also wrote *The Rise of the Goldbergs*, New York: Barse and Co., 1931.

1768. Dickerson, Nancy. *Among Those Present: A Reporter's View of Twenty-Five Years in Washington.* New York: Random House, 1976.

Dickerson's career in the 1950s and 1960s when she was the first female national TV network news correspondent.

1769. Dragonette, Jessica. *Faith Is a Song: The Odyssey of an American Artist.* New York: MacKay, 1951.

Career of Dragonette, woman who was probably NBC radio's first major musical star.

1770. Haralovich, Mary Beth. "Sitcoms and Suburbs: Positioning the 1950s Homemaker." *Quarterly Review of Film and Video.* 11 (1989), pp. 61-83.

One television format (the suburban family sitcom) placed within the historical context from which it drew its conventions, codes of realism, and definitions of family life. The homemaker in the sitcoms was positioned in the "postwar consumer economy by institutions which were dependent on defining her social subjectivity within the domestic sphere."

1771. Heinz, Catharine. "Women Radio Pioneers." *Journal of Popular Culture.* Fall 1979, pp. 305-314.

Experiences of pioneers, from Judith Cary Waller, who produced radio station WGU in 1922, to Fay Wells, White House correspondent in 1964. Concentration on 1920s-1930s, with vignettes of Myrtle Stahl, Hester Kyler, Marjorie Mills, Dorothy Gordon, Madge Tucker, Evadna Hammersley, Edythe J. Meserand, Mae Horne, Agnes Law, Marian Murray, Gertrude Hardeman, Ruth Crane, Fran Harris, Mildred Carlson, Rose Floreyfiorani, Evelyn Walker, Alice Wyman, Hank Fort, Ann Shaffer, and Fay Gillis Wells.

1772. Herzog, Herta. "Daytime Serials." In *Radio Research, 1942-1943*, edited by Paul Lazarsfeld and Frank Stanton. New York: Essential Books, 1944.

1773. Johnson, Hope. "She Okays Famous Last Words: CBS Radio Executive Even Made Molotov Talk." *New York Telegram.* June 2, 1955.

Profile of Helen Sioussat of CBS Radio.

1774. Kennedy, John B. "Ladies of the Air Waves." *Collier's*, July 9, 1932, pp. 14, 44-45.

1775. Kerr, Frances W. *Women in Radio, Illustrated by Biographical Sketches.* Washington, D.C.: U.S. Department of Labor, 1947.

1776. Kretsinger, Geneva. "An Analytical Study of Selected Radio Speeches of Eleanor Roosevelt." Masters thesis, University of Oklahoma, 1941.

1777. McBride, Mary M. *Out of the Air.* Garden City, New York: Doubleday, 1961. 384 pp.

A radio pioneer reminisces.

1778. McCullough, Gordon L. "News Through a Woman's Eyes." Masters thesis, East Texas State University, 1970.

1779. *New York Woman.* "Radio -- A Woman's Game?" November 11, 1936, pp. 16-18, and "Broadcasting Business: From the Bottom Up!" November 18, 1936, pp. 16-17.

1780. *Radio Broadcast.* No. 5, 1924.
    Includes two articles by J.I. Mix: "Are Women Undesirable -- Over the Radio," pp. 333-335 and "For or Against the Woman Radio Speaker," pp. 391-397.

1781. Rouse, Morleen Getz. "Daytime Radio Programming for the Homemaker 1926-1956." *Journal of Popular Culture.* Fall 1979, pp. 315-327.
    Radio as "housewife's electronic liberator," categorizing programs between 1926 and 1956 as companion, teacher, wet nurse, and friend. Shows included were those "that did everything," talk-variety, "one-on-one heart-to-heart," "raising the children," "specific skill show," "fix-it-with-frills show," cooking show, "women on women show," "husband and wife show," domestic problem, and soap opera.

1782. St. John, Jacqueline. "Women in Radio Soap Operas: A Historical Perspective of the Image of Women's 'Sphere' in the 'Golden Age.'" Paper presented at American Theatre Association, Minneapolis, Minnesota, August 7-10, 1983. 22 pp.
    Soap operas of the 1930s and 1940s, particularly those done by Anne and Frank Hummert.

1783. Shurick, E.P.J. *The First Quarter-Century of American Broadcasting.* Kansas City, Missouri: Midland Press, 1946.
    Chapter on "The Women's Role in Broadcasting," discusses early women broadcasters and programming for women.

1784. Sioussat, Helen. *Mikes Don't Bite.* New York: L.B. Fisher, 1943.

1785. Smith, Kate. *Living in a Great Big Way.* New York: Blue Ribbon Books, 1938.
    Three chapters devoted to radio, detailing adjustments a singer had to make when moving into radio.

1786. Spangler, Lynn C. "A Historical Overview of Female Friendships on Prime-Time Television." *Journal of Popular Culture.* Spring 1989, pp. 13-23.
    Prime-time TV drama and how it has depicted female friendships from the 1950s; includes "My Friend Irma," "The Gale Storm Show," "I Love Lucy," "Mary Tyler Moore Show," "Laverne and Shirley," and "Cagney and Lacey," among others.

1787. Williamson, Mary E. "Judith Cary Waller: Chicago Broadcasting Pioneer." *Journalism History.* Winter 1976-77, pp. 111-114.

The story of Waller, who in 1922, was called upon by the Chicago *Daily News* to run a radio station, eventually called WMAQ; based mainly on a 1951 interview with Waller.

Film

1788. Blache, Roberta and Simone Blache, trans.; Anthony Slide, ed. *The Memoirs of Alice Guy Blache.* Metuchen, New Jersey: Scarecrow Press, 1986. 208 pp.

   The career of one of the first significant film directors, Alice Guy Blache, who began her career in France and moved to the U.S. where she established her studio, Solax, in 1910. Includes 99 pages of memoirs, plus 10 appendices.

1789. Brooks, Louise. *Lulu in Hollywood.* New York: Alfred A. Knopf, 1982. 110 pp.

   Seven essays drawn from those written by the author over the years. Brooks' most important film role was in G.W. Pabst's *Pandora's Box* (1929).

1790. Brown, Peter H. and Pamela A. Brown. *The MGM Girls: Behind the Velvet Curtain.* New York: St. Martins, 1983.

   Gossip, interviews, and other sources used to recount the story of female stars at MGM studios in the 1950s.

1791. Cooper, Miriam. *Dark Lady of the Silents: My Life in Early Hollywood.* Indianapolis: Bobbs-Merrill, 1973. 256 pp.

   Cooper's films of 1911-23 and her work with D.W. Griffith.

1792. Creed, Barbara. "Me Jane: You Tarzan! -- A Case of Mistaken Identity in Paradise." *Continuum.* 1:1 (1987), pp. 159-174.

   The role of "Jane" in the history of "Tarzan" films from 1932.

1793. Dyer, Peter John. "The Face of the Goddess." *Films and Filming.* June 1959, pp. 13-15.

   The mythic woman of 1930s' films.

1794. Dyer, Richard. *Stars.* London: British Film Institute, 1979. 204 pp.

   The Hollywood star system and the many actresses who were part of it.

1795. Ford, Charles. "The First Female Producer." *Films in Review.* March 1964, pp. 144-145.

   Alice Guy-Blache.

1796. Gaines, Jane M. "The Popular Icon as Commodity and Sign: The Circulation of Betty Grable, 1941-45." Ph.D. dissertation, Northwestern University, 1982. 625 pp.

1797. Gaines, Jane M. "The Queen Christina Tie-ups: Convergence of Show Window and Screen." *Quarterly Review of Film and Video*. 11 (1989), pp. 35-60.
   The show window and screen analogy applied to the 1933 MGM film, "Queen Christina."

1798. Gaines, Jane M. and Charlotte Herzog. "Puffed Sleeves Before Teatime: Joan Crawford, Adrian and Women Audiences." *Wide Angle*. 6:4 (1985), pp. 24-33.

1799. Harriman, Margaret. "The It-Girl." Part I & II. *New Yorker*. April 20, 1940, pp. 24-30; April 27, 1940, pp. 23-29.

1800. Haymes, Howard. "Movies in the 1950s: Sexism From A to Zapata." *Journal of the University Film Association*. 26:1-2 (1974), pp. 12, 22.

1801. Higashi, Sumiko. "Cinderella vs. Statistics: The Silent Movie Heroine as a Jazz-Age Working Girl." In *Woman's Being, Woman's Place: Female Identity and Vocation in American History*, edited by Mary Kelly, pp. 109-126. Boston: G.K. Hall and Co., 1979.
   Portrayals of the working woman in the 1920s' silent films reinforced the image of the traditionally-dependent woman. By this author: *Virgins, Vamps, and Flappers: The American Silent Movie Heroine*, St. Albans, Vermont: Eden Press Women's Publications, 1978.

1802. Renov, Michael. "Advertising/Photojournalism/Cinema: The Shifting Rhetoric of Forties Female Representation." *Quarterly Review of Film and Video*. 11 (1989), pp. 1-21.
   Ways in which Hollywood films and photographic images functioned as cogs in the U.S. war machine of the 1940s; how females were shown in films, photographs, and advertising.

1803. Renov, Michael. *Hollywood's Wartime Woman: Representation and Ideology*. Ann Arbor, Michigan: UMI Research Press, 1988. 274 pp.
   Hollywood films from World War II that show interest in the representation of women. A general historical survey and a description of the patterns of life and work among American women. Presented as Ph.D. dissertation at University of California, Los Angeles, in 1982 as "Hollywood's Wartime Woman: A Study of Historical/Ideological Determination."

1804. Rosen, Marjorie. "Popcorn Venus." *Ms*. April 1974, pp. 41-47.
   Women's roles in films from the 1920s to the 1970s. The 1920s' movies portrayed flappers who were "working girls"; the 1930s showed women as molls, reporters, secretaries, spies, and con artists, and the 1940s, women working for the war effort. In the 1950s, Hollywood was "mammary mad" but also emphasized the girl-next-door. In the 1960s, when women's lifestyles changed rather drastically, cinematic depiction of them did not.

1805. Rosen, Marjorie. *Popcorn Venus: Women, Movies and the American Dream*. New York: Coward, McCann and Geoghegan, 1973. 416 pp.
Historical view of women in film and what women think of films. The 23 chapters, divided into six chronological periods from before the 1920s through the 1970s, deal with film content, stars, and the impact of filmic portrayals of women.

1806. Ryan, Mary P. "The Projection of a New Womanhood: The Movie Moderns in the 1920s." In *Our American Sisters: Women in American Life and Thought*, edited by Jean E. Friedman and William G. Shade, pp. 366-384. Boston: Allyn and Bacon, 1976.

1807. *Screen Facts*.
Includes: Gene Ringgold, "Deanna Durbin, " (No. 5); Gene Ringgold, "Bette Davis," (No. 9); DeWitt Bodeen, "Geraldine Farrar," (No. 10); Gene Ringgold, "Hedy Lamarr," (No. 11); Gene Ringgold, "Shirley Temple," (No. 12); Jerry Vermilye, "Maria Montez," (No. 13); Ray Hagen, "Ann Sheridan," (No. 14); William J. Pratt, "Esther Williams," (No 21), among others.

1808. Slide, Anthony. *Early Women Film Directors*. New York: De Capo Press, 1984, 119 pp.
The period before sound was a heyday for women directors who virtually controlled the industry.

1809. Viviana, Christian. "Who Is Without Sin? The Maternal Melodrama in American Films, 1930-1939." *Wide Angle*. 4:2 (1980), pp. 4-17.

1810. Waldman, Diane. "'At Last I Can Tell It to Someone!': Feminine Point of View and Subjectivity in the Gothic Romance Film of the 1940's." *Cinema Journal*. Winter 1984, pp. 29-40.
Author's Ph.D. dissertation: "Horror and Domesticity: The Modern Gothic Romance Film of the 1940's," University of Wisconsin, Madison, 1981.

1811. Zierold, Norman. *Sex Goddesses of the Silent Screen*. New York: Regnery, 1973. 207 pp.
Includes Theda Bara, Barbara LaMarr, Pola Negri, Mae Murray, and Clara Bow.

Print Media

1812. Abbott, Edith A. "Printing," In *Women in Industry: A Study in American Economic History*, pp. 246-260. New York: D. Appleton and Co., 1918.
Early source on women printers.

1813. Adams, Elizabeth Kemper. "Information Services: Journalism, Publishing, Advertising, Publicity." In *Women Professional Workers: A Study Made for the Women's Educational and Industrial Union*, pp. 283-291. New York: Macmillan Co., 1921.

1814. Adamson, June. "Nellie Kenyon and the Scopes 'Monkey Trial.'" *Journalism History*. Autumn 1975, pp. 88-89, 97.

    The career of Nellie Kenyon, Tennessee woman journalist who covered the 1925 trial and wrote at length throughout the twentieth century. Based in part on interviews. Author's masters thesis, "Selected Women in Tennessee Newspaper Journalism," University of Tennessee, 1971.

1815. Alexander, Jack. "The Girl From Syracuse." In *Post Biographies of Famous Journalists*, pp. 431-477. Athens, Georgia: University of Georgia Press, 1942.

1816. Alpern, Sara. *Freda Kirchwey: A Woman of The Nation*. Cambridge, Massachusetts: Harvard University Press, 1987. 319 pp.

    Editor, publisher and owner of *The Nation* from 1937-55, Kirchwey began on that magazine in 1918. She helped form national opinion on birth control, free love, McCarthyism, atomic energy, and civil rights. Looks at both her public and private lives.

1817. *American Journalism*. Summer 1983.

    Devoted to women and media: Linda Steiner, "Finding Community in Nineteenth Century Suffrage Periodicals," pp. 1-15; Lewis L Gould, "First Ladies and the Press: Bess Truman to Lady Bird Johnson," pp. 47-62; Maurine H. Beasley, "A 'Front Page Girl' Covers the Lindbergh Kidnaping [sic]: An Ethical Dilemma," pp. 63-74; Anne Messerly Cooper, "Suffrage as News: Ten Dailies' Coverage of the Nineteenth Amendment," pp. 75-91.

1818. Ames, Austine. *Ten Years in Washington: Life and Scenes in the National Capital as a Woman Sees Them*. Hartford, Connecticut: Worthington, 1875.

    Information on nineteenth century Washington correspondent, Austine Ames. Also see her: *Eirene or a Woman's Right*, New York: Putnam, 1871, and *Outlines of Man, Women, and Things*, New York: Hurd and Houghton, 1873.

1819. Anderson, Margaret. *My Thirty Years' War*. New York: Covici-Friede, 1930. 274 pp.

    As editor of the *Little Review*, Anderson made her magazine important by publishing Joyce's *Ulysses* and other pioneer experimental work. The second volume of this autobiography is *The Fiery Fountains*, New York: Horizon, 1969, 242 pp., a reprint of the 1951 original.

1820. Anthony, Katharine S. *Margaret Fuller: A Psychological Biography*. Shores, Michigan: Scholarly Press, 1970. 223 pp.

    Originally brought out in 1920 by Harcourt, Brace and Howe. Seeks to find the influences in Fuller's life that led to views she had about women's role in society.

1821. Baker, Ira L. "Elizabeth Timothy: America's First Woman Editor." *Journalism Quarterly*. Spring 1977, pp. 280-285.

In 1738, Elizabeth Timothy took over the editorship of the *South Carolina Gazette* when her husband died and followed his footsteps as a shrewd business person. Author's masters thesis under same title, University of Illinois, 1963.

1822. Baker, Nina Brown. *Nellie Bly.* New York: Holt, 1956. 125 pp.

Devotes much space to Bly's around-the-world trip, putting it in perspective as a tame affair. Points out the more valuable contribution she made as a crusading "sob sister" during the yellow journalism era.

1823. Ballard, Bettina. *In My Fashion.* New York: McKay, 1960. 312 pp.

Author's 20 years with *Vogue* magazine, beginning in 1930s.

1824. Banks, Elizabeth L. *The Autobiography of a "Newspaper Girl."* New York: Dodd, Mead, 1902. 317 pp.

Story of Wisconsin reporter who represented U.S. papers in South America and Europe, when women normally were not permitted on staffs.

1825. Beasley, Maurine H. "A 'Front Page Girl' Covers the Lindbergh Kidnaping [sic]: An Ethical Dilemma." *American Journalism.* Summer 1983, pp. 63-74.

Covering the Lindbergh kidnapping in 1930s, "front page girl" Lorena Hickok created sentimental human interest stories to satisfy her editors.

1826. Beasley, Maurine H. *Eleanor Roosevelt and the Media, A Public Quest for Self-Fulfillment.* Chicago: University of Illinois Press, 1987. 240 pp.

Eleanor Roosevelt's position as First Lady allowed her to highlight and emphasize women's role in society. Key to her ability was her skillful use of the mass media.

1827. Beasley, Maurine H. "Eleanor Roosevelt's Press Conferences: Symbolic Importance of a Pseudo-Event." *Journalism Quarterly.* Summer 1984, pp. 274-279, 338.

By holding more than 300 meetings with women journalists during 12 years as First Lady of the U.S., Roosevelt changed the newsmaking process of the White House. Most conferences, however, dealt with topics considered women's areas. Also see author's "Eleanor Roosevelt: First Lady as Magazine Journalist," paper presented at Association for Education in Journalism and Mass Communications, Gainesville, Florida, August 5-8, 1984, 38 pp.

1828. Beasley, Maurine H. "Lorena A. Hickok: Woman Journalist." *Journalism History.* Autumn-Winter 1980, pp. 92-113.

The career of Lorena Hickok took off during the Roosevelt administration. A close friend of Eleanor Roosevelt, she carried out some investigative work for the First Lady's activities and speeches, for which she was penalized by the AP.

1829. Beasley, Maurine H. "Mrs. Bush, Meet Ms. Roosevelt." *Washington Journalism Review.* January-February 1989, pp. 39-41.

Eleanor Roosevelt helped create jobs for women reporters by having 350 women-only press conferences. See author's "Mamie Eisenhower as First Lady: Media Coverage of a Silent Partner," paper presented at Association for Education in Journalism and Mass Communication, Gainesville, Florida, August 5-8, 1984, 27 pp.

1830. Beasley, Maurine H. "Pens and Petticoats: Early Women Washington Correspondents." *Journalism History*. Winter 1974-75, pp. 112-115, 136.

Some women fought to be admitted to the press galleries of the U.S. Congress, most notably, Jane G. Swisshelm.

1831. Beasley, Maurine H. "The Curious Career of Anne Royall." *Journalism History*. Winter 1976-1977, pp. 98-102.

Sorts fact from fiction in the career of Anne Royall, a Washington journalist from the 1820s until 1854, who launched *Paul Pry* and *The Huntress* newspapers when she was in her sixties. Author depends upon these newspapers and two biographies of Royall: Bessie Rowland James, *Anne Royall's U.S.A.*, New Brunswick, New Jersey: Rutgers University Press, 1972; and Sarah H. Porter, *The Life and Times of Anne Royall*, Cedar Rapids, Iowa: Torch Press, 1909.

1832. Beasley, Maurine H. *The First Women Washington Correspondents*. Washington, D.C.: George Washington University, George Washington Studies No. 4, 1976.

In the nineteenth century.

1833. Beasley, Maurine H. "The Women's National Press Club: Case Study of Professional Aspirations." *Journalism History*. Winter 1988, pp. 112-121.

Inauguration of the Women's National Press Club in 1919 was preceded by women's first attempts at a national club in 1882. The WNPC struggled to be taken seriously by government officials. In 1970, WNPC admitted men and changed its name to Washington Press Club.

1834. Belford, Barbara. *Brilliant Bylines: A Biographical Anthology of Notable Newspaperwomen in America*. New York: Columbia University Press, 1986. 385 pp.

Lives and careers of 24 newspaperwomen -- Margaret Fuller, Jane Grey Swisshelm, "Jennie June," "Polly Pry," "Dorothy Dix," Ida Wells-Barnett, "Annie Laurie," "Nelly Bly," Elizabeth Jordan, Anne O'Hare McCormick, Emma Bugbee, "Peggy Hull," Sigrid Schultz, Dorothy Thompson, Ishbel Ross, Mildred Gilman, Doris Fleeson, Mary McGrory, Marguerite Higgins, Ada Huxtable, Judith Crist, Georgie Anne Geyer, Ellen Goodman, and Madeleine Blais. Samples of their work and descriptions of problems and influences encountered.

1835. Bell, Margaret. *Margaret Fuller: A Biography*. New York: Charles Boni, 1930. 320 pp.

Romanticized and fictionalized biography, especially in its treatment of Margaret Fuller's final days. Also about Fuller is: Thomas W. Higginson, *Margaret Fuller Ossoli*, Boston: Houghton Mifflin, 1912.

1836. Bennion, Sherilyn Cox. "A Working List of Women Editors of the 19th-Century Frontier." *Journalism History*. Summer 1980, pp. 60-67.

A foundation for a comprehensive catalog of women editors active in 11 U.S. western states and Alaska and Hawaii before 1900. Includes name of editor, publication, periodicity, place of publication, period of editorship, and location of copies.

1837. Bennion, Sherilyn C. "Fremont Older: Advocate for Women." *Journalism History*. Winter 1976-77, pp. 124-127.

Fremont Older of the San Fransisco *Bulletin* was known for fair treatment of women, who became his best reporters, e.g., Pauline Jacobson, Bessie Beatty, Rose Wilder Lane, Elsie McCormick, Cora Older, and Sophi Treadwell.

1838. Bennion, Sherilyn Cox. "*The New Northwest* and *Woman's Exponent*: Early Voices for Suffrage." *Journalism Quarterly*. Summer 1977, pp. 286-292.

Reviews histories and editors of two long-time woman's suffrage newspapers *The New Northwest*, founded in 1871 in Portland, Oregon, and *Woman's Exponent*, 1872-1914, published in Salt Lake City.

1839. Bennion, Sherilyn Cox. "Woman Suffrage Papers of the West, 1869-1914." *American Journalism*. 3:3 (1986), pp. 129-141.

Woman suffrage papers of the West helped frame the ideological and political bases of the movement. By the same author: "*The Pioneer*: The First Voice of Woman's Suffrage in the West," *The Pacific Historian*, Winter 1981, pp. 15-21.

1840. Billington, Mary Frances. "Women and Journalism." In *The Woman's Library. Vol. I. Education and Professions*, edited by Ethel M. McKenna, pp. 173-222. London: Chapman and Hall Ltd., 1903.

Journalism was a good profession for women but as men still controlled the press, even the most successful women had to live through major disappointments. Women must strive for their professional niche through hard work.

1841. Blanchard, Paula. *Margaret Fuller: From Transcendentalism to Revolution*. New York: Delacorte, Seymour Lawrence, 1978. 370 pp.

Dispels myth that she hated men because she competed with them.

1842. Bloomer, Dexter C. *Life and Writings of Amelia Bloomer*. Boston, Massachusetts: Arena Publishing Company, 1895. 387 pp.

The life of journalist Amelia Bloomer, as written admirably by her husband. Describes her writing for his Seneca Falls, New York, paper, her editing for six years of *Western Home Visitor*, and her work for the temperance paper, *Lily*, which she believed was the first paper published on behalf of women.

1843. Blum, Stella, ed. *Victorian Fashion and Costumes from Harper's Bazaar: 1867-1898*. New York: Dover, 1974.

1844. Born, Donna. "The Woman Journalist of the 1920s and 1930s in Fiction and in Autobiography." Paper presented at Association for Education in Journalism, Athens, Ohio, July 25-28, 1982.

    A portrait of the woman journalist through the autobiographies of eight women journalists of the 1920s and 1930s.

1845. Bourke-White, Margaret. *Portrait of Myself*. New York: Simon and Schuster, 1963. 383 pp.

    Autobiography of famous magazine photojournalist who was with *Life* from its 1936 creation. For more on Bourke-White, see: Sean Callahan, *The Photographs of Margaret Bourke-White*, New York: New York Graphic Society, 1972; Vicki Goldberg, *Margaret Bourke-White: A Biography*, New York: Addison-Wesley Publishing Co., 1986; Jonathan Silverman, *For the World To See: The Life of Margaret Bourke-White*, New York: Viking, 1983.

1846. Bradley, Patricia. "Maintaining Separate Spheres: The Career of Margaret Cousins." Paper presented at Association for Education in Journalism and Mass Communication, Memphis, Tennessee, August 3-6, 1985. 45 pp.

    Journalistic career of Margaret Cousins and her concepts of what a home should be.

1847. Bradshaw, James Stanford. "Mrs. Rayne's School of Journalism." *Journalism Quarterly*, Autumn 1983, pp. 513-517, 579.

    In 1886, journalist Martha Louise Rayne established in Detroit, the first U.S. school of journalism aimed at providing practical journalistic instruction for women.

1848. Brady, Kathleen. *Ida Tarbell: Portrait of a Muckraker*. New York: Sea View/Putnam, 1984. 286 pp.

    Letters, scrapbooks, and interviews used to study the famous woman muckraker.

1849. Bridges, Lamar W. "Eliza Jane Nicholson of the 'Picayune.'" *Journalism History*. Winter 1975-76, pp. 110-113.

    Eliza Jane Nicholson, who, in her teens, wrote poetry as "Pearl Rivers," inherited the *New Orleans Picayune* at age 26. She added a number of features, e.g., agricultural news and more sports coverage.

1850. Britt, Albert. *Ellen Browning Scripps: Journalist and Idealist*. London: Oxford University Press for Scripps College, 1961. 134 pp.

    Biography of Ellen B. Scripps, half-sister of E.W. Scripps, especially her role on his Cleveland paper.

1851. Brody, Catharine. "Newspaper Girls." *American Mercury*. March 1926, pp. 273-277.

    "Girl reporters" were changing their tactics in the male-dominated newspapers -- dropping the "stunts" to win the professional respect of the city editor, "concentrating on their appearance and attacking his susceptibility as a male."

1852. Brown, Arthur W. *Margaret Fuller.* New York: Twayne, 1964. 159 pp.
Fuller's life, including that part in journalism.

1853. Brown, Charles B. "A Woman's Odyssey: The War Correspondence of Anna Benjamin." *Journalism Quarterly.* Autumn 1969, pp. 522-530.
Anna Northend Benjamin was one of the first female war correspondents. She covered the Spanish American War, the Philippines, China, and Russia before her death in 1902 at age 27.

1854. Brown, Theodore M. *Margaret Bourke-White, Photo-journalist.* Ithaca, New York: Andrew Dickson White Museum of Art, Cornell University, 1972. 136 pp.
The life of famous photo-journalist, Margaret Bourke-White, in words and photographs, built around photographs that she took in the U.S., India, and elsewhere.

1855. Burmester, William E. "Elizabeth Hauser: Teen Editor of Gaslight Era." *Media History Digest.* Fall-Winter 1988, pp. 17-19.
Nineteen-year-old Hauser's editorship of *Girard* (Ohio) *Grit* reflected her outspoken defense of women's rights in the 1890s.

1856. Burt, Olive. *First Woman Editor: Sarah J. Hale.* New York: Messner, 1960. 191 pp.
Fictionalized biography of Sarah J. Hale, nineteenth century U.S. editor, who aimed for more education for women, better housing for all, greater respect for women's minds, and other causes.

1857. Carpenter, Iris. *No Woman's World.* Boston: Houghton Mifflin, 1946.
Author's experiences as World War II correspondent.

1858. Caswell, Lucy Shelton. "Edwina Dumm: Pioneer Woman Editorial Cartoonist, 1915-1917." *Journalism History.* Spring 1988, pp. 2-7.
Edwina Dumm, believed to be the first fulltime woman cartoonist for a U.S. paper, *Columbus Monitor*, tackled many of same events in her drawings as her male colleagues did.

1859. Chalmers, David M. *The Social and Political Ideas of the Muckrakers.* New York: Citadel, 1964. 127 pp.
Thirteen muckrakers, including Ida Tarbell.

1860. Chapelle, Dickey. *What's a Woman Doing Here?* New York: Morrow, 1962.
War correspondence exploits, from World War II to eve of Vietnam.

1861. Chapin, Howard M. "Ann Franklin, Printer." *American Collector.* September 1926, pp. 461-465.
Her printing activities in colonial Newport, Rhode Island.

1862. Chipperfield, Faith. *In Quest of Love: The Life and Death of Margaret Fuller.* New York: Coward-McCann, 1957. 320 pp.
   Realistic biography of the *Dial* editor and foreign correspondent for Horace Greeley's *New York Tribune.*

1863. Chudacoff, Nancy Fisher. "Woman in the News 1762-1770 -- Sarah Updike Goddard." *Rhode Island History.* Fall 1973, pp. 98-105.
   Career of Sarah Updike Goddard who, either with her son, William, or daughter, Mary Katherine, published the Providence *Gazette* during the pre-Revolutionary War period.

1864. Clark, Emily. *Innocence Abroad.* New York: Knopf, 1931. 270 pp.
   A chapter on the *Reviewer*, a tiny women's magazine in Richmond, Virginia, in the early 1920s.

1865. Coates, Foster. "Women in Journalism." *The Ladies' Home Journal.* September 1892, p. 18.
   Poll of "a number of leading editors" concerning women journalists showed most had very favorable opinions. Author wonders why women should not succeed in journalism, pointing out they have "brains," and answers questions on best journalistic work for women, chances of promotion, and ways to obtain newspaper work.

1866. Conn, Frances G. *Ida Tarbell, Muckraker.* Nashville, Tennessee: Nelson, 1972. 160 pp.
   Life story of muckraker Ida Tarbell who sought to bring about social reform through journalism in early 1900s.

1867. Cooper, Anne M. "Suffrage as News: Ten Dailies' Coverage of the Nineteenth Amendment." *American Journalism.* Summer 1983, pp. 75-91.
   Content of ten U.S. dailies from four regions on the nineteenth amendment's enactment which gave U.S. women the right to vote. No relation existed between type of coverage and region or between status of the nineteenth amendment in a newspaper's home state and coverage of that amendment.

1868. Coy, Patrick, ed. *A Revolution of the Heart: Essays on the Catholic Worker.* Philadelphia: Temple University Press, 1988. 388 pp.
   Eleven essays on one of the longest lived, most deeply radical reform movements of the U.S. -- that of the *Catholic Worker* and its leader, Dorothy Day. Of special interest is Nancy Roberts' essay, "Dorothy Day: Editor and Advocacy Journalist."

1869. Daniels, Elizabeth Adams. "Jessie White Mario: 19th Century Foreign Correspondent." *Journalism History.* Summer 1975, pp. 54-56.
   Story of Jessie White Mario, an Englishwoman chosen by *The Nation* to be its correspondent on Italian affairs in 1866.

1870. Davenport, Walter and James C. Derieux. *Ladies, Gentlemen and Editors.* Garden City, New York: Doubleday, 1960. 386 pp.
    Brief sketches of magazine editors, Mrs. Frank Leslie, Sarah Josepha Hale, Roxie Claflin, and Edward Bok.

1871. Day, Dorothy. *The Long Loneliness. The Autobiography of Dorothy Day.* New York: Harper and Brothers, 1952. 288 pp.
    Day's experiences in Catholic radicalism on the *Catholic Worker* and in work with the poor and dispossessed. Two chapters deal with journalism: "Journalism," pp. 56-66 and "Paper, People and Work," pp. 182-203.

1872. DeMott, John. "Ida B. Wells, Journalist." *Grassroots Editor.* Fall 1989, pp. 5-6, 14.
    Black woman journalist, Ida B. Wells-Barnett, editor of *Memphis Free Speech* during the latter nineteenth century when she editorialized against lynchings and other evils of racism.

1873. Dexter, Elizabeth Anthony. *Colonial Women of Affairs.* New York: Houghton-Mifflin Company, 1924.
    The 17 women who worked in colonial U.S. before 1788, from the earliest, Dinah Nuthead, to Mrs. Nicholas Hasselbach. By the same author: *Career Women of America: 1776-1840*, Francestown, New Hampshire: Jones, 1950.

1874. Dickinson, Susan E. "Women in Journalism." In *Woman's Work in America*, edited by Annie Nathan Meyer, pp. 128-138. New York: Henry Holt and Co., 1891.

1875. Doherty, Amy S. "19th Century Woman Photographers." *The Blatant Image.* 1, 1981, pp. 24-25.

1876. Dorr, Rheta Childe. *A Woman of Fifty.* New York: Funk and Wagnalls, 1924.
    Autobiography of reporter for *New York Evening Mail* who covered Russian Revolution. By the same author: *What Eight Million Women Want*, Boston: Small, Maynard, 1910.

1877. Drewry, John E. *Post Biographies of Famous Journalists.* Athens: University of Georgia Press, 1942.
    Among 22 biographical sketches, the following on women journalists: Hermann B. Deutsch, "Dorothy Dix Talks," pp. 29-47; Stanley Walker, "Cissy Is a Newspaper Lady (Eleanor Patterson)," pp. 346-363; and Jack Alexander, "The Girl From Syracuse (Dorothy Thompson)," pp. 431-477. All originally appeared in the *Saturday Evening Post*.

1878. Dunnigan, Alice E. "Early History of Negro Women in Journalism." *Negro History Bulletin.* Summer 1965, pp. 178-179, 193-197.

1879. Earle, Alice M. *Colonial Dames and Good Wives.* New York: Ungar, 1962.
Women printers included.

1880. Eberhard, Wallace B. "Sarah Porter Hillhouse: Setting the Record Straight." *Journalism History.* Winter 1974-75, pp. 133-136.
Sarah Porter Hillhouse was the first woman editor in Georgia (1803-1812); her paper, Washington *Monitor*, was considered dull.

1881. Ek, Richard A. "Victoria Woodhull and the Pharisees." *Journalism Quarterly.* Autumn 1972, pp. 453-459.
Woodhull's exposé in her weekly newspaper of Rev. Henry Ward Beecher's adulterous affair and her famous speech at New York's Cooper Union.

1882. Ellis, Marc H. *A Year at the Catholic Worker.* New York: Paulist Press, 1978.
Mentions the paper's long-time publisher, Dorothy Day.

1883. Elwood-Akes, Virginia. *Women War Correspondents in the Vietnam War, 1961-1975.* Metuchen, New Jersey: Scarecrow Press, 1988. 274 pp.
Excerpts of works by 12 women correspondents -- Dickey Chappelle, Beverly Deepe, Frances Fitzgerald, Martha Gellhorn, Georgia Ann Geyer, Marguerite Higgins, Jurate Kazickas, Mary McCarthy, Patches (Helen) Musgrove, Elizabeth Pond, Philippa Schuyler, and Kate Webb. Seven chapters that treat the war chronologically; introduction of 28 pages provides background on the correspondents.

1884. Emerson, Gloria. "Hey, Lady, What Are You Doing Here?" *McCall's.* August 1971, pp. 61+.
Her experiences as a Vietnam War correspondent. By the same author: "Arms and the Woman." *Harper's*, Apr. 1973, pp. 35-45 and June 1973, pp. 99-100.

1885. Endres, Kathleen L. "Jane Grey Swisshelm: 19th Century Journalist and Feminist." *Journalism History.* Winter 1975-76, pp. 128-132.
New York Tribune journalist known for opening the U.S. Senate press gallery to women in 1850 and for her anti-slavery and pro-women's rights writing.

1886. Endres, Kathleen L. "The Women's Press in the Civil War: A Portrait of Patriotism, Propaganda, and Prodding." *Civil War History.* March 1984, pp. 31-53.
At least nine publications catered to the female audience in the North during the U.S. Civil War: *Godey's Lady's Book, Peterson's, Lady's Friend, Arthur's Home Magazine, Frank Leslie's Monthly, Mother's Magazine, Family Circle, Ladies' Repository,* and *Sibyl.*

1887. Entrikin, Isabelle Webb. *Sarah Josepha Hale and Godey's Lady's Book.* Philadelphia, Pennsylvania: Author and Lancaster Press, 1946. 160 pp.

Biography of Hale which gives details on magazine journalism from 1825 to 1875.

1888. Ferber, Edna. *A Peculiar Treasure.* Rev. Ed. New York: Doubleday, 1960. 383 pp.
Her life story as novelist and Appleton, Wisconsin reporter. Second volume, covering 1936-1963, entitled, *A Kind of Magic*, New York: Doubleday, 1963, 335 pp.

1889. Ferguson, Charles W. "Americans Not Everyone Knows: Philippa Duke Schuyler." *PTA Magazine.* December 1967, pp. 12-14.
Vietnam War correspondent.

1890. Filler, Louis. *Crusaders for American Liberalism.* New York: Harcourt, Brace, 1939.
Discussion of muckraker Ida Tarbell and war correspondent Rheta Childe Dorr.

1891. Finley, Ruth E. *The Lady of Godey's.* Philadelphia, Pennsylvania: Lippincott, 1931. 318 pp.
Scholarly and popular writing about editor of *Godey's Lady's Book*, Sarah Hale.

1892. Fisher, Andrea, ed. *Let Us Now Praise Famous Women: Women Photographers for the U.S. Government 1935 to 1944.* Winchester, Massachusetts: Unwin and Hyman and Pandora Press, 1987. 160 pp.
Eight women, including Dorothea Lange and Marion Post Wolcott, who participated in U.S. government project to document American life through photographs.

1893. Fisher, Charles. *The Columnists.* New York: Howell, Soskin, 1944. 317 pp.
Includes one woman columnist, Dorothy Thompson.

1894. Flexner, Eleanor. *Century of Struggle.* Cambridge, Massachusetts: Harvard University Press, 1959.
The importance of Susan B. Anthony and Elizabeth Cady Stanton's *The Revolution* to the suffrage movement.

1895. "Foreign Correspondents Self-Reliance in Saigon." *Time.* June 8, 1965.
Exploits of correspondent Beverly Deepe.

1896. Friedman, Stanley. "Dickey Chapelle: Two Wars and Four Revolutions." *Ms.* April 1976, pp. 24-27.
War correspondent who began in World War II and died in Vietnam.

1897. Fryatt, Norma R. *Sara Josepha Hale.* New York: Hawthorne, 1975. 152 pp.

Biography of long-time editor of *Godey's Lady's Book*, based on analysis of magazine's content, interviews with relatives, and other sources.

1898. Furman, Bess. *Washington By-Line.* New York: Knopf, 1949. 357 pp.

Much on Washington political activity but skimpy on Washington journalism or her own work as Washington reporter for Associated Press and *New York Times*.

1899. Garcia, Hazel. "Of Punctilios Among the Fair Sex: Colonial American Magazines, 1741-1776." *Journalism History.* Summer 1976, pp. 48-52, 63.

Nineteen U.S. colonial magazines examined for quantity and content of "what the magazines said to, for, about, and from women." Of 8,300 pages studied, 429 concerned women. Of those, 68 pages came from women during this 35-year period.

1900. Gardener, Virginia. *Friend and Lover: The Life of Louise Bryant.* New York: Horizon Press, 1982.

Biography of correspondent Bryant and her relationship with John Reed, journalist and revolutionary, as they covered workers' movements in the U.S. and the Bolshevik Revolution in Russia.

1901. Garnsey, Caroline John. "Ladies' Magazines to 1850: The Beginnings of an Industry." *Bulletin of the New York Public Library.* February 1954, pp. 74-88.

The development of women's magazines from the first, *The Gentleman and the Lady's Town and Country Magazine*, of 1784, to 1850. Growth by regions and time periods; data on the 110 "ladies" magazines published by 1850.

1902. Garrett, W.E. "What Was a Woman Doing There?" *National Geographic.* February 1966, pp. 270-271.

Dickey Chapelle's war correspondence in Vietnam.

1903. Gies, Dorothy. "Some Early Ladies of the Book Trade." *Publisher's Weekly.* October 5, 1940, pp. 1421-1424.

1904. Goldstein, Cynthia. "The Radical Press and the Beginning of the Birth Control Movement in the United States." Paper presented at Association for Education in Journalism and Mass Communication, Memphis, Tennessee, August 3-6, 1985. 31 pp.

How radical press personnel, mainly socialist women, covered and promoted the birth control movement in early twentieth century U.S.

1905. Gould, Lewis L. "First Ladies and the Press: Bess Truman to Lady Bird Johnson." *American Journalism.* Summer 1983, pp. 47-62.

Four First Ladies between 1945-1969 compared with Eleanor Roosevelt; they did not approach her accessibility to the press.

1906. Gover, C. Jane. *The Positive Image: Women Photographers in Turn of the Century America*. Albany: State University of New York Press, 1988. 191 pp.
    Women photographers of late 1800s and early 1900s in cultural, technological, and historical contexts; they did not represent feminist or alternative viewpoints.

1907. Graham, Sheilah. *The Rest of the Story*. New York: Coward-McCann, 1964. 317 pp.
    Author's life as a Hollywood gossip columnist after the death of her lover, F. Scott Fitzgerald.

1908. Grant, Jane. *Ross, the New Yorker and Me*. New York: Morrow, 1968. 271 pp.
    Some domestic insights about Ross of the *New Yorker*, by a former wife.

1909. Halton, John C., III. "The Women Who Published Newspapers in Colonial and Revolutionary America: Biographies of America's Eleven First Ladies of the Press." Masters thesis, University of Texas -- Austin, 1976.

1910. Hamblin, Dora Jane. *That Was the Life*. New York: Norton, 1977. 320 pp.
    Life on the original *Life* magazine.

1911. Hamilton, Virginia van der Veer. "The Gentlewoman and the Robber Baron." *American Heritage*. April 1970, pp. 78-86.
    Ida Tarbell's career, especially her exposing the monopolistic tendencies of John D. Rockefeller's Standard Oil Trust. Tarbell wrote for *McClure's* and was one of the major "muckrakers" in early twentieth century U.S.

1912. Harrison, Marguerite E. *"There's Always Tomorrow*. New York: Farrar & Rinehart, 1935. 664 pp.
    Baltimore Sun staff member tells the story of her career abroad. By the same author: *Marooned in Moscow: The Story of an American Woman Imprisoned in Russia*, New York: Doran, 1921, 322 pp.

1913. Hatch, Alden. *Ambassador Extraordinary*. New York: Holt, 1955. 254 pp.
    Aspects of Clare Booth Luce's life as a journalist at *Vanity Fair*, the Block and Hearst dailies, and *Life*, and as wife of Publisher Henry Luce.

1914. Hays, Elinor R. *Morning Star: A Biography of Lucy Stone, 1818-1893*. New York: Harcourt, Brace and World, 1961.
    Lucy Stone as suffragist and editor. By the same author: *Those Extraordinary Blackwells: The Story of a Journey to a Better World*, New York: Harcourt, Brace and World, 1967.

1915. Healy, Paul F. *Cissy: The Biography of Eleanor M. 'Cissy' Patterson.* New York: Doubleday, 1966. 421 pp.
    Story of the socialite member of the family that owned Chicago *Tribune*, who, in 1930, joined Hearst-owned daily, Washington *Herald*, and stayed on to become a controversial reporter for nearly two decades.

1916. Henle, Faye. *Au Clare De Luce.* New York: Daye, 1943. 205 pp.
    Clare Luce's literary and political career; chapter on her editorship of *Vanity Fair*.

1917. Henry, Susan. "'Dear Companion, Ever-Ready Co-Worker:' A Woman's Role in a Media Dynasty." *Journalism Quarterly.* Summer/Autumn 1987, pp. 301-312.
    Women's roles in newspaper dynasties; examines the origins of Southern California's Otis-Chandler dynasty in terms of the activities of Eliza A. Otis. Wife of Los Angeles *Times* Publisher Harrison Gray Otis, Eliza wrote for the paper, often offsetting the irritating qualities of her husband, and helping readership.

1918. Henry, Susan. "Exception to the Female Model: Colonial Printer Mary Crouch." *Journalism Quarterly.* Winter 1985, pp. 725-733, 749.
    Mary Crouch, who was unprepared for printing and journalism, entered the profession when her husband died. She differed from other colonial women printers in that she started the Charlestown (S.C.) *Gazette* and Salem (Mass.) *Gazette and General Advertiser*, in 1778 and 1780, respectively.

1919. Henry, Susan. "Margaret Draper: Colonial Printer Who Challenged the Patriots." *Journalism History.* Winter 1974-75, pp. 141-144.
    The nearly two-year battle between Margaret Draper, printer of the *Boston News-Letter*, and the *Boston Gazette*. Draper held strong political opinions and produced a paper more politically partisan than her husband's.

1920. Henry, Susan J. "Private Lives: An Added Dimension for Understanding Journalism History." *Journalism History.* Winter 1979-80, pp. 98-102.
    Some of the ways in which both the new material and the methods used in studying women may affect journalism history. Two approaches to the writing of history about women have dominated: compensatory history and contribution history. Five early women journalists studied to show how their private lives were important to their career achievements.

1921. Henry, Susan. "Reporting 'Deeply and at First Hand': Helen Campbell in the 19th-Century Slums." *Journalism History.* Spring/Summer 1984, pp. 18-25.
    Pioneering work of Helen Campbell, who went into New York's slums and wrote of their inhabitants for the New York *Tribune*. Her work in the 1880s resulted in a series called "Prisoners of Poverty" and "Problems of the Poor." Campbell discussed problems of working women and recommended they organize.

1922. Henry, Susan. "Sarah Goddard: Gentlewoman Printer." *Journalism Quarterly.* Autumn 1982, pp. 23-30.

Colonial woman printer, Sarah Goddard, who took over her son's printshop and prospered from 1765-68. The assumption underlying this article is that "these women did not share the skill in or dedication to printing of the males they replaced."

1923. Henry, Susan. "The Colonial Woman Printer as Prototype: Toward a Model for the Study of Minorities." *Journalism History*. Spring 1976, pp. 20-24.

At least 13 women worked as printers in the U.S. before 1776, yet, historians paid scant attention to them. Content analysis alone allows for drawing limited conclusions, but can be very productive, if combined with an investigation of the individual's life (printers in this case) as revealed through local history.

1924. Henry, Susan. "Work, Widowhood and War: Hannah Bunce Watson, Connecticut Printer." *Connecticut Historical Society Bulletin*. Winter 1983, pp. 24-39.

As printer of *Connecticut Courant* upon death of her husband in 1777.

1925. Hershey, Leonore. "Les Girls." *Dateline*. April 1968.

On Vietnam War female correspondents.

1926. Higgins, Marguerite. *News is a Singular Thing*. New York: Doubleday, 1955. 256 pp.

Pulitzer Prize-winning New York *Herald Tribune* war correspondent, Marguerite Higgins, provided some autobiographical material in these memories of how she started in New York journalism. By the same author and publisher: *War in Korea*, 1961.

1927. Hoekstra, Ellen. "The Pedestal Myth Reinforced: Women's Magazine Fiction, 1900-1920." In *New Dimensions in Popular Culture*, edited by Russel B. Nye, pp. 45-58. Bowling Green, Ohio: Popular Press 1972.

1928. Holtzman, Natalie F., comp. "The Remarkable Speech of Miss Polly Baker." *Journalism History*. Winter 1974-75, p. 116.

Polly Baker's defense in a court case concerning her bastard children, from New York *Weekly Journal* of August 3, 1747, published by Catherine Zenger.

1929. Honey, Maureen. *Creating Rosie the Riveter, Class, Gender and Propaganda*. Amherst: University of Massachusetts Press 1984. 224 pp.

How the strong, competent image of "Rosie the Riveter" became transformed into the childlike, naive, self-alnegating post war woman. In examining why the changed media images of women during the war failed to survive, the author focused on the fiction and advertising of two leading periodicals: the middle-class *Saturday Evening Post* and the working class *True Story*.

1930. Hooper, Leonard J. "Women Printers in America's Colonial Times." *Journalism Educator*. April 1974, pp. 24-27.

Early U.S. women printers who "served successfully as competent managers of print shops left untended by the extended absence or death of the male printer."

1931. Howard, Alice B. *Mary Mapes Dodge of St. Nicholas.* New York: Messner, 1943. 256 pp.
Anecdote-filled story of life of editor of *St. Nicholas Magazine*, Mary Mapes Dodge.

1932. Howard, Jane. "Charlotte Curtis: First Lady of the *New York Times*." *Cosmopolitan.* January 1976, pp. 157-160.

1933. Hubert, Philip G. "Women as Knights of the Quill." In *The Woman's Book. Vol. 1. Occupations for Women*, pp. 55-59. New York: Charles Scribner's Sons, 1894.

1934. Hudak, L.M. *Early American Women Printers and Publishers, 1639-1820.* Metuchen, New Jersey: Scarecrow Press, 1978. 813 pp.

1935. Hudspeth, Robert N. *The Letters of Margaret Fuller: Vol. III: 1842-44.* Ithaca, New York: Cornell University Press, 1984. 272 pp.

1936. Hynes, Terry M. "Magazine Portrayal of Women, 1911-1930." *Journalism Monographs.* May 1981. 56 pp.
Analysis of *Saturday Evening Post, Cosmopolitan, Ladies' Home Journal,* and *Atlantic Monthly* on how they portrayed the emancipation of women. No "marked tendency" by the magazines to "portray the flapper or the politically, economically, and socially liberated woman in the twenties as typical of American women or even as an ideal." A comparison of the 1910s and 1920s found only a "slightly modified" view of the traditional stereotypes. Author's dissertation: "The Portrayal of Women in the Selected Magazines from 1911-1930," University of Wisconsin, Madison, 1975.

1937. Hyser, Sue. "Sarah Hale: A Farm Girl Who Remained a Conservative." *Media History Digest.* Spring/Summer 1988, pp. 36-37.
Sarah J. Hale, a pioneering woman journalist, continued to espouse conservative points of view while editing an important magazine.

1938. Israel, Lee. *Kilgallen.* New York: Delacorte, 1979. 485 pp.
Life of Dorothy Kilgallen, popular writer, with numerous references to her journalist father, James Kilgallen.

1939. Iyer, Pico. "America's First Renaissance Woman: Clare Booth Luce: 1903-1987." *Time.* October 19, 1987, pp. 22-23.
Her many careers, including that of journalist, described at time of her death.

1940. Jakes, John. *Great Women Reporters.* New York: G.P. Putnam's Sons, 1969.
Also by same author and publisher: *Great War Correspondents*, 1967.

1941. James, Bessie Rowland. *Anne Royall's U.S.A.* New Brunswick, New Jersey: Rutgers University Press, 1972. 447 pp.
Facts about nineteenth century journalist, Anne Royall. She was 55 when she started writing; wrote seven travel books, and became a newspaper publisher.

1942. Johnston, Johanna. *Mrs. Satan: The Incredible Saga of Victoria C. Woodhull.* New York: Putnam's, 1967. 319 pp.
Mainly a biography of Woodhull, advocate of free love, U.S. president candidate, orator, and publisher of *Woodhull and Claflin's Weekly* in the 1870s.

1943. Jolliffe, Lee B. and Turner Bond. "Sex-Role Stereotyping in Two Newspapers of 1885: The Influence of the Pioneer Effort." Paper presented at Association for Education in Journalism, Memphis, Tennessee, August 3-6, 1985. 40 pp.
Did the pioneer effort and lifestyle differences affect sex-role stereotypes in the *San Francisco Chronicle* and *New York Times* for 1885?

1944. Jordan, Elizabeth. *Three Rousing Cheers.* New York: Appleton-Century, 1938. 403 pp.
Novelist Elizabeth Jordan's days as newspaperwoman on *New York World* and *Harper's Bazaar*.

1945. *Journalism History.* Winter 1974-1975.
"Women: A Special Issue" includes: "An Editorial: On Ending the Footnote-Syndrome," p. 99; Marion Marzolf, "The Woman Journalist: Colonial Printer to City Desk," pp. 100-107; Anne Mather, "A History of Feminist Periodicals, Part II," pp. 108-111; Maurine Beasley, "Pens and Petticoats: Early Women Washington Correspondents," pp. 112-115; Natalie F. Holtzman, "The Remarkable Speech of Miss Polly Baker," p. 116; Marion Marzolf, "Special 12-Page Supplement: The Literature of Women in Journalism History," pp. 117-128; Ramona R. Rush, "Patterson, Grinstead and Hostetter: Pioneer Journalism Educators," pp. 129-132; Wallace B. Eberhard, "Sarah Porter Hillhouse: Setting the Record Straight," pp. 133-136; Norma Schneider, "Clementina Rind: 'Editor, Daughter, Mother, Wife,'" pp. 137-140; Susan Henry, "Margaret Draper, Colonial Printer Who Challenged the Patriots," pp. 141-144; and "The Woman's History Library," pp. 145-146.

1946. *Journalism History.* Spring 1981.
Special issue on "Journalism History and Women's Experiences" includes: Catherine Covert, "Journalism History and Women's Experience: A Problem in Conceptual Change," pp. 2-6; and Zena Beth McGlashan, "Club 'Ladies' and Working 'Girls': Rheta Childe Dorr and the New York *Evening Post*," pp. 7-13.

1947. Kane, Hartnett T., with Ella Bentley Arthur. *Dear Dorothy Dix: The Story of a Compassionate Woman.* New York: Doubleday, 1952. 314 pp.

The career of Elizabeth Meriwether Gilmer, known as Dorothy Dix, the advice columnist.

1948. Karolevitz, Robert. *Newspapering in the Old West.* Seattle, Washington: Superior Publishing Co., 1965. 191 pp.

"Printers in Petticoats," pp. 173-180, concerning women in frontier journalism of nineteenth century U.S.

1949. Keats, John. *You Might as Well Live: The Life and Times of Dorothy Parker.* New York: Simon & Schuster, 1970. 319 pp.

The world of Dorothy Parker, writer for *New Yorker* and *Vanity Fair,* including the sad aspects.

1950. Kelly, Florence Finch. *Flowing Stream.* New York: Dutton, 1939. 571 pp.

Autobiography of a New York newspaperwoman and critic, with chapters on general journalistic topics.

1951. Kern, Donna Rose Casella. "Sentimental Short Fiction by Women Writers in *Leslie's Popular Monthly.*" *Journal of American Culture.* Spring 1980, pp. 113-127.

1952. Kert, Bernice. *The Hemingway Women.* New York: W.W. Norton, 1983.

Discussion of two of Ernest Hemingway's wives: Martha Gellhorn and Mary Welsh, both World War II correspondents.

1953. Kessler, Lauren. "The Ideas of Woman Suffragists and the Portland *Oregonian.*" *Journalism Quarterly.* Winter 1980, p. 597-605.

All issues of the Portland *Oregonian* examined between June 1, 1869 and October 31, 1905, a period when the battle for woman suffrage in Oregon peaked. Suffrage reported only after it was seen as a legitimate movement by those outside the movement; the woman suffrage association of Oregon was the major source of the ideas, and access was a gradual process. By the same author: "A Siege of the Citadels: Search for a Public Forum for the Ideas of Oregon Woman Suffrage," *Oregon Historical Quarterly,* Summer 1983, pp. 117-149; and "The Ideas of Woman Suffrage in the Mainstream Press," *Oregon Historical Quarterly,* Fall 1983, pp. 257-275.

1954. Kilgore, Margaret. "The Female War Correspondent in Vietnam." *The Quill.* May 1972, pp. 9-12.

Author's experiences as a war correspondent in Vietnam and her determination not to be treated differently than her male colleagues.

1955. Kisner, Arlene, ed. *Woodhull and Claflin's Weekly.* Washington, D.C.: Times Change Press, 1972. 64 pp.

Subtitled, *The Lives and Writings of Notorious Victoria Woodhull and Her Sister Tennessee Claflin. Woodhull and Claflin's Weekly* was published in the 1870s.

1956. Knight, Mary. *On My Own.* New York: Macmillan, 1938. 376 pp.
Author's experiences and career abroad as a United Press reporter.

1957. Kruglak, Theodore E. *The Foreign Correspondents: A Study of the Men and Women Reporting for the American Information Media in Western Europe.* Geneva: Librairie E. Droz, 1955. 163 pp.
Although the book does not contain separate section on women correspondents, it considers them in survey results, which include family backgrounds, training, and other factors.

1958. Kugler, Israel. *From Ladies to Women: The Organized Struggle for Woman's Rights in the Reconstruction Era.* Westport, Connecticut: Greenwood Press, 1987. 221 pp.
"The Woman's Rights Press," documenting the birth of *Revolution, Woman's Journal,* and *Woodhull and Claflin's Weekly* of the 1870s, pp. 157-172.

1959. Kuhn, Irene. *Assigned to Adventure.* London: George G. Harrap and Co., 1938.

1960. Langford, Gerald. *The Richard Harding Davis Years: A Biography of a Mother and Son.* New York: Holt, 1961. 336 pp.
Relationship between journalist/literary figure Richard Harding Davis and his mother, Rebecca Harding Davis, also a writer.

1961. Larsen, Arthur J., ed. *Crusader and Feminist.* St. Paul: Minnesota Historical Society, 1934.
Collection of Jane Grey Swisshelm's correspondence while she was a Washington reporter.

1962. Lenz, Carolyn M. "Newspaperwomen on Metropolitan Dailies: An Historical Survey and Case Study." Masters thesis, University of Wisconsin, 1972.

1963. Lewis, Kathleen Kearny. "Maggie Higgins." Masters thesis, University of Maryland, Baltimore, 1973.

1964. Lewis, Nancy Madison. "A Century of Wisconsin Women Journalists." Masters thesis, University of Wisconsin, 1947.

1965. Lippincott, Sara J. *Greenwood Leaves: A Collection of Sketches and Letters.* Boston: Ticknor, Reed and Fields, 1850. Vol. 2, 1851.
Lippincott's Washington correspondence for the *Saturday Evening Post.* Some autobiographical informaton is in her *Recollections of My Childhood and Other Stories* (1852), *Records of Five Years* (1851), *History of My Pets* (1851), all published by Ticknor, Reed and Fields. Also see: Sarah J. Hale, *"Woman's Record,* New York: Harper, 1853, pp. 624-628, and James Parton et al., *Eminent Women of the Age,* Hartford, Connecticut: Betts, 1869, pp. 147-163.

1966. Liquori, Laura. "Sarah Josepha Hale." *Media History Digest.* Spring/Summer 1988, pp. 32-37.

    Biographic article about Sara J. Hale, the pioneering U.S. woman editor of *Ladies' Magazine*, and later *Godey's Lady's Book*; her many crusades on behalf of women.

1967. List, Karen K. "18th-Century Gender Gap." *Grassroots Editor.* Winter 1984, pp. 6-7.

    Excerpts from the newspapers of Benjamin Franklin Bache and William Cobbett during the latter 18th century on the political coverage of women.

1968. List, Karen K. "Magazine Portrayals of Women's Role in the New Republic." *Journalism History.* Summer 1986, pp. 64-70.

    Messages about women's roles in the new American Republic in three turn-of-the-century magazines. None portrayed women as politically active in any meaningful ways; most messages were that a woman's place was in the home where her primary goal was to be amiable and compliant.

1969. List, Karen K. "The Post-Revolutionary Woman Idealized: Philadelphia Media's 'Republican Mother.'" *Journalism Quarterly.* Spring 1989, pp. 65-75.

    Women's role as represented in periodical literature of the 1790s; they seemed "lacking in their assessment of women's role." When advanced thinking was published, it was quickly contradicted. Publications recognized that women's position in the home gave them power.

1970. List, Karen K. "Two Party Papers' Political Coverage of Women in the New Republic." *Critical Studies in Mass Communication.* June 1985, pp. 152-165.

    The possibility that Philadelphia's leading party newspapers in the latter 1700s contributed to the inclusion of women in politics. Did the *Aurora* and *Porcupine's Gazette* differ in their treatments of women?

1971. *Literature for Ladies. 1830-1930.* Kansas State Agricultural College Bulletin, Industrial Journalism Series 12. Manhattan, Kansas: Kansas State Agricultural College Press, December 1930. 54 pp.

    Historical information on *Godey's Lady's Book*, succeeding women's magazines, and the woman reader of 1830.

1972. Lowell, Joan. *Gal Reporter.* New York: Farrar and Rinehart, 1933. 304 pp.

    One woman's assignment for a metropolitan daily; includes her use of guises to get stories.

1973. Lueck, Therese L. "Text of the Women's Columns in the 'St. Louis Post-Dispatch' of the Early 20th Century as an Example of the 'Reproduction of Mothering.'" Paper presented at Association for Education in Journalism and Mass Communication, Washington, D.C., August 10-13, 1989. 15 pp.

A look at women's pages of the *St. Louis Post-Dispatch*, 1915, 1920, and 1925, to see how they covered women's discourse on functions of daughters in a patriachal structure.

1974. Lutz, Alma. *Created Equal: A Biography of Elizabeth Cady Stanton, 1815-1902.* New York: John Day, 1940.

Suffragist and editor of *Revolution*, Elizabeth Cady Stanton. By the same author: *Susan B. Anthony, Rebel, Crusader, Humanitarian*, Boston: Beacon, 1959. Anthony and Stanton worked together on *Revolution*.

1975. McBride, Sarah E. "Women in the Popular Magazines for Women in America: 1830-1956." Ph.D. dissertation, University of Minnesota, 1966.

The contents of a number of women's magazines analyzed.

1976. McCraken, Elizabeth. "Journalism for the College-Bred Girl." *Independent.* 1912, p. 485.

1977. McGlashan, Zena Beth. "Club 'Ladies' and Working 'Girls': Rheta Childe Dorr and the *New York Evening Post*." *Journalism History.* Spring 1981, pp. 7-11.

The conceptual bridge between "working girls" and "club ladies" named by newswomen, especially Rheta Childe Dorr, whose reporting in the *Post* from 1902 to 1906 was reviewed. Also addressed was Dorr's attitude toward women and their work.

1978. McGlashan, Zena Beth. "Ways of Seeing Women: Challenging Journalism's Past." Paper presented at International Communication Association, Chicago, Illinois, May 22-26, 1986. 17 pp.

Reconstructing of journalism history called for, looking at it from minority (in this case, women's) viewpoints.

1979. McGlashan, Zena Beth. "Women Witness the Russian Revolution: Analyzing Ways of Seeing." *Journalism History.* Summer 1985, pp. 54-61.

The reporting and newspaper treatment of Bessie Beatty (*San Fransisco Bulletin*) and Rheta Childe Dorr (*New York Evening Mail*) as they covered the Russian Revolution of 1917-18. Women's position as journalists discussed. Both wrote books that resulted from their foreign correspondence -- Dorr, *Inside the Russian Revolution*; Beatty, *Red Heart of Russia*. A comparison of the writings of Beatty and Dorr with those of male correspondents showed they were not treated as seriously.

1980. MacKinnon, Janice and Stephen MacKinnon. *Agnes Smedley: The Life and Times of an American Radical.* Berkeley: University of California Press, 1987. 425 pp.

"Maverick" journalist Agnes Smedley, who reported for 20 years from China's cities and countryside; through her writings, the world knew of China's struggles.

1981. Marberry, M.M. *Vicky.* New York: Funk & Wagnalls. 1966. 344 pp.

    The Claflin sisters, Victoria Woodhull and Tennie Claflin, publishers of *Woodhull and Claflin's Weekly* in latter 1800s, stockbrokers, and women liberationists. Woodhull announced her candidacy for president of the U.S., beginning in 1872.

1982. Marken, Edith May. "Women in American Journalism Before 1900." Masters thesis, University of Missouri, Columbia, 1932.

1983. Marschall, Rick and Bill Janocha. "Edwina at 93: Kids and Dogs and an America That We Have Lost." *Nemo.* April 1987, pp. 5-32.

    Interview with 93-year-old Edwina Dumm, a cartoonist for over 70 years; her career with Ohio newspapers, her views on cartooning.

1984. Martin, Ralph G. *Cissy: The Extraordinary Life of Eleanor Medill Patterson.* New York: Simon & Schuster, 1979. 512 pp.

    As editor of the *Washington Herald* and later owner of the *Herald* and *Washington Times.*

1985. Marzolf, Marion. "The Woman Journalist: Colonial Printer to City Desk." *Journalism History.* Winter 1974, pp. 100-107, 146.

    Overview of the history of journalism; part II, which appeared in the Spring 1975 *Journalism History*, took the history from World War II to the present.

1986. Marzolf, Marion. *Up From the Footnote: A History of Women Journalists.* New York: Hastings House, 1977. 310 pp.

    Most media and the women journalists in them; concentration is on the U.S., although author also interviewed in Europe. Historical aspects, as well as background on women's movement.

1987. Marzolf, Marion and Nancy Bock. "The Literature of Women in Journalism History: A Supplement." *Journalism History.* Winter 1976-77, pp. 116-120.

    Supplement to bibliography in the Winter 1974-75 *Journalism History.* Historical and contemporary; categories of "Women Journalists in General Collections," "Black Women in Journalism," "Media Discrimination/Feminist Press," "Foreign Correspondents," "Editors and Publishers and Printers," "Women Reporters," "Washington Correspondents or Press Secretaries," "Women in Broadcasting," "Women's Pages," "Dissertations and Theses," "Film and Photojournalism," "Image," and "Women in Magazines: History and Careers."

1988. Marzolf, Marion, Ramona R. Rush, and Darlene Stern. "The Literature of Women in Journalism History." *Journalism History.* Winter 1974-75, pp. 117-128.

    Topics of "Women Journalists in General Collections," "Women in Journalism: History and Careers," "Black Women in Journalism," "Media Discrimination/Feminist Press," "Foreign Correspondents," "Editors and Publishers," "Washington Correspondents or Press Secretaries," "Women in Broadcasting," "Women's Pages," "Specialists," "Women in Magazines: History and Careers,"

"Magazine Reporters, Editors, Publishers, Careers," "Dissertations and Theses," "Academic Journalism," "Images," "Women's History and Media Archives," "Collected Papers of Women Journalists," and "Selected References."

1989. Masel-Walters, Lynne. "A Burning Cloud by Day: The History and Content of the 'Woman's Journal.'" *Journalism History.* Winter 1976-77.

　　　Feminist newspaper, *Woman's Journal*, over 44 years from its beginnings in 1870. Lucy Stone and Henry Blackwell shouldered most of the editorial duties originally of the paper born of the split in the women's movement.

1990. Masel-Walters, Lynne. "Birth Control as Obscenity: Margaret Sanger and *The Woman Rebel*." Paper presented at Association for Education in Journalism, Seattle, Washington, August 1978.

　　　Sanger's *The Woman Rebel*; contradictions in her career and confusions in the historical record caused by Sanger herself as she fashioned her "image of motivator of and martyr for the birth control movement."

1991. Masel-Walters, Lynne. "For the 'Poor Mute Mothers'? Margaret Sanger and *The Woman Rebel*." *Journalism History.* Spring/Summer 1984, pp. 3-10, 37.

　　　As an organ of the birth control movement.

1992. Masel-Walters, Lynne. "'Their Rights and Nothing More:' A History of *The Revolution, 1868-70*." *Journalism Quarterly.* Summer 1976, pp. 242-251.

　　　The beginnings of women's political journalism in the U.S. traced to the short-lived national newspaper, *The Revolution*, published by Susan B. Anthony and Elizabeth Cady Stanton.

1993. Mather, Anne. "A History of Feminist Periodicals, Part I." *Journalism History.* Autumn 1974, pp. 82-85.

　　　Feminist periodicals from *The Lady's Magazine* of 1792 through the 1950s and 1960s; 560 such periodicals existed between 1968-1973. Author's masters thesis "A History and Analysis of Feminist Periodicals," University of Georgia, 1973.

1994. Mather, Anne. "A History of Feminist Periodicals, Part II." *Journalism History.* Winter 1974-75, pp. 108-111.

　　　U.S. feminist periodicals through the 1960s and 1970s; two catalysts were evident -- the general condition of traditional women's magazines and the proliferation of an underground press. Part 3 was in the Spring 1975 *Journalism History*.

1995. Meaders, Margaret I. "Ida Minerva Tarbell, Journalist and Historian, 1857-1944." Masters thesis, University of Wisconsin, Madison, 1947.

　　　Investigative journalist who wrote about Standard oil, among other topics.

1996. Meyer, Katherine, John Seidler, Timothy Curry, and Adrian Aveni. "Women in July Fourth Cartoons: A 100-Year Look." *Journal of Communication.* Winter 1980, pp. 21-30.

    Political cartoons depicting women in five major dailies over 100 years; the glamour girl and matron have given way to "lifelike women," but subtle cues still show traditional norms in Independence Day cartoons.

1997. Miller, Perry, ed. *Margaret Fuller: American Romantic* Garden City, New York: Doubleday, 1963. 319 pp.

    Collection of the writings and correspondence of Fuller, writer for *Dial* and *New York Tribune*. Among biographies of Fuller are: Joseph J. Deiss, *The Roman Years of Margaret Fuller*, New York: Thomas Y, Crowell, 1969; Mason Wade, *Margaret Fuller: Whetstone of Genius*, New York: Viking, 1940; Katharine Anthony, *Margaret Fuller: A Psychological Biography*, New York: Harcourt, Brace, 1920; Madeline Stern, *The Life Of Margaret Fuller*, New York: Dutton, 1942; Arthur W. Brown, *Margaret Fuller*, New York: Twayne, 1964; Mason Wade, ed., *The Writings of Margaret Fuller*, New York: Viking, 1941; Bell G. Chevigny, ed., *The Woman and the Myth: Margaret Fuller's Life and Writings*, Old Westbury, New York: The Feminist Press, 1977.

1998. Miller, Peter John. "Eighteenth-Century Periodicals for Women. *History of Education Quarterly.* Fall 1971, pp. 279-286.

    The increased rate of literacy among women in the late eighteenth century, which precipitated the development of periodicals for women, demonstrated that increased popular demand often leads to a decline in "taste" and "culture." Although eighteenth century periodicals for women were a product of higher standards of living and increased educational opportunities, they probably cannot be regarded as representing "an advance" in culture or taste.

1999. Miller, William D. *A Harsh and Dreadful Love: Dorothy Day and the Catholic Worker Movement.* New York: Liveright, 1973.

2000. Miner, Ward L. *William Goddard, Newspaperman.* Durham, North Carolina: Duke University Press, 1962.

    Discussion of the roles played in his newspaper life by Mary Katharine Goddard and Sarah Goddard, printers in their own right.

2001. "Miss Mary Winslow: A Camera Heroine of 1895." *Journal of the West.* April 1987, pp. 27-29.

    Reprint of an 1895 *San Fransisco Examiner* article on an early woman traveling photographer.

2002. Mott, Frank Luther. *Journalism in Wartime.* Columbia: University of Missouri, School of Journalism, 1943.

    Includes Genevieve F. Herrick, "The Newspaper Woman Joins Up."

2003. Mrazkova, Daniela. "Legendary Photographer Margaret Bourke-White." *Democratic Journalist.* June 1988, pp. 26-29.

Bourke-White's participation in, and photographing of, many significant events of the twentieth century -- Korean War, liberation of concentration camp prisoners, and Gandhi's compaigns.

2004. Mydans, Carl. "Girl War Correspondent." *Life.* October 2, 1950, pp. 51-56.
Marguerite Higgins.

2005. Nicholson, Eliza Jane. *Pearl Rivers, Publisher of the Picayune.* New Orleans: Tulane University of Louisiana, 1932.

2006. Noble, Iris. *Nellie Bly: First Woman Reporter 1867-1922.* New York: Messner, 1956. 192 pp.
Bly's obsession to compete with male journalists during the yellow journalism and later periods.

2007. "Now is the Time: Men Called it Impossible, But All Woman Recruiting Show Makes Radio History." *New York World Telegram.* April 10, April 11, 1944.

2008. Nunn, Curtis. *Marguerite Clark.* Fort Worth, Texas: Texas Christian University Press, 1981.
Silent film star who made 39 movies, all except one for Famous Players (later Paramount).

2009. O'Connor, Jessie Lloyd, Harvey O'Connor and Susan M. Bowler. *Harvey and Jessie: a Couple of Radicals.* Philadelphia: Temple University Press, 1988. 259 pp.
A type of journalism hard to find today -- independent, radical labor reporting; Jessie became famous writing on the 1929 textile workers' strike of Gastonia, N.C., and on the 1931 Harlan County, Ky., miners' strike.

2010. Oglesby, Catharine. "Women in Journalism." *Ladies' Home Journal.* May 1930, pp. 29, 229.

2011. Oldham, Ellen M. "Early Women Printers of America." *Boston Public Library Quarterly.* July 1958, p. 8.

2012. Overseas Press Club of America. *I Can Tell It Now.* New York: Dutton, 1964.
Information on war correspondent, Dickey Chapelle, and photojournalist Margaret Bourke-White.

2013. Palmquist, Peter E. "Photographers in Petticoats." *Journal of the West.* April 1982, pp. 58-64.
Women photographers of the American West traced to Julia Shannon in 1850, a California midwife and photographer. Other profiles of Abbie E. Cardozo, Mrs. E.W. Withington, Emma Belle Freeman, and Phoebe Train. By the same

author: "California Nineteenth Century Women Photographers," *The Photographic Collector,* Fall 1980, pp. 18-21.

2014. Parker, Cornelia Stratton. *Wanderer's Circle.* Boston, Massachusetts: Houghton Mifflin, 1934. 345 pp.

Author's career as a labor writer and fiction author, recounting her articles for *Ladies' Home Journal, Pictorial Review,* and *Harper's.*

2015. Parsons, Louella O. *The Gay Illiterate.* New York: Doubleday, Doran, 1944. 194 pp.

Autobiography of Hollywood gossip columnist and former newspaper reporter, Louella O. Parsons. Also see her: *Tell It To Louella,* New York: Putnam, 1961, 316 pp.

2016. Patton, Wendy McDonald. "Dorothy Thompson's Way With Hitler." Masters thesis, University of Illinois, Champaign-Urbana, 1965.

2017. "Peggy Hull." *Ladies' Home Journal.* April 1920, p. 83.

Career as a World War I correspondent.

2018. Perry, John W. "Women Leaders of the American Press." *Editor and Publisher.* April 23, 1932, pp. 18-19.

2019. Pichanick, Valerie K. *Harriet Martineau: The Woman and Her Work, 1802-76.* Ann Arbor: University of Michigan Press, 1980. 312 pp.

Her life and writings, including those in periodicals, and on topics such as philosophy, religion, politics, and the rights of women and blacks.

2020. Piehl, Mel. *Breaking Bread. The Catholic Worker and the Origin of Catholic Radicalism in America.* Philadelphia: Temple University Press, 1982.

Dorothy Day and Peter Maurin's Catholic radicalism from the development of their penny paper, *Catholic Worker,* in 1933 to Day's death in 1980. Day pictured as "thoroughly modern and deeply traditional, socially committed yet uninterested in power, devoted to ideas yet absorbed by elemental concerns, ambitious yet unassuming...."

2021. Pierce, Paula. "Frances Benjamin Johnston: Mother of American Photojournalism." *Media History Digest.* Winter 1985, pp. 54-64.

Frances Benjamin Johnston, in the latter nineteenth and early twentieth century, did photographs for various magazines.

2022. Popkin, Zelda. *Open Every Door.* New York: Dutton, 1956. 379 pp.

Author's social causes, reporter days on a Pennsylvania daily, and promotion and public relations work.

2023. Porter, Sarah Harvey. *The Life and Times of Anne Royall.* Cedar Rapids, Iowa: Torch Press, 1909. 298 pp.

Royall's journalistic and political career and troubles with bigoted religionists. Also see: George S. Jackson, *Uncommon Scold*, Boston: Bruce Humphries, 1937.

2024. Potter, Jeffrey. *Men, Money and Magic: The Candid Life Story of Dorothy Schiff.* New York: Coward, McCann & Geohegan, 1976. 352 pp.

Mostly the social life of Dorothy Schiff, but also her career as director, vice president, treasurer, and later, owner and publisher, of the *New York Post*, in the 1930s and 1940s.

2025. Rayne, Mrs. M.L. "Typesettings." and "The Profession of Journalism." In *What Can A Woman Do or Her Position in the Business and Literary World*. Albany, New York: Eagle Publishing Co., 1893, pp. 112-114 and pp. 34-53.

Significance of this work is that it is among the first published about women in media and it is authored by the creator of the first journalism program in the U.S.

2026. Reinholt, Ferdina. "Women in Journalism." *Journalism Quarterly*. November 1925, pp. 38-41.

Author sets out to determine if women were succeeding in journalism and if they possessed any qualities, "inherent in the sex or likely to be developed," which handicapped them. About 10,000 women were members of daily papers' editorial staffs in the mid-1920s. A nationwide survey of women journalists found that women were not accepted in all editorial positions and that the value of a woman's page was doubtful.

2027. Ricciotti, Dominic. "Popular Art in *Godey's Lady's Book*: An Image of the American Woman, 1830-1860." *History of New Hampshire*. 27 (1972), pp. 3-26.

2028. Riley, Sam G., ed. *American Magazine Journalists, 1741-1850.* Dictionary of Literary Biography, Vol. 73. Detroit, Michigan: Gale Research Inc. for Bruccoli Clark Layman, 1988. 430 pp.

Illustrated sketches on women magazine journalists such as Sarah Margaret Fuller (Nora Baker), Caroline H. Gilman (Maurine H. Beasley), Sarah Josepha Hale (Edward Sewell, jr.), Caroline M. Kirkland (Ada Van Gastel), Lydia H. Sigourney (Dorothy A. Bowles), Ann Sophia Stephens (Sam G. Riley), and Frances Wright (Earl L. Conn).

2029. Riley, Sam G., ed. *American Magazine Journalists, 1850-1900.* Dictionary of Literary Biography, Vol. 79. Detroit, Michigan: Gale Research Inc. for Bruccoli Clark Layman, 1989. 387 pp.

Includes illustrated sketches on women magazine journalists such as Louisa May Alcott (Lee Jolliffe), Amelia Bloomer (Linda Steiner), Mary L. Booth (Maurine Beasley), Mary Mapes Dodge (Charles Egleston and Kathleen Keeshen), Jeannette Gilder (W.J. Hug), Josephine St. Pierre Ruffin (Nora Hall), Elizabeth Cady Stanton (Beth M. Waggenspack), Lucy Stone (Lee Jolliffe), and Victoria Woodhull (John A. Lent).

2030. Ringwalt, Jessie E. "Early Female Printers in America." *Printers' Circular.* October 1872, pp. 284-285.

2031. Rittenhouse, Mignon. *The Amazing Nellie Bly.* New York: E.P. Dutton and Co., 1956. 255 pp.
   Biography of Elizabeth Cochrane, "Nelly Bly," the "sob sister" of Pulitzer's *New York World*, who circled the world in fewer than 80 days and performed other stunts to make and report news.

2032. Robb, Inez. *Don't Just Stand There!* New York: McKay, 1962. 309 pp.
   Author's experiences as a syndicated newspaper columnist.

2033. Roberts, Nancy L. "Journalism for Justice: Dorothy Day and the *Catholic Worker.*" *Journalism History.* Spring-Summer 1983, pp. 2-9.
   Dorothy Day's long stay as editor of *Catholic Worker* and her advocacy of uniting Catholicism with a concern for social justice. From author's larger study: *Dorothy Day and the "Catholic Worker,"* Albany: State University of New York, 1984.

2034. Roff, Sandra Shoick. "A Feminine Expression: Ladies' Periodicals in the New York Historical Society Collection." *Journalism History.* Autumn-Winter 1982, pp. 92-99.
   The New York Historical Society's strong, representative collection of nineteenth century "ladies' magazines."

2035. Roosevelt, Eleanor. Rochelle Chadakoff, ed. *Eleanor Roosevelt's My Day: Her Acclaimed Columns, 1936-1945.* New York: Pharos Books, 1989. 402 pp.
   Background and commentary on a sample of the more than 3,000 "My Day" columns.

2036. Ross, Ishbel. *Ladies of the Press. The Story of Women in Journalism by an Insider.* New York: Harper and Brothers, 1936. 622 pp.
   The story of women in the journalism of the nineteenth and twentieth centuries with vignettes of journalists such as Nelly Bly, Anne Royall, Victoria Woodhull, Kate Field, Fanny Fern, Jenny June, Winifred Black, Dorothy Dix, Nixola Greeley-Smith, Rheta Childe Dorr, Ellen B. Simmons, and many more. Treats a variety of subjects, such as the crusaders, war correspondents, woman's pages, society pages, prison reporters, radio broadcasters, tabloid reporters, Washington correspondents, foreign correspondents, columnists, reviewers. Hones in on women at particular newspapers, such as *New York World, New York Times, New York American* and regions such as Boston, Washington, Philadelphia, Buffalo, Detroit, Chicago, Middle West, Denver, California, and the South.

2037. Rosten, Leo C. *The Washington Correspondents.* New York: Harcourt, Brace and Co., 1937.
   Some women correspondents included.

2038. Sanders, Marion K. *Dorothy Thompson: A Legend in Her Time.* Boston, Massachusetts: Houghton Mifflin, 1973. 428 pp.
Career of this magazine journalist from her own recollections.

2039. Sanger, Margaret. *An Autobiography.* New York: Norton, 1938. 504 pp.
The threats to her right to press freedom as she fought for birth control through her newspaper, *Woman Rebel.*

2040. Sanger, Margaret. "Letter from Margaret Sanger." *Mother Earth.* April 1915, pp. 75-78.
Press freedom and her paper's campaign for birth control.

2041. Schilpp, Madelon Golden and Sharon M. Murphy. *Great Women of the Press.* Carbondale, Illinois: Southern Illinois University Press, 1983. 248 pp.
Eighteen women communicators considered to be of international significance: Elizabeth Timothy, Mary Katherine Goddard, Anne Newport Royall, Sarah Josepha Hale, Margaret Fuller, Cornelia Walter, Jane G. Swisshelm, Jane C. Croly, Eliza Nicholson, Ida M. Tarbell, Elizabeth Gilmer, Ida Wells-Bennett, Elizabeth Cochrane Seaman, Winifred Black Bonfils, Rheda Childe Dorr, Dorothy Thompson, Margaret Bourke-White, and Marguerite Higgins.

2042. Schneider, Norma. "Clementina Rind: Editor, Daughter, Mother, Wife." *Journalism History.* Winter 1974-75, pp. 137-140.
Role placed on Clementina Rind, editor of *Virginia Gazette* and head of a large family during a time of tremendous political upheaval in colonial America.

2043. Schofield, Ann. "Rebel Girls and Union Maids: The Woman Question in the Journals of the AFL and IWW, 1905-1920." *Feminist Studies.* Summer 1983, pp. 335-358.
The differences and likenesses between the American Federation of Labor and Industrial Workers of the World approaches to women's issues of 1905-1920: suffrage, female sexuality issues such as birth control, prostitution, and sexual exploitation, union rights for women, and the nature of womanhood. Many union journals analyzed: the *Butcher Workman, Shoe Workers' Journal, Ladies' Garment Worker, Weekly Bulletin, Solidarity, Industrial Worker, Official Journal* of the Amalgamated Meat Cutters and Butcher Workmen, *Cigar Makers' Official Journal, American Federationist, Weekly Bulletin of the Clothing Trades,* and *Glove Workers Monthly Bulletin.*

2044. Shaddeg, Stephen. *Clare Booth Luce.* New York: Simon & Schuster, 1971. 313 pp.
Life and career of journalist and diplomat Clare Booth Luce.

2045. Sheed, Wilfrid. *Clare Booth Luce.* New York: Dutton, 1982. 183 pp.
Luce's career and her life as a wife of *Time* publisher Henry Luce.

2046. Sheehy, Gail. "The Life of the Most Powerful Woman in New York." *New York*. December 10, 1973, pp. 51-69.
  New York Post publisher Dorothy Schiff.

2047. Shi, David. "Edward Bok and the Simple Life." *American Heritage*. December 1984, pp. 100-109.
  Bok's editorship of *Ladies' Home Journal* and his crusades at the turn of the twentieth century, exhorting women to seek peace of mind and body through simplicity.

2048. Shippee, Lester B. "Jane Grey Swisshelm, Agitator." *Mississippi Valley Historical Review*. December 1920, pp. 206-227.
  Nineteenth century Washington correspondent.

2049. Simpson, Carmen McCormack. "Courage and Ingenuity Carried Betty Wason to Europe's Battle Fronts." *Christian Science Monitor*. December 30, 1941.

2050. Smith, C. Zoe. "Great Women in Photojournalism." *News Photographer*. Part I: January 1985, pp. 20-21; Part II: February 1985, pp. 26-29; Part III: April 1985, pp. 22-24.
  The historical basis of women in photojournalism; most were "ambitious, dedicated and self-sacrificing".

2051. Smith, Henry Ladd. "The Beauteous Jennie June: Pioneer Woman Journalist." *Journalism Quarterly*. Spring 1963, pp. 169-174.
  Jane Cunningham Croly, known as Jennie June, worked for 40 years on metropolitan newspapers and magazines after the mid-nineteenth century. Her first work appeared in the New York *Herald* in 1855. Croly was prominent in founding the General Federation of Women's Clubs. See also: Mildred White Wells, *Unity in Diversity*, New York: General Federation of Women's Clubs, 1953; J.C. Croly, *History of the Woman's Club Movement in America*, New York: H.G. Allen and Co., 1898.

2052. Smith, Liz. "The Gossip Columnist." *Gannett Center Journal*. Summer 1989, pp. 83-87.
  The power Hollywood gossip columnists Louella Parsons and Hedda Hopper wielded and the author's encounters with them.

2053. Snyder, Martha (McCoy). "'Hapless Russian': A Revolution." Masters thesis, Pennsylvania State University, 1980.
  Critical picture of Rheta Dorr's role in covering the Russian Revolution.

2054. Snyder, Robert E. "Margaret Bourke-White and the Communist Witch Hunt." *Journal of American Studies*. April 1985, pp. 5-25.
  The controversy of the 1950s over Bourke-White's access to the Strategic Air Command while doing a photo story for *Life* magazine.

2055. Sochen, June. *Movers and Shakers.* New York: Quadrangle/New York Times Book Co., 1973.
Rheta C. Dorr, Freda Kirchway, and Martha Gellhorn included.

2056. Spensley, Sarah A. "Pioneer Women Newspaper Writers in the United States." Bachelor's thesis, University of Wisconsin, 1918.
One of the earliest academic works on the subject.

2057. Stanton, Elizabeth Cady, Susan B. Anthony, and Matilda J. Gage, eds. *History of Woman Suffrage.* Rochester, New York: Susan B. Anthony, 1886. 3 vols.
Information on Stanton and Anthony and their suffrage newspaper, *Revolution.* Also see: Theodore Stanton and Harriot Stanton Blatch, eds., *Elizabeth Cady Stanton as Revealed by Her Letters, Diary and Reminisces*, New York: Harper, 1922. 2 vols.

2058. Stearns, Bertha M. "Before *Godey's*." *American Literature.* 2 (1930), pp. 248-255.

2059. Stein, M.L. *Under Fire: The Story of American War Correspondents.* New York: Julian Messner, 1968.
Mention of women war correspondents in chapter entitled, "Ladies on the Front Line."

2060. Steinberg, Salme Harju. *Reformer in the Marketplace.* Baton Rouge: Louisiana State University Press, 1979. 193 pp.
Newly-discovered papers and records used to illuminate the 30-year reign of Edward W. Bok as editor of *Ladies' Home Journal.*

2061. Steiner, Linda. "Finding Community in Nineteenth Century Suffrage Periodicals." *American Journalism.* Summer 1983, pp. 1-16.
Newspapers and journals produced by suffragists helped women "locate themselves in an exciting and entirely plausible community." Includes history, "symbolic identification with the suffrage community," role of suffrage papers, "loyalty and sisterhood," and symbolic cleavages. Taken from author's Ph.D. dissertation, "The Woman's Suffrage Press, 1850-1900: A Cultural Analysis," University of Illinois, 1969.

2062. Sterling, Dorothy. *Black Foremothers: Three Lives.* Old Westbury, New York: The Feminist Press, 1988. 224 pp.
Among three is journalist Ida B. Wells.

2063. Stern, Madeleine B. *Purple Passage: The Life Story of Mrs. Frank Leslie.* Norman, Oklahoma: University of Oklahoma Press, 1953. 281 pp.
Biography of Miriam Follin, wife of Frank Leslie, engraver-publisher; the rise and fall of the Leslie magazine empire and her roles.

2064. Sterns, Bertha M. "Reform Periodicals and Female Reformers." *American Historical Review.* July 1932, pp. 689-693.
Washington correspondent Jane Grey Swisshelm included.

2065. Swisshelm, Jane Grey. *Half a Century.* Second Ed. New York: Source Book Press, 1970. 363 pp. Originally published in 1880 by Jensen, McClurg of Chicago.
Very little on the journalism of this early nineteenth century woman correspondent; the 80 short chapters are important because this is one of the first books by a U.S. woman journalist.

2066. Tarbell, Ida M. *All in the Day's Work Recollections: 1857-1938.* New York, 1939. 412 pp.
Ida Tarbell's role as a muckraking journalist in the early twentieth century, especially her investigations of Standard Oil.

2067. Tarry, Ellen. *The Third Door.* New York: McKay, 1955. 304 pp.
Career of Ellen Tarry of *Birmingham Truth* and *Catholic World*; the prejudices this black woman journalist experienced.

2068. Taylor, Nancy J. "Women in Illustrations from *Ladies' Home Journal* (1890-1899), *Vanity Fair* (1920-1929)." Masters thesis, University of Illinois, Chicago, 1975.

2069. "The Sower." *Press Woman* June 1976. 44 pp.
The history of the National Federation of Press Women from its 1935 conception by Helen Miller Malloch. Vignettes of Malloch and other pioneers and histories of state chapters.

2070. "The Spectator." *Outlook.* August 17, 1901, pp. 905-906.
Early discussion of women's pages in U.S. dailies.

2071. *The University of Missouri Bulletin.* Journalism Series No. 30, September 10, 1924.
Thematic issue on "Women and the Newspaper" with addresses and discussions by women editors, feature writers, advertising personnel, and women readers. Includes: Sara L. Lockwood, "Introduction," pp. 5-8; Mrs. Marie Weekes, "Journalism as a Career for Women," pp. 9-14; Mrs. Florence Riddick Boys, "The Woman's Page," pp. 15-18; Mrs. W.K. James and Mrs. Elias R. Michael, "What Women Wish From the Newspaper," pp. 19-28; Mrs. Faith G. Sharratt, "Opportunities for Women in Advertising," p. 29.

2072. Thomas, Samuel J. "Catholic Journalists and the Ideal Woman in Late-Victorian America." *International Journal of Women's Studies.* January/February 1981, pp. 89-100.
Catholic press comments of the 1880s and 1890s on the "woman question."

2073. Thompson, Dorothy. "On Women Correspondents and Other New Ideas." *The Nation.* January 6, 1926, pp. 11-12.

2074. Thorp, Margaret F. *Female Persuasion: Six Strong-Minded Women.* New Haven, Connecticut: Yale University Press, 1949.

    Jane Grey Swisshelm reporter who opened Congress press gallery to women, and Sara J. Lippincott of *Saturday Evening Post* and *New York Times* included.

2075. Tien, Joseleyne Slade. "Portrait of a China Reporter: Anna Louise Strong and the Chinese Revolution, 1925-1958." *Asian Profile.* April 1986, pp. 105-117.

    Dean of China reporters from 1921 to 1949 and supporter of Mao Zedong, Strong's name and works regularly appeared on the lists of groups such as the McCarran Subcommittee on Internal Security. She was charged with spying and jailed in the Soviet Union, and later released by Khrushchev. Strong did not achieve the prominence of people such as Edgar Snow, but she outranked them in her diligence and perseverance to get the other side of the China question reported.

2076. Tompkins, Mary E. *Ida M. Tarbell.* New York: Twayne, 1974. 182 pp.

    Her muckraking career, especially her exposé of Standard Oil.

2077. Tumanis, Sue. "The (News)Hen Coops." *The Quill.* January 1971, pp. 21-22.

    A brief history of women journalists from Ann Franklin in 1732.

2078. Underwood, Agness. *Newspaperwoman.* New York: Harper, 1949. 297 pp.

    Author's career on Los Angeles dailies, later as city editor of the *Herald-Express.*

2079. Wade, Mason. *Margaret Fuller.* New York: Viking, 1940. 304 pp.

    Brief account of Fuller's journalistic roles with the *Dial* and *New York Tribune.*

2080. Wagner, Lilya. *Women War Correspondents of World War II.* Westport, Connecticut: Greenwood Press, 1989. 174 pp.

    Interviews with 18 main correspondents on their experiences as World War II correspondents; working conditions, types of stories, and accomplishments. Commonly faced by all were antagonism of certain military officials and jealousy and fear from male colleagues. Featured are: Ann Stringer, Iris Carpenter, Ruth Cowan, Tania Long Daniell, Kathleen McLaughlin, Bonnie Wiley, Lyn Crost, Helen Kirkpatrick, Catherine Coyne, Alice-Leone Moats, Sigrid Schultz, Inez Robb, Sonia Tomara, Martha Gellhorn, Shelley Mydans, Mary Welsh, Virginia Lee Warren, and Lael Laird Wertenbaker.

2081. Wald, Carol. *Myth America: Picturing Women 1865-1945.* New York: Pantheon Books, 1975.

2082. Walker, Alice, ed. *I Love Myself When I Am Laughing...And Then Again When I Am Looking Mean and Impressive. A Zora Neale Hurston Reader.* Old Westbury, New York: The Feminist Press, 1979. 320 pp.
   A collection of the fiction, journalism, and autobiographical sketches of Zora Neale Hurston, intellectual impetus to a generation of Black women writers; anthology of Hurston's work, 1926-1950.

2083. Walker, Stanley. *City Editor.* New York: Stokes, 1934.
   Chapter on women journalists, "A Gallery of Angels."

2084. Waller, Judith Cary. *Radio: The Fifth Estate.* Boston: Mifflin, 1946.
   Early radio history, with substantial section on women in radio and radio journalism, by a radio pioneer.

2085. Waller-Zuckerman, Mary Ellen. "Vera Connolly: Progressive Journalist." *Journalism History.* Summer/Autumn 1988, pp. 80-88.
   Crusading journalist who wrote on Indian affairs, drug abuse, juvenile delinquency, and prison and sweatshop conditions, for *New York Sun*, *World Outlook*, and *McCall's*. She also was a founding editor of *Woman's Day* and woman's page editor of the *Christian Science Monitor*. Connolly's writings provided "evidence of the continuation of a strand of the Progressive movement."

2086. Watson, Lorna. "*The New York Recorder* As a Women's Newspaper, 1891-1894." Masters thesis, University of Wisconsin, Madison, 1939.

2087. Weinberg, Arthur M. and Lila Weinberg, eds. *The Muckrakers: The Era in Journalism That Moved America to Reform -- The Most Significant Magazine Articles of 1902-1912.* New York: Simon and Schuster, 1961. 449 pp.
   Among the 28 articles were those of Ida Tarbell.

2088. Weiss, Margaret R. "The Formidable Frances B. Johnson." *Saturday Review.* August 23, 1976, pp. 51-53.

2089. Wells, Ida B. *Crusade for Justice: The Autobiography of Ida B. Wells.* Edited by Alfreda M. Duster. Chicago Illinois: University of Chicago Press, 1970. 434 pp.
   Activities of Ida Wells, black journalist who wrote against lynching and other mistreatment of blacks; edited by her daughter from an uncompleted autobiography.

2090. Wharton, Don. "Dorothy Thompson." *Scribner's Magazine.* March 1937, pp. 9-14.

2091. Willard, Frances E. "Rationale of Woman's Opportunity in Journalism." *The Independent.* September 16, 1886, p. 4.

2092. Willard, Frances E. and Mary A. Livermore. *American Women: Fifteen Hundred Biographies with over 1,400 Portraits.* Revised ed. New York: Mast, Crowell and Kirkpatrick, 1897. 2 vols.
Some women involved in journalism included.

2093. Winfield, Betty Houchin. "From Washington to Truman: Press Coverage and Images of the 'First Lady.'" Paper presented at Association for Education and Mass Communication, Portland, Oregon, July 2-5, 1988.
The connections between the press coverage of first ladies mainly through the *National Intelligencer* and *New York Times.*

2094. Wingrove, Kendall. "How Three Frontier Newspapers in Michigan Depicted Women." Paper presented at Association for Education in Journalism, Boston, Massachusetts, August 9-13, 1980.
Three Michigan frontier newspapers in 1849-50 and how they depicted women; women's role in courtship and marriage was extremely well covered, women were depicted as hard-working wives and mothers, and famous women merited some coverage.

2095. Winter, Ella. *And Not To Yield, an Autobiography.* New York: Harcourt, Brace & World, 1963. 308 pp.
Self-story of Ella Winter, remembered as the wife of Lincoln Steffens; her books, travels to the USSR, and friendships with world leaders.

2096. Withington, Mrs. E.W. "How a Woman Makes Landscape Photographs." *The Philadelphia Photographer.* 1876, p. 358.

2097. "Women as Printers - A Compositors' Training School." *New York Daily Tribune.* February 6, 1869, p. 5.

2098. Woodward, Helen. *The Lady Persuaders.* New York: Ivan Obolensky, Inc., 1960. 190 pp.
Fifteen chapter, illustrated history of women's magazines written in journalistic style; includes *Godey's Lady's Book, Delineator, Woman's Day, Family Circle, Ladies' Home Journal, Woman's Home Companion, Good Housekeeping, McCall's, Parents' Magazine, Pictorial Review, Mademoiselle, Glamour, Vogue, Charm, Harper's Bazaar, House and Garden,* and *House Beautiful.*

2099. Yeck, Joanne Louise. "The Woman's Film at Warner Brothers, 1935-1950." Ph.D. dissertation, University of Southern California, 1982.

2100. "You Can't Take It With You -- But..." *Forbes.* April 15, 1975, pp. 56-67.
Publisher Helen Copley.

2101. Zang, Barbara. "Society Girl, Sob Sister, Journalism Educator: Mary Paxton Keeley, the First Woman Graduate of the School of Journalism at the University of Missouri." Paper presented at Association for Education in Journalism and Mass Communication, San Antonio, Texas, August 1987. 18 pp.

    Primary research materials left by Mary Paxton Keeley examined; the personal and professional life of the first woman graduate of one of the first journalism schools.

Images of Women

2102. Banta, M. *Imaging American Women: Idea and Ideals in Cultural History.* New York: Columbia University Press, 1987. 844 pp.

    Includes advertising, media, and photography stereotypes.

2103. Bate, Barbara. "Nonsexist Language Use in Transition." *Journal of Communication.* Winter 1978, pp. 139-149.

    Of various communication channels at a U.S. university, the best inducement for changing sexist language habits was a female who encouraged such change.

2104. Bell, Inge Powell. "The Double Standard." *Trans-Action.* November-December 1970, pp. 75-80.

    Media give different age definitions for the sexes: men are considered attractive at middle age, but women must strive to appear younger.

2105. Beuf, Ann. "Doctor, Lawyer, Household Drudge." *Journal of Communication.* Spring 1974, pp. 142-145.

    Interviews with 63 children to determine if the women's movement changed American children's ideas about sex roles. Regardless of the amount of attention the women's movement attracted, children still learned about a role structure which was sex-typed.

2106. Blakely, Mary Kay. "Is One Woman's Sexuality Another Woman's Pornography?" *Ms.* April 1985, pp. 37-38.

    A wide gap exists among those who discuss pornography and what to do with it. Includes sidebars of "A Conflict of Sexual Rights" and "Will Feminist Publications Be Endangered?"

2107. Bond, Jean Carey. "The Media Image of Black Women." *Freedomways.* First Quarter 1975, pp. 34-37.

    The strength and "soulfulness" of black women characters in some TV shows ("Good Times") keeps black men down.

2108. Browne, Pat, ed. *Heroines of Popular Culture.* Bowling Green, Ohio: Bowling Green State University Popular Press, 1987. 184 pp.

    East Lynne's Isabel Vane, Adela Quested of *A Passage to India*, May Welland in *The Age of Innocence*, and Scarlett O'Hara. Soap opera heroines, Black rock music, and Stephen King's modern American heroine bring portrayal up to present.

North America

2109. Busby, Linda Jean. "Mass Media Research Needs: A Media Target for Feminists." *University of Michigan Papers in Women's Studies.* June 1974, pp. 9-29.

    Content analyses of women's images in the media are too limiting and suggests other techniques such as control, media, audience analyses.

2110. Busby, Linda Jean. "Sex-role Research in the Mass Media." *Journal of Communication.* August 1975, pp. 107-131.

    Research on sex-role portrayal in various mass media, broken into content and effects categories. Little research has been done on effects of media on the extension of traditional sex roles.

2111. Butler, Matilda, and William Paisley. *Women and the Mass Media.* New York: Human Sciences Press, 1980. 432 pp.

    The subtitled *A Source Book for Research and Action* is divided into sections of antecedents to the present issues; sexism and media content; institutional sexism and media content; institutional sexism in the media, sexism and media audiences, and indications for research and action.

2112. "Checklist for Entertainment Programming and Advertising." *Media Report to Women.* April 1, 1976, p. 2. Part of *Guidelines for the Treatment of Women in the Media*, National Commission on the Observance of International Women's Year, U.S. Department of State, February 27, 1976.

2113. Cooper, Anne M. and Lucinda Davenport. "Media Coverage of International Women's Decade: Feminism and Conflict." Paper presented at International Communication Association, Chicago, Illinois, May 22-26, 1986. 34 pp.

    Changes in *New York Times* and *Washington Post* treatment of women's issues and feminism from 1975 to 1985, the UN-designated "Women's Decade."

2114. Cooper, Anne M. and Lucinda Davenport. "Newspaper Coverage of International Women's Decade: Feminism and Conflict." *Journal of Communication Inquiry.* Winter 1987, pp. 108-113.

    Significant changes in the coverage of three women's conferences over a decade; latter heavily covered.

2115. Cooper, V.W. "Women in Popular Music: A Quantitative Analysis of Feminine Images over Time." *Sex Roles.* November 1985, pp. 499-506.

    Lyrics of 1,164 popular songs about women that appeared in 12 monthly issues of *Song Hits Magazine*, 1946, 1956, 1966, and 1976.

2116. Cowie, Elizabeth. "The Popular Film as a Progressive Text - A Discussion of 'Coma.'" *M/F.* No. 3, 1979, pp. 59-79.

    Women's images in film and advertising, noting how advertisers have used the "liberated" woman as parts of campaigns.

2117. DeCrow, Karen. *The Young Woman's Guide to Liberation: Alternatives to a Half-Life While the Choice Is Still Yours.* Indianapolis, Indiana: Bobbs-Merrill, 1971.
Sexism on TV and women's magazines are among the topics.

2118. Devore, Mary Ann and James D. Good. "Examining Materials for Sex Fairness: An Instructional Unit." Columbia: University of Missouri, Instructional Materials Lab, 1981. 40 pp.
Compiled for use by Missouri vocational educators to aid students and adults to determine sexism in instructional materials. The same lab brought out: James D. Good and Mary Ann Devore, "Creative Ways to Supplement Biased Materials: An Instructional Unit in Sex Equity," 1981, 27 pp.

2119. Dorenkamp, Angela G., John F. McClymer, Mary M. Moynihan, and Arlene C. Vadum. *Images of Women in American Popular Culture.* San Diego: Harcourt Brace Jovanovich, 1985.

2120. Doyle, Nancy. "Woman's Changing Place: A Look at Sexism." Public Affairs Pamphlet No. 509. New York: Public Affairs Committee, Inc., 1974. 28 pp.
A number of factors, including the mass media, limit women's development and opportunities.

2121. Elwood, Virginia. "A Preliminary Bibliography: Images of Women in the Media, 1971-76." *Journalism History.* Winter 1976-77, pp. 121-123.
Categories used are: "Advertising-General," "Media-General," "Advertising-Magazine," "Advertising-Television," "Film," "Magazine," "Misc.-Public Relations," "Misc.-Music," "Newspaper," and "Television."

2122. Endres, Kathleen L. "Sex Role Standards in Popular Music." *Journal of Popular Culture.* Summer 1984, pp. 9-18.
In periods of 1960, 1970, 1980, males continued to predominate in popular music lyrics and songs were usually written in the first person singular.

2123. Estep, Rhoda. "Women's Roles in Crime as Depicted by Television and Newspapers." *Journal of Popular Culture.* Winter 1982, pp. 151-156.
The most common type of criminal suspect role enacted by females on television and in newspapers was that of murderer. Actions of female murder suspects were often linked to their romantic involvements with men; many other female suspects are shown supporting a man in a leading role.

2124. Fox, Harold W. and Stanley R. Renas. "Stereotypes of Women in the Media and Their Impact on Women's Careers." *Human Resource Management.* Spring 1977, pp. 28-31.
Monitoring of TV and magazine advertising to determine vocational castings. Stereotypes of men and women were reinforced as were the limitations placed upon women in society. Men were almost always the off-camera speakers and outnumbered women 2.5 to 1 as on-camera speakers. One-half of all men and one-fifth of all women were cast in work situations.

2125. Frankel, Judith and Norman Mirsky. "Changing Stereotype of Jewish Women in the Popular Culture." Paper presented at the Popular Culture Association, St. Louis, Missouri, March 20-22, 1975. 10 pp.

    Says media stereotype of the Jewish woman is either of a controlling, guilt-ridden, food-oriented individual or an exotic, seductive person torn between family devotion and pursuit of romantic goals.

2126. Franzone, Dorothy Lawrence. "The Image of Black Women in Films and Television: From 'Mammy' to America's 'No. 1 Mom.'" Paper presented to Conference of Society for Intercultural Education and Training, Amsterdam, The Netherlands, 1986.

    The stereotyped images of black women is "substantively" different from those of white women. Presents black women from the days of silent films to the U.S. TV series, "Cosby Show," of the 1980s.

2127. Friedman, Leslie J. *Sex Role Stereotyping in the Mass Media: An Annotated Bibliography.* New York: Garland Press, 1977.

    Only 12 of the 1,018 annotated items defend sexist portrayals of women. Deals with advertising, children's media, films, print media, and popular culture of comics, science fiction, music, and pornography.

2128. Higgs, Catriona T. and Karen H. Weiller. "The Aggressive Male Versus the Passive Female: An Analysis of Differentials in Role Portrayal." Paper presented at American Alliance For Health, Physical Education, Recreation and Dance, Las Vegas, Nevada, April 13-17, 1987. 18 pp.

    The role of women as portrayed in the mass media.

2129. Hill, Janellen. "Women and Mass Media Course Outline." Paper presented at Western Speech Association, Portland, Oregon, February 16-20, 1980. 22 pp.

    An outline for upper level or graduate course for examining media effects on sex-role stereotyping of women.

2130. Holz, Josephine R. and Charles R. Wright. "Sociology of Mass Communications." *Annual Review of Sociology.* 5 (1979), pp. 193-217.

    Types of research, including work done on media depiction of women.

2131. Hooks, Bell. *Ain't I a Woman: Black Women and Feminism.* Boston: South End Press, 1981.

    Some attention to the negative images of Black women in mass media, especially television.

2132. Hunt, Mary E. "Eve's Legacy: Burden of Blame." *Media and Values.* Winter 1989, pp. 19-20.

    Eve and the rest of the idealized and vilified women of myth and history live on in imaginations of media creators. Ideas on what to do.

2133. Janus, Noreene. "Research and Sex-Roles in the Mass Media: Toward a Critical Approach." *Insurgent Sociologist.* Summer 1977, pp. 19-32.

Images research usually is done by liberal U.S. feminists and assumes sexism can be abolished within the same economic system that created it.

2134. Jewell, Karen S. Warren. "An Analysis of the Visual Development of a Stereotype: The Media's Portrayal of Mammy and Aunt Jemima as Symbols of Black Womanhood." Ph.D. dissertation, Ohio State University, 1976.

2135. Joint Economic Committee, Washington, D.C. *American Women Workers in a Full Employment Economy. A Compendium of Papers Submitted to the Subcommittee on Economic Growth and Stabilization of the Joint Economic Committee, Congress of the United States, 95th Congress, 1st Session, September 15, 1977.* Washington, D.C.: U.S. Government Printing Office, 1977. 304 pp.

Includes paper, "The Impact of Mass-Media Stereotypes upon the Full Employment of Women."

2136. *Journal of Communication.* Spring 1974.

Symposium on "Women: Nine Reports on Role, Image, and Message" includes: Helen H. Franzwa, "Working Women in Fact and Fiction," pp. 104-109; Alice E. Courtney and Thomas W. Whipple, "Women in TV Commercials," pp. 110-118; Nancy Tedesco, "Patterns of Prime Time," pp. 119-125; Helen White Streicher, "The Girls in the Cartoons," pp. 125-129; Mildred Downing, "Heroine of the Daytime Serial," pp. 130-137; Joseph Turow, "Advising and Ordering: Daytime, Prime Time," pp. 138-141; Ann Beuf, "Doctor, Lawyer, Household Drudge," pp. 142-145; Barbara Herrnstein Smith, "Women Artists: Some Muted Notes," pp. 146-149; and Kay Mills, "Fighting Sexism On the Airwaves," pp. 150-156.

2137. Kacerguis, Mary Ann and Gerald R. Adams. "Implications of Sex Typed Child Rearing Practices, Toys, and Mass Media Materials in Restricting Occupational Choices of Women." *Family Coordinator.* July 1979, pp. 369-375.

Review of child-rearing practices, toy materials, mass media literature and TV shows found presence of gender stereotyping.

2138. Kahn, Kim Fridkin and Edie N. Goldenberg. "Evaluation of Male and Female U.S. Senate Candidates: An Investigation of Media Influence." Paper presented at American Political Science Association, Washington, D.C., September 1-4, 1988. 33 pp.

Despite recent gains, women win political office much less frequently than men; one major reason is that media do not give them the same response as provided males.

2139. King, Mae C. "The Politics of Sexual Stereotypes." *Black Scholar.* March-April 1973, pp. 12-23.

Media and women's liberation movement accused of giving too little attention to abuses of black women.

2140. Lavin, Maud. "Welfare, Women and the Media." *Extra.* March/April 1988, p. 5.
When the welfare system is being restructured, media tend to reflect negative stereotypes of women.

2141. Lewis, Jill and Gloria I. Joseph. *Common Differences: Conflicts in Black and White Feminist Perspectives.* Garden City, New York: Anchor Books, 1981.
Images of Black women in media; they must become white in dress and pose before they can have a man.

2142. Luckett, Perry D. "Military Women in Contemporary Film, Television, and Media." *Minerva: Quarterly Report on Women and the Military.* Summer 1989, pp. 1-15.

2143. McCormack, Thelma. "The 'Wets' and the 'Drys': Binary Images of Women and Alcohol in Popular Culture." *Journal of Popular Culture.* 9:1 (1981), pp. 43-64.
Binary images of women and alcohol in popular culture; whether women are drinkers or non-drinkers, they fall below men on attributes of credibility, judgment, and sharing of authority. Analysis of 16 films and 19 novels.

2144. *Media and Values.* Fall 1985.
Includes "Media's New Mood: Sexual Violence," "Where Do You Draw the Line?" "Television Targets Women as Victims," "Erotic Violence Stretches Free Speech," "Time for Research Is Past," and "Resources Offer Tools To Counter Media Sexploitation."

2145. *Media Monitor,* New York. "Images of Women: Curriculum Resources for Teachers and Students." Winter 1978. 22 pp.
Catalogue of media designated to highlight the role of women outside the home.

2146. Melvin, Frances. "Women, AIDS and the Media." *Refractory Girl.* May 1986, pp. 18-29.
The media depiction of the connection between female prostitution and the spread of the AIDS virus; the portrayal is shallow and misses key issues.

2147. Miller, Casey, and Kate Swift. *The Handbook of Nonsexist Writing.* New York: Lippincott & Crowell, 1980. 134 pp. Second edition, 1988, 180 pp.
Guide for writers, editors, and speakers in the use of non-sexist writing, taking up various problems, such as the use of "man" as a generic term. By the same authors: *Women: New Language and New Times,* New York: Anchor Books/Doubleday, 1976.

2148. Noschese, Christine. "The Ethnic Image in the Media: Ethnic Men, and Particularly, Ethnic Women Suffer from Typecasting -- When Cast at All." *Civil Rights Digest.* Fall 1978, pp. 28-34.

Television programs and commercials and films distorted, romanticized, and stereotyped the values, concerns, and lifestyles of ethnic minorities.

2149. Orwant, Jack and Muriel G. Cantor. "How Sex Stereotyping Affects Perceptions of News Preferences." *Journalism Quarterly.* Spring 1977, pp. 99-108.

Among college students, both male and female ratings of audience interest in various types of news reflected sex-role stereotypes.

2150. President's Commission on the Status of Women. *Report on Four Consultations.* Washington, D.C.: President's Commission on the Status of Women, 1963. 43 pp.

Includes discussions of 29 media representatives who discussed the portrayal of women by the mass media.

2151. Quiñones, Wendy B., et al. "Kissing 'The Girls' Good-bye." *Columbia Journalism Review.* May/June 1975, pp. 28-33.

Group of journalists and professor discussed 11 guidelines set down at Stanford University on how to describe a woman in media.

2152. Racism/Sexism Resource Center. "Fact Sheets on Institutional Sexism." New York: Racism/Sexism Resource Center, 1976. 16 pp.

Statistics and statements about the comparative status of men and women in high positions in publishing, films, and broadcasting.

2153. Rivers, Caryl. "Women, Myth, and the Media." In *When Information Counts,* edited by Bernard Rubin, pp. 3-11. Lexington, Massachusetts: Lexington Books, 1985.

Myths about women generated by media, such as superwoman and the notion that the world would go awry if women had political power.

2154. Rodriguez, M. "Do Blacks and Hispanics Evaluate Assertive Male and Female Characters Differently?" *Howard Journal of Communication.* Spring 1988, pp. 101-107.

No significant relationship between racial/ethnic identification and speaker/style and gender.

2155. Salutin, Rick. "The Culture Vulture: Fulfordism and the Media Backlash against the Women's Movement." *This Magazine.* May-June 1979, pp. 29-31.

The backlash against the women's movement was reflected in various ways in mass media. Robert Fulford of *Saturday Night* contended the battle was won at a time when the wage gap between men and women increased nearly threefold (1965-77). The author showed why Fulford's argument was dangerous.

2156. Scott, Joseph E. "Sex References in the Mass Media." *Journal of Sex Research.* 9:3 (1973), pp. 196-209.

2157. Seger, Linda. "How To Evaluate Media Images of Women." *Media and Values.* Winter 1989, p. 21.

Changes occurred concerning TV images of women; "women have yet to be all they can be onscreen, however. Stereotypes are shaded more subtly, but they are still there. Female leads must still be brighter, smarter, funnier and often better looking than their male counterparts."

2158. Seiter, Ellen. "Stereotypes and the Media: A Re-evaluation." *Journal of Communication.* Spring 1986, pp. 14-26.

The failure to account for the evaluative, historical, and descriptive aspects of stereotypes has led to a use of the concept as a "dirty word"; by reevaluating and clarifying the term, the way that media, particularly television, is studied can be improved.

2159. Shoemaker, Pamela J. "Media Treatment of Deviant Political Groups." *Journalism Quarterly.* Spring 1984, pp. 66-75.

Includes League of Women Voters and National Organization for Women.

2160. Silver, Rosalind. "The Many Faces of Media Women." *Media and Values.* Winter 1989, pp. 2-4.

Creators, consumers, and critics discuss the problem of developing believable female characters in film and television.

2161. Silverstein, Brett, et al. "The Role of the Mass Media in Promoting a Thin Standard of Bodily Attractiveness for Women." *Sex Roles.* May 1986, pp. 519-532.

Four studies demonstrated that the standard of attractiveness portrayed on TV and in magazines was slimmer for women than for men; the recent standard for women portrayed in magazines and in movies was slimmer than before.

2162. Smith, Linda Lazier. "Media Images and Ideal Body Shapes: A Perspective on Women with Emphasis on Anorexics." Paper presented at Association for Education in Journalism and Mass Communication, Memphis, Tennessee, August 3-6, 1985. 47 pp.

Media (especially television) influences upon women who strive so hard to be thin that they become anorexic.

2163. Sochen, June. *Enduring Values: Women in Popular Culture.* New York: Praeger, 1987. 173 pp.

Twentieth century treatments of women in media such as film, television, and music.

2164. Spillman, D.M. and C. Everington. "Somatypes Revisited: Have the Media Changed Our Perception of the Female Body Image?" *Psychological Reports.* June 1989, pp. 887-890.

Media's impact on changing images of female body types.

2165. Stewart, Lea P. and Stella Ting-Toomey, eds. *Communication, Gender, and Sex Roles in Diverse Interaction Contexts.* Norwood, New Jersey: Ablex, 1987. 272 pp.

Conceptual and methodological approaches in the study of communication, gender, and sex roles relative to interpersonal, organizational, cultural, and applied interaction contexts. Specific topics included gender differences and loneliness and trait argumentativeness, divorce mediation, stereotypes of stepparents in children's literature, perceptions of women as managers, women's communication in the workplace, gender stereotyping in the comic strips, and others.

2166. Strang, Jessica. *Working Women: An Appealing Look at the Appalling Uses and Abuses of the Feminine Form.* New York: Harry N. Abrams, 1984.

2167. Tarnova, Elizabeth J. "Effects of Sexist Language on the Status and Self-Concept of Women." Paper presented at Association for Education in Journalism and Mass Communication, Portland, Oregon, July 2-5, 1988. 25 pp.

The effects of sexist language on the status and self-concept of women, especially in media.

2168. Tuchman, Gaye. "The Symbolic Annihilation of Women by the Mass Media." In *Hearth and Home: Images of Women in the Mass Media,* edited by Gaye Tuchman, Arlene Kaplan Daniels, and James Benet, pp. 3-38. New York: Oxford University Press, 1978.

Critical of an anti-female ideology of mass media, calling it "the symbolic annihilation of women in the media"; such an ideology devalues women's role and promotes the patriarchy that keeps women invisible.

2169. Tuchman, Gaye. "Women's Depiction by the Mass Media." *Signs.* Spring 1979, pp. 528-542.

Much literature reviewed after asserting, "So angry at the blatant sexism of the mass media as to be blinded, students of the media's presentation of women have been more politically sophisticated than theoretically sound. In part, their research has been crippled by dependence upon the academic study of mass communications, a field hardly known for its intellectual vigor, but one whose problems must be understood in order to see why research on women and the media is theoretically stalled."

2170. Tuchman, Gaye, Arlene Kaplan Daniels, and James Benet, eds. *Hearth and Home: Images of Women in the Mass Media.* New York: Oxford University Press, 1978. 319 pp.

A collection of quantitative analyses (mainly content analysis) of magazines, newspapers, and television presented at a 1975 conference on women in the news media, held in San Francisco. Includes: George Gerbner, "The Dynamics of Cultural Resistance"; Judith Lemon, "Women on Prime-Time Television"; Muriel S. Cantor, "Where Are the Women in Public Broadcasting?" E. Barbara Phillips, "Magazine Heroines: Is *Ms* Just Another Member of the Family Circle?" Marjorie Ferguson, "Imagery and Ideology: The Cover Photographs of Traditional Women's Magazines"; Gladys Engel Lang, "The Most Admired Woman: Image-Making in the News"; Harvey L. Moloteh, "The News of Women and the Work of Men"; Cynthia Fuchs Epstein, "The Women's Movement and the Women's Pages"; G. William Domhoff, "The Women's Page as a Window on the Ruling Class"; James Benet, "Will Media Treatment of Women Improve?"

2171. Tugusheva, M. "Diary of a Girl: Dnevnik Devochki." *Literaturnaya Gazeta.* July 1974, p. 15.
Review of Patricia Dizenzo's novel, *The American Girl*, dealing with the deindividualization effect of mass media on women's liberation.

2172. Ward, Nancy. "Feminism and Censorship." *Language Arts.* May 1976, pp. 536-537.
Texts have a duty to give material that offers a wide variety of optional roles and behavior to both girls and boys.

2173. Ware, M.C. and M.F. Stuck. "Sex-role Messages vis-à-vis Microcomputer Use: A Look at the Pictures." *Sex Roles.* 13:3/4 (1985), pp. 205-214.
Pictorial representation of men, women, boys, and girls in popular computer magazines; women were underrepresented in the illustrations and were not often shown as managers, experts, or repair technicians.

2174. Warner, Marina. *Monuments and Maidens: The Allegory of the Female Form.* New York: Atheneum, 1985.
Western culture as seen through public arts -- status, advertising, and painting, the presence of female symbolism did not mean appreciation for women. TV shows, comic books, and ads used as examples.

2175. Weibel, Kathryn. *Mirror, Mirror: Images of Women Reflected in Popular Culture.* New York: Anchor Books, 1977.
Images since the nineteenth century of women in television, fiction, women's magazines, movies, and magazine ads and fashion; popular culture consistently portrayed them as "housewifely, passive, wholesome, and pretty."

Advertising, Public Relations

2176. Barak, B. and B. Stern. "Women's Age in Advertising: An Examination of Two Consumer Age Profiles." *Journal of Advertising Research.* December 1985-January 1986, pp. 38-47.
Conclusion was that advertisers should listen more carefully to the new ways consumers defined age.

2177. Bardwick, Judith M. and Suzanne I. Schumann. "Portrait of American Men and Women in TV Commercials." *Psychology.* November 1967, pp. 18-23.
Television commercials stereotype women as obsessed with cleanliness and elimination of bad odors in the home, diets, and their appearance; males as knowledgeable, dominating, and sexy outside the home.

2178. Belkaoui, Ahmed and Janice M. Belkaoui. "A Comparative Analysis of the Roles Portrayed by Women in Print Advertisements: 1958, 1970, 1972." *Journal of Marketing Research*. May 1976, pp. 168-172.

Analysis of the portrayal of U.S. women in eight general interest magazines in 1958, 1970, and 1972 shows that the ads did not advance much in their portrayals of women -- they did not keep up with the variety of roles women play.

2179. Benze, James G. and Eugene R. Declercq. "Content of Television Political Spot Ads for Female Candidates." *Journalism Quarterly*. Summer 1985, pp. 278-283.

Study of 113 30-second commercials of 23 male and 23 female candidates from 29 states between 1980 and 1983; 22 advertisements from female statewide candidates did not use a negative approach.

2180. Bretl, David J. and Joanne Cantor. "The Portrayal of Men and Women in U.S. Television Commercials: A Recent Content Analysis and Trends Over 15 Years." *Sex Roles*. May 1987, pp. 595-609.

Men and women were portrayed differently during previous 15 years, but "many of the gaps seem to be narrowing."

2181. Brown, Mary Ellen. "The Dialectic of the Feminine: Melodrama and Commodity in the Ferraro Pepsi Commercial." *Communication*. 9:3/4, 1987, pp. 335-354.

Former U.S. vice presidential candidate Geraldine Ferraro's commercial for Pepsi Cola contained several codes that intersect: her political position, the mother-daughter relationship and its importance to women, and "the advertising conventions which segment and fetishize parts of the female body."

2182. Butler, Matilda, ed. "Image of Women in Advertisements: A Preliminary Study of Avenues of Change." Palo Alto, California: Stanford University, Institute for Communication Research, 1975. 40 pp.

The image of women in advertising and ways of improvement.

2183. Cantor, Muriel G. "Comparison of Tasks and Roles of Males and Females in Commercials Aired by WRC-TV During a Composite Week." In *Women in the Wasteland Fight Back: A Report on the Image of Women Portrayed in TV Programming*, pp. 12-51. Washington, D.C.: NOW, National Capitol Area Chapter, 1972.

2184. Chestnut, Robert W., Charles C. Lachance, and Amy Lubitz. "The 'Decorative' Female Model: Sexual Stimuli and the Recognition of Advertisements." *Journal of Advertising*. April 1977, pp. 11-14.

An increasing prevalence of "decorative" functionless female models were found in print advertising. Models facilitated recognition of model-related information but did little to increase the recognition of brand names.

2185. Courtney, Alice E. and Sarah W. Lockeretz. "A Woman's Place: An Analysis of the Roles Portrayed by Women in Magazine Advertisements." *Journal of Marketing Research.* February 1971, pp. 92-95.

Identification of women's stereotypes in *Life, Look, Newsweek, U.S. News and World Report, Time, New Yorker* and *Saturday Review.*

2186. Courtney, Alice E. and Thomas W. Whipple. *Sex Stereotyping in Advertising.* Lexington, Massachusetts: D.C. Heath, 1983. 239 pp.

A decade of content analyses concerning images of people on television showed that sex stereotyping continued: women were depicted in their homes and either trying to attract a man or to serve him as a housewife and mother.

2187. Culley, James D. and Rex Bennett. "Selling Woman, Selling Blacks." *Journal of Communication.* Autumn 1976, pp. 160-174.

Updating of benchmark studies of women and blacks in mass media advertising shows that negative stereotyping still held: women were overrepresented in ads for cosmetics; underrepresented in commericals for cars, home appliances, banking, and insurance; and shown mainly as housewives/mothers.

2188. Debevec, K. and E. Iyer. "Self-Referencing as a Mediator of the Effectiveness of Sex-role Portrayals in Advertising." *Psychology and Marketing.* Spring 1988, pp. 71-84.

In radio advertising, self-referencing mediated the effect of various product and spokesperson combinations on respondents' attitudes toward the product and its message.

2189. Debevec, K. and E. Iyer. "The Influence of Spokespersons in Altering Products Gender Image: Implications for Advertising Effectiveness." *Journal of Advertising.* 15:4 (1986), pp. 12-20.

Spokespersons' gender proved effective promotional cue in influencing gender images of products.

2190. Dominick, Joseph and Gail E. Rauch. "The Image of Women in Network TV Commercials." *Journal of Broadcasting.* Summer 1973, pp. 259-265.

Females in TV commercials were overrepresented in cosmetic and personal hygiene advertisements and underrepresented in ads for cars, trucks, and related items. Seventy-five percent of the ads showed women in the bathroom or kitchen. Women were placed in decorative (sex objects) or useful (housewife and mother) roles.

2191. Dooley, Janet L. "Effects of the Feminist Movement on Magazine Advertisements." Masters thesis, University of Tennessee, 1975.

2192. Doolittle, John and Robert. "Children's TV Ad Content: 1974." *Journal of Broadcasting.* 19:2 (1975), pp. 131-142.

Male voices predominated in 91 percent of 49 Saturday morning TV commercials; overall, males were shown in authority roles.

2193. England, Paula, Alice Kuhn, and Teresa Gardner. "The Ages of Men and Women in Magazine Advertisements." *Journalism Quarterly*. Autumn 1981, pp. 468-471.

Content analysis of five magazines from 1960 to 1979 showed youthfulness of those portrayed in advertisements; women usually were younger than men.

2194. England, Paula and Teresa Gardner. "Sex Differentiation in Magazine Advertisements: A Content Analysis Using Log-Linear Modeling." In *Current Issues and Research in Advertising 1983*, edited by J.H. Leigh and C.R. Martin, jr., pp. 253-268. Ann Arbor, Michigan: University of Michigan, Graduate School of Business Administration, 1983.

Portrayals of male and female roles in 2,000 advertisements in five U.S. magazines of various specialties revealed much sex-typing.

2195. Feldstein, Jerome H. and Sandra Feldstein. "Sex Differences on Televised Toy Commercials." *Sex Roles*. June 1982, pp. 581-587.

In televised toy commercials during the Christmas 1977 and 1978 advertising seasons, more boys than girls were portrayed (significantly so in 1978) and girls appeared in more passive roles.

2196. Ferrante, Carol, Andrew M. Haynes, and Sarah M. Kinsley. "Image of Women in Television Advertising." *Journal of Broadcasting and Electronic Media*. Spring 1988, pp. 231-237.

Whether the manner in which women are portrayed in TV ads had undergone significant change during the previous 15 years. Women were portrayed in a wider range of occupations and appeared more frequently in settings outside the home.

2197. Ferrante, Karlene. "Making Sense of Sex Stereotypes in Advertising." In *Media Reader*, edited by Shirley Biagi, pp. 239-242. Belmont, California: Wadsworth, 1989.

Questions on advertising and gender addressed by looking at two assumptions made about advertising -- the mirror assumption (advertising reflects society) and the gender assumption (advertising speaks a male voice to female consumers).

2198. Foote, Cone and Belding Marketing Information Service. "A Report on the Way Women View Their Portrayal in Today's Television and Magazine Advertising." New York: Foote, Cone and Belding Marketing Information Service, November 1972.

2199. Forte, Frances L., Daria Mandato, and Wesley A. Kayson. "Effect of Sex of Subject on Recall of Gender-Stereotyped Magazine Advertisements." *Psychological Reports*. 49, 1981, pp. 619-622.

Females recall more details of magazine advertisements, while males recall more details from male-related ads.

2200. Geis, F.L., Virginia Brown, Joyce Jennings (Walstedt), and Natalie Porter. "TV Commercials as Achievement Scripts for Women." *Sex-Roles.* April 1984, pp. 513-525.

Sex stereotypes, "implicitly enacted, but never explicitly articulated, in TV commercials may inhibit women's achievement aspirations." An experimental design was used on 180 men and women. Also see: Florence L. Geis, Virginia Brown, Joyce Jennings, and Denise Corrado-Taylor, "Sex vs. Status in Sex-Associated Stereotypes," *Sex Roles.* 11 (1984), pp. 771-785.

2201. Goffman, Erving. *Gender Advertisements.* Cambridge, Massachusetts: Harvard University Press, 1979. 84 pp.

Data on sexism in U.S. advertisements, detailing picture frame styles, relative size in advertising, the feminine touch, the family in ads, and ritualization of subordination. Over 500 illustrations from newspaper and magazine ads to make the point.

2202. Gornick, Vivian and Barbara Moran, eds. *Women in Sexist Society: Studies in Power and Powerlessness.* New York: Basic Books, 1971.

Includes Lucy Komisar, "The Image of Women in Advertising."

2203. Havens, Beverly and Ingrid Swenson. "Imagery Associated with Menstruation in Advertising Targeted to Adolescent Women." *Adolescence.* Spring 1988, pp. 89-97.

The imagery in advertisements in *Seventeen* magazine for sanitary and menstrual relief products. Menstruation is depicted as a "hygienic crisis" managed by the proper product giving protection and peace of mind.

2204. Hawkins, Joellen W. and Cynthia S. Aber. "The Content of Advertisements in Medical Journals: Distorting the Image of Women." *Women and Health.* 14:2 (1988), pp. 43-59.

Medical journals provide negative and outdated images of women.

2205. Hennessee, J.A. and J. Nicholson. "NOW Says TV Commercials Insult Women." *New York Times Magazine.* May 28, 1972, p. 12+.

T.R. Haskett replies in June 18, 1972 issue (p. 4).

2206. Hiemstra, Roger, Maureen Goodman, Mary Ann Middlemiss, Richard Vosco, and Nancy Ziegler. "How Older Persons Are Portrayed in Television Advertising: Implications for Educators." *Educational Gerontology.* 9 (1983), pp. 111-122.

Less than one percent of characters in 136 network commercials were women more than 59 years old.

2207. *Journal of Communication.* Autumn 1976.

Thematic symposium on "Equality in Advertising" includes: James D. Culley and Rex Bennett, "Selling Women, Selling Blacks," pp. 160-174; Charlotte G. O'Kelly and Linda Edwards Bloomquist, "Women and Blacks on TV," pp. 179-184; Alison Poe, "Active Women in Ads," pp. 185-192; Suzanne Pingree, Robert

288 Women and Mass Communications

Parker Hawkins, Matilda Butler, and William Paisley, "A Scale for Sexism," pp. 193-200.

2208. Kaite, Berkeley. "The Body and Femininity in Feminine Hygiene Advertising." In *Culture & Communication*, edited by Sari Thomas, pp. 159-167. Norwood, New Jersey: Ablex, 1987.

Through the study of changes in women's hygiene products from the 1920s to the 1950s, found that the oppression of women is structural and ideological in complexity.

2209. Kerin, Roger A., William J. Lundstrom, and Donald Sciglimpaglia. "Women in Advertisements: Retrospect and Prospect." *Journal of Advertising*. March 1979, pp. 37-42.

A review of research on the use and reaction to women in advertisements during the preceding decade with intent of projecting future trends. Predicted that the 1980s would exhibit a larger proportion of ads featuring women in "work-related settings in parity occupations with men."

2210. Kern-Foxworth, Marilyn. "Ads Pose Dilemma for Black Women." *Media and Values*. Winter 1989, pp. 18-19.

How Quaker Oats changed its image of the "Aunt Jemima" symbol; called for other advertisers to change their strategies concerning women of color.

2211. Key, Wilson B. *Media Sexploitation*. Englewood Cliffs, New Jersey: Prentice-Hall, 1976. 234 pp.

The American public is constantly media manipulated by subliminal messages. A discussion of women and topics such as body hair, fashion, jewelry, odor, self-image and advertising, and sex objects. See his earlier: *Subliminal Seduction: Ad Media's Manipulation of a Not So Innocent America*, Englewood Cliffs, N.J.: Prentice-Hall, 1973.

2212. Kilbourne, Jean. "Beauty: and the Beast of Advertising." *Media and Values*. Winter 1989, pp. 8-10.

The creator of *Still Killing Us Softly* discussed advertising's portrayal of women (as housewives or sex objects), claiming that the ideal body type portrayed is unattainable by most women, that images created are artificial, and that young people learn a great deal about sexual attitudes from media, particularly from advertising.

2213. Kilbourne, William E. "Female Stereotyping in Advertising: An Experiment on Male-Female Perceptions of Leadership." *Journalism Quarterly*. Spring 1990, pp. 25-31.

Experiment portraying women in several advertisements in two situations -- stereotyped and non-stereotyped; advice to advertisers, avoid stereotyping.

2214. King, Ellie. "Sex Bias in Psychoactive Drug Advertisements." *Psychiatry*. May 1980, pp. 129-137.

Impact of drug advertisements upon sex-role stereotypes affecting physicians' prescription patterns. Psychoactive drug ads in the *American Journal of Psychiatry* over a 17-year period found that females were portrayed as "anxious, neurotic, distorted or ridiculous."

2215. Knill, Barbara J., Marina A. Pesch, George Pursey, Paul Gilpin, and Richard M. Perloff. "Still Typecast After All These Years? Sex Role Portrayals in Television Advertising." *International Journal of Women's Studies*. November-December 1981, pp. 497-506.

   Whether sex portrayals changed since the mid-1970s and whether differences existed between afternoon and evening TV advertising. Men still dominated as voiceovers but women were given more authority, especially in the afternoon.

2216. Komisar, Lucy. "The Image of Woman in Advertising." In *Woman in Sexist Society*, edited by Vivian Gornik and Barbara K. Moran, pp. 304-317. New York: New American Library, 1971.

2217. Leigh, T.W., T.L. Reichenbach, and A.J. Rethans. "Responses to Women's Role Portrayals in Advertisements: A Segmentation Approach." In *Proceedings of the 1985 Conference of the American Academy of Advertising*, edited by N. Stephens, pp. 46-51. Provo, Utah: American Academy of Advertising, 1985.

   Laboratory experiment which manipulated role orientation and portrayal.

2218. Leigh, T.W., A.J. Rethans, and T.R. Whitney. "Role Portrayals of Women in Advertising: Cognitive Responses and Advertising Effectiveness." *Journal of Advertising Research*. October-November 1987, pp. 54-63.

   Women's role portrayals strongly influenced ad effectiveness.

2219. Lundstrom, William J. and Donald Sciglimpaglia. "Sex Role Portrayals in Advertising." *Journal of Marketing*. July 1977, pp. 72-79.

   Whether women and men are critical of how they are shown in ads and how this affects their attitudes toward products.

2220. Lysonski, S. "Female and Male Portrayals in Magazine Advertisements: A Re-examination." *Akron Business and Economic Review*. Summer 1983, pp. 45-50.

   Ads in 22 different men's, women's, and general interest magazines studied; role portrayals changed somewhat between 1974-75 and 1979-80. Stereotypes persisted but women appeared less frequently as dependent upon men and more often as career-oriented.

2221. McArthur, Leslie Zebrowitz and Beth Gabrielle Resko. "The Portrayal of Men and Women in American TV Commercials." *Journal of Social Psychology*. 97:2 (1975), pp. 209-220.

   In 199 commercials televised by the networks on a day in 1971, 43 percent of the 299 main characters were women. Men were usually portrayed as authorities, women as product users.

2222. McCauley, C., K. Thangavely, and P. Rozin. "Sex Stereotyping of Occupations in Relation to Television Representations and Census Facts." *Basic and Applied Social Psychology.* July-September 1988, pp. 197-212.

Two studies (one where people were asked their perceptions of 16 variables; the other where they were asked the amount of their TV viewing and then the 16 variables); very little evidence that television casting contributes to brand judgments.

2223. McIntyre, P., et al. "Effects of Sex and Attitudes Toward Women on the Processing of Television Commercials." *Psychology and Marketing.* 3:3 (1986), pp. 181-190.

"Liberal" viewers objected that women were shown as sex objects and as stupid in TV ads.

2224. Macklin, M.C. and R.H. Kolbe. "Sex Role Stereotyping in Children's Advertising: Current and Past Trends." *Journal of Advertising.* 13:2 (1984), pp. 34-42.

Sixty-four network TV commercials studied on three Saturday mornings; male-oriented ads outnumbered female-oriented ads.

2225. McRee, Christine, Billie F. Corder, and Thomas Haizlip. "Psychiatrists' Responses to Sexual Bias in Pharmaceutical Advertising." *American Journal of Psychiatry.* November 1974, pp. 1273-1274.

Forty-five percent of a sample of 30 psychiatrists perceived pharmaceutical ads in the *American Journal of Psychiatry* as showing "sexual bias that might negatively influence physicians' perceptions of women."

2226. Masse, Michele A. and Karen Rosenblum. "Male and Female Created They Them: The Depiction of Gender in the Advertising of Traditional Women's and Men's Magazines." *Women's Studies International Forum.* 11:2 (1988), pp. 127-144.

Ads in six traditional women's and men's magazines represented a "sex-segregated" world; little real connection existed between the sexes when both were shown.

2227. Masters, Lynn. "Bodies Not Minds." *Women's Studies Newsletter.* Summer 1980, pp. 10-11.

Advertising in the 1960s used a sexually exploitive image of women.

2228. Melton, G.W. and G.L. Fowler, jr. "Female Roles in Radio Advertising." *Journalism Quarterly.* Spring 1987, pp. 145-149.

Female presence in radio commercials was virtually nonexistent -- seven percent of slots.

2229. National Advertising Review Board. *Advertising and Women: A Report of Advertising Portraying or Directed to Women.* New York: National Advertising Review Board, 1975.

Changes recommended in ways women are shown in advertising.

2230. Nelson, Joyce. "Capitalism, Despair and the Media Machine." *This Magazine is About Schools.* February 1985, pp. 16-17.
Disturbed at sexist ads and at the truism that all media deliver people to the advertisers.

2231. O'Donnell, William and Karen J. O'Donnell. "Update: Sex-Role Messages in TV Commercials." *Journal of Communication.* Winter 1978, pp. 156-158.
Traditional stereotypes remained unchanged in TV commercials throughout the 1970s.

2232. Osborn, Suzanne. "Gender Depictions in Television Advertisements: 1988." Memphis, Tennessee: Author, 1988.
Commercials of 1988 compared with studies of the 1970s.

2233. "P and G Stockholders Rebuff Attempt To Change Role of Women in TV Commercials." *Broadcasting.* October 20, 1975, pp. 40-41.

2234. Peterson, Robin T. "Bulimia and Anorexia in Advertising Content." *Journal of Business Ethics.* August 1987, pp. 495-504.
College students' self-image and ideal self-image related to eating disorders and to advertising/marketing practices.

2235. Pingree, Suzanne. "The Effects of Nonsexist Television Commercials and Perceptions of Reality on Children's Attitudes about Women." *Psychology of Women Quarterly.* Spring 1978, pp. 262-277.
Television can teach sex-typed attitudes was tested, using third and eighth graders; children's perceptions of reality were successfully manipulated.

2236. Pingree, Suzanne, Robert Parker Hawkins, Matilda Butler, and William Paisley. "A Scale of Sexism." *Journal of Communication.* Autumn 1976, pp. 193-200.
A majority of the ads portraying women chosen from *Playboy, Time, Newsweek,* and *Ms.* "puts them down" or "keeps them in their place."

2237. Poe, Alison. "Active Women in Ads." *Journal of Communication.* Autumn 1976, pp. 185-192.
There were more numerous and varied magazine ads portraying women in sports in 1928 than in 1956 and 1972.

2238. Prather, Jane and Linda S. Fidell. "Sex Differences in the Content and Style of Medical Advertisements." *Social Science and Medicine.* January 1975, pp. 23-26.
Drug ads from four leading medical journals showed that ads for psychoactive drugs pictured women while those for non-psychoactive drugs showed men.

2239. Rak, D.S. and L.M. McMullen. "Sex-role Stereotyping in Television Commercials: A Verbal Response Mode and Content Analysis." *Canadian Journal of Behavioral Science*. January 1987, pp. 25-39.

Assessment of the degree of sex-role stereotyping in network television commercials using content analysis and Stiles' Taxonomy of Verbal Response Modes.

2240. Reid, Leonard N. and Lawrence C. Soley. "Another Look at the 'Decorative' Female Model: The Recognition of Visual and Verbal Ad Components." In *Current Issues and Research in Advertising 1981*, edited by J.H. Leigh and C.R. Martin, jr., pp. 123-133. Ann Arbor: University of Michigan, Graduate School of Business Administration, 1981.

The presence of women as "decorative" models improves the recognition of advertisements; visual, but not verbal, recognition was significantly affected when female "decorative" models were included in ads.

2241. Reid, Leonard N. and Lawrence C. Soley. "Decorative Models and the Readership of Magazine Ads." *Journal of Advertising Research*. April-May 1983, pp. 27-34.

Are there male readership differences in magazine advertising for sexually-relevant products where decorative female and male models are shown in different settings?

2242. Riffe, Daniel Helene Goldson, Kelly Saxton, and Yang-Chou Yu. "Females and Minorities in TV Ads in 1987 Saturday Children's Programs." *Journalism Quarterly*. Spring 1989, pp. 129-136.

An update of research on females and minorities in children's television advertisements. The number of women and minorities in the three networks' ads was greater, but white males still dominated.

2243. Ruble, Diane N., Terry Balaban, and Joel Cooper. "Gender Constancy and the Effects of Sex-Typed Televised Toy Commercials." *Child Development*. 52 (1981), pp. 667-673.

Only the high gender-constant children were differentially affected by sex-role information under different commercial conditions.

2244. Saunders, Carole S. and Bette A. Stead. "Women's Adoption of a Business Uniform: A Content Analysis of Magazine Advertisements." *Sex Roles*. August 1986, pp. 197-205.

Over 2,500 advertisements surveyed in general interest and business magazines in 1963, 1973, and 1983; businesswomen increasingly were shown attired in the skirted suit.

2245. Scheibe, Cyndy. "Sex Roles in TV Commercials." *Journal of Advertising Research*. 19:1 (1979), pp. 23-27.

An analysis of 6,262 TV commercials broadcast in 1975-76 found that the number of occupations in which female characters were shown had increased, although the number was still only one-half of the total for males; some females were shown in traditional male jobs while the reverse did not hold, and the activities of males and females did not change (even employed females were portrayed as doing the housework).

2246. Schneider, Kenneth C. "Sex Roles in Television Commercials: New Dimensions for Comparisons." *Akron Business and Economic Review.* Fall 1978, pp. 20-24.

2247. Schneider, Kenneth C. and Sharon Barich Schneider. "Trends in Sex Roles in Television Commercials." *Journal of Marketing.* Summer 1979, pp. 79-84.

Trends in role portrayals of men and women characters in television commercials between 1971 and 1976; marketers and society had begun to accept the changing role of women as there was a more equal utilization of male and female characters in both indoor and outdoor settings.

2248. Schuetz, Stephen and Joyce N. Sprafkin. "Portrayal of Prosocial and Aggressive Behaviors in Children's TV Commercials." *Journal of Broadcasting.* 23:1 (1979), pp. 33-40.

In 242 commercials on network and independent TV, females made up 37 percent of all human characters, males performed far more prosocial acts than females, and all aggressive acts were those of males.

2249. Schuetz, Stephen and Joyce N. Sprafkin. "Spot Messages Appearing within Saturday Morning Television Programs." In *Hearth and Home: Images of Women in the Mass Media,* edited by Gaye Tuchman, Arlene Kaplan Daniels, and James Benet, pp. 69-77. New York: Oxford University Press, 1978.

Spot messages analyzed from same data base of the previous entry.

2250. Sciglimpaglia, D., W.J. Lundstrom, and D.T. Vanier. "Psychographic Segmentation by Feminine Role Orientation." In *Current Issues and Research in Advertising 1980,* edited by J.H. Leigh, and C.R. Martin, jr., pp. 201-210. Ann Arbor: University of Michigan, Graduate School of Business Administration, 1980.

Liberal women held negative attitudes toward advertising depicting or directed toward women.

2251. Scott, Patricia Bell. "Advertising's Image of Minorities and Women." *Journal of Home Economics.* 69:1 (1977), pp. 22-23.

Home economists and other educators are aware of racism and sexism in advertising.

2252. Screen Actors Guild. *The Relative Roles of Men and Women in Television Commercials.* New York: SAG, 1974.

A survey of the New York Branch, Women's Conference Committee of the Screen Actors Guild, November 13, 1974.

2253. Sexton, Donald E. and Phyllis Haberman. "Women in Magazine Advertisements.." *Journal of Advertising Research.* August 1974, pp. 41-46.

Good Housekeeping, Look, Newsweek, Sports Illustrated, and *TV Guide* and their advertisements between 1950 and 1971: the images of women reflected in ads were quite narrow, trends over the two decades did not move far from a "limited picture of women as social people appearing in a predictable environment."

2254. Silverstein, Arthur and Rebecca Silverstein. "The Portrayal of Women in Television Advertising." *Federal Communications Bar Journal.* 27:1 (1974), pp. 71-98.

A study of 496 TV commercials during primetime on the three major networks determined the number of women and men depicted, how women were portrayed, and the types of products. A relationship existed between the nature of the product and the portrayal of women; of ads using an announcer, only 5.2 percent had a female voice, and women were portrayed more often as subservient to men, as being homebodies, and as subjects to whom the ads were directed.

2255. Simmons, Marcia K. "The Portrayal of Adult Sex Roles: A Content Analysis of Advertising Pictures in Six Women's Magazines." Masters thesis, Kansas State University, 1974.

2256. Skelly, Gerald U. and William J. Lundstrom. "Male Sex Roles in Magazine Advertising, 1959-1979." *Journal of Communication.* Autumn 1981, pp. 52-57.

Nine magazines analyzed for 1959, 1969, and 1979; men had been portrayed in magazine ads in less stereotyped roles. However, in women's magazines, "the 'manly' activities were replaced by more decorative roles."

2257. Soley, Lawrence C. and Leonard N. Reid. "Effects of Decorative Female Models on Ad Recognition over Time." In *Proceedings of the 1983 Convention of the American Academy of Advertising,* edited by D.W. Jugenheimer, pp. 116-119. Columbia, South Carolina: University of South Carolina, 1983.

Comparison of magazine ads from the 1950s and 1970s, testing for advertising recognition differences.

2258. Soley, Lawrence C. and Leonard N. Reid. "Taking It Off: Are Models in Magazine Ads Wearing Less?" *Journalism Quarterly.* Winter 1988, pp. 960-966.

Was sexual content in magazine advertising proportionately greater in 1984 than in 1964? Yes, there was a substantial increase in sexually explicit content, with women becoming more "sexy" than men over the 20 years.

2259. Stemple, Diane and Jane E. Tyler. "Sexism in Advertising." *The American Journal of Psychoanalysis.* 34:3 (1974), pp. 271-273.

Advertising trends in magazines from 1910 to the 1970s.

2260. Stimson, Gerry. "Women in a Doctored World." *New Society.* May 1, 1975, pp. 265-267.

The medical profession promotes negative stereotypes of women as seen in tranquilizer and birth control ads designed for women.

2261. Stuteville, John R. "Sexually Polarized Products and Advertising Strategy." *Journal of Retailing.* Summer 1971, pp. 3-13.

How consumer products began with "powerful masculine or feminine cathexis"; how they shifted to the opposite sex, and how cultural forces may change the entire process.

2262. Sullivan, Gary L. and P.J. O'Connor. "Women's Role Portrayals in Magazine Advertising: 1958-1983." *Sex Roles.* February 1988, pp. 181-188.

Eight general interest magazines analyzed on the changing nature of women's role portrayals. Findings compared with 1970 and 1958 data; current ads reflect more accurately women's social and occupational roles.

2263. Synnott, Anthony. "The Presentation of Gender in Advertising." In *Media USA: Process and Effect,* edited by Arthur Asa Berger, pp. 436-444. New York: Longman, 1988.

A considerable difference exists between how men and women are portrayed in *New York Times Magazine* ads. Women particularly were stereotyped -- young, extremely beautiful. In ads for men, the body was fully clothed; women were in varying degrees of undress. Men were named more often than women. Women were more likely to be in "bizarre positions."

2264. Tan, Alexis S. "TV Beauty Ads and Role Expectations of Adolescent Female Viewers." *Journalism Quarterly.* Summer 1979,, pp. 283-288.

People exposed to beauty ads showed a cultivation effect in their responses concerning sex appeal, youth, and beauty.

2265. "The Nude in Advertising." *The Forerunner.* January 1916, pp. 54-55.

Women shown in their underwear in ads were "posed inanely" or were "looking in their mirrors," while men were playing tennis or sipping drinks.

2266. "TV Ads for Feminine Hygiene Products Make Progress -- But Barriers Persist." *American Druggist.* August 1, 1974, pp. 31-33.

2267. Venkatesan, M. and Jean Losco. "Women in Magazine Ads: 1959-71." *Journal of Advertising Research.* October 1975, pp. 49-54.

Four each of general interest, men's, and women's magazines analyzed for 1959-71; the portrayal of women as sex objects decreased considerably over these years as did the depiction of women as happy housewives, but the showing of women as dependent upon men remained stable.

2268. Verer, A.M. and L.R. Knupka. "Over-the-Counter Drug Advertising in Gender Oriented Popular Magazines." *Journal of Drug Education.* 16:4 (1986), pp. 367-382.

Study of 111 different gender oriented popular magazines; over seven times more such ads in women's than in men's magazines.

2269. Wagner, Louis C. and Janis B. Banos. "A Woman's Place: A Follow-up Analysis of the Roles Portrayed by Women in Magazine Advertisements." *Journal of Marketing Research.* May 1973, pp. 213-214.

Follow-up of a study by Alice Courtney and Sarah W. Lockeretz in February 1971 *Journal of Marketing Research*; some improvement in how women were depicted in magazine ads over the two years.

2270. Warren, Denise. "Commercial Liberation: What Does 'She' Mean?" *Journal of Communication.* Winter 1978, pp. 169-173.

The power relations, economic contexts, and attitudes about women's roles had not changed in advertising.

2271. Welch, R.L., Aletha Huston-Stein, John C. Wright, and Robert Plehal. "Subtle Sex-Role Cues in Children's Commercials." *Journal of Communication.* Summer 1979, pp. 202-209.

An examination of the more subtle messages denoting sex-role, those found in production techniques. Analysis of 60 television toy commercials in 1977 found that male commercials had abrupt changes of view, more variability, and higher levels of inanimate action, while female ones contained more smooth transitions.

2272. Whipple, Thomas W. and Alice E. Courtney. "Female Role Portrayals of Advertising and Communication Effectiveness: A Review." *Journal of Advertising.* 14:3 (1985), pp. 4-8.

Review of studies concerning model gender-product interactions, female role-setting depictions, and degree of liberation in attitudes.

2273. Whipple, Thomas W. and Alice E. Courtney. "How To Portray Women in TV Commercials." *Journal of Advertising Research.* April 1980, pp. 53-59.

Measurement of the influence of role depictions on effectiveness and irritation of advertising, from both practitioner and consumer viewpoints.

2274. Whipple, Thomas W. and Alice E. Courtney. "Social Consequences of Sex Stereotyping in Advertising." In *Future Directions for Marketing,* edited by George Fisk, Johan Arndt, and Kjell Gronhaug, pp. 332-350. Cambridge, Massachusetts: Marketing Science Institute, 1978.

Survey of the content analyses on the portrayal of women in advertising; advertising showed women in a limited, traditional manner.

2275. Willett, Roslyn. "Do Not Stereotype Women -- An Appeal to Advertisers." *Journal of Home Economics.* October 1971, pp. 549-551.

Comments to a group of representatives of 20 large advertising agencies in January 1971.

2276. Winick, Charles, Lorne G. Williamson, Stuart F. Chusmir, and Mariann Pezella Winick. *Children's Television Commercials: A Content Analysis.* New York: Praeger, 1973.

Analysis of 236 non-toy commercials obtained from advertising agencies in 1971; females were shown more frequently, heroes usually were males, and females' depictions were traditionally stereotyped.

2277. Wortzel, Lawrence H. and John M. Frisbie. "Women's Role Portrayal Preferences in Advertisements: An Empirical Study." *Journal of Marketing.* October 1974, pp. 41-46.

Whether women's liberation changed women's attitudes toward female role portrayals in ads; women sampled preferred roles based on product function, rather than on basis of ideology.

Broadcasting

2278. Abelman, Robert and Kimberly Neuendorf. "Religion in Broadcasting: Demographics." Cleveland, Ohio: Cleveland State University. 1983.

Analyzes three episodes of each of the major 27 religious programs in the U.S.; finds men had 67 percent of all speaking roles and that women were usually shown in lower socio-economic roles.

2279. Adams, William and Susanne Albin. "Public Information on Social Change: TV Coverage of Women in the Workforce." *Policy Studies Journal.* Spring 1980, pp. 717-734.

Analyzes all stories about women in the workforce and about sex discrimination that appeared on the three U.S. networks' early evening news shows, Aug. 1968 to Dec. 1978. During period, a story on working women/sex discrimination appeared every five months.

2280. Allen, S. and R. Heckel. "Social and Demographic Characteristics of Major and Minor Television Characters During Prime Time Viewing in the 1976-77 Season." Columbia, South Carolina: University of South Carolina, 1978.

2281. Alperowicz, Cynthia. *Fighting TV Stereotypes: An ACT Handbook.* Newtonville, Massachusetts: Action for Children's Television, 1983. 24 pp.

Including those of women.

2282. American Association of University Women. *The Image of Women in Television.* Sacramento, California: AAUW, 1974.

Survey by Sacramento branch.

2283. Arliss, Laurie, Mary Cassata, and Thomas Skill. "Dyadic Interaction on the Daytime Serials: How Men and Women Vie for Power." In *Life on Daytime Television: Tuning-in American Serial Drama*, edited by Mary Cassata and Thomas Skill, pp. 147-156. Norwood, New Jersey: Ablex, 1983.

Analysis of 316 dyadic transactions from a month of three U.S. daytime serial dramas; the majority of dyads (62 percent) involved a male and a female. Males were usually part of business-related dyads; females part of social-related dyads.

2284. Atwood, Rita, Susan Brown Zahn, and Gail Webber. "Perceptions of the Traits of Women on Television." *Journal of Broadcasting and Electronic Media.* Winter 1986, pp. 95-101.

Conflicting standards are used by audiences in judging female TV portrayals, the predominant contemporary standards and the traditional ones.

2285. Aylesworth, Margaret F. "American Women on Television: Image and Reality." Masters thesis, University of Maryland, 1968.

2286. Baker, Robert K. and Sandra J. Ball. "The Television World of Violence." In *Violence and the Media*, pp. 313-340. Washington, D.C.: Government Printing Office, 1969. Vol. IX.

Sample of one week of prime-time and weekend and daytime U.S. network drama (1967-68); male characters dominated by four to one and males were at least six times more violent than females.

2287. Bambrot, F.H., D.C. Reep, and D. Bell. "Television Sex Roles in the 1980s: Do Viewers' Sex and Sex Role Orientation Change the Picture?" *Sex Roles.* September 1988, pp. 387-401.

Analysis of four each male and female TV characters; viewers rated all male characters as stereotypical masculine, but only one female character as stereotypical feminine.

2288. Barbatsis, Gretchen S., Martin R. Wong, and Gregory M. Herek. "A Struggle for Dominance: Relational Communication Patterns in Television Drama." *Communication Quarterly.* Spring 1983, pp. 148-155.

The predominant model of interpersonal interaction for both male and female characters in TV drama was a "dominant masculine-style of interaction resulting in the portrayal of a struggle for dominance."

2289. Barcus, F. Earle. *Images of Life on Children's Television: Sex Roles, Minorities, and Families.* New York: Praeger, 1983. 217 pp.

Male dominance prevailed in 38 hours of children's TV, with about three-fourths of the characters being men, with some shows made up almost totally of male characters, and with female characters portrayed as younger, more apt to be married, more likely to be in home or family roles, and less likely to be employed outside the home. Also by Barcus: "Commercial Children's Television on Weekends and Weekday Afternoons: A Content Analysis of Children's Programming and Advertising Broadcasting in October 1977," 1978; "Saturday Children's Television: A Report on Television Programming and Advertising on Boston Commercial Television," 1971, and "Television in the After-School Hours: A Study of Programming and Advertising for Children on Independent Stations Across the United States," 1975, all published by Action for Children's Television, Newtonville, Massachusetts.

2290. Baxter, Leslie A. and Stuart J. Kaplan. "Context Factors in the Analysis of Prosocial and Antisocial Behavior on Prime Time Television." *Journal of Broadcasting.* 27:1 (1983), pp. 25-36.

   In major U.S. dramatic television programs of 1981, more acts by males were antisocial than by females; women were praised when their actions fit sex-roles stereotypes.

2291. Beck, Kay. "Television and the Older Woman." *Television Quarterly.* 15:2 (1978), pp. 47-49.

   Older women did not have much of a TV role, making up only five percent of all female characters. Men were at least ten years older than female partners, and their portrayals showed they aged handsomely. Women did not, hiding their age with dyes and cosmetics.

2292. Berg, Charles M. "Sex, Violence and Rock 'n' Roll: The Manipulation of Women in Music-Videos." Paper presented at Speech Communication Association, Chicago, Illinois,, November 1-4, 1984. 14 pp.

   The exploitation of women as sexual objects that characterizes many music-videos.

2293. Bergman, J. "Are Little Girls Being Harmed by Sesame St.?" In *And Jill Came Tumbling After: Sexism in American Education*, edited by J. Stacey. New York: Dell, 1974.

2294. Blank, David M. and George Gerbner. "The Gerbner Violence Profile." *Journal of Broadcasting.* Summer 1977, pp. 273-279.

   Women are portrayed as victims, rather than aggressors, in TV violence.

2295. Blum, Linda M. "Feminism and the Mass Media: A Case Study of The Women's Room as Novel and Television Film." *Berkeley Journal of Sociology.* 27 (1982), pp. 1-24.

   The novel, *The Women's Room*, and its TV version, are examined to explore the awareness of effects of new family situations and sex roles on women.

2296. Britton, Helen Ann. "Sex Role Stereotyping: A Content Analysis of *Bread and Butterflies*." *ERIC.* 1975. 27 pp. (ED 116 699).

   A 15-program instructional television series on career awareness, "Bread and Butterflies," was produced by the Agency for Instructional Television in 1974-75. The series was analyzed to document how women were portrayed.

2297. Britton, Helen Ann. "The Role of Women in Television: Avenues for Change." Paper presented at Telecommunications Policy Research Conference, Airlie, Virginia, April 21-24, 1976. 22 pp.

   How negative TV portrayals of women may lead to unfulfilling role adaptations, especially among children.

2298. Brown, Jane and Kenneth Campbell. "Race and Gender in Music Videos: The Same Beat but a Different Drummer." *Journal of Communication.* Winter 1986, pp. 94-106.
　　　　Women and blacks remain minorities on MTV.

2299. Busby, Linda Jean. "Defining the Sex-Role Standard in Network Children's Programs." *Journalism Quarterly.* Winter 1974, pp. 690-696.
　　　　A study of 20 U.S. TV network cartoon shows concluded "traditional sex roles are reflected in attributes, attitudes, and behavior of male and female characters."

2300. Butler, Matilda. *Sex Stereotyping in Instructional Materials and Television: Awareness Kit.* San Francisco: Women's Educational Equity Communications Network, 1978. 51 pp.
　　　　The portrayals of women and men in instructional materials and TV and a way to make children aware of sex-stereotyping.

2301. Butsch, Richard and Lynda M. Glennon. "Social Class: Frequency Trends in Domestic Situation Comedy, 1946-1978." *Journal of Broadcasting.* 27:1 (1983), pp. 77-81.
　　　　The working wife appeared in only 13 of 189 series in prime-time network family situation comedies, 1946-1978.

2302. Byars, Jackie L. "Gender Representation in America Family Melodramas of the Nineteen Fifties." Ph.D. dissertation, University of Texas at Austin, 1983. 893 pp.

2303. Cantor, Muriel G. "Feminism and the Media." *Society.* July-August 1988, pp. 76-81.
　　　　The movement to reform U.S. broadcasting in relation to women was strong in the 1970s, but by 1977, it ran out of steam.

2304. Cantor, Muriel G. "Our Days and Our Nights on TV." *Journal of Communication.* Autumn 1979, pp. 66-72.
　　　　Background of daytime and primetime serial dramas discussed, showing the divergent paths they have taken. Although formats have not changed, contents have, from those used by radio to those of TV.

2305. Cantor, Muriel G. "Where Are the Women in Public Broadcasting?" In *Hearth and Home: Images of Women in the Mass Media,* edited by Gaye Tuchman, Arlene K. Daniels, and James Benet, pp. 78-79. New York: Oxford University Press, 1978.
　　　　From a week of U.S. public broadcasting in 1974-75, the authors conclude that "women are not represented as integral to American life."

2306. Cassata, Mary B. "The More Things Change, the More They Are the Same: An Analysis of Soap Operas from Radio to Television." In *Life on Daytime Television: Tuning-in American Serial Drama,* edited by Mary

Cassata and Thomas Skill, pp. 85-100. Norwood, New Jersey: Ablex, 1983.

In both radio and television soap operas, women were the central characters, but in daytime serials, women made up one-half the characters, in prime-time drama, one-fourth.

2307. Cassata, Mary B. and Thomas Skill, eds. *Life on Daytime Television: Tuning-in American Serial Drama.* Norwood, New Jersey: Ablex, 1983. 214 pp.

Surveys U.S. television daytime serial dramas and changes from those of radio. Old age portrayals and other topics included.

2308. Cheles-Miller, Pamela. "An Investigation of Whether the Stereotypes of Husband and Wife Presented in Television Commercials Can Influence a Child's Perception of the Role of Husband and Wife." ERIC. 1974. 13 pp. (ED 094 439).

Whether stereotypes of husbands and wives presented in television commercials can influence a child's perception of the role of husband and wife.

2309. Chulay, Cornell and Sara Francis. "The Image of the Female Child on Saturday Morning Television Commercials." Paper presented at International Communication Association, New Orleans, Louisiana, April 17-20, 1974. 13 pp.

The image of female children in 294 commercials on Saturday morning TV in 1973 tended to orient children to traditional feminine roles in society.

2310. *Communication.* 9:3/4 (1987).

Thematic issue on "Intersections of Power: Criticism - Television - Gender," edited by Paula A. Treichler, Lawrence Grossberg, and John Fiske, includes: Lawrence Gross and Paula A. Treichler, "Intersections of Power: Criticism - Television - Gender"; Jackie Byars, "Reading Feminine Discourse: Prime-Time Television in the U.S."; Andrew Ross, "*Miami Vice*: Selling in"; Mary Ellen Brown, "The Dialectic of the Feminine: Melodrama and Commodity in the Ferraro Pepsi Commercial"; Lisa A. Lewis, "Form and Female Authorship in Music Video," and John Fiske, "*Cagney and Lacey*: Reading Character Structurally and Politically."

2311. Copeland, G.A. "Face-ism and Primetime Television." *Journal of Broadcasting and Electronic Media.* Spring 1989, pp. 209-214.

A composite week of all primetime programming on the three TV networks and Fox Television used to see if there was a pattern of framing men and women. Men were framed from a close-up persepctive.

2312. Dambrot, Faye H., Diana C. Reep, and Daniel Bell. "Television Sex Roles in the 1980s: Do Viewers' Sex and Sex Role Orientation Change the Picture?" *Sex Roles.* September 1988, pp. 387-401.

Viewer perceptions of female and male TV characters as a result of viewer sex and sex role orientation.

2313. Davidson, E., A. Yasuna, and A. Tower. "The Effects of Television Cartoons on Sex-Role Stereotyping in Young Girls." *Child Development.* June 1979, pp. 597-600.

Sex-role stereotyping of five- and six-year-old girls of three TV network cartoons tested. Girls who saw low stereotyped programs had significantly lower sex-role stereotypes than those in high and neutral categories.

2314. Davis, Richard H. *Television and the Aging Audience.* Los Angeles: The Ethel Percy Andrus Gerontology Center, 1980.

Older men outnumbered older women in TV commercials and in dramatic shows; women over 30 years old were less likely to be seen, certainly not as romantic partners.

2315. DeFleur, Melvin L. "Occupational Roles as Portrayed on Television." *Public Opinion Quarterly.* Spring 1964, pp. 57-74.

The world of work as seen in six months of television; "over-all, the world of work on television is a man's world," with the distribution of sexes more unequal on television than in reality.

2316. Deming, Caren J. "Broadcast Networks and the Outsiders: Legal Responsibility from Two Perspectives." Paper presented at Speech Communication Association, San Francisco, California, December 27-30, 1976. 22 pp.

An examination of the legal responsibility of networks to fairly represent outsiders such as women, racial/ethnic minorities, homosexuals, and the elderly.

2317. Dohrmann, Rita. "A Gender Profile of Children's Educational TV." *Journal of Communication.* August 1975, pp. 56-65.

Sex-role analysis of children's educational TV revealed the adult male character had the highest visibility. Educational television reinforces the traditional active-passive roles U.S. society holds.

2318. Dominick, Joseph R. "Crime and Law Enforcement on Prime-Time Television." *Public Opinion Quarterly.* 37:2 (1973), pp. 241-250.

Sex distributions of criminals and murder victims on television compared favorably with FBI reports. Women made up 16 percent of the 96 TV criminals, 20 percent of the 26 murder victims.

2319. Dominick, Joseph R. "The Portrayal of Women in Prime Time, 1953-1977." *Sex Roles.* 5:4 (1979), pp. 405-411.

In sample of prime-time, network drama and comedy drama from 1953 to 1977, women made up 30 percent of starring roles, were more concentrated in situation comedies than men, and were shown less often as housewives (53 percent in 1950s to 39 percent in 1970s).

2320. Donagher, Patricia C., Rita Wicks Poulos, Robert M. Liebert, and Emily C. Davidson. "Race, Sex, and Social Example: An Analysis of Character Portrayals on Inter-Racial Television Entertainment." *Psychological Reports.* 37, 1975, pp. 1023-1034.

A sample of a week of nine prime-time U.S. network series that featured males and females of both races, found that one-third of the major characters were female who were in traditional roles. White women had more non-traditional possibilities than black women.

2321. Downing, Mildred. "Heroine of the Daytime Serial." *Journal of Communication.* Spring 1974, pp. 130-137.

Monitoring of 300 episodes of 15 daytime serials in 1973 showed that despite her handicaps, the daytime heroine may still be the most adequate human on television. The most discriminating factor between male and female portrayals related to occupational level.

2322. Downs, A. Chris. "Sex-Role Stereotyping on Prime-Time Television." *Journal of Genetic Psychology.* 138, 1981, pp. 253-258.

Female and male characters central to 14 prime-time TV programs were monitored to find the frequency of sex-role stereotypic behavior. Few sex differences were shown on most behaviors used in the study, but males usually were portrayed at work, females at home.

2323. Downs, A. Chris and Darryl C. Gowan. "Sex Differences in Reinforcement and Punishment on Prime-Time Television." *Sex Roles.* 6:5 (1980), pp. 683-694.

Analysis of negative and positive behaviors of adult characters in a sample week of network prime-time programming in 1976, found females were more likely than men to give affection, smile, ridicule and receive reinforcement.

2324. Downs, A. Chris and Sheila K. Harrison. "Embarrassing Age Spots or Just Plain Ugly? Physical Attractiveness Stereotyping as an Instrument of Sexism on American Television Commercials." *Sex Roles.* July 1985, pp. 9-19.

From a sample of 4,294 TV network commercials, concluded that attractiveness messages were associated with food, drink, and personal care ads.

2325. Durkin, Kevin. "Children's Accounts of Sex-role Stereotypes in Television." *Communication Research.* July 1984, pp. 341-362.

Seventeen children interviewed had considerable knowledge of sex-role conventions.

2326. Eisenstock, Barbara. "Sex-Role Differences in Children's Identification with Counter-stereotypical Televised Portrayals." *Sex Roles.* 10:5/6, 1984, pp. 417-430.

Television's effectiveness in promoting non-sexist role learning among children with sex-role orientations. Experiment with 238 boys and girls suggested that androgynous children were as likely as feminine children, and more likely than masculine children, to identify with non-traditional TV models.

2327. Ellis Donald G. and G. Blake Armstrong. "Class, Gender, and Code on Prime-Time Television." *Communication Quarterly.* Summer 1989, pp. 157-169.

The nature of codes on prime-time U.S. television as they relate to gender and class are explained. Female middle-class characters were portrayed in a more stereotypical way than males and were not given full access to the syntactic code.

2328. Estep, Rhoda and Patrick T. MacDonald. "How Prime Time Crime Evolved on TV, 1976-1981." *Journalism Quarterly.* 60:2 (1983), pp. 293-300.

Analysis of 50 televised crime studies in 1976-77, 49 in 1978-79, and 30 in 1980-81. In later sample, more women than men were shown as murder victims.

2329. Fife, Marilyn D. "The Black Image in American TV: The First Two Decades." *Black Scholar.* November 1974, pp. 7-15.

2330. Fjeldsted, Margaret, ed. *Guidelines To Update Images of Women in Television.* Sacramento: California State Commission on the Status of Women, 1977. 62 pp.

Input from 25 media groups as part of deliberations about the image of women on radio and TV in public hearings of California Commission on the Status of Women.

2331. Franzwa, Helen. "The Image of Women in Television: An Annotated Bibliography." In *Hearth and Home: Images of Women in the Mass Media,* edited by Gaye Tuchman, Arlene Kaplan Daniels, and James Benet, pp. 273-299. New York: Oxford University Press, 1978.

Annotation of many works of women's images in television revealed that the image did not change much over 20 years.

2332. Gade, Eldon M. "Representation of the World of Work in Daytime Television Serials." *Journal of Employment Counseling.* 8:1 (1971), pp. 37-42.

One month of nine U.S. daytime serials in 1970 analyzed; 62 percent of the women were in professional, technical, or managerial positions, compared to only 19 percent in the actual U.S. workforce.

2333. Gebhardt, Randall E. and James D. Harless. "Television News and Sexist Language: A Study of Television News Effects." Paper presented at Association for Education in Journalism and Mass Communication, Norman, Oklahoma, August 3-6, 1986. 20 pp.

College audience's reactions to two versions of a TV story about a woman -- one in which she is referred to as a woman, the other as a girl.

2334. Geraghty, Christine. *Women in Soap Operas.* Oxford: Polity Press, forthcoming.

Images of the family and women.

2335. Gerbner, George. "Violence in Television Drama: Trends and Symbolic Functions." In *Television and Social Behavior. Vol. I: Media Content and*

Control, edited by G.S. Comstock and E.A. Rubinstein, pp. 28-187. Washington, D.C.: U.S. Government Printing Office, 1972.

In dramatic TV programs, 1967-1969, there was gross underrepresentation of women as major characters -- one-fourth of all leading roles. Women were portrayed in romantic- or family-type plots.

2336. Gerbner, George and Nancy Signorielli. "The World According to Television." *American Demographics*. October 1982, pp. 15-17.

Data showing television to be a male world, with men outnumbering women and appearing in more powerful roles.

2337. Gerbner, George and Nancy Signorielli. "Women and Minorities in Television Drama, 1969-1978." Philadelphia, Pennsylvania: University of Pennsylvania, Annenberg School of Communications, 1979. 44 pp.

Week-long samples of U.S. prime-time and weekend network drama showed that females made up 29 percent of prime-time characters and were mainly in comic, family, or romantic roles.

2338. Giordano, Joseph. "Families: What TV Teaches Children." *Attenzione*. December 1981, pp. 76, 78, 80.

Ethnic stereotypes on television can contribute to children's prejudices against certain groups.

2339. Goff, D.H., L. Dysart, and S.K. Lehrer. "Sex-role Portrayals of Selected Female TV Characters." *Journal of Broadcasting*. Fall 1980, pp. 467-478.

More research needed on the relationshp between viewer sex role and character perception.

2340. Greenberg, Bradley S. *Life on Television: Content Analyses of U.S. TV Drama*. Norwood, New Jersey: Ablex, 1980.

The appearance and portrayal of females, minorities, elderly, and sexual behavior in U.S. television drama. Includes the following with information on TV portrayals of women: "Three Seasons of Television Family Role Interactions," pp. 161-172; "Antisocial and Prosocial Behaviors on Television," pp. 99-128; "Sexual Intimacy on Commercial Television During Prime Time," pp. 129-136; "Trends in Sex-role Portrayals on Television," pp. 65-87; "The Demography of Fictional TV Characters," pp. 35-46.

2341. Greenberg, Bradley S. "Some Uncommon Television Images and the Drench Hypothesis." In *Television as a Social Issue*, edited by S. Oskamp, pp. 88-102. Newbury Park, California: Sage Publications, 1988.

The television images of women. TV programming may have a "drench" effect and to test this hypothesis, research should focus on role portrayals that stand out.

2342. Greenberg, B.S. and C. Heetor. "Television and Social Stereotypes." In *Rx Television: Enhancing the Preventive Impact of TV*, edited by J. Sprafkin, C. Swift, and R. Hess, pp. 37-52. New York: The Haworth Press, 1983.

Multiple content analyses of TV portrayals of roles based on sex, occupation, race, and age. TV consistently has shown the sexes in stereotypical fashion.

2343. Griffin, Robert J. and Shaikat Sen. "Sex and Social Status: Television Use and Occupational Desires Among Adolescents." Paper presented at International Communication Association, San Francisco, California, May 25-29, 1989. 27 pp.

In a sample of 542 Chicago suburban high school students, found that identification with male and female characters in domestic and occupational roles followed traditional lines.

2344. Grossberg, Lawrence and Paula A. Treichler. "Intersections of Power: Criticism, Television, Gender." *Communication.* 9:3/4 (1987), pp. 273-287.

Gender as a "socially and historically constructed category, produced in televised texts through specific representations; these gendered texts do not necessarily 'suceed,' however, as viewers find multiple ways to use them."

2345. Hansen, C.H. and R.D. Hansen. "How Rock Music Videos Can Change What Is Seen When Boy Meets Girls: Priming Stereotypic Appraisals of Social Interactions." *Sex Roles.* September 1988, pp. 287-316.

2346. Harris, Mary B. and Sara D. Voorhees. "Sex-Role Stereotypes and Televised Models of Emotion." *Psychological Report.* 48:3 (1981), p. 826.

From sample of 280 hours of CBS and NBC network television, found that "the pattern of women being more emotional and spending their time on home, romance, and physical appearance while stoic men are at work or sports events with their cars certainly suggests that television continues to perpetuate sex-role stereotypes."

2347. Harvey, Susan E., Joyce N. Sprafkin, and Eli Rubinstein. "Prime-Time TV: A Profile of Aggressive and Prosocial Behaviors." *Journal of Broadcasting.* 23:2 (1979), pp. 179-189.

During one week of network TV programming (prime-time) in 1975-76, women made up 28 percent of characters and were involved in the expression of feelings.

2348. Haskell, Deborah. "The Depiction of Women in Leading Roles in Prime Time Television." *Journal of Broadcasting.* Spring 1979, pp. 191-196.

In 13 U.S. TV series, where women were the leading character or were featured, regular TV characters were rather evenly distributed, but one-time characters were mainly males.

2349. Hawkins, Robert P., et al. "How Children Evaluate Real-Life and Television Women." Paper presented at Association for Education in Journalism, Madison Wisconsin, August 21-24, 1977. 21 pp.

A study of 192 grade school children to determine what they notice.

2350. Head, Sydney W. "Content Analysis of Television Drama Programs." *Quarterly of Film, Radio, and Television.* 9 (1954), pp. 175-194.

In four episodes of 64 network dramas in 1952, one-third of the characters were female. The third most popular occupation of all characters was that of housewife.

2351. Henderson, Katherine Usher and Joseph Anthony Mazzeo, eds. *Meanings of Medium: Perspectives on the Art of Television.* New York: Praeger, 1990.

Includes Harriet Blodgett, "Not Such a Long Way Baby: Women and Televised Myth."

2352. Henderson, Laura and Bradley S. Greenberg. "Sex-Typing of Common Behaviors on Television." In *Life on Television: Content Analyses of U.S. TV Drama*, edited by Bradley S. Greenberg, pp. 89-95. Norwood, New Jersey: Ablex, 1980.

Sample of 1,679 characters from 115 prime-time and 43 Saturday morning television shows (1975-77) found that of speaking characters, only 28 percent were female. At least 46 percent of all behaviors were sex-typed with women performing acts of entertaining, preparing and serving food, and housework.

2353. Henderson, Laura, Bradley S. Greenberg, and C.K. Atkin. "Sex Differences in Giving Orders, Making Plans, and Needing Support on Television." In *Life on Television: Content Analyses of U.S. TV Drama*, edited by Bradley S. Greenberg, pp. 49-63. Norwood, New Jersey: Ablex, 1980.

In a sample of a composite week of fictional TV series from three U.S. networks in 1975, the average depiction was where men were more likely to give orders to other men. Orders given by women were less likely to be followed. Eighty percent of all plans for men and women were made by male characters.

2354. Hess, D.J. and G.W. Grant. "Prime-time Television and Gender-role Behavior." *Teaching Sociology.* April 1983, pp. 371-388.

Use of Bales Interaction Process Analysis System to teach students how to examine gender-role behavior in prime-time TV.

2355. Hodges, Kay Kline, David A. Brandt, and Jeff Kline. "Competence, Guilt, and Victimization: Sex Differences in Attribution of Causality in Television Dramas." *Sex Roles.* 7:5 (1981), pp. 537-546.

Sex differences in attribution of causality in three types of TV programs: prime time family, violent, and daytime serials. There were sex differences in violent shows, with males modeling more "origin" behavior and females more "pawn" behavior. In soap operas, there were no sex differences.

2356. Huston, A.C., et al. "Children's Comprehension of Televised Formal Features with Masculine and Feminine Connotations." *Developmental Psychology.* July 1984, pp. 707-716.

Children in middle childhood understood sex-typed connotations at the subtle level of TV formal features.

2357. Jeffries-Fox, Suzanne and Nancy Signorielli. "Television and Children's Conceptions of Occupations." In *Proceedings of the Sixth Annual Telecommunications Policy Research Conference*, edited by Herbert S. Dordick, pp. 21-38. Lexington, Massachusetts: Lexington Books, 1978.

An analysis of U.S. prime-time network dramatic programming between 1969 and 1976; major characters were female in one-fourth of the instances. The portrayals mirrored reality in the proportion of men and women in six different occupations of medicine, law and police work.

2358. *Journal of Broadcasting*. Summer 1975.

Thematic symposium on "Image of Women on Television: A Dialogue" includes: Jean C. McNeil, "Feminism, Femininity, and the Television Series: A Content Analysis," pp. 259-272; John F. Seggar, "Imagery of Women in Television Drama: 1974," pp. 273-282; Jean C. McNeil, "Imagery of Women in TV Drama: Some Procedural and Interpretive Issues," pp. 283-288; John F. Seggar, "Women's Imagery on TV: Feminist, Fair Maiden, or Maid? Comments on McNeil," pp. 289-294; Jean C. McNeil, "Whose Values?" pp. 295-296; John F. Seggar, "Imagery as Reflected Through TV's Cracked Mirror," pp. 297-300; Mary Ellen Verna, "The Female Image in Children's TV Commercials," pp. 301-305.

2359. Kalisch, Beatrice J., Philip A. Kalisch, and Margaret Scobey. "Reflections on a Television Image: The Nurses, 1962-1965." *Nursing and Health Care*. May 1981, pp. 248-255.

In the TV series, "The Nurses," broadcast 1962-65, images of nurses were compared with nurses in doctor-oriented shows. "The Nurses" provided a more realistic view, picturing nurses as problem solvers, not puppets of doctors.

2360. Kalisch, Philip A. and Beatrice J. Kalisch. "Sex-Role Stereotyping of Nurses and Physicians on Prime-Time Television: A Dichotomy of Occupational Portrayals." *Sex Roles*. April 1984, pp. 533-553.

Sex-role variables in prime-time TV portrayals of nurses and physicians from 1950 to 1980. "Extreme" levels of both sexual and occupational stereotyping existed: TV nurses were 99 percent female, doctors were 95 percent male. Nurses on TV largely served as "window dressing on the set."

2361. Kalisch, Philip A., Beatrice J. Kalisch, and Margaret Scobey. *Image of Nurses on Television*. New York: Springer Publishing Co., 1983. 214 pp.

The development of images of nurses on television, looking at all shows that pictured nurses. Most common stereotype found was that of nurse as doctor's helper. See also: Philip A. Kalisch and Beatrice J. Kalisch, "Nurses on Prime Time Television," *American Journal of Nursing*, 82 (1982), pp. 264-270; Philip A. Kalisch, Beatrice J. Kalisch, Jacqueline Clinton, "The World of Nursing on Prime Time Television, 1950-1980," *Nursing Research*, 31:6 (1982), pp. 258-363.

2362. Kallan, Richard A. and Robert D. Brooks. "The Playmate of the Month: Naked But Nice." *Journal of Popular Culture.* Fall 1974, pp. 328-336.

The playmate of the month in *Playboy* magazine changed from nameless, almost undefined, busty models to brainier, career-oriented women, to "All-American girl," to individualists, etc. Stories that accompanied the nude centerfolds consistently gave two messages: that the women seemed available and that they were morally admirable.

2363. Kalter, Joanmarie. "What Working Women Want from TV." *TV Guide.* January 30, 1988, pp. 2-7.

Working women's disdain for the images created of them by television.

2364. Kaninga, Nancy, Thomas Scott, and Eldon Gade. "Working Women Portrayed on Evening Television Programs." *Vocational Guidance Quarterly.* 23:2 (1974), pp. 134-137.

In a sample of 44 U.S. television evening series in 1972, women made up 31 percent of the characters. Thirty percent of the women were housewives and the 70 percent otherwise employed were young and single. Women were characterized in traditional jobs of nurses and secretaries.

2365. Kaplan, E. Ann. "The Case of the Missing Mother: Maternal Issues in Vidor's *Stella Dallas.*" *Heresies.* 16 (1983), pp. 81-85.

2366. Karp, Walter. "What Do Women Want?" *Channels of Communication.* September-October 1984, pp. 17-19.

The televised woman's world is a "strangely disjointed place," judging from talk shows which indicate that women don't feel at home, at home." Help with real life problems is the shows' concerns, but guests do not sound like practical people.

2367. Kinzer, Nora Scott. "Soapy Sex in the Afternoon." *Psychology Today.* August 1973, pp. 46-48.

Besides insulting viewers' intelligence, soap operas preserve traditional sex roles.

2368. Kirkpatrick, J.T. "Homes and Homemakers on American TV." In *The American Dimension: Cultural Myths and Social Realities*, edited by W. Arens and Susan P. Montague, pp. 69-80. Port Washington, New York: Alfred Publishing Co., 1976.

2369. Lavin, Maud. "Feminization of Poverty and the Media." In *Global Television*, edited by Cynthia Schneider and Brian Wallis, pp. 237-253. Cambridge: MIT Press, 1988.

The growing numbers of poor women during the Reagan administration and the ways mass media covered the feminization of poverty. Analysis of the Moyers show; it typified TV programming, which addressed poverty only in terms of blacks, not other groups such as women.

2370. Lemon, Judith. "Dominant or Dominated? Women on Prime-Time Television." In *Hearth and Home: Images of Women in the Mass Media*, edited by Gaye Tuchman, Arlene Kaplan Daniels, and James Benet, pp. 51-68. New York: Oxford University Press, 1978.

    Characters in occupational interactions in televised situation comedy and crime drama shows of 1975; in such interactions, males were more often dominant.

2371. Lemon, Judith. "Women and Blacks on Prime-Time Television." *Journal of Communication.* Autumn 1977, pp. 70-79.

    All crime dramas and situation comedies broadcast during prime-time in March 1975 analyzed for sex-role portrayals. Results showed that situation comedies provided more favorable portrayals than crime dramas and that men were more frequent participants in interactions and were dominant much more often than women.

2372. Levan, Kathryn. "Television and Sex Roles." Masters thesis, University of Pennsylvania, 1974.

2373. Lewis, Lisa A. "Form and Female Authorship in Music Video." *Communication.* 9:3/4 (1987), pp. 355-377.

    Form and female authorship combine in music videos, negotiating gender inequalities. MTV provides many authorship opportunities for women musicians and an outlet for "strong woman-identified statements."

2374. Lewis, Lisa A. *Gender Politics and MTV: Voicing the Difference.* Philadelphia: Temple University Press, 1990. 300 pp.

    Video and the careers of female musicians Pat Benatar, Cyndi Lauper, Tina Turner, and Madonna; MTV provides more than negative, sexist images of women. Music video is a vehicle of feminist expression.

2375. Lichter, Linda S. and S. Robert Lichter. "Criminals and Law Enforcers in TV Entertainment." *Prime Time Crime.* Washington, D.C.: The Media Institute, 1983.

    Analysis of six weeks of prime-time television in 1980-81, concentrating on shows where at least one crime occurred or a law enforcer appeared. The ratio of male-female criminals on television mirrored real life. By the same authors and Stanley Rothman, "From Lucy to Lacey: TV's Dream Girls," *Public Opinion*, September-October 1986.

2376. Lichter, S. Robert, Linda Lichter, and Stanley Rothman. "1955 to 1985: Women in Prime Time TV Still Traditional, But New Treatment of Women's Rights Themes." *Media Report to Women.* November-December 1986, p. 7.

    Looked at 20 different TV series, 1955-1985.

2377. List, Judith A., W. Andrew Collins, and Sally D. Westby. "Comprehension and Inferences from Traditional and Nontraditional Sex-Role Portrayals on Television." *Child Development.* 54 (1983), pp. 1579-1587.

Relationship between children's sex-role attitudes and memory for televised sex-role-relevant and sex-role-irrelevant information. Among results was that "children's processing of program content was affected by the degree of their stereotypes, but such processing did not necessarily result in biased or distorted memory."

2378. Long, Michele and Rita J. Simon. "The Roles and Statuses of Women on Children and Family TV Programs." *Journalism Quarterly.* Spring 1974, pp. 107-110.

On 22 TV shows for children and families, women were depicted in comic roles or as wives and mothers. Their appearances were prominently played; none worked outside the home.

2379. Lont, Cynthia M. "It's Not What They Play, It's What They Say: A Content Analysis of DJ Chatter." Paper presented at the Study of Communication, Language, and Gender, San Diego, California, October 7-9, 1988. 12 pp.

Two Washington, D.C. radio stations studied to determine DJ references to males and females. The only categories where women were dominant were in traffic reports and as the audience; men were referred to with more respect or authority than women.

2380. Lopate, Carol. "Daytime Television: You'll Never Want To Leave Home." *Feminist Studies.* Spring-Summer 1976, pp. 69-82.

Televised daytime serials, game shows, and commercials played down the power men have over women. In serials, men and women characters were probably more equal than in any other drama form.

2381. Lott, Bernice. "Sexist Discrimination as Distancing Behavior: II Primetime Television." *Psychology of Women Quarterly.* September 1989, pp. 341-355.

Men in TV programs turned away, distanced themselves, from women.

2382. Lull, James T. "Girls' Favorite TV Females." *Journalism Quarterly.* Spring 1980, pp. 146-150.

Girls named these as most popular: Mary Tyler Moore, Rhoda, Jamie Summers, Carol Burnett, Marie Osmond, Farrah Fawcett Majors, LaVerne DeFazio, and Mrs. Cunningham.

2383. Lull, James T., Catherine A. Hanson, and Michael J. Marx. "Recognition of Female Stereotypes in TV Commercials." *Journalism Quarterly.* Spring 1977, pp. 153-157.

From small sample of university students, concluded that young viewers generally are not as sensitive to sex-role stereotypes in TV commercials as feminism advocates might hope.

2384. McArthur, Leslie Zebrowitz and Susan V. Eisen. "Television and Sex-Role Stereotyping." *Journal of Applied Psychology.* 6:4 (1976), pp. 329-351.

In 22 Saturday morning children's TV shows, females made up 32 percent of the characters; they were mainly shown in nurturant roles. Females made up 20 percent of all characters in 161 commercials.

2385. McGhee, P.E. and T. Frueh. "Television Viewing and the Learning of Sex-role Stereotypes." *Sex Roles.* April 1980, pp. 179-188.

Male and female students (grades 1, 3, 5, 7) were classified as heavy or light TV viewers and then tested on the Sex Stereotype Measure; heavy viewers had more stereotyped perceptions than light viewers.

2386. Mackey, W.D. and D.J. Hess. "Attention Structure and Stereotypy of Gender on Television: An Empirical Analysis." *Genetic Psychology Monographs.* 106:2 (1982), pp. 199-215.

Analysis of network evening programs in 1979; males were in scenes twice as often as females and fewer female-female scenes showed task-oriented behavior than did male-male scenes.

2387. McNeil, Jean C. "Feminism, Femininity and the Television Series." *Journal of Broadcasting.* Summer 1975, pp. 259-269.

Whether women were fairly represented and depicted in prime-time TV drama; female characters were fewer, less important, marriage and parenthood were more central to a woman's life than a man's, TV series portrayed traditional division of labor in marriages, women were depicted in traditionally female occupations, TV series females were more personally and less professionally oriented than males, females were far more passive than males, TV series did not acknowledge the feminist movement. By the same author: "Whose Values?" *Journal of Broadcasting,* Summer 1975, pp. 295-296.

2388. McNeil, Jean C. "Imagery of Women in TV Drama: Some Procedural and Interpretive Issues." *Journal of Broadcasting.* Summer 1975, pp. 283-288.

Rebuttal of the views in the same issue by John Seggar, using studies by Turow and Long and Simon; blatant objectification of women is reserved for commercials, while dramas on TV are "more subtly exploitative."

2389. Manes, Audrey L. and Paula Melnyk. "Televised Models of Female Achievement." *Journal of Applied Psychology.* October-December 1974, pp. 365-374.

Models of female achievement portrayed by U.S. television; what is shown about female achievers was not encouraging and might inhibit achievement behavior in women viewers.

2390. Marecek, Jeanne, Jane Allyn Piliavin, Ellen Fitzsimmons, Elizabeth C. Krogh, Elizabeth Leader, and Bonnie Trudell. "Women as TV Experts: The Voice of Authority?" *Journal of Communication.* Winter 1978, pp. 159-168.

A three-year study of television where more women experts sold products for women but were still backed up by an authoritative male voice-over.

2391. Marende, Doreen N. "What is She Like? A Study of Feminine Roles on Saturday Morning Children's Television." Masters thesis, Iowa State University, 1974.

2392. Mariani, John. "Women in Jeopardy: Plot Line of the Year." *New York*. April 14, 1975, pp. 40-43.
"Women in jeopardy," or "wom-jep," was the hottest genre, spawning many books, movies, and TV shows showing young women in situations of terror. Wom-jep shows, where women showed courage, had high ratings of female audiences.

2393. Matelski, Marilyn J. "Image and Influence: Women in Public Television." *Journalism Quarterly*. Spring 1985, pp. 147-150.
Analysis of WGBH-TV for 1983; males outnumbered females two to one in each category of programming.

2394. Mayes, Sandra L. and K.B. Valentine. "Sex-Role Stereotyping in Saturday Morning Cartoon Shows." *Journal of Broadcasting*. Winter 1979, pp. 41-50.
Do children perceive sex-role stereotyping on Saturday morning cartoon shows? Yes, "[T]he girl viewer is permitted to observe a female role model who exhibits attributes different from those the girl usually observes."

2395. Meehan, Diana M. *Ladies of the Evening: Women Characters of Prime-Time Television*. Metuchen, New Jersey: Scarecrow Press, 1983. 202 pp.
Images created by female characters on 33 prime-time television shows from 1950 to 1980: the imp, the good wife, the harpy, the bitch, the victim, the decoy, the siren, the courtesan, the witch, and the matriarch. Each image is treated in a separate chapter.

2396. Meier, Uta. "Masculinity and Femininity in Television Drama." *Sex-Roles within Massmedia Newsletter*. December 1986, pp. 18-20.
Female and male characters in television drama and talk shows (mainly U.S.) to identify assumptions about existence, priorities, values, and relationships.

2397. Miles, Betty. *Channeling Children: Sex Stereotyping on Prime-Time TV*. Princeton, New Jersey: Women on Words and Images, 1975. 84 pp.
Review of the literature on the subject; content analysis of TV shows night-by-night in the Fall of 1973. Considerable underrepresentation of women in all programs.

2398. Miller, M. Mark and Byron Reeves. "Dramatic TV Content and Children's Sex-Role Stereotypes." *Journal of Broadcasting*. Winter 1976, pp. 35-50.
Analysis of one week of 51 TV shows in 1974 to find cross-sex protrayals; survey of Michigan elementary school children. TV helped shape children's sex-role perceptions and did nothing to counter stereotypes on sex-roles.

2399. Morgan, Michael. "Television and Adolescents' Sex Role Stereotypes: A Longitudinal Study." *Journal of Personality and Social Psychology.* November 1982, pp. 947-955.

The relationship over time between TV viewing and adolescents' sex role stereotyping; the amount of TV viewing among girls was associated with sexism scores a year later. TV had no longitudinal effect on boys' sex role attitudes, and lower class boys and girls were more sexist regardless of viewing habits.

2400. Moritz, Marguerite J. "Coming Out Stories: The Creation of Lesbian Images on Prime Time TV." In *Media Reader*, edited by Shirley Biagi, pp. 243-246. Belmont, California: Wadsworth, 1989.

During the television seasons of Fall 1985 through Spring 1988, lesbian characters and story lines began to "come out."

2401. Mulac, Anthony, James J. Bradac, and Susan Karol Mann. "Male/Female Language Differences and Attributional Consequences in Children's Television." *Human Communication Research.* Summer 1985, pp. 481-506.

The language of characters from both PBS and commercial TV children's programs was "clearly gender-differentiated"; the language produced attributions that were stereotypical.

2402. National Commission on Working Women and Wider Opportunities for Women. "Growing Up in Prime Time." Washington, D.C.: NCWW/WOW, 1988. 25 pp.

A study of 200 TV programs in 1988 showed network television had "outmoded and damaging stereotypes of teenage girls" that were "narrow and unrealistic." Girls' looks counted more than their brains, and girls were more passive than boys and represented a narrow range on the socio-economic spectrum.

2403. National Organization for Women, National Capitol Area Chapter. "Women in the Wasteland Fight Back: A Report on the Image of Women Portrayed in TV Programming." Washington, D.C.: NOW, 1972.

Monitoring of composite week of a TV network affiliate showed that women were outnumbered by men; in soap operas and quiz programs, women made up 40 percent of the characters and participants. Women dominated as quiz show participants, but they were often patronized or made the butt of humor.

2404. Nolan, John D., Joann Paley Galst, and Mary Alice White. "Sex Bias on Children's Television Programs." *Journal of Psychology.* 96 (1977), pp. 197-204.

In a month's sample of network and public television, Saturday morning shows and commercials, females made up 26 percent of the characters. Men were considerably more prone to give approval or disapproval than women.

2405. Northcott, Herbert C., John F. Seggar, and James L. Hinton. "Trends in TV Portrayal of Blacks and Women." *Journalism Quarterly.* Winter 1975, pp. 741-744.

The portrayal of women and blacks on the three TV networks; in 1971 and 1973 showed white women became more visible and black women all but disappeared from the screen.

2406. O'Bryant, Shirley L. and Charles R. Corder-Bolz. "The Effects of Television on Children's Stereotyping of Women's Work Roles." *Journal of Vocational Behavior.* April 1978, pp. 233-244.

Sample of 67 elementary school students exposed to specially produced commercials; children do learn about occupations and to stereotype jobs from TV content.

2407. O'Connor, John J. "TV and Civil Rights: The Medium Still Is the Message." *Perspectives: The Civil Rights Quarterly.* Summer 1982, pp. 39-41.

TV aided the civil rights movement; still has limited and biased coverage of women and blacks.

2408. O'Kelly, Charlotte G. "Sexism in Children's Television." *Journalism Quarterly.* Winter 1974, pp. 722-723.

Network children's programs have a strong masculine bias and give off traditional sex-role images.

2409. O'Kelly, Charlotte G. and Linda Edwards Bloomquist. "Women and Blacks on TV." *Journal of Communication.* Autumn 1976, pp. 179-184.

Women on television were numerically underrepresented and shown in roles depicting traditional sex-role divisions of U.S. society.

2410. Peck, Ellen. "Television's Romance with Reproduction." In *Pronatalism: The Myth of Mom and Apple Pie,* edited by Ellen Peck and Judith Senderowitz, pp. 78-97. New York: Thomas Y. Crowell, 1974.

The birthrate on daytime TV seems "to rival that of Latin America!" In many soap operas, women were involved in "competition by conception." Movies, advertisements, and other TV fare surveyed.

2411. Peevers, Barbara H. "Androgyny on the TV Screen? An Analysis of Sex-Role Portrayal." *Sex Roles.* December 1979, pp. 797-809.

Sex-role portrayal in televised drama, its connection to the likeability of characters, and differences in such portrayals between family and non-family viewing times.

2412. Perdue, Lauren and Brett Silverstein. "A Comparison of the Weights and Ages of Women and Men on Television." Paper presented at Eastern Psychological Association, Boston, Massachusetts, March 21-24, 1985. 8 pp.

A rating of 221 male and female characters from 33 popular TV shows found that women were younger and thinner.

2413. Pierce, Chester M., Jean V. Carew, Diane Pierce-Gonzalez, and Deborah Wills. "An Experiment in Racism: TV Commercials." *Education and Urban Society.* 10:1 (1977), pp. 61-87.

Females made up 43 percent of all characters in 190 prime-time network commercials in 1972. Only 6 percent of the commercials featured female voice-overs; females were less likely to be shown in outside-the-home jobs.

2414. Posner, Judith. "Where's Mom?" *Media and Values.* Winter 1989, pp. 6-7.

Television shows, especially sitcoms, ignore mothers as characters; instead, male housekeepers are portrayed, organizing a variety of traditional and reconstituted families. "In television's 40-year history we can find more shows featuring aliens, dogs and horses than shows starring Mom."

2415. Poulos, Rita Wicks, Susan E. Harvey, and Robert M. Liebert. "Saturday Morning Television: A Profile of the 1974-75 Children's Season." *Psychological Reports.* 39 (1976), pp. 1047-1057.

Females constituted 29 percent of the sample; a large number of aggressive acts were recorded, most performed by males.

2416. Ramsdell, M.L. "The Trauma of Television's Troubled Soap Families." *Family Coordinator.* 22 (1973), pp. 299-304.

In eight soap operas telecast by one network in 1971-72, women were portrayed as office and service workers, followed by professionals, and affluent housewives. Misfortunes plagued working women,while housewives were referred to as "real women."

2417. Reep, Diane C. and Faye H. Dambrot. "Effects of Frequent Television Viewing on Stereotypes: 'Drip, Drip' or 'Drench'?" *Journalism Quarterly.* Autumn 1989, pp. 542-550, 556.

The high impact image ("drench') and the frequent viewing effects ("drip, drip") theories are interrelated in explaining TV's effects on viewers.

2418. Reep Diane C. and Faye H. Dambrot. "In the Eye of the Beholder: Viewer Perceptions of TV's Male/Female Working Partners." *Communication Research.* 15 (1988), pp. 51-69.

2419. Reep, Diane C. and Faye H. Dambrot. "Television's Professional Women: Working with Men in the 1980s." *Journalism Quarterly.* Summer/Autumn 1987, pp. 376-381.

2420. Reid, Pamela Trotman. "Racial Stereotyping on Television: A Comparison of the Behavior of Both Black and White Television Characters." *Journal of Applied Psychology.* 64:5 (1979), pp. 465-471.

Females made up 40 percent of the characters in 28 episodes of 10 situation comedies on TV networks in 1977. They were depicted more often than men in nurturant roles, less often in dominating situations.

2421. Repetti, R.L. "Determinants of Children's Sex Stereotyping: Parental Sex-Role Traits and Television Viewing." *Personality and Social Psychology Bulletin.* September 1984, pp. 457-468.

In a study of 40 children and their parents, parental sex roles and the watching of educational TV were related to children's sex typing of toys and occupations; daughters were more influenced by parents' sex roles than were sons.

2422. Roloff, M.E. and B.S. Greenberg. "Sex Differences in Choice of Modes of Conflict Resolution in Real-Life and Television." *Communication Quarterly.* Summer 1979, pp. 3-12.

The uses of modes of conflict resolution by young males and females and the perceived use by their favorite television characters.

2423. Ross, L., D.R. Anderson, and P.A. Wisocki. "Television Viewing and Adult Sex-role Attitudes." *Sex Roles.* June 1982, 589-592.

People who watched more sex-stereotyped TV tended to rate themselves in stereotyped ways.

2424. Schwictenberg, C. "Dynasty: The Dialectic of Feminine Power." *The Central States Speech Journal.* Fall 1983, pp. 151-161.

The ideology and myth of feminine power through analysis of TV show, "Dynasty."

2425. Seggar, John F. "Imagery of Women in Television Drama: 1974." *Journal of Broadcasting.* Summer 1975, pp. 273-282.

Between 1971 and 1973, the distribution of males to females in TV drama changed from four to one to two to one; only 9 percent were major roles and 65 percent "bit parts." Also by same author in this issue: "Imagery as Reflected Through TV's Cracked Mirror," pp. 297-299.

2426. Seggar, John F. "Television's Portrayal of Minorities and Women, 1971-1975." *Journal of Broadcasting.* Fall 1977, pp. 435-446.

Portrayals of women in TV drama in 1971, 1973, and 1975; female gains were greater in numbers and proportion than male gains.

2427. Seggar, John F. "Women's Imagery on TV: Feminist, Fair Maiden or Maid? Comments on McNeil." *Journal of Broadcasting.* Summer 1975, pp. 289-294.

Issue is taken with seven findings Jean C. McNeil reported upon in the same issue; at least five needed further research.

2428. Seggar, John F., Jeffrey Hafen, and Helena Hannonen-Gladden. "Television's Portrayal of Minorities and Women in Drama and Comedy Drama, 1971-80." *Journal of Broadcasting.* Summer 1981, pp. 277-288.

Although the proportional representation of minorities in TV comedy drama and drama declined, that of women increased from 1971-80. Other findings: black females were almost invisible; blacks of both sexes decreased in major roles, and other minority males improved in role significance but minority females lost ground.

2429. Seggar, John F. and Penny Wheeler. "World of Work on TV: Ethnic and Sex Representation in TV Drama." *Journal of Broadcasting.* Spring 1973, pp. 201-214.

The increasing use of minorities in network television programming; differences in dramatic portrayals of minority versus white American roles in a 1971 sample. The number of TV portrayals per group was not aligned with their proportion in the national population; women were particularly underrepresented.

2430. Seiter, Ellen. "Men, Sex, and Money in Recent Family Melodrama." *Journal of University Film and Video Association.* Winter 1982, pp. 17-27.

Family TV melodramas continued to be easy on men and extremely tough on women concerning morality; men were shown as competitive in the business realm, while women were depicted as rewards to be won by men. Also by this author: "The Promise of Melodrama: Recent Women's Films and Soap Operas," Ph.D. dissertation, Northwestern University, 1981.

2431. Serra, Michele R. and Richard A. Kallan. "Sexual Egalitarianism on TV: An Analysis of 'PM Magazine.'" *Journalism Quarterly.* Autumn 1983, pp. 535-538.

Content analysis of ten editions of "PM," a Westinghouse TV production, and surveys of the producers and co-hosts; the show was sexually egalitarian.

2432. "Sexism Still Prevails on/in Television." *Press Woman.* September 1979, pp. 6-7, 15.

The findings of the Commission on Civil Rights report, "Window Dressing on the Set: An Update"; a composite TV portrait of women was that "Females constitute 27.7% of the US population. Half of them are teenagers or in their 20s. They wear revealing outfits, jiggle a lot, but don't do much else. More than a third are unemployed or without any identifiable pursuit or purpose...."

2433. Shaw, Jeffrey. "Interactions on Television: An Analysis of the Interactions of the Main Characters of *All in the Family* and *The Honeymooners*." *Small Group Behavior.* 11:4 (1980), pp. 411-418.

The male leads in these situation comedy shows showed tension and antagonism, while the female partners either reduced tension or remained undisturbed.

2434. Sherman, Barry L. and Joseph R. Dominick. "Violence and Sex in Music Videos: TV and Rock 'n' Roll." *Journal of Communication.* Winter 1986, pp. 79-93.

"Concept" views contained a different type of violence where women, older adults, and nonwhites were more likely to be aggressors than victims.

2435. Signorielli, Nancy. "Marital Status in Television Drama: A Case of Reduced Options." *Journal of Broadcasting.* 26:2 (1982), pp. 585-597.

Network, prime-time dramatic programming between 1975 and 1979 was traditional and stereotyped: males outnumbered females three to one; female characters were less important, young, and more attractive than male counterparts. They also were more apt to be married and as such, not employed outside the home.

2436. Signorielli, Nancy. *Role Portrayal and Stereotyping on Television: An Annotated Bibliography of Studies Relating to Women, Minorities, Aging, Sexual Behavior, Health, and Handicaps.* Westport, Connecticut: Greenwood Press, 1985. 214 pp.

Articles and books relevant to the topics through 1984; the "most striking revelation" of the bibliography was the similarity and stability of the research findings -- in a nutshell, women have been shortchanged in the television portrayals. "Women and Sex-Roles" is the largest section of the book, taking up pages 3-89.

2437. Signorielli, Nancy. "The Demography of the Television World." In *Cultural Indicators: An International Symposium,* edited by Gabrielle Melischek, Karl E. Rosengren, and James Stappers, pp. 137-157. Vienna: The Austrian Academy of Sciences, 1983.

Women in television were underrepresented three-to-one by men. Changes occurred; in 1973, only 25 percent of the characters were female, while in 1980-81, the figure was 31 percent.

2438. Signorielli, Nancy and George Gerbner. "The Image of the Elderly in Prime-time Network Television Drama." *Generations.* Fall 1978, pp. 8-11.

In network drama between 1969 and 1976, the percentage of female characters decreased with age, older women had more negative attributes than older men, and older women were more likely to be killed in the show than males and younger women.

2439. Signorielli, Nancy and George Gerbner. "Women in Public Broadcasting: A Progress Report." Philadelphia, Pennsylvania: University of Pennsylvania, The Annenberg School of Communications, March 1978.

Update of the 1975 Task Force Report on Women in Public Broadcasting; the percentage of women characters increased from 1975, but three-fourths of the announcers and all moderators continued to be male. Females showed a slight increase in the number of characters on children's programming.

2440. Silverman, L. Theresa, Joyce N. Sprafkin, and Eli Rubinstein. "Physical Contact and Sexual Behavior on Prime-Time TV." *Journal of Communication.* Winter 1979, pp. 33-43.

In a 1977-78 sample week of network prime-time programming, females made up 32 percent of the characters and were two-to-one more likely than males to engage in physical forms of affection.

2441. Silverman-Watkins, L. Theresa, Stephen C. Levi, and Meryl A. Klein. "Sex-stereotyping as a Factor in Children's Comprehension of Television News." *Journalism Quarterly.* Spring 1986, pp. 3-11.

Children, 9-13 years old, remembered and liked a special set of news reports; the gender of the newscaster had no discernible impact on children's understanding of news content.

2442. Simson, Eve. "Stereotyping of Women on Television." *USA Today.* September 1978, pp. 14-16.

    Analysis of 157 TV programs; in crime dramas, women were pretty, young, and residents of California.

2443. Smythe, Dallas W. "Reality as Presented by Television." *Public Opinion Quarterly.* 18 (1954), pp. 143-156.

    In a week's sample of dramatic programs on New York City television in 1953, females made up one-third of the characters. Housewives constituted 37 percent of the female sample; women employed in other occupations were more likely to break the law than housewives or employed males. Taken from author's *Three Years of New York Television, 1951-1953*, Urbana, Illinois: National Association of Educational Broadcasters, 1953.

2444. Steenland, Sally. "Prime-Time Girls Just Want To Have Fun." *Media and Values.* Winter 1989, p. 5.

    More than 200 television programs monitored; TV teenage girls are concerned about shopping, grooming, and dating, instead of school or career plans. Excerpted from author's *Growing up in Prime Time: An Analysis of Adolescent Girls on Television.*

2445. Steenland, Sally and Pamela Fujita. "The Picture Improves: A Look at the 1984 Television Season. An Analysis of Female TV Characters on Programs Premiering in 1984." Washington, D.C.: National Commission on Working Women, 1984. 16 pp.

    The 1984 TV season had increases in the number of minority female characters, the percentage of female entrepreneurs and older women characters.

2446. Steenland, Sally and Lisa Schmidt. "Trouble on the Set. An Analysis of Female Characters on 1985 Television Programs." Washington, D.C.: National Commission on Working Women, 1985. 18 pp.

    Some disappointing trends: a decrease in the number of female characters, a return of the two-parent family in situational comedies, and a decrease in the number of minority female characters.

2447. Steenland, Sally and Lauren Whittemore. "Women Out of View. An Analysis of Female Characters on 1987-88 TV Programs." Washington, D.C.: National Commission on Working Women, 1987. 30 pp.

    Female characters on TV compared over two seasons with real-life women.

2448. Steeves, H. Leslie and Marilyn Crafton Smith. "Class and Gender in Prime-Time Television Entertainment: Observations from a Socialist Feminist Perspective." *Journal of Communication Inquiry.* Winter 1987, pp. 43-63.

    Depictions of women in the top ten TV shows from a socialist feminist perspective.

2449. Sternglanz, Sarah Hall and Lisa A. Serbin. "Sex-role Stereotyping in Children's Television Programs." *Developmental Psychology.* September 1974, pp. 710-715.

In commercial television children's programs, a higher percentage of females than males was classified as "good." Females were less likely to make plans or be aggressive and more likely to be punished for much activity.

2450. Stocking, S. Holly, Barry S. Sapolsky, and Dolf Zillman. "Sex Discrimination in Prime Time Humor." *Journal of Broadcasting.* Fall 1977, pp. 447-457.

Prime time programs of the networks for a 1975 week analyzed to determine if women were the butt of comedy more often than men. The opposite was true.

2451. Suls, J. and J.W. Gastoff. "The Incidence of Sex Discrimination, Sexual Contents, and Hostility in Television Humor." *Journal of Applied Communication Research.* Spring 1981, pp. 42-49.

The charge that women are more often made the butt of humor on U.S. prime-time television disproved. The opposite was true probably because males appeared more frequently in TV leads.

2452. Tedesco, Nancy S. "Patterns in Prime Time." *Journal of Communication.* Spring 1974, pp. 119-124.

Women were powerless in prime-time TV drama shows, were lacking in independence, were not found in adventure situations, and were more likely to be younger and married and less likely to be employed. Also see her 1975 M.A. thesis at University of Pennsylvania entitled, "Men and Women in Television Drama: The Use of Two Multivariate Techniques for Isolating Dimensions of Characterizations."

2453. "Television Images of Women." *Intellect.* April 1975, pp. 424-425.

A study by Sharon C. Nash on portrayals of women in TV commercials, soap operas, and prime-time shows, concluded that the female viewer, bombarded by derogatory images, must believe she has very few role options for defining herself.

2454. Tognoli, Jerome and Judith L. Storch. "Inside and Outside: Setting Locations of Female and Male Characters in Children's Television." *EDRA: Environmental Design Research Association.* No. 11 (1980), pp. 288-297.

In 13 most popular children's television programs, women were underrepresented (half as often as men) and portrayed in stereotypically feminine activities.

2455. Tuchman, Gaye. "Mass Media Values." *Society.* November-December 1976, pp. 51-54.

The societal values captured in TV's portrayal of property, violence, and relationships between women and men.

2456. Turow, Joseph. "Advising and Ordering: Daytime, Prime Time." *Journal of Communication.* Spring 1974, pp. 138-141.

    Twelve hours each of daytime and prime-time television drama analyzed; women characters advised and directed men, but usually on "feminine" matters.

2457. Turow, Joseph. "Occupation and Personality in Television Dramas: An Industry View." *Communication Research.* 7:3 (1980), pp. 295-318.

    Personality stereotyping among occupational groups in television drama; females made up 21 percent of blue collar workers and 19 percent of white collar employees.

2458. Uselding, Douglas K. "Assessing the Level of Sex-Role Stereotyping on Children's Preferred Programming." Technical Report No. 1: Children's Use of Television as a Source of Social Role Models. University of South Dakota, Department of Psychology, 1979.

    Rating of characters for "male" and "female" concepts on 64 favorite children's TV programs; female characters were more stereotyped and oriented toward the female concept.

2459. Verna, Mary Ellen. "The Female Image in Children's TV Commercials." *Journal of Broadcasting.* Summer 1975, pp. 301-309.

    Commercials of the three TV networks analyzed for 1973; females exhibited more passive behavior than men, appeared in more independent and cooperative types of activity than men, and almost never were featured in the audio voice-over.

2460. Vincent, Richard. "Clio's Consciousness Raised? Portrayal of Women in Rock Videos Re-examined." *Journalism Quarterly.* Spring 1989, pp. 155-160.

    Analysis of music videos on MTV in the Summer of 1985 and Winter of 1986-87; sexism was still "fairly high," women were used "exclusively as decorative objects" and were portrayed as submissive, passive, and physically attractive.

2461. Vincent, Richard C., Dennis K. Davis, and Lilly Ann Boruszkowki. "Sexism on MTV: The Portrayal of Women in Rock Videos." *Journalism Quarterly.* Winter 1987, pp. 750-755.

    The description of the gender role in media such as rock video was rather traditional and sexist.

2462. Volgy, Thomas J. and John E. Schwarz. "TV Entertainment Programming and Sociopolitical Attitudes." *Journalism Quarterly.* 57:1 (1980), pp. 150-154.

    Male-female relationships in prime-time network entertainment were based on traditional values.

2463. Weigel, Russell and James W. Loomis. "Televised Models of Female Achievement Revisited: Some Progress." *Journal of Applied Social Psychology.* January-February 1981, pp. 58-63.

Replication of a study by Manes and Melnyk, done in 1974; in a week of prime-time network drama in 1978, females were outnumbered two-to-one by males as characters. Concerning employment-happy marriage incompatibility, the percentage of unsuccessful marriages among working women decreased 20 percent, while the percentage of unsuccessful marriages among housewives increased.

2464. Wexler, Marvin and Gilbert Levy. "Women on Television: Fairness and the 'Fair Sex.'" *Yale Review of Law and Social Action.* 2 (1971), pp. 59-68.

Monitoring of 600 hours of television in the Washington, D.C. area; women were the leading characters in 53 hours, men in 508. Women were shown in roles of nurses, housewives, secretaries, witches, maids, dizzy teenagers, and less-than-intelligent starlets, while men were portrayed in more professional roles.

2465. Zeck, Shari. "Female Bonding in *Cagney and Lacey.*" *Journal of Popular Culture.* Winter 1989, pp. 143-154.

"Cagney and Lacey," the network TV series, as an explanation of the ways female bonding is "circumscribed within culture and the threat which women's friendships pose to that culture."

2466. Zemach, Tamar and Akiba Cohen. "Perception of Gender Equality on Television and in Social Reality." *Journal of Broadcasting and Electronic Media.* Fall 1986, pp. 427-444.

The differential perceptions of men and women as they appeared on television as an example of symbolic reality and the way they were perceived in social reality. A marked tendency to regard symbolic reality as more stereotypic than social reality was found in most of the traits, roles, and occupations examined.

2467. Zimmermann, Patricia R. "Good Girls, Bad Women: The Role of Older Women on *Dynasty.*" *Journal of Film and Video.* Spring 1985, pp. 66-74.

Older women made a larger presence in TV drama after 1982-83; Joan Collins and Linda Evans as examples in their roles in "Dynasty."

Film

2468. Adelman, Shonagh. "Representations of Violence Against Women in Mainstream Film." *RFR/DRF New Feminist Research.* June 1989, pp. 21-26.

"Psycho," "Dressed to Kill," "Looking for Mr. Goodbar," and "The Photographer."

2469. Afro-American Studies Program. *Black Images in Films, Stereotyping, and Self-Perception as Viewed by Black Actresses.* Boston: Boston University, Afro-American Studies Program, Occasional Paper No. 2, 1974.

Proceedings of a symposium held in Boston, April 13-14, 1973.

2470. Artel, Linda and Susan Wengraf. *Positive Images: A Guide to Non-Sexist Films for Young People.* San Francisco, California: Bootlegger Press, n.d. 168 pp.
    Alphabetically lists 400 films which "actively challenge sex role stereotypes."

2471. Atkins, Thomas R., ed. *Sexuality in the Movies.* Bloomington: Indiana University Press, 1975.

2472. Baker, M. Joyce. *Images of Women in Film: The War Years, 1941-1945.* Ann Arbor, Michigan: UMI Research Press, 1980. 196 pp.
    Looks at perceptions of women in film on eve of World War II, women behind enemy lines, heroines on the home front, and heroines in military life. Based on Ph.D. dissertation of same title, completed in 1978 at University of California, Santa Barbara.

2473. Bazin, A. "Entomology of the Pin-Up Girl." In *What is Cinema: Essays Selected by Hugh Gray*, pp. 158-162. Berkeley, University of California Press, 1967, 1971.

2474. Betancourt, Jeanne. "Whatever Happened to Women in Film?" *Media and Methods.* October 1975, pp. 25-33.
    Images and roles of women in films from the 1920s to the 1970s. Rather than deal with the emancipated nature of women, 1970s' directors omitted them from films. Also see her *Women in Focus: Guide to 16mm Films by, For and About Women*, Pflaum Standard Publications, 1974.

2475. Bowser, Pearl. "Sexual Imagery and the Black Woman in American Cinema." In *Black Cinema Aesthetics,* edited by Gladstone L. Yearwood, pp. 42-51. Athens, Ohio: Center for Afro-American Studies, Ohio University, 1982.
    Little improvement in opportunities and images. In Black film also, women characters lacked credibility as they were placed on pedestals, used as symbols for black peoples' problems, or treated as love goddesses.

2476. Burrell, Walter. "The Black Woman as a Sex Image in Films." *Black Stars.* December 1972, pp. 32-39.

2477. Cheatwood, Derral and Nijole Benokraitis. "Making the Most of Bad Times: Integrating the Media, Funding, and Teaching." *Teaching Sociology.* April 1983, pp. 337-351.
    Ways of funding and administering courses in sociology during hard times, using as case study, the course, "Images of Women in Film."

2478. Considine, David M. "The Decline and Possible Rise of the Movie Mother." *Journal of Popular Film and Television.* Spring 1985, pp. 4-15.
    Historical and contemporary perspectives on movie mothers.

2479. Cowan, Gloria, Carole Lee, Daniella Levy, and Debra Snyder. "Dominance and Inequality in X-Rated Videocassettes." *Psychology of Women Quarterly.* September 1988, pp. 299-312.
   The extent of domination and sexual inequality in 45 X-rated videocassettes studied; over one-half of sexual themes showed male domination over women.

2480. Cripps, Thomas. "Historical Overview." In *Black Images in Films, Stereotyping, and Self-Perception as Viewed by Black Actresses*, edited by Adelaide Cromwell Gulliver, pp. 9-19. Boston: Boston University, Afro-American Studies Program, 1974.

2481. David, Jane T. "An Investigation of the Image of American Women in Selected American Motion Pictures, 1930-1971." Ph.D. dissertation, New York University, 1975.

2482. Davidman, Joy. "Women: Hollywood Version." *New Masses.* July 14, 1942, pp. 28-31.
   Hollywood films termed male chauvinistic.

2483. Degener, David. "Director under the Influence." *Film Quarterly.* Winter 1975-76, pp. 4-12.
   The dependence of film director John Cassavetes on stereotypic concepts of madness in women for his plots.

2484. DelGuadio, Sybil. "The Mammy in Hollywood Film: I'd Walk a Mile for One of Her Smiles." *Jump Cut.* No. 28, 1983, pp. 23-25.

2485. Donalson, Melvin B. "The Representation of Afro-American Women in the Hollywood Feature Film, 1915-1949." Ph.D. dissertation, Brown University, 1981.

2486. Dworkin, Susan. "Teri Garr: Her Real Role in 'Tootsie': The Behind-the-Scenes Story of the Movie That Helps Men Understand What It's Like To Be a Woman." *Ms.* March 1983, pp. 39-42.
   Director Sydney Pollack and Actor Dustin Hoffman looked deeply into the "sexually political atmosphere" around the U.S. film, "Tootsie."

2487. *Ebony.*
   Black women in films discussed, including: "Movie Maids: Eight New Hollywood Films Backtrack To Hack Racial Stereotypes in Casting Negro Actors as Usual Maids and Menials?" Aug. 1948, pp. 56-59; "Secret of a Movie Maid," Nov. 1949, pp. 52-56; "Black Women in Entertainment," Aug. 1982, pp. 102-108.

2488. Eckert, Charles. "The Carole Lombard in Macy's Window." *Quarterly Review of Film Studies.* Winter 1978, pp. 1-21.

2489. Farber, Stephen. "Violence and the Bitch Goddess." *Film Comment.* November-December 1974, pp. 8-11.

In "woman's pictures" of post-World War II, strong women flourished, e.g. "The Postman Always Rings Twice," "The Strange Love of Martha Ivers," "Sorry Wrong Number," "Double Indemnity," and others.

2490. French, Brandon. *On the Verge of Revolt: Women in American Films of the Fifties*. New York: Ungar, 1978.
Mentions of images of Irish women in U.S. film.

2491. Galerstein, Carolyn L. *Working Women on the Hollywood Screen: A Filmography*. New York: Garland, 1989. 470 pp.
About 4,500 U.S. feature films of 1930-75 listed. Each features the leading female character as a working woman. Divided into occupational categories.

2492. Gerard, Lillian. "Belles, Sirens, Sisters." *Film Library Quarterly*. Winter 1971-72, pp. 14-21.
As women work out their liberation, their screen roles have not changed. Three films analyzed where women are demeaned, denied, or deprived: "McCabe and Mrs. Miller," "Carnal Knowledge," and "Sunday, Bloody Sunday."

2493. Golab, Caroline. "Stellaaaaaa......!!!!!!!!: The Slavic Stereotype in American Film." In *The Kaleidoscopic Lens: How Hollywood Views Ethnic Groups*, edited by Randall M. Miller, pp. 135-155. Englewood Cliffs, New Jersey: Jerome S. Ozer, 1980.

2494. Golden, Daniel S. "Pasta or Paradigm: The Place of Italian-American Women in Popular Film." *Explorations in Ethnic Studies*. January 1979, pp. 3-10.
Images of Italian women in U.S. film (1930s to 1970s), noting either their passive confinement to the kitchen or, occasionally, their "hot-blooded passion."

2495. Gough-Yates, Kevin. "The Heroine." *Films and Filming*. May 1966, pp. 23-27; June 1966, pp. 27-32; July 1966, pp. 38-43; August 1966, pp. 45-50.
The heroine with masculine traits, the anti-heroine, the "good-bad" girls, and the fallen angel discussed.

2496. Grant, Liz. "Ain't Beulah Dead Yet? Or Images of the Black Woman in Film." *Essence*. May 1973, pp. 60-61.

2497. Gray, J. Patrick. "Male Bricolage and the Image of Women: An Analysis of *10*." *International Journal of Women's Studies*. January-February 1982, pp. 75-85.
The film, "10," as an example of a modern myth that affirms the "Mary/Eve" paradigm.

2498. Haskell, Molly. *From Reverence to Rape: The Treatment of Women in the Movies*. New York: Holt, Rinehart and Winston, 1974.

A surgence of film scripts such as "The Eyes of Laura Mars," predicted because such heroines have a passivity that links them to evil, even though they lack any real power. A chronology of images projected in films with explanations on what they have meant to women in society. By the same author: "What's Happening To Women in the Movies," *Family Circle*, February 1976, pp. 36+.

2499. Haskell, Molly. "The Woman Wins in Some New Movies, New Heroines." *Vogue*. April 1972, pp. 66+.

2500. Hooks, Bell. *Yearning. Race and Gender in the Cultural Marketplace.* Boston: South End Press, 1990. 224 pp.
   A look at popular film "uncovers the dangerous ideologies their directors so artfully obscure."

2501. Humboldt, Charles. "Caricature by Hollywood." *New Masses*. July 28, 1942, pp. 29-30.
   U.S. movies distorted the women's position.

2502. Johnston, Claire. "Feminist Politics and Film History." *Screen*. Autumn 1975, pp. 115-124.

2503. Kalisch, Beatrice J., Philip A. Kalisch, and Mary McHugh. "Content Analysis of Film Stereotypes of Nurses." *International Journal of Women's Studies*. November-December 1980, pp. 531-558.
   A study of 200 films from 1930-1979 with nurses as main characters. Their portrayal peaked during the 1940s and declined during the following three decades. They were particularly denigrated in films in the 1970s.

2504. Kaplan, E. Ann, ed. *Women in Film Noir*. Bloomington, Indiana/London: Indiana University Press and British Film Institute, 1980. 132 pp.
   Film noir of the 1940s and 1950s was the exception to the types of stereotypical films that came out of Hollywood; it portrayed women as strong characters.

2505. Kay, K. "Part Time Work of a Domestic Slave." *Film Quarterly*. Fall 1975, pp. 52-57.

2506. Kisner, Ronald E. "What Films Are Doing to the Image of Black Women." *Jet*. June 29, 1972, pp. 56-61.

2507. Koch, Christian and John Powers, comps. *1972 Oberlin Film Conference Selected Essays and Discussion Transcriptions*. Vol. II. Oberlin, Ohio: Oberlin College, 1974. 327 pp.
   Includes "The Image of Women in the Cinema."

2508. Lucas, Bob. "Pam: Why Are Black Women Fading from Films?" *Jet*. November 6, 1980, pp. 58-61.

2509. Mapp, Edward. "Black Women in Films." *Black Scholar.* Summer 1982, pp. 36-40.

    Black women in films of the 1960s. By this author: "Black Women in Films: A Mixed Bag of Tricks," in *Black Films and Film-makers: A Comprehensive Anthology from Stereotype to Superhero,* edited by Lindsay Patterson, pp. 196-205, New York: Dodd, Mead and Co., 1975.

2510. Mellen, Joan. "Bergman and Women: Cries and Whispers." *Film Quarterly.* Fall 1973, pp. 2-11.

    Bergman was noted for his unique affinity for portraying and understanding the female psyche, as evidenced in his 1972 "Cries and Whispers."

2511. Minton, Lynn. "Will Hollywood Ever Discover Women?" *McCall's.* April 1976, p. 150+.

2512. Modleski, Tania. *The Women Who Knew Too Much.* New York: Methuen, 1988.

    In Hitchcock's long film career, woman is never completely obliterated by man. Author makes this point in discussions of the films themselves, which she looks at from a feminist viewpoint.

2513. Movshovitz, Howard. "The Delusion of Hollywood's 'Women's Films.'" *Frontiers: A Journal of Women Studies.* Spring 1979, pp. 9-13.

    Three U.S. films of the 1970s, acclaimed as positive portrayals of women's issues, were actually the same products with new labels.

2514. Pannill, Linda. "The Woman Artist as Creature and Creator." *Journal of Popular Culture.* Fall 1982, pp. 26-29.

    Movies used to show the differences in ways women artists have been depicted by men and by other women.

2515. Schrank, Louise Welsh. "Films for Feminist Consciousness Raising." *Media and Methods.* December 1973, pp. 10-12.

    Films that are good discussion starters on women's issues.

2516. Shaffer, Susan Morris, comp. *Spotlight on Sex Equity: A Filmography.* Washington, D.C.: American University, Mid-Atlantic Center for Sex Equity, 1980. 66 pp.

    Catalog of films, slides, and filmstrips presented at a festival sponsored by the Mid-Atlantic Center for Sex Equity; 17 categories, including sexism in media and language.

2517. Smith, Barbara. "Black Women in Film Symposium." *Freedomway.* 1974, pp. 266-269.

2518. Sobachack, Vivian C. "'The Leech Woman's' Revenge, or a Case for Equal Misrepresentation." *Journal of Popular Film.* 4:3 (1975), pp. 236-257.

Stereotyped roles of women in movies; most critical analyses of women's images are biased. Films can be read differently; "The Leech Woman" is an example.

2519. Sochen, June. "'Mildred Pierce' and Women in Film." *American Quarterly.* Spring 1978, pp. 3-20.
The film, "Mildred Pierce," starring Joan Crawford, made a strong statement against powerful women.

2520. Stephens, Lenora C. "Black Women in Film." *Southern Quarterly.* Spring-Summer 1981, pp. 164-170.

2521. Stern, Lesley. "The Body as Evidence." *Screen.* 23:5 (1982), pp. 38-60.

2522. Stoddard, Karen M. *Saints and Shrews: Women and Aging in American Popular Film.* Westport, Connecticut: Greenwood Press, 1983. 174 pp.
Aging of women in films from 1930 to the early 1980s. Chapters include: "Aging: A Cultural State of Mind," "Maternity and Matriarchy: The Older Woman as Mother, 1930-1945," "Postwar Films: Mom, Apple Pie, and the Crisis Next Door," "Aging as Crisis: The Older Woman in the 1950s," "In the Witch's Castle: The Older Woman in the 1960s," and "Intimidations of Regeneration?: The Older Woman in the 1970s and Beyond."

2523. Turim, Maureen. "Fashion Shapes: Film, the Fashion Industry and the Image of Women." *Socialist Review.* September-October 1983, pp. 79-96.

2524. Tuska, Jon. *The American West in Film: Critical Approaches to the Western.* Westport, Connecticut: Greenwood Press, 1985. 303 pp.
Recorded fantasies about the American West compared with the actual events; includes a part on women under "Types and Stereotypes."

2525. Tyler, Parker. "The Film: Revival of the Matriarchic Spirit." *Accent.* No. 2, 1952, pp. 104-112.
Films that show female wisdom.

2526. Waldman, Diane. "From Midnight Shows to Marriage Vows: Woman, Exploitation, and Exhibition." *Wide Angle.* 6:2 (1984), pp. 40-48.

2527. Wallbott, H.G. "Big Girls Don't Frown, Big Boys Don't Cry -- Gender Differences of Professional Actors in Communicating Emotion Via Facial Expression." *Journal of Nonverbal Behavior.* Summer 1988, pp. 98-106.
Study of 40 "takes" from movies showing facial close-ups of actors and actresses; females were a bit more emotive in communicating via facial expression than males.

2528. Walsh, Andrea S. "'Life Isn't Over Yet': Older Heroines in American Popular Cinema of the 1930s and 1970s/80s." *Qualitative Sociology.* Spring 1989, pp. 72-95.

Analysis of the films, "If I Had a Million" (1932), "Make Way for Tomorrow" (1971), and "The Trip to Bountiful" (1985); critical of the psychoanalytic approaches to the study of female representation in cinema.

2529. West, Ann A. "'Comedie Noire' Thrillers of Alfred Hitchcock: Genres, Psychoanalysis, and Woman's Image." Ph.D. dissertation, University of California, Berkeley, 1982. 172 pp.

2530. White, Maxine Rachofsky. "Images of Women in Contemporary Hollywood Films: Popular Culture, Ideology and Gender." Ph.D. dissertation, University of California, Santa Cruz, 1984. 258 pp.

2531. White, Susan. "Male Bonding, Hollywood Orientalism, and the Repression of the Feminine in Kubrick's *Full Metal Jacket*." *Arizona Quarterly*. Autumn 1988.

2532. Williams, Linda. "'Something Else Besides a Mother': *Stella Dallas* and the Maternal Melodrama." *Cinema Journal*. Fall 1984, pp. 2-27.

2533. Yates, John. "Why There Are No Women in the Movies." *Journal of Popular Film*. 4:3 (1975), pp. 223-233.
How films of the 1930s and 1940s were different from contemporary ones; today's films seldom portray stable male-female relationships.

Print Media

2534. Adams, R.C., et al. "The Effect of Framing on Selection of Photographs of Men and Women." *Journalism Quarterly*. Autumn 1980, pp. 463-467.
Examines validity of the notion that people tend to see men in terms of the face and women in terms of the body. Shows sample of men and women photographs of male and female "candidates."

2535. Anderson, R.E. and E. Jolly. "Stereotyped Traits and Sex Roles in Humorous Drawings." *Communication Research*. 4 (1977), pp. 453-484.

2536. Atkin, David and Jay Moorman. "Portrayals of Women on Television in the 1980s." Paper presented at Association for Education in Journalism and Mass Communication, Minneapolis, Minnesota, 1990.
Longitudinal study focusing on programs in which women were lead characters.

2537. Bailey, Margaret. "The Women's Magazine Short-Story Heroine in 1947 and 1967." *Journalism Quarterly*. Summer 1969, pp. 364-366.
Looks at *McCall's, Ladies' Home Journal,* and *Good Housekeeping*, 1957 to 1967, to see if women's magazine short-story heroines changed from the happy housewives image. For the most part, there was no change, except for the types of problems of the attractive, married woman.

2538. Barcus, Francis E. "The World of Sunday Comics." In *The Funnies: An American Idiom*, edited by David M. White and Robert H. Abel, pp. 190-218. New York: The Free Press of Glencoe, 1963.

   Empirical data on the sex and marital status, as well as goals by sex and marital status, of Sunday comics characters.

2539. Bargainnier, Earl F. "I Disagree!" *Journal of Communication*. Spring 1975, pp. 113-119.

   With Mary Jane Jones' view of the spinster role in Agatha Christie detective novels.

2540. Binns, Catherine A. "Careers and Jobs for American Women as Reflected in the Pages of Mademoiselle, 1935-1975." Masters thesis, University of Mississippi, 1974.

2541. Blackwood, Roy E. "The Content of News Photos: Roles Portrayed by Men and Women." *Journalism Quarterly*. Winter 1983, pp. 710-714.

   In 92 issues of *New York Times* and *Washington Post*, men clearly dominated page one photographs, as well as those of inside news pages, business and sports sections.

2542. Boyer, Peter J. "The Three Phases of Ferraro's Press." *Washington Journalism Review*. November 1984, pp. 24-29.

   The three phases progressed from novelty to notoriety to normal.

2543. Brabant, Sarah. "Sex Role Stereotyping in the Sunday Comics." *Sex Roles*. 2:4 (1976), pp. 333-337.

   Analyzes four family-oriented Sunday comics: in two, female characters overtly dominate the males; in two others, females play passive roles. Claims that "even when overt signs of female dominance are found, traditional sex-role stereotyping persists."

2544. Brabant, Sarah and Linda Mooney. "Sex Role Stereotyping in the Sunday Comics: Ten Years Later." *Sex Roles*. February 1986, pp. 141-148.

   Replication of Brabant's analysis of sex-role stereotyping in Sunday comics, using cartoons for the same six month periods of 1974 and 1984. Females continued to appear less frequently, to remain in the home more often than males, and to be portrayed in stereotypical roles.

2545. Bridge, Junior. "No News Is Women's News." *Media and Values*. Winter 1989, pp. 11-13.

   Findings of a 1989 study on women's roles as newsmakers and creators, chief of which was that women's emerging role in society is not reflected in news media. Female bylines on front pages of ten major U.S. dailies averaged 27 percent; females appeared in only 24 percent of front-page photos, and references to women was an "abysmally low" 11 percent.

2546. Bryant, James. "A Two-Year Selective Investigation of the Female in Sport as Reported in the Paper Media." *ARENA Review.* May 1980, pp. 32-44.

Unequal treatment of females in sports, looking at two Denver newspapers and four sports magazines.

2547. Buresh, Bernice. "Critical Mass." *The Quill.* September 1984, pp. 14-20, 33.

Women's culture emerged in politics and will also find expression in media. Discussion of media reporting of candidate for U.S. vice president in 1984, Geraldine Ferraro.

2548. Burkhart, Ford N. and Carol Sigelman. "Effects of Bias Associated with Author Gender on Evaluations of News Stories." Paper presented at Association for Education in Journalism and Mass Communication, Minneapolis, Minnesota, August 1990.

Two experiments studying the effects of byline gender on news story perception.

2549. Cancian, Francesca M. and Steven L. Gordon. "Changing Emotion Norms in Marriage: Love and Anger in U.S. Women's Magazines Since 1900." *Gender and Society.* September 1988, pp. 308-342.

The "cultural convergence of gender, marriage, and emotion" as viewed in marital advice columns, 1900 to 1979.

2550. Cancian. Francesca M. and Bonnie L. Ross. "Mass Media and the Women's Movement: 1900-1977." *Journal of Applied Behavioral Science.* January-March 1981, pp. 9-26.

News coverage of women was strongly related to the women's movement. Looks at *New York Times* and the periodicals in the *Reader's Guide*, 1900 to 1977.

2551. Chavez, Deborah. "Perpetuation of Gender Inequality: A Content Analysis of Comic Strips." *Sex Roles.* July 1985, pp. 93-102.

Comic strips perpetuate gender inequality and distort reality in ways detrimental to men and women.

2552. Cloud, G.W. "Mr., Ms., and Miss in the Land of Sir and Ma'am: Preference for Newspaper Courtesy Titles in a Southeastern State." *Newspaper Research Journal.* Spring 1989, pp. 11-16.

Of 800 adults in the Carolinas polled on their preferences regarding use of courtesy titles in newspapers, nearly one-half had no preference; 41 percent liked courtesy title use, and 11.6 percent preferred the use of last name only.

2553. Cohen, Anne B. *Poor Pearl, Poor Girl!: The Murdered-Girl Stereotype in Ballad and Newspaper.* Austin: University of Texas Press, 1973. 131 pp.

The influences of ballad stereotypes on "off-white" journalism in the "reinterpretation of legal evidence" as it resurfaces in papers a year later.

2554. Connors, Joanna. "Female Meets Supermale." In *Superman at Fifty! The Persistance of a Legend!*, edited by Dennis Dooley and Gary Engle, pp. 108-115. New York: Collier Books, 1987.

Character "Lois Lane" in "Superman" comics and movies finds "Superman" attractive because he represents freedom.

2555. Cornillon, Susan Koppelman. *Images of Women in Fiction: Feminine Perspective.* Bowling Green, Ohio: Popular Press, 1972. 399 pp.

Fiction as a conditioning agent and art as propaganda.

2556. Davis, Junetta. "Sexist Bias in Eight Newspapers." *Journalism Quarterly.* Autumn 1982, pp. 456-460.

In four Oklahoma, two California, and one each North Carolina and Delaware dailies, only 8.6 percent of all stories had women as the main characters; all papers had a distinct pattern of bias.

2557. Dodd, D.K., B.J. Foerch, and H.T. Anderson. "Content Analysis of Women and Racial Minorities as News Magazine Cover Persons." *Journal of Social Behavior and Personality.* 3:3 (1988), pp. 231-236.

Women were featured on 15 percent of covers of *Time* and *Newsweek* magazines during the preceding four decades. The lowest year was 1963 with 3 percent; the highest was 1977 with 30 percent. Women usually made the covers because of achievement in arts/entertainment.

2558. Dodd, D.K., et al. "Face-ism and Facial Expressions of Women in Magazine Photos." *Psychological Record.* Summer 1989, pp. 325-331.

Face-ism, the tendency for illustrations to emphasize the faces of men and the bodies of women, in *Newsweek* (1938, 1953, 1963, 1975, and 1983) and *Time, Ms., Ebony,* and *Fortune* (1976, 1981, 1986).

2559. Dorris, J.M. "Androgyny and Pedagogy: An Analysis of Interpersonal Communication Textbooks." *Communication Education.* January 1981, pp. 33-43.

How gender identity was presented in 22 interpersonal communication textbooks from 1975-79.

2560. Drew, Dan G. and Susan H. Miller. "Sex Stereotyping and Reporting." *Journalism Quarterly.* Spring 1977, pp. 142-146.

In a small sample of university students, found that the "blatant stereotyping" predicted did not appear in the news stories, questions, or choice of pictures in the study.

2561. Durham, Leona, et al., "APME's 'Guidelines': A Women's Review." *Columbia Journalism Review.* May/June 1971, pp. 55-56.

Group of *Daily Iowan* staff members claim guidelines set down by the Associated Press Managing Editors for newsroom executives were "most blatantly sexist."

2562. East, Catherine and Dorothy Jurney. *New Directions for News. Final Report.* Washington, D.C.: Women's Studies Program and Policy Center, 1983.

"News" definition and assignment editors are keys to news coverage.

2563. Faderman, Lillian. "Lesbian Magazine Fiction in the Early Twentieth Century." *Journal of Popular Culture.* Spring 1978, pp. 800-817.

In early twentieth, and most of the nineteenth century, popular magazine stories often treated lesbianism "totally without self-consciousness and without awareness that such relationships were 'unhealthy' or 'immoral.'" But, the situation changed after the 1920s. Works in many popular and "art" magazines cited.

2564. Feminists on Children's Media. "Little Miss Muffett Fights Back: Recommended Non-Sexist Books About Girls for Young Readers." New York: Feminists on Children's Media, 1971. 48 pp.

List of 200 non-sexist book titles.

2565. Franzwa, Helen H. "Female Roles in Women's Magazine Fiction, 1940-1970." In *Woman: Dependent or Independent Variable?*, edited by Rhoda K. Unger and Florence L. Denmark, pp. 42-53. New York: Psychological Dimensions, 1975.

Depiction of women in three women's magazines: "The only proper role for women was housewife and mother."

2566. Franzwa, Helen H. "Pronatalism in Women's Magazine Fiction." In *Pronatalism: The Myth of Mom and Apple Pie*, edited by Ellen Peck and Judith Senderowitz, pp. 68-77. New York: Thomas Y. Crowell, 1974.

A look at short stories in *McCall's, Ladies' Home Journal,* and *Good Housekeeping*, between 1940 and 1970, to show how the traditional female roles of housewife and mother were portrayed.

2567. Geise, L. Ann. "The Female Role in Middle Class Women's Magazines from 1955 to 1976: A Content Analysis of Non-fiction Selections." *Sex Roles.* February 1979, pp. 51-62.

In 160 nonfiction articles in *Ladies' Home Journal* and *Redbook* between 1955 and 1976, changes found concerning attitudes toward female employment. The image of women as "narrow creatures" was not supported, even during the early years.

2568. Gerbner, George. "The Social Anatomy of the Romance-Confession Cover Girl." *Journalism Quarterly.* Summer 1958, pp. 299-306.

The romance-confession magazine's cover girl appeared oblivious of her surroundings and unrelated to the sin exposed in the magazine's articles. The function of the cover girl was analogous to the inside pages' heroine's function of identification.

2569. Glazer, Nona. "Overworking the Working Woman: The Double Day in a Mass Magazine." *Women's Studies International Quarterly.* 3:1 (1980), pp. 79-93.

Working Woman magazine's portrayal of how employed women combine paid work with unpaid domestic labor.

2570. Gordon, Lynn D. "The Gibson Girl Goes to College: Popular Culture and Women's Higher Education in the Progressive Era, 1890-1920." *American Quarterly.* Summer 1987, pp. 211-230.

During the Progressive Era, magazines portrayed women similarly to the model Charles Dana Gibson drew.

2571. Grauerholz, E., L. Williams, and R.E. Clark. "Women in Comic Strips: What's So Funny?" *Free Inquiry in Creative Sociology.* 10 (1982), pp. 108-111.

2572. Greenwald, Marilyn S. "Gender Representations in Newspaper Business Sections." Paper presented at Association for Education in Journalism and Mass Communication, Portland, Oregon, July 2-5, 1988. 15 pp.

The number of business stories in which women were the main subject in an Ohio and Kentucky daily: in the total of 296 stories, women were the main subject seven times.

2573. Greenwald, Marilyn S. "The Portrayal of Women in Newspapers: A Meta-Analysis." Paper presented at Association for Education in Journalism and Mass Communication, Washington, D.C., August 10-13, 1989. 23 pp.

The role and portrayal of women in newspapers as extracted from 15 published studies, 1973-1988.

2574. Guenin, Zena B. "'Ms.,' 'Miss,' 'Mrs.' as Antiquated as 'Mr.'" *The Quill.* July 1974, p. 29.

Continuation of the argument about the use of marital identification -- or any prefix identification -- for women in news copy.

2575. Harvey, R.C. "More Sexism in Comics." *Comics Journal.* January 1986, pp. 30-36.

Indepth review of Trina Robbins and Cat Yronwode's *Women and the Comics.*

2576. Harvey, R.C. "What's the Beef with Cheesecake?" *Comics Journal.* April 1985, pp. 90-94.

Cartoonists are especially vulnerable to attack for being "sexist perverts." Discusses Mort Walker's "Miss Buxley" and defends artist's right to draw women in sexual poses. Response to Harvey by Andrew Moreton, "Laughter with Captions," *Comics Journal,* November 1985. Harvey also clarified his position.

2577. Hill, C. William. "Ferraro in Cartoon." *Target.* Winter 1987, pp. 14-20.

How cartoonists depicted Geraldine Ferraro, Democratic Party nominee for vice president of U.S. in 1984.

2578. Holder, Dennis. "UPI's Equal Rights Amendment." *Washington Journalism Review*. November 1984, p. 12.

Largely because of Geraldine Ferraro's U.S. vice presidential candidacy, United Press International changed its news treatment of women.

2579. Honey, Maureen. "Images of Women in *The Saturday Evening Post* 1931-1936." *Journal of Popular Culture*. Fall 1976, pp. 352-358.

Although some *Saturday Evening Post* heroines were pictured in successful careers, most were shown in traditional ways. Most were white, middle-class women; images of blacks and lower-class women were seldom positive.

2580. Honey, Maureen. "The Working-Class Woman and Recruitment Propaganda During World War II: Class Differences in the Portrayal of War Work." *Signs*. Summer 1983, pp. 672-687.

The fiction of two magazines, *Saturday Evening Post* and *True Story*, that participated in the U.S. government's propaganda campaigns to recruit women into the work force.

2581. "How 'Ms.' Came To Be (Finally) Adopted by the *New York Times*." *Media Report to Women*. September-October 1986, pp. 1, 9.

The dialogue between Paula Kassell and *Times* editor A.M. Rosenthal, concerning use of the honorific, "Ms."

2582. Hulme, Marylin A. "Sourcebook for Sex Equality: Small Presses. An Annotated Listing of Small Presses and Alternative Sources for Books and Media. Bibliographic Series I." New Brunswick, New Jersey: Rutgers University, 1977. 21 pp.

Guide to non-sexist and non-racist educational materials' suppliers; information on professional, trade, women's organizations, presses, bookstores, etc.

2583. Jarrard, Mary W. "Emerging ERA Patterns in Editorials in Southern Daily Newspapers." *Journalism Quarterly*. Winter 1980, pp. 606-611.

In 61 editorials concerning the Equal Rights Amendment in 29 newspapers of 12 Southern states, conservative rhetoric was evident between 1970 and 1977.

2584. Johnson, Sammye and William G. Christ. "Women Through *Time*: Who Gets Covered?" *Journalism Quarterly*. Winter 1988, pp. 889-897.

Images of women appeared on 482 of 3,386 *Time* magazine covers from 1923 through 1987. The mean age of pictured women was 39; most were from the U.S. and their occupation was usually artist/entertainer.

2585. Jolliffe, Lee B. "Comparing Gender Differentiation in the New York *Times*, 1885 and 1985." *Journalism Quarterly*. Autumn 1989, pp. 683-691.

Stereotyping in *New York Times* in both time periods but improvements in 1985. However, women are not given equal space in the *Times*, nor is the proportion of their working world activities accurately reflected. The paper's portrayal does not reflect reality for either sex. Same author wrote: "Diffusion of Ideas by 19th Century Feminists: The Growth of Women's Magazines," Paper presented at Association for Education in Journalism and Mass Communication, Norman, Oklahoma, August 3-6, 1986. 38 pp.

2586. Jones, Daryl E. "Blood 'n' Thunder: Virgins, Villains, and Violence in the Dime Novel Western." *Journal of Popular Culture.* 4:2 (1970), pp. 507-517.
   How women became romantic, virtuous symbols, under attack by seducers, and how villains became associated with sexual threats women feared.

2587. Jones, Mary Jane. "The Spinster Detective." *Journal of Communication.* Spring 1975, pp. 106-112.
   Detective novels take "only the most conservative view of the independent woman"; the spinster role is necessary to many plots.

2588. *Journal of Communication.* Spring 1975.
   Includes thematic symposium on "Women in Detective Fiction: Three Studies": Agate Nesaule Krouse and Margot Peters, "Why Women Kill?" pp. 98-105; Mary Jane Jones, "The Spinster Detective," pp. 106-112, and Earl F. Bargainnier, "I Disagree!" pp. 113-119.

2589. Kohler, Pam Sebastian. "Objectivity Ends at the Hemline: A Woman's Candid Reply." *The Quill.* October 1972, pp. 25-27.
   Because most editors and reporters are men, photos and stories about women often do not get beyond their bodies -- "her dress, her makeup, her voice and her figure will be evaluated."

2590. Kramer, Cheris. "Stereotypes of Women's Speech: The Word from Cartoons." *Journal of Popular Culture.* Winter 1974, pp. 624-630.
   The manner in which the speech of women and men is presented in cartoons in *The New Yorker, Playboy, Cosmopolitan,* and *Ladies' Home Journal*; the evaluation of that speech made by readers. This composite resulted: "The speech of women is concerned with 'trivial' subjects, inappropriate to many locations, wordy, emotional, unorganized, out of control." The reverses were true of men. By same author: "Women's Rhetoric in 'New Yorker' Cartoons: Patterns for a Mildred Milquetoast," paper presented at Speech Communication Association, New York, November 8-11, 1973, 14 pp., and "Folk Linguistics: Wishy-Washy Mommy Talk: Study of Sex Language Differences Through Analysis of *New Yorker* Cartoons," *Psychology Today,* June 1974, pp. 82-85.

2591. Krouse, Agate Nesaule and Margot Peters. "Why Women Kill." *Journal of Communication.* Spring 1975, pp. 98-105.
   In Agatha Christie novels, one-half of the killers were women; "regardless of finances, women (in detective fiction) kill for love, passion and jealousy."

2592. LaFollette, Marcel C. "Eyes on the Stars: Images of Women Scientists in Popular Magazines." *Science, Technology, and Human Values.* Summer-Fall 1988, pp. 262-275.
   Effects of mass media in giving a negative image of women scientists.

2593. Lasorsa, Dominic L., et al. "Women on the Front Page: A Study of News Roles over 100 Years." Paper presented at Association for Education in Journalism and Mass Communication, Minneapolis, Minnesota, August 1990.

New York Times and *Los Angeles Times* had similar ratios of men to women portrayed on the front page. A substantial increase of women as politically significant informants during past 20 years.

2594. Lawhn, Juanita Luna. "Codes of Behavior for Women in La Prensa vs. Women's Prose: 1913-1920." Paper presented at Conference on Popular Culture in Latin America, New Orleans, Louisiana, April 11, 1986.

Content analysis of *La Prensa* of San Antonio, Texas, 1913-1920, showed women's acceptable code of behavior to be anti-feminist.

2595. Lazer, Charles and S. Dier. "The Labor Force in Fiction: What Does 'She' Mean." *Journal of Communication*. Winter 1978, pp. 174-181.

Discrepancies in female and male occupational roles in *Atlantic Monthly* and *Saturday Evening Post* short stories, 1940-1970; women made up 15 percent of total workforce portrayed.

2596. Lee, John. "Innocent Victim and Evil-doers." *Women's Studies International Forum*. 7:1 (1984), pp. 69-73.

The role of headlines in decoding messages, using one about a girl who is raped as the subject of analysis.

2597. Lee, Stan. *The Superhero Women*. New York: Simon and Schuster, 1977.

The superheroine in comics, written by a popular cartoonist.

2598. Levinson, Richard M. "From Olive Oyl to Sweet Polly Purebread: Sex Role Stereotypes and Televised Cartoons." *Journal of Popular Culture*. Winter 1975, pp. 561-572.

Sex role portrayal of cartoons on Saturday morning television 1973: males outnumbered females three to one, women were neither super-heroes nor arch-villains.

2599. Lisenby, Fay. "American Women in Magazine Cartoons." *American Journalism*. 2:2 (1985), pp. 130-134.

Critical of the prevailing attitude that gave women unfavorable images in magazine cartoons, from 1930 to 1960.

2600. Loughlin, Beverly. "The Women's Magazine Short Story Heroine." *Journalism Quarterly*. Spring 1983, pp. 138-142.

Short stories of *Good Housekeeping, Ladies' Home Journal,* and *McCall's*, November 1979 to April 1981. Of 36 female characters featured, the typical woman was attractive, happily married, and between 26-35 years old. More than half of the women were employed but in insignificant jobs.

2601. Luebke, Barbara F. "News About Women on the A Wire." *Journalism Quarterly*. Summer 1985, pp. 329-333.

On the UPI A wire for a sample week in 1983, 16 percent of the stories were about women and 89 percent were hard news.

2602. Luebke, Barbara F. "News About Women on the Wire." *Media Asia.* 13:2 (1986), pp. 97-98.
There is a scarcity of news about women offered by the wire services; one study indicated that 8.6 percent of the stories featured women as the main character and 51.8 percent featured men. Stories about women commanded smaller headlines, were shorter, and received inadequate play.

2603. Luebke, Barbara F. "Out of Focus: Images of Women and Men in Newspaper Photographs." *Sex Roles.* February 1989, pp. 121-133.
A study of four Connecticut newspapers found far more photos of men than of women; both sexes were highly stereotyped.

2604. Lugenbeel, Barbara Derrick. "Defining Story Patterns in *Good Housekeeping.*" *Journalism Quarterly.* Autumn 1975, pp. 548-550.
The typical *Good Housekeeping* protagonist is female, 26-35 years old with a psychological problem. Her primary goal is social (sex-love); her decisions are moral and end happily.

2605. Lutheran Church of America. *Guidelines for Avoiding Bias for Writers and Editors.* New York: Lutheran Church of America, Office for Communications, 1980. 8 pp.
Concern for sexual bias, as well as racial, ethnic, and religious bias and paternalism.

2606. McBride, Genevieve G. "Women's Crusade, Press Crusaders: The Temperance Campaign in Wisconsin, 1873-74." Paper presented at Association for Education in Journalism and Mass Communication, Minneapolis, Minnesota, August 1990.

2607. McCallum, D.M., et al. "Attraction to Cross-Gender-Role Behavior in Advertising." *Journal of Social Behavior and Personality.* January 1986, pp. 37-46.
Respondents preferred cross-gender stereotyped behavior in magazine ads.

2608. MacDonald, Heidi. "Is Buxley Human?" *Comics Journal.* April 1985, pp. 93-94.
Mort Walker's "Miss Buxley" as sex object in comic strips.

2609. Matacin, Mala L. and Jerry M. Burger. "A Content Analysis of Sexual Themes in *Playboy* Cartoons." *Sex Roles.* August 1987, pp. 179-186.
Cartoons in all 1985 issues of *Playboy* coded according to four themes; when these themes were present, women were more often the victim of sexual coercion, depicted as sexually naive with attractive bodies.

2610. Matera, Fran. "Feminists and the Funnies." *Editor and Publisher.* October 24, 1987, p. 68, 52.

Some women characters in the comic strips should exit the kitchen and get jobs.

2611. Matthews, Mary L. and Carol Reuss. "The Minimal Image of Women in 'Time' and 'Newsweek,' 1940-1980." Paper presented at Association for Education in Journalism and Mass Communication, Memphis, Tennessee, August 3-6, 1985. 21 pp.

The degree of change concerning the image of women in *Time* and *Newsweek*, 1940, 1960, and 1980; no significant change found.

2612. Miller, Edward M. "APME's 'Guidelines' a 'Sexist Document'? An Editor's Reply." *Columbia Journalism Review.* September-October 1971, pp. 62-63.

Former managing editor of *Portland Oregonian* responds to seven woman members of the University of Iowa's *Daily Iowan* who charged that the guidelines of the Associated Press Managing Editors were sexist. Abridged from the official response issued by APME.

2613. Miller, Susan H. "The Content of News Photos: Women's and Men's Roles" *Journalism Quarterly.* Spring 1975, pp. 70-75.

In the *Washington Post* and *Los Angeles Times*, 1973-74, men far outnumbered women as photograph subjects, except in the lifestyle sections.

2614. Mitchel, Delores. "Women Libeled: Women's Cartoons of Women." *Journal of Popular Culture.* Spring 1981, pp. 597-610.

A study of 20 "comix" by women artists in California, 1970-1976, found that women made up 75-100 percent of the character cast, the books were overly autobiographical, and the artists "debunked" themselves.

2615. Mooney, Linda and Sarah Brabant. "Two Martinis and a Rested Woman -- 'Liberation' in the Sunday Comics." *Sex Roles.* October 1987, pp. 409-420.

In three of six family-oriented Sunday cartoons, the wife was a fulltime homemaker; working women differed from non-working women in activities, imaged portrayal, and speaking appearances.

2616. Morris, Monica B. "Newspapers and the New Feminists: Black Out as Social Control?" *Journalism Quarterly.* Spring 1973, pp. 37-42.

In the national newspapers of England and local papers of Los Angeles County, California, the sparse coverage of the feminist movement may have meant that black-out was in effect.

2617. Morris, Monica B. "The Public Definition of a Social Movement: Women's Liberation." *Sociology and Social Research.* July 1973, pp. 526-543.

In the *Los Angeles Times* and *Herald Examiner*, before June 1969 and March 1971, the women's liberation movement was ignored initially by the media. Later, coverage was excessive compared to the moderate growth of the movement.

2618. Nigro, Georgia N., et al. "Changes in the Facial Prominence of Women and Men Over the Last Decade." *Psychology of Women Quarterly.* June 1988, pp. 225-235.

Facial prominence of men and women over the previous decade, analyzing 1,200 photographs in *Time* and *Newsweek* and 640 in *Good Housekeeping* and *Ms.*; women showed a greater increase in facial prominence than men in *Newsweek*.

2619. Nilsen, Alleen-Pace. "Sexism in the Media: Word and Image." Paper presented at National Council of Teachers of English, New York, New York, November 24-26, 1977. 11 pp.

Sexist symbols in editorial cartoons; how thay can affect thought processes and language structure.

2620. Pasley, Kay and Marilyn Ihinger-Tallman. "Portraits of Stepfamily Life in Popular Literature, 1940-1980." *Family Relations.* October 1985, pp. 527-534.

Popular articles on stepfamily life, 1940-1980, were directed primarily to women or general audiences; stepfamily life was viewed optimistically.

2621. Perebinossoff, Philippe. "What Does a Kiss Mean? The Love Comic Formula and the Creation of the Ideal Teen-age Girl." *Journal of Popular Culture.* Spring 1975, pp. 825-835.

In love comics, certain ideals were emphasized: marriage, clothes, and the status quo.

2622. Petruzzello, Marion C. "Image Makers: Reporters or Sources." Paper presented at Association for Education in Journalism and Mass Communication, Corvallis, Oregon, August 6-9, 1983. 24 pp.

The use of news sources by the *New York Times* to create a social image of women during key suffrage events of 1858, 1920, and 1970.

2623. Potter, W.J. "Gender Representation in Elite Newspapers." *Journalism Quarterly.* Autumn 1986, pp. 636-640.

Females were the main characters in only 7.3 percent of front page stories in the *New York Times, Chicago Tribune, Atlanta Constitution, Miami Herald*, and *Christian Science Monitor.*

2624. Preston, Ann E. "The Invisible Woman: Two Decades of Magazine Images of Nurses." Paper presented at Association for Education in Journalism and Mass Communication, Minneapolis, Minnesota, August 1990.

From 1967 to 1987, magazines squeezed nursing off list of perceived career options.

2625. Prisco, Dorothy D. "Women and Social Change as Reflected in a Major Fashion Magazine." *Journalism Quarterly.* Spring 1982, pp. 131-134.

The portrayal of women in *Mademoiselle*, a major fashion magazine; women's issues and current issues ranked fifth in frequency out of 12 categories.

2626. Quam, Jean K. and Carol D. Austin. "Image of Women's Issues in Eight Social Work Journals, 1970-81." *Social Work.* July-August 1984, pp. 360-365.

    A slight increase in social work's attention to women's issues in the 1970s; this trend was not expected to continue in the 1980s.

2627. Rachlin, Susan Kessler and Glenda L. Vogt. "Sex Roles as Presented to Children by Coloring Books." *Journal of Popular Culture.* Winter 1974, pp. 549-556.

    Coloring books severely limit behavioral choices for girls and boys; "Females are definitely encouraged to restrain themselves; males are encouraged *not* to," and leisure activities and occupations have women as "sedate, highly structured, and confining."

2628. Reid, Leonard N. and Lawrence C. Soley. "*Sports Illustrated*'s Coverage of Women in Sports." *Journalism Quarterly.* Winter 1979, pp. 861-863.

    In 424 *Sports Illustrated* articles between 1956 and 1976, the coverage of women's sports had not increased; "[T]he picture presented in *Sports Illustrated* articles, is unchanged -- sports is still a man's domain."

2629. Reinstein, P. Gila. "Sex Roles in Recent Picture Books." *Journal of Popular Culture.* Spring 1984, pp. 116-123.

    In award-winning picture books of 1971-80, there was a lack of sensitivity on the part of the judges concerning the needs of girls and boys to see "examples of people liberated from the confining chains of sexual stereotypes.

2630. Riger, Stephanie. "A Technique for Teaching the Psychology of Women: Content Analysis." *Teaching of Psychology.* December 1978, pp. 221-223.

    Qualitative and quantitative differences found in the portrayal of women and men in comic strips and other media forms.

2631. Riha, Jeanne. "Newspapers' War Against Women -- A '1½ Formula.'" *The Quill.* August 1968, pp. 26-27.

    Mass media reinforce daily the "shield of habitual insignificance" that enshrouds U.S. women by keeping women in place.

2632. Rintala, Jan and Susan Birrell. "Fair Treatment for the Active Female: A Content Analysis of *Young Athlete* Magazine." *Sociology of Sport Journal.* September 1984, pp. 231-250.

    Young Athlete magazine during 1975 to 1982, came closer to meeting its responsibilities of representing women athletes than did other periodicals.

2633. Rivers, Caryl. "Mythogyny." *The Quill.* May 1985, pp. 6-12.

    Lurking behind the interest with biological explanations of social differences between the sexes are the same old myths: "pre-menstrual syndrome got headlines because it validates a long-cherished myth about women -- that they're unpredictable, crazy creatures."

2634. Rivers, William L. *The Mass Media: Reporting, Writing, Editing.* Second Ed. New York: Harper and Row, 1975. 631 pp.
Textbook with guidelines for newswriting about women.

2635. Roberts, Nancy L. "From Pumps, Pearls, and Pleats to Pants, Briefcases, and Hardhats: Changes in the Portrayal of Women in Advertising and Fiction in 'Ladies' Home Journal.'" Paper presented at Association for Education in Journalism, Boston, Massachusetts, August 9-13, 1980. 37 pp.
In *Ladies' Home Journal* in the 1960s and 1970s, fictional treatments remained traditional while advertising changed in its portrayal of women.

2636. Roberts, Robin. "The Female Alien: Pulp Science Fiction's Legacy to Feminists." *Journal of Popular Culture.* Fall 1987, pp. 33-52.
The paradigm of a "large, powerful female alien who is closely associated with nature" appeared regularly in pulp magazine science-fiction of the 1940s and 1950s.

2637. Roesgen, Joan. "How Much Relevance Can a Woman Take?" *American Society of Newspaper Editors Bulletin.* February 1972, pp. 4-5.

2638. Rossi, Lee. "The Whore vs. the Girl-Next-Door: Stereotypes of Woman in *Playboy, Penthouse,* and *Oui.*" *Journal of Popular Culture.* Summer 1975, pp. 90-94.
Penthouse, Playboy, and *Oui* chastised for claiming to liberate women but actually trapping them in a narrowly defined role of sex object.

2639. Ruggierio, Jacqueline A. and Louise C. Weston. "Conflicting Images of Women in Romance Novels." *International Journal of Women's Studies.* January-February 1983, pp. 18-25.
Contrast of the presentation of the heroine in "modern gothic" and "historical romance" novels; in the first, women have options, while in "historical romances," they have fewer but are sexual beings.

2640. Ruggierio, Jacqueline A. and Louise C. Weston. "Sex-Role Characterization of Women in 'Modern Gothic' Novels." *Pacific Sociological Review.* April 1977, pp. 279-300.

2641. Ruggierio, Jacqueline A. and Louise C. Weston. "Work Options for Women in Women's Magazines: The Medium and the Message." *Sex Roles.* March 1985, pp. 535-548.
Differences of six established and four new women's magazines in presenting women's work options. Established magazines were more likely to show women in traditional occupations and less likely to profile women employees as having responsibility or power.

2642. Saenger, Gerhart. "Male and Female Relations in the American Comic Strip." In *The Funnies: An American Idiom*, edited by David M. White and Robert H. Abel, pp. 219-231. New York: The Free Press of Glencoe, 1963.

Comparisons between male and female characters in comics concerning major goals of adult heroes; emphasis on success and leisure, aggression and mastery, the expression of hostility in interpersonal relations, suggestibility, emotionality, and predictability, intelligence and logic, and love. Reprinted from *Public Opinion Quarterly,* Summer 1955, pp. 195-205.

2643. Schrib, June. "Status of Women: Treatment by Selected Consumer Magazines, 1961-1971." Masters thesis, University of Wyoming, 1972.

2644. Scott, Joseph E. and Jack L. Franklin. "The Changing Nature of Sex References in Mass Circulation Magazines." *Public Opinion Quarterly.* 36:1 (1972), pp. 80-86.

2645. Shadoian, Jack. "Yuh Got Pecos! Doggone, Belle, Yuh're As Good As Two Men!" *Journal of Popular Culture.* Spring 1979, pp. 721-736.

The role of women characters in Western comics: young, vigorous women seek the companionship of an old man, concluding that in "these comics, truth, virtue, or gut-knowledge are the property of women and old men in a complex society where mature males lose their way.

2646. Shaw, Donald, Lynda P. Cole, Roy L. Moore, and Richard R. Cole. "Men Versus Women in Bylines." *Journalism Quarterly.* Spring 1981, pp. 103-106.

Whether byline sex was noticed and whether it influenced reader's assessment of news stories.

2647. Silver, Diane. "A Comparison of Newspaper Coverage of Male and Female Officials in Michigan." Paper presented at Association for Education in Journalism and Mass Communication, Gainesville, Florida, August 5-8, 1984. 18 pp.

No real life difference found in how male and female officials were portrayed in 21 Michigan newspapers.

2648. Simon, R.J. and N. Pecora. "Coverage of the Davis, Harris, and Hearst Trials by Major American Magazines." In *Studies in Communications, 3, 1986: News and Knowledge,* edited by T. McCormack, pp. 111-134. Greenwich, Connecticut: JAI Press, 1986.

How three female defendants were covered in feminist, general interest, and traditional women's magazines.

2649. Smith, M. Dwayne and Marc Matre, "Social Norms and Sex Roles in Romance and Adventure Magazines." *Journalism Quarterly.* Summer 1975, pp. 309-315.

Sixteen romance and 14 adventure magazines used to prove that traditional American stereotypes about roles and dispositions of men and women existed.

2650. Smith, Terry and Jack Levin. "Social Change in Sex Roles: An Analysis of Advice Columns." *Journalism Quarterly.* Autumn 1974, pp. 525-527.

Advice columns of Boston dailies studied; women "consistently and overwhelmingly monopolized letter writing" and advice columnists had not made "substantial changes in their general expectations for male and female behavior."

2651. Sonenschein, David. "Love and Sex in the Romance Magazines." *Journal of Popular Culture.* 4:2 (1970), pp. 398-409.

Eight romance or confession magazines and their 73 fictional stories studied; sex linked to non-sexual values in the lives of the characters.

2652. Sparks, Glenn C. and Christine L. Fehlner. "Faces in the News. Gender Comparisons of Magazine Photographs." *Journal of Communication.* Autumn 1986, pp. 70-79.

Time and *Newsweek* photographs of males and females suggest that occupation is related to facial prominence: women in government received the same facial prominence as men, while actresses received substantially less.

2653. Stewart, Penni. "He Admits ... But She Confesses." *Women's Studies International Quarterly.* 3:1 (1980), pp. 105-114.

From examination of *True Story* and *True Confession* magazines, argues that confession is a "female mode of response, reflecting women's position in the private world of home, while admission is more typical of males reflecting their position in the public world of work."

2654. Streicher, Helen White. "The Girls in the Cartoons." *Journal of Communication.* Spring 1974, pp. 125-129.

"Help, save me!" was the most frequent cry of girls pictured in TV cartoons, except in the "teachy-preachy" category. Both women and men were stereotyped in the shows.

2655. Swartz, T.A. "Role Portrayal Preferences For Print Advertisements." In *Proceedings of the 1983 Convention of the American Academy of Advertising,* edited by D.W. Jugenheimer, pp. 112-115. Columbia, South Carolina: University of South Carolina, 1983.

Focus was on print media to determine whether women's role preferences can be predicted on the basis of women's attitudes about their societal roles. The answer -- not usually.

2656. Thaler, Barbara. "Gender Stereotyping in the Comic Strips." In *Communication, Gender, and Sex Roles in Diverse Interaction Contexts,* edited by Lea P. Stewart and Stella Ting-Toomey, pp. 189-199. Norwood, New Jersey: Ablex, 1987.

Gender stereotypes as a source of humor in comic strips; 29 male and eight female title characters analyzed.

2657. Theberge, Nancy and Alan Cronk. "Work Routines in Newspaper Sports Departments and the Coverage of Women's Sports." *Sociology of Sport Journal.* September 1986, pp. 195-203.

Other reasons besides journalists' bias accounted for the limited coverage of women in the sports media.

2658. Tilghman, Romalyn. "A Content Analysis of Goals and Occupations of Heroines in Three Women's Magazines: 1944-1972." Masters thesis, University of Kansas, 1974.

2659. Turk, Judy VanSlyke. "Sex-Role Stereotyping in Writing the News: Another Look at the Influence of Reporter and Source Gender." Paper presented at Association for Education in Journalism and Mass Communication, Norman, Oklahoma, August 3-6, 1986. 30 pp.
   Replication of an experiment conducted in 1984 at Syracuse University to determine whether gender bias and stereotypes filter into reporters' stories about women. Published under that title in *Southwestern Mass Communication Journal*, 3 (1986), pp. 32-44.

2660. Wanta, Wayne and Dawn Leggett. "Gender Stereotypes in Wire Service Sports Photos." *Newspaper Research Journal*. Spring 1989, pp. 105-113.
   Associated Press photographs of female and male tennis players; while photographers did not reinforce gender stereotypes, editors did.

2661. Ward, Jean. "Attacking the King's English: Implications for Journalism in the Feminist Critique." *Journalism Quarterly*. Winter 1975, pp. 699-705.
   Stories that use sexist language; criticism of media for such language use was not as great as was criticism of textbooks. Five implications of sexist language in journalism and recommendations for further study were provided.

2662. Ward, Jean. "The War of Words." *The Quill*. October 1980, pp. 10-12.
   Despite efforts at news coverage equality in the early 1970s, media still practiced sexism; examples from *New York Times* and other media of sexist language use.

2663. Weitzman, Lenore J., et al. "Sex-Role Socialization in Picture Books for Pre-school Children." *American Journal of Sociology*. 77 (1972), pp. 1125-1150.

2664. Whitlow, S. Scott. "How Male and Female Gatekeepers Respond to News Stories of Women." *Journalism Quarterly*. Autumn 1977, pp. 573-579, 609.
   In sample of six newspapers of 39,000 to 300,000 circulation, "some gatekeepers of both sexes tended to reject news items about women and about persons in non-traditional sex roles."

2665. Whitlow, S. Scott. "Private Images Gatekeepers Bring to News of Public Women." *Mass Comm Review*. Winter 1978-79, pp. 10-16.
   Each of 36 editors and reporters in six cities was presented 48 items abstracted from a set of sex-role stereotypes; assessment of cognition of women at three levels, from most job-specific to most general level.

2666. Whitlow, S. Scott. "Women in the Newsroom: A Role Theory View." *Journalism Quarterly*. Summer 1979, pp. 378-383.

From observation of six gatekeepers on six dailies, found that patterns of influence in the newsroom were not clear-cut. But, also found that "Women's section reporters may find news treatment and attitudes toward women by those in the 'hard' news sections to be more acceptable than those of their superiors."

2667. Williams, Donald M. "Don't Call Her Ms. It Was All a Mistake." *The Quill.* July-August 1977, pp. 28-29.

A call for a return to the days when newspapers identified women by marital status; examples given of newspapers that have "yielded" to last-naming women in news copy.

2668. Witaman, Lenore, Deborah Eifler, Elizabeth Hokada, and Catherine Ross. "Sex Role Socialization in Picture Books for Pre-School Children." *American Journal of Sociology.* May 1972, pp. 1125-1150.

Picture books of all kinds underrepresented women in titles, central characters, and illustrations; "where women do appear, their characterization reinforces traditional sex-role stereotypes: boys are active while girls are passive; boys lead and rescue others while girls follow and serve others."

2669. Zimbardo, Philip G. and Wendy Meadow. "Sexism Springs Eternal -- in the Reader's Digest." *ERIC.* 1974. 12 pp. (ED 105 318).

An empirical investigation of anti-women humor appearing in the *Reader's Digest* over three decades, revealing the operation of an unconscious sexist ideology.

Women as Audience

2670. Bandy, Patricia and Patricia A. President. "Recent Literature on Drug Abuse Prevention and Mass Media: Focusing on Youth, Parents, Women and the Elderly." *Journal of Drug Education.* 13:3 (1983), pp. 255-271.

Literature review of mass media campaigns concerning drug abuse prevention aimed at these four groups claims women have been the targets of awareness campaigns.

2671. Bostian, Lloyd R. and John E. Ross. "Functions and Meanings of Mass Media for Wisconsin Farm Women." *Journalism Quarterly.* Winter 1965, pp. 69-76.

Samples farm women in the state of Wisconsin in 1963 to determine functions and meanings of mass media to them.

2672. Bush, Alan J. and John J. Burnett. "Assessing the Homogeneity of Single Females in Respect to Advertising Media and Technology." *Journal of Advertising.* 16:3 (1987), pp. 31-38.

Divorced, never married, and widowed women use media very differently and possess different attitudes about advertising.

2673. Chatman, Elfreda A. "Information, Mass Media Use, and the Working Poor." *Library and Information Science Research.* April-June 1985, pp. 97-113.

Interviews with 50 women in a Comprehensive Employment and Training Act program to determine their use of mass media and the public library.

2674. Darden, Donna K. and William R. Darden. "Middle-Class Females' Media Usage Habits." *Journal of Black Studies.* June 1981, pp. 421-434.

Media usage among females compared to determine differences between black and white middle-class behavior.

2675. Furnham, Adrian and Barrie Gunter. "Sex, Presentation Mode and Memory for Violent and Nonviolent News." *Journal of Educational Television.* 11:2 (1985), pp. 99-105.

Sixty-eight undergraduate students were shown a sequence of violent and nonviolent news stories, either by TV, audio only, or in print, to test their recall. Males recalled violent news better than nonviolent, while the opposite was true for females.

2676. Gamman, Lorraine and Margaret Marshment, eds. *The Female Gaze: Women as Viewers of Popular Culture.* London: The Women's Press, 1988. 224 pp.

Thirteen essays to explore "possibilities and pitfalls of intervention in popular forms in order to find ways of making feminist meanings a part of our pleasures." Includes: "Advertising and the Menstrual Taboo," "The Status of Women Working in Film and Television," and *Cagney and Lacey* and Madonna via feminist soft porn.

2677. Johnson, Carolyn and Lynne Gross. "Mass Media Use by Women in Decision-Making Positions." *Journalism Quarterly.* Winter 1985, pp. 850-854, 950.

Of 11 hypotheses, only one (that decision-making women use media more for professional and work-related information) was proven. Decision-makers spend less time with media in general and less time with TV in particular; they are heavier users of news and trade magazines and large dailies.

2678. Jones, Elise F., James R. Beniger, and Charles F. Westoff. "Pill and IUD Discontinuation in the United States, 1970-1975: The Influence of the Media." *Family Planning Perspectives.* November-December 1980, pp. 293-300.

Data on 3,403 white women on their discontinuance of the use of the pill or IUD; media had significant impact.

2679. Modleski, Tania. *Loving with a Vengeance.* New York: Methuen, 1984. 140 pp.

Analyses of Harlequin romance, female gothics, and soap operas, areas long slighted because they have been "subject to a double critical standard." Author rejects theory that mass art imposes "false needs" on its consumers. These feminine narratives are popular because they satisfy desires all too real in women's lives but which culture has found no adequate way of satisfying. By the same author: "The Disappearing Act: A Study of Harlequin Romances," *Signs*, Spring 1980, pp. 435-448.

2680. Press, Andrea. "New Views on the Mass Production of Women's Culture." *Communication Research*. January 1986, pp. 139-149.

Soap operas and romance novels, both appealing to women, are now taken seriously by scholars, who look at their contents, effects, and audiences.

2681. Smith, Roslyn. "Functions of Mass Media for Wisconsin Farm Women." Ph.D. dissertation, University of Wisconsin -- Madison, 1967.

2682. Sosanie, Arlene K. and George J. Szybillo. "Working Wives: Their General Television Viewing and Magazine Readership Behavior." *Journal of Advertising*. 7:2 (1978), pp. 5-13.

Literature review on married women (non-working, parttime and fulltime employed) and media behavior; primarily on a study of W.R. Simmons and Associates, *1974/1975 Study of Selective Markets and the Media Reaching Them*.

2683. Steeves, H. Leslie, et al. "The Context of Employed Women's Media Use." *Women's Studies in Communication*. Fall 1989, pp. 21-46.

Employed women do other things while using media and use them less often than the general population.

2684. Varga, Karoly. "Achievement, Affiliation and Exposure to Media According to the Sexes." *Society and Leisure*. 8:3 (1976), pp. 223-240.

Only achievement-motivated males allowed themselves to be exposed to media offering immediate gratification for shorter periods.

2685. Venkatesh, Alladi. "Changing Roles of Women -- A Life-style Analysis." *Journal of Consumer Research*. September 1980, pp. 189-197.

Homemaker magazines had a high traditionalist and low feminist appeal; national and international news had high feminist and low traditionalist readership.

Advertising, Public Relations

2686. Alreck, P.L., R.B. Settle, and M.A. Belch. "Who Responds to 'Gendered' Ads, and How?" *Journal of Advertising Research*. April/May 1982, pp. 25-32.

Data from 1980 field study of metropolitan areas of Southern California show women prefer feminine brands, while men do not quickly accept them.

2687. Ascher, Carol. "Selling to Ms. Consumer." In *American Media and Mass Culture: Left Perspectives*, edited by Donald Lazere, pp. 43-52. Berkeley: University of California Press, 1987.

Shows historically that as advertising and consumerism developed in the late 1890s and early 1900s, they did not include the decisions of those most affected by them -- women. Follows up on Christine Frederick, *Selling to Mrs. Consumer*, New York: The Business Course, 1929.

2688. Barry, Thomas, et al. "Advertising to Women with Different Career Orientations." *Journal of Advertising Research.* April-May 1985, p. 26.

Ads featuring career theme miss women in low-desire-to-work-outside-home group.

2689. Berning, Carol A. and Jacob Jacoby. "Patterns of Information Acquisition in New Product Purchases." *Journal of Consumer Research.* September 1974, pp. 18-22.

Examines information acquisition behavior of 86 women for new versus established purchase alternatives. Analyzes print media ads.

2690. Boyenton, William H. "Enter the Ladies -- 86 Proof: A Study in Advertising Ethics." *Journalism Quarterly.* Autumn 1967, pp. 445-453.

The liquor industry began promoting its products for women in 1958; that type of advertising grew quickly and boldly in less than a decade.

2691. Dana, Margaret. "Fear the Facts and Fool the Women." *Atlantic Monthly.* April 1937, pp. 397-405.

Women as a public relations public.

2692. Davis, Ronald M. "Current Trends in Cigarette Advertising and Marketing." *New England Journal of Medicine.* March 1987, pp. 725-732.

Trends in United States cigarette advertising, including campaigns that target women.

2693. Dispenza, Joseph E. *Advertising the American Woman.* Dayton, Ohio: Pflaum Publishing, 1975.

How women have been used in advertising from historical and comtemporary perspectives. Chapters deal with advertisements aimed at facial beauty, domestic matters, early romance and courtship, garments dealing with women's shape, and "spare parts" attitudes toward women.

2694. Easton, Nina. *Women Take Charge, Asserting Your Rights in the Market Place.* Washington, D.C.: Center for Study of Responsive Law, 1983. 201 pp.

Ways offered to assert rights in dealing with ads and their effects.

2695. Ernster, Virginia L. "Women, Smoking, Cigarette Advertising and Cancer." *Women and Health.* Fall-Winter 1986, pp. 217-235.

Cigarette smoking has been the major cause of death of U.S. women, yet the tobacco industry has increased its efforts to sell cigarettes to them. Examples given of media and other campaigns geared to the woman smoker by the tobacco companies. Also in: *Women and Cancer,* edited by S.D. Stellman, pp. 217-236, New York: Haworth Press, 1987.

2696. Fannin, Rebecca. "Women Extend Reach for Media's Brass Ring." *Marketing and Media Decisions.* February 1985, pp. 51+.

2697. Flanley, Mabel G. "Women: A Forgotten Public." *Public Relations Journal.* March 1946, pp. 24-26, 40.
The importance of the women's public to public relations.

2698. Gilly, Mary C. and Thomas E. Barry. "Segmenting the Women's Market: A Comparison of Work-Related Segmentation Schemes." *Current Issues and Research in Advertising.* 9:1/2 (1986), pp. 149-170.
Many important changes have occurred to make the women's market less homogeneous than previously. Researchers attempted to segment the women's market using demographics, psychographics, and combinations of the two. This study attempts to compare the effectiveness of three segmentation bases in advertising to women consumers.

2699. Gould, S.J. "Gender Differences in Advertising Response and Self-consciousness Variables." *Sex Roles.* March 1987, pp. 215-226.
Females were higher in public self-consciousness and social anxiety than males, suggesting they are generally more conscious of themselves as social objects.

2700. Howe, Holly. "An Historical Review of Women, Smoking and Advertising." *Health Education.* May-June 1984, pp. 3-9.
Historical data on relationships between anti-smoking publicity, growth in cigarette advertisers' appeal to women, and change in proportion of women smokers.

2701. Jaffe, L.J. and P.D. Berger. "Impact on Purchase Intent of Sex-role Identity and Product Positioning." *Psychology and Marketing.* Fall 1988, pp. 259-271.
Examination of women's sex-role identity, preferences for modern or traditional product positioning, and intent to purchase.

2702. Jennings (Walstedt), Joyce, Florence L. Geis, and Virginia Brown. "Influence of Television Commercials on Women's Self-Confidence and Independent Judgment." *Journal of Personality and Social Psychology.* 38:2 (1980), pp. 203-210.
The impact of television commercials on women's self-confidence and independence using two matched series of commercials as stimuli. Findings suggested that repeated exposure to non-stereotypic commercials might produce positive behavioral changes in women.

2703. Jordan, W. "Don't Neglect Women in Your Public Relations Effort." *Printers Ink.* November 8, 1946, pp. 92+.

2704. Kanter, Donald and Lawrence Wortzel. "Cynicism and Alienation As Marketing Considerations: Some New Ways to Approach the Female Consumer." *Journal of Consumer Marketing.* Winter 1985, pp. 5-15.

2705. Loken, B. and B. Howard-Pitney. "Effectiveness of Cigarette Advertisements on Women: An Experimental Study." *Journal of Applied Psychology.* August 1988, pp. 378-382.

In a sample of 115 college women, three factors investigated that could influence their reactions to print ads for cigarettes: attractiveness, credibility, and persuasiveness.

2706. Naether, Carl A. *Advertising to Women.* New York: Prentice-Hall, 1928.

2707. Scott, Rosemary. *The Female Consumer.* New York/Toronto: John Wiley and Sons and London: Associated Business Programs, 1976.
Pages 207-299 especially pertinent.

2708. Wolff, Janet L. *What Makes Women Buy: A Guide to Understanding and Influencing the New Woman of Today.* New York: McGraw, 1958. 294 pp.
Textbook directed toward advertisers, copywriters, media editors, and others.

Broadcasting

2709. Brown, Jane D. and Laurie Schulze. "The Effects of Race, Gender, and Fandom on Audience Interpretations of Madonna's Music Videos." *Journal of Communication.* Spring 1990, pp. 88-102.

2710. Budd, M., S. Craig, and C. Steinman. "'Fantasy Island': Marketplace of Desire." *Journal of Communication.* Winter 1983, pp. 67-77.
Dependence is sold to the female audience of the TV show, "Fantasy Island."

2711. Carrillo, Loretta and Thomas A. Lyson. "The *Fotonovela* as a Cultural Bridge for Hispanic Women in the United States." *Journal of Popular Culture.* Winter 1983, pp. 59-64.
Working class women of Mexico are the major audience for *fotonovelas*. Themes of *fotonovelas* are divided as marital/premarital morality, beneficent fate, conflict in family relationships, sexual taboos and social success stories.

2712. Day, Charles W. "The Television Evening Western: Its Meaning for Men and Women." Masters thesis, University of Chicago, 1958.

2713. Fehr, Lawrence A. "Media Violence and Catharsis in College Females." *Journal of Social Psychology.* April 1979, pp. 63-69.
The levels of "manifest hostility and hostility guilt" as functions of the subjects' preferences for violent or non-violent TV shows examined. The catharsis approach to aggression for these college females was not plausible.

2714. Gretchen, Beth. "There Isn't Anything Wishy-Washy about Soaps." *Ms.* August 1974, pp. 42-43+.
Soap operas had changed with a number doing credible jobs educating viewers on drugs, VD, and other issues. People are contemptuous of soap operas because of their audiences of women, an audience that didn't mean much to the industry.

2715. Guest, Pearl E. "Television as a Variable in Citizenship Activities of Women." Ph.D. dissertation, Penn State University, 1954.

2716. Gutman, Jonathan. "Self-Concepts and Television Viewing Among Women." *Public Opinion Quarterly.* Fall 1973, pp. 388-397.

The self-concepts and ideal self-concepts of heavy and light television viewers are compared and related to demographic variables. Data gathered in a *Los Angeles Times* survey in 1970. Self- and ideal self-concept ratings differed significantly for light and heavy female TV viewers; heavy viewers were more socially oriented and light viewers were more oriented to doing things.

2717. Helregel, Brenda K. and James B. Weaver. "Mood-Management During Pregnancy Through Selective Exposure to Television." *Journal of Broadcasting and Electronic Media.* Winter 1989, pp. 15-33.

Focus on pregnant and non-pregnant women and new mothers to determine television program preferences as a function of the physiologically-induced affective stages of pregnancy.

2718. Howard, Shirley J. "An Analysis of the Characteristics of the Women's Audience for Educational Broadcasting in Oregon as a Guide to Programming." Masters thesis, Michigan State University, 1964.

2719. Kiecolt, K. Jill and Marnie Sayles. "Television and the Cultivation of Attitudes Toward Subordinate Groups." *Sociological Spectrum.* 8:1 (1988), pp. 19-33.

The relationship between frequency of viewing television news and crime dramas, and adherence to individualism. Among women, exposure to TV news increased group consciousness; viewing crime dramas decreased personal efficacy.

2720. McCormack, Thelma. "Male Conceptions of Female Audiences: The Case of Soap Operas." In *Mass Communication Review Yearbook*, edited by Ellen Wartella, D. Charles Whitney, and Sven Windahl, pp. 273-283. Beverly Hills, California: Sage, 1983.

A feminist perspective to how women read and use female cultural productions.

2721. Meadowcroft, Jeanne M. and Dolf Zillman. "Women's Comedy Preferences During the Menstrual Cycle." *Communication Research: An International Quarterly.* April 1987, pp. 204-218.

Premenstrual and menstrual women preferred comedy over other choices more strongly than women midway through the cycle.

2722. Ruffner, Marguerite Anne. "Women's Attitudes Toward Progressive Rock Radio." *Journal of Broadcasting.* Winter 1972-73, pp. 85-94.

Attitudes of women, ages 18-34, toward radio are ascertained -- particularly toward a station with a progressive rock format.

2723. Sharits, D. and H.B. Lammers. "Perceived Attributes of Models in Primetime and Daytime Television Commercials: A Person Perception Approach." *Journal of Marketing Research*. February 1983, pp. 64-73.
Study of TV commercials viewing by 32 women and 32 men; perceptions of female and male models differed as a function of time, not the viewer's sex.

2724. Summers, Leda P. "A Study of Daytime Radio Serial Listening by Iowa Women." Masters thesis, Columbia University, 1943.

2725. Tan, Alexis, Jack Raudy, Cary Huff, and Janet Miles. "Children's Reactions to Male and Female Newscasters: Effectiveness and Believability." *Quarterly Journal of Speech*. April 1980, pp. 201-205.
Females perceived the male newscaster to be more powerful than the female newscaster; girls were more susceptible to sex-role stereotyping than boys.

Film

2726. Cantor, Joanne R., Dolf Zillman, and Edna F. Einsiedel. "Female Responses to Provocation after Exposure to Aggressive and Erotic Film." *Communication Research*. October 1978, pp. 395-412.
A study of 60 female undergraduate students to determine their reactions after seeing an aggressive and erotic film.

2727. Ewen, Elizabeth. "City Lights: Immigrant Women and the Rise of the Movies." *Signs: Journal of Women in Culture and Society*. Spring 1980, pp. 45-65.
The interplay between immigrant women moviegoers and silent films about immigrant/ethnic groups; the socialization of immigrants by film.

2728. Fenigstein, Allan. "Does Aggression Cause a Preference for Viewing Media Violence?" *Journal of Personality and Social Psychology*. December 1979, pp. 2307-2317.
Testing in two experiments of the hypothesis that physical aggression and fantasy aggression lead to a preference for viewing violence. Films chosen by men contained more violence than those selected by women.

2729. Frost, Richard and John Stauffer. "The Effects of Social Class, Gender and Personality on Physiological Responses to Filmed Violence." *Journal of Communication*. Spring 1987, pp. 29-45.
Females and males were about equal in their arousal by filmed violence.

2730. Gans, Herbert J. "The Exorcist: A Devilish Attack on Women." *Social Policy*. May-June 1974, pp. 71-73.

2731. Hershey, Lenore. "What Women Think of the Movies." *McCall's*. May 1967, pp. 28+.
Responses to questionnaire on movie preferences.

2732. Hollinger, Karen. "'The Look' Narrative and the Female Spectator in Vertigo." *The Journal of Film and Video.* Fall 1987, pp. 18-27.

Spectators' responses to the filmic test are often biased; they must be recognized as an integration of the visual and narrative elements which make impacts on the spectator's experience of film.

2733. Tamborini, R., J. Stiff, and D. Zillman. "Preference for Graphic Horror Featuring Male Versus Female Victimization: Personality and Past Film Viewing Experiences." *Human Communication Research.* Summer 1987, pp. 529-552.

Print Media

2734. Andreasen, Margaret and H. Leslie Steeves. "Employed Women's Assertiveness and Openness as Shown in Magazine Use." *Journalism Quarterly.* Autumn 1983, pp. 449-457.

Sample of 378 employed women in Wisconsin and Illinois found that assertive employed women read more magazines overall, and more news and hobby and craft magazines than non-assertive employed women.

2735. Andreasen, Margaret and H. Leslie Steeves. "Assertive Response to on-the-job Sex Discrimination as a Possible Predictor of Newspaper Reading Behavior." *Newspaper Research Journal.* Summer 1984, pp. 27-40.

Two samples of employed women used to determine the extent of assertiveness as a predictor of newspaper readership patterns. Assertive women are more interested in news.

2736. Brazelton, Ethel M. Colson. *Writing and Editing for Women.* New York: Funk and Wagnalls, 1927. 258 pp.

Guidelines on writing and editing with a women's audience in mind. Obviously outdated, but useful for historians who wish to see how instruction was geared earlier on.

2737. Brenders, D.A. and J.D. Robinson. "An Analysis of Self-Help Articles: 1972-1980." *Mass Comm Review.* Fall 1985, pp. 29-36.

Analysis of 137 popular magazine articles, 1972 to 1980; 25 percent directed toward women; 74 percent made no distinction.

2738. Geis, Gilbert and Judit Soler. "Response of Female Homicide Offenders to Press Coverage of Their Trials." *Journalism Quarterly.* Autumn 1971, pp. 558-560.

Interviews with 13 women prisoners in California showed they blamed media for poor treatment they claimed they received.

2739. Honey, Maureen. "Recruiting Women for War Work: OWI and the Magazine Industry During World War II." *Journal of American Culture.* Spring 1980, pp. 47-52.

2740. MacLean, Malcolm S., jr. and William R. Hazard. "Women's Interest in Pictures: The Badger Village Study." *Journalism Quarterly.* Spring 1953, pp. 139-162.
Six major appeals accounted for nearly all the variation in interest for 31 of 51 pictures selected from two major news magazines.

2741. Miner, M.M. *Insatiable Appetites: Twentieth-Century American Women's Best Sellers.* Westport, Connecticut: Greenwood Press, 1984. 158 pp.
Women continue to read books where a "women's story" is involved; the five most famous U.S. women's best sellers of the twentieth century are discussed -- *Gone with the Wind, Peyton Place, Forever Amber, Scruples,* and *Valley of the Dolls.*

2742. Rarick, Galen. "Political Persuasion: The Newspaper and the Sexes." *Journalism Quarterly.* Summer 1970, pp. 360-364.
How women used the newspaper, contending that the nearer an event was to the home, the greater was women's concern with it.

2743. Rentz, J.O. and F.D. Reynolds. "Magazine Readership Patterns." *Journal of Advertising.* Spring 1979, pp. 22-25.
Women's magazine exposure, using 1977 survey data of 21 monthly magazines.

2744. Stauffer, John and Richard Frost. "Male and Female Interest in Sexually-Oriented Magazines." *Journal of Communication.* Winter 1976, pp. 25-30.
Male and female responses to *Playboy* and *Playgirl* magazine nudity; women were ambivalent about male nudity.

2745. Urban, Christine D. "Correlates of Magazine Readership." *Journal of Advertising Research.* August 1980, pp. 73-84.
Sample of about 6,000 women and men to determine the factors that influenced magazine readership.

2746. Venkatesh, Alladi and Clint Tankersley. "Magazine Readership by Female Segments." *Journal of Advertising Research.* August 1979, pp. 31-38.
Magazine-readership profiles of three different groups of women and their implications to media segmentation.

2747. Wesson, D.A. and E. Stewart. "Gender and Readership of Heads in Magazine Advertisements." *Journalism Quarterly.* Spring 1987, pp. 189-192.
Analysis of advertisements in *Sports Illustrated* and *Woman's Day*; no relationship between the physical measurements of headlines and readership.

2748. *womenScope Surveys of Women.*
April 1989 issue of this newsletter examines women's interest in and loyalty to newspapers in cover story, "Marketing Newspapers to Women."

Women Practitioners

2749. Agee, Warren K., Phillip H. Ault, and Edwin Emery. *Maincurrents in Mass Communications.* New York: Harper and Row, 1986. 457 pp.

"The Growing Role of Women" includes Katharine Graham's "Women and Power," pp. 261-266, in which she said that women will have "to put their careers and companies first for some part of their working lives." Ellen Stein, in "Careers in Movieland," pp. 266-274, discussed the types of movie work for women and how to obtain it. In second edition (1989), Jean Gaddy Wilson, "Women in the Newspaper Business," pp. 218-222.

2750. Allen, Donna. "From Opportunity to Strategy: Women Contribute to the Communications Future." In *Communications at the Crossroads: The Gender Gap Connection*, edited by Ramona Rush and Donna Allen, pp. 59-79. Norwood, New Jersey: Ablex, 1989.

Explains four circumstances that created a ripe time for women to make contributions to communications: "(a) new technology and rising world demand for more democratic communications have placed us on the threshold of major change in the world communications system; (b) women have built their own worldwide communications media through which their contributions can now be heard; (c) it is newly recognized that women have different and needed contributions to make to communications; and (d) they have developed a strategy to carry their contributions into the media structure."

2751. Artel, Linda and Valerie Wheat. *Women and Work: New Options. A Guide to Nonprint Media.* San Francisco, California: Women's Educational Equity Communications Network, 1979. 86 pp.

Information about 112 films and other audio-visuals dealing with new career options for women.

2752. Barkley, Elizabeth Bookser, ed. *Room at the Top: An Exploration of the Status of Women in Key Communications Jobs.* Austin, Texas: Women in Communications, Inc., 1981.

2753. Beam, Randal A. "Women and Racial Minorities in the Media Labor Force, 1970-80." Paper presented at Association for Education in Journalism and Mass Communication, Norman, Oklahoma, August 3-6, 1986. 24 pp.

The representation of women in the media labor force rose substantially between 1970 and 1980, but women were paid less than men although this difference was shrinking.

2754. Booker, Janice L. "Women in Communications." *Journal of Sociology and Social Welfare.* July 1977, pp. 888-896.

Women's participation in a wide array of communications jobs, as revealed in a U.S. survey done by Women in Communications in 1974.

2755. Borisoff, Deborah and Lisa Merrill. *The Power to Communicate: Gender Differences as Barriers.* Prospect Heights, Illinois: Waveland Press, 1986. 100 pp.

Numerous activities and exercises that can be used in instructional and training situations follow discussions of stereotypes, vocal, verbal and nonverbal behavior, professional image, male dominance as a barrier to change, and effecting change.

2756. Bowman, William W. "Distaff Journalists: Women as a Minority Group in the News Media." Ph.D. dissertation, University of Illinois -- Chicago, 1974.

2757. Brady, Kathleen. "Ladies of the Press." *Gannett Center Journal.* Winter 1989, pp. 42-50.

Description of women who rose to the top of newspapers because they were "born to the right men or connected with the right men" -- Katharine Graham of *Washington Post*, Helen Rogers Reid of *New York Tribune*, Elinor Patterson of *Washington Herald*, and Dorothy Schiff of *New York Post*. Others are Christie Hefner, Gertrude Crain, and Anne Cox Chambers. If not many women are in top management, an encouragement is that more are reaching middle ranks.

2758. Crumley, Wilma and Patricia Sailor. "Working Paper: Careers as Viewed by Five and Ten Year Graduates of Home Economics and Journalism Programs." Paper presented for the Ad Hoc Committee on the Status of Women, Association for Education in Journalism, Ottawa, Canada, August 1975.

2759. Diliberto, Gioia E. "Profiles of Three Newswomen." Masters thesis, University of Maryland, 1975.

Profiles of Pauline Frederick, Meg Greenfield, and Helen Thomas.

2760. Dolan, Darlene J. "The Developing Role of Women in Communications Industries: Can Technology Be the Turning Point?" In *Communications at the Crossroads: The Gender Gap Connection,* edited by Ramona Rush an Donna Allen, pp. 106-119. Norwood, New Jersey: Ablex, 1989.

Case study of Susan W. Leisner, who sued New York Telephone and its parent, AT&T, for job discrimination.

2761. Donovan, Suzanne, ed. *Women in American Journalism Today and in the Future.* Berkeley, California: University of California, Graduate School of Journalism, 1988. 53 pp.

Transcript of four public lectures and panels that looked at women in newspapers and broadcasting. Topics were: "Taking Stock: Women in the Media Before the 21st Century"; "From Lawsuits to Caucuses: Promoting Women in the Newsroom"; "The Only Girl on the Road," and "Stress in the Newsroom: What Can Be Done?"

2762. Downie, Susanna, et al. *Decade of Achievement: 1977-1987.* A Report on a Survey Based on the National Plan of Action for Women. Beaver Dam, Wisconsin: National Women's Conference Center, 1988. 80 pp.
Part II provides data on media and women.

2763. Endres, Kathleen L. "Capitol Hill Newswomen: A Descriptive Study." *Journalism Quarterly.* Spring 1976, pp. 132-135.
Brief history of women as congressional reporters and data resulting from interviews with 43 female and 42 male correspondents.

2764. Fedler, Fred, Tim Counts and Ron F. Smith. "Survey Compares Attitudes of Male, Female Professors." *Journalism Educator.* Autumn 1984, pp. 3-8.
Male and female journalism assistant professors were similar in their responses about job satisfaction, with females more satisfied than males. At the associate professor level, females were less satisfied than males with their lives away from work, their department chairmen, colleagues, and merit allocations.

2765. Filene, Catherine, ed. *Careers for Women: New Ideas, New Methods, New Opportunities -- To Fit a New World.* Boston: Houghton Mifflin Co., 1934.
Includes: Mrs. William Brown Melony, "Newspaper Work," pp. 410-414; Cora G. Lewis, "The Editor of a Weekly Paper," p. 414; Ruth Finney, "The Reporter," pp. 427-430; Catherine Filene, "Radio," pp. 489-507.

2766. Fins, Alice. *Women in Communications.* Skokie, Illinois: National Textbook Co., 1979. 151 pp.
Sketches of and interviews with a number of women in a variety of communication positions. Lists associations and degree programs and gives information on practical aspects (salaries, financial aid for training).

2767. Fishburn, Katherine. *Women in Popular Culture: A Reference Guide.* Westport, Connecticut: Greenwood Press, 1982. 267 pp.
Numerous annotated references on women's roles and participation in fiction, magazines, film, and comics.

2768. Golden, L.L.L. "The Opening Door." *Saturday Review.* July 10, 1971, pp. 47-48.
New opportunities for women.

2769. Grunig, Larissa A. "Sex Discrimination in Promotion and Tenure in Journalism Education." *Journalism Quarterly.* Spring 1989, pp. 93-100, 229.
Discrimination exists, perhaps not intentional, but structural in nature. Analysis of a department as a case study; requested a panel of women educators in various universities to react to the case. Few direct effects of sex discrimination on promotion and tenure in the department existed, but there were examples of bias, misunderstanding, and insensitivity.

2770. Harwood, Kenneth. "Earnings and Education of Men and Women in Selected Media Occupations." *Journal of Broadcasting.* Spring 1976, pp. 233-237.
Sexual differences in rates of pay, using census data.

2771. Jensen, Marlene. *Women Who Want To Be Boss.* New York: Doubleday, 1987.
Among 22 top managers included were: Cathleen Black, *USA Today* publisher; Helen Gurley Brown, *Cosmopolitan* editor-in-chief, and Kay Koplovitz, USA Network president.

2772. Kelly, James D. "Gender, Pay and Job Satisfaction of Faculty in Journalism." *Journalism Quarterly.* Summer 1989, pp. 447-452.
Women journalism faculty members are definitely paid less than men and are less satisfied with their jobs. Yet, "gender does not ... seem to predict or interact with job satisfaction."

2773. McKerns, Joseph P., ed. *Biographical Dictionary of American Journalism.* Westport, Connecticut: Greenwood Press, 1989. 820 pp.
Sketches of 500 important U.S. journalists from 1690 to the late 1980s including 71 women. Each entry has works by and about the journalist.

2774. Maryland State Commission for Women. Baltimore. *In the Public Interest: Law, Government, and Media. Maryland Women's History Resources Packet -- 1986.* Baltimore: Maryland State Department of Education, 1986. 342 pp.
Maryland women who made their marks on government, law, and public interest media.

2775. *MediaFile*, San Francisco.
December-January 1987-1988 issue devoted to women and media, highlighting experiences from women hired as "tokens," studies on the number of women in broadcasting, and interviews with six media women "who have made a difference."

2776. Merrill, John C., John Lee, and Edward J. Friedlander. *Modern Mass Media.* New York: Harper and Row, 1990. 452 pp.
Some limited information on women: "Black Women as Writers," p. 143; "Minorities and Women in the Newspaper Business," p. 126; "Ida Tarbell: Queen of the Muckrakers," p. 154; "Minorities and Women in Radio," p. 186; "Minorities and Women in Television," p. 213, and "Women in Public Relations," p. 309.

2777. Mills, Kay. *A Place in the News: From the Women's Pages to the Front Pages.* New York: Dodd, Mead, 1988. 378 pp.
The history of the role of women in U.S. journalism; goes back to 1930s to provide collective biography and interview-based history. All professional roles in news journalism, from reporting to publishing; sexual discrimination in journalism.

2778. *Newsweek.*
Hundreds of news items about women journalists; a few of some historical interest listed: "Women Reporters on Alert To Cover New European War," October 23, 1939, p. 44; "Ladies of Washington's Working Press: They Get Their Copy -- and Their Rights," March 1, 1943, p. 64; "81 Men and a Girl," December 2, 1959, p. 82 (Elaine Shephard, only woman reporter on President Eisenhower's global tour).

2779. Ott, Louise. "Sexual Harassment in the Workplace." *The Professional Communicator.* June-July 1988, pp. 25-27.

2780. "Pay Gap/Power Gap Still Apparent for Media Women in USA." *Gender and Mass Media Newsletter.* November 1989, pp. 22-24.
Three studies released at a Women, Men and Media Conference. Junior Bridge and Kathy Bonk analyzed front pages of 10 major U.S. dailies in 1989, and found that coverage of and by women was "shockingly low." A second study showed women were making very small steps toward equality on network newscasts, and a third, that women fared less well in all media in pay.

2781. Reed, Barbara Straus. "On the Margin: A Look at Part-Time Journalism Faculty with Special Emphasis on the Status of Women." Paper presented for the Ad Hoc Committee on the Status of Women, Association for Education in Journalism, Ottawa, Canada, August 1975.

2782. Reskin, Barbara F. and Patricia A. Roos. *Job Queues, Gender Queues. Explaining Women's Inroads into Male Occupations.* Philadelphia, Pennsylvania: Temple University Press, 1990. 368 pp.
Book editor, public relations specialist, and compositor included.

2783. Russ, Joanna. *How to Suppress Women's Writing.* Austin: University of Texas Press, 1983. 159 pp.
Discussion of prohibitions, bad faith, denial of agency, pollution of agency, double standard of content, false categorizing, isolation, anomalousness, and lack of models.

2784. Russell, Becky, D.J. Cline, Judith Sylvester. "Women in Sports Communication." *Press Woman.* April 1984, pp. 1-6.
Three women discuss their ideas and experiences about women sportswriters in three different articles.

2785. Russman, Linda. "Women, Men and Media Update." *Professional Communicator.* Summer 1989, pp. 8-10.
The lack of progress in hiring, promotion, and portrayal of women.

2786. Sharp, Nancy, et al. "Faculty Women in Journalism and Mass Communications: Problems and Progress." Columbia, South Carolina: Association for Education in Journalism and Mass Communication and Gannett Foundation of Rochester, New York, 1985, 74 pp.

Women's progress in mass communications education programs in 1983 as a follow-up to a 1972 study.

2787. Shepard, Elaine. *Forgive Us Our Press Passes.* Englewood Cliffs, New Jersey: Prentice-Hall, 1962. 301 pp.

Author's careers as movie actress, writer-photographer for Women's News Service, North American Newspaper Alliance, and magazines, and foreign correspondent.

2788. Sigma Delta Chi. "The Big Story: Ten Questions and Answers About the Booming Career Field of Journalism and Communications." Chicago: Sigma Delta Chi, 1973. 13 pp.

One question was: What about opportunities for women?

2789. Snyder, Jerome and Bill Tara. "Women in the Communication Arts." *Communication Arts.* 13:2 (1971), pp. 70-95.

Women in art design, ad direction, and magazines.

2790. Strainchamps, Ethel, ed. *Rooms with No View: A Woman's Guide to the Man's World of the Media.* New York: Harper & Row, 1974. 333 pp.

The conditions for women working in book, magazine, and newspaper publishing, broadcasting, and auxiliary professions; women are paid less for the same work done by men, discriminated against in promotions, salary raises, and jobs with more responsibilities. Based on 1971-73 experiences.

2791. Westmoreland, Reg, Douglas P. Starr, Keith Shelton, and Yorgo Pasadeos. "New Writing Styles of Male and Female Students." *Journalism Quarterly.* Autumn 1977, pp. 599-601.

Analysis of the writing of 18 male and 20 female journalism students; females were "more wordy, use more imprecise words, use more personal words, use more adjectives and use more 'ly' adverbs."

2792. Wheeler, Helen Rippier. *Getting Published in Women's Studies: An International Interdisciplinary Professional Development Guide Mainly for Women.* Jefferson, North Carolina: McFarland, 1989. 241 pp.

Women in academia given a number of resources for their work, including publication in periodicals, thematic journal issues, and audiovisuals.

2793. Wilson, Jean Gaddy. "Future Directions for Females in the Media." In *Communications at the Crossroads: The Gender Gap Connection*, edited by Ramona Rush and Donna Allen, pp. 160-174. Norwood, New Jersey: Ablex, 1989.

Women *are* increasing their percentages of employees in the media, making up one-third of the newspaper newsrooms and broadcasting stations; but, there is a "woman's place" in employment, as well as in coverage, and it is not in management.

2794. Wilson, Jean Gaddy. "What It Takes to Be a Pro." *Working Woman.* October 1985, pp. 130-132.

2795. Wilson, Jean Gaddy. "Women in the United States Media: Opportunities Today in Employment and Promotion." *Sex-Roles within Massmedia Newsletter.* November 1988, pp. 38-39.
There are 79 women publishers among 1,658 dailies, and "at least" 13 women general managers of TV stations; solutions offered for problems of women in the media.

2796. Wilson, Vincent, jr. *The Book of Distinguished American Women.* Brookeville, Maryland: American History Research Associates, 1984.
More than one-half of the 50 women featured had worked in media.

2797. Wood, Mary Ann. "Profile of the Woman Journalism Teacher in the Two-Year College." Paper presented for the Ad Hoc Committee on the Status of Women, Association for Education in Journalism, Ottawa, Canada, August 1975.

Advertising, Public Relations

2798. Akamatsu, Muriel. "Liberating the Media: Advertising." Columbia: University of Missouri, School of Journalism, Freedom of Information Center Report No. 290, 1972.
Rounds up research about women in advertising.

2799. Alderman, Royal. "My Hectic Times with 'Mr. Charles' Revson: Master Promoter." *Advertising Age.* March 8, 1976, pp. 39-40.
Describes association with marketer of glamor to U.S. women.

2800. Faulkner, Melissa, et al. "Advertising Students See Field as Less Gender-Focussed Than Other Business Careers." *Journalism Educator.* Winter 1989, pp. 4-10.
Male and female students see most advertising jobs as "androgynous," but females believe they will have fewer advancement possibilities than men.

2801. Fitz-Gibbon, Bernice. *Macy's, Gimbels, and Me: How To Earn $90,000 a Year in Retail Advertising.* New York: Simon and Schuster, 1967. 380 pp.
Memoirs of woman who created slogans for the department stores and became the highest paid U.S. advertising woman.

2802. Grunig, Larissa A. "A Research Agenda for Women in Public Relations." *Public Relations Review.* Fall 1988, pp. 48-57.
Women must set their own research agenda on their own concerns separate from those of men.

2803. Hartman, John K. "Assessing Women in the Creative Department: What Creative Directors Think." Paper presented at Association for Education in Journalism and Mass Communication, Portland, Oregon, July 2-5, 1988. 15 pp.
The status of women in the creative departments of 196 advertising agencies in Detroit studied through questionnaires.

2804. Henry, Susan. "In Her Own Name?: Public Relations Pioneer Doris Fleischman Bernays." Paper presented at Association for Education in Journalism and Mass Communication, Portland, Oregon, July 2-5, 1988.

Public relations pioneer Edward Bernays had much help from his wife, Doris Fleischman Bernays, a partner in his firm for 58 years.

2805. Hunt, Todd and David W. Thompson. "Bridging the Gender Gap in PR Courses." *Journalism Educator.* Spring 1988, pp. 49-51.

Rutgers University of New Jersey sought to attract more males into PR courses and the profession.

2806. Iketon, Barbara. "The Female Practitioner Talks about Her Status." *Public Relations Journal.* September 1967, pp. 14-15.

2807. Joseph, Ted. "The Women Are Coming, The Women Are Coming." *Public Relations Quarterly.* Winter 1985, pp. 21-22.

Results of a survey showed women concerned about lower salaries and public relations treated as a "women's field" such as nursing and teaching.

2808. Kingman, Merle and Pat Sloan. "101 of the Best and Brightest Women in Advertising/Marketing." *Advertising Age.* December 12, 1988, pp. 1+.

Even though the industry was still male-oriented, women made much progress as shown here.

2809. Lance, Elizabeth P. "Survey Finds That Few Women Are Teaching in PR Programs." *Journalism Educator.* Winter 1986, pp. 7-8, 48.

Although nearly 70 percent of undergraduate public relations majors are women, only about 131 women teach those courses. Of these, most "started late, didn't originally plan teaching careers and have not progressed far up the academic ladder."

2810. Lukowitz, Karlene. "Women Practitioners: How Far, How Fast?" *Public Relations Journal.* May 1989, pp. 15-22.

Interviews with 30 high-level public relations executives; much optimism about the future of women in the field, mainly among male respondents.

2811. Pollock, John C. and Michael Winkleman. "Salary Survey." *Public Relations Journal.* June 1987, pp. 15-17.

Although males usually have salaries 65 percent higher than females in public relations, the difference results because of age and experience.

2812. Post, Linda Currey. "Where Do We Go from Here?" *Communication World.* May 1988, pp. 30-33.

The stories of four top women public relations practitioners and how they achieved.

2813. Russell, Victor. "Salary Survey." *Public Relations Journal.* June 1988, pp. 26-30.

The median difference in male and female salaries in public relations was $12,000.

2814. Santi, Tina. "Today's Women Explodes Yesterday's Ad Dream World." *Advertising Age.* March 18, 1974, pp. 49-53.
Advertisers must take into account changes in women's lives, careers, and attitudes.

2815. Sattler, John E. "Career Opportunities in Public Relations." *Public Relations Quarterly.* Fall 1970, p. 28.
Including those for women.

2816. Selnow, G.W. and S. Wilson. "Sex Roles and Job Satisfaction in Public Relations." *Public Relations Review.* Winter 1985, pp. 38-47.
Nationwide survey of 300 public relations practitioners found that women were less likely than men to be satisfied with the creative challenges and salaries of their jobs.

2817. Smith, Rea. "Women in Public Relations." *Public Relations Journal.* October 1968, pp. 26-29.
Achievements and expectations of women in public relations.

2818. Taylor, Ron and Roxanne Hovland. "Women Likely To Face Salary Discrimination in Advertising." *Journalism Educator.* Winter 1989, pp. 11-16.
Despite their higher grade point averages, female graduates received consistently lower salaries upon entering advertising.

2819. *Tips and Tactics.*
Supplement to weekly *pr reporter* devoted March 27, 1989 issue to problems women face in public relations. Among commentators were Vivian Deuschl and Rose Sexton.

2820. Weber, W.J. and W.W. Seifert. "National Survey Explores Role of Women in Public Relations." *Public Relations Journal.* July 1966, pp. 33-34.

Broadcasting

2821. Alter, Jonathan. "'Looksism' in TV News." *Newsweek.* November 6, 1989, pp. 72-73.
"Brainless beauties" believed to populate TV shows; progress made to change.

2822. Balon, Robert E., Joseph C. Philport, and Charles F. Beadle. "How Sex and Race Affect Perceptions of Newscasters." *Journalism Quarterly.* Spring 1978, pp. 160-163.
Sex was an affective condition of race only in the presence of the black male.

2823. Barnard, Charles N. "Some Questions for Miss Walters." *TV Guide.* December 30, 1972, pp. 26-30.

2824. Barrett, Marvin, ed. *Survey of Broadcast Journalism 1970-1971: A State of Siege.* New York: Grosset and Dunlap, 1971. 183 pp.
Supplementary essay on women on the air.

2825. Bennetts, Leslie. "The Prime Time of Mary Alice Williams." *Vanity Fair.* September 1989, pp. 256-259.

2826. Biagi, Shirley. *Newstalk II: State-of-the-Art Conversations with Today's Broadcast Journalists.* Belmont, California: Wadsworth, 1987. 256 pp.
Interviews with Marlene Sanders, CBS News; Susan Spencer, CBS News; Judy Woodruff, MacNeil/Lehrer News Hour, and Susan Wornick, WCVB-TV, Boston.

2827. Blair, Gwenda. *Almost Golden: Jessica Savitch and the Selling of Television News.* New York: Simon and Schuster, 1988. 352 pp.
The short, successful career of Jessica Savitch, from her Philadelphia days to NBC, including personal traits.

2828. Buchman, P. "Title VII Limits on Discrimination Against Television Anchorwomen on the Basis of Age-Related Appearance." *Columbia Law Review.* January 1985, pp. 190-215.
The requirement of "youthful appearance" for TV anchorwomen constituted unlawful employment discrimination.

2829. Cantor, Muriel G. "A TV License Challenge -- Women and Media Research." Paper presented at Society for the Study of Social Problems, New York, August 25, 1973.
Research in support of a NOW petition that challenged Washington, D.C.'s WRC-TV license in 1972, claiming the station did not treat women fairly.

2830. Cantor, Muriel G. "Women and Public Broadcasting." *Journal of Communication.* Winter 1977, pp. 14-19.
An analysis of the results and recommendations of the Report of the Task Force on Women in Public Broadcasting (Corporation for Public Broadcasting, 1975) showed women were underemployed or underpaid at CPB, and Task Force recommendations were not implemented.

2831. Carlinsky, Dan. "New Careers for Women in TV and Radio." *Seventeen.* October 1972, pp. 132, 194.

2832. Carter, Jimmy. "The White House Proposals for Public Broadcasting." *Public Telecommunications Review.* September-October 1977, pp. 58-60.
Participation by women in public broadcasting included in president's message to Congress.

2833. Carter, Linda. "New Spirit Beginning To Change Old Male Media Attitudes and Practices." *Media Report to Women*. January-February and March-April 1987, p. 11.

Excerpted from author's "On the Air, The Fight of Women Broadcasters To Be Seen and Heard!" in Fall 1986 *Changing Woman*.

2834. Castro, Janice. "Women in Television: An Uphill Battle." *Channels*. January 1988, pp. 42-52.

Claims that "Despite the broad gains made by women during the past 10 to 15 years, the evidence of a persistent pattern of discrimination against women in the television industry is far more than anecdotal."

2835. Causey, Betty Jo. "A Study of the Radio-TV Workshop at the Texas State College for Women from September 1953 to June 1954." Masters thesis, Texas Women's University, 1954.

2836. Cobb-Reiley, Linda. "Minority Voices in the Marketplace of Ideas: A Case Study of Women and the Fairness Doctrine." *Freedom of Speech Newsletter*. June 1979, pp. 3-13.

National Organization for Women's monitoring of network and local TV in 1971 and onwards, and its arguments for fairness before the Federal Communications Commission.

2837. Corporation for Public Broadcasting. *1979 Annual Report*. Washington, D.C.: CPB, 1980. 38 pp.

Includes human resources development (minority and women's affairs) and inservice training for women and minorities.

2838. Craft, Christine. *Christine Craft. An Anchorwoman's Story*. Santa Barbara, California: Capra Press, 1986. 220 pp.

Christine Craft was fired by Metromedia, Inc. and its Kansas City TV station in 1983 because she was "too old, too unattractive and not deferential enough to men." Craft sued and won the case, but the verdict was later overturned.

2839. Crist, Judith. "Job Opportunities for Women in Television Still Found Good." *New York Tribune*. May 30, 1948.

An early reference to the topic.

2840. Cronkite, Walter. "On Choosing -- and Paying -- Anchorpeople." *Columbia Journalism Review*. July/August 1976, pp. 24-25.

2841. Darrach, Brad. "Goodbye *Today*, Hello Tomorrow." *Life*. December 1989, pp. 46-53, 56.

TV personality Jane Pauley's quitting her *Today* slot to spend more time at home.

2842. DeGooyer, Janice and F. Borah. "What's Wrong with This Picture? A Look at Working Women on Television." Washington, D.C.: National Commission on Working Women, 1982.

Twenty-five top-rated TV shows compared between 1972 and 1981; the image of women changed very little. Young women were shown; older and black women were frequently shown in situation comedies. By the senior author: DeGooyer, Janice, "Women, Work and Age Discrimination," Washington, D.C.: National Commission on Working Women, 1981, 12 pp.

2843. Dreyfuss, Joel. "Public Television: Toward a Redefinition of Minority Roles." *Public Telecommunications Review.* January-February 1976, pp. 70-72.

Public television's record in helping blacks, women, and Hispanics has been worse than that of commercial TV.

2844. Ellerbee, Linda. *And So It Goes: Adventures in Television.* New York: Putnam, 1986.

2845. Feldman, Orna. "Terry Gross of NPR." *Washington Journalism Review.* June 1989, pp. 34-38.

National Public Radio's Terry Gross, who does daily show, "Fresh Air."

2846. Ferri, Anthony J. "Perceived Career Barriers of Men and Women Television News Anchors." *Journalism Quarterly.* Fall 1988, pp. 661-667, 732.

Women TV anchors perceived more barriers than their male counterparts in a 1984 sample of 68 anchors.

2847. Ferri, Anthony J. and Jo E. Keller. "Perceived Career Barriers for Female Television News Anchors." *Journalism Quarterly.* Autumn 1986, pp. 463-467.

Responses of 78 TV news anchors used to identify the forces that female anchors perceived as obstacles to their advancement.

2848. Fife, Marilyn D. "A Critical Assessment of Equal Employment Opportunity Policy in U.S. Telecommunication Industries." *Mass Comm Review.* Winter-Spring 1988-89, pp. 3-9.

The implementation and enforcement of equal opportunities left much to be desired.

2849. Flander, Judy. "Women in Network News. Have They Arrived Or Is Their Prime Time Past?" *Washington Journalism Review.* March 1985, pp. 39-43.

Network women are pessimistic about progress of the women's role in network news.

2850. Flinn, John. "On Location with Pay TV." *Channels.* November 1988, pp. 36-42.

Bridget Potter, Home Box Office television official, who has taken risks doing documentaries and dramas that have paid off.

2851. Fung, Victoria M. "Anchor Jobs Go to Young Women and Experienced Men." *Washington Journalism Review.* October 1988, pp. 20-24.
Women remain underpaid at networks, rewarded for their youth and attractiveness and not so much for their expertise.

2852. Gay, Verne. "Is There Room at the Top for the Women of TV News?" *Variety.* May 10-16, 1989, p. 86.
Report on women in executive positions in television. "There are more women producers and bureau chiefs than ever before. It just cuts off at a certain point. For vice presidents, it is still an old boys' club," claims Marlene Sanders.

2853. Gelfman, Judith S. *Women in Television News.* New York: Columbia University Press, 1976. 186 pp.
Interviews with 30 successful women in television news accompanied by observations on that data. Topics include: breaking ground, background for career, expectations of a career, being a woman in TV news, "double tokenism," career versus home life, and career guidance and advice.

2854. Gielow, L.S. "Sex Discrimination in Newscasting." *Michigan Law Review.* December 1985, pp. 443-474.
Judicial deference to viewer surveys in the hiring of television newspeople is unwarranted.

2855. Gladstone, Brooke. "Sonia Landau." *Washington Journalism Review.* January 1986, pp. 41-45.
Chair of the Corporation for Public Broadcasting.

2856. Gottehrer, Barry. "Television's Princess of the Press Corps." *Saturday Evening Post.* September 1964, pp. 36-37.
Television newswoman, Nancy Dickerson.

2857. Gray, Nancy K. "Before Barbara Walters There was Dorothy Fuldheim." *Ms.* December 1976, pp. 40-45.

2858. Guider, Elizabeth. "Networks Dragging Femme Anchors." *Variety.* February 28, 1990, pp. 1, 4.
Discussion of Connie Chung, Diane Sawyer, and Jane Pauley; networks pay them highly but the problem remains of finding a proper niche for them.

2859. Hansen, Audrey B. "A Descriptive Survey of Career Women in United States Television Stations and Various Job and Attitude Factors Affecting Their Employment." Masters thesis, Sul Ross State College, 1965.

2860. Harwood, Kenneth. "Women in Broadcasting 1984-1990." *Feedback.* Spring 1984, pp. 18-21.

Figures on the proportion of women in the broadcasting labor force -- .316 in 1980, compared to .351 predicted for 1984 and .389 for 1990.

2861. Heinz, Catharine. "The Voice of Authority; or, Hurrah for Christine Craft." *Feedback.* Spring 1984, pp. 3-6.

Part of a special issue on women in broadcasting, this article discusses Craft, female TV anchor fired for lack of attractiveness, as launching point for history of women in TV and radio.

2862. Hennessee, Judith. "The Press's Very Own Barbara Walters Show." *Columbia Journalism Review.* July-August 1976, pp. 22-25.

The press and broadcasting's uproar over ABC's offer of a five-year, U.S. $5 million TV anchor slot to Barbara Walters. Media reaction to the offer.

2863. Hill, George H. and Sylvia Saverson Hill. *Blacks on Television: A Selectively Annotated Bibliography.* Metuchen, New Jersey: Scarecrow Press, 1985. 223 pp.

Includes sections, "Actresses," pp. 86-97 and "Women," pp. 176-177.

2864. Hodgetts, Victoria. "Will ABC's Eight-Million Dollar Baby Pay Off?" *New York.* December 23, 1974, pp. 38-41.

Reference to Stephanie Edwards of television's "AM America."

2865. Holcomb, Betty. "The ABC's of Sexism." *Columbia Journalism Review.* May-June 1986, pp. 8-9.

Women at ABC television worked from within to change their salaries and positions.

2866. Horne, Sandra. "How Policies on Jobs for Women Could Be Put into Practice." *Television Today.* October 25, 1984, pp. 16-17.

2867. Hosley, David H. and Gayle K. Yamada. *Hard News: Women in Broadcast Journalism.* Westport, Connecticut: Greenwood Press, 1987. 207 pp.

Exclusively deals with women broadcast journalists; begins with Ruth Crane of WJR (Detroit) in 1929 and ends with Carolyn Wean, vice president of KPIX (San Francisco). The evolution of women broadcasters from "women's home companion" to their role in top management. Focus on pioneers: Sigrid Schultz, Helen Sioussat, Dorothy Fuldheim, Pauline Frederick, and Barbara Walters. Delineation of issues facing broadcast women, i.e., equal pay, aging, opportunity, and sexual harassment.

2868. Joy, Patricia. "Hearts and Minds." *News Photographer.* December 1988, p. 31.

The problems a news film camerawoman faced in the 1970s.

2869. Kienzle, Kathleen J. "A Study of the Employment Opportunities for Women in Broadcast News." Masters thesis, Ohio State University, 1965.

2870. Klever, Anita. *Women in Television.* Philadelphia, Pennsylvania: Westminster Press, 1975. 142 pp.
Interviews with 37 women in many different television jobs who relate their accomplishments.

2871. Kuney, Jack. *Take One. Television Directors on Directing.* Westport, Connecticut: Greenwood Press, 1990.
The insights of ten television directors through interviews, one with Emily Squires, entitled, "Directing *Sesame Street*."

2872. Landsberg, Michele. "TV Women: How They're Doing in Male-Chauvinist TV-Land." *Chatelaine.* May 1974, pp 39+.
Women in television must work twice as hard as men; they cannot move into managerial positions or those involving researching or reporting.

2873. Leonard, Mary. "Cassie Mackin: No Ambitions To Be a Brinkley or Cronkite." *The Quill.* January 1973, pp. 16-17.
Profile of NBC News correspondent Catherine (Cassie) Mackin.

2874. "McCall's Golden Mike Awards for 7 Women in Radio and TV." *McCall's Magazine.* January 1952, January 1954, January 1955, May 1956, May 1957, May 1958, May 1959, May 1960, May 1961, May 1962, May 1963, May 1964, May 1965.

2875. McCleneghan, J. Sean. "TV Newswomen in Texas." *Journalism Quarterly.* Spring 1982, pp. 122-124.
Two themes emerged concerning the number of women employed as first-year reporters in Texas television operations in 1980 -- women did not hold managerial news jobs and most continued to do features ("puff balls") instead of hard news reporting.

2876. McCormick-Pickett, Nancy, ed. *Women on the Job: Careers in the Electronic Media.* Washington, D.C.: American Women in Radio and Television, Inc., Women's Bureau, 1984. 32 pp.
Some career opportunities for women in the electronic media. Main areas described: administration, art, engineering, legal, news, personnel, production, programming, promotion, and sales.

2877. Marting, Leeda and Sue Foley. "Women in Broadcast Education." *Journal of Broadcasting.* 19:1 (1975), pp. 31-42.
Rank, salary, and discrimination levels of women educators in broadcasting. By the senior author: "An Empirical Study of the Images of Males and Females During Prime-Time Television Drama," Ph.D. dissertation, Ohio State University, 1973.

2878. Matusow, Barbara. *The Evening Stars: The Making of the Network News Anchor.* Boston: Houghlin Mifflin, 1983. 302 pp.
Barbara Walters included; the status of women in broadcasting to 1976.

2879. Mentzler, Carolyn A. "The Role of Women Employees in Educational Television Stations in 1964." Masters thesis, Ohio State University, 1964.

2880. Miller, Mark Crispin. "Sex, Lies and Videotape." *Savvy Woman.* October 1989, pp. 70-72.
    On TV personality, Barbara Walters.

2881. Mills, Kay. "Fighting Sexism on the Airwaves." *Journal of Communication.* Spring 1974, pp. 150-155.
    Women represent 22 percent of the television workforce; 75 percent of them are clerical. Thirty percent of those in noncommercial broadcasting were women; 54 percent of them in clerical jobs.

2882. Morris, Michele. "The St. Joan of Television." *Working Woman.* May 1986, pp. 70-76.
    Joan Ganz Cooney of Children's Television Workshop, labeled the "conscience of television."

2883. Nash, Abigail Jones. "The Status of Women in Broadcast Journalism: A National Survey." Masters thesis, University of Wisconsin, 1974.

2884. Nash, Abigail Jones, et al. "Minorities and Women in Broadcast News: Two National Surveys." Paper presented at Association for Education in Journalism, San Diego, California, August 18-21, 1974. 23 pp.
    A survey of newswomen in radio and TV; only 14 percent thought being female helped them to get their jobs; 89 percent received "good" or "excellent" job ratings from their news directors.

2885. National Commission on Working Women. Washington, D.C. "The Status of Women in the Broadcasting Industry Today." Proceedings of a Symposium (Washington, D.C., December 5, 1984). Washington, D.C.: National Commission on Working Women, 1985. 22 pp.
    Topics such as employment, programming, and funding; special attention given to the lack of women radio talk show hosts, wages, insufficient power for women, and many more subjects. By the same commission: *Women in Focus: An Analysis of TV's Female Characters and Their Jobs*, 1986; *Women Out of View: An Analysis of Female Characters on 1987-88 TV Programs*, 1987.

2886. Nelson, Malcolm and Diana George. "Interview with Linda Kelsey and Michele Gallery." *Journal of Popular Culture.* Spring 1981, pp. 683-.
    Linda Kelsey, who played the role of "Billie Newman" on the TV "Lou Grant" show, and the story editor for the show, Michele Gallery.

2887. Oettinger, Mal. "Women's Lib Is Not a Laughing Matter for Offending Broadcasters." *Television/Radio Age.* October 15, 1973, pp. 69-70.
    Efforts of the National Organization for Women and American Women in Radio and Television to get the Federal Communication Commission to standardize methods for targeting broadcast licensees who might be discriminating.

2888. O'Keefe, John. "Recruiting Women -- Why We Must Continue To Review the Process." *Television Today.* August 16, 1984, pp. 40-41.

2889. Orenstein, Peggy. "Women on the Verge of a Nervy Breakthrough." *Mother Jones.* June 1989, pp. 28-31, 46, 48-50, 52.
   The success women have attained as network television anchors through a forum of Ann Rubenstein (NBC), Marion Goldin (formerly CBS), Linda Ellerbee (NBC and ABC), and Meredith Vieira (CBS). Some of the all-too-usual questions were asked -- what would you tell an aspiring woman reporter, are you as women journalists concerned about aging?

2890. Paisner, Daniel. *The Imperfect Mirror: Inside Stories of Television Newswomen.* New York: Morrow, 1989. 270 pp.
   The struggles of women to succeed in TV: Lesley Stahl, Diane Sawyer, Connie Chung, Marlene Sanders, Jane Pauley, Christine Craft, some lesser-known newswomen.

2891. Parsons, Harriet. "What Producers Do." *Films in Review.* October 1954, pp. 404-408.
   Author's production work with "I Remember Mama" and "The Enchanted Cottage."

2892. Pogrebin, Letty Cottin. "The Working Woman." *Ladies' Home Journal.* April 1975, pp. 18, 20, 34.
   Working women of television.

2893. Press, Tina. "News Woman in a Man's World." *Public Telecommunications Review.* February 1975, pp. 28-30.
   WCBS Radio executive producer discussed roles, images, and stereotypes of women in broadcasting.

2894. Quinn, Sally. *We're Going to Make You a Star.* New York: Dell, 1975. 286 pp.
   Her brief career at CBS Morning News.

2895. Reep, Diane C. and Faye H. Dambrot. "Having It All? Career Conflicts for TV's Women." *Journal of Studies in Technical Careers.* 9 (1987), pp. 217-233.

2896. Reid, Charlotte T. "Women Forging Ahead in Broadcast Management." *Television/Radio Age.* March 31, 1975, pp. 48-50.

2897. Sanders, Marlene. "Are Women Reporters Better Than Men?" *TV Guide.* March 18, 1989, pp. 15-20.
   As a group, no; as some individuals, yes.

2898. Sanders, Marlene. "'I Can Do Anything Better Than You' -- Well Almost, Says a Lady Who Reached the TV Peak." *Journalism Educator.* Spring 1968, pp. 17-20.

Author's reporting experiences and advice to women aspiring for journalism careers.

2899. Sanders, Marlene. "The Long-Term Solution: Time." *The Quill.* February 1990, pp. 23-25.
Women journalists in the three networks.

2900. Sanders, Marlene. "Women in TV News -- Where We've Been and Where We're Going." *Television Quarterly.* Spring 1981, pp. 49-56.
In her early career of the early 1950s, Sanders was the only woman in her category of TV work. Now a CBS correspondent, she provides information on her career and offers a yardstick by which to measure the progress of women in TV.

2901. Sanders, Marlene. "Yes, It's True: *We* Don't Look Like *Them*." *The Quill.* January 1986, pp. 38-39.
A new roadblock -- "comfort factor" -- keeps women from moving as far as they can in broadcasting.

2902. Sanders, Marlene and Marcia Rock. "Marlene Sanders Has Done It All." *Quill.* November 1988, pp. 24-31.
CBS News journalist Marlene Sanders talked about her career and shared insights, warnings, and hope with women broadcasters.

2903. Sanders, Marlene and Marcia Rock. *Waiting for Prime Time: The Women of Television News.* Urbana: University of Illinois Press, 1988. 214 pp.
Autobiography of Sanders, who worked in broadcasting since 1955, and interviews with Lesley Stahl, Faith Daniels, Diane Sawyer, Lynn Sherr, Pauline Frederick, and Susan Spencer. Subtle pressures on women broadcasters emphasized.

2904. Savitch, Jessica. *Anchorwoman.* New York: Berkley Books, 1982. 192 pp.
Author's climb to the top reaches of network newscasting, shattering the myth of no place for "broads in broadcasting."

2905. Segaloff, Nat. "Peggy Charren and 'Action for Children's Television.'" *Animation.* Fall 1989, pp. 41-42.
Peggy Charren, who for over 20 years, has tried to straighten out children's television.

2906. Sherman, Ellen. "Femme Scribes Cop Top Jobs." *Ms.* December 1974, pp. 84-92.
Women's roles as TV scriptwriters had improved, but only 6.5 percent of stories and 1.5 percent of the pilots for the 1973-74 season were written by women.

2907. Simpson, Peggy. "The Revolutionary of Radio." *Working Woman.* August 1986, pp. 46-50.

Dorothy Bruson, one of few black female broadcast owners pioneered "urban contemporary" radio.

2908. Singleton, Loy A. and Stephanie Cook. "Television Network News Reporting by Female Correspondents: An Update." In *Mediamerica*, edited by Edward Jay Whetmore, pp. 311-316. Third edition. Belmont, California: Wadswroth, 1985.

A content analysis of 1,247 network news reports; there is a significant difference between male- and female-related topics on network news reports. Women reported fewer stories than men about foreign affairs, the economy, business, sports, disasters, and features, and more about the U.S. government, environment, women's issues, and social problems. Published in *Journal of Broadcasting*, Winter 1982, pp. 487-491.

2909. Smith, Conrad, Eric S. Fredin, and Carroll Ann Ferguson. "Sex Discrimination in Earnings and Story Assignments Among TV Reporters." *Journalism Quarterly*. Spring 1988, pp. 3-11.

Data from a national survey to examine the nature and extent of pay and story-assignment discrimination against female reporters at network-affiliated television stations.

2910. Smith, Don D. and Kenneth Harwood. "Women in Broadcasting." *Journal of Broadcasting*. Fall 1966, pp. 399-455.

Women and men broadcasters compared.

2911. Solomon, Sybil R. "A Survey of the Employment of Women in Certain Phases of Television Production." Masters thesis, University of Houston, 1955.

2912. Stone, Vernon A. "Attitudes Toward Television Newswomen." *Journal of Broadcasting*. Winter 1973-74, pp. 49-61.

Acceptance of on-air television newswomen indicated by the results of five surveys of different audience groups and TV news directors.

2913. Stone, Vernon A. "Newswomen's Numbers Level Off, More Become News Directors." *RTNDA Communicator*. July 1984, pp. 122-123.

2914. Stone, Vernon A. "Pipelines and Dead Ends: Jobs Held by Minorities and Women in Broadcast News." Paper presented at Association for Education in Journalism and Mass Communication, Portland, Oregon, July 2-5, 1988. 20 pp.

Minority women filled a number of broadcast production jobs and were as likely as non-minority men and women to be reporting or anchoring; white women also made up a substantial share of the work force. See his paper given at the same conference in 1986: "The Changing Profiles of Broadcast News Directors," 18 pp.

2915. Stone, Vernon A. "Trends in the Status of Minorities and Women in Broadcast News." *Journalism Quarterly*. Summer 1988, pp. 288-293.

Over the period, 1976-1986, the minority share of the broadcast news workforce decreased slightly; minority women"s share had very little change. Author has conducted analyses of newswomen's careers; see his *Careers in Broadcast News*, East Lansing, Mich.: Radio and Television News Directors Association, 1972.

2916. Tabacsko, Ken. "Gayle Gardner's Lament." *The Quill.* January 1987, pp. 25-27.

    Female sportscaster of ESPN television, her trying times in a traditionally male career.

2917. Trotta, Liz. "Hey, Fellows, Chet and David Have Sent a Woman." *TV Guide.* April 19, 1969, pp. 6-10.

2918. "TV Director." *Glamour.* February 1975, pp. 130-131.

2919. Tyler, Ralph. "Cooney Cast Light on a Vision." *Variety.* December 13, 1989, pp. 63, 72.

    Creator of "Sesame Street," Jane Ganz Cooney. Other stories on the show, pp. 63-79.

2920. Wade, Margaret H. "A Descriptive Study of the Jobs Held by Women in the Radio-Television Industry in Los Angeles." Masters thesis, University of Southern California, 1952.

2921. Walker, Connecticut. "Newswomen and Television Beauty on the Tube." *Parade.* February 16, 1975, pp. 4-5.

2922. Whittaker, Susan and Ron Whittaker. "Relative Effectiveness of Male and Female Newscasters." *Journal of Broadcasting.* Spring 1976, pp. 177-184.

    In a 1974 study, a sample audience found no statistically-significant differences in the perceived acceptance, believability, or effectiveness of male and female newscasters.

2923. Wilson, Jean Gaddy. "Are Newswomen Changing the News?" *Ms.* December 1984, pp. 45-50, 124.

    A number of TV newswomen responded to the question: Is the power of Diane Sawyer and her colleagues less than meets the eye?

2924. "Women in Key TV Posts 'Sharply Diminished': May Be Departing out of Frustration in Upward Mobility." *Media Report to Women.* July-August 1986, p. 6.

    Reprinted from January-February 1986 Emmy, "Women Execs ... Up, Up ... and Out?" by Carole S. Schneider. Also in Spring 1986 *Women in Film Newsmagazine.*

Film

2925. Bonderoff, Jason. *Shortakes ... Sally Field: A Biography.* New York: St. Martin's Press, 1988.
   The career of actress Sally Field. Also see his *Barbara Walters: Today's Woman*, New York: Leisure Books, 1975.

2926. Bucher, Felix. "Women, Film Direction and Vocation." *Camera.* September 1967, p. 46.
   Various women directors discussed.

2927. Carrier, Jeffrey L. *Jennifer Jones: A Bio-Bibliography.* Westport, Connecticut: Greenwood Press, 1990. 160 pp.
   Highlights of the life of actress Jennifer Jones includes a complete filmography, list of her radio, TV, and theatre performances, and an annotated bibliography.

2928. Chen, Amy. "Asian American Cinema: Women Directors at the Forefront." *Bridge.* 9:3/4 (1984), pp. 14-19.
   Women directors whose cinema is described as a "means to examine our roles and perspectives on society."

2929. Citron, Michelle. "Comic Critique: The Films of Jan Oxenberg." In *Jump Cut: Hollywood, Politics and Counter Cinema*, edited by Peter Steven, pp. 315-325. Toronto: Between the Lines, 1985.

2930. Clarke, Shirley and Storm De Hirsch. "'Female' Film-Making." *Arts Magazine.* April 1967, pp. 23-24.
   The woman as filmmaker "transcends subjectivity."

2931. Condon, Frank. "Not a Lady in Sight." *Saturday Evening Post.* August 13, 1932, pp. 26+.
   Women not visible among film assistant directors, makeup and other personnel.

2932. Cook, Pam. "Approaching the Work of Dorothy Arzner." In *Sexual Stratagems: The World of Women in Film,* edited by Patricia Erens, pp. 224-235. New York: Horizon Press, 1979.

2933. Dunn, Reina Wiles. "Off-Stage Heroines of the Movies." *National Business Woman.* July 1934, pp. 202-203+.
   Women in film production.

2934. Eberly, Stephen L. *Patty Duke: A Bio-Bibliography.* Westport, Connecticut: Greenwood Press, 1988. 144 pp.
   Biography of actress Duke, along with complete discography, filmography, and lists of plays, television appearances, and award.

2935. Edwards, Anne. *Shirley Temple: American Princess.* New York: William Morrow, 1988.
    The movie career and Republican Party activities of Shirley Temple.

2936. Emerson, Mark and Eugene E. Pfaff. *Country Girl: The Life of Sissy Spacek.* New York: St. Martin's Press, 1988.
    A short description of the life and career of the actress, Sissy Spacek, star of "Coal Miner's Daughter" and "Crimes of the Heart."

2937. Erens, Patricia. "Interview with Jill Godmilow." *Women and Film.* 2:7 (1975), pp. 34-43.
    Interviews director Jill Godmilow on the making of "Antonia: A Portrait of a Woman."

2938. Erens, Patricia, ed. *Sexual Stratagems: The World of Women in Film.* New York: Horizon Press, 1979.

2939. Erens, Patricia. *The Films of Shirley MacLaine.* South Brunswick, New Jersey: A.S. Barnes, 1978. 202 pp.

2940. Farber, Stephen. "The Vanishing Heroine." *Hudson Review.* Winter 1974-1975, pp. 570-576.
    The lack of women in films of early 1970s commented upon; books about women in film, Marjorie Rosen's *Popcorn Venus* and Molly Haskell's *From Reverence to Rape*, reviewed.

2941. Ferlita, Ernest and John R. May. *The Parables of Lina Wertmüller.* New York: Paulist Press, 1977. 104 pp.
    Commentary on films of Wertmüller from Christian perspective; interview with Wertmüller.

2942. *Film Library Quarterly* Staff. "An Interview with Madeline Anderson on the Making of 'I Am Somebody.'" Winter 1971-72, pp. 39-41.
    An interview with Madeline Anderson on her film, "I Am Somebody," the story of 500 black women who took on the powerful white establishment in Charleston, South Carolina, and won.

2943. Fischer, Lucy. *Shot/Countershot. Film Tradition and Women's Cinema.* Princeton, New Jersey: Princeton University Press, 1989. 320 pp.
    How film critics believe women filmmakers present from a "countershot" vision, and how counter-cinema is related to theories of intertextuality.

2944. Fraser, Laura. "Nasty Girls." *Mother Jones.* February-March 1990, pp. 32-35, 48-50.
    Erotic videos made explicity for women and couples by self-proclaimed feminist pornographers such as Candida Royalle of Femme Productions, Susie Bright of *On Our Backs* and Fatale Films, Annie Sprinkle, and Vera Veronica.

2945. Freedland, Michael. *Jane Fonda: A Biography.* New York: St. Martin's Press, 1988.
>The life and career of U.S. actress, Jane Fonda, who starred in award-winning movies, and promoted civil rights in the 1960s and physical fitness in the 1980s.

2946. Gallagher, John Andrew. *Film Directors on Directing.* Westport, Connecticut: Greenwood Press, 1989. 313 pp.
>Interviews with 21 filmmakers, including Susan Seidelman and Joan Micklin Silver, on the craft of directing, including preparing the screenplay, working with actors, and dealing with distributors.

2947. Gustafson, Robert. "The Power of the Screen: The Influence of Edith Head's Film Designs on the Retail Fashion Market." *The Velvet Light Trap.* 19 (1982), pp. 8-15.

2948. Haskell, Molly. "Women in the Movies Grow Up." *Psychology Today.* January 1983, pp. 18-26.
>Leading men have dominated the film world; is it now the turn of Streep, Fonda, Lange, or Redgrave?

2949. Level, Hildegard. "Women Behind the Screen." *Independent Woman.* June 1948, pp. 170-172.
>The film producer, "script girl," costume designer, and others discussed.

2950. Lupino, Ida. "Me, Mother Directress." *Action.* May-June 1967, pp. 14-15.
>Her acting and directing careers.

2951. McClelland, Doug. *Eleanor Parker, Woman of a Thousand Faces: A Bio-Bibliography and Filmography.* Metuchen, New Jersey: Scarecrow Press, 1989. 291 pp.
>Film actress Parker.

2952. McCreadie, Marsha. *Women on Film: The Critical Eye.* New York: Praeger, 1983.
>The work of women film critics; women's acceptance in such roles resulted from film criticism being considered a fringe art form. Thirty-two women critics reviewed in eight chapters. By the same author: *The American Movie Goddess*, New York: John Wiley and Sons, 1973.

2953. Madsen, Axel. *Gloria and Joe.* New York: Arbor House, 1988.
>The three-year romance of Joseph Kennedy and Gloria Swanson.

2954. "Man's World, Woman's Place." *Film Library Quarterly.* Winter 1971-72, pp. 26-27.
>Women active in film comment on their careers and feelings about women in film; among them, Eleanor Perry, Anita Loos, Suzanne E. Bauman, and Lillian Gish.

2955. Matzen, Robert D. *Carole Lombard: A Bio-Bibliography.* Westport, Connecticut: Greenwood Press, 1988. 181 pp.

New information on this successful Hollywood star of the 1930s, including a published interview, an article by her, investigative report on the airplane crash that took her life, unpublished photographs, and detailed bibliography.

2956. Miller, Lynn Fieldman. *The Hand That Holds the Camera: Interviews with Women Film and Video Directors.* New York: Garland, 1988. 271 pp.

Interviews with women film and TV directors who challenge the traditional depictions of women in the mass media. Includes a brief introductory essay about each director and a list of her films and/or videos. The directors are Doris Chase, Michelle Citron, Kavery Duta, Tami Gold, Amalie Rothschild, Meg Switzgable, and Linda Yellen.

2957. Mordden, Ethan. *Movie Star: A Look at the Women Who Made Hollywood.* New York: St. Martin's Press, 1983.

Influential Hollywood actresses from the casting side -- the images they projected and the conflicts between their career plans and audience expectations.

2958. Murphy, Mary. "Sexual Harassment in Hollywood." *TV Guide.* March 29, 1986, pp. 2-11.

Sexual harassment of young actresses is still a serious problem in the entertainment business.

2959. Parish, James R. *The Paramount Pretties.* New Rochelle, New York: Arlington House, 1972. 587 pp.

Biographies, filmographies, and stills of Paramount stars, Gloria Swanson, Clara Bow, Claudette Colbert, Carole Lombard, Paulette Goddard, Marlene Dietrich, Miriam Hopkins, Sylvia Sidney, Mae West, Dorothy Lamour, Veronica Lake, Diana Lynn, Betty Hutton, Joan Crawford, Lizabeth Scott, and Shirley MacLaine.

2960. Parish, James R. *The RKO Gals.* New Rochelle, New York: Arlington House, 1974. 896 pp.

Fourteen RKO female stars, among whom were, Ann Harding, Irene Dunne, Ginger Rogers, Katherine Hepburn, Jane Russell, and Lupe Velez.

2961. Parish, James R. *The Slapstick Queens.* New York: A.S. Barnes and Co., Inc., 1973.

Five comediennes, their careers and contributions to American culture. Each chapter includes a detailed filmography with cast, credits, character names, synopses, reviews, and photos.

2962. Parish, James R. and Don E. Stanke. *The Glamour Girls.* New Rochelle, New York: Arlington House, 1975. 736 pp.

Biographies and filmographies of ten stars, Audrey Hepburn, Rita Hayworth, Jennifer Jones, Kim Novak, Merle Oberon, and Joan Bennett among them.

2963. Pfaff, Eugene E., jr. and Mark Emerson. *Meryl Streep: A Critical Biography.* Jefferson, North Carolina: McFarland, 1987.
Her career and a filmography.

2964. Pitts, Michael R. *Kate Smith: A Bio-Bibliography.* Westport, Connecticut: Greenwood Press, 1988. 276 pp.
Entertainer Kate Smith's life, discography, filmography, song index, and list of appearances.

2965. Rabinovitz, Lauren Holly. "Radical Cinema: The Films and Film Practices of Maya Deren, Shirley Clarke, and Joyce Wieland (New York)." Ph.D. dissertation, University of Texas, Austin, 1982. 352 pp.

2966. Rainey, Buck. *Those Fabulous Serial Heroines: Their Lives and Films.* Metuchen, New Jersey: Scarecrow Press, 1990. 537 pp.
Forty-six serial movie heroines of 1912-1956 era, including Pearl White, Marie Walcamp, Carol Forman, Mary Fuller, Allene Ray, Ruth Rolland, and Linda Stirling.

2967. Ralston, Esther. *Some Day We'll Laugh: An Autobiography.* Metuchen, New Jersey: Scarecrow Press, 1985. 244 pp.
Hollywood and Esther Ralston.

2968. Rivadue, Barry. *Alice Faye: A Bio-Bibliography.* Westport, Connecticut. Greenwood Press, 1990. 240 pp.
Biography of Alice Faye, actress of film, stage, broadcasting, and recording, with annotated bibliography on her life and career from 1933 through 1989, filmography, discography, and specialized appendices.

2969. Sarthe, Jean. "She Makes Movies." *National Business Woman.* October 1934, pp. 315+.
Director Vyvyan Donner.

2970. Schanke, Robert A. *Eva LeGallienne: A Bio-Bibliography.* Westport, Connecticut: Greenwood Press, 1989. 218 pp.
LeGallienne's career from 1914 debut; Broadway, film, television, and radio work.

2971. Scholtes, Mary C. "A Study of the Careers of 100 Women Who Prepare and Present Television Programs for Homemakers." Ph.D. dissertation, Columbia University, 1957.

2972. Schoonmaker, Mary Ellen. "TV News and the Face-Lift Factor." *Columbia Journalism Review.* March-April 1987, pp. 48-50.
Because of the effects of the Christine Craft trial, local TV women anchors were not as pressured to look like beauty queens.

2973. Schultz, Margie. *Ann Sothern: A Bio-Bibliography.* Westport, Connecticut: Greenwood Press, 1990, 276 pp.

The 60-year career of actress of stage, film, radio, television, and recordings; includes bibliography of articles by and about Sothern, as well as a filmography, discography, and list of her appearances.

2974. *Sepia.*

Articles on black movie actresses, such as, "Hollywood's New Black Beauties," March 1973, pp. 37-44, and "Is Hollywood Afraid To Star a Sexy Actress?" June 1969, pp. 10-15.

2975. Smith, Sharon. *Women Who Make Movies.* New York: Hopkinson and Blake, 1975. 307 pp.

Three major parts: an overview of women filmmakers worldwide since 1896, the new filmmakers who make films outside Hollywood, and a listing of U.S. women filmmakers.

2976. Spindle, Les. *Julie Andrews: A Bio-Bibliography.* Westport, Connecticut: Greenwood Press, 1989. 163 pp.

The professional career of actress Julie Andrews.

2977. *The Screen Guild Magazine.*

Includes Mary Astor, "Why I Prefer the Stage to Pictures," 1:3 (1934), and Genevieve Tobin, "An Actress' Working Day," 1:7 (1934).

2978. Tildesley, A.L. "She Stepped Down To Step Up." *Independent Woman.* November 1953, pp. 402-403.

Film director Dorothy Arzner.

2979. Ward, Carol M. *Mae West: A Bio-Bibliography.* Westport, Connecticut: Greenwood Press, 1989. 241 pp.

Mae West's life and career in three major phases: the early theater years, her meteoric film career in the 1930s, and her life as a popular culture legend.

2980. Zucker, Carole, ed. *Making Visible the Invisible: An Anthology of Original Essays on Film Acting.* Metuchen, New Jersey: Scarecrow Press, 1990. 440 pp.

Film performance from different perspectives, including feminist. Among contributors: Zucker, Angela della Vache, Lucy Fischer, Marian Keene, and Roberta Pearson.

Print Media

2981. Alburn, Miriam. "A Word About Women." *The Quill.* November 1966, pp. 26-27.

Several female stereotypes, largely fiction, steered high school and college women from journalism.

North America 383

2982. Alter, Jonathan. "Monitoring the News." *Savvy.* June 1988, pp. 46-53.
Traces career of Kay Fanning, from being wife of a newspaper publisher to owner of an Alaskan paper, editor of *Christian Science Monitor*, and president of the American Society of Newspaper Editors.

2983. American Society of Newspaper Editors. *Achieving Equality for Minorities in Newsroom Employment. ASNE's Goal and What It Means.* Washington, D.C.: ASNE, 1986. 101 pp.
Offers listings with percentage of the "minority population for the counties in which each newspaper has at least 5 percent of its circulation." Data from the 1980 U.S. Census, the 1984 ABC reports and American Newspaper Markets, Inc.

2984. *ASNE Bulletin.*
January 1986 issue of American Society of Newspaper Editors organ devoted much space to "Women in Management." Authors included Judy Clabes and Deborah Howell on differences between male and female editors, Stan Strick on working for a woman, Dorothy Jurney on the number of women editors, Maurine Beasley on a "pink-collar ghetto" study, Susan Miller and Maryle C. Levine on keeping careers on track, Janet Brandt on one woman's network, Sue Burzynski on family and career, Janet Chusmir on mobility of women journalists, Linda Cunningham on media myths about women, Angus McEachran and Madelyn Ross on one metro's experience of making a woman managing editor, eight managers on "things we wish we had known," and John Seigenthaler on why newsroom management must take women seriously. In September 1989 issue of *ASNE News*: Duncan McDonald, "A Return to Courtesy Titles? Most Editors Say No"; Susan Miller, "The Latest Editorial Challenge Is To Regain Women Readers," and an annual study of women in policy-making press jobs written by Dorothy Jurney.

2985. "ASNE Panelists Poles Apart on Status of Women Journalists." *Media Report to Women.* May-June 1988, pp. 1-2.
Discussion of impact of women on U.S. dailies at American Society of Newspaper Editors panel.

2986. Atkins, Paul A. "It's Here, Men. Women Are Invading Newsrooms." *The Quill.* February 1965, pp. 14-15.
Women's presence in newspapers will increase, based on number of female students in journalism at author's university.

2987. Baker, John F. "Gloria Emerson." *Publishers Weekly.* January 10, 1977, pp. 8-9.
Vietnam War correspondent.

2988. Barrett, G.H. "Job Satisfaction Among Newspaper Women." *Journalism Quarterly.* Autumn 1984, pp. 593-599.
In a survey of 239 newswomen, intrinsic and extrinsic satisfaction levels were found to be crucial to overall job satisfaction.

2989. Barron, John B. "The Paper Dolls Are Paper Tigers -- But They're Crowding Journalism Schools." *The Quill.* September 1965, pp. 12-15.
    Spoof of the increasing numbers of women journalism majors.

2990. Benedek, Elissa P. "Editorial Practices of Psychiatric and Related Journals: Implications for Women." *American Journal of Psychiatry.* January 1976, pp. 89-92.
    Of 37 professional journals in psychiatry, only a few actively tried to increase the number of women contributing authors or editorial board members.

2991. Biagi, Shirley. *Newstalk I: State-of-the-Art Conversations with Today's Print Journalists.* Belmont, California: Wadsworth, 1987. 240 pp.
    Satisfactions, frustrations, and excitement of working as a print journalist revealed through interviews with a dozen reporters, feature writers, and columnists, including Madeleine Blais of *Miami Herald*; Rheta Grimsley Johnson, Memphis *Commercial Appeal*; Marilyn Schwartz, *Dallas Morning News*; Helen Thomas, UPI; and Linda Williams, *Wall Street Journal*.

2992. Boucher, Bill. "Woman Edits Alaska's Oldest Newspaper." *The Quill.* May 1959, pp. 15-16.
    Emily Boucher, editor-publisher of the *Nome Nugget*.

2993. Bowles, Dorothy. "Women in the Newsroom: Pink-Collar Ghetto or Brave New World?" In *Seeing Female: Social Roles and Personal Lives*, edited by Sharon Brehn. Westport, Connecticut: Greenwood Press, 1988.

2994. Boylan, James. "Another Male Enclave Besieged." *Columbia Journalism Review.* March/April 1977, pp. 56-58.

2995. Brumagin, Vicki Lee. "A Study of Women in American Journalism from 1696 to 1972." Masters thesis, California State University, Northridge, 1972.

2996. Burroughs, Elise. "Opinions Differ on Why Progress Lags for Women News Managers." *ASNE Bulletin.* January 1988, pp. 16-17.

2997. Cantarow, Ellen. "Don't Throw That Old Diaphragm Away!" *Mother Jones.* June-July 1987, pp. 22-26, 43.
    Nicole Hollander and her comic strip, "Sylvia."

2998. Caswell, Lucy Shelton. "Women Practitioners of 'The Ungentlemanly Art.'" *1989 Festival of Cartoon Art.* Columbus, Ohio: Ohio State University Libraries, 1989, pp. 67-93.
    Profiled female cartoonists: Edwina Dumm, Lillian Weckner Meisner, Etta Hulme, Kate Salley Palmer, Signe Wilkinson, M.G. Lord, and Linda Frances Boileau.

2999. Cavalieri, Joey. "Jewish Mice, Bubblegum Cards, Comic Art, and Raw Possibilities." *Comics Journal.* August 1981, pp. 98-125.

Art Spiegelman and Françoise Mouly and their comic art, "Maus," depicting the fate of the Jews during World War II.

3000. Chang, Won H. "Characteristics and Self Perceptions of Women's Page Editors." *Journalism Quarterly.* Spring 1975, pp. 61-65.

   A survey of 335 women's page editors of daily newspapers who receive lower pay than male journalists but believe their situation is improving.

3001. Cheshire, Maxine, with John Greenya. *Maxine Cheshire, Reporter.* Boston, Massachusetts: Houghton Mifflin, 1978. 307 pp.

   Career of outspoken Washington reporter, Maxine Cheshire, and her biggest exposé, "Koreagate."

3002. Christy, Karen. "Women Fight for Equal Rights." *News Photographer.* November 1987, pp. 10-12.

3003. Cirillo, Joan J. "Suit Suite." *The Quill.* December 1984, pp. 14-18.

   Associated Press efforts to percolate women and minorities up through the ranks after a U.S. $2 million discrimination suit and threats of federal law hanging over it.

3004. Clabes, Judith G., ed. *New Guardians of the Press.* Indianapolis, Indiana: R.J. Berg & Co., 1983. 140 pp.

   Biographies of 12 women editors and publishers, written by the women themselves and prefaced with information about them.

3005. Cline, D.J. "Back to School (Graduate School, That Is)." *Press Woman.* September 1980, pp. 2-5.

   Difficulties of women journalists returning to school for a master's degree as perceived by a couple of journalism professors.

3006. Coburn, Marcia Froelke. "Inside the *Ebony* Empire." *Savvy Woman.* December 1989, pp. 55-57.

   President, chief operating officer and heir-apparent of Johnson publications, Linda Johnson Rice.

3007. Coram, Robert. "New Life at the *Monitor*." *The Quill.* April 1987, pp. 18-23.

   Katherine Fanning's efforts to change the *Christian Science Monitor.*

3008. Cronin, Mary M. "An Analysis of a Wartime Agenda: The Korean War Reporting of Marguerite Higgins." Paper presented at Association for Education in Journalism and Mass Communication, Minneapolis, Minnesota, August 1990.

   Higgins' goals to make Americans more aware of dangers of poorly-trained troops, of "evils" of communism, and of what Korean War was about.

3009. Czerniejewski, Halina J. "Then Came Lansden: Hitting the Road with Pamela's String of Perils." *The Quill.* February 1974, pp. 23-26.

Syndicated columnist Pamela Lansden, known for taking risks and odd occupations to get a story: Playboy bunny, logger, forest ranger, and raspberry picker.

3010. Dalton, Terry A. "A Story of Love and Marriage." *The Quill.* November 1988, pp. 42-44.

The "cut-throat competition" of Vermont reporters, David Karvelas and Deborah Sline, who are husband and wife.

3011. Davis, Deborah. *Katharine the Great: Katharine Graham and the Washington Post.* New York: Harcourt, Brace, Jovanovich, 1979. 290 pp.

Katharine Graham, publisher of the Washington *Post* and *Newsweek*, changed from a champion of liberal causes out of principle in her college days to a supporter of liberal causes out of "expediency and personal whim" in her publishing days.

3012. Davis, Lenwood G. "A History of Journalism in the Black Community: A Preliminary Survey. Exchange Bibliography No. 862." Monticello, Illinois: Council of Planning Librarians, 1975. 37 pp.

Six sections include citations about black women in journalism.

3013. Davis, Linda H. *Onward and Upward: A Biography of Katharine S. White.* New York: Fromm International Publishing Corporation, 1989. 300 pp.

The story of Katharine S. White, influential editor of the *New Yorker's* fiction department for more than 30 years, based on letters and correspondence with family members.

3014. Dryfoos, Susan W., ed. *Iphigene: Memoirs of Iphigene Ochs Sulzberger of the New York Times Family.* New York: Dodd, Mead and Co., 1981. 312 pp.

Iphigene Ochs Sulzberger, daughter of the "founder" of the *Times*, and wife, mother-in-law, and mother of publishers of that paper. Dryfoos is Iphigene's granddaughter.

3015. Eason, David L. "On Journalistic Authority: The Janet Cooke Scandal." *Critical Studies in Mass Communication.* December 1986, pp. 429-447.

Janet Cooke's forfeiting of the Pulitzer Prize she was awarded for what was discovered as a fabricated story.

3016. Eberhard, Wallace B. and Margaret L. Myers. "Beyond the Locker Room: Women in Sports on Major Daily Newspapers." *Journalism Quarterly.* Fall 1988, pp. 595-599.

The number of women on sports staffs of large U.S. dailies is small, but they cover major sports.

3017. Edelman, Scott. "A Comic of One's Own." *Comics Journal.* April 1986, pp. 91-95.

Discrimination against women in the comics industry, using Naomi Basner's story.

3018. Edwards, Julia. *Women of the World: The Great Foreign Correspondents.* Boston: Houghton Mifflin, 1988. 275 pp.

The stories of the many women journalists working abroad, including Dickey Chapelle, Marguerite Higgins, Mary Rinehart, Ann Stringer, Margaret Bourke-White, and Dorothy Thompson.

3019. Ellis, Frederick R. "Dickey Chapelle: A Reporter and Her Work." Masters thesis, University of Wisconsin, 1968.

3020. Engel, Margaret. "Women and Minorities Win Big Victory From AP." *Nieman Reports.* Autumn 1988, pp. 25, 44.

The Associated Press, the world's largest news gathering organization, agreed in an out-of-court settlement to pay $2 million in back wages and to improve its hiring of women, blacks, and Hispanics.

3021. Fitzgerald, Mark. "Many Women Leaving Newspapers." *Editor and Publisher.* October 17, 1987, p. 9.

Low pay and failure to get promotions cited as reasons.

3022. Fleener, Nickieann. "Without Bias? How Selected Employee Publications Depict the Roles of Women and Men within the Corporate Structure." Paper presented at Association for Education in Journalism and Mass Communication, Corvallis, Oregon, August 6-9, 1983. 40 pp.

How the presentation of men and women by selected internal business publications changed from 1978 to 1982 -- not for the better for women.

3023. Flenniken, Shary. "Fixations and Vexations: A Panel of Women Cartoonists." *Comics Journal.* February 1985, pp. 87-92.

Comments of women cartoonists on a panel on "Women in Cartooning," held in New York, November 4, 1982. Cartoonists were Shary Fenniken, Nicole Hollander, M.G. Lord, Wendy Pini, Trina Robbins, Avis Rosenberg, and Mary Wilshire.

3024. Frizzi, Ginny. "An Open Door for Women Sports Reporters." *Scholastic Editor.* 56:6 (1977), pp. 28-29.

High school girls' preparation for a sports writing career.

3025. Fruhauf, Aline. *Making Faces: Memoirs of a Caricaturist.* Washington, D.C.: Seven Locks Press, 1987. 254 pp.

Insights into the life and career of caricaturist Aline Fruhauf, noted for her caricatures of celebrities in theater, fashion, and music. Fruhauf's work appeared in New York City dailies and periodicals such as *Vogue, Vanity Fair, Esquire,* and *Musical America.*

3026. Gersh, Debra. "Advice to Women Journalists." *Editor & Publisher.* February 22, 1986, pp. 16-17.

On how to advance to managerial levels.

3027. Geyer, Georgie Anne. *Buying the Night Flight.* New York: Delacorte Press, 1983. 338 pp. (New York: Laurel Books, 1985.)
    An autobiography of author as foreign correspondent, relating her coverage of many of the world's newsmakers and hot spots.

3028. Gieber, Walter. "The 'Lovelorn' Columnist and Her Social Role." *Journalism Quarterly.* Spring 1960, pp. 499-514.
    Analysis of letters to a popular, syndicated "lovelorn" columnist. Believes columnist helps "groupless" readers "make contact with a wider world in which there are other anxious persons ... and friendly authority." Excerpts from a number of letters categorized into groups.

3029. Goldin, Marion. "Father Times: Who's on the Op-Ed Page?" *Mother Jones.* January 1990, p. 51.
    On *New York Times* op ed pages, five of the six regular columnists and 90 percent of the outside writers were male. The *Times* op ed page "perpetuates the myth that only men are the reliable experts in this society."

3030. Goodrick, Evelyn Trapp. "Women on Editorial Pages: Characteristics and Attitudes." Paper presented at the Association for Education in Journalism, Portland, Oregon, July 2-5, 1988. 34 pp.
    Women had not made significant progress on editorial page staffs, according to survey.

3031. Gran, Martin. "Sylvia by Nicole Hollander." *Cartoonist PROfiles.* March 1987, pp. 58-63.
    Interview with cartoonist who self-syndicates her seven-times-a-week strip.

3032. Greene, Gael. *Don't Come Back Without It.* New York: Simon and Schuster, 1960. 214 pp.
    A "typical" newswoman's life, probably written by male staffers of the *New York Post.* A female reporter's life was oriented around her loves and diets in this spoof.

3033. Groth, Gary. "Slaughter on Greene Street." *Comics Journal.* August 1982, pp. 70-82.
    Interview with Art Spiegelman and Françoise Mouly about their comic magazine work, "Raw."

3034. Harman, Jeanne Perkins. *Such a Life.* New York: Crowell, 1956. 210 pp.
    Author's seven years as reporter, researcher, or writer for *Life* magazine.

3035. Harris, George. "Lady Editor: Helen Brannon Smith." *Look.* November 16, 1965, pp. 121-122.

3036. Hedgepeth, Julia. "A Quiet Revolution." Paper presented at Association for Education in Journalism and Mass Communication, Minneapolis, Minnesota, August 1990.

Elizabeth Timothy, Cornelia Bradford, and Catherine Zenger, the first three female newspaper editors, had interests in female issues but did not lose sight of news as defined by the era.

3037. Hempel, Amy. "Laugh Lines." *New York Times Magazine.* November 27, 1988, pp. 44-45, 62-66.
Work of women cartoonists Linda Barry of "Pets in Our Lives" and Roz Chast of *New Yorker.*

3038. Hilliard, S. Lee. "Pressing for Power." *Black Enterprise.* April 1985, pp. 42-50.
The work of the "most influential" black woman in newspaper publishing, Pam Johnson, of the *Ithaca Journal.*

3039. Hoffman, Ellen. "Women in the Newsroom." *Columbia Journalism Review.* Winter 1970/1971, pp. 53-55.

3040. Hoge, Alice Albright. *Cissy Patterson.* New York: Random House, 1966. 237 pp.
Written by relative of famed publisher of the *Washington Times-Herald.*

3041. Holly, Susan. "Women in Management of Weeklies," *Journalism Quarterly.* Winter 1979, pp. 810-815.
On 182 weeklies surveyed, one-third of the editors were women. Yet, women were still underrepresented in management jobs.

3042. Hopper, Hedda, with James Brough. *The Whole Truth and Nothing But.* New York: Doubleday, 1963. 331 pp.
Autobiography of Hedda Hopper, gossip columnist in mid-twentieth century.

3043. Howard, Margo. *Eppie: The Story of Ann Landers.* New York: G.P. Putnam's Sons, 1982. 253 pp.
Life of advice columnist and her relationship with her daughter, the author of this book.

3044. Janensch, Gail. "'We've Come a Long Way, Baby, in Journalism.'" *The Quill.* November 1970, pp. 30-32.
Editors had given women more opportunities but not enough; women journalists were being "liberated" by specialization.

3045. Jeffers, Dennis W. "A Descriptive Study of Perceived Impact of Gender on Employment Status, Type of Work, Industry Relationships, Working Environment and Job Satisfaction in Livestock Industry Magazines." Paper presented at Association for Education in Journalism and Mass Communication, San Antonio, Texas, August 1-4, 1987. 25 pp.
Women are underrepresented on staffs of livestock magazines although the situation changed favorably for them in the 1980s.

3046. Jenkins III, Henry. "Star Trek Rerun, Reread, Rewritten: Fan Writing as Textual Poaching." *Critical Studies in Mass Communication.* June 1988, pp. 85-107.
Women who write fiction and fan literature based on the "Star Trek" universe are discussed.

3047. Johnson, Burges. "Preparing College Women for Journalism." *Outlook.* September 28, 1921, pp. 128-129.

3048. Jones, Adelaide H. "Women Journalism Graduates in the 1941-51 Decade." *Journalism Quarterly.* Winter 1953, pp. 49-54.
Women finishing in the class of 1941 at 13 journalism schools averaged better "financially and maritally" than college and professional women generally.

3049. Jurney, Dorothy. "When Was the Last Time You Hired a Homely Woman?" *ANPA Bulletin.* April 1974, p. 20.

3050. Jurney, Dorothy. "Women Editors Advance to 11.1 Per Cent -- But the Numerical Total Barely Moves." *ASNE Bulletin.* November/December 1984, pp. 32-35.

3051. Lanyi, Ronald Levitt. "Trina, Queen of the Underground Cartoonists: An Interview." *Journal of Popular Culture.* Spring 1979, pp. 739-754.
Interview with Trina Robbins, one of the cartoonists who created *Wimmen's Comix*, an underground women's comic magazine.

3052. Lawrence, David. "The Myth of the Pink Collar Ghetto." *Washington Journalism Review.* January 1986, pp. 21-23.
The growing numbers of women in journalism will not devalue the profession; such a claim is a "red herring."

3053. Lawrenson, Helen. *Whistling Girl.* Garden City, New York: Doubleday, 1978. 182 pp.
Author's work in magazine journalism.

3054. Lazar, Kay. "Gender Gap." *News Inc.* June 1990, pp. 15-16, 18-20.
How the women of the Daniels family "cashed out" on the family's newspapers in Raleigh, North Carolina.

3055. Leavitt, Judith A., ed. *American Women Managers and Administrators: A Selective Biographical Dictionary of Twentieth-Century Leaders in Business, Education, and Government.* Westport, Connecticut: Greenwood Press, 1985. 317 pp.
Media women included were Katharine Graham, Christie Hefner, and others.

3056. Lewis, Kathleen K. "Maggie Higgins." Masters thesis, University of Maryland, 1973.

3057. Lewis, Nancy Madison. "A Century of Wisconsin Women Journalists." Masters thesis, University of Wisconsin, 1947.

3058. Lockridge, Kay. "An Interview with Katharine Graham." *The Quill.* January 1980, pp. 29-32.
　　　Interview with the chair and chief executive officer of the Washington Post Co.

3059. Lublin, Joann S. "Discrimination Against Women in Newsrooms: Fact or Fantasy?" *Journalism Quarterly.* Summer 1972, pp. 357-361.
　　　Survey of 152 women journalists and 80 daily newspaper executives on discrimination. Two-thirds of the women reported they "hardly" perceived sex discrimination on their papers. Between one-third and one-half of all the women perceived sex bias in hiring, job status, and promotability, and to a lesser extent, in salary. Based on author's masters thesis at Stanford University, 1971.

3060. Lublin, Joann S. "Women in the Newsroom." *The Quill.* November 1972, pp. 45-47.
　　　Her own experiences, and those of others, to show the progress made concerning women's entry into newsrooms. But, as a survey showed, sex discrimination continued.

3061. Lumby, Malcolm E. "Ann Landers' Advice Column: 1958 and 1971." *Journalism Quarterly.* Spring 1976, pp. 129-132.
　　　Ann Landers' columns in 1958 and 1971; in latter year, more evidence that she listened to her readers and that she had become more tolerant of variant sexual behavior.

3062. McCall, Patricia Ellen. "The Current Status of Newspaperwomen in Wisconsin." Paper presented at Association for Education in Journalism, San Diego, California, August 18-21, 1974. 20 pp.
　　　A survey of women on all 35 Wisconsin dailies found they perceived their jobs as not different in performance than those of men; they believed they had poor opportunities to advance and were under-utilized according to their abilities.

3063. "McCall's." *Cartoonist PROfiles.* March 1986, pp. 16-19.
　　　Interview with cartoon editor of *McCall's*, Barbara Sloane.

3064. McDonnell, Lynda. "There's Been a Change in the Newsroom." *Nieman Reports.* Winter 1989, pp. 24-27.
　　　Women's newsroom careers; asks questions, such as: "Since few men reduce their hours when they become fathers, does a woman who works part-time permanently stunt her career?" Editors from many U.S. newspapers mentioned.

3065. McLendon, Winola, and Scottie Smith. *Don't Quote Me!* New York: Dutton, 1971. 208 pp.
　　　The work of a few dozen successful women journalists in Washington; emphasis on their scoops, especially about gossip.

3066. McLeod, Merikay. *Betrayal, The Shattering Sex Discrimination Case of Silver vs. Pacific Press Publishing Association.* Loma Linda, California: Mars Hill Publications, 1985. 356 pp.

Diary-like, first hand account of Merikay Silver (McLeod) and her discrimination in publishing suit.

3067. MacPherson, Myra. "Janet Chusmir and the *Miami Herald.*" *Washington Journalism Review.* April 1989, pp. 30-35.

The power of editor Chusmir.

3068. "Magazine Cartoonist: Martha Campbell." *Cartoonist PROfiles.* June 1989, pp. 66-69.

Campbell's career and the daily routine of doing gag cartoons for magazines.

3069. Millner, C. "How Cartoonist Cathy Guisewite Makes Us Laugh at Life's Little Frustrations." *Seventeen.* May 1983, pp. 42-43.

3070. Mills, Kay. "Beyond the Women's Pages." *The Professional Communicator.* March-April 1989, pp. 12-15.

Roles played by women journalists and her own experiences with job hunting.

3071. Mills, Kay. "New Perspectives, Different Voices." *The Quill.* April 1989, pp. 22-24.

The role of women in journalism and profiles of some contemporary female journalists.

3072. Mills, Kay. "We've Come a Long Way, Maybe." *The Quill.* February 1990, pp. 20-23.

Her 30 years' newspaper experience and that of other women journalists used to show the difficulties women have had getting established in the profession.

3073. Mills, Kay. "Women Shaping the News: A Continuing Revolution." *Washington Journalism Review.* January-February 1988, pp. 40-42.

The increased number of women in newsrooms changed news coverage, with different topics coming to the fore.

3074. Morgan, Margaret Knox. "Women in Photojournalism." *Popular Photography.* February 1964, pp. 41, 80-83.

Abstracted from the author's masters thesis by the same title, University of Missouri, 1962.

3075. Morris, Gloria C. "Two Black Women in Media: A Minority Within a Minority." Paper presented at the Association for Education in Journalism, Madison, Wisconsin, August 21-24, 1977. 36 pp.

The contributions of Ida Baker Wells and Ethel L. Payne.

3076. Muir, Florabel. *Headline Happy.* New York: Holt, 1950. 248 pp.
Author's Pacific Coast journalistic experiences, as well as those in New York, Chicago, and Salt Lake City.

3077. Nash, Alana. "The Woman Who Overturned an Empire." *Ms.* June 1986, pp. 44-46, 48-50+.
Sallie Bingham's actions that forced the sale of the family's *Louisville Courier Journal* and its properties.

3078. Newfield, Jack. "Goodbye Dolly." *Harper's.* September 1969, pp. 92-98.
Dorothy Schiff, *New York Post* publisher.

3079. Ogan, Christine L. "Life at the Top for Men and Women Newspaper Managers: A Five-Year Update of Their Characteristics." *Newspaper Research Journal.* Winter 1983, pp. 57-68.
Professional and personal characteristics of women and men newspaper managers had not undergone major changes between 1977 and 1982.

3080. Ogan, Chrstine L. "On Their Way to the Top? Men and Women Middle-Level Newspaper Managers." *Newspaper Research Journal.* May 1980, pp. 51-62.
In a sample of 364 middle-level newspaper managers, women received less compensation than men even though their education and experience levels were comparable.

3081. Ogan, Christine L., Charlene J. Brown, and David H. Weaver. "Characteristics of Managers of Selected U.S. Daily Newspapers." *Journalism Quarterly.* Winter 1979, pp. 803-809.
A composite picture of the typical top-level manager on 433 newspapers surveyed: white, Protestant, married man; only 2.4 percent were women.

3082. Ogan, Christine L. and David H. Weaver. "Job Satisfaction in Selected U.S. Daily Newspapers: A Study of Male and Female Top-Level Managers." *Mass Comm Review.* Winter 1978-1979, pp. 20-26.
Responses of 558 top-level managers of daily newspapers on their job satisfaction; only 27 were female. Their salaries were "consistently and substantially lower" than men's average salaries, yet, their average levels of satisfaction were equally as high as those for males.

3083. Olson, Alma Louise. *Free-lance Writing as an Occupation for Women.* Northampton, Massachusetts: Smith College, 1927. 93 pp.
Women writers' views used to provide answers to some of the queries about free-lance writing in the 1920s.

3084. Paul, Charlotte. *And Four To Grow.* New York: Random, 1961. 308 pp.
Author's newspaper career with a weekly newspaper in Snoqualmie, Washington.

3085. Pinsky, Mark. "Reflections on Joan Little." *Columbia Journalism Review.* March/April 1976, pp. 30-31.

3086. Powers, Thom. "Lynda Barry." *Comics Journal.* November 1989, pp. 60-75.
   Alternative newspaper comic strip artist Lynda J. Barry, known for her works depicting male-female relationships.

3087. Prendergast, Alan. "Best in the West." *Washington Journalism Review.* July-August 1987, pp. 21-25.
   Mary Hargrove, investigative journalist of *Tulsa Tribune.*

3088. *Press Woman.* February 1983.
   Thematic issue on women in journalism education in U.S. included a survey on hiring practices and nine other articles.

3089. Reed, Charles Gordon. "Tenure/Pay Rough Battle for Women." *Press Woman.* January 1988, pp. 8-9.
   Faculty women at universities, citing legal cases.

3090. Reiner, John. "The Laughter Lives On." *Cartoonist PROfiles.* September 1989, pp. 12-17.
   Bunny Hoest carries on the comic strip career of her late husband, Bill Hoest, of "Lockhorns" and other strips.

3091. Robbins, Trina and Catherine Yronwode. *Women and Comics.* New York: Eclipse Books, 1985. 127 pp.
   The careers of the hundreds of women who created and worked in the field of comic strips, comic books, and cartooning, such as, Rose O'Neill, Nell Brinkley, Grace Drayton, and Dale Messick.

3092. Rook, Susan. "Working Girl." *Gannett Center Journal.* Winter 1989, pp. 51-57.
   The status of women journalists as perceived by male employers; author's experiences with Cable Network News.

3093. Rottenberg, Dan. "Ann and Abby's Lessons for Journalists." *The Quill.* January 1984, pp. 20-24.
   How twin-sister advice columnists, Abigail Van Buren and Ann Landers, handle questions submitted by readers -- find out what's bothering people and get some professional help.

3094. Rowland, Mary. "The Mastermind of a Media Empire." *Working Woman.* November 1989, pp. 114-120.
   Washington Post Company's Katharine Graham.

3095. Rykken, Rolf. "Female Editors Offer Different View of News." *Presstime.* June 1989, pp. 16-18.
   Women newspaper editors have helped to expand how news is defined.

3096. Sammon, Virginia. "Surviving the *Saturday Evening Post.*" *The Antioch Review.* Spring 1969, pp. 103-109.

3097. Samra, Risë. "Helen Thomas: Veteran White House Reporter." *The Professional Communicator.* November-December 1988, pp. 21-22.
   White House veteran correspondent Helen Thomas, from her years on the *Washington Daily News* to the UPI.

3098. Schoonmaker, Mary Ellen. "The Baby Bind: Can Journalists Be Mothers?" *Columbia Journalism Review.* March-April 1988, pp. 33-39.
   Case studies of women journalists and their difficulties maintaining careers while caring for small children; most pay a high price for having babies, while some thrive. The lack of employer-supplied child care centers by the U.S. press and the better conditions under which journalist-mothers work in Japan, France, Finland, England, and other parts of Europe related in sidebars.

3099. Schreider, Rosemary. "Education and Training of Fashion Magazine Editors." *Journalism Quarterly.* June 1949, p. 203.
   Four "leading" women's fashion magazines surveyed; two-thirds of the employees were college graduates and most held other jobs before their current editorships. No indication on how many were women.

3100. Schultz-Brooks, Terri. "Getting There: Women in the Newsroom." *Columbia Journalism Review.* March-April 1984, pp. 25-31.
   Fifty dailies had women publishers while 120 had women managing editors; a number of prominent women journalists were interviewed about their difficulties in achieving equal treatment and other experiences.

3101. Schultz-Brooks, Terri. "Is the News Business Fair to Women?" *Working Woman.* December 1984, pp. 119-128.
   Not very.

3102. Sheehy, Gail. "Cinderella West." *New York.* May 17, 1976, pp. 46-52, 57-64.
   Publisher Helen Copley.

3103. Shessel, Sheila. "Elizabeth Cady Stanton and the Woman's Bible." Paper presented at Association for Education in Journalism and Mass Communication, Minneapolis, Minnesota, August 1990.
   Editor Stanton published controversial "The Woman's Bible."

3104. "Signe Wilkinson." *Bull's Eye: The Magazine of Editorial Cartooning.* December 1988, pp. 16-20.
   Wilkinson, one of the few women editorial cartoonists, expresses some strong views in *Philadelphia Daily News.*

3105. Simpson, Peggy. "The Meek Shall Not Inherit the Newsroom." *The Quill.* February 1990, pp. 32-34.
   Legal skirmishes of the 1970s that opened newsrooms wider for women.

3106. Slatterly, Karen and Jim Fosdick. "Professionalism in Photojournalism: A Female/Male Comparison." *Journalism Quarterly.* Summer 1979, pp. 243-247.

Survey of 116 male and 91 female news photographers indicated women photographers were as professional as men.

3107. Smith, Ron and Cheryl Bennett Weber. "Spectator Sports ... Women on Athletic Turf." *The Quill.* November 1980, pp. 18-19.

Interviews with female sportswriters who discuss problems of interviewing in locker rooms, their strengths as reporters, and the discrimination they face.

3108. Snow, Carmel, and Mary Louise Aswell. *The World of Carmel Snow.* New York: McGraw-Hill, 1962. 213 pp.

Career of fashion journalist Carmel Snow of *Harper's Bazaar.*

3109. Sohn, Ardyth B. "Goals and Achievement Orientations of Women Newspaper Managers." *Journalism Quarterly.* Autumn 1984, pp. 500-505.

Female newspaper managers were strongly committed to their jobs, were setting goals different than those of their companies, and were pessimistic that they would advance two positions above that at which they were then, within five years.

3110. Sohn, Ardyth B. "Women in Newspaper Management: An Update." *Newspaper Research Journal.* October 1981, pp. 94-106.

A survey of 546 managers of newspapers in five Rocky Mountain states found that more than three-fourths were male, and only 17 percent of the 130 women qualified as managers by job tasks as well as by titles.

3111. Sohn, Ardyth B. and Leonard H. Chusmir. "The Motivational Perspectives of Newspaper Managers." *Journalism Quarterly.* Summer 1985, pp. 296-303.

3112. Spurgeon, Dolores F. *Magazine Journalism as a Career for Women.* New York: Magazine Publishers Association, 1969. 57 pp.

Questionnaire data from 1,065 magazine publishers and editors to determine vocational opportunities and working conditions for women journalists.

3113. Stein, M.L. "Who Was First?" *Editor and Publisher.* June 17, 1987, pp. 12-13.

Janet Chusmir, executive editor of the *Miami Herald*, was not the first woman in charge of a major daily newsroom; Mary Anne Dolan of *Los Angeles Herald Examiner* was in 1981-1985.

3114. Steiner, Linda and Susanne Gray. "Genevieve Forbes Herrick: A Front-Page Reporter 'Pleased To Write About Women.'" *Journalism History.* Spring 1985, pp. 8-16.

Long-time reporter and columnist for the *Chicago Tribune* and *New York Daily News* served as a model for women journalists as she proudly focussed on the women's angle in her hard news stories.

3183. Greenwald, Marilyn S. "'All Brides Are Not Beautiful': The Influence of Charlotte Curtis on Women's News at the New York Times." Paper presented at Association for Education in Journalism and Mass Communication, Minneapolis, Minnesota, August 1990.
Role of *Times* associate editor, Charlotte Curtis, on "women's pages," 1961-1987.

3184. Gross, Harriet Engel and Sharyne Merritt. "Social Issues and the Women's Page." *Press Woman.* April 1979, pp. 2-4.
The changing concepts of the content of women's pages in daily newspapers.

3185. Guenin, Zena B. "Women's Pages in American Newspapers: Missing out on Contemporary Content." *Journalism Quarterly.* Spring 1975, pp. 66-69, 75.
Comparison of three dailies' modernized women's sections with three dailies' traditional women's pages; although some dailies changed their women's pages to attract a wider audience, the content was not as broad as suggested. By the same author: "Women's Pages in the 1970s," *Montana Journalism Review*, 16 (1973), p. 30. Both based on her "Women's Pages in Transition," Masters thesis, California State University, Northridge, 1974.

3186. Harrington, Stephanie. "*Ms.* Versus *Cosmo*: Two Faces of the Same Eve." *New York Times Magazine.* August 11, 1974, pp. 10-11, 36, 74-76.

3187. Hatch, Mary G. and David L. Hatch. "Problems of Married Working Women as Presented by Three Popular Working Women's Magazines." *Social Forces.* 37 (1958), pp. 148-153.

3188. Henry, Nancy. "We Zipped it Low This Year: Women's Magazines, The Chic Sell." *Nation.* June 5, 1972, pp. 710-712.

3189. Henry, Susan. "Juggling the Frying Pan and the Fire: The Portrayal of Employment and Family Life in Seven Women's Magazines, 1975-1982." *Social Science Journal.* October 1984, pp. 87-107.
The interaction between women's paid work and family lives in seven women's magazines. Charges against these magazines of presenting a "Superwoman" myth were only partly accurate. None of the magazines was successful in providing alternatives to the "double day" of working women with families.

3190. *Heresies.* January 1986.
Thematic issue on media included Jane Gaines, "War, Women, and Lipstick: Fan Magazines in the 1940's" and Sally A. Stein, "The Graphic Ordering of Desire: Modernization of a Middle-Class Women's Magazine, 1914-1939."

3191. Herriman, Nancy Gibbs, ed. *Burrelle's Women's Media Directory 1983-84.* Livingston, New Jersey: Burrelle's Media Directories, 1983. 72 pp.

More than 500 listings of radio and TV stations and networks, state and local newspapers, nationally syndicated columns, college publications, wire services, advertising representatives, and national, state, and local periodicals.

3192. Hesterman, Vicki. "You've Come a Long Way, Baby -- Or Have You? Women's Magazines, Cigarette Advertisements, Health Articles and Editorial Autonomy." Paper presented at Association for Education in Journalism and Mass Communication, San Antonio, Texas, August 1-4, 1987. 32 pp.
How women's magazines, *Ms.*, *Good Housekeeping,* and *Seventeen*, handled stories on smoking-related health problems and cigarette advertising. Editorial autonomy for women's magazines disappeared when they were dependent upon advertising; the bottom line rules.

3193. Humphreys, Nancy. *American Women's Magazines: An Annotated Historical Guide.* New York: Garland Publishing Co., 1989. 303 pp.
Alternative periodicals of early women's rights and feminism causes, and mainstream publications from the eighteenth to twentieth centuries.

3194. Hurd, Jud. "New Woman." *Cartoonist PROfiles.* December 1985, pp. 32-35.
Interview with cartoon editor of *New Woman*, Rosemarie Lennon.

3195. Joan, Polly, and Andrea Chesman. *Guide to Women's Publishing.* Paradise, California: Dustbooks, 1978. 296 pp.
Media in which women publish or to which they can submit manuscripts and receive a sympathetic response; emphasizes women's publications, presses, and distributors.

3196. Kaiser, Kathy. "The New Women's Magazines: It's the Same Old Story." *Frontiers.* Spring 1979, pp. 14-17.
Most newer women's magazines directed at liberated women have not changed their contents drastically, still depending upon fashion, family relations, or recipes.

3197. Kelly, Katie. *The Wonderful World of Women's Wear Daily.* New York: Saturday Review Press, 1972. 247 pp.
A gossipy history of this fashion newspaper.

3198. Kessler, Lauren. *The Dissident Press, Alternative Journalism in American History.* Beverly Hills, California: Sage, 1984. 160 pp.
In chapter on feminist press, contends that from 1840s to 1980s, feminist periodicals were the backbone of the women's movement.

3199. Kessler, Lauren. "Women's Magazines' Coverage of Smoking Related Health Hazards." *Journalism Quarterly.* Summer 1989, pp. 316-322, 445.
Six major women's magazines -- *Cosmopolitan, McCall's, Good Housekeeping, Mademoiselle, Ms., Woman's Day* -- carried virtually no content about smoking and cancer.

3200. Kline, Helen G. "The Old and the New: *Ladies' Home Journal* and *New Woman*, June 1971 Through May 1972." Masters thesis, Murray State University, 1972.

3201. Koch, Beverly Stephen. "The History and Evolution of Women's Pages in American Newspapers." Masters thesis, University of California, Berkeley, 1974.

3202. Kranich, Kimberlie A. "Catalysts for Change: Periodicals by U.S. Women of Color, 1968-1988." *Feminist Teacher*. Spring 1990.
Description of 100 newspapers, newsletters, and magazines published or edited by women of color.

3203. Lamont, Helen Otis, ed. *A Diamond of Years: The Best of The "Woman's Home Companion."* Garden City, New York: Doubleday, 1961. 640 pp.
The 75th anniversary of this large women's magazine.

3204. Laner, Mary R. "Media Mating II: 'Personals' Advertisements of Lesbian Women." *Journal of Homosexuality*. Fall 1978, pp. 41-61.
"Personals" advertisements for lesbian partners in two issues of a lesbian newsletter; the ads emphasized positive characteristics.

3205. Langham, Barbara. "Movers, Shakers, Read *Ms.*" *Matrix*. Fall 1975, pp. 8-9, 30.
Pat Carbine of *Ms.* magazine.

3206. Lentz, Rose Mary. "What's This 'Women's Editor' To Do?" *The Quill*. February 1975, p. 29.
The changes made in women's pages; they had become undefinable and catch-alls for all types of news and information.

3207. McCracken, Ellen. "Critical Approaches to Mass Culture: The Case of Advertising." *Media Development*. February 1984, pp. 11-14.
Advertisements are such a large part of our daily lives that little thought is given to the professional techniques of hard and soft sell. Discussion of the "tricks of the trade" using examples from U.S. women's magazines.

3208. McCracken, Ellen. "Demystifying *Cosmopolitan*: Five Critical Methods." *Journal of Popular Culture*. Fall 1982, pp. 30-42.
Methods relating to ideology, infrastructure, semiology, feminism, and reception to analyze *Cosmopolitan* magazine.

3209. McGlashan, Zena Beth. "Woman's Day Editor Tells About Her Readers." *Press Woman*. September 1985, pp. 4-5.
Associate editor Sally Platkin Koslow on readers of *Woman's Day* magazine and tips for freelance writers.

3210. Masel-Walters, Lynne. "To Hustle with the Rowdies: The Organization and Functions of the American Woman Suffrage Press." *Journal of American Culture.* Spring 1980, pp. 167-183.

3211. Matkov, Rebecca Roper. "*Ladies' Home Journal* and *McCalls* in 1960 and 1970: A Content Analysis." Masters thesis, University of North Carolina, 1972.

3212. Merritt, Sharyne and Harriet Gross. "Women's Page/Lifestyle Editors: Does Sex Make a Difference?" *Journalism Quarterly.* Autumn 1978, pp. 508-514.
   Yes, differences exist in terms of section goals, content, and coverage: "women editors of women's/lifestyle pages are more likely than men editors to use stories about women's movement and club and social events."

3213. Miller, Susan H. "Changes in Women's/Lifestyle Sections." *Journalism Quarterly.* Winter 1976, pp. 641-647.
   Of *New York Times, Washington Post, Chicago Tribune,* and *Los Angeles Times,* only the *New York Times* substantially changed the amount of lifestyle and consumer coverage in the previous decade; at some papers, there was more talk than change.

3214. Milligan, Susan. "Has *Ms.* Undergone a Sex Change?" In *Media USA: Process and Effect,* edited by Arthur Asa Berger, pp. 87-96. New York: Longman, 1988.
   Ms. magazine underwent a radical transformation, abandoning its feminist philosophy and accepting a new one: "the way for women to succeed is the same as it has long been for men: acquire money and status."

3215. Newkirk, Carole Ruth. "Female Roles in Non-Fiction of Three Women's Magazines." *Journalism Quarterly.* Winter 1976, pp. 779-782.
   Of *Mademoiselle, Redbook,* and *Ms.,* the latter showed the most portrayals of women in non-domestic roles; neither *Mademoiselle* nor *Redbook* increased its non-domestic portrayals from 1966 to 1974.

3216. O'Reilly Jane. "Whatever Happened to *Ms.*?" *New York.* June 26, 1972, pp. 39-42.

3217. Ortiz, Jeanne A. and Larry P. Ortiz. "Do Contemporary Women's Magazines Practice What They Preach?" *Free Inquiry in Creative Sociology.* May 1989, pp. 51-55.
   Most women were portrayed in stereotypical, sexist roles, in 288 advertisements in *Ms., Self, Working Mother,* and *Working Woman,* 1981-1984.

3218. Pool, Gail. "Women's Periodicals: Some Issues." *Massachusetts Review.* Summer 1983, pp. 467-473.

3219. Pool, Gail Levy. "Women's Magazines' Male Monopoly on Women's Communication Is Being Broken by Women's Own Media." *Media Report to Women.* November-December 1984, p. 9.

   Excerpts from author's "How To Cook Your Goose, A Survey of Women's Magazines," in March 1984 *Radcliffe Quarterly*; the removal of the male presence in editorships of women's magazines results in a different product.

3220. Probert, Christina. *Lingerie in Vogue Since 1910.* New York: Abbeville Press, 1981.

3221. Reed, Barbara Straus. "The Link Between Mobilizing Information and Service Journalism as Applied to Women's Magazine Coverage of Eating Disorders." Paper presented at Association for Education in Journalism and Mass Communication, Minneapolis, Minnesota, August 1990.

   Believes women's magazines could provide mobilizing information for eating disorder addictive women.

3222. Sedlak, Robert A. and Denise M. Sedlak. "Special Education Information in Women's Magazines: A Five-Year Analysis." *Journal for Special Educators.* Spring 1983, pp. 72-77.

   Five popular women-oriented magazines, 1976 and 1980, and their special education content; *Good Housekeeping* had the highest.

3223. Seebohm, Caroline. *The Man Who Was Vogue: The Life and Times of Condé Nast.* New York: Viking Press, 1982. 390 pp.

   Condé Nast publications writer tells the story of the man who built *Vogue* into a leading magazine of appeal to women.

3224. "Sharp Increase Seen in New Women's Periodicals, Black and Women of Color Papers; Greater Political Emphasis." *Media Report to Women.* September-October 1984, pp. 1, 15.

   Extracts from 1985 *Index/Directory of Women's Media*.

3225. Sherman, Bill. "Trina in the Mainstream." *Comics Journal.* September 1986, pp. 54-56.

   Three Trina Robbins' comic strips reviewed: "Meet Misty," "The Legend of Wonder Woman," and "Silver Metal Lover."

3226. Silver, Sheila J. "Covering Women: Women's Publications and the Mass Media." Paper presented at Association for Education in Journalism, Madison, Wisconsin, August 21-24, 1977. 24 pp.

   How 210 editors of women's publications felt about communication for women. See author's paper at the previous year's meeting of AEJ: "Then and Now: Women's Roles in 'McCall's Magazine' in 1964 and 1974," 42 pp., published as "The Suburban Woman: Women's Roles in McCall's in 1964 and 1974," *Magazine Studies Quarterly*, Summer 1977.

3227. Smilgis, Martha. "A Maturing Woman Unleashed." *Time*. May 15, 1989, pp. 70-72.
   The success of Frances Lear's magazine for women over 40.

3228. Smith, Barbara. "A Press of Our Own: Kitchen Table: Women of Color Press." In *Communications at the Crossroads: The Gender Gap Connection*, edited by Ramona Rush and Donna Allen, pp. 202-207. Norwood, New Jersey: Ablex, 1989.
   The work of Kitchen Table: Women of Color Press, which since the early 1970s, has worked to make visible the writing, culture, and history of women of color.

3229. Spieczny, Sandra. "Dancing Backward: Women's Magazines and the Equal Rights Amendment, 1970-1979." Paper presented at Association for Education in Journalism and Mass Communication, San Antonio, Texas, August 1-4, 1987. 36 pp.
   How 13 women's magazines covered the Equal Rights Amendment between 1970 and 1979; *Ms.* led with 45 articles, followed by *Redbook* with 14.

3230. "The *Ms.* Magazine Success Story: An Interview with Pat Carbine." *Folio: The Magazine for Magazine Management*. April 1975, pp. 29-34.

3231. Tortora, Phyllis. "Fashion Magazines Mirror Changing Role of Women." *Journal of Home Economics*. March 1973, pp. 19-29.
   The history of fashion magazines and how they changed to represent women's issues; *Godey's Lady's Book, Peterson's Magazine, Harper's Bazar* [sic], *The Delineator,* and *Vogue* dealt with in some depth.

3232. Trahey, Jane, ed. *Harper's Bazaar: 100 Years of the American Female*. New York: Random House, 1967.

3233. "Women in and Escaped from Systems of Prostitution Begin National Paper -- 'We Will Write the Truth.'" *Media Report to Women*. July-August 1986, pp. 1, 11.
   W.H.I.S.P.E.R., started with Winter 1985-86 issue.

3234. "Women's International News Gathering Service Broadcasts by Satellite to Radio Stations in U.S. and Abroad." *Media Report to Women*. July-August 1986, pp. 1, 4.
   Women's International News Gathering Service (WINGS), founded out of Western Public Radio of San Francisco in 1986.

3235. Zube, Margaret J. "Changing Concepts of Morality: 1948-1969." *Social Forces*. March 1972, pp. 385-392.
   In the *Ladies' Home Journal*.

APPENDIX: ORGANIZATIONS, PERIODICALS, OTHER RESOURCES

1. *Ad Lib.* Sydney: The Coming Out Show, Australian Broadcasting Corporation. Newsletter of a group of ABC women fighting against discriminatory language and imagery in broadcasting.

2. *Aegis: Magazine on Ending Violence Against Women.* Washington, D.C.: Feminist Alliance Against Rape. Quarterly feminist magazine that regularly covers pornography and abuse of women in the media.

3. AFFIRM (Alliance for Fair Images and Representation in the Media). Central body through which women can channel their complaints. Issues *Women's Media Action Bulletin.* c/o Women's Arts Alliance, 10 Cambridge Terrace News, London NWI England.

4. Association for Education in Journalism and Mass Communication. Columbia, South Carolina. Has a Committee on the Status of Women that solicits papers for presentation at its sessions during annual AEJMC conferences.

5. Association Internationales des Journalistes de la Presse Féminine et Familiale. Takes up the issue of women's treatment by the media. Published a 1978 survey, *How the Press Treats Women,* covering France, Hungary, Israel, Italy, the Netherlands, Canada, Great Britain, and Switzerland.

6. *Broadsheet.* Auckland, New Zealand. Women's monthly has had articles on media, including Debra Reweti, "Polynesian Women in Television," Oct. 1985.

7. *Camera Obscura.* A journal of feminism and film theory dating to 1974, published thrice yearly for the University of Rochester by the Johns Hopkins University Press.

8. Centre for Development of Instructional Technology. Indian development group experimenting in media alternatives; has a program of activities called "Women and Media in Development." D-1 Soami Nagar, New Delhi, India.

9. Cine Mujer. Organization of Colombian professional women who make films to promote different images of women. Started in 1979. Apartado Aereo 2758, Bogota, Colombia.

10. *Coming Out Newsletter.* Published by Australian Women's Broadcasting Cooperative. ABC Radio, GPO Box 994, Sydney, NSW 2001, Australia.

11. Deutscher Frauenrat. A German women's council that has worked for better presentation and representation of women in the media. Augustastrasse 42, D-5300 Bonn-Bad Godesberg 1, West Germany.

12. *Federation of Africa Media Women Newsletter.* Marare, Zimbabwe. Quarterly which shares news and information about developments within mass media and women's roles in them.

13. *Feminist Japan International Issue.* Tokyo. International edition of a bimonthly in Japanese. No. 2 carried articles on women and media in Asia and elsewhere. Feminist Inc., Seien Bldg. No. 502, 1-3-2, Kita-Aoyama, Minato-ku, Tokyo, Japan 107.

14. *Feminist Periodicals: A Current Listing of Contents.* Madison, Wisconsin: University of Wisconsin System, Office of the Women's Studies Librarian-at-Large. 1981 to present.

15. *Feminist Studies.* College Park, Maryland. Published thrice yearly to encourage analytical responses to feminist issues and to open new areas of research, criticism, and speculation. Includes articles on women and media, such as: Jessica Benjamin, "The Bonds of Love: Rational Violence and Erotic Domination," 6:1 (1980); Kristen Drotner, "English Girls and Their Magazine Reading Between the Wars," and Janice A. Radway, "Women Read the Romance," both Spring 1983; Ann Scofield, "The Woman Question in the Journals of the AFL and IWW, 1905-1920," Summer 1983. Women's Studies Program, University of Maryland, College Park, Md. 20742.

16. *Frauen und Film.* Berlin, West Germany. Quarterly in German since 1974; includes thematic issues, catalogues of new women's films, and articles on film politics, theory, and criticism.

17. *Gender and Mass Media Newsletter.* Annual published by Madeleine Kleberg, Ulla B. Abrahamsson, Charly Hulten, and Iris Nilsson, of University of Stockholm and Swedish Broadcasting Corporation. Each issue deals with forthcoming events, reports from conferences, articles,

papers, projects, and reports. First nine issues, from August 1981, with two in 1983, called *Sex-Roles within Mass Media Newsletter*; title change with No. 10 (1989).

18. *Genders: Art, Literature, Film, History.* Three times yearly periodical focussing on "theoretical issues relating sexuality and gender to social, political, racial, economic, or stylistic concerns." Published by University of Texas Press, Austin, with University of Colorado.

19. International Association for Mass Communication Research. Has section on "Gender and Mass Communication." From 1982, section (originally working group) has presented many panels on sex-roles. After 1990, IAMCR also has had a working group on Gender and New Information Technologies (GRANITE), which has presented papers at the IAMCR biennial conferences.

20. International Communication Association. Has an interest group on "Feminist Scholarship" that holds panels at annual conference. Created in 1985.

21. International Interdisciplinary Congress on Women. Dublin, Ireland. Includes papers on women and media at its triennial congresses, first in Israel in 1981, followed by The Netherlands in 1984 and Ireland, 1987. Sessions on "Women and the Electronic Mass Media" at the Dublin Congress included: "Internationalization of the Media Industry and the Consequences for Women," "Women in Television Programmes -- Changing Images?" and roundtable on research and theory concerning the study of women and media.

22. *International Women's Tribune Center Newsletter.* Regularly listed resources and literature on women; Spring 1981 issue dealt with women and media. 305 E. 46th St., New York, New York 10017.

23. *Isis International Women's Journal.* Rome. Produced twice yearly in conjunction with women's groups of developing countries. In English and Spanish, dealing with different issues, including women and media. Has bi-annual supplement, *Women in Action*; succeeds *Isis Bulletin*, of which there were 29 between 1974 and 1983. Via Santa Maria dell'Anima 30, 00186 Rome, Italy.

24. *Journalism and Women Symposium Newsletter.* Estes Park, Colorado. Includes short articles; Spring 1987 (1:2) featured Judy Mann on information women need and Pam Johnson on "What? Me Manage?"

25. *Jump Cut.* Berkeley, California. Quarterly carrying news, reviews, and criticism of commercial and alternative film. Each issue includes a special thematic section.

26. *Manushi.* New Delhi. Monthly journal about women and society that has dealt with images of women in media. Published alternately in English and Hindi. C1/202 Lajpat Nagar, New Delhi 110024, India.

27. *Matrix.* Austin, Texas. Quarterly magazine of Women in Communications, Inc. Carries news, history, instructional articles on communications. WICI, P.O. Box 9561, Austin, Texas 78766.

28. *Matrix.* Santa Cruz. Monthly magazine with a different theme each issue. November 1980 issue was on women and media. 418 Cedar St., Santa Cruz, California 95060.

29. *Media and Values.* Contains one or two pages each issue devoted to women, dealing with topics such as video and women, ethnic sensitivity on TV, women's images. Has had special issues devoted to women and media.

30. *Media Report to Women.* Washington, D.C.: Women's Institute for Freedom of the Press. Monthly periodical with facts and stories on extent and progress of women's media nationally and internationally. Includes facts about existing media (monitoring studies), changes (legal actions, agreements, etc.). Other publications of the institute are *The Directory of Women's Media* and *Syllabus Source Book on Media and Women.* Since 1972.

31. Medienkartie. Contains files on media, particularly addresses of women working in various German media. c/o Rita Schmidt, Haupstrasse 97, 1 Berlin 62, West Germany.

32. *Mujer Ilet.* Santiago, Chile: Unidad de Comunicación Alternativa de la Mujer. Monthly publication of Latin American Institute of Transnational Studies (ILET), with news clippings and features from FEMPRESS. The Women's Alternative Communication Unit helps create alternative media to counteract the perpetuation of traditional stereotypes about women.

33. *Mujer y Comunicación.* Caracas, Venezuela: Sindicato Nacional de Trabajadores de la Prensa. Magazine founded and continued by Venezuelan women journalists to encourage emancipation and liberation. Centers its attention on the problems of current journalism and communication as seen in the special context of Venezuelan women. "Democratization of communication" is a key goal.

34. National Watch on Images of Women in the Media (MediaWatch) Inc. Independent Canadian feminist group promoting an improved portrayal and presence of women in the mass media. 250-1820 Fir St., Vancouver, B.C. V6J 3BI, Canada.

35. National Women and Media Collection, University of Missouri. Documents the roles women have played in media fields. First collection of personal papers in U.S. devoted exclusively to women and media. Among papers collected since 1987 inauguration are those of Donna Allen, NOW Legal Defense and Education Fund, Tad Baritimus, Jo Hartley, Susan Miller, Dorothy Jurney, Carol Kleiman, Beth Campbell, Carol Richards, Joye Patterson, among other. Women in Media Research, School of Journalism, University of Missouri, Columbia, Missouri 65205.

36. *News and Views.* Newsletter published ten times annually by the American Women in Radio and Television, 1321 Connecticut Ave. N.W., Washington, D.C. 20036.

37. *Press Woman.* Official monthly organ of the National Federation of Press Women with conference and organization news, profiles of successful women journalists, articles of technical and professional nature. Includes directory of women journalists annually. Volume 52 in 1989. NFPW, Box 99, Blue Springs, Missouri 64015.

38. *RFR/DRF. Resources for Feminist Research/Documentation sur la recherche féministe.* Published four times yearly as a Canadian journal for feminist scholarship. Annual indices provide number of sources on women and media.

39. *Scarlet Woman.* Fitzroy, Australia. A socialist feminist magazine that has dealt with women and media. 193 Smith St., Fitzroy VIC 3065, Australia.

40. *Serpentine.* Amsterdam. Monthly magazine of a group of feminist journalists working with weekly magazines, radio, and television.

41. *Studies on Women Abstracts.* Oxford: Carfax Publishing. Quarterly with abstracts of 200 journals, including topics dealing with women and media. P.O. Box 25, Abingdon, Oxfordshire, Oxford 143UE England.

42. The Depthnews Women's Features Syndicate. Manila: Press Foundation of Asia. Network of independent women journalists, organized in 1979, to cover non-traditional women's issues. Features are distributed to Asian newspapers.

43. *The Professional Communicator.* Published by Women in Communications Inc. six times a year since 1980. Many articles of an inspirational or reminiscing character. P.O. Box 17460, Arlington, Virginia 22216.

44. *The Tribune: A Women and Development Quarterly.* New York: International Women's Tribune Centre. Issues newsletters, some of which deal with media. Newsletter No. 14, 1981, covers "Women and Media"; No. 21, 1982, "Women and Graphics: A Beginner's Kit"; No. 23, 1983, "Women and Media 2"; and March 1989, "Women Using Media To Effect

Change." The latter discusses the absence of women on newspaper front pages and in media positions of power, and images of women in media.

45. Unidad de Comunicación Alternativa de la Mujer. Instituto Latinoamericano de Estudios Transnacionales. Santiago, Chile. Publishes regular periodicals on women, including *Especial-Mujer*, which consists of articles about special themes relating to women, such as prostitution, abortion, tension between males and females, women and formal education, young women, women and communications; and *Mujer* (later *Mujer/Fempress*), which consists of reports and articles pertaining to women, broken down by country. The latter is monthly.

46. Voice of Women Group. Started in Sri Lanka in 1980 to monitor press in its campaign against sexism in advertising.

47. *Wiplash*. Contains articles on subtle forms of discrimination against women's issues in British publishing. *Wiplash* is monthly of Women in Publishing in England.

48. *Women Against Pornography Newsreport*. New York. Newsletter dealing with actions taken against pornography and violence against women in the media.

49. *Women and Film*. Santa Monica, California. Published between 1972 and 1975 as leftist organ for dissemination of information on women in film. Dealt with images of women in film and female filmmakers. Seven issues with following frequencies: Nos. 1 and 2, 1972; 3/4, 1973; 5/6, 1974; 7, Summer 1975. Some notable articles were: Sharon Smith, "The Image of Women in Film," No. 1; Gretchen Bataille, "Early Suffrage Films," No. 3/4; interviews with Nelly Kaplan, No. 2; Lina Wertmüller, No. 5/6; Agnes Varda, No. 5/6; Eleanor Perry, No. 7.

50. *WomeNews*. Hollywood, California. Periodical of the American Federation of Television and Radio Artists National Women's Committee. 1717 North Highland Ave., Hollywood, California 90028.

51. Women in Communications Inc. Has chapters in many cities and on many campuses. 2101 Wilson Blvd., Suite 417, Arlington, Virginia 22201.

52. Women in Film. Has chapters in several U.S. cities. 8489 W. 3rd St., Los Angeles, California 90048.

53. Women in Media. Group of women working in media in Britain; established in 1970. First campaigns directed at British Broadcasting Corporation. Works for fairer images of women in media and more and better jobs in the media. Published report, "The Packaging of Women" and book, *Is This Your Life? Images of Women in the Media*. 22 Torbay Rd., London NW6 England.

54. Women's Institute for Freedom of the Press. Founded in 1972 as research and publishing organization of women concerned with reordering mass media to be in all peoples' hands, not just those of a few wealthy, male media owners. Publishes annual media directory concerning women. Publishes *Media Report to Women* (monthly), *the Index/Directory of Women's Media* (every five years), *The Directory of Women's Media* (annually), *Women in Media: A Documentary Source Book* (by Beasley and Gibbons), and *Syllabus Source Book on Media and Women.*

55. *Women's Studies in Communication.* Periodical of Organization for Research on Women and Communication (Dept. of Communication, University of Oklahoma, Norman, Oklahoma 73019). Provided a forum for research, teaching strategies, and book reviews concerning gender and communication. Featured perspectives on gender and communication in areas of interpersonal communication, rhetorical theory and criticism, small group communication, and organizational communication. Existed from 1978 to 1981. Volume 7 (1984) included proceedings of a conference on women and communication. Articles included: H.L. Goodall, jr., "Research Priorities for Investigations of Gender and Communication: Rediscovering the Human Experience of Sexuality and Talk," pp. 91-97; L.M. Jackson, "Available Research Methods To Study Gender Role in Communication," pp. 86-90; F.L. Johnson, "Positions for Knowing About Gender Differences in Social Relationships," pp. 77-82; W.K. Rawlins, "Interpretive Stance and Gender-Role Research," pp. 69-72; M. Solomon, "A Prolegomenon to Research on Gender Role Communication," pp. 98-100; J.T. Wood and G.M. Phillips, "Rethinking Research on Gender and Communication: An Introduction to the Issues," pp. 59-60, and B. Bate, "Submerged Concepts in Gender/Communication Research," pp. 101-104.

56. *Women's Studies Newsletter.* Quarterly publication of The Feminist Press and The National Women's Studies Association. Includes some articles on women and the media throughout the world. Since 1972. The Feminist Press, Dept. ZN, Box 334, Old Westbury, New York 11568.

57. World Association of Women Journalists and Writers. Has had world congresses in continental U.S., Israel, Korea, France, Puerto Rico, Canada, and Egypt. 1200 Allen, Chomedey, Laval, Quebec, Canada H7W 1G9.

AUTHOR INDEX

References to sources in the appendix are prefixed with "A."

Aaron, D., 1464
Abbott, Edith A., 1812
Abdel Kadar, Soha, 303
Abdel-Rahman, Awatef, 368
Abdullayeva, Irada, 893
Abdul-Rahman, Asma, 304
Abel, John D., 1648, 3139
Abel, Robert H., 2538, 2642
Abelman, Robert, 1654, 2278
Aber, Cynthia S., 2204
Abeysekera, Sunila, 399, 743
Abrahamsson, Ulla B., 78, 83, 904-905, 1024-1028, 1161
Abramo, Lélia, 1425
Abramson, Paul R., 1712
Accad, E., 299
Adams, C., 134
Adams, Elizabeth Kemper, 1813
Adams, Gerald R., 2137
Adams, Margaret, 268
Adams, R. C., 2534
Adams, William, 2279
Adamson, June, 1814
Adburgham, Alison, 978
Adelman, Shonagh, 2468
Adeogun, Modupe F., 320
Agardy, Susanna, 135
Agarwal, Bina, 398-399, 404, 498, 582
Agee, Warren K., 2749
Agger, Gunhild, 1030
Aghi, Mira B., 417
Agrawal, Binod C., 406, 417, 424, 460, 610-611, 744-745
Agreda, Consuela C., 612
Agren, Annika, 1162

Aho, William R., 1359
Akamatsu, Muriel, 2798
Akhileshwari, R., 613
Akpan, Emmanuel D., 321
Akudinobi, Emmanuel, 322
Al-Abd, Atif Adli, 300, 369
Alberdi, Inés, 964
Albin, Susanne, 2279
Albistur, Maïté, 979
Alburn, Miriam, 2981
Alderman, Royal, 2799
Alegría Ortega, Idsa E., 1360, 1366-1367
Alexander, Jack, 1815, 1877
Alexander, Sandra, 840
Alford, Katrina, 808
Al-Hadeedy, Muna, 370
Ali, S. M., 614
Allen, Donna, 21, 27, 96, 208, 283, 293, 1074, 1240, 1339,1363, 2750, 2760, 2793, 3133, 3142, 3228
Allen, Gina, 1728
Allen, Isobel, 1184
Allen, Jeanne, 1705
Allen, Martha L., 3132
Allen, Robert, 61, 206, 1634-1635
Allen, S., 2280
Alloo, Fatma, 364
Allouche, Richard, 371
Almquest, June, 1722
Al Mujahid, Sharif, 433, 450
Alpern, Sara, 1816
Alperowicz, Cynthia, 2281
Al-Qazzaz, Ayad, 301
Alreck, P. L., 2686

Alter, Jonathan, 2821, 2982
Altman, Karen E., 1561, 1764
Amadieu, Georges, 1031
American Society of Newspaper Editors, 2983-2984
Ames, Austine, 1818
Ames, Katrine, 1625
Amin, Amina, 50, 485-486
Amin Manzurul, 417
Anand, Anita, 487
Anant, Victor, 1265
Ancheta, Herminia M., 668
Anderman, Linda, 1587
Anderson, Betty, 1570
Anderson, D. R., 2423
Anderson, H. T., 2557
Anderson, Madeline, 227
Anderson, Margaret, 239, 1819
Anderson, Paul Bunyon, 980
Anderson, R. E., 2535
Andoh, Isaac Fritz, 348
Andrassy, Maria, 881
Andreasen, Margaret, 2734-2735
Andrén, Gunnar, 1032-1033
Andrén, Kiell, 1033
Andujar, Sonia, 1368
Ang, Ien. 15, 189
Angelusz, Róbert, 875
Anklesaria, Shahnaz, 399-400
Ansah, Paul, 45
Anthony, Katharine S., 1820, 1997
Anthony, Susan B., 2057
Antrobus, Peggy, 1369
Anu, Mini, 488
Anuradha, Sushma Kepoor, 401
Applewhite, Harriet B., 1005
Arboleda Cueva, Esmeralda, 136
Archibald, Linda, 1465
Arell, Ruth, 1765
Arens, Agna, 1266
Arens, W., 1639, 2368
Arliss, Laurie, 2283
Armatage, Kay, 129, 255
Armogathe, Daniel, 979
Armstrong, G. Blake, 2327
Arndt, Johan, 2274
Arnold, June, 77
Artel, Linda, 2470, 2751
Arthur, Ella Bentley, 1947
Asante, Molefi Kete, 316
Ascher, Carol, 2687
Ashley, Barbara Renchkovsky, 3
Ashley, David, 3

Ashworth, Georgina, 907
Asian Broadcasting Union, 402
Asian Institute of Journalism, 489
Association of Women for Action and Research, 403
Astelarra, Judith, 964
Astor, Mary, 2977
Aswell, Mary Louise, 3108
Ata, A. W., 302
Athar, Najma, 394
Atkin, C. K., 2353
Atkin, David, 2536
Atkin, Elsa, 841
Atkins, Paul A., 2986
Atkins, Thomas R., 2471
Atkinson, D., 888
Atwood, Rita, 2284
Augusto, Sérgio, 1426
Ault, Phillip H., 2749
Austin, Carol D., 2626
Australia Council, 842
Australian Broadcasting Corporation, 843
Australian Film and Television School, 846-848
Australian Film Commission, 844-845
Australian Women's Broadcasting Co-operative, 849
Aveni, Adrian, 1996
Avery, Robert K., 1636
Avilade O'Farrill, Hilda, 240
Awasthy, G. C., 747
Aylesworth, Margaret F., 2285
Ayree, Joyce, 259, 349
Azarcon-dela Cruz, Pennie S., 490
Azevedo, Christiane D. de, 1413

Baacke, Dieter, 1119
Bachy, Victor, 165
Bader, Eleanor, 77
Baehr, Helen, 4-6, 78, 83, 909, 943, 1036-1037, 1164-1165
Baerns, Barbara, 1038
Bagheri, Abbas S., 383
Bahadur, Satish, 669
Bahi, Sushil, 190
Bahri, Muna Vonnis, 372
Bailey, Bruce, 3160
Bailey, Margaret, 2537
Baird, Jo, 1714
Bajaj, S. S., 616
Baker, Ira L., 1821

Author Index 421

Baker, John F., 2987
Baker, M. Joyce, 2472
Baker, Nina Brown, 1822
Baker, Nora, 2028
Baker, Robert K., 2286
Baker, Suzanne, 846
Bal, Vidya, 748
Balaban, Terry, 2243
Balaguer-Callejon, M. Luisa, 7
Balasubrahmanyam, Vimal, 408
Baldes, Ingrid, 1166-1167
Baldwin, Wayne, 850
Ball, Sandra J., 2286
Ballard, Bettina, 1823
Balon, Robert E., 2822
Balsamo, Anne, 22, 1561
Baltera, Lorraine, 1624
Bambrot, F. H., 2287
Banchare, Ishwar, 616
Bandy, Patricia, 2670
Banerji, Prava, 404
Banks, Asiah Sarji, 491
Banks, Elizabeth L., 1824
Banks, Jane, 1561
Banos, Janis B., 2269
Banta, M., 2102
Barak, B., 2176
Baraka, Iqbal, 373
Baran, Stanley J., 1637
Baranay, Inez, 851
Barat, François, 1168
Barbatis, Gretchen S., 23, 2288
Barcus, F. Earle, 2289, 2538
Bardwick, Judith M., 2177
Bargainnier, Earl F., 2539, 2588
Bargh, Liz, 1169
Barkley, Elizabeth Bookser, 2752
Barnard, Charles N., 2823
Baron, Deneen, 1446
Barr, P., 1102
Barrell, Joan, 1268
Barreno, M. I., 1039
Barreto, Marien S., 1311
Barrett, G. H., 2988
Barrett, Gregory, 492
Barrett, Marvin, 1638, 2824
Barron, John B., 2989
Barros, Sonia Miceli Passoa de, 1398
Barrowclough, Susan, 8
Barry, Thomas E., 2688, 2698
Barthel, Diane, 1626
Bartos, Rena, 191-193
Baruch, Grace, 9

Barwick, Linda, 15, 140
Bat-Ada, Judith, 77, 374
Bataille, Gretchen, A-49
Bate, Barbara, 211, 1559, 2103, A-55
Bathrick, Serafina Kent, 1687
Batt, Sharon, 292
Baum, Chris, 1427
Baur, Elke, 919
Bautista, Paulina F., 493
Baxter, Leslie, A., 2290
Baytion, Maria Corazon E., 670
Bazilli, Susan, 292
Bazin, A., 2473
Beadle, Charles F., 2822
Beahan, Charlotte L., 468
Beam, Randal A., 2753
Bean, Susan, 1639
Beardsell, Susan, 1040
Beasley, Maurine H., 1522-1523, 1535,
    1746, 1754, 1766, 1817, 1825-1833,
    1945, 2028-2029, 2984
Beath, Linda, 129
Beauchamp, Collette, 10
Beck, Kay, 2291
Becker, Jorg, 1213
Begum, Hasna, 617
Behera, Sunil Kanta, 494-495
Behrens, Thorkild, 933
Békés, Ferenc, 875
Belch, M. A., 2686
Belford, Barbara, 1834
Belgrade, Paul, 1766
Belkaoui, Ahmed, 2178
Belkaoui, Janice M., 2178
Bell, D., 2287
Bell, Daniel, 2312
Bell, Inge Powell, 2104
Bell, J. H., 175, 809
Bell, Margaret, 1835
Bellour, Raymond, 17, 60
Benedek, Elissa P., 2990
Benegal, Shyam, 496
Benet, James, 2168, 2170, 2249, 2305,
    2331, 2370
Beniger, James R., 2678
Benjamin, Jessica, A-15
Bennett, Arnold, 981
Bennett, E. A., 982
Bennett, Rex, 2187, 2207
Bennett, Shelley M., 983
Bennett, Tony, 1293
Bennetts, Leslie, 2825
Bennion, Sherilyn C., 1754, 1836-1839

Benoît, N., 910
Benokraitis, Nijole, 2477
Benston, Margaret, 11, 1579
Bentson, M. L., 65
Benze, James G., 2179
Berckman, Edward M., 137
Berg, Charles M., 2292
Berg, Elisabeth, 919
Berg, Gertrude, 1767
Berger, Arthur Asa, 2263, 3214
Berger, P. D., 2701
Bergman, J., 2293
Bergstrom, Janet, 60, 245
Berkowitz, Leonard, 1691
Berlan, Martine, 1041
Bermann, Tamar, 911
Bernheim, Nicole-Lise, 1170
Berning, Carol A., 2689
Bernstein, Henry, 1624
Berrian, B., 350
Berry, Chris, 749
Berry, Sarah, 1679
Berryman, C. L., 1524
Bershen, Wanda, 221
Besha, R. M., 319
Betancourt, Jeanne, 2474
Betterton, Rosemary, 138
Beuf, Ann, 2105, 2136
Bhagat, Rekha, 618-620
Bharti, 621
Bhasin, Kamla, 398-399, 404, 497-498, 582
Bhaskar, Ira, 399, 499
Biagi, Shirley, 1525, 2197, 2400, 2826, 2991
Biber, Ayala, 381
Billings, V., 1571
Billington, Mary Frances, 1840
Binford, Mira Reym, 139
Binns, Catherine A., 2540
Bird, M., 1623
Birrell, Susan, 2632
Bishnoi, Indu, 681
Bishop, Robert L., 1627
Bisplinghoff, Gretchen Deanna, 1688
Blache, Roberta, 1788
Blache, Simone, 1788
Black, Maggie, 365
Black, Sheila, 3161
Blackmar, Beatrice, 3179
Blackwood, Roy E., 2541
Blair, Gwenda, 2827
Blakely, Julie, 240

Blakely, Mary Kay, 2106
Blanchard, Paula, 1841
Blanchard, Rae, 984
Blanchard, Simon, 1171
Blanco, Patricia, 1383
Bland, M. Susan, 1466
Blank, David M., 2294
Blatch, Harriot Stanton, 2057
Blonski, Annette, 852, 867
Bloomer, Dexter C., 1842
Bloomquist, Linda Edwards, 1615, 2207, 2409
Blum, Linda M., 2295
Blum, Stella, 1843
Boafo, S. T. Kwame, 346
Bock, Nancy, 1987
Bodeen, DeWitt, 1807
Boethius, Gunilla, 905
Bolle, Hans-Jurgen, 894
Bond, Jean Carey, 2107
Bond, Richmond, 995
Bond, Turner, 1943
Bonderoff, Jason, 2925
Bonilla de Ramos, Elssy, 1312
Bonk, Kathy, 2780
Bonnerjea, Lucy, 907
Bonvoisin, S. M., 1269
Booker, Janice L., 2754
Booth, Jane, 5, 1042
Bop, Codou, 324
Borah, F., 2842
Borges, Adelia, 1327
Borisoff, Deborah, 2755
Born, Donna, 1844
Borquez, Julio, 1732
Boruszkowski, Lilly Ann, 2461
Bosanac, Gordana, 872
Boserup, Ester, 12
Bossart, Louis, 1172
Bostian, Lloyd R., 2671
Bostick, Theodora P., 985
Boucher, Bill, 2992
Boucher, Sandy, 77
Boughner, Genevieve, 1747-1748
Bouillon, Antoine, 13
Bouraoui, H. A., 1270
Bourgeois, Bea, 1587
Bourke-White, Margaret, 1845
Bouthilet, Lorraine, 1676
Bowler, Susan M., 2009
Bowles, Dorothy A., 2028, 2993
Bowman, William W., 1558, 2756
Bowser, Pearl, 500, 2475

Author Index 423

Boyenton, William H., 2690
Boyer, Peter J., 2542
Boylan, James, 2994
Boynton, Gregory J., 1738
Boys, Mrs. Florence Riddick, 2071
Brabant, Sarah, 2543-2544, 2615
Brack, O. M., jr., 131
Bradac, James J., 2401
Bradley, Patricia, 1846
Bradshaw, James Stanford, 1847
Brady, Kate, 750
Brady, Kathleen, 1848, 2757
Braithwaite, Brian, 1268
Brandt, David A., 2355
Brandt, Janet, 2984
Branningan, A., 798
Brayfield, C., 1102
Brazelton, Ethel M. Colson, 2736
Brehn, Sharon, 2993
Brenders, D. A., 2737
Bretl, David J., 2180
Bridge, Junior, 1579, 1587, 2545, 2780
Bridges, Lamar W., 1849
Brie, Sonja, 14
Briere, John, 1572
Britt, Albert, 1850
Britton, Helen Ann, 2296-2297
Brodber, E., 1361
Brody, Catharine, 1851
Broihier, Mary C., 1563
Brooks, Louise, 1789
Brooks, Robert D., 2362
Brophy, Chris, 867
Brough, James, 3042
Brown, Arthur W., 1852, 1997
Brown, Betsy, 1744
Brown, Charlene J., 3081
Brown, Charles B., 1853
Brown, Jane Delano, 179, 1526, 2298, 2709
Brown, Judith, 1117
Brown, Mary Ellen, 15, 140, 212, 2181, 2310
Brown, Pamela A., 1790
Brown, Peter H., 1790
Brown, Robert U., 1722
Brown, Theodore M., 1854
Brown, Virginia, 2200, 2702
Browne, Pat, 2108
Browner, Carole, 1377
Bruggerman, Theodor, 1043
Brumagin, Vicki Lee, 2995
Brunet, Jean, 1560

Bruno, Giuliana, 1173
Brunsdon, Charlotte, 61, 78, 83, 206, 265
Bryant, James, 2546
Bryant, Jennings, 1622
Bryceson, Deborah, 319
Buch, Hans-Christoph, 1044
Bucher, Felix, 2926
Buchman, P., 2828
Buck, Elizabeth B., 177, 1640
Buck, Macky, 16
Buckmann, Peter, 130
Budd, M., 2710
Buerkel-Rothfuss, Nancy L., 1641, 1661
Bufwack, Mary, 1527
Buhle, Paul, 1527
Bulcher, Graf, 1147
Bullwinkle, Davis A., 305-307
Bunce, Jenny, 810
Buonanno, Milly, 1045
Burchfield, Stephanie, 1174
Buresh, Bernice, 2547
Burgard, Andrea M., 1528
Burger, Jerry M., 2609
Burkhart, Ford N., 2548
Burkhart, Fred, 1722
Burmester, William E., 1855
Burnett, John J., 2672
Burrell, Walter, 2476
Burroughs, Elise, 2996
Burston, J., 246
Burstyn, Varda, 1447
Burt, Olive, 1856
Burton, Clare, 835
Burton, Julianne, 1433
Burzynski, Sue, 2984
Busby, Linda Jean, 1529, 1642, 2109-2110, 2299
Bush, Alan J., 2672
Bussy Genevois, Danielle, 986
Butalia, Urvashi, 399, 672, 751-752
Butler, Matilda, 1559, 1715-1716, 2111, 2182, 2207, 2236, 2300
Butsch, Richard, 2301
Byars, Jackie, 247, 1643, 2302, 2310
Byerly, Carolyn M., 266
Byrne, Pamela R., 1313

Cabau, Michèle, 944
Cadman, Eileen, 213
Caillods, Francoise, 210
Calderon, Carola Garcia, 1314

Callahan, Genevieve, 1742
Callahan, Sean, 1845
Calvert, Catherine, 1570
Campbell, Karlyn Kohrs, 23
Campbell, Kenneth, 2298
Campbell, Richard, 1717
Camps, Victoria, 964
Canadian Advertising Foundation, 1467-1468
Canadian Broadcasting Corporation, 1496
Canadian Radio-Television and Telecommunications Commission, 1469-1470
Cancian, Francesca M., 2549-2550
Candelas, Laura, 1347
Cano, Ana María, 1411
Cantarow, Ellen, 2997
Cantor, Joanne, 2180, 2726
Cantor, Muriel G., 125, 1615, 1644-1645, 1658, 1660, 2149, 2170, 2183, 2303-2305, 2829-2830
Capek, Mary Ellen S., 3133
Carden, Maren Lockwood, 1718
Cardinale, Susan, 1719
Cardoso, Irede, 1425, 1434
Care, Helen, 847
Careem, Nicky, 673
Carew, Jean V., 2413
Carlin, John C., 165
Carlinsky, Dan, 2831
Carlson, Marifran, 1417
Carlson, Pamela, 1722
Carpenter, Iris, 1857
Carr, E. A., 1530
Carreon, B. A., 623
Carreon, Estella, 444
Carrier, Jeffrey L., 2927
Carrillo, Loretta, 2711
Carter, Erica, 1148
Carter, Jimmy, 2832
Carter, Kathryn, 140, 1531, 1543, 1604
Carter, Linda, 2833
Carty, James W., jr., 77, 674, 1315, 1386-1387
Carty, Marjorie T., 76, 214, 1315
Casey, Ralph D., 1753
Cassata, Mary B., 125, 1646, 1660, 2283, 2306-2307
Castro, Janice, 2834
Castronovo, V., 941
Caswell, Lucy Shelton, 1858, 2998
Causey, Betty Jo, 2835

Cavalieri, Joey, 2999
Ceulemans, Mieke, 19, 912, 1251
Chalfant, H. Paul, 3162
Chalmers, David M., 1859
Chambon, Jacques, 1046
Chandiram, Jai, 405-406
Chandralekha, 399, 407
Chang, Gypsy, 675
Chang, Sung-ja, 501
Chang, Won H., 3000
Chapelle, Dickey, 1860
Chapin, Howard M., 1861
Charney, Ann, 1497
Charnley, Mitchell V., 3140
Charriere, Jacques, 221
Chase, Edna Woolman, 3163
Chase, Ilka, 3163
Chatman, Elfreda A., 2673
Chatterji, Jyotsna, 502
Chatterji, Shoma A., 503, 676, 679
Chauvel Carlsson, Susanne, 804
Chavez, Deborah, 2551
Cheatwood, Derral, 2477
Check, James V. P., 1703
Cheles-Miller, Pamela, 2308
Chelli, Mounira, 303
Chen, Amy, 2928
Chen, Anne M. Cooper, 215
Cheshire, Maxine, 3001
Chesler, Phyllis, 1621
Chesman, Andrea, 3195
Chester, Gail, 213
Chester, Giraud, 3141
Chestnut, Robert W., 2184
Cheung Man-Yee, 677
Chevigny, Bell G., 1997
Chhabra, Rami, 457, 678
Chhachhi, Amrita, 399, 753
Ching, Liu Mei, 469
Chipperfield, Faith, 1862
Chodorow, Nancy, 1643
Christ, William G., 2584
Christian, Harry, 273, 1242, 1720
Christian, Leona, 1465
Christopher, Maurine, 1624
Christopher, R., 141
Christy, Karen, 3002
Chu, Leonard L., 467
Chudacoff, Nancy Fisher, 1863
Chudakoff, Rochelle, 2035
Chulay, Cornell, 2309
Chusmir, Janet, 2984
Chusmir, Leonard H., 3111

Chusmir, Stuart F., 2276
Cirillo, Joan J., 3003
Cirksena, Kathryn, 21, 1561
Citron, Michele, 247, 2929
Clabes, Judy, 2984, 3004
Claire, Roxanne, 54, 142
Clardy, Andrea Fleck, 296, 1272
Clark, Danae, 15
Clark, Emily, 1864
Clark, R. E., 2571
Clark, Rebecca L., 3164
Clarke, A. C., 1049
Clarke, Patricia, 805
Clarke, Peter, 3165
Clarke, Shirley, 2930
Clason, C., 1435
Clayton, Sue, 1171
Clift, Elayne, 194
Clifton, T., 1175
Cline, D. J., 2784, 3005
Clinton, Catherine, 1527
Clinton, Jacqueline, 2361
Cloud, G. W., 2552
Coates, Foster, 1865
Cobb-Reiley, Linda, 2836
Coburn, Julia, 1739
Coburn, Marcia Froelke, 3006
Cockburn, Cakau, 394
Cohen, Akiba A., 384, 2466
Cohen, Anne B., 2553
Coke, Andree, 682
Cole, Barry G., 1644
Cole, Johnetta B., 69
Cole, Lynda P., 2646
Cole, Richard R., 2646
Coleman, Kit, 1456
Colle, Royal D., 195
Collins, Jean E., 240, 1749
Collins, W. Andrew, 2377
Colomina de Rivera, Marta, 1399
Colton, Helen, 1728
Comer, Nancy A., 1570
Commission of the European Communities, 913-914
Comstock, G. S., 2335
Condon, Frank, 2931
Cong Cong, 683
Conn, Earl L., 2028
Conn, Frances G., 1866
Connors, Joanna, 2554
Considine, David M., 2478
Constantino, Renato, 754
Consumer's Association of Penang, 504

Cook, Pam, 143, 233, 2932
Cook, Stephanie, 2908
Cooper, Anne M., 220, 308, 1561, 1817, 1867, 2113-2114
Cooper, Joel, 2243
Cooper, Miriam, 1791
Cooper, Nancy, 3166
Cooper, Pamela, 1721
Cooper, V. W., 2115
Copeland, G. A., 2311
Coram, Robert, 3007
Corboud, Adrienne, 1177
Corder, Billie F., 2225
Corder-Bolz, Charles R., 2406
Corea, Gena, 1722
Cornillon, Susan Koppelman, 2555
Cornwell, Regina, 221, 227
Corpuz, Lavinia F., 625
Corrado-Taylor, Denise, 2200
Cortinas, Laura, 1430
Cosetang, Alicia M. L., 467
Cosgrave, Jack, 1169
Costello, Michael, 1753
Cotten-Huston, A. L., 26
Cottingham, Jane, 27
Council for Better Programming, Tokyo, 626
Council on Interracial Books for Children, 505
Counts, Tim, 2764
Courtney, Alice E., 1441, 1633, 2136, 2185-2186, 2269, 2272-2274
Cousins, Jane, 811
Covarrubias, Paz, 1401
Covert, Catherine L., 1750, 1762, 1946
Cowan, Gloria, 2479
Cowie, Elizabeth, 144, 2116
Coxon, Kirby, 506
Coy, Patrick, 1868
Craft, Christine, 2838
Craig, S., 2710
Cramer, Judith A., 1535
Crawshay, Myfanwy, 987
Crean, Susan, 1498-1500
Creed, Barbara, 852, 1792
Creedon, Pamela J., 1535
Cregeen, Jane, 461
Cremen, Christine, 853
Crescioni, Gladys, 1366
Cripps, Thomas, 2480
Crist, Judith, 2839
Cristall, Ferne, 1442
Croll, Elisabeth, 470-471

Croly, J. C., 2051
Cronberg, Tarja, 507
Cronin, Mary M., 3008
Cronk, Alan, 2657
Cronkite, Walter, 2840
Crowther, Claire, 907
Crumley, Wilma, 2758
Cruz, Neal H., 755
Cudjoe, Selwyn R., 1370
Cuenca de Herrera, Gloria, 1436
Culley, James D., 2187, 2207
Cunningham, Linda, 1722, 2984
Curran, James, 1048
Curry, T. J., 1049
Curry, Timothy, 1996
Cuthbert, Marlene, 76, 1348-1349, 1362-1364, 1369, 1371
Cutlip, Scott M., 1628
Cutrufelli, Maria Rosa, 145, 309
Czerniejewski, Halina J., 3009

Daisley, Jenny, 1178
Dajani, Karen Finlon, 388
Dalton, Pen, 5, 28
Dalton, Terry A., 3010
Dambrot, Faye H., 2312, 2417-2419, 2895
Dana, Margaret, 2691
Dancyger, Irene, 269
Dangugo, H. S., 363
Daniels, Arlene Kaplan, 2168, 2170, 2249, 2305, 2331, 2370
Daniels, Elizabeth Adams, 1869
Danzig, Fred, 1624
Darden, Donna K., 2674
Darden, William R., 2674
Dardigna, Anne-Marie, 1273
Darrach, Brad, 2841
Darroch, Dorothy B., 820
Darschin, Wolfgang, 915
Dasgupta, Chidananda, 457
Dasgupta, Shibani, 508
Daswani, T. C., 409, 417, 460
Davenport, Lucinda, 1561, 1587, 2113-2114
Davenport, Walter, 1870
David, Jane T., 2481
Davidman, Joy, 2482
Davidson, E., 2313
Davidson, Emily C., 2320
Davies, Katherine, 146
Davies, Margery, 29

Davies, Michael, 1722
Davis, Deborah, 3011
Davis, Dennis K., 2461
Davis, Junetta, 2556
Davis, Lenwood G., 3012
Davis, Linda H., 3013
Davis, Patricia E., 1570
Davis, Richard H., 2314
Davis, Ronald M., 2692
Dawit, T., 344
Dawson, Bonita, 222
Day, Charles W., 2712
Day, Dorothy, 1871
Dayal, Abha, 509
Debevec, K., 2188-2189
de Bock, Harold, 1568
de Camargo, Nelly, 1428
de Claricini, S., 1274
Declercq, Eugene R., 2179
DeCrow, Karen, 2117
DeFleur, Melvin L., 2315
Degener, David, 2483
DeGooyer, Janice, 2842
de Grass, Jan, 1275, 1515
de Guevara, Licenciada Miriam Lynch, 1318
De Hirsch, Storm, 2930
Deiss, Joseph J., 1997
Deitch, Cindy, 16
Dejanikus, Tacie, 1437
De Keyser, E., 1050
De Kunst, R., 1051
de la Garde, Roger, 1501
de la Luz Hurtado, Maria, 30
de la Peña, Patricia, 259, 1388
de la Peña Sobarzo, Patricia, 1376
De La Roche, Catherine, 196
De Lauretis, Teresa, 31, 247
deLeon, Anna Leah, 684
DelGuadio, Sybil, 2484
Delorme, Charlotte, 57, 1276
Demac, Donna, 3167
Deming, Caren J., 15, 1372, 2316
Deming, Robert, 17, 1679
DeMott, John, 351, 1872
Denault, Jocelyn, 18, 1689
Denisoff, R. S., 1577
Denmark, Florence L., 2565
Deocampo, Nick, 685
de O'Farrill, Hilda Avila, 1389
Derieux, James C., 1870
Derry, Charles, 147
Derryck, Vivian Lowery, 148

Author Index

Dervin, Brenda, 32, 1640
Desai, Neera, 394, 410
Deshpande, Anjali, 582
de Souza, E., 457
Desser, David, 510
Deterding, Karen, 1465
Deuschl, Vivian, 2819
Deutsch, Hermann B., 1877
Devore, Mary Ann, 2118
Dewey, Langdon, 223
Dexter, Elizabeth Anthony, 1873
Diamond, Edwin, 3168
Diaz-Abaya, Marilou, 496
Díaz de Landa, Marta, 1319
Dickerson, Nancy, 1768
Dickey, Julienne, 146, 149
Dickinson, Susan E., 1874
Diekerhof, Els, 916
Dier, S., 2595
Dighe, Anita, 51, 539, 632
Dijkstra, Bram, 150
Diliberto, Gioia E., 2759
Dispenza, Joseph E., 2693
Dissanayake, Wimal, 575, 581, 597, 686
di Stadio, Patrizia, 1052
Doane, Mary Ann, 60, 151, 197, 988, 1705, 3148-3149
Dodd, D. K., 2557-2558
Doherty, Amy S., 1875
Dohrmann, Rita, 2317
Dolan, Darlene J., 2760
Dolliver, Mark, 1625
Domhoff, G. William, 2170
Dominguez, Juan, Milagros, 271
Dominick, Joseph, 2190, 2318-2319, 2434
Donagher, Patricia C., 2320
Donalson, Melvin B., 2485
Donath, B., 1624
Doneson, Judith E., 375
Donnerstein, Edward, 1536, 1690-1691, 1701-1702
Donovan, Suzanne, 2761
Dooley, Dennis, 2554
Dooley, Janet L., 2191
Doolittle, John, 2192
Doolittle, Robert, 2192
Dordick, Herbert S., 2357
Dorenkamp, Angela G., 2119
Door, Rheta Childe, 1876
Dorris, J. M., 2559
Dotan, Judith, 384
Doughan, David T. J., 296, 1277

Douglas, Ann, 1537
Doumbia, Terez, 366
Dowling, G. R., 812
Downie, Susanna, 2762
Downing, John, 1053, 1589, 3169
Downing, Mildred, 2136, 2321
Downs, A. Chris, 2322-2324
Doyle, Nancy, 2120
Dozier, David M., 1630
Dragonette, Jessica, 1769
Drain, Dorothy, 846
Drakulich, Slavenka, 873
Drath, J., 1187
Dravie, Kayissan, 303
Drew, Dan G., 2560
Drewry, John E., 1877
Dreyfuss, Joel, 2843
Drotner, Kirsten, 1278, A-15
Dryfoos, Susan W., 3014
Dua, M. R., 511
Dubois-Jallais, Denise, 1179
Dunn, Reina Wiles, 2933
Dunne Carolyn, 868
Dunnigan, Alice E., 1878
Durham, Leona, 2561
Durkin, Kevin, 1054-1058, 2325
Duster, Alfreda M., 2089
Dutt, Prabha, 688
Dutta, Neelam, 457
Duus, Masayo, 689
Dworkin, Andrea, 34
Dworkin, Susan, 2486
Dyer, Carolyn Stewart, 1535
Dyer, Gilliam, 6
Dyer, Peter John, 1793
Dyer, Richard, 1794, 3150
Dysart, L., 2339

Eakins, B. W., 35
Eakins, R. G., 35
Earl, Claudette, 1350
Earle, Alice M., 1879
Earnshaw, Stella, 1279-1280
Eason, David L., 3015
East, Catherine, 2562
Easton, G., 1059
Easton, Nina, 2694
Eberhard, Wallace B., 1880, 1945, 3016
Eberly, Stephen L., 2934
Eckersley, Robyn, 917
Eckert, Charles, 2488
Eddings, Barbara M., 5, 224

Edelman, Scott, 3017
Edgar, Patricia, 813-814, 834
Edmondson, Madeleine, 1647
Edwards, Anne, 2935
Edwards, Emily D., 1586
Edwards, Julia, 3018
Edwards, Sandra, 1369, 1373
Edwards-Stuart, Fiona, 1169
Efrat, Roni Ben, 376
Egleston, Charles, 2029
Eide, Elisabeth, 1060
Eifler, Deborah, 2668
Einsiedel, Edna F., 2726
Einstein, Dan, 17, 1679
Eisen, Arlene, 412
Eisen, Susan V., 2384
Eisenstein, Zillah R., 29
Eisenstock, Barbara, 2326
Ek, Richard A., 1881
Elias, Mirjam, 916
Ellerbee, Linda, 2844
Ellis, Albert, 1728
Ellis, Dickie Lou, 1538
Ellis, Donald G., 2327
Ellis, Frederick R., 3019
Ellis, Kate, 1723
Ellis, Marc H., 1882
Ellis, Pat, 1350
Ellison, Katherine, 1390
El Saadawi, Nawal, 377
Elsas, Diana, 1539
Elvinia, Lutgarda R., 512
Elwood, Virginia, 1754, 2121
Elwood-Akes, Virginia, 1883
Eman, V. A., 1524
Emanuel, Barbara, 1442
Embree, Alice, 1580
Emerson, Gloria, 1884
Emerson, Mark, 2936, 2963
Emery, Edwin,1751, 2749
Emery, Michael, 1751
Emmison, Michael, 835
Emond, Ariane, 1502
Endres, Kathleen L., 1758, 1885-1886, 2122, 2763
Engel, Margaret, 3020
England, Paula, 2193
Engle, Gary, 2554
Entrikin, Isabelle Webb, 1887
Epple, Ron, 1692
Epstein, Cynthia Fuchs, 2170
Epstein, Laurily Keir, 1443
Epstein, T., Scarlett, 198

Erausquin, Estela, 1327
Erazo, Viviana, 54, 1342, 1396
Erens, Patricia, 287, 2932, 2937-2939
Ergas, Yasmine, 1062
Ericson, Richard V., 1493
Ernster, Virginia L., 2695
Escario, Pilar, 964
Escoto, José Augusto, 1355
Esposito, Virginia, 3165
Estabaya, D. M., 690
Estep, Rhoda, 2123, 2328
Eubben, M. C., 152
Evans, Richard J., 989
Everington, C., 2164
Ewen, Elizabeth, 2727
Eyal, C. H., 378

Fachel Leal, Ondina, 1402
Faderman, Lillian, 2563
Fagoaga, Concha, 1063
Fahim, Fawzia, 352
Faithfull, Emily, 990
Fallon, Martine, 1281
Falloon, Mary, 847
Fannin, Rebecca, 2696
Fanshel, Susan, 1374
Farber, Stephen, 2489, 2940
Farges, Joël, 1168
Farley, Jennie, 3170
Fasting, Kari, 1064-1065
Fauconnier, Guido, 19
Faulder, C., 1102
Faulkner, Melissa, 2800
Fedler, Fred, 2764
Fehlner, Christine L., 2652
Fehr, Lawrence A., 2713
Feinstein, Adam, 1182
Fejes, Fred, 37, 541
Feldman, Harry, 226
Feldman, Joseph, 226
Feldman, Orna, 2845
Feldstein, Jerome, 2195
Feldstein, Sandra, 2195
Feliciano, Gloria D., 413
Fellman, Anita Clair, 1449
Fenigstein, Allan, 2728
Ferber, Edna, 1888
Fergus, Jan, 131
Ferguson, Carroll Ann, 2909
Ferguson, Charles W., 1889
Ferguson, Marjorie, 272-273, 1284, 2170
Ferguson, Ted, 1456

Ferlita, Ernest, 2941
Fernandes, Vic, 1369
Fernandez, Doreen G., 433, 691
Fernández, Norman, 1285
Fernández Violante, Marcela, 1327
Fernon, Christine, 854
Ferrante, Carol, 2196
Ferrante, Karlene, 2197
Ferrarotti, Franco, 1540
Ferri, Anthony J., 2846-2847
Fewster, W. Jean, 627
Fidell, Linda S., 2238
Fife, Marilyn D., 2329, 2848
Fifita, Nanise, 259, 855
Figueroa, Blanca, 1405
Filene, Catherine, 2765
Filler, Louis, 1890
Fine, Marlene G., 1649, 1661
Fink, Conrad, 1541
Fink, Margaret, 863
Finke, Blythe Foote, 240
Finlayson, A., 1503
Finley, Ruth E., 1891
Finney, Ruth, 2765
Fins, Alice, 2766
Fischer, Arlene, 3171
Fischer, Lucy, 2943
Fischer, Raymond L., 1650
Fishburn, Katherine, 1542, 2767
Fisher, Andrea, 1892
Fisher, Charles, 1893
Fisher, June, 3172
Fisher, Sue, 257
Fishman, Gideon, 382
Fisk, George, 2274
Fisk, Margaret, 1722
Fiske, John, 15, 1651-1652, 2310
Fitzgerald, Mark, 1722, 3021
Fitz-Gibbon, Bernice, 2801
Fitzsimmons, Ellen, 2390
Fjeldsted, Margaret, 2330
Flander, Judy, 2849, 3173
Flanley, Mabel G., 2697
Fleener, Nickieann, 3022
Fleeson, Doris, 1739
Fleetwood, Cynthia, 1563
Flenniken, Shary, 3023
Flexner, Eleanor, 1894
Flick, Marian, 50, 153, 1067-1078, 1183
Flick, Marjan, 950
Flinn, John, 2850
Flitterman-Lewis, Sandy, 17, 1079, 1679

Flora, Cornelia Butler, 5, 154-156, 1320-1322, 1334, 1418
Florika, 1580
Flynn, Elizabeth A., 1013
Foerch, B. J., 2557
Fogarty, Michael P., 1184
Foldvári, Eva, 875
Foley, Sue, 2877
Folkerts, Jean, 3174
Ford, Charles, 1795
Forte, Frances L., 2199
Forte, Jeanie K., 1542
Fortin, Nina E., 1255
Forum for Children's Television, 628
Fosdick, Jim, 3106
Foss, Karen A., 1543-1544, 1724
Foss, Sonja K., 1543-1544, 1724
Fougeyrollas, Pierre, 345
Fowler, G. L., jr., 2228
Fox, Harold W., 2124
Francis, Sara, 2309
Franco, Rolando, 1401
Frank, Shirley, 1714
Frankel, Judith, 2125
Franklin, Jack L., 2644
Frankovic, Kathleen A., 1732
Franks, Lucinda, 1186
Franquet, Rosa, 964
Franzblau, Susan, 1653
Franzone, Dorothy Lawrence, 2126
Franzwa, Helen H., 2136, 2331, 2566, 3175
Fraser, Laura, 2944
Fraser, Nancy, 21
Frazer, Elizabeth, 1287
Fredin, Eric S., 1535, 2909
Freedland, Michael, 2945
Freedman, Marcia, 389
Freeman, Barbara M., 1457-1460
Freiberg, Freda, 516, 852
Freise, H., 1187
French, Brandon, 2490
Frenkel, C., 325
Freyer, E., 1694
Frey-Vor, Gerlinde, 24-25
Friedan, Betty, 3176
Friedberg, Anne, 60
Friedlander, Edward J., 2776
Friedlander, Madeline, 227, 3151
Friedman, Barbara, 1545
Friedman, Jean E., 1806
Friedman, Leslie J., 2127

Friedman, Stanley, 1896
Friendly, Sheryl, 1721
Fries, M., 1080
Frisbie, John M., 2277
Frisof, Jamie Kelem, 1618
Fritz, Leah, 1288
Fritz, Paul, 997
Frizzell, Alan, 1495
Frizzi, Ginny, 3024
Frost, Richard, 165, 2729, 2744
Frueh, T., 2385
Fruhauf, Aline, 3025
Fryatt, Norma R., 1897
Fudger, M., 1102
Fujita, Pamela, 2445
Fukao, Tokiko, 444, 467
Fukuda, Jun, 548
Fulle, Isis, 1081-1082
Fung, Victoria M., 2851
Furian, M., 1083
Furman, Bess, 1898
Furnham, Adrian, 1084-1085, 1090, 1149, 2675

Gabor, Mark, 157
Gaborone, Samora, 210
Gade, Eldon M., 2332, 2364
Gage, Mitilda J., 2057
Gagnard, Alice, 1535
Gaines, Jane M., 275, 1546, 1705, 1796-1798, 3190
Gajendragadkar, Nikhil, 693
Galerstein, Carolyn L., 2491
Gallagher, Margaret, 39-45, 50, 54, 76, 78, 83, 158, 188, 228-229, 268, 352, 354, 517, 705, 921-923, 931, 1086-1087, 1188-1189, 1428, 1500, 2946
Galst, Joann Paley, 2404
Gamman, Lorraine, 2676
Gandy, Oscar H., jr., 3172
Ganguly, Shailaja, 433, 518
Gans, Herbert J., 2730
Garcia, Hazel, 1899
Garcia, Maria Isabel, 1327
García Calderón, Carola, 1394
García Flores, Margarita, 1323
Gardener, Virginia, 1900
Gardner, Jo Ann, 1618
Gardner, Mary A., 240
Gardner, Teresa, 2194
Garnsey, Caroline John, 1901
Garrett, Carolyn, 1535

Garrett, W. E., 1902
Garrison, Garnet R., 3141
Gasca, Luis, 1088
Gaspar-Ruppert, Walburga, 159
Gassen, Gisela, 929
Gastoff, J. W., 2451
Gaudart, Dorothea, 958
Gay, Jill, 1324
Gay, Verne, 2852
Gebhardt, Randall E., 2333
Geis, Florence L., 1600, 2200, 2702
Geis, Gilbert, 2738
Geise, L. Ann, 2567
Geissbler, Rainer, 924
Geist, Kathe, 46
Gelbart, Nina Rattner, 991
Gelfman, Judith S., 2853
Gentile, Mary C., 230
George, Diana, 2886
Geracimos, Ann, 3177
Geraghty, Christine, 2334
Gerard, Lillian, 227, 2492
Gerbner, George, 2170, 2294, 2335-2337, 2438-2439, 2568
Gersh, Debra, 3026
Geyer, Georgie Anne, 1587
Ghosh, Akhila, 399, 629
Giacomini, Stefania, 1115
Gibbons, Keith, 925
Gibbons, Sheila, 1522, 1547, 1552, 1620
Gieber, Walter, 3028
Gielow, L. S., 2854
Gies, Dorothy, 1903
Gietson, G., 1149
Gill, Donna, 18, 1474
Gill, Rina, 417
Gilliatt, Penelope, 1570
Gilligan, Carol, 1643
Gilly, Mary C., 160, 2698
Gilmer, Elizabeth, 1739
Gilpin, Paul, 2215
Giordano, Joseph, 2338
Girija, Devi, 519
Gish, Lillian, 1695
Gladstone, Brooke, 2855
Glazer, Nona, 5, 2569
Glazer Schuster, Isa, 326
Gledhill, Christine, 247, 276
Glenn, Judith A., 1548
Glennon, Lynda M., 2301
Gloria, Amelia J., 757
Glouden, Barbara, 1369
Goddard, T., 1102

Goff, D. H., 2339
Goffman, Erving, 2201
Gokhale, L. N., 414, 417, 460
Golab, Caroline, 2493
Goldberg, Vicki, 1845
Golden, Daniel S., 2494
Golden, L. L. L., 2768
Goldenberg, Edie, 1732, 2138
Goldin, Marion, 3029
Goldstein, Cynthia, 1904
Golmakani, Houshang, 390
Gomes, Jaina, 457
Gonzalez, Michaela B., 668
Good, James D., 2118
Goodall, H. L., jr., A-55
Goodman, Kathleen, 630
Goodman, Maureen, 2206
Goodrick, Evelyn Trapp, 3030
Goonatilake, Hema, 394, 415, 520
Gopaldas, Tara, 417
Gordon, Ann D., 1527
Gordon, Lorna, 1369
Gordon, Lynn D., 2570
Gordon, Steven L., 2549
Gordon, Thomas F., 1549
Gornick, Vivian, 2202, 2216
Gosling, L. A. Peter, 521
Gottehrer, Barry, 2856
Gottlieb, Agnes Hooper, 3178
Gough-Yates, Kevin, 2495
Gould, Bruce, 3179
Gould, Lewis L., 1817, 1905
Gould, S. J., 2699
Goulden, Joseph C., 3180
Gover, C. Jane, 1906
Gowan, Darryl C., 2323
Graham, Cooper C., 1191
Graham, Katharine, 2749
Graham, Sheila, 1907
Graham-Brown, Sarah, 379
Gran, Martin, 3031
Grant, G. W., 2354
Grant, Jane, 1908
Grant, Linda M., 1593
Grant, Liz, 2496
Grauerholz, E., 2571
Gray, Elizabeth Dodson, 3142
Gray, J. Patrick, 2497
Gray, Nancy K., 2857
Gray, Susanne, 3114
Green, Nancy L., 1587
Green, Norma, 1624, 3181

Greenberg, Bradley S., 1654, 1661, 2340-2342, 2352-2353, 2422
Greene, Gael, 1570, 3032
Greenfield, Meg, 3182
Greenfield, Thomas Alan, 1655
Greenwald, Marilyn S., 2572-2573, 3183
Greenya, John, 3001
Gregg, Nina, 1561
Gretchen, Beth, 2714
Grewe-Partsch, Marianne, 231
Grieve, Mary, 992
Grieve, Norma, 808
Griffin, Robert J., 2343
Griffith, Alison, 1475
Grilikhes, Alexandra, 132
Grimshaw, Allen, 1550
Grimshaw, Patricia, 808
Grjebine, Lois, 522
Gronhaug, Kjell, 2274
Gross, Charles W., 1736
Gross, Harriet Engel, 3184, 3212
Gross, Lynne, 2677
Grossberg, Lawrence, 2310, 2344
Groth, Gary, 3033
Grunig, Larissa S., 1535, 1630, 2769, 2802
Grunwald, Mary, 1289
Guénette, Françoise, 1502
Guenin, Zena B., 2574, 3185
Guerra-Cunningham, Lucia, 1323
Guest, Pearl E., 2715
Guider, Elizabeth, 2858
Guimary, Donald L., 3143
Guitar, Mary Ann, 1570
Gulliver, Adelaide Cromwell, 2480
Gunawardene, Hema, 694
Gunter, Barrie, 50, 161, 1089-1090, 1149, 2675
Gupta, J. P., 523
Gustafson, Robert, 2947
Gutcheon, Beth, 1581
Gutierrez y Villalobos, Sonia, 1338
Gutman, C., 1126
Gutman, Jonathan, 2716
Guzda, M. K., 1722
Gwynn, Tonya K., 925

Haagen, Bernd-Ulrich, 1192
Haberman, Phyllis, 2253
Habert, Angeluccia Bernardes, 1404
Habib, Miriam, 524, 695

Hafen, Jeffrey, 2428
Haffey, Joan, 1405
Hagen, Ray, 1807
Hahner, June E., 1414-1415
Haig, Kenneth M., 1461
Haizlip, Thomas, 2225
Hale, Sarah J., 1965
Hall, Nora, 2029
Hall, Stuart, 926, 1142, 1152
Hall, Susan, 310
Halliday, Jon, 232
Halonen, A., 1091
Halonen, Irma Kaarina, 162, 1091
Halopainen, Irma, 930, 950
Halton, John C., III, 1909
Hamblin, Dora Jane, 1910
Hamilton, Robert, 1092
Hamilton, Virginia van der Veer, 1911
Hamima, Dona Mustafa, 467, 631
Hamlin, John E., 163
Hammeluddin, Mehmood, 457
Hammouche, Abdelkader, 371
Hanák, Katalin, 875, 882-883, 885, 895
Haniff, Nesha Z., 1375
Hanitra, Tiana, 366
Hannonen-Gladden, Helena, 2428
Hansen, Audrey B., 2859
Hansen, C. H., 2345
Hansen, R. D., 2345
Hanson, Catherine A., 2383
Hansson, Carola, 896
Hansson, Lennart, 1093
Havalovich, Mary Beth, 1705, 1770
Hardy, Phil, 143, 233
Harkness, Shirley, 1418
Harless, James D., 2333
Harman, Jeanne Perkins, 3034
Harms, Joan, 927
Harp, D. A., 1656
Harp, S. H., 1656
Harriman, Margaret, 1799
Harrington, Stephanie, 1581, 3147, 3186
Harris, Anne, 696
Harris, George, 3035
Harris, Mary B., 2346
Harris, P. R., 1094
Harris, Rosemary J., 869, 871
Harrison, Brian, 993
Harrison, Cynthia Ellen, 3134
Harrison, Marguerite E., 1912
Harrison, Sheila K., 2324
Harrop, Lori, 1488
Hartley, John, 15

Hartman, John K., 2803
Hartmann, Paul, 632
Hartnett, Sally, 824
Harvey, R. C., 2575-2576
Harvey, Susan E., 2347, 2415
Harwood, Kenneth, 2770, 2860, 2910
Haskell, Deborah, 2348
Haskell, Molly, 1581, 2498-2499, 2940, 2948
Hatano, Ruriko, 433, 697
Hatch, Alden, 1913
Hatch, David L., 3187
Hatch, Mary G., 2187
Haugh, Louis J., 1624
Havens, Beverly, 2203
Hawkins, Joellen W., 2204
Hawkins, Robert P., 1674, 2207, 2236, 2349
Haworth, Brian, 1092
Haymes, Howard, 1800
Haynes, Andrew M., 2196
Hays, Elinor R., 1914
Hays, Lora, 227, 1193
Hazard, William R., 2740
Head Sydney W., 2350
Healy, Paul F., 1915
Hebert, Brenda, 1599
Heckel, R., 2280
Heck-Rabi, Louise, 234
Hedgepeth, Julia, 3036
Heetor, C., 2342
Heinz, Catharine, 1648, 1771, 2861
Heinzelmann, Herbert, 1194
Heiskala, Risto, 1095
Helfand, Judy, 1713
Hellwig, T., 542
Helregel, Brenda K., 2717
Hempel, Amy, 3037
Henderson, Katherine Usher, 2351
Henderson, Laura, 2352-2353
Hendrick, Dianne, 1465
Henle, Faye, 1916
Henley, Nancy M., 49, 185
Hennessee, J. A., 2205
Hennessee, Judith, 1581, 2862
Henry, Nancy, 3188
Henry, Susan, 1535, 1551, 1917-1924, 1945, 2804, 3189
Henstra, P., 928
Herbert, Ralph, 835
Herd, Harold, 994
Herek, Gregory M., 23, 2288
Hering, Heide, 1096

Author Index

Hermes, Joke, 1290
Hernández Torres, Elizabeth, 1365-1366
Herouy, Alem Seged, 316
Herrera, Alicia, 1325
Herrick, Genevieve F., 2002
Herriman, Nancy Gibbs, 3191
Hershey, Leonore, 1925, 2731
Herstein, Sheila R., 1022
Herzberger-Fofana, Pierrette, 303
Herzog, Charlotte, 275, 1798
Herzog, Herta, 1772
Hess, D. J., 2354, 2386
Hess, R., 2342
Hesterman, Vicki, 3192
Heygster, Anna-Luise, 919
Heyn, Leah, 1618
Hiebert, Ray Eldon, 1552
Hiemstra, Roger, 2206
Higashi, Sumiko, 1801
Higgins, Marguerite, 1926
Higginson, Thomas W., 1835
Higgs, Catriona T., 2128
Hill, C. William, 2577
Hill, George H., 2863
Hill, Jane H., 1377
Hill, Janellen, 2129
Hill, Sylvia Saverson, 2863
Hilliard, S. Lee, 3038
Hilton, Lesley, 1171
Himebaugh, Glenn A., 1722
Hinds, Harold E., jr., 1378
Hino, Jiro, 633
Hinton, David B., 1195
Hinton, James L., 2405
Hirschfeld, Mary, 235
Hitchens, Gordon, 1196
Hjort, Anne, 1150
Hoar, Nancy, 1611
Hobson, Dorothy, 15, 125, 206, 926, 1151-1152
Hodge, Esther, 277
Hodge, Merle, 1351
Hodges, James, 995
Hodges, Kay Kline, 2355
Hodgetts, Victoria, 2864
Hodson, Jeannette, 1752
Hoekstra, Ellen, 1927
Hoffman, Ellen, 3039
Hoffman, Marta, 50
Hoffmann Márta, 884-885
Hoge, Alice Albright, 3040
Hokada, Elizabeth, 2668

Holcomb, Betty, 2865
Holder, Dennis, 2578
Hole, Judith, 1553
Hollinger, Karen, 58, 2732
Holly, Susan, 3041
Holmlund, Christine Anne, 1197
Holopainen, Irma, 1097
Holtzman, Natalie F., 1928, 1945
Holy, Renate, 1198
Holz, Josephine R., 2130
Honey, Maureen, 1929, 2579-2580, 2739
Hooks, Bell, 2131, 2500
Hooper, Leonard J., 1930
Hopper, Hedda, 3042
Horn, Maurice, 1098, 1726
Horne, Sandra, 2866
Horowitz, D., 1554
Hosken, Fran, 77
Hosley, David H., 2867
Houston, Beverle, 86
Hovland, Roxanne, 2818
Howard, Alice B., 1931
Howard, Jane, 1932
Howard, Margo, 3043
Howard, Shirley J., 2718
Howard-Pitney, D., 2705
Howe, Florence, 1714
Howe, Holly, 2700
Howell, Deborah, 2984
Hoyte, Harold, 1369
Hubert, Philip G., 1933
Hudak, L. M., 1934
Hudson, Pat, 846
Hudspeth, Robert N., 1935
Huff, Cary, 2725
Hug, W. J., 2029
Hulme, Marylin A., 2582
Hulston, Linda, 698
Humboldt, Charles, 2501
Humphreys, Nancy, 3193
Hunt, Felicity, 296
Hunt, Margaret, 996
Hunt, Mary E., 2132
Hunt, Todd, 2805
Hunter, Jean, 997
Hurd, Jud, 3194
Hurt, Karen, 127
Huston, A. C., 2356
Huston-Stein, Aletha, 2271
Hutnik, Nimmi, 699
Huyssen, Andreas, 1696
Hynes, Terry M., 1936

Hyser, Sue, 1937

Ide, Sachiko, 316, 525
Ihinger-Tallman, Marilyn, 2620
Ijaz Gul, 700
Iketon, Barbara, 2806
Imam, Ayesha, 303
Imamura, Taihei, 527
Indra, Doreen, 1476
Infield, Glenn B., 1199
Inge, M. Thomas, 1542, 1555
Inoue, Teruko, 278, 702
International Association of Mass Communication Research, 931
International Organization of Journalists, 703, 874
Intintoli, Michael J., 1657
Iqbal Masud, 679
Irukwu, Enoh, 354
Isaacs, Gayla C., 327
Isber, Caroline, 1658
Ishikawa, S., 529
Israel, Lee, 1581, 1938
Iwao, S., 530
Iyer, E., 2188-2189
Iyer, Pico, 1939

Jabbar, Javed, 421
Jacobs, Lea, 17
Jackson, Darryl, 1446
Jackson, George S., 2023
Jackson, L. M., A-55
Jacoby, Jacob, 2689
Jaddou, Liliane, 164, 943
Jaffe, L. J., 2701
Jahan, Roushan, 399, 760
Jakab, Zoltán, 885
Jakes, John, 1940
James, Bessie Rowland, 1831, 1941
James, C. L. R., 1527
James, Mrs. W. K., 2071
Janensch, Gail, 3044
Jang, Hoonsoon Kim, 704
Janocha, Bill, 1983
Jansen, Lies, 50, 931
Jansen, Sue Curry, 1556, 1560
Janus, Noreene, 2133, 3172
Japan Broadcasting Co., 761
Jarrad, Mary W., 2583
Jaschok, Maria, 531
Jayamanne, Laleen, 473

Jayaweera, Swarna, 210
Jeffers, Dennis W., 3045
Jeffrey, Liss, 1659
Jeffries-Fox, Suzanne, 2357
Jelinkova, L., 56
Jenkins, Henry, 3046
Jennings (Walstedt), Joyce, 2200, 2702
Jensen, Else, 50-51, 70, 78, 83, 199, 931-932, 950, 1099, 1200-1201
Jensen, Margaret Ann, 1452
Jensen, Marlene, 2771
Jersenius, Bosse, 1093
Jewell, Karen S. Warren, 2134
Jimenez David, Rina, 423
Joan, Polly, 3195
Johannesson, Jan, 1202
John, George, 1369
Johnson, Burges, 3047
Johnson, Carolyn, 2677
Johnson, Fern L., 23, 1557, A-55
Johnson, Hope, 1773
Johnson, Lynda D., 634
Johnson, Mary D., 1005
Johnson, Pam, A-24
Johnson, Robert C., 1727
Johnson, Rolland C., 1644
Johnson, Sammye, 1535, 2584
Johnston, Claire, 60, 143, 233, 245, 280-281, 1203, 2502
Johnston, Johanna, 1942
Johnston, Lynn, 1505
Johnstone, John W. C., 1558
Jolliffe, Lee B., 1943, 2029, 2585
Jolly, E., 2535
Jones, Adelaide H., 3048
Jones, Daryl E., 2586
Jones, Elise F., 2678
Jones, Lee, 399, 815
Jones, Mary Jane, 2587-2588
Jones, Patricia, 966
Jordan, Elizabeth, 1944
Jordan, W., 2703
Joseph, Gloria I., 2141
Joseph, Ted, 2807
Josephine, 762
Joshi, Hansa, 424
Joshi, Ila S., 635
Joshi, S. R., 51, 424, 705-706
Joshi, Shashi, 488
Joubert, Jacqueline, 998
Joy, Patricia, 2868
Joyrich, Lynne, 17, 1679
Jugenheimer, D. W., 2257, 2655

Author Index

Julien, Fabienne, 1502
Jung, Yung-ae, 636
Juno, Pia, 933
Junyk, Myra, 1477
Jurney, Dorothy, 77, 2562, 2984, 3049-3050
Jyrkiainen, Jyrki, 1205

Kacerguis, Mary Ann, 2137
Kahn, Kim Fridkin, 1732, 2138
Kaiser, Addy, 50-51, 1206
Kaiser, Kathy, 3196
Kaite, Berkeley, 2208
Kalisch, Beatrice J., 1600, 2359-2361, 2503
Kalisch, Philip A., 1600, 2359-2361, 2503
Kallan, Richard A., 2362, 2431
Kalonen, Irma Kaarina, 1100
Kalter, Joanmarie, 2363
Kalwachwala, Dinaz, 764
Kane, Hartnett T., 1947
Kaneko, Yoshimi, 478
Kaninga, Nancy, 2364
Kanter, Donald, 2704
Kanzleiter, Gerda, 919, 935, 1222
Kapardis, A., 798
Kaplan, E. Ann, 59-61, 78, 83, 237, 247, 532, 605, 1697, 2365, 2504
Kaplan, Stuart J., 2290
Kapoor, Coomi, 688
Kapoor, Nina, 582
Karkal, Malini, 637
Karl, Marilee, 54, 166
Karlekar, Malavika, 765
Karolevitz, Robert, 1948
Karoui, Naima, 311
Karp, Walter, 2366
Karpf, Anne, 5, 61-62
Kassell, Paula, 283
Katana, Kazungu, 355
Kato, Hidetoshi, 527
Katsutoshi, Yamashita, 707
Katumba, Rebecca, 353
Katz, Elihu, 206
Katzman, Natan, 1662
Kaufman, Debra Renee, 9
Kaufman, Susan J., 283
Kaunda, Josina N., 303
Kaur, Anita, 533
Kaur, Ranbir, 638
Kay, K., 2505

Kay, Karyn, 237
Kayson, Wesley A., 2199
Keats, John, 1949
Keeler, Suzanne, 175, 816
Keeshen, Kathleen, 2029
Keller, Jo E., 2847
Kelly, Florence Finch, 1950
Kelly, Gail P., 69
Kelly, James D., 2772
Kelly, Katie, 3197
Kelly, Mary, 17, 1801
Kelly, Peggy, 18, 1506
Kelly, S., 1722
Kennedy, John B., 1774
Kerin, Roger A., 2209
Kern, Donna Rose Casella, 1951
Kernan, Margot, 1698
Kern-Foxworth, Marilyn, 2210
Kerr, Dennis, 1672
Kerr, Frances W., 1775
Kert, Bernice, 1952
Kessler, Lauren, 1953, 3198-3199
Kessler, Lori, 1552
Kettner, Britta, 1101
Key, Wilson B., 2211
Khanum, Saleema, 439
Khileshwari, R. A., 417
Kiecolt, K. Jill, 2719
Kienzle, Kathleen J., 2869
Kilbourne, Jean, 1579, 2212
Kilbourne, William E., 2213
Kilgore, Margaret, 1954
Kilguss, Anne F., 1663
Kimball, M. M., 1478
Kim Jae Hee, 766
Kim Sook-hyun, 534
Kindem, Gorham A., 58, 1207
King, Ellie, 2214
King, J., 1102
King, Katie, 1534
King, Linda, 1507
King, Mae C., 2139
King, S. S., 26
Kingman, Merle, 2808
Kinikar, Shashikant, 681
Kinross, Felicity, 897
Kinsley, Sarah M., 2196
Kinzer, Nora Scott, 2367
Kippax, Susan, 200
Kirby, Malcolm, 1669
Kirkendall, Lester, 1728
Kirkpatrick, J. T., 2368
Kishwar, Madhu, 425, 535

Author Index

Kisner, Arlene, 1955
Kisner, Ronald E., 2506
Kitman, Marvin, 3147
Klapper, Zina, 3144
Kleberg, Madeleine, 167, 932, 1201, 1208
Klein, Marie Luise, 1103
Klein, Meryl A., 2441
Kleipool, Hans, 297
Klenicki, Ana R., 63
Klever, Anita, 2870
Klimpel, Alvarado Felícitas, 1429
Kline, Helen, G., 3200
Kline, Jeff, 2355
Klingbeil, Julie A., 1738
Knapp, Sharon, 1515
Knight, Annette, 64
Knight, Mary, 1956
Knightley, Philip, 238
Knill, Barbara J., 2215
Knopp, S., 886
Knudson, Jerry, 240
Knupka, L. R., 2268
Koch, Beverly Stephen, 3201
Koch, Christian, 2507
Kodama, M., 536
Kodesh, Wolfie, 356
Koerber, C., 1102
Kohler, Pam Sebastian, 2589
Kokohiwa, Milda, 201
Kolbe, R. H., 2224
Komisar, Lucy, 2202, 2216
Kon, Hidemi, 767
Kong, A. C., 168
Konie, Gwendoline, 268
Koon, Helene, 999
Korabik, Karen, 537
Korzenny, Betty Ann, 1379
Korzenny, Felipe, 1379
Kotelmann, Joachim, 1104
Kotz, Liz, 169
Koumba-Tessa, Albertine, 312
Kovacs, Midge, 1624
Kowalski, Rosemary Ribich, 1699
Kramarae, Cheris, 23, 65, 257, 1562
Kramer, Cheris, 2590
Kranich, Kimberlie A., 3135, 3202
Krendl, Kathy, 1560, 1563
Kretsinger, Geneva, 1776
Krichmar, Albert, 66
Krippendorff, Sultana, 538
Krishnan, Prabha, 51, 539, 582
Krogh, Elizabeth C., 2390

Kroll, Becky Swanson, 23
Kronhausen, Eberhard, 1564
Kronhausen, Phyllis, 1564
Krouse, Agate Nesaule, 2588, 2591
Kruglak, Theodore E., 1957
Kuchendoff, 1083
Kuchenhoff, E., 936
Kugler, Israel, 1958
Kuhn, Annette, 170, 284-285, 937
Kuhn, Irene, 1959
Kulkarni, V. G., 426, 444, 467
Kumar, Jai, 708
Kundya, Hilda L., 316
Kuney, Jack, 2871
Kunzle, David, 1000-1001
Kurokochi, Paul, 768
Kurtz, Camille, 313
Kuusela, Leila, 1105
Kweka, Aikael, 210
Kyaruzi, Agnes, 319, 328

Lachance, Charles C., 2184
Lafferty, William, 1679
Lafky, Sue, 1535
LaFollette, Marcel C., 2592
La Guardia, Robert, 1664, 1677
Laine, P., 1106
Lal, Rama Shanker, 457
Lammers, H. B., 2723
Lamont, Helen Otis, 3203
Lamoureux, Diane, 1516
Lamphere, Louise, 286
Lance, Elizabeth P., 2809
Landsberg, Michele, 2872
Landy, Marcia, 57
Laner, Mary R., 171, 3204
Lang, Gladys Engel, 2170
Lang, Marjory, 1462
Langford, Gerald, 1960
Langham, Barbara, 3205
Lanot, Marra P., 427
Lant, Antonia, 1131
Lanyi, Ronald Levitt, 3051
Lapin, Jackie, 240
La Place, Maria, 1700
Larkin, Alile Sharon, 247
Larrain, Bárbara, 1381
Larsen, Arthur J., 1961
Larsson, Lisbeth, 1153-1154
Lasagni, M. Cristina, 964
Lasorsa, Dominic L., 2593
Lauffer, Jurgen, 1119

Author Index 437

Laurikietis, R., 134
Lavaerts, C., 939
Laverde Toscano, María Cristina, 1328
Lavin, Maud, 2140, 2369
Lavoisier, Bénédicte, 1107
Lavrin, Asunción, 1415
Lawhn, Juanita Luna, 2594
Lawrence, David, 3052
Lawrenson, Helen, 3053
Lazar, Joyce, 1676
Lazar, Kay, 3054
Lazaro, Cecilia L., 259, 709
Lazarsfield, Paul, 1772
Lazer, Charles, 2595
Lazere, Donald, 1546, 1673, 1723, 2687
Lazier-Smith, Linda, 1535
Lazreg, Marnia, 329
Leader, Elizabeth, 2390
Lealand, Geoff, 856
Leavitt, Judith A., 3055
Lebra, Joyce, 428, 540
Ledden, Sean, 541
Leder, Gilah C., 817-818
Lee, Carole, 2479
Lee, John, 2596, 2776
Lee, Kyong-ja, 474
Lee, Marilyn, 1002-1003
Lee, Myong-ha, 769
Lee, Philip, 41
Lee, Stan, 2597
Lee, Wai Keong, 770
Leggett, Dawn, 2660
Lehrer, S. K., 2339
Leidholdt, Dorchen, 1565
Leigh, J. H., 1633, 2194, 2240, 2250
Leigh, T. W., 2217-2218
Leinfellner, Christine, 958
Leman, Joy, 5, 1004
Lemmer, Eleanor M., 330
Lemon, Judith, 2170, 2370-2371
Lent, John A., 429-430, 710, 1356, 2029
Lentz, Rose Mary, 3206
Lenz, Carolyn M., 1962
Leonard, Mary, 2873
Lerner, M., 1554
Lesage, Julia, 287, 711, 1433
Levan, Kathryn, 2372
Level, Hildegard, 2949
Levelt, Peter, 1108
Levere, June, 1722
Levi, Stephen C., 2441
Levin, Jack, 2650
Levin, Tobe, 771

Levine, Ellen, 1553
Levine, Maryle C., 2984
Levinson, Richard, 2598
Levy, Daniella, 2479
Levy, Darline, 1005
Levy, Gilbert, 2464
Lewartowska, Zofia, 876
Lewis, Cherie S., 1665
Lewis, Cora G., 2765
Lewis, Jack, 1459
Lewis, Jill, 2141
Lewis, Kathleen Kearny, 1963, 3056
Lewis, Lisa A., 15, 1561, 1666, 2310, 2373-2374
Lewis, Nancy Madison, 1964, 3057
Lewis, Paula Gilbert, 1508
Lichter, Linda, 2376
Lichter, S. Robert, 2376
Liden, Karin, 896
Lieberman, Leonard, 1667
Lieberman, Leslie, 1667
Liebert, Robert M., 2320, 2415
Liebes, Tamar, 206
Liebman, Nina, 1679
Liehm, Mira, 1210
Lihamba, Amandina, 331
Li Li, 712
Liljencrantz, Christina, 12
Lilli, Laura, 941
Lim, Linda Y. C., 431
Limbacher, James L., 68
Lind, Agneta, 210
Linden-van Ruiten, Ank, 1212
Linderman, Deborah, 60
Lindfors, Bernth, 332
Lindsay, Beverly, 69
Lindsay, Malvina, 1739
Linné, Olga, 1213
Linz, David, 1536, 1701-1702
Lippe, G., 1065
Lippincott, Sara J., 1965
Lipsitz, George, 17, 1679
Liquori, Laura, 1966
Lisenby, Fay, 2599
List, Judith A., 2377
List, Karen K., 1967-1970
Lista, Carlos Alberto, 1319
Littell, Joseph F., 1668
Livermore, Mary A., 2092
Lloyd, Jerome, 1566
Locher-Scholten, Elsbeth, 542
Lockeretz, Sarah W., 2185, 2269
Lockridge, Kay, 3058

438 Author Index

Lockwood, Audrey E., 593
Lockwood, Sara L., 2071
Logarta, Lita Torralba, 475
Loken, B., 2705
Long, Michele, 2378
Longo, Gioia, 78, 83
Longo di Cristofaro, Gioia, 1110
Longreen, Hanne, 70
Lonial, S. C., 1629
Lont, Cynthia M., 2379
Loomis, James W., 2463
Lopate, Carol, 1759, 2380
Loree, M., 172
Losco, Jean, 2267
Lott, Bernice, 2381
Lott, Sylvia, 1006
Loughlin, Beverly, 2600
Love, Gail, 1669
Lovelock, Molly, 1744
Lowe, Andrew, 926
Lowell, Joan, 1972
Lowell, Sandra, 255
Lowry, Dennis T., 1661, 1669
Lubitz, Amy, 2184
Lublin, Joann S., 3059-3060
Lucas, Bob, 2508
Luckett, Perry D., 2142
Luebke, Barbara F., 2601-2603
Lueck, Therese L., 1973
Lugenbeel, Barbara Derrick, 2604
Luisi, Paulina, 1430
Lukowitz, Karlene, 2810
Lull, J., 1567
Lull, James T., 2382-2383
Lumby, Malcolm E., 3061
Lund, Sissel, 78, 83, 950, 1155-1156
Lundstrom, William J., 2209, 2219, 2250, 2256
Lupino, Ida, 2950
Lutz, Alma, 1974
Lyon, Elisabeth, 1214
Lyson, Thomas A., 2711
Lysonski, S., 1111, 2220

McAnany, Emile G., 3172
McArthur, Leslie Zebrowitz, 2221, 2384
McBride, Genevieve G., 1760, 2606
McBride, Mary Margaret, 1755, 1777
McBride, Sarah E., 1975
MacBride, Sean, 173
McCabe, Trisha, 1294
McCaffrey, Kathleen M., 314, 333

McCall, Patricia Ellen, 3062
McCallister, Linda, 209
McCallum, D. M., 2607
McCauley, C., 2222
McClelland, Doug, 2951
McClelland, W. D., 1292
McCleneghan, J. Sean, 2875
McCormack, Thelma, 124, 1534, 1568, 2143, 2648, 2720
McCormick, Ruth, 713
McCormick-Pickett, Nancy, 2876
McClymer, John F., 2119
McCracken, Ellen, 1329, 3207-3208
McCraken, Elizabeth, 1976
McCreadie, Marsha, 2952
McCullough, Caroline, 1114
McCullough, Gordon L., 1778
McCullum, Pamela, 1517
McDermott, Stan, 1408
MacDonald, David, 1456
McDonald, Duncan, 2984
MacDonald, Heidi, 2608
MacDonald, Kenneth, 1729
MacDonald, Patrick T., 2328
McDonnell, Lynda, 1587, 3064
McEachran, Angus, 2984
Macek, Carl, 1734
McGarry, Eileen, 288
McGhee, P. E., 2385
McGillivray, Katherine, 239
McGlashan, Zena Beth, 1946, 1977-1979, 3209
McGough, Barbara, 847
McGuigan, Dorothy G., 1569
McHugh, Mary, 2503
McIntyre, P., 2223
McKay, A., 65
McKenna, Ethel M., 1840
McKerns, Joseph P., 2773
Mackey, W. D., 2386
MacKinnon, Janice, 1980
MacKinnon, Stephen, 1980
Macklin, M. C., 2224
MacLachlan, Colin, 1395
MacLean, Malcolm S., jr., 2740
McLellan, Iain, 334
McLendon, Winola, 3065
McLeod, Merikay, 3066
McMullen, L. M., 2239
McMullen, Lorraine, 1462
McNeil, Jean C., 2358, 2387-2388, 2427
McPhee, Hilary, 814
MacPherson, Myra, 3067

McRae, Christine, 2225
McReynolds, Louise, 898
McRobbie, Angela, 71, 124, 1148, 1293-1294
Madhok, Sujata, 399, 543, 582, 714
Madjdi, Sofia, 335
Madrigal, Margaret, 95
Madsen, Axel, 2953
Maes, L., 942
Mahmood, H., 583
Maignien, M., 1269
Majumder, Kumar Sankar, 857
Makhijani, Savitri, 715
Makita, Tetsuo, 544-545
Malamuth, Neil M., 1571-1572, 1703, 1730
Malay, Armando, 476, 716, 772
Mallick, Amal Kumar, 639
Mamonova, Tatyana, 877, 887
Mandato, Daria, 2199
Manduit, Jean, 1112
Manes, Audrey L., 2389
Mangeskar, Lata, 681
Mann, Denise, 17, 1679, 1705, 1763
Mann, Judy, A-24
Mann, Margaret, 1157
Mann, Patricia, 175, 819
Mann, Susan Karol, 2401
Manns, Ulla, 1113
Manstead, A. S. R., 1114
Mant, Andrea, 820
Manushi Collective, 774
Mapp, Edward, 2509
Marberry, M. M., 1981
March, Robert M., 836
Marchetti, Gina, 546, 1561
Marecek, Jeanne, 1559, 2390
Marende, Doreen N., 2391
Mareuil, Chantal, 48
Mariani, John, 2392
Marine, Gene, 1573
Mariño, Nery, 1406
Marken, Edith May, 1982
Marques de Melo, Jose, 1407
Marquez, Floredelindo T., 547
Marrades, M. Isabel, 952
Marschall, Rick, 1983
Marsh, Marion, 858
Marshall, Jane P., 1587
Marshall, V. W., 1484
Marshment, Margaret, 2676
Martin, C. R., jr., 1633, 2194, 2240, 2250

Martin, Graham, 1293
Martin, Marcel, 1215
Martin, Michèle, 18, 72, 1463, 1574
Martin, Ralph G., 1984
Martin, Richard R., 1408
Martineau, Barbara Halpern, 73, 255
Martinelli, Adriana, 1115
Marting, Leeda, 2877
Martyna, Wendy, 1575
Marx, Michael J., 2383
Marzolf, Marion, 1576, 1754, 1945, 1985-1988
Masel-Walters, Lynne, 1754, 1989-1992, 3210
Mashita, Shin'ichi, 548
Masse, Michele A., 2226
Masterman, L., 265
Masters, Lynn, 2227
Matabane, Paula, 1535
Matacin, Mala L., 2609
Matelski, Marilyn J., 1670, 2393
Matera, Fran, 2610
Mathai, Rabia, 640
Mather, Anne, 1945, 1993-1994
Mathew, Rae, 799
Mathews, Wilma, 1630
Mathu, Eunice Njambi, 268, 353
Mathur, J. C., 641
Mathur, P. N., 619-620
Matkov, Rebecca Roper, 3211
Matre, Marc, 2649
Matsui, Y., 549
Matsuzawa, Kazuko, 432, 642
Mattelart, Armand, 203, 1420
Mattelart, Michèle, 74-75, 78, 83, 202-203, 241, 1330, 1419-1420
Matthews, Daniel G., 313
Matthews, Mary L., 2611
Matusow, Barbara, 2878
Matzen, Robert D., 2955
Mauriac, Claude, 1116
Mawby, Rob I., 1117
May, John R., 2941
Mayer, Henry, 175, 289, 821-822
Mayes, Sandra L., 1641, 2394
Maykovich, M. K., 174
Mayne, Judith, 1295
Mayorca, E., 1408
Mazuera, Migdaléder, 1331
Mazumdar, Vina, 643
Mazzeo, Joseph Anthony, 2351
Meade, M., 1577
Meaders, Margaret I., 1995

Meadow, Wendy, 2669
Meadowcroft, Jeanne M., 2721
Mechanic, Mindy R., 1712
Meehan, Diana M., 2395
Meeks, Corina, 1369
Mehta, Subhash C., 550
Meier, Uta, 51, 1118, 1158, 2396
Meijer, Maaike, 1305
Melcher, Dale, 16
Melischek, Gabrielle, 2437
Mellen, Joan, 551-553, 2510
Melnyk, Paula, 2389
Melony, Mrs. William Brown, 2765
Melton, G. W., 2228
Melville, Joy, 1296
Melvin, Frances, 2146
Menezes, Ervell E., 1216
Mentzler, Carolyn A., 2879
Mercadier, Marthe, 944
Merrill, John C., 2776
Merrill, Lisa, 2755
Merritt, Sharyne, 3184, 3212
Messaris, Paul, 1672
Metz, Augst, 17
Meulenbelt, Anja, 1266
Mevissen, Annemarie, 935
Meyer, Annie Nathan, 1874
Meyer, Katherine, 1996
Mhaiki, P. J., 315
Michael, Mrs. Elias R., 2071
Michel, Andrée, 172, 945, 1217
Middlemiss, Mary Ann, 2206
Mielke, Keith W., 1644
Mikhail, M. N., 380
Mikos, Lothar, 1104, 1119
Miles, Betty, 2397
Miles, Janet, 2725
Miles, Virginia, 204
Miller, Beth, 1357
Miller, Casey, 2147
Miller, Debra A., 1630
Miller, Edward M., 2612
Miller, Francesca, 1332
Miller, Lynn Fieldman, 2956
Miller, M. Mark, 179, 2398
Miller, Mark Crispin, 2880
Miller, Perry, 1997
Miller, Peter, 1998
Miller, Randall M., 2493
Miller, Susan H., 2560, 2613, 2984, 3213
Miller, William D., 1999
Milligan, Susan, 3214

Millner, C., 3069
Mills, J., 1600
Mills, Janet, 1731
Mills, Kay, 1587, 2136, 2777, 2881, 3070-3073
Millum, Trevor, 290
Miner, M. M., 2741
Miner, Ward L., 2000
Minervini, Estela Marip, 1318
Minney, Doris, 1753
Minton, Lynn, 2511
Mirsky, Norman, 2125
Mitchel, Delores, 2614
Mitra, Sumit, 681
Mix, J. I., 1780
Miyazaki, Toshiko, 644
Mizejewski, Linda, 58, 1704
Mlama, Penina M., 303, 346
Moan, Pat, 1122
Modig, Maria, 905
Modleski, Tania, 61, 80, 1673, 2512, 2679
Mohammadi, Ali, 1589
Mohd. Hamdan Adnan, 433, 554, 718
Möhrmann, Renate, 1218
Mojumdar, Modhumita, 582
Molloy, Vicki, 853, 863
Moloteh, Harvey L., 2170
Monji, Jana, 555
Montague, Susan P., 1639, 2368
Monteiro, Anjali, 2
Monteiro, Rita, 127
Moody, John, 1391
Mooney, Linda, 2544 2615
Moore, Roy L., 2646
Moorehead, Caroline, 966
Moorman, Jay, 2536
Mora, Carl J., 1380
Moran, Albert, 802
Moran, Barbara, 2202, 2216
Mordden, Ethan, 2957
Moreton, Andrew, 2576
Morgan, Elaine, 296
Morgan, Janice M., 1219
Morgan, Margaret Knox, 3074
Morgan, Michael, 2399
Morgan, Robin, 1580
Morin, E., 910
Moritz, Marguerite J., 2400
Morley, Ann, 1302
Morley, David, 1171
Morris, Gloria C., 3075
Morris, Michele, 2882

Author Index 441

Morris, Monica B., 2616-2617
Morton, Richard, 997
Moslem, Shima, 434, 719
Moto, Hagio, 789
Mott, Frank Luther, 2002
Movido, Monica S., 645
Movshovitz, Howard, 2513
Moynihan, Mary M., 2169
Mrazkova, Daniela, 243, 1392, 2003
Mueller, Carol, 1732
Muir, Anne Ross, 1220
Muir, Florabel, 3076
Mulac, Anthony, 1567, 2401
Mulay, Vijaya, 556
Mulhern, Chieko Irie, 435, 478
Müller, Jutta, 946
Mulvey, Laura, 60, 245, 947
Muramatsu, Yasuko, 436, 544-545, 557-559, 646, 720
Murphy, Mary, 2958
Murphy, Sharon M., 1582, 1587, 2041
Murray, Ellen M., 23
Murray, Janet Horowitz, 990
Murthy, P. V. S., 647
Musa, A. B. M., 433, 450
Muskens, G. J., 948
Mussell, K., 1733
Musser, Charles, 1131
Mwenda, Deborah, 319
Mwendamseke, Nancy, 127
Mydans, Carl, 2004
Myers, Margaret L., 3016
Myers, Mildred S., 1620

Nadler, Lawrence B., 1583
Nadler, Marjorie Keeshan, 1583
Nadotti, Maria, 1173
Naether, Carl A., 2706
Naga, Nihal, 351
Nagelschmidt, Ana M., 1409
Nagy, Márta, 875
Nakajima, Iwao, 648
Nakashira, Tumiko, 479
Nakpil, Carmen Guerrero, 775
Narciso, Minnie, 794
Nardone, Carroll Ann Ferguson, 1535
Nash, Abigail Jones, 2883-2884
Nash, Alana, 3077
Nash, June, 1419
Nash, Sharon C., 2453
Nasha, Margaret, 357
Nathan, D. V., 560, 721

National Commission on the Role of Filipino Women, 561-564
National Press Club, Philippines, 722
Natkin, Ritva, 1121
Nava, Mica, 1148
Ndulo, Winnie N., 347
Nelson, Beth, 296
Nelson, Joyce, 2230
Nelson, Malcolm, 2886
Nelson, Sharon H., 1453
Nettler, Lydia, 16
Neuendorf, Kimberly, 1654, 2278
Neumann, A. Lin, 724
Neustatter, Angela, 1297
Nevard, Jacques, 725
Neverla, Irene, 919, 935, 1222
Newfield, Jack, 3078
Newkirk, Carole Ruth, 3215
Newland, Kathleen, 81, 176
Newsom, Doug, 1630
Newton, Barbara J., 177, 1640
Newton, Nancy, 1405
NiCarty, Ginny, 1713
Nicholls, Jill, 1122
Nichols, Bill, 1710
Nicholson, Eliza Jane, 2005
Nicholson, J., 2205
Niehof, Anke, 542
Nightingale, Virginia, 15
Nigro, Georgia N., 2618
Nilsen, Alleen-Pace, 2619
Nimmo, D., 1526
Nirmala, 20, 777
Nlomo, Jacqueline Abema, 336
Noble, Iris, 2006
Noelle-Neumann, Elisabeth, 82, 1229
Nolan, John D., 2404
North, Sandre, 1585
Northcott, Herbert C., 2405
Noschese, Christine, 2148
Nowak, Kjell, 1250
Nozkova, Marta, 358
NSW Women's Advisory Council, 801
Nugent, Andrea, 1509
Nuita, Yoko, 650
Nunn, Curtis, 2008
Nweke, T., 363
Nye, Russel B., 1298

Oakley, A., 90
O'Bryan, K., 1510
O'Bryant, Shirley L., 2406

O'Connor, Harvey, 2009
O'Connor, Jessie Lloyd, 2009
O'Connor, John E., 1635
O'Connor, John J., 2407, 3147
O'Connor, P. J., 2262
O'Donnell, Karen J., 1559, 2231
O'Donnell, William J., 1559, 2231
Oduyoye, Marcy Amba, 76
Oehler, Carolyn Henninger, 84
Oermann, Bob, 1527
Oettinger, Mal, 2887
Office of the Status of Women, Canberra, 823-824
Office of Women's Affairs, Canberra, 825
Ogan, Christine, 293, 3079-3082
Oglesby, Catharine, 2010
Ohashi, Terue, 651
Ohkum, Yukiko, 726
O'Keefe, John, 2888
O'Kelly, Charlotte G., 1615, 2207, 2408-2409
Okigbo, Charles, 51, 244, 337
Okwenje, Elizabeth, 268
Oldham, Ellen M., 2011
Oliven, Ruben G., 1402
Olson, Alma Louise, 3083
Olson, George L., 432
Ontiveros, Suzanne R., 1313
Opole, Monica, 359
Oppenheim, Beatrice, 1753
O'Reilly, Jane, 3216
Orenstein, Peggy, 2889
Ortiz, Jeanne A., 3217
Ortiz, Larry P., 3217
Orwant, Jack, 2149
Osborn, Suzanne, 2232
Osborne, Graeme, 95
Osei Boadu, Samuel, 1646, 1660
Oskamp, S., 2341
Osman, Mariam, 304
Ostman, Ronald E., 616
Ott, Louise, 2779
Oukrop, Carol, 77
Overstreet, Robert M., 1734

Padgaonkar, Latika, 1224
Padilla, Dolores, 1421, 1439
Paillard, B., 910
Paisley, William, 1559, 1715-1716, 2111, 2207, 2236
Paisner, Daniel, 2890

Palmegiano, E. M., 951
Palmer, Patricia, 837
Palmquist, Peter E., 2013
Palys, T. S., 1482
Panday, Narendra R., 433, 450
Pandey, U. S., 175, 809
Pannill, Linda, 2514
Pantzer, Sara, 848
Parish, James R., 2959-2962
Park, Yong-Sang, 433, 440
Parker, Cornelia Stratton, 2014
Parker, Douglas, 1459
Parkes, Bessie Rayner, 1007
Parkinson, Laura, 1483
Parsons, Harriet, 2891
Parsons, Louella O., 2015
Parton, James, 1965
Pasadeos, Yorgo, 2791
Pasha, Shireen, 439
Pasley, Kay, 2620
Patel, Vibhuti, 399, 566
Pathak, Ila, 50, 399, 567-569, 779-780
Patil, B. R., 632
Patterson, Elizabeth L., 1735
Patterson, Lindsay, 2509
Patton, Wendy McDonald, 2016
Paul, Charlotte, 3084
Paulson, Joy, 428, 540
Pauwels, Anne, 826
Payne, Ethel L., 240
Peacocke, Nora E., 1369
Pearl, David, 1676
Peary, Gerald, 237
Peck, Ellen, 2410, 2566
Peckham, Linda, 60
Pecora, N., 2648
Pedersen, Vibeke, 50, 70, 78, 83
Peeradina, Saleem, 178
Peevers, Barbara H., 2411
Peirce, Kate, 1586
Pellegrini, Sylvia, 1401
Pelletier, Francine, 18, 1502
Pendleton, John, 1617
Penley, Constance, 245
Penolidis, Tina, 1225
Penrod, S., 1701-1702
Perdue, Lauren, 2412
Perebinossoff, Philippe, 2621
Pereira, Regina Paranhos, 1416
Peres, B., 1410
Perinat, Adolfo, 952
Perini, Maria-Grazia, 48
Perkins, Roberta, 175, 827

Perlmutter, Ruth, 57
Perloff, Richard M., 179, 2215
Pernito, Virgilio L., 652
Perry, Eleanor, 1570
Perry, John W., 2018
Pervez, Seema, 570, 653
Pescatello, Ann, 1321, 1334
Pesch, Marina A., 2215
Peters, Margot, 2588, 2591
Petersen, Angela, 338
Peterson, R. A., 1577
Peterson, Robin T., 1736, 2234
Petersson, Birgit, 1008
Petro, Patrice, 1009
Petruzzello, Marion C., 2622
Petty, Sheila, 18, 339
Peyrinaud, Franck, 944
Pfaff, Eugene E., 2936, 2963
Pfeiffer, Sarah Fields, 1753
Phadnis, Urmila, 441
Pham-Tung, 728
Phillips, E. Barbara, 2170
Phillips, G. M., A-55
Phillips, Susana, 1446
Philport, Joseph C., 2822
Pichanick, Valerie K., 2019
Picó, Isabel, 1367
Picon Garfield, Evelyn, 1358
Piehl, Mel, 2020
Pierce, Chester M., 2413
Pierce, Paula, 2021
Pierce-Gonzalez, Diane, 2413
Pierre, 1226
Piliavin, Jane Allyn, 2390
Pinckaers, L., 928
Pineda, Magaly, 54, 1352
Pines, Ayala M., 1601
Pingree, Suzanne, 125, 1645, 1674, 2207, 2235-2236
Pinsky, Mark, 3085
Pip, Chris, 858
Pitts, Michael R., 2964
Piva, Paola, 964
Pivot, Agnes, 213
Place, J., 246
Plehal, Robert, 2271
Poe, Alison, 2207, 2237
Pogrebin, Letty Cottin, 2892
Polini, Anne, 944
Pollarola, Giovanna, 1432
Pollock, John C., 1102, 2811
Pool, Gail, 3218-3219
Popkin, Nancy, 240

Popkin, Zelda, 2022
Porter, Natalie, 2200
Porter, Sarah Harvey, 1831, 2023
Portuges, Catherine E., 1123
Posner, Judith, 1484, 1579, 2414
Post, Linda Currey, 2812
Poteet Bussard, Lavonne C., 1353
Potkay, Catherine E., 1737-1738
Potkay, Charles R., 1737-1738
Potter, Jeffrey, 2024
Potter, W. J., 2623
Poulos, Rita Wicks, 2320, 2415
Powers, Elizabeth, 428
Powers, Janet, 571
Powers, John, 2507
Powers, Thom, 3086
Poynten, Beverly, 15
Prather, Jane, 2238
Pratt, William J., 1807
Prendergast, Alan, 3087
President, Patricia A., 2670
Press, Andrea, 15, 37, 1675, 2680
Press, Tina, 2893
Preston, Ann E., 2624
Prevratilova, Gabriela, 85
Pribram, E. Deidre, 247
Prieto de Zegarra, Judith, 1440
Prisco, Dorothy D., 2625
Probert, Christina, 3220
Probyn, Elspeth, 18, 1485
Proulx, Serge, 1560
Provencher, Raymonde, 1502
Punwani, Jyoti, 572
Purnell, Sandra E., 1620
Purohit, Madhavi, 680
Pursey, George, 2215
Putnam, Linda L., 180
Pyes, C., 1554
Pyke, S. W., 1486

Quam, Jean K., 2626
Quart, Barbara K., 249, 899
Quimpo, Candy, 729
Quinn, Sally, 2894
Quiñones, Wendy B., 2151
Quiroz, María Teresa, 1411
Quiroz, Teresita, 1381

Rabinovitz, Lauren Holly, 2965
Raborg, Frederick A., 1722
Rachlin, Susan Kessler, 2627

Author Index

Radecki, Thomas, 20
Radio Telefís Eireann, 954-955
Radway, Janice A., 1534, 1740, A-15
Rai, Kumkum, 611
Raices, M., 1510
Rainer, Yvonne, 60, 3152
Rainey, Buck, 2966
Rak, D. S., 2239
Rakos, Richard F., 1597
Rakow, Lana, 37, 1534-1535, 1588-1590
Ralston, Esther, 2967
Ramanathan, Kamala, 781
Ramazanova, Nelia, 291, 900
Ramesh, Asha, 582
Ramírez Berg, Charles, 1382
Ramsdell, M. L., 2416
Ramsey, Cynthia, 3153
Ramzi, Nahid, 385
Randall, Margaret, 1335
Rao, Leela, 51, 573-574
Rao, Purnima, 51, 445, 539
Rapping, Elayne, 3154
Rarick, Galen, 2742
Ratnavibhushana, Ashley, 730
Rauch, Gail E., 2190
Raudy, Jack, 2725
Rawie, Mrijke, 1266
Rawlins, W. K., A-55
Rawnsley, David E., 1741
Ray, L., 1591
Ray, Michèle, 1228
Raymond, Janice G., 1565
Rayne, Mrs. M. L., 2025
Rayns, Tony, 575
Red, Isagani V., 654
Reed, Barbara Straus, 2781, 3221
Reed, Charles Gordon, 3089
Reed, Linda, 1592
Reed, Rex, 1706
Reep, Diane C., 2287, 2312, 2417-2419, 2895
Reeves, Byron, 2398
Reeves, Jimmie L., 1717
Reichenbach, T. L., 2217
Reid, Alison, 255
Reid, Charlotte T., 2896
Reid, Leonard N., 2240-2241, 2257-2258, 2628
Reid, Pamela Trotman, 2420
Reid, Thomas R., 576
Reimann, Helga, 205
Reiner, John, 3090
Reinholt, Ferdina, 2026

Reinstein, P. Gila, 2629
Renas, Stanley R., 2124
Renov, Michael, 1705, 1802-1803
Rentz, J. O., 2743
Repetti, R. L., 2421
Reskin, Barbara F., 2782
Resko, Beth Gabrielle, 2221
Rethans, A. J., 2217-2218
Reumann, K., 1229
Reuss, Carol, 1552, 2611
Revett, J., 1624
Reweti, Debra, A-6
Reyes, Elma, 1350
Reyes, Emmanuel A., 577
Reyes-Matta, Fernando, 1341
Reynaud, Bérénice, 3152
Reynolds, Barbara, 1587
Reynolds, F. D., 2743
Reynolds, Kimberley, 1010
Reynolds, Lessie M., 1124
Rhodes, Jane, 1535
Ribeiro, Jorge, 782
Ricciotti, Dominic, 2027
Rice, James H., 1753
Rich, B. Ruby, 3152
Rich, Carole, 1722
Richardson, Anna Steele, 1739
Richardson, John, 806
Richardson, L., 184
Richardson, Lou, 1742
Richer, William L. 578
Richter, Linda K., 578
Rickel, Annette U., 1593
Riffe, Daniel Helene Goldson, 2242
Riger, Stephanie, 2630
Riha, Jeanne, 2631
Rihani, M., 181
Riley, Sam G., 2028-2029
Ringgold, Gene, 1807
Ringwalt, Jessie E., 2030
Rinnert, Ulrike, 956
Rintala, Jan, 2632
Riti, M. D., 579
Rittenhouse, Mignon, 2031
Rivadue, Barry, 2968
Rivers, Caryl, 77, 1552, 2153, 2633
Rivers, William L., 2634
Robarts, Sadie, 1230
Robb, Inez, 1739, 2032
Robbins, Jim, 1612
Robbins, Trina, 1734, 3091
Roberts, Elizabeth J., 1676
Roberts, Helen, 90

Roberts, Nancy L., 1761, 1868, 2033, 2635
Roberts, Robin, 2636
Robertson, E. Arnot, 1125
Robins, Marjorie A., 3145
Robinson, Gertrude J., 78, 83, 91-92, 124, 231, 1231, 1444-1445, 1455, 1466, 1511
Robinson, J. D., 2737
Robinson, Lillian S., 93
Rocard, G., 1126
Rock, Marcia, 2902-2903
Rodenhuis, Ynske, 1266
Rodi, Rob, 1743
Rodriguez, M., 2154
Rodríguez Calderón, Mirta, 1336-1337
Roesgen, Joan, 2637
Roff, Sandra Shoick, 2034
Rokeach, Milton, 1615
Rolland, Asle, 1127
Roloff, M. E., 2422
Romanow, Walter I., 1489
Romero, Patricia W., 1232
Rook, Susan, 3092
Roos, Patricia A., 2782
Roosevelt, Eleanor, 2035
Root, Jane, 94, 182
Rose, Brian, 1660, 1677
Rose, Jacqueline, 245
Rosen, Marjorie, 1804-1805, 2940, 3155
Rosen, S. L., 1567
Rosenbaum, Mitchell, 3152
Rosenberg, Jan, 3156
Rosenblum, Karen, 2226
Rosengren, Karl Erik, 1250, 2437
Rosenham, Mollie, 888
Rosolato, Guy, 60
Ross, Andrew, 183, 2310
Ross, Bonnie L., 2550
Ross, Catherine, 2668
Ross, Ishbel, 1753, 2036
Ross, John E., 2671
Ross, L., 2423
Ross, M., 1102
Ross, Madelyn, 2984
Rossi, Lee, 2638
Rossiter, John R., 1631
Rossler, Patrick, 1159
Rosten, Leo C., 2037
Roth, Morry, 1612
Rothman, Stanley, 2376
Rottenberg, Dan, 3093
Rounds, David, 1647

Rouse, Morleen Getz, 1781
Rowland, Mary, 3094
Royale, Gloria, 1369
Royes, Heather, 1369
Rozin, P., 2222
Rubin, B., 1594
Rubin, Bernard, 2153
Rubin, Donald R., 23
Rubinstein, Eli A., 1653, 2335, 2347, 2440
Ruble, Diane N., 2243
Ruffner, Marguerite Anne, 2722
Ruggierio, Jacqueline A., 2639-2641
Rupp, Leila J., 184
Rush, Ramona, 21, 27, 95-96, 208, 283, 293, 1074, 1240, 1338-1339, 1363, 1756, 1945, 1988, 2750, 2760, 2793, 3133, 3142, 3228
Russ, Joanna, 2783
Russell, Becky, 2784
Russell, Victor, 2813
Russman, Linda, 2785
Ruths, May Britt, 919
Ryan, Mary P., 1806
Ryan, Michele, 909
Rykken, Rolf, 3095
Rysman, Alexander, 1757

Sadoul, Jacques, 957
Saenger, Gerhart, 2642
Safa, Helen Icken, 1419
Safilios-Rothschild, Constantina, 1128, 1591
Sagan, Leontine, 1233
Sailor, Patricia, 2758
St. John, Jacqueline, 1782
Saito, Kenji, 655
Salber, Wilhelm, 1129
Salmon, Claudine, 783
Salutin, Rick, 2155
Sammon, Virginia, 3096
Samra, Risë, 2097
Sanborn, Sara, 1581
Sanchez de Rota, Gilda, 1379
Sanders, Marion K., 2038
Sanders, Marlene, 77, 240, 1587, 2897-2903
Sandler, Joanne, 97
Sanford, David, 1234
Sanger, Margaret, 2039-2040
Sangregorio, Inga-Lisa, 507
Sanna, Caterian Porcu, 1115

Santa Cruz, Adriana, 54, 1339-1342, 1396, 1412
Santi, Tina, 1624, 2814
Santiago-Marazzi, Rosa, 1354
Santos, Rubens de Costa, 1422
Sapolsky, Barry S., 2450
Sardar, Nazli, 1092
Sargent, Alice G., 185
Sarthe, Jean, 2969
Sasidharan, Rekha M., 580
Sassi, Sinikka, 360
Sathe, V. P., 679
Sato, Tadao, 581
Sattler, John E., 2815
Saunders, Carole S., 2244
Saunders, Eileen, 98
Savitch, Jessica, 2904
Sax, Marjan, 916
Saxton, Kelly, 2242
Sayles, Marnie, 2719
Scantlebury, Marcia, 1383
Schaap, Jetty, 1305
Schaffer, Kay, 828
Schamber, Linda, 1535
Schanke, Robert A., 2970
Schanne, Michael, 1177
Scheibe, Cyndy, 2245
Schiller, Patricia, 1595
Schilpp, Madelon Golden, 2041
Schmidt, Lisa, 2446
Schmidt, Nancy J., 340
Schneider, Carole S., 2924
Schneider, Cynthia, 1433, 2369
Schneider, Kenneth C., 2246-2247
Schneider, Norma, 1945, 2042
Schneider, Sharon Barich, 2247
Schnitman, Jorge, 3172
Schodt, Frederik L., 446
Schofield, Ann, 2043, A-15
Schofield, S., 1084
Scholand, Hildegard, 919
Scholtes, Mary C., 2971
Scholtz-Klink, Gertrud, 1011
Schoonmaker, Mary Ellen, 2972, 3098
Schrank, Louise Welsh, 2515
Schreiber, E. M., 1596
Schreider, Rosemary, 3099
Schrib, June, 2643
Schroeder, Harold E., 1597
Schudson, Michael, 1762
Schuetz, Stephen, 2248-2249
Schultz, Margie, 2973
Schultz-Brooks, Terri, 1552, 3100-3101

Schulz, W., 1229
Schulz, Wolfgang, 958
Schulze, Laurie, 2709
Schumann, Suzanne I., 2177
Schwarz, John E., 2462
Schwarzer, Alice, 1235
Schweickart, Petrocinio P., 1013
Schwichtenberg, Cathy, 37, 2424
Sciglimpaglia, Donald, 2209, 2219, 2250
Scobey, Margaret, 2359, 2361
Scott, Jim, 1722
Scott, Joseph E., 2156, 2644
Scott, Patricia Bell, 2251
Scott, Rebecca Dare, 1753
Scott, Rosemary, 2707
Scott, Thomas, 2364
Secanella, Petra Maria, 1063
Sedlak, Denise M., 3222
Sedlak, Robert A., 3222
Seebohm, Caroline, 3223
Segaloff, Nat, 2905
Seger, Linda, 1579, 2157
Seggar, John F., 2358, 2405, 2425-2429
Seidler, John, 1996
Seifert, W. W., 2820
Seigenthaler, John, 2984
Seiter, Ellen, 57, 206, 1236, 1276, 1678, 2158, 2430
Seligman, Ruth, 251
Sellari, Maricla, 1327
Sellen, Betty-Carol, 1598
Selnow, G. W., 2816
Semenov, V. S., 889
Sempere, Pedro, 1300
Sen, Geeti, 457
Sen, Shaikat, 2343
Senderowitz, Judith, 1599, 2410, 2566
Sengupta, Ranjana, 457
Sepstrup, P., 1130
Serbin, Lisa A., 2449
Serra, Michele R., 2431
Sethi, Renu, 583
Settle, R. B., 2686
Sewell, Edward, jr., 2028
Sexton, Donald E., 2253
Sexton, Rose, 2819
Shaddeg, Stephen, 2044
Shade, William G., 1806
Shadoian, Jack, 2645
Shaffer, Susan Morris, 2516
Shaheed, Farida, 399, 784
Shannon, Kathleen, 1519, 1579
Shardwaj, Prabha, 359

Author Index 447

Sharits, D., 2723
Sharma, K., 418
Sharma, Sheila, 731
Sharma, Sima, 433, 450
Sharp, Nancy, 2786
Sharratt, Mrs. Faith G., 2071
Shaw, Donald, 2646
Shaw, Jeffrey, 2433
Shawkat, Faiza, 304
Shear, Marie, 165
Sheed, Wilfrid, 2045
Sheehan, Helena, 959
Sheehy, Gail, 2046, 3102
Shelton, Keith, 2791
Shepard, Elaine, 2787
Sherman, Barry L., 2434
Sherman, Bill, 3225
Sherman, Ellen, 2906
Sherwood, Peter, 732
Shessel, Sheila, 3103
Shevelow, Kathryn, 1012-1014
Shi, David, 2047
Shigekawa, Joan, 3146
Shimanoff, Susan B., 23, 108
Shin, Young-Il, 769
Shinar, Dov, 381
Shippee, Lester B., 2048
Shoemaker, Pamela J., 2159
Shrivastava, K. M., 451
Shurick, E. P. J., 1783
Shyam, R., 418
Sicam, Paulynn P., 733
Sidharta, Myra, 785
Siegelaus, S., 203
Siemer, Nan, 1587
Sigelman, Carol, 2548
Signorielli, Nancy, 2336-2337, 2357, 2435-2439
Sigurd, Bengt, 1250
Sigurdson, Karen, 1488
Silberman, Marc, 17, 1237
Silbert, Mimi H., 1601
Silva Torres, Vanda M., 1327
Silver, Diane, 77, 2647
Silver, Rosalind, 1579, 2160
Silver, Sheila J., 1522, 3226
Silvera, Makeda, 1520
Silverman, Jonathan, 1845
Silverman, Kaja, 60, 109, 3149
Silverman, L. Theresa, 2440
Silverman-Watkins, L. Theresa, 2441
Silverstein, Arthur, 2254
Silverstein, Brett, 2161, 2412

Silverstein, Rebecca, 2254
Sim Foo Gaik, 662
Simmons, Marcia K., 2255
Simmons, W. R., 2682
Simon, Rita J., 2378, 2648
Simpson, Carmen McCormack, 1753, 2049
Simpson, Peggy, 1587, 2907, 3105
Sims, Monica, 1238, 1267
Simson, Eve, 2442
Singhpatboonporn, Urai, 584
Singleton, Loy A., 2908
Sinha, Arbind K., 424, 744-745
Sioussat, Helen, 1784
Siu, Yvonne, 585
Skard, Torild, 960, 1239-1241
Skelly, Gerald U., 2256
Skill, Thomas D., 125, 1646, 1660, 2283, 2306-2307
Sklar, Robert, 1131
Slater, Marty M., 23
Slatterly, Karen, 3106
Slawski, Edward J., 1558
Slide, Anthony, 1788, 1808
Sloan, Kay, 133
Sloan, Margaret, 1581
Sloan, Pat, 2808
Small, Vernon, 1570
Smelik, Anneke, 1305
Smiley, Virginia, 3136
Smilgis, Martha, 3227
Smith, Babette, 846
Smith, Barbara, 2517, 3228
Smith, Barbara Herrnstein, 2136
Smith, C. Zoe, 2050
Smith, Charles, 1722
Smith, Conrad, 1535, 2909
Smith, Don D., 165, 1602, 2910
Smith, Dorothy, 110
Smith, Henry Lad, 2051
Smith, Kate, 1785
Smith, Linda Lazier, 2162
Smith, Liz, 2052
Smith, M. Dwayne, 2649
Smith, Marilyn Crafton, 1535, 1561, 2448
Smith, Mary Ann Yodelis, 124, 1603
Smith, Paul, 17
Smith, Prudence, 252
Smith, R., 1242
Smith, Rea, 2817
Smith, Ron F., 2764, 3107
Smith, Roslyn, 2681

Smith, Scottie, 3065
Smith, Sharon, 2975, A-49
Smith, Terry, 2650
Smyth, Ailbhe, 1301
Smythe, Dallas W., 2443
Snow, Carmel, 3108
Snyder, Debra, 2479
Snyder, Jerome, 2789
Snyder, Martha (McCoy), 2053
Snyder, Robert E., 2054
Sobachack, Vivian C., 2518
Sochen, June, 2055, 2163, 2519
Soderlund, Walter C., 1489
Soderström, Lars, 1202
Sofia, Zoe, 111
Soh Mi-ja, 480
Sohn, Ardyth B., 2109-3111
Sohoni, A. W., 656
Sokologska, Magdalena, 890-891
Soler, Judit, 2738
Soley, Lawrence C., 2240-2241, 2257-2258
Solomon, M., A-55
Solomon, Martha, 23
Solomon, Sybil R., 2911
Sonenschein, David, 1745, 2651
Song, Yu-jae, 452, 586
Soriano, Marcelo B., 734
Sosanie, Arlene K., 2682
Southerwood, Marion, 453
Spain, Nancy, 1243
Spangler, Lynn C., 1786
Sparks, Glenn C., 2652
Speed, Sally, 859
Spender, Dale, 4, 90, 112, 253
Spender, Lynne, 113, 254, 296
Spensley, Sarah A., 2056
Spieczny, Sandra, 3229
Spiegel, Lynn, 17, 1679
Spielman, Edie, 16
Spigel, Lynn, 1679, 1705, 1763
Spillman, D. M., 2164
Spindle, Les, 2976
Spindler-Brown, Angela, 50
Spinner, Barry, 1730
Spitzack, Carole, 140, 1531, 1543, 1604
Sprafkin, Joyce N., 1653, 2248-2249, 2342, 2347, 2440
Spurgeon, Dolores F., 3112
Sreberny-Mohammadi, Annabelle, 1589
Srinivasan, K. S., 587
Srivastava, U. K., 417, 787
Stacey, J., 2293

Stafford, Beth, 1714
Stanke, Don E., 2962
Stanley, Liz, 1302
Stanton, Elizabeth Cady, 2057
Stanton, Frank, 1772
Stanton, Theodore, 2057
Stappers, James, 2437
Starr, Douglas P., 2791
Stauffer, John, 165, 2729, 2744
Stead, Bette A., 2244
Stearns, Bertha, 1015-1016, 2058
Stedman, Ralph, 1677
Steele, Cynthia, 1384
Steenland, Sally, 2444-2447
Steeves, H. Leslie, 51, 341, 1535, 1561, 1605, 2448, 2683, 2734-2735
Stein, Ellen, 2749
Stein, M. L., 1722, 2059, 3113
Stein, Sally A., 3190
Steinberg, Salme Harju, 2060
Steinem, Gloria, 1621
Steiner, Linda, 1817, 2029, 2061, 3114
Steinman, C., 2710
Stellman, S. D., 2695
Stemple, Diane, 2259
Stephens, Evelyn P., 1334
Stephens, Lenora C., 2520
Sterling, Dorothy, 2062
Stern, B., 2176
Stern, Carol Simpson, 23
Stern, Darlene, 1988
Stern, Lesley, 2521
Stern, Madeleine B., 2063
Stern, Madeline, 1997
Sternberg, Janet, 227, 3157
Sternglanz, Sarah Hall, 2449
Sterns, Bertha M., 2064
Steven, Lawrence, 1459
Steven, Peter, 2929
Stevens, John D., 1762
Stevenson, Rosemary M., 1606
Stewart, E., 2747
Stewart, J. C., 1486
Stewart, Lea P., 1721, 2165, 2656
Stewart, Lynda J., 1630
Stewart, Penni, 5, 2653
Stiff, J., 2733
Still, L. V., 860
Stimson, Gerry, 2260
Stirling, Lesley, 826
Stobart, J., 1094
Stockbridge, Sally, 15
Stocker, Laura J., 829

Stocking, S. Holly, 2450
Stoddard, Karen M., 2522
Stone, Vernon A., 2912-2915
Storch, Judith L., 2454
Stott, M., 1102
Stow, Mary, 1739
Strainchamps, Ethel, 2790
Strang, Jessica, 2166
Stratford, Teresa, 146
Straube, Gabi, 961
Streicher, Helen White, 2136, 2654
Streitmatter, Roger, 3115
Stressac, Alfreda, 799
Stretch, S. M., 1656
Strick, Stan, 2984
Stromquist, Nelly P., 207
Struck, Karin, 1303
Strzyz, Klaus, 1244
Stuart, Martha, 208, 657
Stuck, M. F., 2173
Studlar, Gaylyn, 57, 1707
Stuteville, John R., 2261
Sullerot, Evelyne, 1017
Sullivan, Ann, 3116
Sullivan, Gary L., 2262
Sullivan, Kaye, 294
Sullivan, Patricia A., 1561
Suls, J., 2451
Summerhill, Audrey, 962
Summers, Leda P., 2724
Surlin, Stuart H., 1489
Suter, Jacqueline, 17
Sutheim, S., 1607
Suyoko, Threes S., 788
Suzuki, Midori F., 588
Swartz, T. A., 2655
Swenson, Ingrid, 2203
Swift, C., 2342
Swift, Kate, 2147
Swisshelm, Jane Grey, 2065
Sylvester, Judith, 2784
Synnott, Anthony, 2263
Szanton, Cristina Blanc, 454
Szilágyi, Erzsébet, 892
Szostak, Jutta, 935, 963
Szybillo, George J., 2682

Tabacsko, Ken, 2916
Taibo, Paco Ignacio, 1393
Tajima, Renee, 500
Takemiya, Keiko, 789
Tamborini, R., 2733

Tamez, Elsa, 76
Tammes, Diane, 5, 1248
Tan, Alexis S., 2264, 2725
Tangen, Jan O., 1064-1065
Tankersley, Clint, 2746
Tanwar, Taruna, 589
Tara, Bill, 2789
Taraporevala, Sooni, 680
Tarbell, Ida M., 2066
Tarnova, Elizabeth J., 2167
Tarry, Ellen, 2067
Tatum, Charles, 1378
Tauskey, Thomas, 1512
Taylor, Anita, 211
Taylor, D. B., 1304
Taylor, Nancy J., 2068
Taylor, Ron, 2818
Taylor, Sandra, 839
Taylor, V., 184
Teale, Ruth, 807
Tebbutt, Margaret W., 836
Tedesco, Nancy, 2136, 2452
Teeter, Dwight L., 3174
Thaler, Barbara, 2656
Thangavely, K., 2222
Theberge, Nancy, 2657
Theus, Kathryn, 1523
Thiruchandran, Selvy, 461
Thoman, Elizabeth, 1579
Thomas, Helen, 3118
Thomas, Samuel J., 2072
Thomas, Sari, 2208
Thompson, Bill, 713
Thompson, David W., 2805
Thompson, Dorothy, 2073
Thompson, Kim, 1249
Thompson, Meg, 682
Thoms, Patience, 846
Thorne, Barrie, 185
Thorp, Margaret F., 2074
Thoveron, Gabriel, 923, 1132
Thunberg, Anne-Marie, 1250
Tidhar, Chava E., 392
Tielens, M., 1251
Tien, Joseleyne Slade, 2075
Tiercelin, Marie-France, 1252
Tildesley, A. L., 2978
Tilghman, Romalyn, 2658
Timár, János, 875
Ting-Toomey, Stella, 2165, 2656
Tipace, Amada R., 792
Tobin, Genevieve, 2977
Tobin, Joan, 77

Author Index

Todd, Alexandra Dundas, 257
Todd-Mancillas, William, 1583
Toeplitz, Jerzy, 847
Tognoli, Jerome, 2454
Tohamy, Mochtar, 386
Tokgöz, Oya, 50, 1160, 1253
Tolentino, Mercy Therese S., 735
Tomeh, Aida K., 387
Tomer, Adrian, 381
Tompkins, Mary E., 2076
Toner, C., 1059
Torrevillas-Suarez, Domini, 736
Torsh, Daniela, 853
Tortora, Phyllis, 3231
Toth, Elizabeth Lance, 1630
Toubia, Nahid, 373
Tower, A., 2313
Towler, Robert, 1133-1134
Toyo, Rose, 317
Traber, Michael, 1344
Trahey, Jane, 3232
Tranfaglia, N., 941
Traore, Myriam, 303
Travis, Lisa, 1446
Treichler, Paula A., 23, 1534, 1608, 2310, 2344
Tremblay, Gisele, 1502
Treole, Victoria, 853
Trillin, Calvin, 3119
Trinh T. Minh-ha, 17
Trömel-Plotz, Senta, 1254
Trommsdorff, G., 968
Trotta, Liz, 2917
Trudell, Bonnie, 2390
Tsudor, A., 1135
Tuchman, Gaye, 1255, 2168-2170, 2249, 2305, 2331, 2370, 2455
Tufte, Birgitte, 70, 78
Tugusheva, M., 2171
Tulloch, John, 802
Tumanis, Sue, 2077
Tunstall, Jeremy, 969, 1256
Turim, Maureen, 458, 1709-1710, 2523
Turk, Judy VanSlyke, 3120
Turow, Joseph, 2136, 2456-2457
Tuska, Jon, 2524
Tyler, Jane E., 2259
Tyler, Parker, 1711, 2525
Tyler, Ralph, 2919
Tysoe, Maryon, 1609

Umiker-Sebeok, Jean, 1068

Underwood, Agness, 2078
Unesco, 114-117, 258, 361, 402, 878
Unger, Rhoda K., 2565
United Nations, 118-122
United States Commission on Civil Rights, 1680-1681
Urban, Christine D., 2745
Uselding, Douglas K., 2458
Utreras, Rosario, 1327

Vadum, Arlene C., 2119
Valentine, Carol Ann, 1611
Valentine, K. B., 2394
Valicha, Kishore, 594
Valenzuela, Carmen, 794
Vanarase, Shyamala, 669
Van Auken, S., 1629
Van de Maele, B., 970
Vanderhaeghen, C., 152
Vanderwey, Judy K., 595
Van Dijck, Bernadette, 1305
Van Gastel, Ada, 2028
Van Gelder, Lindsy, 1581
Vani, M. N., 51, 574
Vanier, D. T., 2250
Vankeirsbilck, L, 1251
VanSlyke Turk, Judy, 1587, 2659
Van Zandt, Lydia, 738
Van Zoonen, Liesbet, 51, 971-972, 1257, 1290
Varga, Karoly, 879, 2684
Vargas Roma, Maria Antonieta, 1423
Vasikova, Irina, 901
Vasudev, Aruna, 399, 596-598, 739
Vaughan-Rees, Michael, 1020
Venkatesan, M., 2267
Venkatesh, Alladi, 2685, 2746
Venugopal, 770
Vera Irizarry, Jesús, 1366
Verbrugge, Lois M., 660
Verer, A. M., 2268
Verghese, Joseph, 599
Vergne, E., 1258
Vermilye, Jerry, 1807
Verna, Mary Ellen, 1549, 2358, 2459
Vervaet-Clays, Els, 973
Vibas, Danny T., 600
Vidmar, Neil, 1615
Viezzer, Moema, 1344
Vilanilam, John V., 601
Villamar, Sonia S., 795
Villar-Gaviria, Alvaro, 1345

Author Index 451

Vincent, Richard C., 2460-2461
Viviana, Christian, 1809
Vogel, Jean, 1136
Vogel-Polsky, Eliane, 923
Vogt, Glenda L, 2627
Voight, Melvin J., 1640
Volgy, Thomas J., 2462
Voli, Virginia, 1085
Voltoline, Nanete, 1425
Voorhees, Sara D., 2346
Vorlat, E., 974
Vosco, Richard, 2206
Voumakis, Sophia E., 1493
Voyenne, Jeanne Maud, 944

Wade, Mason, 1997, 2079
Wadsworth, A. J., 1632
Wage, Margaret H., 2920
Waggenspack, Beth M., 2029
Wagley, Mana, 630
Wagner, Lilya, 2080
Wagner, Louis C., 2269
Wahab, Eileen, 462
Waites, Bernard, 1293
Wakem, Beverley, 861
Walb, Lore, 935
Wald, Carol, 2081
Waldman, Diane, 1810, 2526
Walker, Alice, 2082
Walker, Connecticut, 2921
Walker, Janet, 60
Walker, Mort, 48
Walker, Nancy A., 1613
Walker, Stanley, 1877, 2083
Walkowitz, Judith R., 1137
Wallbott, H. G., 2527
Waller, Jane, 1020
Waller, Judith Cary, 2084
Waller, Margaret, 268
Waller-Zuckerman, Mary Ellen, 2085
Wallis, Brian, 1433, 2369
Walsh, Andrea S., 2528, 3158
Walter, Pat, 846
Walters, Chris, 1614
Walters, Patricia, 1184
Wander, Philip, 1660, 1682
Wang, Yeujin, 602
Wanta, Wayne, 2660
Ward, Bill, 1734
Ward, Carol M., 2979
Ward, Ed, 3121
Ward, Jean, 2661-2662

Ward, Lea, 740
Ward, Nancy, 2172
Ward, Walter, 1576
Ware, M. C., 2173
Warken, Bettina, 1192
Warner, Marina, 2174
Warren, Denise, 2270
Wartella, Ellen, 124, 1445, 1534, 1603, 1608, 2720
Wartovo, John, 661
Wassell, Ann, 16
Wassenaar, I., 975
Watanabe, Haruko K., 862
Watkins, Charlotte C., 1022
Watson, Lorna, 2086
Watson-Rouslin, Virginia, 3122
Wattz, Susan, 342
Weaver, David H., 3081-3082
Weaver, Emily, 1456
Weaver, James B., 2717
Webb, R. K., 1021
Webber, Gail, 2284
Weber, Cheryl Bennett, 3107
Weber, W. J., 2820
Webster, Edna Robb, 1753
Weekes, Mrs. Marie, 2071
Weerackody, Irvin, 433, 450
Weerasinghe, Amila, 461
Weibel, Kathryn, 2175
Weider-Hatfield, Deborah, 23
Weigel, Russell, 2463
Weiller, Karen H., 2128
Weimann, Gabriel, 382
Weinberg, Arthur M., 2087
Weinberg, Lila, 2087
Weiner, Joel H., 1022
Weiss, Margaret R., 2088
Weitzman, Lenore J., 2663
Welch, R. L., 2271
Weller, Saulwick, 824
Wells, Alan, 1615, 3175
Wells, Ida B., 2089
Wells, Lana, 846
Wells, Mildred White, 2051
Wells, Troth, 662
Wen, Wendy H. L., 796
Wengraf, Susan, 2470
Werner, Anita, 1138, 1259
Wesson, D. A., 2747
West, Ann A., 2529
West, Celeste, 3123
Westby, Sally D., 2377
Westmoreland, Reg, 2791

Westoff, Charles F., 2678
Weston, Louise C., 2639-2641
Wexler, Marvin, 2464
Wharton, Don, 2090
Wheat, Valerie, 2751
Wheeler, Helen Rippier, 604, 1616, 2792
Wheeler, Penny, 2429
Whetmore, Edward Jay, 2908
Whipple, Thomas W., 1441, 1633, 2136, 2186, 2272-2274
White, Cynthia Leslie, 1306
White, David Manning, 1617, 2538, 2642
White, Jean M., 3147
White, Mary Alice, 2404
White, Maxine Rachofsky, 2530
White, Patricia, 3152
White, Paul, 1683
White, Susan, 2531
Whitehead, Helen, 1570
Whitehouse, Mary, 1260
Whitlow, S. Scott, 2664-2666
Whitney, D. Charles, 124, 1445, 1603, 2720
Whitney, T. R., 2218
Whittaker, Ron, 2922
Whittaker, Susan, 2922
Whittemore, Lauren, 2447
Wieser, Nora Jacquez, 69
Wiggins, Ana, 1490
Wiio, Osmo A., 209
Wilder, Frances Farmer, 1677
Wilhelm, Klaus, 902
Wilhoit, Cleveland, 1568
Willard, Frances E., 2091-2092
Willer, Thomas, 606
Willett, Roslyn, 2275
Williams, Donald M., 2667
Williams, Jon, 164, 943
Williams, L., 2571
Williams, Linda, 247, 2532
Williams, Tannis MacBeth, 51, 1446, 1478
Williamson, Janice, 1514
Williamson, Judith, 1140
Williamson, Lenora, 1722
Williamson, Lorne G., 2276
Williamson, Mary E., 1754, 1787
Willis, Paul, 926
Willis, Sharon, 1261
Wills, Deborah, 2413

Wilson, Jean Gaddy, 77, 1587, 2749, 2793-2794, 2923, 3124-3127
Wilson, Rosalind, 607
Wilson, S., 2816
Wilson, Vincent, jr., 2796
Wilson, W. C., 1595
Windahl, Sven, 124, 1445, 1603, 2720
Winfield, Betty Houchin, 2093
Wingrove, Kendall, 2094
Winick, Charles, 2276
Winick, Mariann Pezella, 2276
Winkleman, Michael, 1625, 2811
Winship, Janice, 295, 1141-1142, 1307-1308
Winter, Ella, 2095
Wischermann, Ulla, 1023
Wisocki, P. A., 2423
Wistrand, Birgitta, 1262
Witaman, Lenore, 2668
Withington, Mrs. E. W., 2096
Wober, Mallory, 125
Wolfe, Lois Lauer, 3128
Wolff, Janet L., 2708
Women's Advisory Council, 1684-1685
Women's Film Fund, Sydney, 864
Women's Institute for Freedom of the Press, 3137-3138
Wong, Martin R., 23, 2288
Wood, Ananda, 465
Wood, J., 865
Wood, Julia T., 23, A-55
Wood, Mary Ann, 2797
Woodhead, Jane, 1454
Woodward, Helen, 2098
Wortzel, Lawrence H., 2277, 2703
Wright, Charles R., 2130
Wright, John C., 2271
Wyndham, Diane, 77, 175, 803, 830-833, 866

Yadava, J. S., 664
Yamada, Gayle K., 2867
Yasuna, A., 2313
Yates, John, 2533
Yau, Esther C. M., 483, 605, 609
Yearwood, Gladstone, 2475
Yeck, Joanne Louise, 2099
Yem, Chan-Huy, 797
Yeo, Mary Chuan-Hua, 466
Yonezawa, Hiroshi, 665
Yonezawa, Yoshihiro, 484

Yoshida, Maki, 593
Young, Patricia A., 1598
Yronwode, Catherine, 3091
Yu, Jen, 666
Yu, Timothy, 467
Yu Yang-Chou, 2242

Zagarell, Sandra Abelson, 1310
Zahn, Susan Brown, 2284
Zaid, Lydia, 1136
Zang, Barbara, 2101
Zavitz, Carol, 297
Zeck, Shari, 2465
Zemach, Tamar, 2466

Zhao, Xiaoyan, 667
Ziegler, Nancy, 2206
Zierold, Norman, 1811
Zilliacus-Tikkanen, Henrika, 1263-1264
Zillman, Dolf, 1622, 2450, 2721, 2726, 2733
Zimbardo, Philip G., 2669
Zimmermann, Patricia R., 57, 1561, 2467
Zinn, Deborah, 343
Ziska, Deborah, 63, 298
Zornosa, Anna Lucia, 1346, 1385
Zube, Margaret J., 3235
Zucker, Carole, 2980
Zuñiga Escobar, Miriam, 1424
Zureik, Elia T., 1495

SUBJECT INDEX

ABC, 77
Acción Cultural Popular, 1435
"A Country Practice," 802
Action, 1
Action for Children's Television, 2905
Ad Age, 77
advertising, 1, 19, 47, 77, 103, 190-193, 290, 461, 914, 928, 1580, 1631, 1633, 1758; audiences, 614, 649, 807, 1345, 1347, 1349, 1624, 1632, 2672, 2686-2708; images of women in, 77, 107, 153, 172, 175, 202-203, 325, 399, 459, 485-486, 490, 498, 504, 506, 509, 511, 513, 515, 518, 530, 533, 547, 550, 560, 563-565, 572, 580, 583, 587, 599-600, 608, 808, 812, 816, 819-825, 830-833, 884, 967, 969, 1008, 1029, 1032-1033, 1040, 1047-1050, 1059, 1067-1073, 1075-1078, 1084-1085, 1092, 1094, 1096, 1102, 1107, 1111, 1114, 1122, 1126, 1130, 1140-1142, 1363, 1365, 1385, 1422, 1441, 1464, 1466-1468, 1491, 1494, 1535, 1579, 1624, 1626, 1705, 2102, 2112, 2116, 2121, 2124, 2148, 2174, 2176-2277, 2607; pharmaceutical, 2214, 2225, 2238, 2268; subliminal, 2211; women in advertising, 77, 239, 860, 1549, 2071; women practitioners of, 77, 1623-1625, 2798-2801, 2803, 2808, 2814, 2818
AFFIRM, 2122
Africa, 207, 299-319; images of women in, 320-343; women and film in, 286; women in communication in, 18, 44, 51, 76-77, 107, 117, 128, 260; women practitioners in, 77, 117, 311, 348-363; women's audience in, 344-347; women's media in, 464-467
Agence de coopération culturelle et technique, 1
aging (older women), 77, 381, 1479, 1484, 2176, 2193, 2206, 2291, 2307, 2314, 2412, 2438, 2467, 2522, 2528, 2828, 2838, 2851, 2867, 2889
Ahmedabad Women's Action Group, 779
AIDS, 2146
Akman, Nisan, 1224
Alberta, 1518
Album Cubano de lo Bueno y lo Bello, 1355, 1358
alcohol, 1121, 1534, 2143, 2690, 3162
Alcott, Louisa May, 2029
Alfon, Estrella D., 668
Algeria, 329
Allen, Donna, 3167
Allende, Salvador, 1330
Allfrey, Phyllis, 1370, 1375
All India Radio, 607, 613, 615, 656, 747
"All in the Family," 2433
"Ally Sloper," 1000-1001
Almy, Max, 17
alternative media, 54, 107, 225, 250, 267, 303, 364, 399, 1209, 1320, 1326, 1337, 1339, 1341, 1343-1344, 1438-1439, 1532, 1558, 2582, 3051, 3169, 3195, 3198
Althusser, Louis, 230
Alvarez, Julia, 222
Amaral, Susana, 249
Amazonen-Frauenverlag, 1289
American Federation of Labor, 2043

American Girl, The, 2171
American Journal of Psychiatry, 2214, 2225
American Newspaper Guild, 3117
American Society of Newspaper Editors, 2985, 3125
American Women in Radio and Television, 2887
Ames, Austine, 1818
anchorwomen, 2828, 2838, 2840, 2846, 2851, 2858, 2861, 2878, 2889, 2904, 2972
Anderson, Madeline, 227, 2942
Anderson, Margaret, 1819
Andrews, Julie, 2976
androgyny, 185, 1090, 1524, 2411, 2559
Angola, 14
anorexia, 2162, 2234, 3221
Anson-Rosa, María, 668
Anthony, Susan B., 1894, 1974, 1992, 2057
"Antonia: A Portrait of a Woman," 2937
Apostol, Eugenia, 729
Arab States, 44; portrayals of women in, 101; women in communication in, 117, 127; women practitioners in, 117; women's magazines in, 77
Ara, Shamin, 700
Ardakani, Tahmineh, 390
Argentina, 100, 1313, 1315, 1327, 1343, 1417, 1438
Arguelles, Gloria, 1374
"Army Nurse," 532
Army Talks, 1752
Arthur's Home Magazine, 1886
Arzner, Dorothy, 226, 234, 245, 249, 1203, 2932, 2978
Asahi Shimbun, 768
Asia, 128, 207; historical studies in, 468-484; images of women in, 485-609; women and media in, 44, 77, 105, 107, 191, 286; women practitioners in, 117, 668-742; women's audience in, 610-667; women's media in, 743-797
Asian American, 2928
Asian Mass Communication Research and Information Centre, 449
Asia-Pacific Broadcasting Union, 861
Asociación Peru-Mujer, 1405
assertiveness, 1597, 2154, 2734-2735
Associated Press, 2660, 3003, 3020

Associated Press Managing Editors, 2561, 2612
Association for Education in Journalism and Mass Communication, 1582
Association of Media Women in Kenya, 359
Athenian Mercury, 1014
Atlanta Constitution, 2625
Atlantic Monthly, 1936, 2595
A Tribuna do Ribeira, 1431
audiences, 15, 17, 70, 77-78, 83, 189-210; in Africa, 344-347; in Asia, 424, 429, 435, 610-667; in Australia, 834-839; in Western Europe, 1009, 1147-1160; in Middle East, 383-387; in Latin America, 1345, 1347, 1349; in United States, 2670-2748
audiovisual, 279, 650, 881, 944, 1349
"Aunt Jemima," 2134, 2210
Aurora, 1970
Australia, 258, 261, 399, historical studies in, 804-807; images of women in, 77, 101, 160, 175, 798, 808-833; women and media in, 15, 77, 100, 105-106, 212; women practitioners in, 687, 799-801, 840-866; women's audience in, 834-839; women's media in, 867-871
Australian Broadcasting Corporation, 841, 843, 849
Australian Family Physician, 820
Australian Film Commission, 844, 863
Australian Women's Broadcasting Co-Operative, 801, 868
Austria, 129, 958, 976, 1034, 1101
AWAG, 399
Azmi, Shabana, 708

Bache, Benjamin Franklin, 1967
Baker, Polly, 1928, 1945
Bales Interaction Process Analysis System, 2354
Ballad of Halo Jones, The, 1743
Ballard, Bettina, 1823
"Bandhana," 218, 579
Bangladesh, 14 394, 434, 538, 617, 719, 760
Bangla Readers, 538
Banks, Elizabeth L., 1824
Bara, Theda, 1811
Barbados, 1373
Barry, Linda, 3037

Barry, Lynda, 3087
Barskaya, Margarita, 226
Basner, Naomi, 3017
Bauman, Suzanne E., 2954
"Bazar," 83
Beatty, Bessie, 1837, 1979
Behn, Aphra, 978
Belgium, 77, 939, 942, 1047
Belles Lettres, 77
Bemberg, Maria Luisa, 216, 249
Benegal, Shyam, 496, 556
Benin, 1
Benjamin, Anna, 1853
Bennett, Joan, 2962
Bennett, Louise, 1375
Berg, Gertrude, 1767
Bergman, Ingmar, 2510
Bermuda, 1356
Bermuda Gazette, 1356
Bernays, Doris Fleischman, 2804
Bernays, Edward, 2804
Besant, Annie, 721
Best, 1309
Bhanumathi, 218
bibliographies, 64, 66, 88, 102, 106, 108, 116, 181, 289, 301, 305-307, 350, 429-430, 867, 919, 940, 951, 1017, 1127, 1157, 1313, 1403, 1545, 1549, 1587, 1598, 1606, 1627-1628, 1636, 1655, 1699, 1705, 1714, 1754, 1763, 1945, 1987-1988, 2121, 2127, 2331, 2436, 2582, 2863, 2927, 2934, 2951, 2955, 2959, 2968, 2970, 2973, 2979
Bihar Press Law, 425
Bingham, Sallie, 3077
Birmingham Truth, 2067
birth control, 1758, 1816, 1904, 1990-1991, 2040, 2260, 2678
Bitter Tears of General Yen, The, 1561
Blache, Alice Guy, 234, 249, 1788, 1795
Black, Cathleen, 2771
Black, Winifred, 2036, 2041
Blackmar, Beatrice, 3179
Blais, Madeleine, 1834, 2991
Blandon, Nelba, 1390
Bloomer, Amelia, 1842, 2029
Bly, Nellie, 898, 1722, 1822, 1834, 2006, 2036
body language, 49
Boileau, Linda Frances, 2998
Bok, Edward, 1870, 2047, 2060
Bolivia, 240, 1323, 1438
Bondarchuk, Natalia, 217

Booth, Mary L., 2029
Borden Lizzie, 216
Boston News-Letter, 1919
Botswana, 210, 357-358
Boucher, Emily, 2992
Bourke-White, Margaret, 1522, 1753, 1845, 1854, 2003, 2012, 2041, 2054, 3018
Bow, Clara, 1811, 2959
Bradford, Cornelia, 3036
Branching Out, 77
Bravo, Estela, 1325
Brazil, 100, 261, 1327, 1341, 1343-1344, 1398, 1402-1403, 1407, 1409-1410; historical studies in, 1413-1416; images of women in, 1422; women practitioners in, 218, 248, 270, 1315, 1425-1427, 1431; women's media in, 1420, 1433-1434, 1438
"Bread and Butterflies," 2296
Breien, Anja, 58, 1207
Bretécher, Claire, 1249
"Bride of the Andes," 713
Bright, Susie, 2944
Brinkley, Nell, 3091
Brisbane *Courier-Mail*, 869, 871
British Advertising Standards Authority, 1122
British Broadcasting Corporation, 77, 1164, 1178, 1238, 1267
broadcasting, 78-79, 92, 250, 402, 517, 936, 946, 1615, 1638, 1671; audience, 2709-2725; for women, 747, 868, 927, 1267, 3139-3147; images of women in, 1444, 1469-1473, 1480, 1483, 1487, 1490, 2278-2467; religious, 2278; women in, 5, 50, 77, 106-107, 224, 240, 260, 354, 420, 422, 451, 921, 1263-1264, 1658, 1683, 1987, 2170; women practitioners in, 677, 717, 720, 861, 865, 902, 904-905, 909, 953-955, 1161-1162, 1178, 1180, 1189, 1192, 1245-1248, 1496, 1500, 1506, 1510, 1648, 2821-2924
Brocka, Lino, 546
Brooks, Louise, 1789
Brown, Helen Gurley, 2771
Bruckner, Jutta, 1190
Bruson, Dorothy, 2907
Bryant, Louise, 1900
Buchanan, Annette, 3116
Buchanan, Edna, 3119
Buenhogar, 1436

Bugbee, Emma, 1834
bulimia, 2234, 3221
Bulletin Today, 722, 724, 733
Bunker, Archie, 1615
Burda Moden, 873
Burkina Faso, 1
Burnett, Carol, 2382

"Cabaret," 58, 1704
Cable Network News, 3092
"Cagney and Lacey," 15, 1651, 1786, 2465, 2676
calypso, 1350, 1359
Cameroon, 336
Campbell, Helen, 1921
Campbell, Martha, 3068
Canada: images of women in, 830, 1441, 1444-1446, 1453, 1464-1495; women and film in, 129, 218, 222, 248, 255, 270, 286, 1447-1448, 1450; women and media in, 47, 51, 70, 99, 105-106, 239, 258, 261; women practitioners in, 1451, 1455-1462, 1496-1514; women's media in, 77, 1449, 1452, 1515-1520
Canadian Association of Broadcasters, 1487
Canadian Broadcasting Corporation, 1469, 1471, 1487, 1500
Canadian Radio-Television and Tele-Communications Commission, 1468-1469, 1471, 1473, 1487, 1515
"candy-sex" magazines, 171
Capital Radio, London, 1084
Carbine, Pat, 3205, 3230
Cardiff Broadcasting Company, 909
Cardozo, Abbie E., 2013
careers: in broadcasting, 2751, 2831, 2846-2847, 2859, 2876, 2895, 2898, 2915, 2971; in film, 2954, 2971; in magazines, 3112; in mass media, 2749, 2758, 2765, 2788; in newspapers, 2984, 3064; in public relations, 2815
Caribbean: historical studies in, 1355-1358; images of women in, 1311, 1359, 1366; women and communication in, 44, 76, 96, 207, 1317; women as audience in, 1347, 1349; women in communication in, 117, 128, 260, 1350; women practitioners in, 1367-1375; women's media in, 1352-1353
Caribbean Women's Feature Syndicate, 1369, 1373
Carlson, Mildred, 1771
"Carnal Knowledge," 2492
Carpenter, Iris, 1857, 2080
Cartwright, Marguerite, 240
Cassavetes, John, 2484
Castillo, Celso Ad., 600
Castro, Luz Mat, 481
Catholic Worker, 1868, 1871, 1882, 1999, 2020, 2033
Catholic World, 2067
Cavani, Lilliana, 218, 1210
Cebu, 690
censorship, 267, 367, 711, 937, 991, 1390, 1447, 1729, 1744, 2172
Central America: images of women in, 1376-1385; women practitioners in, 1386-1393; women's media in, 1394-1396
Centro de Información y Apayo de la Mujer, 1439
Chadimova, Karla, 217
Chambers, Anne Cox, 2757
Chamorro, Violeta, 1391
Channel Four, 1171
chapbooks, 332, 340
Chapelle, Dickey, 1860, 1883, 1896, 1902, 2012, 3018-3019
Charleston (S.C.) *Gazette*, 1918
Charm, 2098
Charren, Peggy, 2905
Chase, Dorris, 1956
Chast, Roz, 3037
Chauvel, Charles, 804
Chauvel, Elsa, 804
Chen Rujin, 468
Chen Xie-fen, 468
Cheshire, Maxine, 3001
Cheung Man-Yee, 677, 740
Chicago Liberation School for Women, 3136
Chicago Tribune, 77, 2625, 3114, 3213
children's books, 186, 324, 505, 810, 826, 886, 888, 1010, 1138, 1544, 1618, 2564, 2663, 2668
children's media, 77, 378, 628, 787, 837, 839, 889, 1055, 1093, 1105, 1278, 1287, 1293-1294, 1629, 1644, 1671, 2192, 2224, 2242, 2248-2249, 2271, 2276, 2289, 2293, 2299, 2309, 2313,

2317, 2358, 2378, 2384, 2391, 2394, 2401, 2404, 2408, 2415, 2439, 2449, 2454, 2458-2459, 2598, 2621, 2627, 2629, 2663, 2668, 2905
Children's Television Workshop, 2882
Chile, 75, 235, 240, 1401, 1412, 1419, 1429, 1438
China, 2, 47; images of women in, 137, 471, 483, 505, 513, 531-532, 537, 575, 585, 602, 605, 609; women and film in, 46, 411, 458; women as audience in, 667; women practitioners in, 77, 218, 469-470, 683, 687, 712; women's media in, 468, 477, 749, 758
Chinese Women's Journal, 468
Ch-iu Chin, 469
Chodorow, Nancy, 1643
Chopra, Joyce, 249
Chow, Selina, 732
Christian Science Monitor, 2625, 3007
Christie, Agatha, 2539
Christie, Julie, 216-217
"Christopher Strong," 16
Chung, Connie, 2858, 2890
Chusmir, Janet, 3067, 3113
Chytilová, Vera, 223, 249
cigarettes, 1762, 2692, 2695, 2700, 2705, 3192, 3199
citizens' groups, 3143
Citron, Michelle, 2956
Claflin, Roxie, 1870
Claflin, Tennessee, 1981
Clark, Marguerite, 2008
Clarke, Shirley, 234, 255, 2965
Cláudia, 1410
Cleveland Plain Dealer, 1758
clothes, 925, 1656, 1843, 2244, 3220
Cobbett, William, 1967
Colbert, Claudette, 2959
Coleman, Kathleen Blake, 1456, 1459-1460
Collins, Joan, 2467
Colombia, 100, 155, 215, 220, 222, 1315, 1418, 1424, 1435
coloring books, 2627
Columbia Broadcasting Company, 77
Columbus Monitor, 1858
"Coma," 2116
comics (cartoons), 48, 77, 446, 484, 623, 645, 789, 850, 1000-1001, 1244, 1249, 1285, 1503-1505, 1734, 1743, 1858, 1982, 2997-2999, 3017, 3023, 3025,

3031, 3033, 3037, 3051, 3063, 3068-3069, 3087, 3090-3091, 3104, 3121, 3129, 3160, 3194, 3225; images in, 137, 141, 490, 527, 541, 1031, 1043-1044, 1046, 1088, 1096, 1098, 1116, 1320, 1378, 1384, 1726, 1737-1738, 1996, 2136, 2165, 2174, 2299, 2313, 2394, 2535, 2538, 2543-2544, 2551, 2554, 2571, 2575-2577, 2590, 2597-2599, 2608-2610, 2614-2615, 2619, 2621, 2630, 2642, 2645, 2654, 2656
"Coming Out Show," 868
Commission of the European Communities, 921
Commission on Obscenity and Pornography, 1568
Committee on the Portrayal of Women in the Media, 398
Common Ground/Different Planes, 3135
communication, 1531, 2751-2752, 2754, 2760, 2766, 2784; women and, 114, 127, 968, 1379; women in, 117, 2788
Communication Monographs, 1543
Compropolitan, 1329, 1396
computers, 236, 1560, 1563, 2173
Concio, Lupita A., 546
Congo, 317
Connecticut, 2603
Connecticut Courant, 1924
Connolly, Vera, 2085
consumerism and women, 17, 70, 74-75, 190-193, 399, 624, 636, 662, 774, 793, 1148, 1314, 1705, 1759, 1763, 2643, 2687, 2694, 2704, 2707-2708
Consumers' Association of Penang, 624
Cooke, Janet, 3015
Cooke, Kaz, 850
Coolidge, Martha, 249
Cooney, Joan Ganz, 2882, 2919
Cooper, Miriam, 1791
Co-op Radio, Vancouver, 1515
Copley, Helen, 240, 2100, 3102
Corporation for Public Broadcasting, 2830, 2837, 2855
correspondents, 215, 220, 238, 240, 1228, 1457-1458, 1751, 1753, 1818, 1824, 1830, 1832, 1853, 1857, 1860, 1869, 1876, 1883-1884, 1889, 1895-1896, 1898, 1900, 1925-1926, 1945, 1952, 1954, 1979-1980, 1987, 2002, 2004, 2017, 2036-2037, 2048-2049, 2059, 2064-2065, 2073, 2075, 2080, 2763, 2778, 2787, 2908, 2987, 3008, 3018-

3019, 3027, 3056
Cosmo, 1142
Cosmopolitan, 1281, 1324, 1436, 1936, 2590, 3165, 3186, 3199, 3208
Costa Rica, 1315, 1381, 1383, 1386
Courage, 77, 1310
courtesy titles, 2552, 2574, 2581, 2667, 2984
Cousins, Margaret, 1846
Covert, Catherine L., 1551
Cowan, Ruth, 2080
Coyne, Catherine, 2080
Crackenthorpe, Mrs., 980
Craft, Christine, 77, 1648, 2838, 2861, 2890, 2972
Crain, Gertrude, 2757
Crane, Ruth, 1522, 1771, 2867
Crawford, Joan, 1798, 2519, 2959
"Cries and Whispers," 2510
Crist, Judith, 1834
Critical Studies in Mass Communication, 1543
criticism: film, 17, 86, 246-247, 276, 287, 2952, 3149; television, 15, 78, 83
Crocker, Betty, 1607
Crossing Press, 1272
"Crossroads," 61, 1151
Crost, Lyn, 2080
Crouch, Mary, 1918
Cuba, 69, 217, 1355, 1357-1358, 1372, 1374
cultural industries, 42, 74, 202, 1095
Cunningham, Mary, 1620
Curtis, Charlotte, 1932, 3183
Curtis Publishing Company, 3179-3180
Czechoslovakia, 79, 129, 217, 703, 1209

Dagens Nyheter, 1113
Daily Courant, 1002-1003
Daily Iowan, 2561, 2612
"Dallas," 189, 1150, 1159
Daniell, Tania Long, 2080
Daniels, Faith, 2903
Daniels family, 3054
Dansereau, Mireille, 222
Davis, Bette, 1700, 1807
Davis, Rebecca Harding, 1960
Davis, Richard Harding, 1960
Dawn, The, 476
Day, Dorothy, 1868, 1871, 1882, 1997, 2020, 2033
de Beauvoir, Simone, 1270

Debi, Suprabha, 218
Deepe, Beverly, 1883, 1895, 3131
Deitch, Donna, 216, 249
de Izcue, Nora, 1432
de la Cruz, Katy, 668
de la Rama-Hernandez, Atang, 668
de la Riviere Manley, Mary, 994
de Leon, Mike, 546
Delineator, The, 2098, 3231
de Montanclos, Madam, 991
Denmark, 165, 248, 267; images of women in, 101, 965, 1030, 1130; women and media in, 70, 101-102, 107, 933; women as audience in, 1150; women practitioners in, 1200-1201
Derakhshandeh, Puran, 390
Derech Hanitzotz, 376
Deren, Maya, 221, 227, 2965
"Detruire, Dit-Elle," 1197
development programs, 9, 12, 51, 121, 123, 194-195, 198, 201, 205, 208, 251, 293, 298, 341, 344-345, 365, 386, 399, 401, 467, 497, 535, 611, 645, 723, 1312, 1348, 1362, 1364, 1368, 1373, 1405
Dhanraj, Deepa, 711
Dharmayug, 578
Dial, 1862, 1997, 2079
Diaz-Abaya, Marilou, 496, 546
Dickerson, Nancy, 1768, 2856
Dietrich, Marlene, 2959
Ding Chuo-o, 468
disk jockey, 2379
Dix, Dorothy, 1834, 1877, 1947, 2036
Dizenzo, Patricia, 2171
Dodge, Mary Mapes, 1931, 2029
Dolan, Mary Anne, 3113
Dominica, 1370, 1375
Dominica *Herald*, 1375
Dominican Republic, 1341, 1343, 1353, 1368
Dominica *Star*, 1375
Dong-A Ilbo, 534
Donner, Vyvyan, 2969
Doordarshan, 51, 408, 417, 539, 569, 596, 706, 787
Dorr, Rheta Childe, 1522, 1876, 1890, 1946, 1977, 1979, 2036, 2041, 2053, 2055
Dorrie, Doris, 249
"Double Indemnity," 2489

Downs, Claire, 218, 1216
Dragonette, Jessica, 1769
Draper, Margaret, 1919, 1945
Drayton, Grace, 3091
"drench" hypothesis, 2341, 2417
"Dressed to Kill," 2468
"drip, drip" hypothesis, 2417
drug abuse, 2670, 2714
Duke, Patty, 2934
Dulac, Germaine, 132, 221, 226-227, 234, 249
Dumm, Edwina, 1858, 1983, 2998
Duncan, Sara Jeannette, 1512
Dunne, Irene, 2960
Dunnigan, Alice Allison, 3115
Duras, Marguerite, 217, 1168, 1170, 1197, 1214, 1219, 1261
Durbin, Deanna, 1807
Duta, Kavery, 2956
Dutch Broadcasting System, 931
Duval, Marie, 1000-1001
"Dynasty," 15, 57, 2424, 2467
DZWS, 756

Ebony, 2558, 3006
Echo Magazine, 738
Ecuador, 1327, 1343, 1428, 1439
editors, women, 77, 721, 728, 1836, 1856, 1914, 1916, 2984, 3004, 3035-3036, 3041, 3050, 3064, 3095, 3099, 3124-3125, 3128, 3219, 3226
editorials, 2583, 2984, 3030
Educational Broadcasting Review, 1636
education and training, 77, 313, 337, 467-468, 840, 866, 1454, 1523, 1535, 1551, 1558, 1576, 1582, 1642, 1746, 1756, 1847, 1945, 2101, 2769, 2772, 2781, 2786, 2805, 2809, 2877, 2989, 3005, 3048, 3089, 3099
Edwards, Stephanie, 2864
Egypt, 14, 44, 248, 303, 307, 323, 335, 351-352, 368, 370, 388
Eisenhower, Mamie, 1829
El Bello Sexo, 475
electronic media, 77, 135, 363, 1369, 2751, 2876
El Espectador, 1424
"11 P.M.," 576
El Hogar, 475
Elle, 1179
Ellerbee, Linda, 2889
El Mundo, 1343

El Payo, 1378
Emerson, Gloria, 1884, 2987
Emma, 1310
employment of women, 967, 1538, 1545, 2780, 2785, 2793, 2795, 3089; in broadcasting, 99, 103, 923, 969, 1144, 1188-1189, 1388, 1428, 1480, 1496, 1500, 1507, 1658, 2839, 2843, 2854, 2859-2860, 2869-2870, 2879, 2883-2885, 2896-2897, 2899-2901, 2910-2911, 2913-2915, 2920; in film, 2931, 2933; in media, 43, 70, 78, 83, 117, 214, 347, 1169, 1205, 1220, 2135, 2567; in newspapers, 47, 50-51, 77, 1427, 1535, 1747, 2983, 2986, 2988, 2991, 2993, 3025, 3039, 3044-3045, 3060, 3070, 3073, 3100; in public relations, 2810; in television, 51, 705
England, 24, 37, 47, 50, 70, 138, 183, 225, 258, 907, 925, 934, 937, 943, 951, 969; images of women in, 101, 107, 177, 917, 927, 966-967, 983-985, 997, 1008, 1010, 1014, 1018, 1029, 1035-1037, 1040, 1042, 1048, 1053-1059, 1084, 1086, 1088-1089, 1092, 1094, 1102, 1109, 1111, 1114, 1117, 1120, 1122, 1125, 1131, 1133-1134, 1137, 1140-1142; women in broadcasting in, 77, 130, 909; women and film in, 133, 217, 248, 270, 962; women as audience in, 1013, 1090, 1149, 1151-1152, 1157; women filmmakers in, 59, 218, 237, 947, 1203, 1216; women practitioners in, 982, 993-994, 996, 1000-1003, 1021, 1164-1165, 1169, 1171, 1178, 1184, 1220-1221, 1223, 1230, 1232, 1238, 1242-1243, 1248, 1255-1256, 1260; women's media in, 296, 978, 980-981, 987, 990, 992, 995, 999, 1004, 1007, 1012, 1015-1016, 1019-1020, 1022, 1265, 1267-1268, 1272, 1277-1280, 1284, 1287-1288, 1292-1294, 1296-1297, 1302, 1304, 1306-1308
English Woman's Journal, 1007, 1019, 1022
equal opportunity, 77, 422, 841, 843-844, 904-905, 1245-1247, 1250, 1500, 2780, 2836, 2848, 2867, 2983, 3002, 3101
equal rights, 1715-1716
ERA, 23, 2583, 3170, 3229

eroticism, 1410, 1416, 1690-1691, 1730, 2144, 2726, 2944
Essentials, 1309
Etemad, Rakhshan Bani, 390
Ethiopia, 14, 316
ethnicity, 1476, 1557, 1610, 1679, 2125, 2148, 2154, 2338, 2429, 2490, 2493-2494
European Economic Community, 1132, 1136, 1188
Europe, Eastern, 44, 872-880; images of women in, 881-892; women practitioners in, 893-902
Europe, Western: historical studies in, 978-1023; images of women in, 1024-1146; women and media in, 44, 77, 102, 105, 117, 126, 175, 191, 286, 903-977, 1624; women as audience in, 1147-1160; women practitioners in, 1161-1264; women's media in, 1265-1310
Evans, Linda, 2467
Eve's Weekly, 578, 765, 781
"Exorcist, The," 2730
"Eyes of Laura Mars, The," 2498

face ism (framing), 2311, 2534, 2558, 2652
faculty, women, 77, 2764, 2772, 2781, 2786, 2792, 2797, 2809, 3084
Fallaci, Oriana, 1174-1175, 1186, 1227 1234
family-career balance, 77, 714, 2463, 2853, 3098, 3189
Family Circle, 1886, 2098
Fanning, Katherine (Kay), 2982
"Fantasy Island," 2710
farm women, 616, 618-620, 638, 641, 1488, 2671, 2681
Farrar, Geraldine, 1807
"Far Road, The," 713
fashion, 2523, 2624, 2947, 3099, 3108, 3220, 3231
Faye, Alice, 2968
Federal Communications Commission, 77
Félix, María, 1393
Fellini, Federico, 1124
FEM, 1341
Fem, 1343
female bonding, 2465
Female Spectator, The, 995, 999, 1014
Female Tatler, 980

Femina, 578, 765, 781
feminine hygiene, 2208, 2266
Feminine Mystique, The, 1270
"Femininio Plural," 1433
femininity, 23, 51, 75, 80, 138, 272, 1141, 1307, 1652, 1764, 2358, 2387, 2391, 2396
feminism, 28, 67, 604, 829, 1217, 1294, 1447, 1508, 1530-1531, 1565, 1598, 2113, 2141; and advertising, 107, 275, 917, 1067; and communication research, 21, 70-71, 78, 83, 91, 96, 341, 1724; and communication studies, 37, 39, 107, 1543-1544, 1561, 1605, 1608, 3123; and film, 18, 31, 86, 108, 211, 216, 230, 237, 245-247, 276, 285, 457, 516, 600, 711, 730, 887, 947, 962, 1207, 1226, 1237, 1295, 1442, 1519, 1693, 1696-1697, 2502, 2512, 2944, 2980, 3153, 3156; and media, 3-5, 10, 15, 22-23, 51, 124, 1037, 1535, 1557, 1567, 1603, 2172, 2303, 2585; and popular culture, 1534, 1588-1589; and press, 77, 295, 468, 470, 634, 771, 877, 986, 993, 1052, 1177, 1257, 1283, 1296-1297, 1301-1302, 1307, 1315, 1549, 1553, 1723, 1728, 2594, 2610, 2616, 2661, 2685, 3178, 3214; and technology, 236; and television, 106, 189, 1109, 1171, 1290, 1433, 1673, 2131, 2295, 2358, 2387, 2427, 2720
Feminisme in de Mediamangel, 1283
Feminist, 292
feminist press, 53, 77-78, 254, 277, 292, 296, 389, 752, 952, 969, 979, 986, 1052, 1269, 1288-1289, 1291, 1413-1415, 1436, 1744, 1945, 1959, 1987, 1990-1994, 3166, 3198
feminization of poverty, 2369
Femmes du Viet-Nam, 703
Ferber, Edna, 1888
Fern, Fanny, 2036
Ferraro, Geraldine, 77, 1561, 1732, 2310, 2542, 2547, 2577-2578
Field, Kate, 2036
Field, Sally, 2925
Fiji, 394, 855
film, 17-18, 38, 46, 86, 93, 178, 252, 282, 284-288, 294, 408, 410-411, 938, 1079, 1539, 1579, 1686, 1689, 1693, 1698-1699, 1706, 1708-1710;

audiences, 629, 834, 1009, 1798, 2726-2733; by women, 20, 55, 57, 59, 73, 126, 132, 215, 222, 237, 248, 263, 270, 920, 1692; distribution, 270; for women, 265, 267, 280-281, 749, 762, 777, 791, 797, 867, 947, 962, 1010, 1271, 1276, 1295, 1303, 1305, 1516, 1519, 3148-3159; images of women in, 59, 68, 133, 139, 143-144, 151-152, 169-170, 175, 187, 233, 314, 329, 333, 335, 338-340, 370, 373, 375, 399, 419, 424, 457, 459, 461, 483, 488, 490-492, 496, 499-500, 503-504, 510, 516, 519, 526, 531-532, 535, 546, 548, 551-553, 556, 561-562, 569, 573, 575, 577, 579, 581, 589, 594-595, 597-598, 601-602, 605, 609, 811, 827-828, 887, 892, 937, 988, 1035, 1123-1125, 1128-1129, 1131, 1380, 1382, 1416, 1442, 1450, 1561, 1570, 1610, 1617, 1687-1688, 1690-1691, 1704, 1707, 1712, 1792-1793, 1797, 1802-1806, 1809-1810, 2116, 2121, 2148, 2160-2161, 2163, 2430, 2468-2533; music, 681, 693; theory, 17, 31, 60, 109, 111, 230, 245-247, 276, 1643, 1696-1697; women directors of, 77, 218-219, 221, 223, 226, 230, 234, 249, 390, 679-680, 804, 1808; women in, 55, 129, 217-219, 227, 242, 255, 258, 265, 437, 454, 458, 473, 480, 1448, 1581, 1694; women practitioners in, 669, 673, 676, 679-681, 683, 685-686, 693, 695, 700-701, 704, 707-708, 711-713, 739, 844-848, 851-853, 857-859, 863-864, 866, 875, 895, 899, 1168, 1170, 1173, 1181, 1185, 1190-1191, 1193-1197, 1199, 1203, 1207, 1210, 1214-1220, 1224, 1226, 1233, 1235-1237, 1248, 1258, 1261, 1325, 1327, 1374, 1393, 1425-1426, 1432, 1497, 1514, 1612, 1695, 1699-1700, 1788-1791, 1794-1796, 1798-1799, 1801, 1807-1808, 1811, 1987, 2925-2980
film festivals, 3155
film noir, 2504
filmography, 2491, 2516, 2927, 2934, 2951, 2959, 2961-2964, 2968, 2973
Filmotsav '86, 791
Finland, 248; images of women in, 1091, 1095, 1097, 1100, 1105, 1121; women and media in, 100-101; women practitioners in, 927, 930, 950, 1205, 1263-1264
Finnish Broadcasting Company, 927, 1263
Fireweed, 1520
First, Ruth, 356
First Ladies, 1817, 1826-1829, 1905, 2093
Fitzgerald, Frances, 1883
Fitz-Gibbon, Bernice, 2801
Fleeson, Doris, 1834
Fleet Street, 1221
Flenniken, Shary, 3023
Flick, Marian, 135
Flor, Lina, 481
Flores-Trinidad, Carolina, 668
Floreyfiorani, Rose, 1771
Fonda, Jane, 217, 2945, 2948
"For Better or for Worse," 1503-1505
Forever Amber, 2741
Forman, Carol, 2966
Fort, Hank, 1771
Fortune, 2558
fotonovelas, 5, 1300, 1399, 1404, 2711; images in, 155, 176, 1320, 1322, 1330, 1377, 1401
Foucault, Michel, 1181
France, 24, 908, 910, 940, 945, 957; images of women in, 152, 171, 186, 1031, 1041, 1046, 1050, 1098, 1106-1107, 1112, 1116, 1123, 1126; women and media in, 938, 944, 998, 1079; women filmmakers in, 59, 129, 217-218, 221, 1168, 1170, 1214-1215, 1217; women practitioners in, 1005, 1179, 1181, 1185, 1228, 1249, 1252, 1258; women's media in, 979, 981, 1017, 1269-1271, 1273, 1281, 1285, 1298
Frank Leslie's Monthly, 1886
Franklin, Ann, 1861, 2077
Frauenbuchverlag, 1289
Frauen-Film Produktion, 949
Frauenoffensive Verlag, 1289
Frauenselbstverlag, 1289
Frederick, Pauline, 2759, 2867, 2903
freelance writing, 3083
Freeman, Emma Belle, 2013
Free-Thinker, 1014
Friedan, Betty, 1270

Friends of Women, 790
Friends of Women Group (Puen Ying), 399, 790
Fruhauf, Aline, 3025
Fujin no tomo, 478
Fuldheim, Dorothy, 2857, 2867
Fulford, Robert, 2155
Fuller, Margaret, 1522, 1820, 1834-1835, 1841, 1852, 1862, 1935, 1997, 2028, 2041, 2079
Fuller, Mary, 2966
"Full Metal Jacket," 2531
Furman, Bess, 1753, 1898

Gabon, 312
"Gale Storm Show, The," 1786
Gallagher, Margaret, 922
Gallery, Michele, 2886
Gannett, 3173
Garbo, Greta, 217
García, Sara, 1380
Gardner, Gayle, 2916
Garr, Teri, 2486
Gartenlaube, 1023
gatekeepers, 2664-2666
Gearhart, Sally Miller, 829
Gellhorn, Martha, 1883, 1952, 2055, 2080
gender, 180, 342, 908, 1013, 1148, 1338, 1485, 1521, 1535, 1544, 1556, 1560-1561, 1583, 1586, 1590, 1626, 1629, 1640, 1652, 1929, 1967, 2165, 2268, 2527, 2652, 2686, 2699, 2709, 2729, 2747, 2755; communication, 26, 37, 209, 257; equality, 635, 698, 706, 2551, 2772, 2800, 2805; media portrayals of, 23, 101, 106-107, 337, 435, 483, 494-495, 501, 541, 809, 816, 826, 828, 950, 1024, 1032-1033, 1049, 1068-1078, 1085-1086, 1131, 1133, 2189, 2197, 2199, 2201, 2226, 2232, 2263, 2298, 2302, 2308, 2310, 2317, 2327, 2344, 2354, 2374, 2386, 2448, 2466, 2500, 2530, 2548-2549, 2572, 2585, 2607, 2625, 2656
Gentleman and the Lady's Town and Country Magazine, The, 1901
Gentleman's Magazine, 997
Gerbner, George, 2294
Germany, East, 218, 703, 886, 894, 902
Germany, West, 24, 184, 261, 267, 915, 961, 1083; images of women in, 886, 989, 1009, 1038, 1043, 1096, 1103-1104, 1119 1129, 1145; women and media in, 99, 929, 948-949, 956, 968; women as audience in, 1148, 1159; women broadcasters in, 101, 919, 935-936, 946, 963, 1011, 1066, 1192; women filmmakers in, 17, 59, 218, 1190-1191, 1194-1199, 1218, 1226, 1233, 1235-1237; women's media in, 77, 873, 1006, 1023, 1276, 1289, 1291, 1295, 1303, 1310; women practitioners in, 1163, 1187, 1211, 1222, 1229, 1231, 1244, 1249, 1254
Geyer, Georgie Anne, 1834, 1883, 3027, 3131
Ghana, 14, 259, 307, 333, 348-349
"Ghar Bar," 751
Ghatak, Ritwik, 399, 499, 556
Ghosh, Parvati, 218
Gibson, Charles Dana, 2570
Gibson Girl, 2570
Gilder, Jeannette, 2029
Gilligan, Carol, 1643
Gilman, Caroline H., 2028
Gilman, Mildred, 1834
Gilmer, Elizabeth, 2041
Girard (Ohio) *Grit*, 1855
"girlie" magazines, 157
Girls of the White Orchid, The, 1561
Gish, Dorothy, 1695
Gish, Lillian, 1695, 2954
Glamour, 2098, 3164
Glasnost, 873
Godard, Jean-Luc, 17
Goddard, Mary Katherine, 1522, 1863, 2000, 2041
Goddard, Paulette, 2959
Goddard, Sarah Updike, 1863, 1922, 2000
Goddard, William, 2000
Godey's Lady's Book, 1886-1887, 1891, 1897, 1966, 1971, 2027, 2058, 2098, 3231
Godmilow, Jill, 2937
Gold, Tami, 2956
Goldin, Marion, 2889
Gómez de Avellaneda, Gertrudis, 1355, 1357-1358
Gone with the Wind, 2741
Good Housekeeping, 1324, 2098, 2253, 2537, 2566, 2600, 2604, 2618, 3192, 3199, 3222
Goodman, Ellen, 1834
Gordon, Dorothy, 1771

Gorris, Marlene, 230, 249
gossip, 15, 1757, 1907, 2015, 2052, 3042, 3065
Gould, Bruce, 3179
Grable, Betty, 1796
Graham, Katharine, 2757, 3011, 3055, 3058, 3094
Graham, Sheilah, 1907
Grant, Jane, 1908
Greece, 1, 217, 1128, 1286
Greeley-Smith, Nixola, 2036
Greenfield, Meg, 2759
Greenwood, Irene, 806
Grewe-Partsch, Marianne, 1231
Grinstead, Frances, 1756, 1945
Gross, Terry, 2845
"Growing up Female: As Six Become One," 3157
Guatemala, 1315
Guerrero-Nakpil, Carmen, 668
"Guiding Light, The," 1645, 1657
Guisewite, Cathy, 3069
Gusher, Iris, 218
Guyana, 251

Ha'aretz, 378
Hakim, Christine, 739
Hakim, Shafi, 857
Hale, Sarah Josepha, 1522, 1856, 1870, 1887, 1891, 1897, 1937, 1965-1966, 2028, 2041
Halliday, Jon, 232
Hammersley, Evadna, 1771
Han, Michelle, 737
Hardeman, Gertrude, 1771
Harding, Ann, 2960
Hargrove, Mary, 3088
Harlequin, 2679
Harlequin Enterprises, 1452
Harman, Jeanne Perkins, 3034
Harper's Bazaar, 1843, 1944, 2098, 3108, 3231-3232
Harris, Fran, 1771
Harrison, Marguerite E., 1912
Hasegawa, Machiko, 527
Haskell, Molly, 216
Hasselbach, Mrs. Nicholas, 1873
Hauser, Elizabeth, 1855
Hawa, 388
Hawn, Goldie, 249
Hayes, Kate Simpson, 1459
Haywood, Eliza, 999
Hayworth, Rita, 2962

Head, Edith, 2947
Hearst, 1324, 1335
Hefner, Christie, 2757, 3055
Hello!, 1309
Hénaut, Dorothy, 1514
"Henrietta the Homemaker," 1466
Hepburn, Audrey, 2962
Hepburn, Katherine, 2960
HERA, 77
Herland, 829
Herrick, Genevieve Forbes, 3114
Her World, 770
He Zhen, 468
Hickok, Lorena, 1825, 1828
Hidari, Sachiko, 249, 713
Higgins, Marguerite, 1834, 1883, 1926, 1963, 2004, 2041, 3008, 3018, 3056
Hillhouse, Sarah Porter, 1880, 1945
Hind, E. Cara, 1459, 1461
Hispanic women, 2711
history, 29, 47, 129-133, 951; in Asia, 468-484; in Australia, 804-807; in Canada, 1456-1463; in Caribbean, 1355-1358; in Western Europe, 978-1023; in South America, 1413-1416; in United States, 1535, 1746-2101, 2700, 3012; of women and film, 129, 132-133
Hitchcock, Alfred, 2512, 2529
Hite, Shere, 77
Hochin Shinbun, 478
Honey, 1142
Hoest, Bunny, 3090
Holland, Agnieszka, 249
Hollander, Nicole, 2997, 3023, 3031
Holocaust, 375
homemakers (housewives), 612, 614, 625-626, 628, 633, 645, 648-650, 652, 655, 658-659, 666, 750, 835-836, 926, 1111, 1152, 1345, 1705, 1742, 1770, 1781, 2190, 2212, 2267, 2350, 2368, 2414, 2416, 2443, 2537, 2565-2566, 2615, 2685, 2971
Honduras, 1315
"Honeymooners, The," 2433
Hong Kong, 235, 444, 467; women practitioners in, 218, 673-674, 677, 687, 732, 737, 740
Hontiveros-Avellana, Daisy, 668
Hopkins, Miriam, 2959
Hopper, Hedda, 2052, 3042
Horne, Mae, 1771
Hostetter, Helen P., 1756, 1945

House and Garden, 2098
House Beautiful, 2098
Hudson Valley Women's Times, 77
Huffzky, Hans, 1006
Hui, Ann, 216, 218, 249
Hull, Peggy, 1834, 2017
Hulme, Etta, 2998
Human Communication, 1543
Hu Mei, 749
Hummert, Anne, 1782
Hummert, Frank, 1782
humor, 1524, 1527, 1613, 1633, 2450-2451, 2535, 2669
Hungary: images of women in, 50, 103, 107, 881-885; women and media in, 99-100, 105, 875; women as audience in, 879; women practitioners in, 892, 895
"Hunlog," 574
Huong, Nguyen Thi Than, 703
Hurston, Zora Neale, 2082
Hutton, Betty, 2959
Huxtable, Ada Louise, 1566, 1834
Hyde, Helen Patterson, 1756, 1945
Hymsa, 107, 1282

"I Am Curious (Yellow)," 1698
"I Am Somebody," 227, 2942
ICAIC, 1374
Iceland, 77, 1275
"If I Had a Million," 2528
ILET, 1326, 1341
Illinois, 2734
Illustrated Weekly, The, 578
Illustrierte Zeitung Leipzig, 1023
"I Love Lucy," 1786
images of women, 18-19, 42-44, 47, 53, 134-188, 290; in advertising, 50, 77, 101, 107, 160, 171, 202-203; in Africa, 300, 303, 319-343, 347, 357; in Asia, 398-399, 408-410, 416-418, 424, 429, 434-437, 441, 443-444, 446, 454, 457, 459, 461, 470, 483, 719; in Australia, 808-833; in broadcasting, 50-51, 101, 103, 106-107, 135, 140; in Canada, 830, 1441, 1444-1446, 1464-1495; in Caribbean, 1359-1366; in Central America, 1376-1386; in comics, 137-141; in Europe, 881-892, 1024-1146; in film, 54, 57-58, 139, 143-144, 151; in media, 66, 70, 77, 107, 115, 127-128, 136-137, 145-146, 158, 166, 171, 176; in Middle East, 368-382; in newspapers, 77, 207; in South America, 1311, 1318-1323, 1331, 1333, 1335-1336, 1338, 1340, 1417-1424; in United States, 2102-2669
Imai, Tadashi, 551
Imamura, Shohei, 510, 551
immigrant women, 2727
Indecent Representation of Women (Prohibition) Bill 1986, 518
India: images of women in, 77, 103, 107, 400, 409, 443, 488, 494-495, 497-499, 502-503, 508-509, 511, 515, 518-519, 522-523, 526, 528, 533, 535, 539, 543, 550, 556, 560, 566-569, 571-574, 578-580, 582-583, 587, 589, 591, 594, 596-599, 601, 607; women and film in, 46, 54, 178, 399; women and media in, 1, 2, 14, 44, 50, 100, 127, 251, 394, 397-401, 404, 407-408, 410, 417, 425, 456-457, 459, 465, 467; women and television in, 24, 36, 51, 107, 406, 424; women as audience in, 610-611, 613, 615-616, 618-621, 627, 629, 632, 634-635, 637-641, 643, 647, 656, 664; women in media of, 107, 414, 418-419, 441, 451; women practitioners in, 218, 248, 669, 672, 676, 678-681, 686, 688, 693, 698, 701, 705-706, 708, 711, 714-715, 721, 731; women's media in, 744-745, 747-748, 751-753, 759, 762-765, 771, 773-774, 777, 779-781, 787
Indian Press Council, 583
Indonesia, 122, 208, 542, 739, 783, 785, 788
Industrial Workers of the World, 2043
INSTRAW, 77
International Association for Mass Communication Research (IAMCR), 47, 50-51, 103, 105-106, 167
International Association of Women in Radio and Television, 897
International Bulletin, 27
International Commission for the Study of Communication Problems, 173
international communication, 45, 96, 3138
interpersonal communication, 631, 1526, 2559
International Feminist Network, 27

Inter Press Service, 284
Iowa, 2724
Iran, 1, 235, 384, 390
Iraq, 14, 372
Ireland, 954-955, 959, 1301
Irish women, 2490
ISIS, 27, 1343-1344
ISIS Journal, 77
Israel, 248; images of women in, 77, 374-375, 378, 381-382; women in media in, 107, 376, 392; women's media in, 389
Italian-American women, 2494
Italy, 57, 70, 79, 155, 218, 903, 941, 1045, 1052, 1062, 1085, 1110, 1115, 1124, 1173-1175, 1186, 1210, 1227, 1274 1299, 1327

Jackie, 1287, 1293-1294
"Jack the Ripper," 1137
Jacobson, Pauline, 1837
Jahr, John, 1006
Jakubowska, Wanda, 226
Jamaica, 100, 215, 220, 1349, 1364, 1375
Jamaica *Gleaner*, 1375
Jang Jan-yun, 468
Japan, 174, 176, 186, 215, 220, 270, 278, 436, 467, 507; images of women in, 101-102, 106-107, 177, 435, 444, 510, 514, 516, 525, 527, 529-530, 536, 541, 544-545, 548-549, 551-553, 555, 557-559, 576, 581, 588, 590, 593, 604; women and media in, 77, 100, 411, 428, 433, 446, 458, 492; women as audience in, 626, 628, 632-634, 646, 648-651, 655, 657, 659, 663, 665; women practitioners in, 416, 420, 422, 482, 682, 707, 713, 720, 1612; women's media in, 478-479, 484, 750, 761, 767-768, 782, 789
JAWS (Journalism and Women Symposium), 77, 1587
"Jenny Distaff," 1014
Jewish women, 2125
Jimenez-Magsanoc, Letty, 734
Johnson, Pam, 3038
Johnson, Rheta Grimsley, 2991
Johnston, Frances Benjamin, 2021, 2088
Johnston, Lynn, 1503-1505
Jóia, 1410
Jones, Jennifer, 2927, 2962
Joplin, Janis, 1527

Jordan, Elizabeth, 1834, 1944
Jornal das Famílias, 1413
Joubert, Jacqueline, 998
journalism, 261-261, 678, 682, 694, 714, 719, 721, 726-728, 731, 733-735, 742, 805, 856, 900-901, 948, 987, 991, 994, 1038, 1091, 1166-1167, 1174, 1183, 1186-1187, 1204, 1221-1222, 1227-1229, 1232, 1234, 1239-1241, 1257, 1259, 1263-1264, 1315, 1336, 1375, 1386, 1456-1462, 1509, 1511-1513, 1592, 1638, 1718, 1747-1750, 1753, 1976, 2025-2026, 2756, 2761, 2773, 2777-2778, 3012, 3044, 3047-3048
Journalist, The, 1522
journalists, 235, 262, 264, 350, 355, 357-358, 434, 478-479, 678, 682, 688, 690-692, 694, 702, 714, 719, 721, 726-728, 731, 733-735, 805, 807, 856, 871, 874-875, 893, 898, 901, 948, 994, 1005, 1038, 1166-1167, 1174-1175, 1177, 1183, 1204, 1206, 1220-1221, 1227-1229, 1232, 1234, 1239-1241, 1257, 1259, 1263-1264, 1315, 1370, 1375, 1386, 1389, 1429-1431, 1456-1462, 1498, 1501-1502, 1511-1513, 1522, 1558, 1747-1750, 1815, 1850, 1865, 1877, 1945, 1985-1986, 2026, 2071, 2077, 2085, 2756, 2985, 3026, 3057, 3065, 3071, 3092-3093, 3098, 3126
Journal of Communication, 1543
Journal of the New Woman of China, 468
Journal of Women's Studies, 468
June, Jennie (Jane C. Croly), 1834, 2036, 2041, 2051
Junkerseeliger, Hilde, 1163

Kalima, 367
Kaliman, 1378
Kantha Handa, 743
Kantha Maga, 743
Karath, Prema, 218, 249, 686
Karvelas, David, 3010
Kassell, Paula, 2581
"Kate and Allie," 17, 1679
Kazickas, Jurate, 1883
Keeley, Mary Paxton, 2101
Keller, Marjorie, 17
Kelly, Florence Finch, 1950
Kelsey, Linda, 2886

Kena, 1436
Kennedy, Joseph, 2953
Kenya, 44, 225, 308, 341, 359
Kenyon, Nellie, 1814
"Khandaan," 574
Kheda TV, 745
Kilgallen, Dorothy, 1938
Kilgore, Maggie, 1722
Kilman, Charlotte Perkins, 829
Kindem, Gorham A., 58
Kirchwey, Freda, 1816, 2055
Kirk, Susie, 3131
Kirkland, Caroline M., 2028
Kirkpatrick, Helen, 2080
Kitchen Table: Women of Color Press, 3228
Klein, Bonnie Sherr, 216
Klimova, Rita, 1209
Knight, Mary, 1956
Koplovitz, Kay, 2771
Korea, 235, 467, 636; images of women in, 77, 101, 177, 501, 534, 586, 592; women and media in, 46, 100, 105, 433, 440, 452; women practitioners in, 480, 704; women's media in, 474, 766, 769, 797, 870
Korean Woman's Magazine, 474
Koslow, Sally Platkin, 3209
Kuhn, Irene, 1959
Kurosawa, Akira, 551
Kuroyanagi, Tetsuko, 1612
Kurys, Diane, 249
Kvennalistinn, 1275
Kyler, Hester, 1771

La Cacerola, 1343
Lacan, Jacques, 230
Ladies' Home Journal, 1936, 2047, 2060, 2068, 2098, 2537, 2566-2567, 2590, 2600, 2635, 3164, 3172, 3179-3180, 3200, 3211, 3235
Ladies' Magazine, 1966
Ladies' Repository, 1886
Lady's Friend, 1886
Lady's Magazine, The, 983, 1993
Lady's Museum, 1012, 1014
La familia Burrón, 1378
Lagrimas, 1378
Lake, Veronica, 2959
La Mala Vida, 1343
La Marr, Barbara, 1811
Lamarr, Hedy, 1807

Lambert, Susan, 853
Lamour, Dorothy, 2959
La Mujer Trampa, 1285
La Tortuga, 1437
Lanctot, Micheline, 218
Land, The, 175
Landau, Sonia, 2855
Landers, Ann, 3043, 3061, 3093
Lane, Rose Wilder, 1837
Lange, Dorothea, 1892
Langham Place Circle, 1022
language, 23, 35, 84, 112, 416, 826, 1524, 1559, 2103-2104, 2147, 2151, 2167, 2333, 2401, 2516, 2590, 2605, 2661-2662
Lansden, Pamela, 3009
La Prensa (Nicaragua), 1391
La Prensa (United States), 2594
La Presse Feministe, 292
"La Signora di tutti," 988
La Solidaridad, 472
Latin America, 5, 44, 54, 69-70, 77, 96, 191, 207, 1324; images of women in, 156, 176, 1318-1319, 1322-1323, 1331, 1333, 1335-1336, 1338, 1340, 1342-1343; women and media in, 5, 44, 54, 70, 77, 96, 105, 1311, 1316-1317, 1320, 1327, 1337; women as audience in, 1345; women practitioners in, 117, 1315, 1325, 1343; women's media in, 24-25, 36, 78, 83, 1321, 1326, 1329-1330, 1332, 1334, 1339, 1341, 1343-1344, 1346
Laurie, Annie, 1834
"Laverne and Shirley," 1786
"LaVerne DeFazio," 2382
Law, Agnes, 1771
Lawrenson, Helen, 3053
Lazareff, Hélène, 1179
League of Women Voters, 2159
Lear, Frances, 3227
Lebanon, 77, 100, 371, 387
Le Deuxième Sexe, 1270
"Leech Woman, The," 2518
LeGallienne, Eva, 2970
"Legend of Tian Yun Mountain, The," 532
"Legend of Wonder Woman, The," 3225
Leisner, Susan W., 2760
Le Journal des Dames, 991
Lennon, Rosemarie, 3194
Lennox, Charlotte, 1012

Lerche, Doris, 1244
Leroy, Cathy, 3131
lesbians, 1524, 1534, 2400, 2563, 3204; and films, 55, 73, 126, 282, 3150
Leslie, Mrs. Frank (Miriam Follin), 1870, 2063
Leslie's Popular Monthly, 1951
Leslie's Weekly, 77
Levi-Strauss, Claude, 143
License To Rape, 77
Lidové Noviny, 1209
Life, 1909, 1913, 2185, 3034
Lilith Video, 1433
Lily, 1842
Lindblom, Gunnel, 249
Lin Tai-yi, 675
Lippincott, Sara J., 1965, 2074
literacy, 207, 210, 345, 365, 617
Literary Xpress, 3135
Little, Joan, 3086
Little Review, 1819
"Lockhorns," 3090
"Lois Lane," 2554
Lokkeberg, Vibeke, 58, 1207
Lombard, Carole, 2488, 2955, 2959
Look, 2185, 2253
London Daily Sketch, 1243
London Mercury, 1014
"Looking for Mr. Goodbar," 2468
"looksism," 2821, 2851, 2921, 2972
Loos, Anita, 2954
Lord, M. G., 2998, 3023
Los Angeles, 2920
Los Angeles Herald Examiner, 2617, 3113
Los Angeles Times, 2593, 2613, 2617, 2716, 3213
Louisville Courier-Journal, 3077
Love and Rockets, 1743
lovelorn columnist, 3028
Lowell, Joan, 1972
Lo Yan-bin, 468
Luce, Clare Booth, 1913, 1916, 1939, 2044-2045
Luce, Henry, 2045
"Lucecita," 1300
Lupino, Ida, 226, 234, 249, 2950
Lu Xiaoya, 249
Lynn, Diana, 2959

McBride, Mary Margaret, 1755, 1777, 3141
"McCabe and Mrs. Miller," 2492

McCall's, 2098, 2537, 2566, 2600, 2874, 3063, 3164, 3199, 3211, 3226
McCarthy, Mary, 1883
McClure's, 1911
McCormick, Anne O'Hare, 1834
McCormick, Elsie, 1837
McGrory, Mary, 1581, 1834
Machar, Agnes Maule, 1459
Mackin, Catherine (Cassie), 2873
MacLaine, Shirley, 2939, 2959
McLaughlin, Kathleen, 240, 2080
MacLean's Magazine, 1466
McMurray, Mary, 218
Madagascar, 366
Mademoiselle, 2098, 2540, 2624, 3165, 3199, 3215
Madonna, 2676, 2709
magazines, 131, 183, 278, 1549, 1719, 1736, 1908; audiences, 622, 634, 645, 2682, 2685, 2734, 2737, 2743-2747; for women, 5, 77, 268-269, 272-273, 277, 290, 295-297, 366-367, 388, 399, 408, 469, 474-477, 743, 748, 750-751, 753, 757-759, 763, 765, 767, 770-771, 773-774, 781-783, 785, 790, 792-793, 795-796, 870, 873, 898, 969, 978-980, 983, 991-992, 995, 999, 1004, 1006-1007, 1012-1017, 1019-1020, 1265, 1268-1270, 1272-1274, 1277-1284, 1286-1287, 1293-1294, 1297-1298, 1304, 1306-1310, 1314, 1324, 1329-1330, 1332, 1339, 1346, 1353, 1355, 1357-1358, 1394-1396, 1399, 1413-1415, 1436-1437, 1517, 1520, 1522, 1552, 1624, 1745, 1864, 1886, 1901, 1989-1994, 1998, 2034, 2038-2039, 2047, 2058, 2060-2061, 2098, 3161-3168, 3170, 3172, 3174-3176, 3179-3181, 3186-3193, 3196-3200, 3202-3203, 3205, 3208-3209, 3211, 3214-3224, 3226-3227, 3229-3232, 3235; images of women in, 5, 102, 107, 154, 156, 165, 171, 338, 378, 459, 490, 578, 582, 876, 889, 997, 1023, 1030, 1052, 1105, 1111, 1321, 1330, 1333-1334, 1410, 1445, 1466, 1495, 1559, 1715-1716, 1728, 1730, 1899, 1927, 1936, 1968, 1971, 1975, 2027, 2043, 2068, 2117, 2121, 2161, 2170, 2362, 2537, 2540-2541, 2549, 2557-2558, 2563, 2565-2569, 2579-2580, 2584, 2592, 2595, 2599-

2600, 2604, 2611, 2618, 2623-2624, 2626, 2628, 2632, 2635-2636, 2638, 2641, 2643-2644, 2648-2649, 2651-2653, 2658, 2669; women practitioners on, 675, 699, 714, 738, 846, 1179, 1355-1358, 1535, 1570, 1869-1870, 1887, 1890-1891, 1897, 1910-1911, 1913, 1916, 1931, 1951, 1965, 1995, 2014, 2019, 2028-2029, 2044-2046, 2063, 2066, 2087, 2090, 2789, 3006, 3013, 3022, 3034, 3045, 3053, 3096, 3099, 3108, 3112, 3129
Majority Report, 3166
Majors, Farrah Fawcett, 2382
"Make Way For Tomorrow," 2528
Malayalam, 601
Malaysia, 236, 431, 433, 467, 770; images of women in, 399, 491, 504, 522, 554, 565; women as audience in, 624, 631, 660, 662; women practitioners in, 671, 674, 687, 717-718
male chauvinism, 188, 2482, 2872
male gazing, 15, 50, 59, 78, 83, 103
Mali, 303
Mallet, Elizabeth, 1002-1003
Malloch, Helen Miller, 2069
"Mammy," 2126, 2134, 2484
Manchete, 1410
Mangeskar, Lata, 681, 693
Manila Chronicle, 493
Manila Daily Bulletin, 493, 710
Manila Times, 493
Manushi, 399, 763, 771, 773-774
Manushi Collective, 54
"Ma Perkins," 1664
Marcos, Ferdinand, 546, 709-710, 724, 729, 734, 736
Marcos, Imelda R., 668
Maria, Liberacion del Pueblo, 1343
Marianismo, 1334
"Marianne and Juliane," 57, 1236, 1276
Marie-Claire, 1270, 1281
Mario, Jessie White, 1869
marketing to women, 77, 190-193, 202-204, 836
Martineau, Harriet, 1021, 2019
Martinez, Norma, 217
Marvel Comics, 77
"Mary Hartman," 1647, 1664
"Mary Noble," 1647
"Mary Tyler Moore Show," 1786
masochistic aesthetic, 1704, 1707

mass media, 1, 5, 14, 53, 63-64, 241, 319, 799, 801, 803, 808, 814, 823, 825, 835-836, 874, 907, 934-935, 949-950, 1041, 1061, 1064-1065, 1102, 1110, 1121, 1127, 1137, 1155-1156, 1331, 1343, 3132, 3134-3135, 3137; audience, 2670-2674, 2677-2678, 2681, 2683-2684; women and, 76, 96-97, 99, 102, 104-107, 116-120, 878, 958, 966; women in, 75, 85, 259, 303, 862, 894, 896-897, 900, 956, 971, 973, 1163, 1172, 1212-1213, 1251, 1253, 1260, 1262, 1317-1319, 2770-2771, 2773, 2775, 2780, 2785, 2790, 2793, 2795, 3094
Maurin, Peter, 2020
"Maus," 2999
May, Elaine, 249
media ownership, 77, 1648, 2907, 3054, 3077, 3139
Media Report to Women, 3167
media research and women, 18, 21, 32, 70, 78, 83, 108, 179, 460, 610, 1231, 1531, 1590, 1599, 1721, 1724, 2110; feminist, 90, 1543-1544, 2109
MediaWatch, 77, 1481
MediaWatch Collective, 603
Medical Journal (Australia), 820
medical journals, 2204, 2238, 2990
Mediterranean Women, 1286
"Meet Misty," 3225
"Meghe Dhaka Tara," 399, 499
Mehta, Vijaya, 676, 679, 686
Meiselas, Susan, 1392
Meisner, Lillian Weckner, 2998
Menken, Marie, 132
menstruation, 2203, 2633, 2676, 2721
Menzi, Hans, 724
Mercouri, Melina, 217
Meserand, Edythe J., 1771
Messick, Dale, 3091
Meszaros, Marta, 230, 249
Mexico, 2, 240, 259, 267, 278, 1313, 1341; images of women in, 155, 160, 1323, 1376-1380, 1382, 1384-1385; women and film in, 270, 1327; women practitioners in, 1315, 1387-1389, 1393; women's media in, 1314, 1343, 1346, 1394-1396
MGM, 1790, 1797
Miami Herald, 2625, 3067, 3113, 3119
"Miami Vice," 183, 2310

Michigan, 2094, 2398, 2647
Middle East: images of women in, 368-382; women practitioners in, 388-393; women's audience in, 383-387
Mikkelsen, Laila, 1207
"Mildred Pierce," 2519
military, 2142
Miller, Sadie, 77
Mills, Marjorie, 1771
minority women (women of color), 77, 126, 240, 500, 1256, 1535, 1541, 1581, 1587, 1872, 1878, 1987, 2067, 2082, 2089, 2863, 2907, 2974, 3006, 3012, 3038, 3075, 3115, 3202, 3224, 3228; images of, 2107, 2126, 2131, 2134, 2139, 2141, 2210, 2251, 2319-2320, 2329, 2405, 2426, 2428, 2469, 2475-2476, 2480, 2484-2485, 2487, 2496, 2506, 2508-2509, 2517, 2520
Miró, Pilar, 1182
Mishmar Li 'Yladim, 378
"Miss Buxley," 2576, 2608
Mizoguchi, Kenji, 510, 516, 551
Moats, Alice-Leone, 2080
models, 171, 530, 2240-2241, 2257-2258, 2723
"Modesty Blaise," 1116
Monroe, Marilyn, 217
Montaner, Rita, 217
Montez, Maria, 1807
Monthly Extract, 3166
Moore, Mary Tyler, 2382
Morita, Yoshimitsu, 411
Morocco, 367
Mosadi, 358
Mother's Magazine, 1886
Motoko, Hani, 478
Mouly, Françoise, 2999, 3033
Moyers, Bill, 2369
Mr. and Ms., 729
"Mrs. Cunningham," 2382
Ms., 77, 1522, 1715, 2170, 2236, 2558, 2618, 3164, 3181, 3186, 3192, 3199, 3205, 3214-3217, 3229-3231
MTV, 2298, 2373-2374, 2460
muckraking, 1848, 1859, 1866, 1890, 1911, 1995, 2066, 2076, 2087, 2776, 3001, 3088
Muir, Florabel, 3076
Mujer, 1339
Mujer-FEMPRESS, 1339
Mujer ILET, 1439
Mujer-Tec, 1368
Mukti, 751
Mulherio, 1341, 1343
multinational corporations, 431, 466, 945, 1324, 1335, 1346, 1396
Mulvey, Laura, 242
Murray, Mae, 1811
Murray, Marian, 1771
Musgrove, Patches (Helen), 1883
music, 681, 693, 1350, 1359, 1362-1363, 1527, 1666, 2115, 2122, 2163
music video, 15, 1477, 1561, 2292, 2298, 2310, 2345, 2373-2374, 2434, 2460-2461, 2709
Muslim, The, 692
Mydans, Shelley, 2080
"My Day," 2035
"My Friend Irma," 1786

Nable de Avellano, Florentina, 472
NAEB Journal, 1636
Nair, Mira, 680
Nancy Kwan Films Ltd., 673
"Nari Tu Narayani," 764
Nast, Condé, 3163, 3223
Nation, The, 1816, 1869
National Broadcasting Company, 77
National Commission on the Causes and Prevention of Violence, 1568
National Council for Research on Women, 3133
National Federation of Press Women, 2069
National Film Board, Studio D, 211, 1514, 1519
National Intelligencer, 2093
National Public Radio, 2845
NCWW, 77
Negri, Pola, 1811
Nepal, 33, 630, 723
Netherlands, 248, 939, 970, 975, 1158; images of women in, 50, 104, 1108, 1118; women and media in, 100, 106-107, 928, 971-972, 1071, 1075, 1266; women practitioners in, 51, 107, 916, 1176, 1180, 1206, 1212, 1257; women's media in, 1283, 1290, 1305
New Age, 356
New Dawn, 1715
New Northwest, The, 1838
New Orleans Picayune, 1849, 2005

news, 1149, 1443, 1581, 2149, 2441, 2548, 2562, 2634, 2646; audience for, 2675, 2680, 2725; decision making of, 77 162, 871, 1164-1165, 1200-1201, 3095; women in, 77, 176, 220, 244, 266, 326, 392, 399, 493, 508, 972, 1061, 1369, 1418, 1579, 1612, 1867, 2170, 2333, 2545, 2560, 2574, 2659, 2664-2666, 3140
news directors, 77, 2913, 2918, 2996
newspaper managers, 3079-3082, 3109-3111, 3113, 3120, 3124-3125
newspapers, 47, 274, 424, 871, 1453, 1729, 1833; audiences, 639, 643, 649, 1153, 2735-2736, 2740, 2748; for women, 79, 755, 768, 775, 780, 786, 788, 794, 869, 981-982, 985, 1297, 1518, 1722, 1739, 1838-1839, 1894, 1958, 2070-2071, 2086, 3171, 3173, 3177-3178, 3182, 3185, 3191, 3201, 3204, 3206, 3210, 3212-3213, 3233; images of women in, 77, 319, 321, 328, 382, 418, 520, 534, 547, 549, 564, 567-568, 593, 606, 826, 828, 876, 996, 1060, 1103, 1112-1113, 1117, 1465, 1493, 1535, 1727, 1837, 1943, 1967, 1970, 1973, 2072, 2093-2094, 2121, 2123, 2541, 2550, 2552-2553, 2572-2574, 2581, 2583, 2585, 2589, 2593-2594, 2596, 2603, 2612, 2616-2617, 2622, 2625, 2647, 2657, 2662, 2664-2667; women in, 50-51, 53, 376, 416, 419-420, 438, 477-479, 1063, 1390, 1826-1827, 1829, 1917; women practitioners in, 688, 690-692, 710, 722, 724, 727-728, 729, 731, 733-736, 846, 854, 856, 898, 900-901, 1002-1003, 1021-1022, 1206, 1209, 1375, 1391, 1427, 1429-1431, 1456-1462, 1552, 1570, 1587, 1747, 1749, 1753, 1814-1825, 1828, 1830-1832, 1834-1836, 1840-1842, 1844-1866, 1868, 1871-1874, 1876-1878, 1880-1885, 1887-1896, 1900, 1902, 1909, 1912-1915, 1918-1919, 1921-1926, 1932-1933, 1935, 1937-1942, 1944-1950, 1952-1957, 1959-1964, 1966, 1972, 1974, 1976-1977, 1979-1988, 1997, 1999-2000, 2002, 2004-2006, 2009-2010, 2012, 2015-2018, 2020, 2022, 2024, 2031-2033, 2035-2038, 2040, 2042, 2046, 2048-2049, 2051-2053, 2055-2057, 2059, 2062, 2064-2065, 2067, 2073-2080, 2083, 2085, 2089, 2100, 2757-2759, 2765, 2776, 2981-2989, 3000-3001, 3004, 3007-3011, 3014-3016, 3021, 3026-3030, 3032, 3035-3036, 3038-3073, 3075-3082, 3085, 3088, 3092, 3100-3102, 3105, 3109-3111, 3113-3117, 3119-3120, 3124-3128, 3131
news services: for women, 77, 283, 293, 846, 1369, 1373, 3234; images of women in, 2578, 2601-2602, 2660; women practitioners in, 1956, 3003, 3020, 3097, 3118
Newsweek, 77, 2185, 2236, 2253, 2557-2558, 2611, 2618, 2652
New Woman, 3194, 3200
New Women, 770
New Women's Movement, 1183
New Words, 77
New York American, 2036
New York Daily News, 77, 3114
New Yorker, 1908, 2185, 2590, 3013, 3037
New York *Herald*, 2051
New York Historical Society, 2034
New York Post, 1977, 2024, 2046, 3032, 3078
New York Recorder, 2086
New York Times, 77, 1932, 1943, 2036, 2074, 2093, 2541, 2550, 2581, 2585, 2598, 2622, 2625, 2662, 3014, 3029, 3177, 3183, 3213
New York Times Magazine, 2263
New York Times Women's Caucus, 77
New York *Tribune*, 1921, 1997, 2079
New York Woman, 1624
New York World, 1944, 2036
New Zealand, 248, 261, 267, 810, 826, 856, 861
Nicaragua, 248, 1390-1392
Nicholson, Eliza Jane, 1849, 2005, 2041
Niger, 1, 323
Nigeria, 225, 261, 307, 321, 354, 363; images of women in, 107, 303, 320, 322, 332, 337, 340
19, 1142
Nippon Hoso Kyokai, 761
Noelle-Neumann, Elisabeth, 21
Nogueira Lima, Monica, 1431
Nome Nugget, 2992

North America, 117, 191, 1441-1446
Norway, 47, 107; images of women in, 47, 1060, 1064-1065, 1067-1078, 1135, 1138-1139, 1146; women and media in, 70, 96, 99, 102, 950; women as audience in, 1155-1156; women broadcasters in, 103, 911; women filmmakers in, 58, 248, 1207; women journalists in, 50, 961 1183, 1239-1241, 1259
Norwegian Broadcasting Corporation, 1139
Novak, Kim, 2962
NOW (National Organization of Women), 77, 1624, 2159, 2205, 2829, 2836, 2887
"Now Voyager," 17, 1700
nudity, 2265, 2744
Nueva Mujer, 1341, 1343
"Nurses, The," 2359
nurses, 77, 1600, 2359-2361, 2503, 2623
Nuthead, Dinah, 1873
NWICO (New World and International Communication Order), 40-41, 76, 102, 225

O Bello Sexo, 1414
Oberon, Merle, 2962
O'Connor, Harvey, 2009
O'Connor, Jessie Lloyd, 2009
Office of War Information, 2739
"Official Story, The," 3153
off our backs, 1522, 3135
O Jorno das Senhoras, 1414
Older, Cora, 1837
Older, Fremont, 1754, 1837
"Olympia," 1191
O'Neill, Rose, 3091
Ontario Educational Communications Authority, 1510
Ophul, Max, 988
Options, 1308
Oregon, 2718
Oregonian, 1953
ORF, 1101
Orosa, Rosalinda L., 668
Osmond, Marie, 2382
Otis, Eliza A., 1917
Ottinger, Ulrike, 1190
Oui, 2638
Outlook, The, 476
Outwrite, 751

Oxenberg, Jan, 2929
Ozu, Yasujiro, 411, 551

Pacific, 259, 394-396, 405, 462, 682, 776, 838, 855, 862
"Pacific Women," 776
Pacquet-Sévigny, Thérèse, 256
Páginas, 1436
Pakistan, 653, 784; images of women in, 107, 524, 570; women and media in, 100, 421, 439; women practitioners in, 218, 692, 695, 700
Palcy, Euzhan, 249
Palma, Tina Monzon, 737
Palmer, Kate Salley, 2998
Pan Am, 77
Pankhurst, Sylvia, 1232
Panorama, 722, 733-734
Papua New Guinea, 855
Paraguay, 1438
Paramount, 2959
Paranjpye, Sai, 218
Parents' Magazine, 2098,
Parker, Cornelia Stratton, 2014
Parker, Dorothy, 1949
Parker, Eleanor, 2951
Parra, Violeta, 217
Parry, Natasha, 217
Parsons, Harriet, 2891
Parsons, Louella O., 2015, 2052
"Pattern of Marriage," 1042
Patterson, Eleanor M. "Cissy," 1877, 1915, 1984, 2757, 3040
Paul, Charlotte, 3085
Pauley, Jan, 2841, 2858, 2890
Payne, Ethel L., 3075
Peking Women's News, 468
Peng Xiaolian, 749
Penthouse, 1730, 2638
Pepsi Cola, 2181, 2310
Peries, Sumitra, 730
Perincioli, Christina, 1190
Perry, Eleanor, 2954
Persephone Press, 1744
Peru, 107, 225, 235, 248, 1315, 1341, 1405, 1410, 1423, 1432, 1437-1438, 1440
Petersburg Leaf, 898
Peterson's Magazine, 1886, 3231
Peyton Place, 2741
Philadelphia, 1969-1970

Philadelphia Daily News, 3104
Philippine Daily Inquirer, 729
Philippine Press Institute, 755
Philippines, 46, 77, 225, 411, 437-438, 467; images of women in, 101, 107, 177, 413, 427, 490, 493, 512, 522, 546-547, 561-564, 577, 595, 600, 603; women and media in, 107, 259, 423, 433, 454, 458, 472; women as audience in, 612, 623, 625, 645, 652, 654; women in communication in, 128, 475-476, 481, 496; women practitioners in, 668, 670, 684-685, 690-691, 709-710, 716, 722, 724, 729, 733-737; women's media in, 754-757, 772, 775, 778, 786, 792, 794-495
Philippines Herald, 493
"Photographer, The," 2468
photography, 5, 107, 170, 243, 268, 1392, 2740; history of, 77, 1753, 1845, 1854, 1875, 1906; images in, 379, 884, 1600, 1731, 2102, 2534, 2541, 2584, 2603, 2613, 2652; women practitioners of, 1892, 2001, 2003, 2013, 2021, 2050, 2054, 2096, 3002, 3074, 3106, 3130
photoroman, 1298
Pictorial Review, 2098
Piercy, Marge, 829
Pini, Wendy, 3023
Pintong, Khun Nilawan, 699
pin-up girl, 2473
Pioneer, The, 1839
Playboy, 1730, 2236, 2362, 2590, 2609, 2638, 2744
Playgirl, 1715, 2744
"Plays for Today," 1036, 1109
"PM Magazine," 2431
Poirier, Anne-Claire, 216
Poland, 248, 703, 876, 890-891
"Polly Maggoo," 1116
Polotan-Tuvera, Kerima, 668
Pond, Elizabeth, 1883
Popkin, Zelda, 2022
popular culture, 1527, 1534, 1542, 1555, 1588-1589, 1608, 1617, 1723, 1733, 1740, 1745, 2108, 2119, 2125, 2143, 2163, 2175, 2530, 2570, 2676, 2767
Popular Unity, 1330
Porcupine's Gazette, 1970
pornography, 3, 17, 34, 54, 77, 138, 142, 165, 374, 798, 917, 1482, 1530, 1536, 1564-1565, 1568, 1571, 1591, 1598, 1601-1602, 1622, 1728, 1735, 2106, 2676; in film, 20, 170, 399, 815, 1546, 1690-1691, 1703, 2944
"porn-vertising," 107
Portugal, 914, 1039
"Postman Always Rings Twice, The," 2489
Potter, Bridget, 2850
pregnancy, 2717
press, 18, 240, 291, 464, 911, 916, 940, 942, 957, 960-961, 986, 1291-1292, 1620, 1720, 2738; history of, 468, 990-991, 994; images of women in, 107, 337, 343, 371, 441, 443, 554, 818, 887, 918, 952, 1018, 1039, 1096, 1361-1363, 1417, 1474-1475, 1732, 1904, 2542, 2582, 2606, 2637, 2655; practitioners, 703, 714-715, 719, 1242-1243, 1389, 1889, 2041
Press, Tina, 2893
"Preying Mantis," 77
Prima, 1309
printing, 1812, 1861, 1879, 1918-1919, 1922-1924, 1930, 1934, 1945, 2000, 2011, 2023, 2030, 2097
professionalism, 51, 115, 244, 848, 1251, 1257, 2025, 3106
pronatalism, 2410, 2566
propaganda, 184, 725, 989, 993, 1011, 1232, 1434, 1627, 1752, 1929, 2555, 2580
prostitution, 522, 827, 1380, 1601, 2146, 3233
Pry, Polly, 1834
"Psycho," 2468
psychoanalysis, 1571, 1643; and film, 60, 109, 111, 1123, 2528-2529, 3148
public broadcasting, 2305, 2393, 2439, 2830, 2832, 2837, 2843, 2845, 2855, 2885
Public Broadcasting Service, 1658
public relations, 77, 1421, 1509, 1535, 1625, 1627-1628, 1630, 1760, 2121, 2691, 2697, 2703, 2776, 2802, 2804-2807, 2809-2813, 2815-2817, 2819-2820
Public Telecommunications Review, 1636
publishing, 1735, 2741, 3066; by women, 77, 213, 253-254, 267-268, 296, 389, 696, 729, 1169, 1223, 1255, 1288-

474   Subject Index

1289, 1296, 1301-1302, 1325, 1744, 1813, 1903, 1934, 3103; for women, 752, 3195; images in, 373, 399, 542, 1120, 1453, 2586-2588
Puerto Rico, 77, 126, 1315, 1347, 1360, 1365-1367
Pulitzer Prizes, 77

Qiu Jin, 468
Quarterly Journal of Speech, 1543
Quebec, 1501-1502, 1513-1514, 1516
Queen, 1022
"Queen Christina," 1797
Quinn, Sally, 2894
quiz shows, 15, 2380, 2403

racism, 2413, 2420, 2487, 2582
radio, 165, 229, 1655; audiences, 615, 620, 627, 630, 656, 658, 661, 879, 1160, 2722, 2724; for women, 1299-1300, 1434, 1438, 1772, 3139-3141, 3143, 3145; images of women in, 5, 62, 103, 319, 490, 498, 607, 882, 885, 1084, 1093, 1139, 1146, 1362-1363, 2304-2306, 2379; women and, 33, 102, 104, 106, 257; women in, 258, 303, 352, 391; women practitioners, 689, 723, 725, 727, 806, 840-841, 843, 846-849, 855, 865, 929, 1428, 1535, 1570, 1753-1755, 1765-1767, 1769, 1771, 1773-1780, 1782-1785, 1787, 2085, 2765, 2776, 2855, 2893, 2907; women's programs, 77, 201, 756, 761, 772, 778, 1515, 1781
Radio Donna, 1299
Radio Educación México, 1343
Radio Education Teacher Training Project, 630
Rádio-Mulher, 1434
Radio New Zealand, 861
Radio Telefís Eireann, 100, 954-955
Radio Television Hong Kong, 677
Radio Tuvalu, 855
Rainer, Yvonne, 230, 3152
Rajkumari, 681
Ralston, Esther, 2967
Ramlee, P., 491
Rangoonwala, Feroze, 556
"Raosaheb," 679
rape, 542-543, 798, 800, 1622, 1701, 2498; in press, 77, 163, 566-567
Ray, Allene, 2966

Ray, Michèle, 1228
Ray, Satyajit, 457, 556
Rayne, Martha Louise, 1847
Reader's Digest, 675, 2669
Reader's Guide to Periodical Literature, 1716
reading, 1154, 1157, 1278, 2735
Realidade, 1410
REAL Women, 1474
"Rear Window," 57
Redbook, 1715, 2567, 3164, 3215, 3229
Rede Mulher, 1344
Redgrave, Vanessa, 217, 2948
Red Radiofónica de Mujeres, 1343
"Red Sorghum," 602
Reform Bill of 1867, England, 985
Reidemeister, Helga, 1190
Reid, Helen Rogers, 2757
resources on women and media, 88-89, 297, 799, 801, 803, 867, 1176, 1545, 1548-1549, 1576, 1616, 1686, 1741, 2145, 2152, 2470, 2767, 2774, 2792, 3132, 3134-3135, 3137, 3159, 3191, 3195
Reuppel, Carol Hope, 1541
Reviewer, 1864
Revolution, The, 1894, 1958, 1974, 1992, 2057
Revson, Charles, 2799
"Rhoda," 2382
Rice, Linda Johnson, 3006
Riefenstahl, Leni, 226, 1191, 1195-1196, 1199
Riffaud, Madeleine, 238
Rind, Clementina, 1945, 2042
Rinehart, Mary, 3018
risa y amor, 1378
RKO, 2960
Robb, Inez, 2032, 2080
Robbins, Trina, 3023, 3051, 3121, 3225
Rogers, Ginger, 2960
Rolland, Ruth, 2966
Roosevelt, Eleanor, 1766, 1777, 1826-1829, 1905, 2035
Ropars, Marie-Claire, 17
Rosema, Patricia, 216
Rosenberg, Avis, 3023
Rosenthal, A. M., 2581
"Rosie the Riveter," 184, 1466, 1705, 1929
Ross, Ishbel, 1522, 1834
Rothschild, Amalie, 2956

Roy, Bimal, 503
Royall, Anne, 1522, 1754, 1831, 1941, 2023, 2036, 2041
Royalle, Candida, 2944
RTVE, 1182
Rubenstein, Ann, 2889
Ruffin, Josephine St. Pierre, 2029
Runge, Erika, 1190
rural women, 195, 198, 201, 344, 386, 399, 406, 418, 611, 618, 620, 629, 632, 637, 640, 656, 661, 744-745, 1435
Russell, Jane, 2960

Saddam Hussein, 372
Sagan, Leontine, 132, 226, 1233
SAGE, 77
St. Louis Post-Dispatch, 1973
St. Nicholas Magazine, 1931
"Salaam Bombay!" 680
Salem (Mass.) *Gazette and General Advertiser*, 1918
"Salt of the Earth," 3153
Sander, Helke, 1190
Sanders, Marlene, 77, 2826, 2852, 2890, 2898, 2900, 2902-2903
Sanders-Brahms, Helma, 218, 1194
San Francisco Chronicle, 1943
Sangeeta, 218, 700
Sanger, Margaret, 1990-1991, 2039-2040
Sangre India: Chamula, 1384
Saraste, Leena, 243
Sarita, 578
Sassy, 1671
Satri Sarn, 699
Saturday Evening Post, 1929, 1936, 1965, 2074, 2579, 2595, 3096
Saturday Review (England), 1019
Saturday Review (United States), 2185
Sauder, Helke, 230
Savitch, Jessica, 2827, 2904
Savvy, 77
Sawyer, Diane, 2858, 2890, 2903, 2923
"Sazae-san," 527
Scandinavia, 1127
Schiff, Dorothy, 2024, 2046, 2757, 3078
Schloendorff, Volker, 1226
Schmidt, Evelyn, 218
Schneemann, Carolee, 242
School Friend, 1278
Schultz, Sigrid, 1834, 2080, 2867
Schuyler, Philippa, 1883, 1889

Schwartz, Marilyn, 2991
"Schwarzwaldklinik," 1159
science fiction, 17, 67, 829, 1451, 2636, 3046
scientists, 2592
Scott, Lizabeth, 2959
Screen Actors Guild, 77
Scripps, Ellen Browning, 1850
Seaman, Elizabeth Cochrane, 2041
Seidelman, Susan, 218, 249, 2946
Self, 3217
Sen, Aparna, 218, 686
Senegal, 1, 303, 324, 333, 366
Service Woman, 1752
"Sesame Street," 1618, 2293, 2919
"seven sisters' magazines," 77
Seventeen, 1671, 2203, 3192
Sevilla de Alvero, Rosa, 272
sex, 1650, 1653, 1661, 1669, 1671, 1711-1712, 1729, 2223, 2292, 2312, 2320, 2340, 2343, 2353, 2422, 2429-2430, 2434, 2440, 2476, 2582, 2644, 2651, 2675, 2744, 2822, 3212
sex discrimination, 77, 229, 2404, 2450-2451, 2479, 2735, 2760, 2769, 2777, 2790, 2818, 2828-2830, 2834, 2854, 2872, 2875, 2877, 2887, 2909, 3003, 3017, 3020, 3059-3060, 3066, 3072, 3084
sexism, 408, 512, 582, 603, 815, 1053, 1549, 2103; in advertising, 77, 325, 565, 583-584, 608, 816, 825, 832, 1122, 1494, 1524, 1624, 2104, 2202, 2207, 2216, 2227, 2230, 2235-2236, 2251, 2259; in films, 535, 1193, 1800, 2516; in media, 2111, 2117, 2120, 2133, 2147, 2151-2152, 2156, 2167, 2169, 2576, 2619; in newspapers, 77, 1722, 2556, 2612, 2661-2662, 3049; in publishing, 1120, 2582, 2669, 3218; in television, 77, 1108, 1477, 2293, 2324, 2333, 2381, 2408, 2432, 2460-2461, 2865, 2881; in textbooks, 66, 148-149, 505, 591, 886, 2564
sex objects, 19, 504, 598, 1111, 1365, 1624, 2190, 2211-2212, 2223, 2267, 2292, 2608, 2638-2639
sex roles, 23, 47, 51, 104, 112, 134, 167, 179-180, 301, 569, 589, 1075, 1078, 1087, 1127, 1130, 1262, 1423, 1478, 1526, 1569, 2105, 2110, 2122, 2173, 2219, 2255-2256, 2271, 2627, 2629, 2649-2650, 2655, 2701; and

television, 77, 168, 177, 539, 557, 1025-1028, 1054-1058, 1118, 1132, 1134-1135, 1385, 1446, 1559, 1644, 2245-2247, 2287, 2295, 2299, 2312, 2340, 2367, 2371-2372, 2423, 2436
sex-role stereotyping, 101, 116, 161, 185-187, 524, 563, 670, 695, 810, 919, 1084-1085, 1101, 1114, 1361; in Australia, 160, 809, 812; in Canada, 47, 1465, 1467-1468, 1470-1471, 1473, 1481, 1487, 1490, 1496, 1500, 1515; in India, 441, 498, 503, 566, 580; in Japan, 186, 444, 514, 537, 544, 588; in Mexico, 160, 1376-1377; in United States, 47, 77, 160, 1593, 1673, 1680-1681, 1943, 2124-2129, 2134-2137, 2139, 2149, 2157-2158, 2177, 2185-2188, 2194-2195, 2197, 2200, 2213-2215, 2220, 2222, 2224, 2231, 2239, 2243, 2263, 2274-2275, 2281, 2290, 2296, 2300, 2313, 2322, 2325-2326, 2339, 2342, 2345-2346, 2352, 2356, 2360-2361, 2377, 2383-2386, 2394, 2397-2399, 2401-2402, 2406, 2409, 2411, 2417, 2421, 2435-2436, 2441-2442, 2449, 2454, 2458, 2469-2470, 2475, 2480, 2483, 2501, 2503, 2518, 2524, 2535, 2543-2544, 2553, 2560, 2638, 2640, 2654, 2659-2660, 2663, 2665, 2668, 2702, 2725, 2981
Sex-Roles within Massmedia Newsletter, 99-107
sexual harassment, 2779, 2867, 2958
sexuality, 138, 165, 182, 506, 550, 926, 1040, 1142, 1622, 1637, 1764, 2043, 2106, 2258; in cinema, 68, 169-170, 457, 553, 594, 602, 937, 1129, 1393, 2471
sexual politics, 133, 183, 216, 1708, 2139, 2374, 2504
Shaffer, Ann, 1771
Shannon, Julia, 2013
Shelanu, 378
Shephard, Elaine, 2778, 2787
Shepitko, Larissa, 216, 218, 249, 899
Sheridan, Ann, 1807
Sherr, Lynn, 2903
Sibyl, 1886
Sidney, Sylvia, 2959
Sierra Leone, 307, 323
Sigourney, Lydia H., 2028
Silveira, Helena, 1431

Silver, Joan Micklin, 249, 2946
Silver (McLeod), Merikay, 3066
"Silver Metal Lover," 3225
Simmons, Ellen B., 2036
"Simplemente Maria," 176
Singapore, 403, 431, 453, 466-467, 606, 608, 727
Sioussat, Helen, 1773, 1784, 2867
S.I.T.E., 611
situation comedy, 17, 1705, 1770, 2319, 2370-2371, 2414, 2420, 2428, 2446
SKILLS, 407
Slavic women, 2493
Sline, Deborah, 3010
Sloane, Barbara, 3063
Smedley, Agnes, 1980
Smith, Helen Brannon, 3035
Smith, Kate, 1785, 2964
Smutna, Dana, 217
Snow, Carmel, 3108
soap operas, 13, 15, 17, 24-25, 61, 78, 83, 126, 130, 140, 147, 174, 189, 206, 212, 265, 490, 644, 652, 802, 839, 906, 959, 1109, 1119, 1150-1151, 1159, 1399, 1402, 1449, 1531, 1581, 1634-1635, 1639, 1641, 1645-1647, 1649, 1654, 1657, 1660-1664, 1673, 1677-1679, 1682, 1705, 1772, 1781-1782, 2108, 2136, 2283, 2304, 2306-2307, 2321, 2332, 2334, 2367, 2380, 2403, 2410, 2416, 2430, 2679-2680, 2714, 2720, 2724
"sob sister," 1822, 2101
socialist-feminism, 16, 2448
social work, 2626
Society for Cinema Studies, 18, 1689
society pages (women's pages), 754-755, 766, 768, 775, 780, 786, 788, 846, 869, 1551, 1581, 1722, 1739, 1987, 2036, 2070-2071, 2170, 2666, 2777, 3000, 3070, 3178, 3182-3185, 3201, 3206, 3212-3213
somatypes, 2164
"Something Different," 1698
Song Hits Magazine, 2115
"Sorry, Wrong Number," 2489
Sothern, Ann, 2973
South Africa, 306, 356; images of women in, 127, 325, 330, 338, 343
South America: historical studies in, 1413-1416; images of women in, 1401, 1417-1424; women practitioners in, 1425-1432; women's

media in, 1398-1400, 1402, 1404-1405, 1407, 1433-1440
South Asia, 433, 445, 450, 742
Southeast Asia, 540, 614
Soviet Union, 129, 217, 703, 873, 877, 887-888; women practitioners in, 218, 248, 893, 896, 898-901, 1205
Spacek, Sissy, 2936
Spain, 155, 952, 964, 1147; images of women in, 986, 1088; women practitioners in, 106, 1063, 1182; women's media in, 107, 1282, 1300
Spain, Nancy, 1243
Spectator, 1014
Spencer, Susan, 2826, 2903
Spiegelman, Art, 2999, 3033
spiral of silence, 21, 82
Spokeswoman, The, 3166
sports, 77, 1064-1065, 1103, 2546, 2628, 2632, 2657, 2660, 2784, 2916, 3016, 3024, 3107, 3122, 3181
Sports Illustrated, 2253, 2628, 2747
Spring, Sylvia, 222
Sprinkle, Annie, 2944
Squires, Emily, 2871
Sri Lanka, 100, 210, 215, 220, 458, 461; images of women in, 399, 520; women practitioners in, 473, 694, 730, 743
Stahl, Lesley, 2890, 2903
Stahl, Myrtle, 1771
Stanhope, Mrs., 1012
Stanton, Elizabeth Cady, 1894, 1974, 1992, 2029, 2057
Steele, Richard, 984
Steffens, Lincoln, 2095
Steinem, Gloria, 1722
"Stella Dallas," 2365, 2532
Stephens, Ann Sophia, 2028
Stiles' Taxonomy of Verbal Response Modes, 2239
Still Killing Us Softly, 2212
"Still Sane," 77
Stirling, Linda, 2966
Stockdale, Joseph, 1356
Stockdale sisters, 1356
Stockl, Ula, 1190
Stone, Lucy, 1914, 1989, 2029
Straits Times, 606
"Strange Love of Martha Ivers, The," 2489
Streep, Meryl, 1581, 2948, 2963
Streisand, Barbra, 249

"Stress of Our Lives," 1449
Stri Mukti, 127
Stringer, Ann, 2080, 3018
Strong, Anna Louise, 2075
Sturm, Hertha, 1231
Sudan, 304
suffrage, 985, 1018, 1522, 1760, 1817, 1838-1839, 1867, 1914, 1953, 2043, 2057, 2061, 2622, 3174, 3210
Sulzberger, Iphigene Ochs, 3014
"Summer of the Seventeenth Doll, The," 811
Summers, Jamie, 2382
"Summers Sun," 1402
"Sunday, Bloody Sunday," 2492
Sundsvalls Tidning, 1008
Surgeon General's Report on Television and Social Behavior, 1568
Sveriges Radio, 904-905, 1245-1246
Swanson, Gloria, 2953
Sweden, 128, 248; images of women in, 1008, 1024-1028, 1032-1033, 1061, 1093, 1113, 1143; women and broadcasting in, 77-78, 83, 102-104, 107, 932, 953, 965; women and media in, 47, 70, 99, 105; women as audience in, 1153-1154; women practitioners in, 904-905, 1161-1162, 1201-1202, 1204, 1208, 1245-1247, 1250, 1262
Swedish Broadcasting Corporation, 99, 953, 1161-1162, 1247
Swedish Television Corporation, 1143, 1208
Swisshelm, Jane G., 1522, 1830, 1834, 1885, 1961, 2041, 2048, 2064-2065, 2074
Switzerland, 101, 107, 270, 918, 920; women practitioners in, 1166-1167, 1172, 1177
Switzgable, Meg, 2956
Sydney Women's Radio Group, 801
"Sylvia," 2997
Syria, 14

"tabloid TV," 77
Taiwan, 458, 463, 467, 506, 585, 622, 658, 666, 674-675, 687, 696, 725, 738, 793, 796
talk shows, 78, 83, 1118, 1781, 2366, 2396, 3142
Tamara, Sonia, 2080
Tammes, Diane, 1248

Subject Index

Tanzania, 107, 210, 225, 306, 315, 319, 341, 346; images of women in, 127, 328, 331
Tarbell, Ida, 1522, 1525, 1848, 1859, 1866, 1890, 1911, 1995, 2041, 2066, 2076, 2087, 2776
Tarrosa-Subido, Trinidad, 668
Tarry, Ellen, 2067
"Tarzan," 1792
Tatler, 1013-1014
technology: information, 11, 53, 65, 96, 236, 431, 507, 903, 908, 1556, 2672, 2760; television, 18, 1506
telecommunications, 964, 1252, 2848
telenovela, 24, 30, 36, 54, 78, 83, 1311, 1352, 1397-1398, 1400, 1407, 1411, 1420
telephone operators, 1463, 1574
Televisa, 1385
television, 7, 17-18, 61, 94, 183, 247, 923, 959, 1397, 1539, 1637, 1659, 1665, 1667, 1672, 1674, 1676, 1685; and women's culture, 15, 125, 345, 439; audiences, 610-611, 613, 620, 625-626, 628, 633, 635, 638, 644, 646, 648, 652, 655, 657-659, 665-666, 837-838, 879, 1150-1152, 1156, 1158-1160, 1578, 1641, 1675, 1679, 1770, 2710, 2712-2720, 2723; educational, 2317, 2421, 2718, 2879; portrayals of women in, 5-6, 51, 54, 101-104, 106-107, 140, 161, 168, 177, 303, 322, 334, 371, 381, 459, 490, 494-495, 501, 504, 512, 514, 521, 523, 529, 539, 544-545, 557-559, 563, 574, 576, 580, 585-586, 588, 590, 592, 596, 813, 821, 881, 883, 930-931, 965, 972, 1024-1028, 1036, 1045, 1047, 1054-1058, 1061, 1064, 1066, 1082-1083, 1085-1087, 1089-1090, 1094, 1097, 1100-1102, 1104, 1108-1109, 1114-1115, 1118-1119, 1132-1136, 1139, 1143-1144, 1146, 1360, 1362-1363, 1365-1366, 1369, 1446, 1469-1470, 1478, 1485-1487, 1489-1490, 1492, 1561, 1579, 1600, 1615, 1617-1618, 1640, 1643-1644, 1650-1653, 1668, 1680-1681, 1684, 1786, 2107, 2117, 2121, 2123, 2126, 2136-2137, 2148, 2157, 2160-2163, 2170, 2174, 2279-2291, 2293-2297, 2299-2302, 2304, 2306-2315, 2317-2344, 2346-2361, 2363-2372, 2375-2378, 2380-2438, 3440-2459, 2462-2467, 2536, 2598; programs for women, 417, 744-745, 764, 787, 1266, 1290, 1433, 1634-1635, 1639, 1645-1647, 1649, 1654, 1657, 1660-1664, 1669-1670, 1677-1678, 3139, 3141-3142, 3144, 3146-3147; women in, 102, 104, 106, 215, 220, 229, 258-259, 296, 352, 391-392, 406, 408-410, 424, 463, 932, 1327, 1549, 1559, 1610; women practitioners in, 670, 684, 705-706, 709, 732, 737, 740, 840-841, 843, 845-849, 851, 858, 865-866, 913, 919, 929, 998, 1164-1165, 1171, 1176, 1182, 1188-1189, 1198, 1200-1201, 1208, 1217, 1220, 1225, 1230, 1388, 1506, 1535, 1570, 1578, 1612, 1656, 1680-1681, 1764, 1768, 2776, 2821-2823, 2825-2829, 2834-2836, 2838-2847, 2849-2854, 2856-2859, 2861-2868, 2870-2875, 2878-2883, 2887-2892, 2894-2895, 2897-2906, 2908-2912, 2916-2924, 2972
Televisione Italiana, 1327
temperance, 1842, 2606
Temple, Shirley, 1807, 2935
"10," 2498
Tennessee, 1814
Texas, 2875
textbooks, 1, 116, 148, 300, 459, 538, 591-592, 1618, 2559
Thailand, 399, 467, 547, 584, 790; women practitioners in, 77, 464, 699, 746
Third Reich, 1006, 1011, 1191, 1195-1196, 1199
Third World, 59, 64, 69, 181, 791, 1324
33 Women and One Man, 901
Thomas, Helen, 2759, 2991, 3097, 3118
Thompson, Dorothy, 1834, 1877, 1893, 2016, 2038, 2041, 2090, 3018
Throsby Report, The, 842
Tianyi, 468
Time, 77, 2185, 2236, 2557-2558, 2584, 2611, 2618, 2652
Timothy, Elizabeth, 1821, 2041, 3036
Toeplitz, Jerzy, 847
Togo, 303
Toguri d'Aquino, Iva ("Tokyo Rose"), 689
Tomorrow: Politics and High Fashion, 183
Tongo, 855
"Tootsie," 2486

"Torchy," 1734
Toronto *Globe and Mail*, 1493
Toronto Mail, 1457-1458, 1460
Toronto Star, 1452, 1493
Toronto *Sun*, 1493
Train, Phoebe, 2013
Treadwell, Sophi, 1837
Trinidad, 1359, 1369
"Trip to Bountiful, The," 2528
"Triumph of the Will," 1196
Trotta, Liz, 2917, 3131
True Confession, 2653
True Story, 1929, 2580, 2653
Trujillo, Marisol, 1374
Tucker, Madge, 1771
Tulsa Tribune, 3088
Tunisia, 248, 303, 342
Turkey, 50, 100, 103, 107, 1158, 1160, 1224, 1253
Turkiewicz, Sophia, 853
TV Guide, 2253

Uganda, 306, 353
Underwood, Agness, 2078
Unesco, 846-848, 862, 874, 880, 1326
Unidad de Comunicación Alternativa de la Mujer, 1341
Union Wage, 3169
Union Women's Alliance To Gain Equality, 3169
United Arab Emirates, 393
United Nations, 159, 240, 256, 274
United Press International, 2578, 2601, 3097, 3118
United States: historical studies in, 1522, 1525, 1535, 1746-2101, 2700; images of women in, 101, 137, 160, 171, 175, 177, 527, 1441, 1444-1446, 2102-2669; women and media in, 24, 37, 46-47, 51, 59, 70, 79, 96, 99-100, 105, 107, 126, 129-130, 133, 174, 183-184, 212, 215, 217, 258, 261, 270, 278, 286, 1623-1745; women as audience in, 2670-2748; women practitioners in, 218, 221, 682, 900, 2749-3131; women's media in, 1616, 3132-3235
United States Information Agency, 77
University of Maryland, 1523, 1528, 1547
UN Radio Service, 77
Uruguay, 1315, 1343, 1430, 1438
USA Today, 77

U.S. News and World Report, 2185

Valley of the Dolls, 2741
Van Buren, Abigail, 3093
Vanity Fair, 1913, 1916, 2068
Van Trotter, Margarethe, 55, 57
Varda, Agnes, 216-218, 222, 234, 249, 1215
Velez, Lupe, 2960
Venezuela, 155, 1343, 1397, 1399-1400, 1406, 1408, 1436, 1438
Vera, Dolores H., 668
Verlag Frauenpolitik, 1289
Veronica, Vera, 2944
"Vertigo," 58, 2732
video, 33, 50, 55, 251, 298, 399, 760, 815, 845, 858, 867, 1099, 1433, 1442, 1477, 1482, 1516, 1624, 2374, 2460-2461, 2479, 2709
Vidéo Femmes, 1516
Video Sewa, 251
Vieira, Meredith, 2889
Vietnam, 69, 412, 703, 728
Vijayanirmala, 218
Vilasis, Mayra, 1374
violence of women (crime): in advertising, 1624; in film, 77, 282, 777, 834, 1450, 1690-1691, 1701-1703, 2468, 2489, 2728-2730, 2733; in media, 77, 543, 1137, 1493, 1536, 1568, 1571, 1653, 1713, 1730, 2144, 2591, 2675; in television, 2286, 2292, 2294, 2318, 2328, 2355, 2375, 2434, 2713, 2719
Virginia Gazette, 2042
Visiter, 1014
visual images, 53, 55, 2240
Viva, 1343
Vogue, 1823, 2098, 3163, 3220, 3223, 3231
Voice of Women's Liberation, 3166
von Trotta, Margarethe, 216, 218, 249, 1226, 1235-1236, 1276

Walcamp, Marie, 2966
Walker, Evelyn, 1771
Walker, Mort, 2576, 2608
Waller, Judith Cary, 1754, 1787, 2084
Walsh, Raoul, 143, 233, 245
Walter, Cornelia, 2041
Walters, Barbara, 2823, 2857, 2862, 2867, 2878, 2880, 2925

Subject Index

Wanderground, The, 829
Wanita, 770
Warner Brothers, 2099
Warren, Virginia Lee, 2080
Washington Daily News, 3097
Washington *Herald*, 1915, 1984
Washington *Monitor*, 1880
Washington Post, 77, 2541, 2613, 3011, 3058, 3094, 3178, 3213
Washington Press Club Foundation, 77
Washington Woman, 77
Wason, Betty, 2049
Watashi Wa Onna, 176
Watkins, Kathleen Blake, 1458
Watson, Hannah Bunce, 1924
Wean, Carolyn, 2867
Webb, Kate, 1883, 3131
Weber, Lois, 249
Webspinner, 1518
Weekly Women's Magazine, 792
Weiland, Joyce, 222
Weill, Claudia, 222, 249
Wells, Fay Gillis, 1771
Wells, Ida Baker, 1872, 2062, 2089, 3075
Wells-Barnett, Ida, 1834, 2041
Welsh, Mary, 1952, 2080
Wertenbaker, Lael Laird, 2080
Wertmüller, Lina, 38, 249, 1210, 2941
West, Mae, 2959, 2979
Western Home Visitor, 1842
Western Samoa, 855
WGBH-TV, 2393
Wheeler, Helen R., 77
W.H.I.S.P.E.R., 3233
White, Katharine S., 3013
White, Pearl, 2966
Whitehouse, Mary, 1260
Wieland, Joyce, 2965
Wilding, Emily, 1302
Wiley, Bonnie, 2080
Wilkinson, Signe, 2998, 3104
Williams, Esther, 1807
Williams, Linda, 2991
Williams, Mary Alice, 2825
Willis, Catherine Ferguson, 1457
Wilshire, Mary, 3023
Wilson, Lady Sarah, 238
Wimmen's Comix, 3051
Winslow, Mary, 2001
Winter, Ella, 2095
Wisconsin, 1760, 1824, 1964, 2671, 2681, 2734, 3057, 3062

Withington, Mrs. E. W., 2013
"Without a Roof Nor Law," 1215
Wolcott, Marion Post, 1892
Woman (England, 19th century), 981
Woman (England, 20th century), 992, 1304, 1307
Woman, The (Taiwan), 796
"Woman Alive!" 3146-3147
Woman and Russia: An Almanac to Women about Women, 877
Woman Rebel, The, 1990-1991
Woman's Day, 2085, 2098, 2747, 3129, 3199, 3209
Woman's Exponent, 1838
Woman's Home Companion (Philippines), 795
Woman's Home Companion (United States), 2098, 3203
Woman's Journal, 1754, 1958, 1989
Woman's Own, 1265, 1304
Woman's Press of England, 1302
Woman's Realm, 1304
Woman's Weekly, 1304
"Woman to Woman," 3142, 3144
Women, 770
Women Against Violence and Exploitation, 815
Women: A Journal of Liberation, 3166
women and media courses, 77, 1547, 1698, 2129, 2477
Women for Women: A Research and Study Group, 760
Women in Broadcasting Technology, 117
Women in Communication Inc., 77
Women in Film and Television, 801
"women in jeopardy," 2392
Women in the News (WIN), 77
Women Make Movies, Inc., 117
Women of China, 758
Women on the Edge of Time, 829
women politicians, 77, 1465, 1561, 1596, 1632, 1732, 2138, 2179, 2434, 2547, 2577-2578, 2647
women practitioners, 19, 42, 44, 58-59, 77, 101, 106-107, 115, 211-264; in Africa, 323, 348-363; in Asia, 394, 404, 406, 408, 414, 416-417, 419-420, 436, 439-441, 450-451, 457-458, 463-464, 467, 469, 472-473, 475-476, 478-482, 540, 668-742; in Australia, 840-866; in Canada, 1451, 1455-1462, 1496-1514; in Caribbean, 1315,

1350, 1367-1375; in Central America, 1315, 1386-1393; in Eastern Europe, 893-902; in Western Europe, 1161-1264; in Middle East, 388-393; in South America, 1315, 1325, 1343, 1424-1432; in United States, 2749-3131
Women's Action Forum (Khawateen Mahaz-e-Amal), 784
Women's Army Corps, 1752
women's bookstores, 77, 389
Women's Center Library, Oregon State University, 1548
Women's Community Video Group, 117
Women's Daily, 794
Women's Features Service, 77, 117, 266, 293
Women's Film Fund, 801
Women's Information Centre, Bangkok, 746
Women's Information Network for Asia and the Pacific, 117
Women's International News Gathering Service, 3234
Women's International News Service, 77, 283
Women's Journal, 757
women's liberation (feminist movement), 21, 66, 77, 218, 373, 571, 989, 1023, 1068, 1070, 1074, 1076, 1183, 1275, 1417, 1436, 1534, 1553, 1573, 1585, 1718, 2105, 2155, 2170-2171, 2191, 2277, 2550, 2616-2617, 2887, 3136, 3151
women's media, 77, 96, 265-298; in Africa, 364-367; in Asia, 429, 459, 468, 474-475, 477, 484, 743-797; in Australia, 867-871; in Canada, 1449, 1452, 1515-1520; in Caribbean, 1352-1353; in Central America, 1394-1396; in Europe, 1265-1310; in Middle East, 388-393; in South America, 1314, 1324, 1326-1327, 1329, 1332, 1334, 1339, 1341, 1343-1344, 1346, 1402, 1404-1405, 1407, 1433-1440; in United States, 3132-3235
Women's Media Circle Foundation, 684
Women's Monthly, 469
Women's National Press Club, 1833
Women's National Radio Committee, 3143
Women's News, 1624, 3181
Women Speaking, 277

Women's Radio Collective, 117
Women's Review of Books, 77
Women's Room, The, 2295
Women's Studies in Communication, 1543
Women's Studies International, 1714
Women's Studies Newsletter, 1714
Women's Studies Quarterly, 1714
women's talk, 23, 35, 65, 211, 257, 1562, 1611
Women's Wear Daily, 3197
Women's World, 468
Womym's Braille Press, 77
Wong Chen Quan, 477
Woodhull, Victoria, 1881, 1942, 1981, 2029, 2036
Woodhull and Claflin's Weekly, 1942, 1955, 1958, 1981
Woodruff Judy, 2826
Working Mother, 3217
Working Woman, 2569, 3217
working women, 2363-2364, 2416, 2419, 2457, 2491, 2569, 2580, 2615, 2641, 2682-2683, 2688, 2734, 2842, 2892, 3165, 3175, 3187, 3215
World Association for Christian Communications, 2, 107, 127-128
World of Ginger Fox, The, 1743
World War II, 1761, 1802-1803, 2472, 2580, 2739
Wornick, Susan, 2826
WRC-TV, 2183, 2829
Wright, Frances, 2028
Wu, Linda, 738
Wyman, Alice, 1771

Xu Shouli, 712

Yamasaki, Tizuka, 218
Yellen, Linda, 2956
"Yellow Earth," 609
Yemen, People's Democratic Republic of, 14
Yomiuri Shimbun, 768
Young Athlete Magazine, 2632
Yugoslavia, 248
Yunzhu, Shangguan, 683

Zambia, 1, 77, 104, 303, 326, 347
Zenger, Catherine, 3036
Zetterling, Mai, 223
Zhang Nuanxin, 218, 249, 749
Zimbabwe, 267, 316

About the Compiler

JOHN A. LENT is a pioneer in the study of Third World mass communications and popular culture. He has authored or edited thirty-seven books and monographs and hundreds of articles; most have dealt with mass communications in Asia and the Caribbean. This is his eighth book-length bibliography. Dr. Lent was the first coordinator of the mass communications program at Universiti Sains Malaysia, which inaugurated the discipline in Malaysia, was a Fulbright Scholar in the Philippines and a professor at universities throughout the United States.